Reality,
Knowledge,
and the
Good Life

REALITY, KNOWLEDGE, AND THE GOOD LIFE

A Historical Introduction to Philosophy

Willem A. deVries
University of New Hampshire

St. Martin's Press, New York

Senior editor: Don Reisman
Project management: Denise Quirk
Text design: Gene Crofts
Cover design: Doug Steel

For information, write:
St. Martin's Press, Inc.
175 Fifth Avenue
New York, NY 10010

ISBN: 0-312-03657-4

Photo credits: Socrates, p. 11 (left), The Bettmann Archive; Plato, p. 11
(right), The Granger Collection; Aristotle, p. 87, The Granger Collection;
Saint Augustine (Raphael), p. 155, Culver Pictures, Inc.; Saint Thomas
Aquinas, p. 174, Culver Pictures, Inc.; René Descartes (Frans Hals), p. 203,
The Bettmann Archive; Thomas Hobbes, p. 240, The Bettmann Archive;
John Locke, p. 265, The Bettmann Archive; Gottfried Wilhelm Leibniz, p.
317, The Granger Collection; David Hume (engraving based on painting by
Allen Ramsay), p. 336, The Bettmann Archive; Immanuel Kant (E. Hader),
p. 372, The Bettmann Archive; Karl Marx, p. 447, The Bettmann Archive;
John Stuart Mill, p. 467, The Bettmann Archive; Friedrich Nietzsche (Carl
Korig), p. 491, The Bettmann Archive; Charles Sanders Peirce, p. 517, The
Bettmann Archive; Edmund Husserl, p. 539, The Granger Collection; Lud-
wig Wittgenstein, p. 566, The Granger Collection; Simone de Beauvoir, p.
601, UPI/Bettmann Newsphotos; John Rawls, p. 619, Harvard University
Office of News and Public Affairs.

To my son Hadriel

Preface

Reality, Knowledge, and the Good Life presents in historical sequence core readings from the Western philosophical tradition. These readings are substantial selections rather than short extracts in order to present a more comprehensive view of the philosophers represented and to allow the complexity and nuance of their work to shine through. The decision to include lengthy extracts entailed including fewer authors, but this is a small price for greater depth and comprehensiveness. Nevertheless, abridgments have been made in order to allow for a greater variety of readings and to clarify the structure of the arguments presented.

Reality (metaphysics), knowledge (epistemology), and reflections about the good life provide the focus for the collection, but the variety of philosophical issues addressed in the readings is ample for constructing topic-centered courses or modules. Suggested topics and a guide to the relevant selections have been included in the Topical Table of Contents. While this book is aimed at historical introductions to philosophy, its material is also sufficient for a survey of the history of philosophy.

Each part introduction provides an overview of the development of philosophical thought in the historical period: the prominent philosophers, the important questions addressed and the mode of inquiry used, and, in particular, the treatment of the questions of reality, knowledge, and the good life. In addition, each introduction explores the social, political, and economic forces that shaped the context in which the questions relevant to the era were discussed.

Anthologies of classical readings often contain translations that are old and neither terribly reliable nor easily readable. In this collection I have attempted to include the best translations available. Deciding which translations to use was not easy, and I have many people to thank for their suggestions. The texts of Locke and Hume are based on the recent critical editions; the Locke texts have been edited to conform with current spelling and punctuation. Whenever there is a standard citation format for an author or a work, those reference numbers have been included with the text here.

Several kinds of pedagogical aids supplement the readings. The point of these aids is to enhance students' encounter with the text, not to substitute for it. The *headnote* for each author contains a short biography and overview of his or her philosophy. These should help orient students to the author's historical position and central theses, but are not an attempt to provide detailed guidance to the content of the readings. Students are encouraged to develop their own insights.

Each *reading context* offers a brief, focused commentary to help introductory students approach the texts. These commentaries may describe the historical setting that influenced the work or outline the ongoing debate to which the selection contributes. Some concentrate on specific arguments presented in the selection or on the methodology used to address them.

Reading questions also accompany the selections. Most beginning philosophy students start out not knowing what to look for in a text and consequently become disoriented. By keeping the reading questions in mind while studying a text, students should more easily grasp some of the questions that need to be answered in understanding the text. The reading questions, while not exhaustive, are intended to make the point that philosophy texts need to be aggressively challenged, sympathetically but critically, in order for learning to take place.

Notes on the texts lend further background on the readings while also emphasizing the literary and philological dimensions of these classical texts. *Selected bibliographies* include primary sources as well as prominent pieces in the secondary literature. The bibliographies focus on books rather than articles because I have found that books tend to provide fuller expositions that are more intelligible to introductory students than do journal articles.

A project like this involved a great amount of work, and there are many people whom I must thank for making the task easier. Andrea Guidoboni first encouraged me to undertake the project; she has since left St. Martin's to become an educator. Don Reisman picked up the banner after Andrea and was very helpful. Denise Quirk saw the book through production and was a pleasure to work with.

Many of my colleagues offered assistance and criticism, all of it valuable. Dan Lloyd, with whom I shared an office at Harvard when this project was first conceived, lent both suggestions and encouragement. My colleagues at Tufts University the following year, Dan Dennett, Norman Daniels, Hugo Bedau, Helen Cartwright, Steve White, and Jody Azzouni, were also extremely supportive of a visitor in their midst. The philosophy department here at the University of New Hampshire is a very special place, for my colleagues have been extraordinarily supportive and fun to argue with. I am grateful to them for bearing with me patiently as I grilled them about which readings they prefer or which translations were strongest and as I complained about the time and effort I was spending on the book. Paul Brockelman, Drew Christie, Val Dusek, Paul McNamara, Bob Scharff, Ken Westphal, and Yutaka Yamamoto all helped. I am especially indebted to Charlotte Witt, whose aid with the ancient philosophers was absolutely indispensable. The Center for the Humanities at the University of New Hampshire also provided support for some of the research involved in compiling the materials.

I also wish to acknowledge the many reviewers who offered helpful suggestions at various stages of this project: James E. Bayley, The City College of the City University of New York; Barry Curtis, University of Hawaii at Hilo; Ellen Haring, University of Florida; Jasper Hopkins, University of Minnesota—Twin Cities; Yeager Hudson, Colby College; Murray Kiteley, Smith College; James J. Lee, John Jay College; Michael Levin, The City College of the City University of New York; Catherine Ludlum, Moorhead State University; Randy L. Maddox, Sioux Falls College; John J. McDermott, Texas A&M University; Clyde Lee Miller, State University of New York at StonyBrook; James Risser, Seattle University. In addition, I am grateful to the questionnaire respondents for their valuable comments: Robert V. Andelson, Auburn University; Cyrus W. Banning, Kenyon College; William M. Bethea, Rogers State College; Martin Bunzl, Rutgers University; Eva Cadwallader, Westminster College; Marte Chandler, DePauw University; Thomas A. Duggan, Regis College; Marilynn Fleckenstein, Niagara University; Charles Griswold, Howard University; Charles E.

Hornbeck, Keene State College; Willard Hutcheon, The City College of the City University of New York; Peter Kosso, Northwestern University; Robert Leisey, University of Detroit; Sally Markowitz, Willamette University; Jorge L. Nobo, Washburn University of Topeka; Carl Page, Emory University; Louis P. Pojman, University of Mississippi; Avrum Stroll, University of California at San Diego; Terry Winant, Wesleyan University.

My wife, Dianne, has read every word I've written and more often than not forced me to rewrite them. Her scrutiny is the toughest test I pass in bringing something to print, but also the most valuable. My mother advised me on German translations, as well as offered maternal support. I dedicated my first book to Dianne, so this one is for our son Hadriel. I hope he'll read this one and begin to understand what I do behind closed doors and why I love philosophy.

Contents

Topical Table of Contents

Reading titles are followed by standard reference numbers; page numbers are in parentheses.

INTRODUCTION

What is philosophy? It is the disciplined exercise of wonder—a groping for clarity about the questions we ask, the concepts we use, and our right to use them. It is the search for meaning and for the ultimate truths about reality, knowledge, and the good life. It is whatever philosophers do and have done with excitement, even passion, and intellectual commitment for more than two millennia. It is a rich and worthy tradition —an ongoing, interwoven pattern of problems and answers, claims and objections, puzzles and insights. That no sharper and clearer definition can here be offered is only as it should be, for the field of philosophy simply is neither sharp nor clear, and this is part of its enduring fascination.

The works of Plato, Aristotle, Saint Thomas Aquinas, René Descartes, John Locke, and Immanuel Kant, among others, roughly define the core of the Western philosophical tradition. Anyone who continues the conversation of the core philosophers is "doing philosophy." Yet that cannot be a definition of philosophy, for cosmology, physics, psychology, politics, economics, and almost every other field of intellectual pursuit enter into the conversation of philosophers. Philosophy itself becomes whatever is left over after all the other special disciplines have been subtracted.

Philosophy traces the shifting borders of our intellectual life, asking the questions that lie outside the special competencies of other disciplines, the questions that either are not well enough defined for a particular discipline or, because they are in some way *about* the discipline, cannot be answered *within* it.

Many find such a characterization of philosophy puzzling: It seems a grab bag, a miscellaneous collection of unanswerable questions. But isn't it tremendously exciting that there is a discipline—a sometimes confusing discipline, but a discipline nonetheless, with all the attendant intellectual standards—into which fall the questions that no one else knows how to handle?

1

The questions of philosophy can be characterized a bit more precisely than this. A distinction long familiar to philosophers separates *empirical* from *nonempirical* questions. Those that can, in principle, be answered experimentally—that is, questions that necessitate the use of sensory perception—are empirical. Consider the following questions: What did the thirty-second president of the United States serve at his inaugural ball? What color socks did I put on this morning? How fast can a cheetah run? Will it rain on July 4, 1999? What are the basic physical forces in the universe? These are very different questions, but in each case the answer entails looking at, smelling, hearing, tasting, or feeling the world. Some of the answers require more than just sensing; they involve remembering, drawing on the knowledge of others, or even constructing elaborate theories. But in each case the evidence of the senses plays an essential role in justifying the answer.

Questions to which sensory evidence is not relevant are considered nonempirical. The fact that the two apples in your right hand, together with the two in your left hand, make four apples total is not grounds for the claim that 2 plus 2 equals 4. We know the truth of this mathematical equation without having to verify it by counting things. Similarly, if someone proposes to give an example in which 2 plus 2 does not equal 4, we immediately know that a trick is being prepared. That 2 plus 2 equals 4 is not open to refutation through sensory evidence.

Paper and pencil or sophisticated computers may be employed to arrive at the solution to a mathematical equation, but those devices do not provide evidence in the way a laboratory experiment does, for there is an essential difference between a calculation and an experiment. Calculations are not open-ended; if the rules are followed, the correct answer will be produced, and the answer arrived at follows strictly from the definitions of the system employed. Experiments are always open-ended; there are myriad ways in which an experiment can go wrong no matter how carefully the rules are followed. Most important, a successful experiment can force revision of the theory being tested.

This is not the case with a calculation: no arithmetic calculation is going to persuade us to revise arithmetic. Arithmetic is simply not subject to testing in the way a scientific hypothesis or a prediction about the weather is. Of course, not all mathematical questions are answered by calculation; proofs play an extremely important role in mathematics. But proofs share with calculations the important property of *formality*: like a calculation, a proof always involves the employment of a limited and well-defined set of rules, and nothing else is relevant. Whether something is a good proof should involve nothing more than checking to see whether the rules have been strictly followed.

The questions asked by philosophers are not straightforwardly empirical questions; if they were, philosophy would turn into an experimental discipline like physics or psychology. Does that mean that philosophical questions must be nonempirical? They are not formal questions like those in arithmetic or set theory: there is no system of agreed definitions and axioms to be explored, no calculations to be made, no clearly delimited formal proofs to be constructed. So we conclude that philosophical questions are neither empirical nor formal.

This negative definition falls short of a positive characterization of philosophical questions. Furthermore, it creates a paradox and raises a philosophical question itself. The evidence of our senses *does* seem relevant to answering many of the questions philosophers ask, even if in a very indirect way. For instance, the general character of our sensory experience may have a good deal to do with the reliability of induction, a problem philosophers have often considered. We have good reasons, then, to believe each of the following theses: (1) philosophical questions are nonempirical, since philosophy is not an experimental discipline; (2) sensory evidence is not relevant to nonempirical questions; and (3) sensory evidence is relevant to at least some philosophical questions. Every possible position has been argued: some people have claimed that every question (even whether 2 plus 2 equals 4) is empirical; others have argued that every question is at least in principle susceptible to a nonempirical answer (even if not by beings like us); still others have attacked the idea that the distinction itself makes sense, claiming that any attempt to delimit the two classes turns out to be arbitrary and indefensible. The dispute is not about what is going on in the world or about the consequences of the fundamental theorems of some formal system. The dispute is about the nature and meaning of several concepts we use to understand the world—namely, the empirical/nonempirical distinction—and about our right to use them. This particular dispute may seem narrow and technical, but it has far-ranging consequences, for consider these questions: Is a moral judgment an empirical or a nonempirical statement? How are the judgments that all humans have inalienable rights or that the state ought not to control a woman's access to an abortion known? How one draws the empirical/nonempirical distinction affects not only our conception of the empirical sciences but also our conception of moral and aesthetic judgments as well.

The prospect of a world without philosophy is depressing, even frightening. It would be a world in which questions outside the special disciplines could not be treated with any intellectual rigor at all, or rather a world in which they did not even arise, in which there were no haunting questions to entice us to reach beyond our grasp. Can you fathom a world in which the meaning of human existence is never questioned, the nature and validity of scientific method is never challenged, and fundamental human rights and obligations are never debated? There is thus something especially human about asking the kinds of questions that philosophy deals with. Although traits such as the making of tools and the use of language have often been cited as the distinguishing human characteristics, surely no mere animal has engaged in philosophy. Being human *is* being the kind of thing that asks such questions. The answers we accept depend on our fundamental conceptions of ourselves and our world, and they have a tremendous influence on what we do and who we are.

Reading the classic works of philosophy is the best way to understand what philosophy is. It also provides a front-row-center seat on the epic drama of the growth of humanity. Through the classic works one learns that philosophy is not just the default discipline where we throw all the questions that cannot be handled elsewhere. It is the stubborn attempt "to understand how things in the broadest sense of the term hang together in the broadest sense of the term."[1] To read the history of philosophy is to watch humankind attempt to make sense of the world. More important, it is to join the process oneself.

---

1. Wilfrid Sellars, "Philosophy and the Scientific Image of Man," *Science, Perception, and Reality* (New York: Humanities Press, 1963), p. 1.

This book assembles some of the core works in the history of Western philosophy. It is not exhaustive, for philosophy's core is too rich to be stuffed into one text. But it is representative. These texts will give a well-rounded introduction to the history of philosophy and therefore to philosophy itself.

I have also chosen the readings with an eye on three problem areas that have been at the center of philosophical concern through the ages: reality, knowledge, and the good life.

Metaphysical questions about the nature of reality have taken many forms over the past 2,500 years: Is the way things seem to be to our ordinary perception the way they *really* are? Are there things that lie beyond the reach of the senses? Is there anything that has to exist no matter what, a necessary existent? What is the ultimate stuff of which everything is made? How do minds or souls differ from bodies, and what relationships to bodies do they have? If my thoughts and sensations are the only things I know for sure, why think that there is anything outside them, any external reality at all? What is it for a judgment of mine to be *true*, to correspond with the facts?

The questions raised by philosophy are diverse, and they have changed somewhat over the millennia. For example, the early Milesian philosophers worried a great deal about the ultimate stuff of the universe; modern philosophers are willing, by and large, to leave that problem to the physicists. Questions that depend on drawing a sharp contrast between subjectivity and objectivity have been particularly important since Descartes. Understanding the transformation of the ruling questions governing philosophical reflection is at least as revealing and important as understanding the answers given to those questions and usually requires insight of a broad scope, not just into the philosophical trends but also into the developments in religion, science, and world politics.

It is often difficult to keep the questions of epistemology (the study or theory of knowledge) separate from those of metaphysics (the study of the nature of reality), for as soon as we ask about what there really is, it seems almost automatic to go on to ask how we know. Epistemology is concerned not only with how much we can legitimately claim to know but with what it is to know anything at all in the first place. Just what is the difference between knowledge and mere opinion? How can we tell which we have? Can the senses, ever changing and not fully reliable as they are, give us knowledge? Conversely, how can we know something that we cannot see, hear, or touch? Can there be any knowledge apart from the senses? Are there some things I cannot be mistaken about? If I can be mistaken about something, does that mean that I do not know it? We often distinguish between someone's having good and bad reasons for believing something, but what constitutes a good reason? If I have a good reason for believing something, must it be a good reason for you as well? Finally, many of the beliefs we have are built on other beliefs—what we know or believe forms a kind of structure. What kind of structure is it? Is it like a great house, resting on a foundation firmly anchored in bedrock, or is it like a ship at sea, holding together despite the buffeting of the waves but without any firm tie to the world?

Knowing what kind of world we live in and how much we can know about it is not enough; we also seek the good life. For some people this denotes simply a life of material well-being. Most, however, recognize that a good life must be lived with integrity and in harmony with others. We need to know how we should act and what kind of life to strive for. Should one seek to satisfy whatever desires one has? But not all one's desires are compatible, nor are the desires of different people compatible. Are there rules for choosing which desires to satisfy or how to resolve conflicts? Are there desires no one should have? What kind of legitimate claims do other people have on us for attention, care, respect, or love? Can I choose to live any way I please? Are there any rules that everyone ought to obey, come what may? If we must associate together to survive as a species, by what principles should that association be organized?

Wittingly or unwittingly, we face the problems of practical philosophy every day, making choices that shape our lives and the lives of those around us. In philosophy more than any other discipline, those choices are brought to consciousness and reflected on, assessed, reaffirmed, or rejected. The effort to assess and control the shape of our lives is essentially human, and philosophy is the discipline in which those very efforts at assessment and control come into question.

ANCIENT GREEK PHILOSOPHY

Western philosophy began with the Greeks, in Miletus, a Greek colony on the western coast of what is now Turkey, around 600 B.C.E.[1] Why it was that the first recognizable efforts at a *philosophical* understanding of the world emerged there at that time remains a matter of conjecture, but several factors probably played a crucial role. Miletus was an active, seafaring, trading culture that came into contact not just with other Greek colonies but also with the Phoenicians, the Egyptians, the Babylonians, and other societies as well. The Milesians thus had ready access to the new forms of knowledge and inquiry developed elsewhere (e.g., mathematics in Egypt, astronomy in Babylonia), and they must have been struck by the widely differing religious and mythological accounts of the world. For some reason, in this place before all others, these factors combined to generate philosophical attempts to explain and understand the world.

Tradition identifies Thales as the first philosopher, but we know very little about him. The evidence we have about his thought is all secondhand, consisting mostly of reports by later writers, many of whom relied on a long (and unreliable) oral tradition. This generally defines the limits of our knowledge of pre-Socratic philosophers: in the absence of primary sources and reliable secondary accounts, little can be said about their beliefs with a high degree of certainty.

Thales is best known for his belief that water is the principle of all things. What are we to make of such a claim? It could mean many different things. It could be a poetic evocation of water as the nurturing medium of life, or it could serve to announce the

---

1. Throughout this book, dates before the Common Era will be so marked; unmarked dates can be assumed to be in the Common Era unless clearly established otherwise. This notation seems preferable to the sectarian B.C. and A.D.

ascendancy of a particular god and hence of the clan, city, or trade most closely associated with that deity. But seen in its context, Thales' pronouncement is neither poetic nor religious nor political: he was reaching for some broad-ranging theory of the fundamental elements of reality. Thales claims that everything is made of water! Thales could with equal justice be considered the first physicist, but his methodology (so far as we can tell) seems speculative rather than observational.

Thales' pupil Anaximander objected that the primacy of any one kind of thing would entail the nonexistence of its opposites (the Greeks had a strong tendency to view the world in terms of various opposites—hot and cold, wet and dry, and so on). If water, the wet and cold, were the principle of all things, how could there be anything of an opposite nature, such as fire, the dry and hot? Anaximander therefore concluded that the principle of things could not be some one particular thing but must be the *apeiron*, the "unbounded" or "indefinite," out of which the particular qualities discoverable in the world emerge. The order of the world is best understood as a kind of political order, suggests Anaximander, wherein the opposites that have separated out from the *apeiron* vie with each other for dominance and thus account for the changing seasons, weather, and even objects themselves by their constant battles and coalitions.

Anaximander's pupil Anaximenes in turn rejected his teacher's proposal and attempted to explain the changes in the world as different processes of condensation and rarefaction of air, his candidate for the principle of all things.

Philosophy, the attempt to plumb the roots of existence without reliance on tradition, mythology, or religious authority, remained at the edges of the Greek world for the next two hundred years, for the figures who rose up after the Milesians also came from colonies on the rim of the Greek Mediterranean. Heraclitus, from Ephesus in Turkey, who held that the nature of the world is constant flux; Pythagoras of Samos, who migrated to Croton in southern Italy to found a cult in which mathematics played a primary role; Parmenides and Zeno of Elea, also in southern Italy not far from Croton, who rejected the changing world we experience through our five senses as mere illusion in favor of the eternal, unchanging One—all these early philosophers worked in the dynamic, mercantile hinterlands of Greek society, and each left a deep mark on philosophy. Empedocles, again from the Italian colonies, and Leucippus, another later Milesian, also contributed. Not until Anaxagoras, born in Clazomenae in Turkey, did philosophy move to the political center of Grecian culture, Athens, where we pick it up with Socrates and Plato.

The pre-Socratics mentioned so far are united by a common search for the fundamental elements of reality. Another group of intellects, commonly called Sophists ("the wise"), also had a tremendous influence on Greek thinking. The Sophists do not comprise a homogenous group. Some, like Protagoras, were men of true intellectual stature; others were skillful wranglers lacking any real depth to their thought. The Sophists professed to teach valuable skills: grammar, literary interpretation, mnemonics, and skill in oral argumentation. In a small society where numerous issues were settled in the courts, the power to convince others was true power indeed. With this emphasis on argumentative skill the Sophists developed extraordinary critical acumen. They seemed capable of defeating any argument.

Thus the Sophists became skeptical of the efforts of the natural philosophers who had preceded them. Gorgias, for instance, composed a treatise arguing that (1) nothing exists, (2) if anything did exist, it would be unknowable, and (3) if it were knowable, it would be incommunicable. Skepticism of a different nature also became rampant. The Sophists tended to be moral skeptics. The most challenging brand of moral skepticism depended on a distinction between *physis*, or nature, and *nomos*, or convention. Humans, they argued, are by nature rapacious; it is only by the conventions of society that humans are restrained from thoroughly self-seeking behavior. Given this assumption, all the constraints of morality look to be merely arbitrary impositions of a social group, impositions to be evaded whenever possible. Perhaps this moral skepticism was but a natural outgrowth of the cosmopolitan culture that first gave rise to philosophy, but much of Plato's philosophy was a response to the dangerous notions of the Sophists.

Because the interpretation of the pre-Socratic philosophers is especially difficult, requiring careful, scholarly study of fragmentary and unreliable texts, none have been included in this book. Nevertheless, studying this time period affords the special thrill of watching philosophy slowly create itself. In addition to the textual problems of pre-Socratic philosophy, it is important to keep in mind that philosophy and physics— philosophy and science generally—were not clearly distinguished or distinguishable in these early days. The differences between hypotheses tested by their ability to illuminate our understanding and hypotheses tested as well against controlled observation were slow in being recognized. Watching the birth of Western civilization is both exciting and humbling.

SELECTED BIBLIOGRAPHY

Brumbaugh, Robert S. *The Philosophers of Greece.* New York: Crowell, 1964.

Frankfort, Henri, et al. *Before Philosophy.* Harmondsworth, England: Penguin, 1949.

Guthrie, W.K.C. *A History of Greek Philosophy.* Cambridge: Cambridge University Press, 1962–.

Irwin, Terence. *Classical Thought: A History of Western Philosophy,* vol. 1. New York: Oxford University Press, 1988.

Jaeger, Werner. *Paideia.* 2nd ed. Trans. Gilbert Highet. New York: Oxford University Press, 1945.

Robinson, John Mansley. *An Introduction to Early Greek Philosophy.* Boston: Houghton Mifflin, 1968.

Socrates and Plato

For over two millennia Socrates has been esteemed as the model of a philosopher, yet he never wrote a word, so far as we know. Everything we know about him has come to us secondhand, mostly through the writings of his student Plato. Plato's dialogues captured the essence of Socrates, revealing a character who personifies the philosophical life because of his intellect, his honesty, his sense of humor, and his unwillingness to ignore the important questions that so many people shun out of intellectual indolence or cowardice.

Socrates was born in Athens in 469 B.C.E. Little is known of the details of his life. We do not know whether he practiced a trade, though we do know that he served in the army with distinction, which means that he had sufficient money to provide his own arms. In his later years, though, he was apparently quite poor.

Socrates was born during the golden age of Athens. Persia had been defeated in 479 B.C.E., leaving Athens at the head of a confederation of states that evolved into an Athenian empire. As a large trading center, Athens also became the preeminent cultural hub. Drama, poetry, and science all flourished as never before in cosmopolitan, democratic (at least for male landowners) Athens.

This golden age was not to last, however. In 431 Athens became embroiled in a war with its great rival city-state, Sparta. The Peloponnesian War lasted almost thirty years, subjecting Athens to great strains and ultimately breaking its cultural and political hegemony.

Socrates exerted tremendous influence on Western intellectual culture by simply making a habit of hanging around in public places and asking difficult questions about issues of moral concern. According to the story passed down, his friend Chaerophon once asked the Oracle at Delphi whether there was anyone wiser than Socrates. The Oracle said there wasn't, a fact Socrates could not believe. Socrates then sought to show that others were wiser than he and began asking questions of all and sundry to elicit their wisdom. To his surprise, he found that they knew no more than he—in fact, his wisdom consisted in his realization of his own ignorance.

Socrates gathered around him a group of mostly younger men with whom he routinely discussed and argued. Among this group were Plato and his older brothers, Glaucon and Adeimantus, who are later portrayed in *The Republic*. The principal topics of discussion were moral concepts—what is piety? what is courage? what is justice?—and the sharpness of Socrates' wit honed the minds of his followers. There were at the time a number of professional teachers of rhetoric (the art of persuasive argument), for in the Athenian democracy persuasive speaking was an important form of power. These teachers, the Sophists, also claimed to be able to teach virtue, for the person who won the day—in the courts, on the battlefield, in business affairs—was the virtuous person. Socrates steadfastly refused to accept that a glib tongue and an ability to prevail constituted virtue. Instead, he looked for a deeper knowledge of the good and the right that would enable us to choose our actions wisely and, just as important, to raise our children to be good people.

In 399, however, Socrates was charged with impiety and corrupting the young. For those who knew Socrates, his integrity was beyond reproach. Many Athenians, however, found his questioning distinctly uncomfortable; others may have been misled by Aristophanes' unfavorable caricature of Socrates in his comedy *The Clouds*. It is probably true that there was a group of cynical young men who liked to listen to Socrates question others and demonstrate their ignorance to them but who took from Socrates' conversations none of the deeper lessons he intended to impart. Singled out as an example of destructive questioning of authority, Socrates was found guilty and sentenced to death. The recording of his work and death fell to Plato.

Plato was more than forty years Socrates' junior, born in 427 B.C.E. His family was patrician and very well connected in Athenian politics. Plato would have expected to play an active role in Athenian civic life, but its increasingly disordered state conspired to drive him away from any active participation.

In many ways Plato should be considered the first Western philosopher. Prior to Plato's writings, the work of the pre-Socratics was part mythology, part religious practice, part poetry, and, of course, part philosophy. Although Socrates left most of the mythology, poetry, and religion behind, focusing on the rational practice of dialectic, Plato developed philosophy into its own unique discipline and gave it a body of writings that solidified the problems and many of the methods that form the core of Western philosophy.

We don't know exactly when Plato made the decision to devote himself to philosophy, but surely his earliest dialogues, among them the *Apology* (an account of Socrates' defense in his trial) and the *Euthyphro* (which employs the method of question and refutation attributed to Socrates), must have had among their aims restoring

Socrates' reputation and preserving his style and method. A number of Socrates' disciples created other such dialogues, most of which have been lost to us except for a few by Xenophon. Xenophon's dialogues seem explicitly concerned with recording the historical Socrates, but Plato's quickly grow beyond the bounds of biography, focusing increasingly on the philosophical issues themselves, slowly evolving into statements of a recognizably Platonic philosophy.

In 388 B.C.E., at the age of forty, Plato visited the Grecian settlements in Italy and Sicily, perhaps to discuss his views with some of the Pythagorean philosophers there. He visited the court of Dionysius I of Syracuse, where he became good friends with the ruler's brother-in-law, Dion. Upon Plato's return to Athens in 386, he founded his school, the Academy. This school was dedicated to the pursuit of the good, much as Socrates would have wanted, in stark contrast to the competing schools of a more sophistical bent, in which rhetoric and style were uppermost. The Academy endured for centuries, leaving its mark not just through its founder but also in a long line of distinguished students, especially Aristotle.

In 367 Dionysius I of Syracuse died and Dion persuaded Plato to come to Syracuse to teach his nephew, Dionysius II. Plato apparently hoped to shape young Dionysus into the philosopher-king of *The Republic*. But Dionysius, already twenty-eight years old, did not take to the instruction Plato offered, particularly the mathematics. He banished Dion, and Plato soon left Syracuse, returning briefly in 361 at Dionysius' invitation but again failing in his efforts to mold Dionysius into a philosopher-king. From then until his death in 347, Plato devoted himself to the Academy and to his writing.

Philosophy

The early dialogues of Plato—including the *Euthyphro* and the *Apology*—are thought to be fairly accurate representations of Socrates and his opinions and methods. Socrates steadfastly refuses to claim knowledge; he professes an ignorance that he hopes his interlocutor can help to alleviate, but in fact the interlocutor, confident of his own knowledge of the right thing to do, ends up confounded. Socrates is never looking for particular advice about what to do in a specific situation; he is seeking definitions and principles that would be applicable in any number of cases, usually in questions of ethics. The major Socratic convictions that seem to emerge from the early dialogues are that the unexamined life is not worth living, that the attempt to understand the principles by which we ought to live is a tremendously important enterprise, and that it is always wrong to harm another person—that is, people must be treated with respect.

Plato's writings are usually divided into three periods. In the early period, the dialogues are Socratic in tenor, often inconclusive explorations of the nature of piety or courage or the duties we owe the state. There is little, if any, attempt to construct a grand philosophical theory to resolve such questions or even to give a unified position on the nature of those questions. The give-and-take between Socrates and his interlocutors is fairly natural in these dialogues. (The twentieth-century English philosopher Gilbert Ryle has even suggested that Plato's dialogues were performed, with Plato himself always playing Socrates.)

The ruling questions in the early dialogues are always fundamentally ethical, and Socrates is always seeking a clear formulation of either a definition or a principle that will provide a touchstone for resolving doubtful or borderline cases and will also guide our efforts at moral education. Plato, like (we can assume) Socrates before him, concerned himself with the problem of teaching virtue, for despite our ability to teach skills and factual knowledge, he notes, we have not had noticeable or consistent success teaching people to be good.

As Plato pondered these questions, especially within the pedagogical context of the Academy, he must have begun developing his own theories to explain and support his methodology and to answer questions in a more systematic and definitive fashion. In his middle period, the dialogues seem primarily aimed at the exposition and justification of Plato's own theories. The Republic is probably the best known of these dialogues. In it, as in the other middle-period works, the dialogic form is more superficial. Socrates argues and questions, but his interlocutors are generally limited to voicing assent and dissent. In The Republic we meet a compendious treatment of most of Plato's major concerns: the theory of Ideas, which explains the possibility of objective judgment and knowledge; the connection between virtue and knowledge; the form of a proper moral education; the true nature of humanity; the nature and structure of a properly run state.

Plato believed that there is a realm of purely intelligible entities—the Ideas or Forms—not accessible through sense perception (which can afford access only to changeable and imperfect sensible things). These Ideas are eternal, unchanging, and perfect; sensible things can copy or participate in these forms, thereby fixing, at least for a while, the ever-shifting indeterminacy of material things. Among the Ideas or Forms are forms of natural objects such as geraniums and horses, forms of artifacts such as beds and houses, and especially forms of properties and actions such as courage and, most important, the Good. Sensible things, for example, are beds because they share in the form of the bed. Whatever is good is so because it participates in the form of the Good. These Ideas are the true objects of knowledge (sensible things are too changeable and indeterminate to be true objects of knowledge), and that is the knowledge the philosopher strives for. In parts of The Republic not included here, Plato sketches out the educational program that he thinks would best prepare citizens of an ideal state to master the world of Ideas. In other parts that are included, especially the stories of the divided line and the cave, Plato discusses the value of the knowledge of the Ideas and how he envisions the realm of Ideas to be structured. The metaphysical theory of Ideas became the central supporting structure of Plato's philosophy.

In the late-period dialogues, Plato went much deeper into such philosophical problems as the nature of nonbeing, the nature of knowledge, and the constitution of a proper state, even to the point of criticizing his earlier theory of Ideas, which he does with sometimes devastating effect in the Parmenides. In the last of these dialogues, Socrates begins to recede as the major figure in favor of other players—the Eleatic Stranger in the Sophist or the Athenian Stranger in Plato's final work, the Laws. These dialogues are much more intricately argued than their predecessors and pose difficult interpretive challenges.

Often cited is English philosopher Alfred North Whitehead's remark that all of Western philosophy is but a series of footnotes to Plato. Indeed, Plato is to philosophy as Homer is to the epic, Aeschylus to tragedy, Newton to physics, or Darwin to evolutionary theory. Each had notable, even great predecessors, but each of these men was able to formulate a vision that drew together theretofore disparate activities, beliefs, and observations into a new, unified form or discipline for succeeding generations.

The Reading Context

Euthyphro

The *Euthyphro* takes place just before the trial of Socrates. (Nevertheless, it was probably written after the *Apology*.) Euthyphro's understanding of piety is perhaps representative of the views of those who brought charges of impiety against Socrates. The dialogue reaches no final answer to the central question. How, then, is Socrates to be judged guilty or innocent?

Apology

The *Apology* is thought to be a relatively faithful portrayal (though undoubtedly idealized to some extent) of Socrates' actual plea before the court. If you had been a member of the jury, how would you have voted? Does Socrates adequately distinguish himself from those to whom he believes the charges apply?

The Republic

One of the most influential books of the Western world, *The Republic* starts with an important question—what is justice?—and discusses virtually every important philosophical question before its end. But more than in the earlier dialogues, Socrates encounters relatively little resistance. As you read Plato, and especially as you read *The Republic*, extend the dialogues along the lines *you* would have followed had you been Socrates' interlocutor.

A Note on the Texts

As influential in the Western tradition as they have been, Plato's works have not always been available. Plato's school, the Academy, remained open several hundred years after his death, but the early Church fathers often knew of Plato's thought only indirectly, for example, through Plotinus. Medieval thought became deeply impregnated with the Neoplatonism inherited from Plotinus. Plato's own works, other than the *Timaeus*, were unavailable to medieval thinkers. They were reintroduced to the West at a relatively late date and constituted a major inspiration to Renaissance thinkers.

There remain today numerous manuscripts of Platonic works, but none go all the way back to Plato himself. Each differs in various ways from the others, so that constructing (or reconstructing) a reliable text from the manuscripts is a difficult enterprise. Citations of Platonic texts standardly refer to the pagination of the 1578 edition of Plato's works edited by Henri Estienne (in Latin, *Stephanus*). These Stephanus numbers appear in the margins of the following texts.

Reading Questions

Euthyphro

1. What kind of answer to the question "What is pious?" is Socrates looking for?
2. Euthyphro makes four major attempts to answer Socrates' question. What are they?
3. What is wrong with Euthyphro's answer that the pious is what is loved by the gods?
4. Is Euthyphro pious?
5. What lesson about piety emerges from this dialogue?

Apology

1. How does Socrates distinguish himself from the Sophists?
2. What is the meaning of the pronouncement by the Oracle at Delphi?
3. How does Socrates defend himself against the charge of corrupting the youth?
4. Why does Socrates philosophize?

The Republic

1. How many different definitions of justice are voiced in the first book?
2. Is it a good strategy to defend being just by trying to show that it is in one's own best interest?
3. What is the purpose of the story of Gyges?
4. Are justice in an individual and justice in a state sufficiently similar to permit inference from the nature of one to the nature of the other?
5. Where does Socrates locate temperance, wisdom, courage, and justice in the city? In the soul?
6. For what purpose or purposes does a state educate its citizens?
7. What are the differences among reason, understanding, belief, and conjecture? How do their objects differ?
8. What role does Socrates envision for the form of the Good?
9. How do the categories of the divided line correspond with the levels in the parable of the cave?

Euthyphro

EUTHYPHRO:[1] What's new, Socrates, to make you leave your usual haunts in the 2
Lyceum and spend your time here by the king-archon's court? Surely you are not
prosecuting anyone before the king-archon as I am?

SOCRATES: The Athenians do not call this a prosecution but an indictment,
Euthyphro.

E: What is this you say? Someone must have indicted you, for you are not going b
to tell me that you have indicted someone else.

S: No indeed.

E: But someone else has indicted you?

S: Quite so.

E: Who is he?

S: I do not really know him myself, Euthyphro. He is apparently young and
unknown. They call him Meletus, I believe. He belongs to the Pitthean deme, if you
know anyone from that deme called Meletus, with long hair, not much of a beard, and
a rather aquiline nose.

E: I don't know him, Socrates. What charge does he bring against you?

S: What charge? A not ignoble one I think, for it is no small thing for a young c
man to have knowledge of such an important subject. He says he knows how our young
men are corrupted and who corrupts them. He is likely to be wise, and when he sees
my ignorance corrupting his contemporaries, he proceeds to accuse me to the city as
to their mother. I think he is the only one of our public men to start out the right way, d
for it is right to care first that the young should be as good as possible, just as a good
farmer is likely to take care of the young plants first, and of the others later. So, too,
Meletus first gets rid of us who corrupt the young shoots, as he says, and then after- 3
wards he will obviously take care of the older ones and become a source of great blessings for the city, as seems likely to happen to one who started out this way.

E: I could wish this were true, Socrates, but I fear the opposite may happen. He
seems to me to start out by harming the very heart of the city by attempting to wrong
you. Tell me, what does he say you do to corrupt the young?

S: Strange things, to hear him tell it, for he says that I am a maker of gods, and b
on the ground that I create new gods while not believing in the old gods, he has
indicted me for their sake, as he puts it.

E: I understand, Socrates. This is because you say that the divine sign keeps coming to you.[2] So he has written this indictment against you as one who makes innova-

---

From Plato, *Five Dialogues*, trans. G. M. A. Grube (Indianapolis: Hackett, 1981), pp. 6–22. With permission
by Hackett Publishing Co., Inc., Indianapolis and Cambridge.

1. We know nothing about Euthyphro except what we can gather from this dialogue. He is obviously a professional priest who considers himself an expert on ritual and on piety generally and, it seems, is generally so
considered. One Euthyphro is mentioned in Plato's *Cratylus* (396d) who is given to *enthousiasmos*, inspiration
or possession, but we cannot be sure that it is the same person. [Trans. note]

2. In Plato, Socrates always speaks of his divine sign or voice as intervening to prevent him from doing or
saying something (e.g., *Apology* 31d), but never positively. The popular view was that it enabled him to foretell the future, and Euthyphro here represents that view. Note, however, that Socrates dissociates himself from
"you prophets" (3e). [Trans. note]

tions in religious matters, and he comes to court to slander you, knowing that such things are easily misrepresented to the crowd. The same is true in my case. Whenever
c   I speak of divine matters in the assembly and foretell the future, they laugh me down as if I were crazy; and yet I have foretold nothing that did not happen. Nevertheless, they envy all of us who do this. One need not worry about them, but meet them head-on.

S: My dear Euthyphro, to be laughed at does not matter perhaps, for the Athenians do not mind anyone they think clever, as long as he does not teach his own wis-
d   dom, but if they think that he makes others to be like himself they get angry, whether through envy, as you say, or for some other reason.

E: I have certainly no desire to test their feelings towards me in this matter.

S: Perhaps you seem to make yourself but rarely available, and not to be willing to teach your own wisdom, but I'm afraid that my liking for people makes them think that I pour out to anybody anything I have to say, not only without charging a fee but even glad to reward anyone who is willing to listen. If then they were intending to
e   laugh at me, as you say they laugh at you, there would be nothing unpleasant in their spending their time in court laughing and jesting, but if they are going to be serious, the outcome is not clear except to you prophets.

E: Perhaps it will come to nothing, Socrates, and you will fight your case as you think best, as I think I will mine.

S: What is your case, Euthyphro? Are you the defendant or the prosecutor?

E: The prosecutor.

S: Whom do you prosecute?

4   E: One whom I am thought crazy to prosecute.

S: Are you pursuing someone who will easily escape you?

E: Far from it, for he is quite old.

S: Who is it?

E: My father.

S: My dear sir! Your own father?

E: Certainly.

S: What is the charge? What is the case about?

E: Murder, Socrates.

S: Good heavens! Certainly, Euthyphro, most men would not know how they
b   could do this and be right. It is not the part of anyone to do this, but of one who is far advanced in wisdom.

E: Yes, by Zeus, Socrates, that is so.

S: Is then the man your father killed one of your relatives? Or is that obvious, for you would not prosecute your father for the murder of a stranger.

E: It is ridiculous, Socrates, for you to think that it makes any difference whether the victim is a stranger or a relative. One should only watch whether the killer acted
c   justly or not; if he acted justly, let him go, but if not, one should prosecute, even if the killer shares your hearth and table. The pollution is the same if you knowingly keep company with such a man and do not cleanse yourself and him by bringing him to justice. The victim was a dependent of mine, and when we were farming in Naxos he was a servant of ours. He killed one of our household slaves in drunken anger, so my father bound him hand and foot and threw him in a ditch, then sent a man here to
d   enquire from the priest what should be done. During that time he gave no thought or

care to the bound man, as being a killer, and it was no matter if he died, which he did. Hunger and cold and his bonds caused his death before the messenger came back from the seer. Both my father and my other relatives are angry that I am prosecuting my father for murder on behalf of a murderer when he hadn't even killed him, they say, and even if he had, the dead man does not deserve a thought, since he was a killer. For, they say, it is impious for a son to prosecute his father for murder. But their ideas of the divine attitude to piety and impiety are wrong, Socrates.

    e

S: Whereas, by Zeus, Euthyphro, you think that your knowledge of the divine, and of piety and impiety, is so accurate that, when those things happened as you say, you have no fear of having acted impiously in bringing your father to trial?

E: I should be of no use, Socrates, and Euthyphro would not be superior to the majority of men, if I did not have accurate knowledge of all such things.

    5

S: It is indeed most important, my admirable Euthyphro, that I should become your pupil, and as regards this indictment challenge Meletus about these very things and say to him: that in the past too I considered knowledge about the divine to be most important, and that now that he says that I am guilty of improvising and innovating about the gods I have become your pupil. I would say to him: "If, Meletus, you agree that Euthyphro is wise in these matters, consider me, too, to have the right beliefs and do not bring me to trial. If you do not think so, then prosecute that teacher of mine, not me, for corrupting the older men, me and his own father, by teaching me and by exhorting and punishing him." If he is not convinced, and does not discharge me or indict you instead of me, I shall repeat the same challenge in court.

    b

E: Yes, by Zeus, Socrates, and, if he should try to indict me, I think I would find his weak spots and the talk in court would be about him rather than about me.

    c

S: It is because I realize this that I am eager to become your pupil, my dear friend. I know that other people as well as this Meletus do not even seem to notice you, whereas he sees me so sharply and clearly that he indicts me for ungodliness. So tell me now, by Zeus, what you just now maintained you clearly knew: what kind of thing do you say that godliness and ungodliness are, both as regards murder and other things; or is the pious not the same and alike in every action, and the impious the opposite of all that is pious and like itself, and everything that is to be impious presents us with one form[3] or appearance in so far as it is impious?

    d

E: Most certainly, Socrates.

S: Tell me then, what is the pious, and what the impious, do you say?

E: I say that the pious is to do what I am doing now, to prosecute the wrongdoer, be it about murder or temple robbery or anything else, whether the wrongdoer is your father or your mother or anyone else; not to prosecute is impious. And observe, Socrates, that I can quote the law as a great proof that this is so. I have already said to others that such actions are right, not to favour the ungodly, whoever they are. These people themselves believe that Zeus is the best and most just of the gods, yet

    e

    6

---

3. This is the kind of passage that makes it easier for us to follow the transition from Socrates' universal definitions to the Platonic theory of separately existent eternal universal Forms. The words *eidos* and *idea*, the technical terms for the Platonic Forms, commonly mean physical stature or bodily appearance. As we apply a common epithet, in this case *pious*, to different actions or things, these must have a common characteristic, present a common appearance or form, to justify the use of the same term, but in the early dialogues, as here, it seems to be thought of as immanent in the particulars and without separate existence. The same is true of 6d where the word "Form" is also used. [Trans. note]

they agree that he bound his father because he unjustly swallowed his sons, and that he in turn castrated his father for similar reasons. But they are angry with me because I am prosecuting my father for his wrongdoing. They contradict themselves in what they say about the gods and about me.

S: Indeed, Euthyphro, this is the reason why I am a defendant in the case, because I find it hard to accept things like that being said about the gods, and it is likely to be the reason why I shall be told I do wrong. Now, however, if you, who have full knowl-
b edge of such things, share their opinions, then we must agree with them too, it would seem. For what are we to say, we who agree that we ourselves have no knowledge of them? Tell me, by the god of friendship, do you really believe these things are true?

E: Yes, Socrates, and so are even more surprising things, of which the majority has no knowledge.

S: And do you believe that there really is war among the gods, and terrible enmi-
c ties and battles, and other such things as are told by the poets, and other sacred stories such as are embroidered by good writers and by representations of which the robe of the goddess is adorned when it is carried up to the Acropolis? Are we to say these things are true, Euthyphro?

E: Not only these, Socrates, but, as I was saying just now, I will, if you wish, relate many other things about the gods which I know will amaze you.

S: I should not be surprised, but you will tell me these at leisure some other time.
d For now, try to tell me more clearly what I was asking just now, for, my friend, you did not teach me adequately when I asked you what the pious was, but you told me that what you are doing now, prosecuting your father for murder, is pious.

E: And I told the truth, Socrates.

S: Perhaps. You agree, however, that there are many other pious actions.

E: There are.

S: Bear in mind then that I did not bid you tell me one or two of the many pious actions but that form itself that makes all pious actions pious, for you agreed that all
e impious actions are impious and all pious actions pious through one form, or don't you remember?

E: I do.

S: Tell me then what this form itself is, so that I may look upon it, and using it as a model, say that any action of yours or another's that is of that kind is pious, and if it is not that it is not.

E: If that is how you want it, Socrates, that is how I will tell you.

S: That is what I want.
7 E: Well then, what is dear to the gods is pious, what is not is impious.

S: Splendid, Euthyphro! You have now answered in the way I wanted. Whether your answer is true I do not know yet, but you will obviously show me that what you say is true.

E: Certainly.

S: Come then, let us examine what we mean. An action or a man dear to the gods is pious, but an action or a man hated by the gods is impious. They are not the same, but quite opposite, the pious and the impious. Is that not so?

E: It is indeed.

S: And that seems to be a good statement?

E: I think so, Socrates.   b

S: We have also stated that the gods are in a state of discord, that they are at odds with each other, Euthyphro, and that they are at enmity with each other. Has that, too, been said?

E: It has.

S: What are the subjects of difference that cause hatred and anger? Let us look at it this way. If you and I were to differ about numbers as to which is the greater, would this difference make us enemies and angry with each other, or would we proceed to count and soon resolve our difference about this?   c

E: We would certainly do so.

S: Again, if we differed about the larger and the smaller, we would turn to measurement and soon cease to differ.

E: That is so.

S: And about the heavier and the lighter, we would resort to weighing and be reconciled.

E: Of course.

S: What subject of difference would make us angry and hostile to each other if we were unable to come to a decision? Perhaps you do not have an answer ready, but examine as I tell you whether these subjects are the just and the unjust, the beautiful and   d the ugly, the good and the bad. Are these not the subjects of difference about which, when we are unable to come to a satisfactory decision, you and I and other men become hostile to each other whenever we do?

E: That is the difference, Socrates, about those subjects.

S: What about the gods, Euthyphro? If indeed they have differences, will it not be about these same subjects?

E: It certainly must be so.

S: Then according to your argument, my good Euthyphro, different gods consider   e different things to be just, beautiful, ugly, good, and bad, for they would not be at odds with one another unless they differed about these subjects, would they?

E: You are right.

S: And they like what each of them considers beautiful, good, and just, and hate the opposites of these?

E: Certainly.

S: But you say that the same things are considered just by some gods and unjust by others, and as they dispute about these things they are at odds and at war with each   8 other. Is that not so?

E: It is.

S: The same things then are loved by the gods and hated by the gods, and would be both god-loved and god-hated.

E: It seems likely.

S: And the same things would be both pious and impious, according to this argument?

E: I'm afraid so.

S: So you did not answer my question, you surprising man. I did not ask you what same thing is both pious and impious, and it appears that what is loved by the gods is   b also hated by them. So it is in no way surprising if your present action, namely punishing your father, may be pleasing to Zeus but displeasing to Kronos and Ouranos, pleasing to Hephaestus but displeasing to Hera, and so with any other gods who differ from each other on this subject.

E: I think, Socrates, that on this subject no gods would differ from one another, that whoever has killed anyone unjustly should pay the penalty.

c   S: Well now, Euthyphro, have you ever heard any man maintaining that one who has killed or done anything else unjustly should not pay the penalty?

E: They never cease to dispute on this subject, both elsewhere and in the courts, for when they have committed many wrongs they do and say anything to avoid the penalty.

S: Do they agree they have done wrong, Euthyphro, and in spite of so agreeing do they nevertheless say they should not be punished?

E: No, they do not agree on that point.

S: So they do not say or do anything. For they do not venture to say this, or dispute that they must not pay the penalty if they have done wrong, but I think they deny

d   doing wrong. Is that not so?

E: That is true.

S: Then they do not dispute that the wrongdoer must be punished, but they may disagree as to who the wrongdoer is, what he did and when.

E: You are right.

S: Do not the gods have the same experience, if indeed they are at odds with each other about the just and the unjust, as your argument maintains? Some assert that they

e   wrong one another, while others deny it, but no one among gods or men ventures to say that the wrongdoer must not be punished.

E: Yes, that is true, Socrates, as to the main point.

S: And those who disagree, whether men or gods, dispute about each action, if indeed the gods disagree. Some say it is done justly, others unjustly. Is that not so?

E: Yes, indeed.

9   S: Come now, my dear Euthyphro, tell me, too, that I may become wiser, what proof you have that all the gods consider that man to have been killed unjustly who became a murderer while in your service, was bound by the master of his victim, and died in his bonds before the one who bound him found out from the seers what was to be done with him, and that it is right for a son to denounce and to prosecute his father on behalf of such a man. Come, try to show me a clear sign that all the gods

b   definitely believe this action to be right. If you can give me adequate proof of this, I shall never cease to extol your wisdom.

E: This is perhaps no light task, Socrates, though I could show you very clearly.

S: I understand that you think me more dull-witted than the jury, as you will obviously show them that these actions were unjust and that all the gods hate such actions.

E: I will show it to them clearly, Socrates, if only they will listen to me.

c   S: They will listen if they think you show them well. But this thought came to me as you were speaking, and I am examining it, saying to myself: "If Euthyphro shows me conclusively that all the gods consider such a death unjust, to what greater extent have I learned from him the nature of piety and impiety? This action would then, it seems, be hated by the gods, but the pious and the impious were not now defined, for what is hated by the gods has also been shown to be loved by them." So I will not insist on this point; let us assume, if you wish, that all the gods consider this unjust and that they all hate it. However, is this the correction we are making in our discussion, that what all the gods hate is impious, and what they all love is pious, and that what some gods love and others hate is neither or both? Is that how you now wish us to define piety and impiety?

E: What prevents us from doing so, Socrates?

S: For my part nothing, Euthyphro, but you look whether on your part this proposal will enable you to teach me most easily what you promised.

E: I would certainly say that the pious is what all the gods love, and the opposite, what all the gods hate, is the impious.

S: Then let us again examine whether that is a sound statement, or do we let it pass, and if one of us, or someone else, merely says that something is so, do we accept that it is so? Or should we examine what the speaker means?

E: We must examine it, but I certainly think that this is now a fine statement.

S: We shall soon know better whether it is. Consider this: Is the pious loved by the gods because it is pious, or is it pious because it is loved by the gods?

E: I don't know what you mean, Socrates.

S: I shall try to explain more clearly: we speak of something being carried[4] and something carrying, of something being led and something leading, of something being seen and something seeing, and you understand that these things are all different from one another and how they differ?

E: I think I do.

S: So there is something being loved and something loving, and the loving is a different thing.

E: Of course.

S: Tell me then whether that which is being carried is being carried because someone carries it or for some other reason.

E: No, that is the reason.

S: And that which is being led is so because someone leads it, and that which is being seen because someone sees it?

E: Certainly.

S: It is not seen by someone because it is being seen but on the contrary it is being seen because someone sees it, nor is it because it is being led that someone leads it but because someone leads it that it is being led; nor does someone carry an object because it is being carried, but it is being carried because someone carries it. Is what I want to say clear, Euthyphro? I want to say this, namely, that if anything comes to be, or is affected, it does not come to be because it is coming to be, but it is coming to be because it comes to be; nor is it affected because it is being affected but because something affects it. Or do you not agree?

---

4. This is the present participle form of the verb *pheromenon*, literally *being-carried*. The following passage is somewhat obscure, especially in translation, but the general meaning is clear. Plato points out that this participle simply indicates the object of an action of carrying, seeing, loving, etc. It follows from the action and adds nothing new, the action being prior to it, not following from it, and a thing is said to be loved because someone loves it, not vice versa. To say therefore that the pious is being loved by the gods says no more than that the gods love it. Euthyphro, however, also agrees that the pious is loved by the gods because of its nature (because it is pious), but the fact of its being loved by the gods does not define that nature, and as a definition is therefore unsatisfactory. It only indicates a quality or affect of the pious, and the pious is therefore still to be defined (11a7). [Trans. note]

E: I do.

S: What is being loved is either something that comes to be or something that is affected by something?

E: Certainly.

S: So it is in the same case as the things just mentioned; it is not loved by those who love it because it is being loved, but it is being loved because they love it?

E: Necessarily.

d   S: What then do we say about the pious, Euthyphro? Surely that it is loved by all the gods, according to what you say?

E: Yes.

S: Is it loved because it is pious, or for some other reason?

E: For no other reason.

S: It is loved then because it is pious, but it is not pious because it is loved?

E: Apparently.

S: And because it is loved by the gods it is being loved and is dear to the gods?

E: Of course.

S: The god-beloved is then not the same as the pious, Euthyphro, nor the pious the same as the god-beloved, as you say it is, but one differs from the other.

e   E: How so, Socrates?

S: Because we agree that the pious is beloved for the reason that it is pious, but it is not pious because it is loved. Is that not so?

E: Yes.

S: And that the god-beloved, on the other hand, is so because it is loved by the gods, by the very fact of being loved, but it is not loved because it is god-beloved.

E: True.

S: But if the god-beloved and the pious were the same, my dear Euthyphro, and

11 the pious were loved because it was pious, then the god-beloved would be loved because it was god-beloved, and if the god-beloved was god-beloved because it was loved by the gods, then the pious would also be pious because it was loved by the gods; but now you see that they are in opposite cases as being altogether different from each other: the one is of a nature to be loved because it is loved, the other is loved because it is of a nature to be loved. I'm afraid, Euthyphro, that when you were asked what piety is, you did not wish to make its nature clear to me, but you told me an affect or quality of it, that the pious has the quality of being loved by all the gods, but you have not

b yet told me what the pious is. Now, if you will, do not hide things from me but tell me again from the beginning what piety is, whether loved by the gods or having some other quality—we shall not quarrel about that—but be keen to tell me what the pious and the impious are.

E: But Socrates, I have no way of telling you what I have in mind, for whatever proposition we put forward goes around and refuses to stay put where we establish it.

c S: Your statements, Euthyphro, seem to belong to my ancestor, Daedalus. If I were stating them and putting them forward, you would perhaps be making fun of me and say that because of my kinship with him my conclusions in discussion run away and will not stay where one puts them. As these propositions are yours, however, we need some other jest, for they will not stay put for you, as you say yourself.

E: I think the same jest will do for our discussion, Socrates, for I am not the one who makes them go round and not remain in the same place; it is you who are the Daedalus; for as far as I am concerned they would remain as they were.   d

S: It looks as if I was cleverer than Daedalus in using my skill, my friend, in so far as he could only cause to move the things he made himself, but I can make other people's move as well as my own. And the smartest part of my skill is that I am clever without wanting to be, for I would rather have your statements to me remain unmoved than possess the wealth of Tantalus as well as the cleverness of Daedalus. But enough   e
of this. Since I think you are making unnecessary difficulties, I am as eager as you are to find a way to teach me about piety, and do not give up before you do. See whether you think all that is pious is of necessity just.

E: I think so.

S: And is then all that is just pious? Or is all that is pious just, but not all that is just pious, but some of it is and some is not?   12

E: I do not follow what you are saying, Socrates.

S: Yet you are younger than I by as much as you are wiser. As I say, you are making difficulties because of your wealth of wisdom. Pull yourself together, my dear sir, what I am saying is not difficult to grasp. I am saying the opposite of what the poet said who wrote:
You do not wish to name Zeus, who had done it, and who made all things grow, for
where there is fear there is also shame.   b
I disagree with the poet. Shall I tell you why?

E: Please do.

S: I do not think that "where there is fear there is also shame," for I think that many people who fear disease and poverty and many other such things feel fear, but are not ashamed of the things they fear. Do you not think so?

E: I do indeed.

S: But where there is shame, there is also fear. For is there anyone who, in feeling shame and embarrassment at anything, does not also at the same time fear and dread   c
a reputation for wickedness?

E: He is certainly afraid.

S: It is then not right to say "where there is fear there is also shame," but that where there is shame there is also fear, for fear covers a larger area than shame. Shame is a part of fear just as odd is a part of number, with the result that it is not true that where there is number there is also oddness, but that where there is oddness there is also number. Do you follow me now?

E: Surely.

S: This is the kind of thing I was asking before, whether where there is piety there is also justice, but where there is justice there is not always piety, for the pious is a part   d
of justice. Shall we say that, or do you think otherwise?

E: No, but like that, for what you say appears to be right.

S: See what comes next: if the pious is a part of the just, we must, it seems, find out what part of the just it is. Now if you asked me something of what we mentioned just now, such as what part of number is the even, and what number that is, I would say it is the number that is divisible into two equal, not unequal, parts. Or do you not think so?

E: I do.

e   S: Try in this way to tell me what part of the just the pious is, in order to tell
Meletus not to wrong us any more and not to indict me for ungodliness, since I have
learned from you sufficiently what is godly and pious and what is not.

        E: I think, Socrates, that the godly and pious is the part of the just that is con-
cerned with the care of the gods, while that concerned with the care of men is the
remaining part of justice.

        S: You seem to me to put that very well, but I still need a bit of information. I do
13   not know yet what you mean by care, for you do not mean the care of the gods in the
same sense as the care of other things, as, for example, we say, don't we, that not everyone knows how to care for horses, but the horse breeder does.

        E: Yes, I do mean it that way.

        S: So horse breeding is the care of horses.

        E: Yes.

        S: Nor does everyone know how to care for dogs, but the hunter does.

        E: That is so.

        S: So hunting is the care of dogs.

b   E: Yes.

        S: And cattle raising is the care of cattle.

        E: Quite so.

        S: While piety and godliness is the care of the gods, Euthyphro. Is that what you
mean?

        E: It is.

        S: Now care in each case has the same effect; it aims at the good and the benefit
of the object cared for, as you can see that horses cared for by horse breeders are
benefited and become better. Or do you not think so?

        E: I do.

        S: So dogs are benefited by dog breeding, cattle by cattle raising, and so with all
c   the others. Or do you think that care aims to harm the object of its care?

        E: By Zeus, no.

        S: It aims to benefit the object of its care?

        E: Of course.

        S: Is piety then, which is the care of the gods, also to benefit the gods and make
them better? Would you agree that when you do something pious you make some one
of the gods better?

        E: By Zeus, no.

        S: Nor do I think that this is what you mean—far from it—but that is why I asked
d   you what you meant by the care of gods, because I did not believe you meant this kind
of care.

        E: Quite right, Socrates, that is not the kind of care I mean.

        S: Very well, but what kind of care of the gods would piety be?

        E: The kind of care, Socrates, that slaves take of their masters.

        S: I understand. It is likely to be a kind of service of the gods.

        E: Quite so.

        S: Could you tell me to the achievement of what goal service to doctors tends? Is
it not, do you think, to achieving health?

        E: I think so.

e   S: What about service to shipbuilders? To what achievement is it directed?

E: Clearly, Socrates, to the building of a ship.

S: And service to housebuilders to the building of a house?

E: Yes.

S: Tell me then, my good sir, to the achievement of what aim does service to the gods tend? You obviously know since you say that you, of all men, have the best knowledge of the divine.

E: And I am telling the truth, Socrates.

S: Tell me then, by Zeus, what is that excellent aim that the gods achieve, using us as their servants?

E: Many fine things, Socrates.

S: So do generals, my friend. Nevertheless you could easily tell me their main concern, which is to achieve victory in war, is it not?

14

E: Of course.

S: The farmers too, I think, achieve many fine things, but the main point of their efforts is to produce food from the earth.

E: Quite so.

S: Well then, how would you sum up the many fine things that the gods achieve?

E: I told you a short while ago, Socrates, that it is a considerable task to acquire any precise knowledge of these things, but, to put it simply, I say that if a man knows how to say and do what is pleasing to the gods at prayer and sacrifice, those are pious actions such as preserve both private houses and public affairs of state. The opposite of these pleasing actions are impious and overturn and destroy everything.

b

S: You could tell me in far fewer words, if you were willing, the sum of what I asked, Euthyphro, but you are not keen to teach me, that is clear. You were on the point of doing so, but you turned away. If you had given that answer, I should now have acquired from you sufficient knowledge of the nature of piety. As it is, the lover of inquiry must follow his beloved wherever it may lead him. Once more then, what do you say that piety and the pious are? Are they a knowledge of how to sacrifice and pray?

c

E: They are.

S: To sacrifice is to make a gift to the gods, whereas to pray is to beg from the gods?

E: Definitely, Socrates.

S: It would follow from this statement that piety would be a knowledge of how to give to, and beg from, the gods.

d

E: You understood what I said very well, Socrates.

S: That is because I am so desirous of your wisdom, and I concentrate my mind on it, so that no word of yours may fall to the ground. But tell me, what is this service to the gods? You say it is to beg from them and to give to them?

E: I do.

S: And to beg correctly would be to ask from them things that we need?

E: What else?

S: And to give correctly is to give them what they need from us, for it would not be skillful to bring gifts to anyone that are in no way needed.

e

E: True, Socrates.

S: Piety would then be a sort of trading skill between gods and men?

E: Trading yes, if you prefer to call it that.

S: I prefer nothing, unless it is true. But tell me, what benefit do the gods derive from the gifts they receive from us? What they give us is obvious to all. There is for us

15   no good that we do not receive from them, but how are they benefited by what they
      receive from us? Or do we have such an advantage over them in the trade that we
      receive all our blessings from them and they receive nothing from us?

          E: Do you suppose, Socrates, that the gods are benefited by what they receive from
      us?

          S: What could those gifts from us to the gods be, Euthyphro?

          E: What else, do you think, than honour, reverence, and what I mentioned just
      now, gratitude?

b   S: The pious is then, Euthyphro, pleasing to the gods, but not beneficial or dear
      to them?

          E: I think it is of all things most dear to them.

          S: So the pious is once again what is dear to the gods.

          E: Most certainly.

          S: When you say this, will you be surprised if your arguments seem to move about
      instead of staying put? And will you accuse me of being Daedalus who makes them
      move, though you are yourself much more skillful than Daedalus and make them go
      round in a circle? Or do you not realize that our argument has moved around and come
c   again to the same place? You surely remember that earlier the pious and the god-
      beloved were shown not to be the same but different from each other. Or do you not
      remember?

          E: I do.

          S: Do you then not realize now that you are saying that what is dear to the gods
      is the pious? Is this not the same as the god-beloved? Or is it not?

          E: It certainly is.

          S: Either we were wrong when we agreed before, or, if we were right then, we are
      wrong now.

          E: That seems to be so.

          S: So we must investigate again from the beginning what piety is, as I shall not
d   willingly give up before I learn this. Do not think me unworthy, but concentrate your
      attention and tell the truth. For you know it, if any man does, and I must not let you
      go, like Proteus, before you tell me. If you had no clear knowledge of piety and impiety
      you would never have ventured to prosecute your old father for murder on behalf of a
      servant. For fear of the gods you would have been afraid to take the risk lest you should
      not be acting rightly, and would have been ashamed before men, but now I know well
e   that you believe you have clear knowledge of piety and impiety. So tell me, my good
      Euthyphro, and do not hide what you think it is.

          E: Some other time, Socrates, for I am in a hurry now, and it is time for me to go.

          S: What a thing to do, my friend! By going you have cast me down from a great
      hope I had, that I would learn from you the nature of the pious and the impious and
16   so escape Meletus' indictment by showing him that I had acquired wisdom in divine
      matters from Euthyphro, and my ignorance would no longer cause me to be careless
      and inventive about such things, and that I would be better for the rest of my life.

Apology

I do not know, men of Athens, how my accusers affected you; as for me, I was almost 17
carried away in spite of myself, so persuasively did they speak. And yet, hardly anything of what they said is true. Of the many lies they told, one in particular surprised
me, namely that you should be careful not to be deceived by an accomplished speaker
like me. That they were not ashamed to be immediately proved wrong by the facts, b
when I show myself not to be an accomplished speaker at all, that I thought was most
shameless on their part—unless indeed they call an accomplished speaker the man
who speaks the truth. If they mean that, I would agree that I am an orator, but not after
their manner, for indeed, as I say, practically nothing they said was true. From me you
will hear the whole truth, though not, by Zeus, gentlemen, expressed in embroidered c
and stylized phrases like theirs, but things spoken at random and expressed in the first
words that come to mind, for I put my trust in the justice of what I say, and let none
of you expect anything else. It would not be fitting at my age, as it might be for a young
man, to toy with words when I appear before you.

One thing I do ask and beg of you, gentlemen: if you hear me making my defence
in the same kind of language as I am accustomed to use in the market place by the
bankers' tables,[1] where many of you have heard me, and elsewhere, do not be surprised
or create a disturbance on that account. The position is this: this is my first appear- d
ance in a lawcourt, at the age of seventy; I am therefore simply a stranger to the manner of speaking here. Just as if I were really a stranger, you would certainly excuse me
if I spoke in that dialect and manner in which I had been brought up, so too my present 18
request seems a just one, for you to pay no attention to my manner of speech—be it
better or worse—but to concentrate your attention on whether what I say is just or not,
for the excellence of a judge lies in this, as that of a speaker lies in telling the truth.

It is right for me, gentlemen, to defend myself first against the first lying accusations made against me and my first accusers, and then against the later accusations
and the later accusers. There have been many who have accused me to you for many b
years now, and none of their accusations are true. These I fear much more than I fear
Anytus and his friends, though they too are formidable. These earlier ones, however,
are more so, gentlemen; they got hold of most of you from childhood, persuaded you
and accused me quite falsely, saying that there is a man called Socrates, a wise man,
a student of all things in the sky and below the earth, who makes the worse argument c
the stronger. Those who spread that rumour, gentlemen, are my dangerous accusers,
for their hearers believe that those who study these things do not even believe in the
gods. Moreover, these accusers are numerous, and have been at it a long time; also,
they spoke to you at an age when you would most readily believe them, some of you
being children and adolescents, and they won their case by default, as there was no
defence.

From Plato, *Five Dialogues*, trans. G. M. A. Grube (Indianapolis: Hackett, 1981), pp. 24–44. With permission
by Hackett Publishing Co., Inc., Indianapolis and Cambridge.

1. The bankers or money-changers had their counters in the market place. It seems that this was a favourite
place for gossip. [Trans. note]

What is most absurd in all this is that one cannot even know or mention their
d   names unless one of them is a writer of comedies.[2] Those who maliciously and slanderously persuaded you—who also, when persuaded themselves then persuaded others—
all those are most difficult to deal with: one cannot bring one of them into court or
refute him; one must simply fight with shadows, as it were, in making one's defence,
and cross-examine when no one answers. I want you to realize too that my accusers are
of two kinds: those who have accused me recently, and the old ones I mention; and
to think that I must first defend myself against the latter, for you have also heard their
e   accusations first, and to a much greater extent than the more recent.

Very well then. I must surely defend myself and attempt to uproot from your minds
19 in so short a time the slander that has resided there so long. I wish this may happen,
if it is in any way better for you and me, and that my defence may be successful, but
I think this is very difficult and I am fully aware of how difficult it is. Even so, let the
matter proceed as the god may wish, but I must obey the law and make my defence.

Let us then take up the case from its beginning. What is the accusation from which
b   arose the slander in which Meletus trusted when he wrote out the charge against me?
What did they say when they slandered me? I must, as if they were my actual prosecu-
tors, read the affidavit they would have sworn. It goes something like this: Socrates is
guilty of wrongdoing in that he busies himself studying things in the sky and below the
earth; he makes the worse into the stronger argument, and he teaches these same
c   things to others. You have seen this yourselves in the comedy of Aristophanes, a
Socrates swinging about there, saying he was walking on air and talking a lot of other
nonsense about things of which I know nothing at all. I do not speak in contempt of
such knowledge, if someone is wise in these things—lest Meletus bring more cases
against me—but, gentlemen, I have no part in it, and on this point I call upon the
majority of you as witnesses. I think it right that all those of you who have heard me
d   conversing, and many of you have, should tell each other if anyone of you has ever
heard me discussing such subjects to any extent at all. From this you will learn that the
other things said about me by the majority are of the same kind.

Not one of them is true. And if you have heard from anyone that I undertake to
teach people and charge a fee for it, that is not true either. Yet I think it a fine thing
e   to be able to teach people as Gorgias of Leontini does, and Prodicus of Ceos, and Hippias of Elis.[3] Each of these men can go to any city and persuade the young, who can
keep company with anyone of their own fellow-citizens they want without paying, to
20 leave the company of these, to join with themselves, pay them a fee, and be grateful
to them besides. Indeed, I learned that there is another wise man from Paros who is
visiting us, for I met a man who has spent more money on Sophists than everybody
else put together, Callias, the son of Hipponicus. So I asked him—he has two sons—
"Callias," I said, "if your sons were colts or calves, we could find and engage a supervisor

---

2. This refers in particular to Aristophanes, whose comedy, *The Clouds*, produced in 423 B.C., ridiculed the
(imaginary) school of Socrates. [Trans. note]

3. These were all well-known Sophists. Gorgias, after whom Plato named one of his dialogues, was a
celebrated rhetorician and teacher of rhetoric. He came to Athens in 427 B.C., and his rhetorical tricks took
the city by storm. Two dialogues, the authenticity of which has been doubted, are named after Hippias, whose
knowledge was encyclopedic. Prodicus was known for his insistence on the precise meaning of words. Both
he and Hippias are characters in the *Protagoras* (named after another famous Sophist). [Trans. note]

for them who would make them excel in their proper qualities, some horse breeder or b
farmer. Now since they are men, whom do you have in mind to supervise them? Who
is an expert in this kind of excellence, the human and social kind? I think you must
have given thought to this since you have sons. Is there such a person," I asked, "or is
there not?" "Certainly there is," he said. "Who is he?" I asked, "What is his name, where
is he from? and what is his fee?" "His name, Socrates, is Evenus, he comes from Paros,
and his fee is five minas." I thought Evenus a happy man, if he really possesses this art, c
and teaches for so moderate a fee. Certainly I would pride and preen myself if I had this
knowledge, but I do not have it, gentlemen.

One of you might perhaps interrupt me and say: "But Socrates, what is your occupation? From where have these slanders come? For surely if you did not busy yourself with
something out of the common, all these rumours and talk would not have arisen
unless you did something other than most people. Tell us what it is, that we may not
speak inadvisedly about you." Anyone who says that seems to be right, and I will try d
to show you what has caused this reputation and slander. Listen then. Perhaps some
of you will think I am jesting, but be sure that all that I shall say is true. What has
caused my reputation is none other than a certain kind of wisdom. What kind of wisdom? Human wisdom, perhaps. It may be that I really possess this, while those whom
I mentioned just now are wise with a wisdom more than human; else I cannot explain e
it, for I certainly do not possess it, and whoever says I do is lying and speaks to slander
me. Do not create a disturbance, gentlemen, even if you think I am boasting, for the
story I shall tell does not originate with me, but I will refer you to a trustworthy source.
I shall call upon the god at Delphi as witness to the existence and nature of my wisdom, if it be such. You know Chairephon. He was my friend from youth, and the friend 21
of most of you, as he shared your exile and your return. You surely know the kind of
man he was, how impulsive in any course of action. He went to Delphi at one time
and ventured to ask the oracle—as I say, gentlemen, do not create a disturbance—he
asked if any man was wiser than I, and the Pythian replied that no one was wiser.
Chairephon is dead, but his brother will testify to you about this.

Consider that I tell you this because I would inform you about the origin of the b
slander. When I heard of this reply I asked myself: "Whatever does the god mean?
What is his riddle? I am very conscious that I am not wise at all; what then does he
mean by saying that I am the wisest? For surely he does not lie; it is not legitimate for
him to do so." For a long time I was at a loss as to his meaning; then I very reluctantly
turned to some such investigation as this: I went to one of those reputed wise, thinking
that there, if anywhere, I could refute the oracle and say to it: "This man is wiser than c
I, but you said I was." Then, when I examined this man—there is no need for me to tell
you his name, he was one of our public men—my experience was something like this:
I thought that he appeared wise to many people and especially to himself, but he was
not. I then tried to show him that he thought himself wise, but that he was not. As d
a result he came to dislike me, and so did many of the bystanders. So I withdrew and
thought to myself: "I am wiser than this man; it is likely that neither of us knows anything worthwhile, but he thinks he knows something when he does not, whereas when
I do not know, neither do I think I know; so I am likely to be wiser than he to this small
extent, that I do not think I know what I do not know." After this I approached
another man, one of those thought to be wiser than he, and I thought the same thing, e
and so I came to be disliked both by him and by many others.

After that I proceeded systematically. I realized, to my sorrow and alarm, that I was getting unpopular, but I thought that I must attach the greatest importance to the god's oracle, so I must go to all those who had any reputation for knowledge to examine

22   its meaning. And by the dog,[4] gentlemen of the jury—for I must tell you the truth—I experienced something like this: in my investigation in the service of the god I found that those who had the highest reputation were nearly the most deficient, while those who were thought to be inferior were more knowledgeable. I must give you an account of my journeyings as if they were labours I had undertaken to prove the oracle irrefutable. After the politicians, I went to the poets, the writers of tragedies and dithyrambs

b   and the others, intending in their case to catch myself being more ignorant then they. So I took up those poems with which they seemed to have taken most trouble and asked them what they meant, in order that I might at the same time learn something from them. I am ashamed to tell you the truth, gentlemen, but I must. Almost all the bystanders might have explained the poems better than their authors could. I soon

c   realized that poets do not compose their poems with knowledge, but by some inborn talent and by inspiration, like seers and prophets who also say many fine things without any understanding of what they say. The poets seemed to me to have had a similar experience. At the same time I saw that, because of their poetry, they thought themselves very wise men in other respects, which they were not. So there again I withdrew, thinking that I had the same advantage over them as I had over the politicians.

Finally I went to the craftsmen, for I was conscious of knowing practically nothing,

d   and I knew that I would find that they had knowledge of many fine things. In this I was not mistaken; they knew things I did not know, and to that extent they were wiser than I. But, gentlemen of the jury, the good craftsmen seemed to me to have the same fault as the poets: each of them, because of his success at his craft, thought himself very wise in other most important pursuits, and this error of theirs overshadowed the

e   wisdom they had, so that I asked myself, on behalf of the oracle, whether I should prefer to be as I am, with neither their wisdom nor their ignorance, or to have both. The answer I gave myself and the oracle was that it was to my advantage to be as I am.

As a result of this investigation, gentlemen of the jury, I acquired much unpopular-

23   ity, of a kind that is hard to deal with and is a heavy burden; many slanders came from these people and a reputation for wisdom, for in each case the bystanders thought that I myself possessed the wisdom that I proved that my interlocutor did not have. What is probable, gentlemen, is that in fact the god is wise and that his oracular response

b   meant that human wisdom is worth little or nothing, and that when he says this man, Socrates, he is using my name as an example, as if he said: "This man among you, mortals, is wisest who, like Socrates, understands that his wisdom is worthless." So even now I continue this investigation as the god bade me—and I go around seeking out anyone, citizen or stranger, whom I think wise. Then if I do not think he is, I come to the assistance of the god and show him that he is not wise. Because of this occupation, I do not have the leisure to engage in public affairs to any extent, nor indeed to look after my own, but I live in great poverty because of my service to the god.

---

4. A curious oath, occasionally used by Socrates, it appears in a longer form in the *Gorgias* (482b) as "by the dog, the god of the Egyptians." [Trans. note]

Furthermore, the young men who follow me around of their own free will, those c who have most leisure, the sons of the very rich, take pleasure in hearing people questioned; they themselves often imitate me and try to question others. I think they find an abundance of men who believe they have some knowledge but know little or nothing. The result is that those whom they question are angry, not with themselves but with me. They say: "That man Socrates is a pestilential fellow who corrupts the d young." If one asks them what he does and what he teaches to corrupt them, they are silent, as they do not know, but, so as not to appear at a loss, they mention those accusations that are available against all philosophers, about "things in the sky and things below the earth," about "not believing in the gods" and "making the worse the stronger argument;" they would not want to tell the truth, I'm sure, that they have been proved to lay claim to knowledge when they know nothing. These people are ambitious, violent and numerous; they are continually and convincingly talking about me; they e have been filling your ears for a long time with vehement slanders against me. From them Meletus attacked me, and Anytus and Lycon, Meletus being vexed on behalf of the poets, Anytus on behalf of the craftsmen and the politicians, Lycon on behalf of the orators, so that, as I started out by saying, I should be surprised if I could rid you 24 of so much slander in so short a time. That, gentlemen of the jury, is the truth for you. I have hidden or disguised nothing. I know well enough that this very conduct makes me unpopular, and this is proof that what I say is true, that such is the slander against b me, and that such are its causes. If you look into this either now or later, this is what you will find.

Let this suffice as a defence against the charges of my earlier accusers. After this I shall try to defend myself against Meletus, that good and patriotic man, as he says he is, and my later accusers. As these are a different lot of accusers, let us again take up their sworn deposition. It goes something like this: Socrates is guilty of corrupting the young and of not believing in the gods in whom the city believes, but in other new divinities. Such is their charge. Let us examine it point by point. c

He says that I am guilty of corrupting the young, but I say that Meletus is guilty of dealing frivolously with serious matters, of irresponsibly bringing people into court, and of professing to be seriously concerned with things about none of which he has ever cared, and I shall try to prove that this is so. Come here and tell me, Meletus. Surely you consider it of the greatest importance that our young men be as good as d possible?[5] —Indeed I do.

Come then, tell the jury who improves them. You obviously know, in view of your concern. You say you have discovered the one who corrupts them, namely me, and you bring me here and accuse me to the jury. Come, inform the jury and tell them who it is. You see, Meletus, that you are silent and know not what to say. Does this not seem shameful to you and a sufficient proof of what I say, that you have not been concerned with any of this? Tell me, my good sir, who improves our young men? —The laws. e

That is not what I am asking, but what person who has knowledge of the laws to begin with? —These jurymen, Socrates.

---

5. Socrates here drops into his usual method of discussion by question and answer. This, no doubt, is what Plato had in mind, at least in part, when he made him ask the indulgence of the jury if he spoke "in his usual manner." [Trans. note]

[The answers Socrates receives are preceded by a dash, which indicates a change in speaker.]

How do you mean, Meletus? Are these able to educate the young and improve them? —Certainly.

All of them, or some but not others? —All of them.

Very good, by Hera. You mention a great abundance of benefactors. But what about
25 the audience? Do they improve the young or not? —They do, too.

What about the members of Council? —The Councillors, also.

But, Meletus, what about the assembly? Do members of the assembly corrupt the young, or do they all improve them? —They improve them.

All the Athenians, it seems, make the young into fine good men, except me, and I alone corrupt them. Is that what you mean? —That is most definitely what I mean.

b   You condemn me to a great misfortune. Tell me: does this also apply to horses do you think? That all men improve them and one individual corrupts them? Or is quite the contrary true, one individual is able to improve them, or very few, namely the horse breeders, whereas the majority, if they have horses and use them, corrupt them? Is that not the case, Meletus, both with horses and all other animals? Of course it is, whether you and Anytus say so or not. It would be a very happy state of affairs if only one person corrupted our youth, while the others improved them.

c   You have made it sufficiently obvious, Meletus, that you have never had any concern for our youth; you show your indifference clearly; that you have given no thought to the subjects about which you bring me to trial.

And by Zeus, Meletus, tell us also whether it is better for a man to live among good or wicked fellow-citizens. Answer, my good man, for I am not asking a difficult question. Do not the wicked do some harm to those who are ever closest to them, whereas good people benefit them? —Certainly.

d   And does the man exist who would rather be harmed than benefited by his associates? Answer, my good sir, for the law orders you to answer. Is there any man who wants to be harmed? —Of course not.

Come now, do you accuse me here of corrupting the young and making them worse deliberately or unwillingly? —Deliberately.

What follows, Meletus? Are you so much wiser at your age than I am at mine that
e   you understand that wicked people always do some harm to their closest neighbours while good people do them good, but I have reached such a pitch of ignorance that I do not realize this, namely that if I make one of my associates wicked I run the risk of being harmed by him so that I do such a great evil deliberately, as you say? I do not
26 believe you, Meletus, and I do not think anyone else will. Either I do not corrupt the young or, if I do, it is unwillingly, and you are lying in either case. Now if I corrupt them unwillingly, the law does not require you to bring people to court for such unwilling wrongdoings, but to get hold of them privately, to instruct them and exhort them; for clearly, if I learn better, I shall cease to do what I am doing unwillingly. You, however, have avoided my company and were unwilling to instruct me, but you bring me here, where the law requires one to bring those who are in need of punishment, not of instruction.

And so, gentlemen of the jury, what I said is clearly true: Meletus has never been
b   at all concerned with these matters. Nonetheless tell us, Meletus, how you say that I corrupt the young; or is it obvious from your deposition that it is by teaching them not to believe in the gods in whom the city believes but in other new divinities? Is this not what you say I teach and so corrupt them? —That is most certainly what I do say.

Then by those very gods about whom we are talking, Meletus, make this clearer to me and to the jury: I cannot be sure whether you mean that I teach the belief that   c
there are some gods—and therefore I myself believe that there are gods and am not altogether an atheist, nor am I guilty of that—not, however, the gods in whom the city believes, but others, and that this is the charge against me, that they are others. Or whether you mean that I do not believe in gods at all, and that this is what I teach to others. —This is what I mean, that you do not believe in gods at all.

You are a strange fellow, Meletus. Why do you say this? Do I not believe, as other   d
men do, that the sun and the moon are gods? —No, by Zeus, jurymen, for he says that the sun is stone, and the moon earth.

My dear Meletus, do you think you are prosecuting Anaxagoras? Are you so contemptuous of the jury and think them so ignorant of letters as not to know that the books of Anaxagoras[6] of Clazomenae are full of those theories, and further, that the young men learn from me what they can buy from time to time for a drachma, at most,   e
in the bookshops, and ridicule Socrates if he pretends that these theories are his own, especially as they are so absurd? Is that, by Zeus, what you think of me, Meletus, that I do not believe that there are any gods? —That is what I say, that you do not believe in the gods at all.

You cannot be believed, Meletus, even, I think, by yourself. The man appears to me, gentlemen of the jury, highly insolent and uncontrolled. He seems to have made this deposition out of insolence, violence and youthful zeal. He is like one who com-   27
posed a riddle and is trying it out: "Will the wise Socrates realize that I am jesting and contradicting myself, or shall I deceive him and others?" I think he contradicts himself in the affidavit, as if he said: "Socrates is guilty of not believing in gods but believing in gods," and surely that is the part of a jester!

Examine with me, gentlemen, how he appears to contradict himself, and you, Meletus, answer us. Remember, gentlemen, what I asked you when I began, not to cre-   b
ate a disturbance if I proceed in my usual manner.

Does any man, Meletus, believe in human affairs who does not believe in human beings? Make him answer, and not again and again create a disturbance. Does any man who does not believe in horses believe in equine affairs? Or in flute music but not in flute-players? No, my good sir, no man could. If you are not willing to answer, I will tell you and the jury. Answer the next question, however. Does any man believe in divine   c
activities who does not believe in divinities? —No one.

Thank you for answering, if reluctantly, when the jury made you. Now you say that I believe in divine activities and teach about them, whether new or old, but at any rate divine activities according to what you say, and to this you have sworn in your deposition. But if I believe in divine activities I must quite inevitably believe in divine beings. Is that not so? It is indeed. I shall assume that you agree, as you do not answer. Do we not believe divine beings to be either gods or the children of gods? Yes or no?   d
—Of course.

---

6. Anaxagoras of Clazomenae, born about the beginning of the fifth century B.C., came to Athens as a young man and spent his time in the pursuit of natural philosophy. He claimed that the universe was directed by Nous (Mind), and that matter was indestructible but always combining in various ways. He left Athens after being prosecuted for impiety. [Trans. note]

Then since I do believe in divine beings, as you admit, if divine beings are gods, this is what I mean when I say you speak in riddles and in jest, as you state that I do not believe in gods and then again that I do, since I believe in divine beings. If on the other hand the divine beings are children of the gods, bastard children of the gods by nymphs or some other mothers, as they are said to be, what man would believe children of the gods to exist, but not gods? That would be just as absurd as to believe the young of horses and asses, namely mules, to exist, but not to believe in the existence of horses and asses. You must have made this deposition, Meletus, either to test us or because you were at a loss to find any true wrongdoing of which to accuse me. There is no way in which you could persuade anyone of even small intelligence that it is not the part of one and the same man to believe in the activities of divine beings and gods, and then again the part of one and the same man not to believe in the existence of divinities and gods and heroes.

I do not think, gentlemen of the jury, that it requires a prolonged defence to prove that I am not guilty of the charges in Meletus' deposition, but this is sufficient. On the other hand, you know that what I said earlier is true, that I am very unpopular with many people. This will be my undoing, if I am undone, not Meletus or Anytus but the slanders and envy of many people. This has destroyed many other good men and will, I think, continue to do so. There is no danger that it will stop at me.

Someone might say: "Are you not ashamed, Socrates, to have followed the kind of occupation that has led to your being now in danger of death?" However, I should be right to reply to him: "You are wrong, sir, if you think that a man who is any good at all should take into account the risk of life or death; he should look to this only in his actions, whether what he does is right or wrong, whether he is acting like a good or a bad man." According to your view, all the heroes who died at Troy were inferior people, especially the son of Thetis who was so contemptuous of danger compared with disgrace.[7] When he was eager to kill Hector, his goddess mother warned him, as I believe, in some such words as these: "My child, if you avenge the death of your comrade, Patroclus, and you kill Hector, you will die yourself, for your death is to follow immediately after Hector's." Hearing this, he despised death and danger and was much more afraid to live a coward who did not avenge his friends. "Let me die at once," he said, "when once I have given the wrongdoer his deserts, rather than remain here, a laughing-stock by the curved ships, a burden upon the earth." Do you think he gave thought to death and danger?

This is the truth of the matter, gentlemen of the jury: wherever a man has taken a position that he believes to be best, or has been placed by his commander, there he must I think remain and face danger, without a thought for death or anything else, rather than disgrace. It would have been a dreadful way to behave, gentlemen of the jury, if, at Potidaea, Amphipolis and Delium, I had, at the risk of death, like anyone else, remained at my post where those you had elected to command had ordered me, and then, when the god ordered me, as I thought and believed, to live the life of a philosopher, to examine myself and others, I had abandoned my post for fear of death or anything else. That would have been a dreadful thing, and then I might truly have

---

7. The scene between Thetis and Achilles is from *Iliad* (18, 94ff.). [Trans. note]

justly been brought here for not believing that there are gods, disobeying the oracle, fearing death, and thinking I was wise when I was not. To fear death, gentlemen, is no other than to think oneself wise when one is not, to think one knows what one does not know. No one knows whether death may not be the greatest of all blessings for a man, yet men fear it as if they knew that it is the greatest of evils. And surely it is the most blameworthy ignorance to believe that one knows what one does not know.   b
It is perhaps on this point and in this respect, gentlemen, that I differ from the majority of men, and if I were to claim that I am wiser than anyone in anything, it would be in this, that, as I have no adequate knowledge of things in the underworld, so I do not think I have. I do know, however, that it is wicked and shameful to do wrong, to disobey one's superior, be he god or man. I shall never fear or avoid things of which I do not know, whether they may not be good rather than things that I know to be bad. Even if you acquitted me now and did not believe Anytus, who said to you   c
that either I should not have been brought here in the first place, or that now I am here, you cannot avoid executing me, for if I should be acquitted, your sons would practise the teachings of Socrates and all be thoroughly corrupted; if you said to me in this regard: "Socrates, we do not believe Anytus now; we acquit you, but only on condition that you spend no more time on this investigation and do not practise philosophy, and if you are caught doing so you will die;" if, as I say, you were to acquit me on those   d
terms, I would say to you: "Gentlemen of the jury, I am grateful and I am your friend, but I will obey the god rather than you, and as long as I draw breath and am able, I shall not cease to practise philosophy, to exhort you and in my usual way to point out to any one of you whom I happen to meet: Good Sir, you are an Athenian, a citizen of the greatest city with the greatest reputation for both wisdom and power; are you not ashamed of your eagerness to possess as much wealth, reputation and honours as possi-   e
ble, while you do not care for nor give thought to wisdom or truth, or the best possible state of your soul?" Then, if one of you disputes this and says he does care, I shall not let him go at once or leave him, but I shall question him, examine him and test him, and if I do not think he has attained the goodness that he says he has, I shall reproach him because he attaches little importance to the most important things and greater   30
importance to inferior things. I shall treat in this way anyone I happen to meet, young and old, citizen and stranger, and more so the citizens because you are more kindred to me. Be sure that this is what the god orders me to do, and I think there is no greater blessing for the city than my service to the god. For I go around doing nothing but per-
suading both young and old among you not to care for your body or your wealth in   b
preference to or as strongly as for the best possible state of your soul, as I say to you: "Wealth does not bring about excellence, but excellence brings about wealth and all other public and private blessings for men."

Now if by saying this I corrupt the young, this advice must be harmful, but if anyone says that I give different advice, he is talking nonsense. On this point I would say to you, gentlemen of the jury: "Whether you believe Anytus or not, whether you acquit me or not, do so on the understanding that this is my course of action, even if   c
I am to face death many times." Do not create a disturbance, gentlemen, but abide by my request not to cry out at what I say but to listen, for I think it will be to your advantage to listen, and I am about to say other things at which you will perhaps cry out. By no means do this. Be sure that if you kill the sort of man I say I am, you will not

harm me more than yourselves. Neither Meletus nor Anytus can harm me in any way;
d   he could not harm me, for I do not think it is permitted that a better man be harmed
by a worse; certainly he might kill me, or perhaps banish or disfranchise me, which he
and maybe others think to be great harm, but I do not think so. I think he is doing
himself much greater harm doing what he is doing now, attempting to have a man
executed unjustly. Indeed, gentlemen of the jury, I am far from making a defence now
on my own behalf, as might be thought, but on yours, to prevent you from wrongdoing
e   by mistreating the god's gift to you by condemning me; for if you kill me you will not
easily find another like me. I was attached to this city by the god—though it seems a
ridiculous thing to say—as upon a great and noble horse which was somewhat sluggish
because of its size and needed to be stirred up by a kind of gadfly. It is to fulfill some
such function that I believe the god has placed me in the city. I never cease to rouse
31   each and every one of you, to persuade and reproach you all day long and everywhere
I find myself in your company.

    Another such man will not easily come to be among you, gentlemen, and if you
believe me you will spare me. You might easily be annoyed with me as people are when
they are aroused from a doze, and strike out at me; if convinced by Anytus you could
easily kill me, and then you could sleep on for the rest of your days, unless the god, in
his care for you, sent you someone else. That I am the kind of person to be a gift of
the god to the city you might realize from the fact that it does not seem like human
b   nature for me to have neglected all my own affairs and to have tolerated this neglect
now for so many years while I was always concerned with you, approaching each one
of you like a father or an elder brother to persuade you to care for virtue. Now if I
profited from this by charging a fee for my advice, there would be some sense to it, but
you can see for yourselves that, for all their shameless accusations, my accusers have
c   not been able in their impudence to bring forward a witness to say that I have ever
received a fee or ever asked for one. I, on the other hand, have a convincing witness
that I speak the truth, my poverty.

    It may seem strange that while I go around and give this advice privately and inter-
fere in private affairs, I do not venture to go to the assembly and there advise the city.
You have heard me give the reason for this in many places. I have a divine sign from
d   the god which Meletus has ridiculed in his deposition. This began when I was a child.
It is a voice, and whenever it speaks it turns me away from something I am about to
do, but it never encourages me to do anything. This is what has prevented me from taking part in public affairs, and I think it was quite right to prevent me. Be sure, gentlemen of the jury, that if I had long ago attempted to take part in politics, I should have
e   died long ago, and benefited neither you nor myself. Do not be angry with me for
speaking the truth; no man will survive who genuinely opposes you or any other crowd
32   and prevents the occurrence of many unjust and illegal happenings in the city. A man
who really fights for justice must lead a private, not a public, life if he is to survive for
even a short time.

    I shall give you great proofs of this, not words but what you esteem, deed. Listen to
what happened to me, that you may know that I will not yield to any man contrary
to what is right, for fear of death, even if I should die at once for not yielding. The
things I shall tell you are commonplace and smack of the lawcourts, but they are true.
b   I have never held any other office in the city, but I served as a member of the Council,
and our tribe Antiochis was presiding at the time when you wanted to try as a body

the ten generals who had failed to pick up the survivors of the naval battle.[8] This was illegal, as you all recognized later. I was the only member of the presiding committee to oppose your doing something contrary to the laws, and I voted against it. The orators were ready to prosecute me and take me away, and your shouts were egging them on, but I thought I should run any risk on the side of law and justice rather than join   c
you, for fear of prison or death, when you were engaged in an unjust course.

This happened when the city was still a democracy. When the oligarchy was established, the Thirty[9] summoned me to the Hall, along with four others, and ordered us to bring Leon from Salamis, that he might be executed. They gave many such orders to many people, in order to implicate as many as possible in their guilt. Then I showed   d
again, not in words but in action, that, if it were not rather vulgar to say so, death is something I couldn't care less about, but that my whole concern is not to do anything unjust or impious. That government, powerful as it was, did not frighten me into any wrongdoing. When we left the Hall, the other four went to Salamis and brought in Leon, but I went home. I might have been put to death for this, had not the government fallen shortly afterwards. There are many who will witness to these events.   e

Do you think I would have survived all these years if I were engaged in public affairs and, acting as a good man must, came to the help of justice and considered this the most important thing? Far from it, gentlemen of the jury, nor would any other man. Throughout my life, in any public activity I may have engaged in, I am the same man   33
as I am in private life. I have never come to an agreement with anyone to act unjustly, neither with anyone else nor with any one of those who they slanderously say are my pupils. I have never been anyone's teacher. If anyone, young or old, desires to listen to me when I am talking and dealing with my own concerns, I have never begrudged this to anyone, but I do not converse when I receive a fee and not when I do not. I am equally ready to question the rich and the poor if anyone is willing to answer my questions and listen to what I say. And I cannot justly be held responsible for the good or   b
bad conduct of these people, as I never promised to teach them anything and have not done so. If anyone says that he has learned anything from me, or that he heard anything privately that the others did not hear, be assured that he is not telling the truth.

Why then do some people enjoy spending considerable time in my company? You have heard why, gentlemen of the jury, I have told you the whole truth. They enjoy   c
hearing those being questioned who think they are wise, but are not. And this is not unpleasant. To do this has, as I say, been enjoined upon me by the god, by means of oracles and dreams, and in every other way that a divine manifestation has ever ordered a man to do anything. This is true, gentlemen, and can easily be established.

If I corrupt some young men and have corrupted others, then surely some of them   d
who have grown older and realized that I gave them bad advice when they were young

---

8. This was the battle of Arginusae (south of Lesbos) in 406 B.C., the last Athenian victory of the war. A violent storm prevented the Athenian generals from rescuing their survivors. For this they were tried in Athens and sentenced to death by the assembly. They were tried in a body, and it is this to which Socrates objected in the Council's presiding committee which prepared the business of the assembly. He obstinately persisted in his opposition, in which he stood alone, and was overruled by the majority. Six generals who were in Athens were executed. [Trans. note]

9. This was the harsh oligarchy that was set up after the final defeat of Athens in 404 B.C. and that ruled Athens for some nine months in 404–403 before the democracy was restored. [Trans. note]

should now themselves come up here to accuse me and avenge themselves. If they were unwilling to do so themselves, then some of their kindred, their fathers or brothers or other relations should recall it now if their family had been harmed by me. I see many
e of these present here, first Crito, my contemporary and fellow demesman, the father of Critoboulos here; next Lysanias of Sphettus, the father of Aeschines here; also Antiphon the Cephisian, the father of Epigenes; and others whose brothers spent their time in this way; Nicostratus, the son of Theozotides, brother of Theodotus, and
34 Theodotus has died so he could not influence him; Paralios here, son of Demodocus, whose brother was Theages; there is Adeimantus, son of Ariston, brother of Plato here; Acantidorus, brother of Apollodorus here.

I could mention many others, some one of whom surely Meletus should have brought in as witness in his own speech. If he forgot to do so, then let him do it now; I will yield time if he has anything of the kind to say. You will find quite the contrary, gentlemen. These men are all ready to come to the help of the corruptor, the man who
b has harmed their kindred, as Meletus and Anytus say. Now those who were corrupted might well have reason to help me, but the uncorrupted, their kindred who are older men, have no reason to help me except the right and proper one, that they know that Meletus is lying and that I am telling the truth.

Very well, gentlemen of the jury. This, and maybe other similar things, is what I
c have to say in my defence. Perhaps one of you might be angry as he recalls that when he himself stood trial on a less dangerous charge, he begged and implored the jury with many tears, that he brought his children and many of his friends and family into court to arouse as much pity as he could, but that I do none of these things, even though I may seem to be running the ultimate risk. Thinking of this, he might feel resentful
d toward me and, angry about this, cast his vote in anger. If there is such a one among you—I do not deem there is, but if there is—I think it would be right to say in reply: My good sir, I too have a household and, in Homer's phrase, I am not born "from oak or rock" but from men, so that I have a family, indeed three sons, gentlemen of the jury, of whom one is an adolescent while two are children. Nevertheless, I will not beg you to acquit me by bringing them here. Why do I do none of these things? Not through
e arrogance, gentlemen, nor through lack of respect for you. Whether I am brave in the face of death is another matter, but with regard to my reputation and yours and that of the whole city, it does not seem right to me to do these things, especially at my age and with my reputation. For it is generally believed, whether it be true or false, that
35 in certain respects Socrates is superior to the majority of men. Now if those of you who are considered superior, be it in wisdom or courage or whatever other virtue makes them so, are seen behaving like that, it would be a disgrace. Yet I have often seen them do this sort of thing when standing trial, men who are thought to be somebody, doing amazing things as if they thought it a terrible thing to die, and as if they were to be immortal if you did not execute them. I think these men bring shame upon the city
b so that a stranger, too, would assume that those who are outstanding in virtue among the Athenians, whom they themselves select from themselves to fill offices of state and receive other honours, are in no way better than women. You should not act like that, gentlemen of the jury, those of you who have any reputation at all, and if we do, you should not allow it. You should make it very clear that you will more readily convict a man who performs these pitiful dramatics in court and so makes the city a laughingstock, than a man who keeps quiet.

Quite apart from the question of reputation, gentlemen, I do not think it right to supplicate the jury and to be acquitted because of this, but to teach and persuade   c them. It is not the purpose of a juryman's office to give justice as a favour to whoever seems good to him, but to judge according to law, and this he has sworn to do. We should not accustom you to perjure yourselves, nor should you make a habit of it. This is irreverent conduct for either of us.

Do not deem it right for me, gentlemen of the jury, that I should act towards you in a way that I do not consider to be good or just or pious, especially, by Zeus, as I am   d being prosecuted by Meletus here for impiety; clearly, if I convinced you by my supplication to do violence to your oath of office, I would be teaching you not to believe that there are gods, and my defence would convict me of not believing in them. This is far from being the case, gentlemen, for I do believe in them as none of my accusers do. I leave it to you and the god to judge me in the way that will be best for me and for you.

[The jury now gives its verdict of guilty, and Meletus asks for the penalty of death.]

There are many other reasons for my not being angry with you for convicting me,   e gentlemen of the jury, and what happened was not unexpected. I am much more surprised at the number of votes cast on each side, for I did not think the decision would   36 be by so few votes but by a great many. As it is, a switch of only thirty votes would have acquitted me. I think myself that I have been cleared on Meletus' charges, and not only this, but it is clear to all that, if Anytus and Lycon had not joined him in   b accusing me, he would have been fined a thousand drachmas for not receiving a fifth of the votes.

He assesses the penalty at death. So be it. What counter-assessment should I propose to you, gentlemen of the jury? Clearly it should be a penalty I deserve, and what do I deserve to suffer or to pay because I have deliberately not led a quiet life but have neglected what occupies most people: wealth, household affairs, the position of general or public orator or the other offices, the political clubs and factions that exist in the city? I thought myself too honest to survive if I occupied myself with those things. I did not follow that path that would have made me of no use either to you or   c to myself, but I went to each of you privately and conferred upon him what I say is the greatest benefit, by trying to persuade him not to care for any of his belongings before caring that he himself should be as good and as wise as possible, not to care for the city's possessions more than for the city itself, and to care for other things in the same way. What do I deserve for being such a man? Some good, gentlemen of the jury, if I   d must truly make an assessment according to my deserts, and something suitable. What is suitable for a poor benefactor who needs leisure to exhort you? Nothing is more suitable, gentlemen, than for such a man to be fed in the Prytaneum,[10] much more suitable for him than for any one of you who has won a victory at Olympia with a pair or a team of horses. The Olympian victor makes you think yourself happy; I make you   e be happy. Besides, he does not need food, but I do. So if I must make a just assessment of what I deserve, I assess it at this: free meals in the Prytaneum.   37

When I say this you may think, as when I spoke of appeals to pity and entreaties, that I speak arrogantly, but that is not the case, gentlemen of the jury; rather it is like

---

10. The Prytaneum was the magistrates' hall or town hall of Athens in which public entertainments were given, particularly to Olympian victors on their return home. [Trans. note]

this: I am convinced that I never willingly wrong anyone, but I am not convincing you of this, for we have talked together but a short time. If it were the law with us, as it is

b elsewhere, that a trial for life should not last one but many days, you would be convinced, but now it is not easy to dispel great slanders in a short time. Since I am convinced that I wrong no one, I am not likely to wrong myself, to say that I deserve some evil and to make some such assessment against myself. What should I fear? That I should suffer the penalty Meletus has assessed against me, of which I say I do not know whether it is good or bad? Am I then to choose in preference to this something that

c I know very well to be an evil and assess the penalty at that? Imprisonment? Why should I live in prison, always subjected to the ruling magistrates, the Eleven? A fine, and imprisonment until I pay it? That would be the same thing for me, as I have no money. Exile? for perhaps you might accept that assessment.

I should have to be inordinately fond of life, gentlemen of the jury, to be so unreasonable as to suppose that other men will easily tolerate my company and conversation when you, my fellow citizens, have been unable to endure them, but found

d them a burden and resented them so that you are now seeking to get rid of them. Far from it, gentlemen. It would be a fine life at my age to be driven out of one city after another, for I know very well that wherever I go the young men will listen to my talk

e as they do here. If I drive them away, they will themselves persuade their elders to drive me out; if I do not drive them away, their fathers and relations will drive me out on their behalf.

Perhaps someone might say: But Socrates, if you leave us will you not be able to live quietly, without talking? Now this is the most difficult point on which to convince some of you. If I say that it is impossible for me to keep quiet because that means dis-

38 obeying the god, you will not believe me and will think I am being ironical. On the other hand, if I say that it is the greatest good for a man to discuss virtue every day and those other things about which you hear me conversing and testing myself and others, for the unexamined life is not worth living for man, you will believe me even less.

What I say is true, gentlemen, but it is not easy to convince you. At the same time,

b I am not accustomed to think that I deserve any penalty. If I had money, I would assess the penalty at the amount I could pay, for that would not hurt me, but I have none, unless you are willing to set the penalty at the amount I can pay, and perhaps I could pay you one mina of silver.[11] So that is my assessment.

Plato here, gentlemen of the jury, and Crito and Critoboulus and Apollodorus bid me put the penalty at thirty minae, and they will stand surety for the money. Well then, that is my assessment, and they will be sufficient guarantee of payment.

[*The jury now votes again and sentences Socrates to death.*]

c It is for the sake of a short time, gentlemen of the jury, that you will acquire the reputation and the guilt, in the eyes of those who want to denigrate the city, of having killed Socrates, a wise man, for they who want to revile you will say that I am wise even if I am not. If you had waited but a little while, this would have happened of its own accord. You see my age, that I am already advanced in years and close to death. I am

d saying this not to all of you but to those who condemned me to death, and to these

---

11. One mina was 100 drachmas, equivalent to, say, twenty-five dollars, though in purchasing power probably five times greater. In any case, a ridiculously small sum under the circumstances. [Trans. note]

same jurors I say: Perhaps you think that I was convicted for lack of such words as might have convinced you, if I thought I should say or do all I could to avoid my sentence. Far from it. I was convicted because I lacked not words but boldness and shamelessness and the willingness to say to you what you would most gladly have heard from me, lamentations and tears and my saying and doing many things that I say are unworthy of me but that you are accustomed to hear from others. I did not think then that the danger I ran should make me do anything mean, nor do I now regret the nature of my defence. I would much rather die after this kind of defence than live after making the other kind. Neither I nor any other man should, on trial or in war, contrive to avoid death at any cost. Indeed it is often obvious in battle that one could escape death by throwing away one's weapons and by turning to supplicate one's pursuers, and there are many ways to avoid death in every kind of danger if one will venture to do or say anything to avoid it. It is not difficult to avoid death, gentlemen of the jury, it is much more difficult to avoid wickedness, for it runs faster than death. Slow and elderly as I am, I have been caught by the slower pursuer, whereas my accusers, being clever and sharp, have been caught by the quicker, wickedness. I leave you now, condemned to death by you, but they are condemned by truth to wickedness and injustice. So I maintain my assessment, and they maintain theirs. This perhaps had to happen, and I think it is as it should be.

Now I want to prophesy to those who convicted me, for I am at the point when men prophesy most, when they are about to die. I say gentlemen, to those who voted to kill me, that vengeance will come upon you immediately after my death, a vengeance much harder to bear than that which you took in killing me. You did this in the belief that you would avoid giving an account of your life, but I maintain that quite the opposite will happen to you. There will be more people to test you, whom I now held back, but you did not notice it. They will be more difficult to deal with as they will be younger and you will resent them more. You are wrong if you believe that by killing people you will prevent anyone from reproaching you for not living in the right way. To escape such tests is neither possible nor good, but it is best and easiest not to discredit others but to prepare oneself to be as good as possible. With this prophecy to you who convicted me, I part from you.

I should be glad to discuss what has happened with those who voted for my acquittal during the time that the officers of the court are busy and I do not yet have to depart to my death. So, gentlemen, stay with me awhile, for nothing prevents us from talking to each other while it is allowed. To you, as being my friends, I want to show the meaning of what has occurred. A surprising thing has happened to me, judges— you I would rightly call judges. At all previous times my usual mantic sign frequently opposed me, even in small matters, when I was about to do something wrong, but now that, as you can see for yourselves, I was faced with what one might think, and what is generally thought to be, the worst of evils, my divine sign has not opposed me, either when I left home at dawn, or when I came into court, or at any time that I was about to say something during my speech. Yet in other talks it often held me back in the middle of my speaking, but now it has opposed no word or deed of mine. What do I think is the reason for this? I will tell you. What has happened to me may well be a good thing, and those of us who believe death to be an evil are certainly mistaken. I have convincing proof of this, for it is impossible that my customary sign did not oppose me if I was not about to do what was right.

Let us reflect in this way, too, that there is good hope that death is a blessing, for it is one of two things: either the dead are nothing and have no perception of anything, or it is, as we are told, a change and a relocating for the soul from here to another place. If it is complete lack of perception, like a dreamless sleep, then death would be a great advantage. For I think that if one had to pick out that night during which a man slept soundly and did not dream, put beside it the other nights and days of his life, and then see how many days and nights had been better and more pleasant than that night, not only a private person but the great king would find them easy to count compared with the other days and nights. If death is like this I say it is an advantage, for all eternity would then seem to be no more than a single night. If, on the other hand, death is a change from here to another place, and what we are told is true and all who have died are there, what greater blessing could there be, gentlemen of the jury? If anyone arriving in Hades will have escaped from those who call themselves judges here, and will find those true judges who are said to sit in judgement there, Minos and Radamanthus and Aeacus and Triptolemus and the other demi-gods who have been upright in their own life, would that be a poor kind of change? Again, what would one of you give to keep company with Orpheus and Musaeus, Hesiod and Homer? I am willing to die many times if that is true. It would be a wonderful way for me to spend my time whenever I met Palamedes and Ajax, the son of Telamon, and any other of the men of old who died through an unjust conviction, to compare my experience with theirs. I think it would be pleasant. Most important, I could spend my time testing and examining people there, as I do here, as to who among them is wise, and who thinks he is, but is not.

What would one not give, gentlemen of the jury, for the opportunity to examine the man who led the great expedition against Troy, or Odysseus, or Sisyphus, and innumerable other men and women one could mention. It would be an extraordinary happiness to talk with them, to keep company with them and examine them. In any case, they would certainly not put one to death for doing so. They are happier there than we are here in other respects, and for the rest of time they are deathless, if indeed what we are told is true.

You too must be of good hope as regards death, gentlemen of the jury, and keep this one truth in mind, that a good man cannot be harmed either in life or in death, and that his affairs are not neglected by the gods. What has happened to me now has not happened of itself, but it is clear to me that it was better for me to die now and to escape from trouble. That is why my divine sign did not oppose me at any point. So I am certainly not angry with those who convicted me, or with my accusers. Of course that was not their purpose when they accused and convicted me, but they thought they were hurting me, and for this they deserve blame. This much I ask from them: when my sons grow up, avenge yourselves by causing them the same kind of grief that I caused you, if you think they care for money or anything else more than they care for virtue, or if they think they are somebody when they are nobody. Reproach them as I reproach you, that they do not care for the right things and think they are worthy when they are not worthy of anything. If you do this, I shall have been justly treated by you, and my sons also.

Now the hour to part has come. I go to die, you go to live. Which of us goes to the better lot is known to no one, except the god.

The Republic

Book I

Yesterday I went down to the Piraeus with Glaucon, Ariston's son, to offer my devotions to the goddess.[1] I also wanted to see how their new festival would turn out. Our own citizens staged a fine parade, but even the Thracians were good.

Once we had made our devotions and seen the whole festival, we started home. But at that moment Polemarchus, Cephalus's son, saw us hurrying on and had his boy run to stop us. He grabbed my cloak from behind and said that Polemarchus hoped that we would wait for him to catch up. . . .

Soon, Polemarchus joined us along with Glaucon's brother Adeimantus, Nicias's son, Niceratus, and a few others who had apparently marched in the procession.

Then Polemarchus said: Socrates, it looks as though you and Glaucon are hurrying to leave us and return to Athens.

That is a good guess.

But do you see how many there are of us?

Of course.

Well, you are going to have to choose between staying here peacefully or fighting us if you try to get away.

How about a third choice in which we persuade you that you ought to let us go?

But could you persuade us if we don't listen?

Obviously not, said Glaucon.

Then you might as well know right now that we won't listen. . . .

It looks like we had better change our minds, Socrates.

Well, if you say so, Glaucon, I suppose we must.

So we went to Polemarchus's house. Polemarchus's brothers, Lysias and Euthydemus, were there. So was Thrasymachus of Chalcedon, as well as Charmantides the Paeanian and Cleitophon, the son of Aristonymus.

Cephalus, Polemarchus's father, was also at home. . . . Cephalus greeted me as soon as he saw me. . . .

[*Socrates engages Cephalus in a discussion of his attitudes toward aging and wealth.*]

Yes, but let me ask one more question. What do you think is the greatest benefit wealth has conferred upon you?

Something that will once again provoke a skeptical response from many people. But let me tell you, Socrates, when death comes near, a man will begin to fear and worry about things that before seemed innocuous. If he once laughed at stories of the netherworld and the punishments said to be in store for earthly misdeeds, his unbelief now retreats before his fears that the stories may be true. . . . He reflects on his past

327

b

c

328b

330d

e

From Plato, *The Republic*, trans. Richard W. Sterling and William C. Scott (New York: Norton, 1985), pp. 25–214, by permission of W.W. Norton & Co., Inc. All rights reserved.

1. The Piraeus, about six miles from Athens, was the seaport for the city. As such it was open to many exotic influences. Socrates is present for the festival of Bendis, a moon goddess whose cult was imported from abroad. [Trans. note]

and ponders what wrong he has done to others. If his burden of guilt is heavy, he will
wake up at night in terror, like a child. Dark forebodings will cloud his life. But the
man with a clear conscience will have Pindar's "sweet hope" as the constant companion of his age.... This is the reward of virtue, and the chief value of wealth is to
strengthen virtue—if not in every man, then in the good man. Money makes it easier
for a man to shun cheating and fraud. Money enables him to pay his debts, so that he
need not fear the next world because of what he owes to gods or men in this one.
Money obviously has other uses, too. All in all, however, I believe that wealth's chief
service to the reasonable man is what I have just described.

You have nobly praised both honesty and honor as essential virtues in the good
man. But are these the same as justice itself? To tell the truth and pay one's debts—are
these invariably equivalent to just behavior? Or may it sometimes be more just not to
pay a debt, or not to tell the truth? Consider an example: a friend who is sound in
mind and body lends you his weapons. Then, when he returns to claim them, you see
that he has gone mad. Would it not be wrong to give them back to him? Would that
not be an injustice? Would it not also be unjust to tell your mad friend the exact truth
of his condition and situation?

Your questions are to the point, Socrates.

Then we must say that telling the truth and repaying one's debts cannot serve as an
adequate definition of justice.

Polemarchus broke in. Yes, they can, Socrates. At least that is what Simonides
says....

Then tell us, Polemarchus, how the heir to the argument understands Simonides
on justice and why you think him right.

I think Simonides speaks rightly when he says that justice is giving to each man his
due.

Simonides is a man of both intelligence and inspiration. It is difficult to doubt him.
Yet I must say this his meaning may be clear to you, Polemarchus, but not to me. Were
he to address himself to our recent example, he would certainly not advocate the
indiscriminate return of property to someone who had gone mad. Yet the property was
on loan and due on demand, wasn't it?

Yes.

But on no account must one return weapons to a madman?

True.

Then when Simonides said it is just to render that which is due, he must have had
something else in mind.

He certainly did. He wanted to explain what is due from friend to friend: something good and nothing evil.

You mean that if a friend borrows money from another friend, he ought not to
return it if, for some reason, repayment should harm the lender? Would repayment
under these circumstances actually violate the rule that only good is due from friend
to friend? Is that Simonides' meaning?

Yes.

This proposition evidently implies another: enemies must receive their due.

Of course. Enemies must receive what is owing them, and the debt from enemy to
enemy is nothing good but something evil.

Then, as poets so often will, Simonides talks in riddles about justice. He seems to   c
have wanted to say that justice requires that everyone be given his due. But what he
actually said is that everyone has the right to collect what is owed him.

What is the matter with that?

We shall see what's the matter. Supposing we were to ask Simonides what obligation the art of medicine has to its patients. What is the patient's due? How do you
think he would answer?

That is obvious. Medicine is an art obligated to provide patients with proper drugs,
food, and drink. . . .

Excellent. Now tell me what does the art of justice properly confer and upon   d
whom?

If we are to follow the earlier reasoning, Socrates, justice is an art that benefits
friends and injures enemies.

So Simonides defines justice as doing good to friends and evil to enemies?

I think so.

Then who is best able to benefit friends and injure enemies in times of sickness?

A doctor.

Or on a voyage when all aboard face the perils of the sea?   e

A captain.

And how about a just man? In what situation is he best able to help his friends and
harm his enemies?

In war, Socrates, when he joins his fellow countrymen in battle against the foe.

I see. All this leads me to conclude that when we are well and safely on dry land,
we have no use for doctors or captains.

True.

But how about justice? Will it be useless in peacetime?

I don't want to say that.

Then justice has its uses in times of peace?   333

Yes.

Just like farming and shoemaking?

Yes.

Just how is justice useful in peacetime?

It is useful in business, in drawing up contracts and in forming partnerships.

But if you were competing in a game, whom would you prefer as a partner? A skillful
player or a just man?   b

A skillful player. . . .

Then for what kind of partnership is the just man best suited?

In a partnership involving money.

But surely not where money is changing hands. If we wanted to buy or sell horses,
it would be better to have a canny judge of horse-flesh as our partner. If ships were the   c
commodity, we should want a shipbuilder or sea captain on our side.

No doubt.

Then in what kinds of money transactions will the just man be the best partner?

When one wants to deposit money for safekeeping.

You mean that the just man is useful only when money lies idle?

Exactly. . . .

d   Then it must follow that justice is useful whenever you want to put thing in storage, whether they are pruning hooks, shields, or harps. But when you want to put these things to use, you apply the art of viniculture, of warfare, or of music, as the case may be.
Yes. . . .

e   Then justice can't be worth much. But let us try another approach. The boxer who is most skilled in offense will also be most skilled in defense. The doctor who is most
334 capable of protecting us from disease is also most capable of infecting us. The soldier who guards the fort well will also be good at raiding the enemy's camp. Would you agree?
Yes.

So one who guards well is also good at stealing? The just man, who guards money well, will also be good at stealing it?
Evidently.

Then it seems we have revealed the just man to be a kind of thief. . . . Apparently
b   you agree with Homer and Simonides that justice sanctions even the art of stealing so long as a man steals things to benefit friends or injure enemies. Is that what you meant?

Certainly not, although I confess I no longer know what I said. But I am still sure of one thing: the just man is one who benefits friends and injures enemies.

c   Then another question comes up. Whom do you call friends? Those you think are good and honest people, or those who really are? And are your enemies really bad, or are they men you only think are bad?

Well, a man's judgments naturally depend on what he thinks and believes.

But don't people often misjudge the good and the bad, so that good people are mistaken for bad and bad people for good?
Clearly.

Then misjudgment can transform good people into enemies and evil people into friends?
That follows.

This also must follow: in such circumstances the just man will find himself defending bad people and injuring the good.
d   Evidently.

Yet the just man is good and would not do evil.
Yes.

But according to your previous reasoning, it is just to injure one who does no wrong.

No, no. That is certainly false doctrine, Socrates.

Is it then better to say that one should harm those who do wrong and help those who are honest and just?
That sounds better.

e   The truth is that Simonides' definition doesn't work. Someone who is a poor judge of people will often have friends who are bad friends; in this case it turns out that Simonides' definition would have him do his friends injury. Conversely, he will have enemies who in fact are good men; and these the definition bids him support. But now we have come around to the exact opposite of Simonides' original position.

You are right. The error seems to be connected with our use of the terms *friend* and *enemy*.

What error, Polemarchus?

We defined a friend as one who seems to us to be good.

And what definition should we use instead?

A friend is one who is good in fact and not merely in our opinion. If he only seems good, he will be only a seeming friend. The same must be said for enemies.   335

With this we arrive at the proposition that the good are our friends and the bad our enemies?

Yes.

You add something, then, to Simonides' original definition of justice as helping friends and punishing enemies. Now you want to say that justice requires that we do good to friends who really are good and harm enemies who really are bad.

That clarifies it.   b

But is it right for the just person to inflict injury on anyone?

Of course. He is right to injure bad men who are his enemies.

But what about injury itself? If you injure, say, horses or dogs, will you not make them less excellent animals?

Yes.

Does that not also hold for human beings? If you injure them, will they not be less   c
excellent as men?

Yes.

Is justice a human excellence, Polemarchus?

Yes.

So if you injure a man you make him less just?

I guess so.

Now consider musicians or riding masters. Are their purposes achieved if their students become less musical or less able to ride horseback?

No.

How about the just man? Will it be his purpose to behave justly in order to make other men less just? Will the virtuous behavior of good men make other men bad?   d

No.

Then the good cannot corrupt any more than heat can generate cold or dryness water. If justice and goodness are the same, then the just man injures no one. It is his opposite, the unjust man, who inflicts injury on his fellows.

Socrates, I think you are right.   e

So it cannot be wise to say that justice is giving to each his due, if what is due includes injury to enemies as well as benefits to friends. It cannot be true because we have proved that the just man never injures anyone.

I agree. . . .

Well, our success in disproving one definition of justice can only lead us to ask   336
whether anyone can come up with another.

Thrasymachus had often tried to break into the argument but had been restrained   b
by the others who wanted to hear it to the end. But when Polemarchus and I had reached this point in the conversation, there was a brief pause, and Thrasymachus could no longer be held back. He rose up like a beast and leaped at us as if he would tear us to pieces. Polemarchus and I recoiled in terror.

Then he bellowed at us and the whole company. What idiocy is this, Socrates?   c
Why do the two of you behave like dolts, solemnly deferring to each other's vacuous

notions? If you really want to know what justice is, you should be able not only to ask the question but also to answer it. You should not try to score points simply by refuting your opponent's efforts; you ought to provide your own definition. After all, there are

d   many who ask but cannot answer. So now say what you think justice is. Say it at last with clarity and precision, and spare us your ponderous analogies with duty or interest or profit or advantage. They produce only nonsense, and I don't put up with nonsense.

I was thunderstruck and could hardly look at Thrasymachus without trembling.

e   Indeed, as in the proverb, I should have been speechless had I not already spotted this wolf before he saw me. In fact, I was watching him all the while his temper was waxing hot, and so I was able to reply.

Spare me your anger, Thrasymachus. If there were errors in the argument, believe me, they were not intentional. Had we been searching for gold, we surely would not have played games with each other and risked letting the treasure slip from our hands. But here we have been looking for justice, something far more precious than gold. How could you suppose that we would waste time pretending to defer to false opinions rather than devoting all our energy to finding the truth? We have been in earnest, my friend, even though our explorations have not been successful. In this situation superior minds like yours should respond with sympathy rather than with scorn.

337   Thrasymachus responded with sarcastic laughter: A fine sample of your famous irony, Socrates. I know how you argue, as I warned everyone here at the outset. Whatever Socrates is asked, he refuses to answer. He will resort to irony or to any other

d   stratagem in order to avoid being pinned down.... What if I formulate a definition of justice superior to any you have offered? What penalty would you accept?

The penalty appropriate to ignorance: I must make the effort to learn from the wise....

e   Yes, and then Socrates will go through his well-known routine, refusing to answer anything himself but demolishing the answers of everybody else.

But, Thrasymachus, how can anyone who admits he doesn't know the answer then try to answer anyway? The difficulty is compounded if some august intelligence tells him that even the few things he might know something about have no place in the

338   argument. Be more flexible, Thrasymachus. Since you both know and profess to know, it is entirely proper that you should be the teacher and provide the definition. The rest of us are eager to hear you teach.

Glaucon and the others seconded my request. As for Thrasymachus, he was obviously flattered; he was convinced that his definition could not be refuted. He was eager to speak and still more eager for the acclaim he assumed would reward his discourse....

c   Then here is my answer: justice is simply the interest of the stronger. Well, why don't you praise me? But of course you won't.

First I have to understand you. What do you mean by saying that justice is the interest of the stronger? An athlete like Polydamas is far stronger than we are, and it

d   is in his interest to eat great amounts of beef to keep himself in shape. You are not going to argue that we nonathletes have a like interest in such a diet or that it would be good for us to follow it?

Socrates, you are a buffoon. But though your methods are clumsy, you are effective enough in sabotaging other people's arguments.

Not at all. I am simply trying to understand them.

Well, try again. You must know that tyrannies, democracies, and aristocracies are different forms of government. . . .

Yes.

Now governments use their power to make tyrannical, democratic, or aristocratic laws, as suits their interests. These laws, then, designed to serve the interests of the ruling class, are the only justice their subjects are likely to experience. Transgressors will be punished for breaking the laws and sullying justice. This is why I say that justice operates on the same principle everywhere and in every society. Justice is what advantages the interest of the ruling class. Since the ruling class is also the strongest class, the conclusion should be evident to anyone who reasons correctly: justice is the same in every case—the interest of the stronger.

Now I understand your meaning. But whether it is true or not is something I must still ascertain. I note you used the word "interest" in defining justice, a word you were unwilling to let me use. I admit, however, that in your definition you add the words "of the stronger."

A trifling addition, no doubt.

Trifle or not, our chief business is to discover whether your definition is true. First, I will agree that justice is an interest of some sort. But then you add that it is the interest of the stronger. I question that. We must examine that point.

Go ahead.

I will. Tell me, do you think that it is just and right to obey men in power?

Yes.

How about those in power? Are they always right, or do they sometimes make mistakes?

They will certainly make some mistakes. . . .

When the rulers legislate rightly, the laws will conform to their interest. But to the extent that they miscalculate in their lawmaking, the laws will be contrary to their interest. Is that right?

Yes.

The subjects must nevertheless obey all the laws enacted by the rulers? You call that justice?

Yes.

Then it follows from your argument that it is just to serve the interest of the stronger but equally just not to.

What are you saying?

Exactly what you have been saying. But let us look at the matter more closely. You have just made two points. One is that the rulers may sometimes be mistaken about their best interests and that their laws may reflect those mistakes. The other is that justice requires the subjects to obey whatever laws there may be. Did you not make these two propositions?

Yes.

All of which amounts to admitting that it can be just and right to do that which contradicts the interest of the stronger. When the rulers blunder in devising their policies, they damage their own interests. The requirement that subjects must unquestioningly support all the rulers' policies compounds the damage. Now, most wise

Thrasymachus, can you see how you contradict yourself? Your indiscriminate equation of justice with what the strong command and the weak obey leads only to its own negation; it actually requires the weak to injure the interests of the strong. . . .

340b   What Thrasymachus meant, said Cleitophon, is that justice is what the stronger believes to be in his interest. Obedience to this belief, in turn, is the just duty of the subject.

But he didn't say that, objected Polemarchus.

c   It doesn't matter, Polemarchus, said I. If that is the position Thrasymachus now wants to take, let us accept it. Is that what you want to say, Thrasymachus? Is justice what the stronger thinks is his interest, whether it really is or not?

Of course not. Do you think I would call someone stronger at the very moment he is making a mistake?

d   Your admission that rulers are sometimes fallible led me to that inference.

That's because you are addicted to quibbling, Socrates. Would you call a man a doctor at the very moment he errs in diagnosing his patient? Does his error confirm his status as a doctor? Do we apply the same measure to mathematicians or grammarians, calling them by these names even when they make mistakes? True, it is customary to say that the doctor or mathematician or grammarian makes a mistake.

e   But this is a loose way of speaking. I contend that none of these ever makes a mistake so long as his conduct accords with professional standards. When he does err, his skill has deserted him, and his professional status is in default. To be precise, then—and I know you are a great lover of precision—any craftsman ceases to be a craftsman when he makes mistakes. Just so with rulers. The moment the ruler makes

341   a mistake, he nullifies his status as a ruler. But so long as he is a proper ruler he never makes mistakes and always decrees what is in his own interest, and his subjects are always required to obey. Thus we return to what I said at the outset: justice is the interest of the stronger. . . .

b   Tell me, when we speak of the ruler, should we now understand the term in what you called its customary, or loose, sense? Or should we define the ruler more precisely in the way you advocated a moment ago?

I speak of a ruler in the most precise sense. Now go ahead and quibble and set out

c   your snares. I am not afraid of you for the simple reason that you are no match for me.

But of course. Do you think I should be so mad as to imagine I could outwit a Thrasymachus? . . . Tell me, is the doctor, in your strict sense of the word, one whose first business is to make money? Or is it to heal the sick?

The doctor is a healer of the sick.

In the same strict sense, what of the ship's captain? Is he an ordinary sailor or is he commander of the crew?

d   He commands the crew.

Then his mere presence on board does not define his status. He is called captain not because he sails but because of his skill in commanding the crew.

True.

Therefore, specific professions or arts seek to discover something useful for other men.

Yes. . . .

342c   Medicine pays no heed to its own interest but only to that of the diseased body?

That's right.

And the horse trainer attends not to himself but to the horse? Is it not then the same with all the arts? They have no needs; they care only for their subjects.

I agree.

Then we must conclude, Thrasymachus, that the arts are superior to their subjects and have authority over them.

Thrasymachus conceded as much, but with great reluctance.

Another conclusion: none of the arts, professions, or sciences serves the interest of the stronger; instead, all promote the advantage of the weaker.

After much hesitation and inward struggle Thrasymachus also agreed to this.   d

So the true doctor concerns himself with the patient's interest and not his own. The true doctor is like a ruler whose subject is the human body; he is not a mere money maker. Are we agreed?

Agreed. . . .

So too with government. The governor—or ruler—insofar as he is true to his call-   e
ing, will never consider what is to his own interest. He will take into account only the interest of his subjects and the requirements connected with the art of governing. These are the sole criteria by which he plans and governs.

By now it was clear that Thrasymachus's definition of justice had been stood on its   343
head. But instead of replying, Thrasymachus asked whether I had a nurse.

Why ask such a question? You owe an answer to a question of mine.

Because your nurse evidently neglects to wipe your nose and leaves you sniveling. What's more, she leaves you ignorant of the difference between shepherd and sheep.

Why do you say that?

Because you fancy that the shepherd or cowherd has the interests of his charges at   b
heart, grooming and fattening them for their own sakes and not to serve the master's profit or his own. You carry this illusion into politics with the consequence that you fail to see how rulers really behave. The actual ruler or governor thinks of his subjects as sheep, all right, but his chief occupation, day and night, is how he can best fleece them to his own benefit. You have strayed so far from reality that you cannot even   c
understand that what is just is simply something that is good for someone else. He who behaves justly does not benefit himself. It follows that a just subject properly serves the interests of the ruler but does so to his own injury. The dynamics of justice, then, con- sistently operate to advantage the ruler but never the subjects. The result is that injustice lords it over those who are truly simple and truly just. Because the unjust ruler is stronger, his subjects serve his interests and his happiness at the expense of   d
their own.

The just man is always a loser, my naïve Socrates. He always loses out to the unjust. Consider private business. If a just man takes an unjust man for a partner and the part- nership is later dissolved, it is invariably the unjust man who walks away with the lion's share of the assets. Consider their dealings with government. When taxes fall due, the just man will pay more and the unjust less on the same amount of property. . . .

The unjust man is in exactly the opposite situation. I mean the same man as the   e
one I spoke of before, the man of injustice who exploits others on a grand scale. I   344
speak, namely, of the tyrant and of tyranny, the highest form of injustice. If you want to see how unjust acts benefit the tyrant, watch how he makes his crimes pay off. Watch how his own happiness and prosperity impoverish his subjects. Watch how he persecutes those who reject injustice and continue to act justly. . . .

b   Any one of these acts perpetrated by a private individual would be condemned and
punished. The guilty one would be branded a thief, swindler, housebreaker, cheat, or
robber of temples. But if a man not only steals from his fellows but also uses the powers
of government to enslave them, one hears no such unfriendly epithets. All the world
c   applauds every instance of triumphant injustice; all the world calls the unjust ruler
happy and blessed.

The reason for this is that people censure injustice only because they fear to be its
victims and not because they have scruples about being unjust themselves. So it is,
Socrates, that injustice, when practiced on a large enough scale, is stronger and freer
and more successful than justice. What I said at the outset, then, remains true. Justice
is whatever serves the interest of the stronger; injustice, on the other hand, is whatever
serves the personal advantage of any man.

d   Like a bath attendant pouring buckets of water on our heads, Thrasymachus had
nearly drowned us with his oratory. Now he wanted to leave. But we all demanded that
he stay and defend his position. . . .

e   You seem not to care about us. You don't seem to care whether our ignorance of
what you claim to understand will make our lives better or worse. Please, Thrasyma-
345   chus, share your knowledge with us. There are quite a number of us here. Any benefit
you confer will surely be rewarded.

I should add that for my own part I am not convinced by your argument. I do not
believe that injustice, even if it operates free of all restraint, is more profitable than
justice. I grant that there might be an unjust man who uses force and fraud and gets
away without a reckoning. Even so, I remain unconvinced that injustice has the
b   advantage over justice, and there may be others who agree with me. But we may also
be wrong; so let us benefit from your wisdom, and show us where we are mistaken.

How should I do that if you are not convinced by what I have just said? What else
can I do? Are you asking to be spoon-fed?

God forbid. But I do ask you to be consistent. A while ago you offered an exact defi-
c   nition of the doctor, but you were not nearly so exact when subsequently you defined
the shepherd. You said that the shepherd's purpose was to fatten sheep, not to benefit
the sheep but to satisfy the banqueter who loves the pleasures of the table. Or else you
d   wanted the shepherd to play the businessman whose aim is to sell the sheep profitably
in the market. But shepherding is an art in itself and so requires nothing beyond fidelity to its own rules. Hence the shepherd, properly defined, is concerned with nothing
else than the welfare of his charges.

Drawing on these observations I concluded that the same holds true for all kinds
e   of authority, whether public or private. To the extent that the ruler conforms to the
strict definition of his function, he is concerned solely with the good of those he
rules. . . .

346   Now let me ask you a question, my friend. Are not the several arts differentiated
by the specific functions each performs? . . .

Yes, I agree that function explains their differentiation.

b   And each art benefits us in a particular way? Medicine restores our health, navigation secures our safety at sea?

Yes.

And earning a living brings us wages; that is its specific function. Therefore, earning a living ought not to be confused with other functions any more than navigation

ought to be confused with medicine simply because the sea captain has improved his health during a voyage. . . . We must make the same judgment concerning the doctor himself. The fact that he takes fees for healing the sick does not mean that medicine is the same as money-making.

I agree.

And we are also agreed that each art, profession, or skill produces its own distinctive benefit. At the same time, all who practice these diverse arts also receive a common benefit called wages. Thus all must share a common quality different from the diverse qualities of their specialized skills. That is, they each provide distinctive benefits in their capacity as members of a specific profession, and they all receive wages in their common role of wage earners.

Possibly.

So wages benefit the wage earner's account and do not derive directly from his art. In his professional role the doctor nurtures health; in his wage-earning role he collects his pay. The same with the architect who builds a house, and the same with all the others. Each art performs the functions proper to it and benefits its proper objects.

Now, if the person who performs professional services is not paid, can he be said to benefit from his labors?

Apparently not.

But don't those same services constitute a benefit, whether they are paid or not?

Clearly they do.

Then, Thrasymachus, we must return to an earlier proposition. No art, craft, skill, or profession is designed to serve itself or its practitioners. Instead, its proper function is to serve its clients. In the case of politics this means that governors should serve the governed and not the other way round. That is, the stronger ought to seek the advantage of the weaker and not their own. . . .

For this reason alone I would not assent to Thrasymachus's argument that justice is the interest of the stronger. But let us return to that question later. More important is Thrasymachus's most recent statement that the unjust live better lives than the just. . . .

Thrasymachus, can we return to the beginning of the argument? Your initial position was that perfect injustice is more profitable than perfect justice. . . . But I would like to consider it from another perspective. I presume you would agree that a city or a state can be unjust, that it may try to enslave other cities unjustly and hold them in subjection.

Of course. This is exactly what the best state will do, the state which most nearly achieves complete injustice. . . .

Could a city, an army, a gang of bandits or thieves, or, for that matter, any group seeking to realize common purposes succeed if the group members were constantly trying to wrong each other?

No.

Would they be more likely to achieve their objectives if their members refrained from being unjust to one another?

Yes.

This is because injustices generate hatred, quarrels, and factions. Only justice can create unity and love. Is that not true?

If you insist. I don't want to contradict you.

How good of you. Tell me more. If injustice invariably implants hatred, whether among groups of free men or slaves, will it not cause them to hate and injure each other, making it impossible for them to cooperate in common enterprises?

e   Yes.

So will it be also with any two individuals. Injustice will make them hate each other and so divide them. They will be enemies to one another and to all just men as well.

Agreed.

The same will hold for a single individual. Injustice will once again manifest its divisive effects and will put a man at odds with himself.

Let it be as you say.

Then it becomes apparent that wherever injustice appears—in the city, in the
352   family, or in the individual—it first spawns factions and disunion and then excites enmity among the divided parts. Finally, anything so at odds with itself must become its own enemy as well as the enemy of all who are just. . . .

d   But now we come to the question we postponed earlier: whether the just have a better and happier life than the unjust. From what we have said up to this point I think the answer is already clear that they do. Still, it bears closer examination, for we are considering no ordinary matter. We are, in fact, inquiring into the right rules for the conduct of life.

Inquire away.

Tell me, then—does a horse have a specific function?

e   Yes.

And would you define the function as something only a horse can do or, at least, as something a horse does best?

I don't understand.

Look at it this way. Do we see only with our eyes and hear only with our ears?
Yes.

So that we can properly say that seeing and hearing are the respective specific functions of the eyes and the ears?

Clearly. . . .

353   Then the specific function of anything is that which it alone can do or which it can do better than anything else.

b   I understand you now. You have explained the meaning of specific functions to my satisfaction.

Can we then agree that everything performing a function must be measured by the excellence or deficiencies of its performance? Can we not say that the eye will perform either well or deficiently?

Yes. . . .

Then we may generalize to say that all things have a function which is measured in terms of the excellence or defectiveness of its performance.

Very well. . . .

c   Here I would like to ask whether you agree with the proposition that things function adequately because of the excellence of their own qualities or inadequately because these qualities are defective.

I agree.

And our agreement would apply to eyes, ears, and all other things?

Yes.   d

Well, then, has not the soul a specific function which cannot be performed by any-thing else, a function which would include such things as reasoning, willing, and governing? Are these not functions specific to the soul? Could they ever be performed by something other than the soul?

No.

Does the soul not govern the conduct of life?

Certainly.

And the soul is to be measured in terms of its excellence and defects?

Yes.

If the soul lacks excellence, it cannot perform well?

That follows.

Then a person with a bad soul will govern his life badly. The person with a good soul will govern his life well.

That follows.

Do you recall our agreement that justice is the peculiar excellence or virtue of the soul and injustice its defect?

Yes.   e

Can we now agree that the just will live well but that it will go ill with the unjust?

Your argument makes it appear so.

Can we go further? He who lives well is happy, and he who lives ill is not?

Yes.

Hence the just man is happy and the unjust man miserable.

So be it.

And happiness pays well, but misery pays poorly.   354

Yes.

At last, then, my worthy Thrasymachus, we have discovered that injustice can never be more profitable than justice.

Then consider your entertainment complete, Socrates, on this feast day of Bendis.

You are the one who provided the feast, Thrasymachus, after you ceased to be angry with me and began to speak gently. Nevertheless—and through no fault of yours—I have not dined well. It strikes me that I have been like a glutton, snatching at one dish b after another and eating in such haste that I had no time to savor the food. I am afraid this is the way I have gone about our inquiry. We had not finished defining justice before I was off to examine. . .the comparative profitability of justice and injustice. So I must confess that the outcome of the discussion is that I know nothing. After all, if justice still remains undefined, I can hardly know whether it is in fact a virtue or a vice. Nor can I know whether the just man is in fact happy or miserable.

Book II

All this having been said, I thought the discussion was at an end. But on the contrary, 357 the end turned out to be the beginning. With his usual energy, Glaucon objected to Thrasymachus's withdrawal from the contest. He went on to ask: Socrates, do you b really want to convince us that justice is preferable to injustice, or will you be content if we only seem to be persuaded?

I would really like to persuade you.

Well, so far you haven't succeeded. Consider this question. Is there some kind of good we ought to strive for, not because we expect it to bring about profitable results but simply because we value the good for its own sake? Joy might be an example, or those sorts of harmless pleasures that leave nothing behind except the memory of enjoyment.

These are good pleasures to savor.

c   And can we agree that there is a second and different kind of good, valuable not only for its own sake but also for the desirable effects it produces? I think of sight, of knowledge, of health.

Of course.

How about a third kind of good? Gymnastic, medicine, the art of making money— all these yield benefits but are tiresome in the doing. Hence we think of them not as
d   goods in themselves but value them only for their effects.

Yes, this is certainly another kind of good. But what is your point?

I want to know in which of these three categories or classes of goods you locate justice.

358   Justice belongs in the most valuable category. It is the good that the happy man loves both for its own sake and for the effects it produces.

But the multitude does not think so. Most people consider the practice of justice a burdensome affair. They think it a task to be avoided, if possible, and performed only if necessary to maintain one's reputation for propriety—and to collect whatever
b   rewards such a reputation may be worth. . . . I think Thrasymachus conceded the argument before he should have. He reminded me of a snake, too soon charmed by the sound of your voice. As for me, neither the nature of justice or injustice is yet clear. I want to consider both of them quite apart from their effects or the rewards they might bring. What are they in themselves? What power do they exert within the confines of a man's soul?

c   To begin with, Socrates, I should like to revive Thrasymachus's argument. So I will speak first of all of the common view of the nature and origin of justice. Second, I shall argue that all who practice justice do so against their own will. This is so because they regard just behavior as something necessary but not as something good. Third, I shall stress that the rationale for such attitudes is rooted in the common view that the life of the unjust man is far better and happier than the life of the just man.

I do not believe these things myself, Socrates. But I admit that I become perplexed when I listen to the arguments of Thrasymachus and all those who believe as he does.
d   My uncertainty is all the greater when I reflect that I have never yet heard an unambiguous proof that justice is always superior to injustice.

What I desire most, Socrates, is to hear someone praise justice for its own sake, and you are the one most likely to do so. Thus my purpose in praising the unjust life is to provoke a response from you that will effectively repudiate injustice and vindicate justice. Does my proposal please you?

What else could please me more? . . .

e   Excellent. I shall begin by discussing the nature of justice and its origin. Most men say that to be unjust is good but to suffer injustice is bad. To this opinion they add another: the measure of evil suffered by one who is wronged is generally greater than the good enjoyed by one who does wrong. Now, once they have learned what it is to

wrong others—and also what it is to be wronged—men tend to arrive at this conclu-   359
sion: justice is unattainable and injustice unavoidable.

Those so lacking in strength that they can neither inflict injustice nor defend themselves against it find it profitable to draw up a compact with one another. The purpose of the compact is to bind them all neither to suffer injustice nor to commit it. From there they proceed to promulgate further contracts and covenants. To all of these they attach the name of justice; indeed, they assert that the true origin and essence of justice is located in their own legislation.

Their lawmaking is clearly a compromise, Socrates. The compromise is between what they say is best of all—to do wrong without incurring punishment—and what is worst of all—to suffer wrong with no possibility of revenge. Hence they conceive of   b
justice not as something good in itself but simply as a midway point between best and worst. Further, they assert that justice is praised only by those too weak to do injustice and that anyone who is a real man with power to do as he likes would never agree to refrain from doing injustice in order not to suffer it. He would be mad to make any such agreement.

As you very well know, Socrates, this is the orthodox account of the nature and origin of justice. Its corollary is that when people practice justice, they do so against their own wills. Only those are just who lack the power to be unjust. Let us test this proposition by altering the power distribution and assigning the just and the unjust equal power to do what they please. We shall then discover that the just man and the unjust   c
man will follow precisely the same path. They will both do what all nature decrees to be good. They will pursue their own interests. Only if constrained by law will they be confined to the path of justice.

The test I propose makes the assumption that both the just and the unjust enjoy the peculiar liberty said to have been granted to Gyges, ancestor of Croesus the   d
Lydian. Tradition has it that Gyges was a shepherd in the service of the king of Lydia. While he was feeding his flock one day, there was a great storm, after which an earthquake opened a chasm directly in front of the place where Gyges stood with his flock. Marveling at the sight, Gyges descended into the chasm. There he beheld many wonders, among them a hollow bronze horse fitted with doors. When he opened one of the doors and looked within, he saw the corpse of a huge man, nude except for a gold ring on his finger. Gyges removed the ring and made his way up and out of the chasm.

Now when the shepherds next met to prepare their customary monthly report to   e
the king concerning their flocks, Gyges attended wearing the ring. While there, he chanced to turn the stone of the ring on his finger inward, toward the palm of his hand. Instantly he became invisible to all eyes. He was amazed to hear those who sat   360
near him speak of him as if he were absent. Fumbling with the ring again, he turned the stone outward, away from the palm, and became visible once more. Now he began to experiment, turning the ring this way and that and always with the same results— turning it inward he became invisible, turning it outward he became visible again. Once he discovered the ring's power, he hastily managed to have himself appointed one of the messengers to the king's court. On arrival he seduced the queen and then,   b
with her help, murdered the king. Thus it was that he became king of Lydia.

Supposing now there were two such rings, the just man wearing one and the unjust man the other. No man is so unyielding that he would remain obedient to justice and c   keep his hands off what does not belong to him if he could steal with impunity in the very midst of the public market itself. The same if he could enter into houses and lie with whom he chose, or if he could slay—or release from bondage—whom he would, behaving toward other men in these and all other things as if he were the equal of a god. The just man would act no differently from the unjust; both would pursue the same course. . . .

e   Next, if we are to choose between the lives of justice and injustice, we must be precise in distinguishing the one from the other. Otherwise we cannot choose rightly. We can make the distinction only by treating the two as strictly separate. We must assume the just man to be entirely just and the unjust man entirely unjust. Each must possess all the qualities appropriate to his character and role as a just—or unjust—man.

         First, the unjust man: his behavior must be like that of a clever craftsman. Like any good physician or pilot, he must practice his art with an intuitive sense for what is possible and what is impossible, holding fast to the first and shunning the latter. When he makes a mistake, he must be able to recover and correct himself. This means that the unjust man must pursue injustice in the proper way. If he is altogether unjust, he must possess an unerring capacity to escape detection; otherwise, if he fails and is caught, he shows himself to be a mere bungler. After all, the highest form of injustice is to appear just without being so.

361   Perfect injustice denotes the perfectly unjust man. Nothing belonging to injustice must be withheld from him. He must be allowed to enjoy the greatest reputation for justice all the while he is committing the greatest wrongs. . . .

b   Having constructed a model of the unjust man, we must now do the same for the just man. He will be noble and pure—in Aeschylus's words, one who wants to be good rather than to seem good. Accordingly, he must be deprived of the seeming. Should

c   he retain the appearance of being just, he would also enjoy an esteem that brings with it honors and gifts. In that case we could not know whether he serves justice for its own sake or because he covets the honors and gifts. He must therefore be stripped of everything but justice; his situation must be the opposite of his unjust counterpart. Though the best of men, he must be thought the worst. Then let him be put to the test to see whether he will continue resolute in the service of justice, even though all

d   the while he must suffer the opprobrium of an evil reputation. Let him so persevere—just in actuality but unjust in reputation—until death itself. . . .

e   They will tell you that every man who is just, but whose reputation stamps him as unjust, will learn what it is to feel the lash, the rack, the chains, and the branding iron

362 burning out his eyes. And after suffering all the other agonies he will be impaled on spikes, there finally to learn his lesson that it is better to seem just than to be so. . . .

366c   If there is a convincing rebuttal to these arguments, it could come only from a man with enough trust in the superiority of justice to be gentle with the unjust. . . .

d   Socrates, there is a single cause that impels the flow of all these words from me and from by brother, Glaucon. We are astonished at all your self-professed advocates of

e   justice—from the heroes of ancient times and their surviving discourses down to the present day. None has ever awarded blame to injustice or praise to justice except in terms of the gifts, honors, or reputation each of them attracts. Both verse and prose have failed to convey their intrinsic qualities. They do not tell us how justice and injustice do their work within the human soul, out of the sight of both gods and men. No one has ever provided proof that the one is the greatest of goods and the other the

greatest of evils. Why did all of you not do this from the beginning and convince us   367
from our youth up? Had you done so, we would not now be guarding against one
another's injustices. Instead, each would first of all guard himself; each would banish
injustice from his own conduct, so that his own soul might be safeguarded from the
taint of evil. . . .

You have said that justice belongs to that highest class of good things which not   c
only produce good effects but which are, above all, valuable in themselves. Some of   d
these are sight, hearing, health, and intelligence, things whose value is innate and not
a matter of opinion. So tell us how justice benefits a man intrinsically, and in the same
way how injustice harms him. Let others praise or blame the respective rewards and
reputations. I don't say I wouldn't listen to others debate these issues, including the
matter of reputation. But you have spent all your life studying the question, and I
expect better fare from you, Socrates, unless you tell me in your own words that you
are unable to offer it. I repeat, then, disregard outward appearances, and prove to us   e
that justice is better than injustice by showing us the effects each has on a man's soul
and how and why each effect can properly be called either good or evil.

I have always admired the brilliance of Glaucon and Adeimantus, but on this occasion their words gave me special pleasure. . . . There must indeed be some divine spark   368
at work in your natures that you should be able to make such formidable arguments on
behalf of injustice and yet resist being convinced by your own reasoning. And I believe
that you are really not convinced. I infer this, however, from my knowledge of your
characters; if I had to deal with your words alone, I would be suspicious of you.   b

But the greater my trust in you, the more difficult becomes my task. What can I say
when I doubt my ability to offer you satisfactory answers to your questions? And my
doubt is well founded, for you have refused to accept the arguments I used against
Thrasymachus and which I thought had amply proved the superiority of justice to
injustice. Yet I cannot remain silent; that would be a shameful course to take when   c
justice is under attack. As long as there is voice and breath in me, then, I think it is
best to give to justice all the help that I can offer. . . .

Well, I think all of you are pressing for an inquiry that is by no means an easy under-   d
taking. We must keep our wits about us. And since our wits are not always sharp, we
should do well to adopt a method of examination similar to that used when people
without very keen vision are required to read small letters from a distance. This
method would draw their attention to the same letters writ large, and I think they
would count it a godsend if they could read the larger letters first then check the
smaller letters against them to see if they correspond.

Agreed, said Adeimantus, but what kind of analogy are you trying to draw with   e
justice?

I will tell you. We sometimes speak, do we not, of a just man and also of a just city?
Of course.
And the city is larger than the man?
Yes.
Perhaps, then, there would be more of justice in the city; it might also be easier to
observe it there. So if it is agreeable to you, let us first inquire into the nature of justice   369
and injustice in the city, and only after that in the individual. In this way we could
begin with the larger and then return to the smaller, making comparisons between
the two.

A good suggestion.

If we begin our inquiry by examining the beginning of a city, would that not aid us also in identifying the origins of justice and injustice?

Perhaps it would.

So that when our analysis is complete, we should be in a better position to find what we are seeking?

b   Much better. . . .

Very well. A city—or a state—is a response to human needs. No human being is self-sufficient, and all of us have many wants. Can we discover the origins of the state in any other explanation?

I can imagine no other.

c   Since each person has many wants, many partners and purveyors will be required to furnish them. One person will turn to another to supply a particular want, and for a different want or need he will seek out still another. Owing to this interchange of services, a multitude of persons will gather and dwell together in what we have come to call the city or the state.

Right.

And so one man trades with another, each assuming he benefits therefrom.

Right.

Come, then, let us construct a city beginning with its origins, keeping in mind that the origin of every real city is human necessity.

That is evident.

d   Now the first and greatest necessity, on which our very life depends, is food.

Certainly.

Next is a place in which to live; third, clothing and the like.

Yes.

Then we must ask how our city will provide these things. A farmer will be needed, and a builder and a weaver as well. I suppose we should add a shoemaker and still another who can care for the needs of the body.

I agree.

Hence the simplest city or state would count at least four or five people?

e   Evidently.

Then how should they proceed? Should what each produces be made available to all? I mean, should the individual farmer produce food for himself and also for the rest? That would require him to produce, say, four times as much food as he could use himself. Correspondingly, he would invest four times as much labor in the land than if he were supplying only himself. Or should he decline to concern himself with the others?

370   Should he produce food for his own needs alone, devoting only a fourth of his total effort to that kind of work? Then he could allot the other three-fourths of his time to building a house, making clothes, and cobbling shoes. Choosing the latter, he wouldn't have to bother about associating with others; he could supply his own wants and be his own man.

I don't think he should try to do everything, said Adeimantus. He should concentrate on producing food.

I agree that this would probably be the better way. Your words remind me that we
b   are not all alike. There is a diversity of talents among men; consequently, one man is best suited to one particular occupation and another to another. What do you think?

I think you are right.

Then a man would do better working at one task rather than many?

I think so. . . .

We can conclude, then, that production in our city will be more abundant and the   c
products more easily produced and of better quality if each does the work nature has
equipped him to do, at the appropriate time, and is not required to spend time on other
occupations.

A sound conclusion.

Then, Adeimantus, we shall need more than our four original citizens to produce
all that will be required. If the farmer's plow and hoe and other implements are to be
of good quality, he will not be able to make them himself. The builder will also need
equipment and supplies, and so will the shoemaker and the weaver.   d

True.

With carpenters, smiths, and other craftsmen joining our city, it will begin to grow
considerably. . . . And we must also note that it would be very difficult to establish a   e
city that would not require imports. That means there must be still another class of
citizens who import goods from other cities.

Clearly.

It follows that we must have goods to export. If our traders go forth empty-handed,
with nothing to exchange for what they want from other cities, they must come home   371
empty-handed.

Inevitably.

Then domestic production must exceed domestic demand, so that there will be a
surplus of quality products to exchange with traders from abroad.

True.

Then we shall need more farmers and artisans. There must also be importers and
exporters, those whom we call merchants. . . .

Supposing the farmer or other craftsman brings his produce to market but does not   c
arrive at the same time as those who would buy from him. Would he sit idly in the market place, wasting time he could otherwise devote to productive work?

Not at all. There will be men at the market who will offer their services to remedy
the situation by acting as salesmen. . . .

So the need for money in the exchange of goods produces the class we know as   d
tradesmen. Is this not the name we give to those who buy and sell in the agora, just
as we give the name merchants to those who perform the same function in trade
between cities?

Yes.

Then there is still another class of workers whose intellects are perhaps too   e
weak to count them as full partners in the city but whose bodily strength enables
them to perform hard physical labor. They sell their strength for a price, and the
price is called wages. Hence they are called wage earners, and they, too, will be part
of our city.

True.

Well, Adeimantus, has our city now reached its full growth? Could we call it complete?

Perhaps.

Where, then, do we find justice and injustice? How do they gain entry into the city?
Are they brought in by one or more of the groups we have just included among the
city's constituents?

372   I don't know, Socrates. Perhaps they have their origins in the mutual needs of the city's inhabitants.

You may well be right. We must pursue the matter further and not let up now. First, then, let us consider the way of life of the people in the city we have just described. . . . They will work in the summer for the most part without clothes or
b   shoes, but in the winter they will want to wear both. They will grind meal from barley and flour from wheat; then they will knead and bake cakes and loaves of fine quality and serve them on mats of reeds or on clean leaves. . . .

d   But this is fare for a city of pigs, Socrates. Would you provide nothing else?

What do you suggest, Glaucon?

The usual things. If the people are not to be uncomfortable, they must be able to recline on couches and dine from tables. They ought to have sauces and sweetmeats
e   the way we do.

Now I understand what you mean. We are to consider the origins not simply of a city as such but of a luxurious city. Your suggestion is probably a good one because it is in the luxurious city that we are more likely to discover the roots of justice and injustice.

I believe the city I have just described is well founded and that it will prove to be robust. But if you also want to examine a city in a state of fever, we can do that, too. It is in any case evident that many will not be content with simple fare and
373 simple ways. They will want couches and tables and other types of furniture. Sweets and perfumes, incense, courtesans, and cakes—all must be furnished in quantity and variety. . . .

True.

b   Then we must further enlarge our city. The well-founded city we started with will no longer be big enough. It must be extended and filled up with superfluities. There will, for example, be hunters in plenty. There will be crowds of imitators—those who paint and sculpt. Others will make music: there will be poets and their attendants,
c   rhapsodizers, players, dancers, and impresarios. . . . Will not tutors be in demand as well, along with wet nurses and dry nurses, barbers and beauticians, cooks and bakers? . . .

You are right.

d   And this way of life will require many more doctors than were needed before.

That is certain.

Must we also assume that the territory which was at one time sufficient to feed the city will no longer be adequate?

Yes.

So we shall covet some of our neighbor's land in order to expand our pasture and tillage. And if our neighbor has also disregarded the limits set by necessity and has given himself over to the unlimited acquisition of wealth, he will, in turn, covet what belongs to us.

e   Inevitably.

Then the next step will be war, Glaucon. Or do you see some other outcome?

There can be no other, Socrates.

This is not the time to speak of the good or ill effects of war. What we can say is that we find war originating from the same causes that generate most of the private and public evils in the city.

Agreed.

So our city must be enlarged once more, this time by nothing less than a whole army. We must have it march out to fight our enemies in defense of all the wealth and luxury we have just described. 374

Does this necessarily follow? Cannot the people defend themselves?

Not if our initial assumptions about constructing the city still hold. Surely you remember our agreement that no man can perform many tasks well?

Yes.

And don't you think that war is an art and fighting a profession? b

Yes. . . .

Now it is obviously of the first importance that soldiers should do their work well. c But is the art of war so easily learned that a soldier can at the same time be a farmer, a shoemaker, or active in some other employment? . . . Is it credible that a man who d takes up a shield or any other instrument of war for the first time should forthwith become a competent soldier, ready to fight on line where heavy armor is used or in other forms of warfare? . . .

But now we approach the most important business in the city, the task of the guardians. Accordingly, a guardian would have to spend more time than any other in education—in learning and practice. By the same token, he would have to be freer e than any other from tasks extraneous to his work.

I should think so.

And he would also have to have a nature suited to his calling?

Of course. . . .

If we think of an aptitude for guarding, could we imagine there would be any difference between the nature of a noble young man and the nature of a young thorough- 375 bred dog?

What is your point?

I mean that each must be keen in perceiving an enemy, swift in pursuit and capture, and strong if he must then subdue him.

Yes, those are certainly necessary qualities.

And in order to fight well each must be brave as well as strong. . . . And essential to bravery is spirit. Neither a horse, a dog, nor anything else is brave without being high-spirited. . . . So now we know what the physical qualities of the guardian's nature b must be.

Yes.

And we also know something of his quality of soul. He must be spirited.

Yes.

But, Glaucon, will not these high-spirited natures be likely to be quick-tempered and savage with one another, and with everyone else as well?

That is undeniably a difficulty.

The difficulty is compounded by the requirement that they be fierce to their ene- c mies but gentle to their friends. If they fail in this respect they will destroy one another before their enemies ever get at them.

Right. . . .

In fact, combinations of opposites are a universal phenomenon, but it is especially d evident in the natures of those we chose to compare. Consider our thoroughbred hounds e again: they are gentle to their friends and those they recognize but not to strangers.

That is true.

Then that which we thought impossible before proves now to be perfectly possible. And so the standards we set for the guardian's nature turn out to be perfectly reasonable.

It seems so.

Does it also seem to you that the guardian should have another quality in addition to that of spirit? Should he not be a philosopher?...

376b   A what?

A lover of wisdom. Do you not see that knowing and not knowing are the sole criteria the dog uses to distinguish friend from enemy? Does it not follow that any animal that verifies his likes and dislikes by the test of knowledge and ignorance must be a lover of learning?

Oh, indeed.

And is not the love of learning the same as the love of wisdom which, in turn, is philosophy?

All are identical.

c   Then let us be bold. Having made the case for the dog, let us make the case for man as well: he who is gentle to friends and to those he knows must by nature be a philosopher.

Let us assume so.

Then we may conclude that the true guardian of city or state is one who is strong, swift, high-spirited, and a lover of wisdom.

Without doubt....

Book IV

427c   Then, son of Ariston, we have finished with founding the city. Next, you, your
d   brother, and Polemarchus, and all the others must find something that will illuminate the city. The light must be clear and strong so that we may discover where justice and injustice are located. We must be able to see what is the difference between them. We want to know whether it is justice or injustice that brings a man happiness. We want to know if justice and injustice are qualities that affect happiness differently according to whether they are practiced openly or in secret....

e   I believe we can find what we are looking for by making the following assumption: the city we have founded—if we have built rightly—will be good in the fullest sense of the word.

That is certain.

It means that the city is wise, courageous, temperate, and just.

Necessarily.

Now, if we find some of these qualities in the city, can we assume the ones not yet found will nonetheless be present?

428   Let us assume it.

Then we can proceed as we would if we were seeking any one element in a set of four. If we discover that one element before the others, we shall have accomplished our task. But if we find the other three first, the one we are looking for will necessarily be the remaining one in the set.

That seems right.

Then let us apply this method as we inquire into the four virtues in our city. Of these virtues, wisdom is evidently the first. But I must add that there appears to be some peculiarity connected with it.   b

What?

Well, let us see. The city is certainly wise, for it abounds in good counsel. Good counsel, in turn, is a sort of skill or proficiency, something generated from knowledge and not from ignorance. . . .

All right, then. Is there any form of skill or knowledge possessed by some of the   c
citizens of the city we recently founded that attends not to particular interests but to the general interest, to the city as a whole in both its domestic and foreign policies?   d

Yes.

What is it, and where is it to be found?

It is the art of guardianship practiced by the city's rulers whom we recently described as guardians in the fullest sense.

What description will fit the city possessing this kind of knowledge?

A city that is prudent and truly wise. . . .

Apparently, then, our discussion of wisdom as one of the four virtues in the city has   429
given us some understanding of its nature and where it is to be found.

If we follow the same approach, I think we can discover the nature of courage, where it is situated, and how it imparts its spirit to the entire city. Now whoever calls   b
a city brave or cowardly will think first about its armed forces. This is so because the character of the city is not determined by the bravery or cowardice of the citizenry as a whole. The city is brave because there is a part of it that is steadfast in its convictions about what is to be feared and what is not to be feared. These convictions constitute   c
an integral part of the education prescribed by the city's founder. They also define the meaning of courage.

Would you please say that again? I don't think I understand.

Courage is a preservative. Strengthened by education, it preserves convictions about the things that are legitimately to be feared and those that are not. Courage makes a man hold fast to these convictions no matter whether he is threatened by danger or lured by desire. Neither pain nor pleasure will move him. . . .

Well, then, after wisdom and courage we wanted to search out two further virtues   430c
in the city. One is temperance—or moderation. The other is justice, the grand object   d
of all our inquiries.

Agreed.

Now, do you think we could go ahead and move directly to a consideration of justice without first inquiring into the nature of temperance?

I don't know. What I do know is that I should regret turning immediately to justice if that meant missing the opportunity for a better understanding of temperance and self-control. So let us look at these first. . . .

I will. To begin with, temperance seems more clearly related to peace and harmony   e
than to wisdom and courage.

How so?

It appears to me that temperance is the ordering or controlling of certain pleasures and desires. This is what is implied when one says that a man is master of himself. It is a curious expression because it suggests that a man is both his own master and his   431 own servant. But I believe the proper meaning of the phrase is that there is both good and bad in the soul of man. When the good part governs the bad, a man is praised for being master of himself. But if bad education or bad company subjects the good (and smaller part) of the soul to the bad (and larger) part, a man will be blamed for being unprincipled and a slave of self.

Now look at our newly founded city. If temperance and self-mastery are in charge, if the better part rules the worse, we may well say that the city is master of itself.

I agree.

We may say that the mass of diverse appetites, pleasures, and pains is to be found chiefly among children, women, slaves, and the many so-called freemen from the lower classes. But the simple and temperate desires governed by reason, good sense, and true opinion are to be found only in the few, those who are the best born and the best educated.

Yes.

Both the few and the many have their place in the city. But the meaner desires of the many will be held in check by the virtue and wisdom of the ruling few. It follows that if any city may claim to be master of its pleasures and desires—to be master of itself—it will be ours. For all these reasons, we may properly call our city temperate.

I agree.

There is another point. In our city, if anywhere, rulers and subjects will share a common conviction as to who should rule. What does this agreement suggest about the location of temperance? Will we find it among the rulers or the subjects?

In both, I should think.

Then we were not wrong in detecting a similarity between temperance and some kind of harmony. Temperance is different from wisdom and courage, each of which is associated with a particular part of the city. Temperance, on the other hand, pervades the entire city, producing a harmony of all its parts and inhabitants, from the weakest to the strongest. And this holds true however you want to measure strength and weakness: by force, or numbers, or wealth, or wisdom. Hence we may properly conclude that temperance is a consensual agreement between superior and inferior as to which should rule. And we should note that our conclusion applies both to individuals and to societies.

Agreed.

Now we have inquired into three of the four chief qualities of our city. The fourth and final quality is justice. But here we must take care that it does not elude us. We must be like hunters who surround a thicket to make sure that the quarry doesn't escape. Justice is clearly somewhere hereabouts. Look sharp, and call me if you see it first.

I wish I could. But I am only your follower, with sight just keen enough to see what you show me. . . .

The wood is dark and almost impenetrable. We will have a hard time flushing out the quarry. Still, we must push on . . . . There, I see something. Glaucon! I think we're on the track. Now it won't escape us.

Good news.

But we have really been stupid.

How so?

Because a long time ago, at the beginning of our inquiry, justice was right in front of us, and we never saw it. . . .

What do you mean?. . .   e

Tell me now whether I am right or wrong. You remember the original principle we   433
laid down at the founding of the city: each citizen should perform that work or function for which his nature best suits him. This is the principle, or some variation of it,
that we may properly call justice.

We often said that.

We also said that justice was tending to one's own business and not meddling in   b
others'.

Yes.

So minding one's own business really appears, in one sense, at least, to be justice.
Do you know how I reached this conclusion?

No.

You remember we were inquiring into the four cardinal virtues of a city. We examined temperance, courage, and wisdom; now justice remains the one still to be considered. What we will find is that justice sustains and perfects the other three; justice   c
is the ultimate cause and condition of their existence.

Now that we have wisdom, courage, temperance, and justice fairly before us, it
would be hard to decide which of the four virtues effectually contributes most to the
excellence of the city. Is it the harmony existing between rulers and subjects? Is it the
soldier's fidelity to what he has learned about real and fictitious dangers? Or wisdom
and watchfulness in the rulers? Or, finally, is it the virtue that is found in everyone—   d
children, women, slaves and freemen, craftsmen, rulers, and subjects—which leads
them each to do his own work and not to interfere with others? These are questions
not easily answered.

Yes. They are very perplexing.

But we can at least accept the conclusion that the fourth virtue of minding one's
own business rivals the other three virtues in contributing to the city's excellence.
That is to say that justice is at least the equal of wisdom, courage, and temperance. . . .   e

We can be certain about the nature of justice only if its role in the individual turns   434d
out to be identical to its role in the city. If we cannot establish the identity, we must
make a fresh start. But let us first finish what we have already started.

Remember that we began with the proposition that if we first examined justice on
a larger scale, it would be easier to understand justice in the individual. We used the   e
city as our larger measure. We founded the best city we could because we were confident that in a good city we would find justice. Now let us apply our findings to the
individual. If they hold for both city and citizen, we will rest our case. But if justice
in the individual is shown to be different, we must return to the city for further investi-   435
gations. Perhaps if we adopted procedures to examine city and citizen simultaneously,
we could rub them up against one another and generate enough friction to light the
countenance of justice and fix it firmly and forever in our own minds.

The approach seems promising, said Glaucon. Let's try it.

All right. If we use the same name for two things, city and man, one large and one
small, they will be alike in that quality to which their common name refers. It follows
that as far as the quality of justice is concerned there will be no difference between the   b
just man and the just city.

I agree. The man will resemble the city.

But we must remember that we deemed the city just when each of its three classes
attended to its own business. We also called the city temperate, brave, and wise

because of the particular qualities and dispositions of the classes. If we now assess the individual in the same way, we must demonstrate that the same three elements from which they spring are actually present in the individual and have the same effects and consequences. In order to do this, of course, we have to halt for a moment to deal with a minor question. Does the individual soul have these three elements or not?

Hardly a minor question, Socrates. But what is worth questioning is seldom easy.

You are right, Glaucon. I must say then that I don't think that our present procedures of inquiry will lead us to the truth of this matter. We need to follow another more difficult and much longer path. But perhaps we can reach at least some useful conclusions based on what we have said so far. . . .

Then don't hold back.

Very well. Surely we must admit that the same qualities we observed in the city are also to be found in the individual. Indeed, it is obvious that the individual transmits them to the city. . . .

So much is easy to see. But the next step is more difficult. Is our whole soul involved in whatever we do? Or is bravery, intellectual effort, and bodily appetite each the exclusive product of a distinct and separate part of the soul? Is our nature an undivided entity, or is it a set of disconnected components?

This is a tricky question. But let's begin by trying to ascertain whether the parts of the soul are identical to each other or different. An example may help. Can something be both at rest and in motion at the same time?

Never.

Then we can infer that nothing acts in opposite ways at the same time. Nor can anything exist simultaneously in two opposing states. If, then, we seem to perceive the soul behaving in contradictory ways or reflecting two opposing states at once, we must conclude that the soul is many and not one. . . .

Then should we say that the following kinds of pairs are composed of opposites: attraction and repulsion, desire and aversion, agreement and disagreement? And should we observe that any proper discussion of opposites applies to actions as well as emotions?

Yes.

Keeping in mind the pairs we just described, would we not say that thirst, hunger, willing and wishing, and desires in general are examples of the active element in the pairs? The one who desires something actively searches for the object of his desire; he tries to draw to himself the thing he wants to possess. Seeking satisfaction, he will put the question to himself and then answer yes.

That's the way it happens.

What about not wanting, not desiring, not willing? Shall we class them with the passive components of our pairs, along with rejection and repulsion?

Of course. . . .

Thus a thirsty man, insofar as he is only thirsty, desires only to drink. This is what he wants and seeks.

Clearly.

But if a thirsty man refrains from drinking, it must be due to a part of him different from the thirsty part that pulls every animal to water. This conclusion is in accord with our earlier finding that nothing can behave in opposite ways at the same time. . . .

There must be something in these people that urges them to drink and something else that bids them abstain, something that overpowers and inhibits the initial urge.

Yes.

And what is the inhibiting agent? Is it not reason and reflection? And does not the agent that urges and attracts find its source in passion and sometimes in disease?   d

Evidently.

Then it would be reasonable to conclude that the soul is composed of at least two distinct parts. One is the reasoning part. The other is appetite or desire, where hunger, thirst, and sexual passion have their abode along with other irrational drives.

The conclusion is reasonable.   e

Then we are agreed about these two parts of the soul. But is there a third? What about the spirited part which enables us to feel anger or indignation? Is this something separate, or is it identical with one of the other two parts?

I should think it is akin to the desiring part.

A story I once heard may help us find an answer. One day Leontius, the son of Aglaion, was coming up from the Piraeus alongside the north wall when he saw some dead bodies fallen at the hand of the executioner. He felt the urge to look at them; at the same time he was disgusted with himself and his morbid curiosity, and he turned away. For a while he was in inner turmoil, resisting his craving to look and covering his eyes. But finally he was overcome by his desire to see. He opened his eyes wide and   440
ran up to the corpses, cursing his own vision: "Now have your way, damn you. Go ahead and feast at this banquet for sordid appetites."

I have heard that story, too.

Leontius's behavior shows clearly that desire and anger are two different things and sometimes go to war with one another.

Yes, the meaning of the story is obvious.

We often see this kind of behavior where a man's desires overmaster his reason. This   b
results in his reproaching himself for tolerating the violence going on within himself. In this situation a man's soul can resemble a city riven by two warring factions. The spirited part, here in the guise of anger or indignation, will ally with reason against the passions. Indeed, every time reason rejects what the passions propose, neither anger nor indignation nor any other expression of spirit will desert to passion's cause. I don't believe you or anyone else could cite a single instance where spirit and the passions have united against a confident reason.

I could not. . . .

We understand each other well. But do you see how our position has changed? Just   e
minutes ago the spirited element of the soul appeared to be the ally of the appetites and desires. But now, when the soul is torn by internal divisions, we see spirit arrayed alongside reason.

Yes.

Hence we must now ask whether spirit is distinct from reason or only a function of reason? If the latter, the soul must consist of no more than the two elements of   441
reason and appetite. Or does the soul in fact resemble the city as we have described it, held together by the three classes of craftsmen, auxiliaries, and guardians? . . .

No question about it. The soul must be composed of three parts.

Right, but only if spirit, which has already been distinguished from appetite, can now be distinguished from reason.

That is easily proved. Even young children display spirit almost from birth—that is, they frequently display indignation or anger. On the other hand, many of them never seem to discover where it is that reason rules, and most manage it only late in life.   b c   At last, then, strenuous effort has helped us to reach agreement that the structure of the city corresponds to the structure of the soul; both are composed of three basic elements.

Yes.

Wisdom is the same in the man and in the city. Courage in the city is the same as
d   courage in the individual. Virtue is the same quality in both. A man and a city will be deemed just or unjust according to the same standards.

Yes.

Let us not forget that justice in the city is founded in the good order to which each citizen doing his own work contributes. . . .

442d   I see no difference between the two, said Glaucon. . . .

443b   Then justice is nothing else than the power that brings forth well-governed men and well-governed cities. Our dream has come true. We have made real what we only
c   surmised at the outset of our inquiry when we suspected that some divine power was drawing our attention to a basic pattern of justice.

I agree. This is what we have accomplished. . . .

But the early model was analogy, not reality. The reality is that justice is not
d   a matter of external behavior but the way a man privately and truly governs his inner self. The just man does not permit the various parts of his soul to interfere with one another or usurp each other's functions. He has set his own life in order. He is his own master and his own law. He has become a friend to himself. He will
e   have brought into tune the three parts of his soul: high, middle, and low, like the three major notes of a musical scale, and all the intervals between. When he has brought all this together in temperance and harmony, he will have made himself one man instead of many.

Only then will he be ready to do whatever he does in society: making money, training the body, involving himself in politics or in business transactions. In all the public activities in which he is engaged he will call just and beautiful only that conduct which harmonizes with and preserves his own inner order which we have just described. And the knowledge that understands the meaning and importance of such conduct he will call wisdom.

444   Conversely, behavior that subverts the inner order he will deem unjust. The kind of intellect that sanctions such behavior he will condemn as ignorant and foolish.

Socrates, you have said the exact truth. . . .

d   Justice, like health, depends upon the presence of a natural order governing the soul in the relations of its parts and in the conduct of the whole. With injustice, as with illness, the natural order has vanished from the soul, giving place to its opposite.

Agreed.

e   Then we can agree that virtue is the very health, beauty, and strength of the soul, while vice makes the soul sick, ugly, and weak?

Yes.

What is beautiful, then, must lead to virtue and what is ugly to vice?

Yes.

445   Well, then, we have only one other matter to consider. Is it profitable to live one's life in the cause of justice and beauty, whether or not anyone takes notice? Or is it more profitable to be unjust, provided you can escape punishment and thus escape repentance, too?

But, Socrates, now you are really asking a ridiculous question. We all know that when our health is irreparably ruined, life is no longer worth living, no matter how much wealth, power, and luxury may be ours. No more would one wish to cling to life   b
if the soul's paramount principle were to be corrupted. With the principle of justice in ruins men are condemned to do whatever they like—except to banish evil and restore themselves to virtue.

Yes, the question is ridiculous. But it has helped us to reach the point where we may see truth clearly with our own eyes. . . .

Book VI

We have said that philosophers are those capable of comprehending what is eternal and   484b
unchanging. Those who are not philosophers lack this capability; instead they wander about inspecting swarms of irrelevancies. So who ought to be the leaders in a city?

How would one give a fair answer to the question?

By deciding who appear competent to guard the laws and the activities of society: c
these should be made the guardians. . . . What we need to ascertain is whether it is   485
possible for any people to have all the necessary qualities.

True.

As we noted earlier, the first thing we have to understand is the nature of the persons with whom we are concerned. If we sufficiently agree about this, then we shall likely agree also that the combination of qualities we seek is to be found in this kind of person. Then we need seek no further for guardians for our cities.

How do you mean?

We must first agree that one trait of the philosophical nature is ever to be in love with knowledge—not the kind caught up in the never-ending round of birth and   b
death, but the knowledge that discloses something of the eternal.

We do agree.

And such a nature loves and wants all of that knowledge. He does not willingly renounce any part of it, small or large, more valuable or less. In this he is like those covetous of love and of honor whom we described earlier.

Yes.

Must not those natures who are to meet our qualifications exhibit a further quality?   c

Which quality have you in mind?

Truthfulness: an unwillingness to countenance falsehood of any kind, a hatred of untruth, a love of truth.

Probably.

Not probably, but necessarily. . . . At the same time, we know that when a man's   d
desires strongly incline to any one thing, they are weaker with respect to other things. It is like a stream being diverted to another channel.

Yes.

So if a man's desires have been taught to flow into the channel of learning, he will become caught up in the pleasures of the soul. If he is a true and not a counterfeit   e
philosopher, he will become indifferent to the pleasures of the body. . . .

And do you think a mind of true grandeur, fixed on eternity and on all being, will   486
assign much importance to the life of man?

Impossible.

b Death will not be terrible to such a man?

To him least of all. . . .

Would a man who has put his soul in order, who is generous and . . . who is neither braggart nor coward—would he ever be unjust? . . .

Impossible. . . .

487 Can you, then, find any fault with a course of study that can be followed only by him whose nature learns quickly and whose memory is long, who displays the qualities of magnificence and grace, who is friend and kin to truth, justice, courage, and temperance?

Momus himself couldn't fault such a combination.[2]

Well, then, when they are matured by education and age, are these not the kind of men who alone should rule the city?

b At this point Adeimantus intervened: No one would be able to dispute these statements of yours, Socrates. Nonetheless, when your listeners hear you argue in this way, they think that because they are inexperienced in your method of question and answer, each question leads them ever so slightly astray until they reach the end of the argument when the sum of these divergences amounts to serious error and self-

c contradiction. They feel like unskilled players in a game contending with masters; they are finally cornered and can't make a move. So it is with your game, played with words instead of counters: finally their mouths are stopped, and they don't know what to say. Yet the truth of the matter has by no means been settled. Our present subject of discussion is a case in point. Someone might say that as far as words are concerned, he is unable to contradict you in any of your questions. But when he looks at the facts, he sees that of those who turn to philosophy—not the people who are merely acquiring a nodding acquaintance with it by way of rounding off their education but rather those

d who linger with the study of philosophy too long—the majority become cranks, not to say completely debased. And for even the best among them, the studies you yourself prescribe finally render them useless to society.

Do you suppose the men who say this are lying?

I don't know, but I should be glad to hear your opinion.

You shall hear it. I think they are telling the truth.

e Then how can it be right to say that our cities will have no respite from their ills until they are ruled by philosophers who, in turn, are of no use to them?

Your question needs to be answered with a parable. . . .

488 Now, nothing in all of nature can be found to match the cruelty with which society treats its best men. If I am to plead their cause, I must resort to fiction, combining a multitude of disparate things like painters do when they concoct fantastic progeny of stags and goats and the like. Let us imagine, then, a set of events happening aboard many ships or even only one. Imagine first the captain. He is taller and stronger than

b any of the crew. At the same time, he is a little deaf and somewhat short-sighted. Further, his navigation skills are about on a par with his hearing and and his vision. The sailors are quarreling with each other about who should take the helm. Each insists he has a right to steer the ship though he has never mastered the art of navigation and

---

2. Momus is the god of ridicule, censure, or blame. [Trans. note]

cannot say who taught him or when he learned. Pushing the matter further, they will assert that it cannot be taught anyway; anyone who contradicts them they will cut to pieces. Meanwhile, they crowd around the captain, badgering him and clamoring for the tiller. Occasionally some will succeed with their entreaties and get the captain's ear, but they will, in turn, fall victim to those who did not and will be put to death or be cast off the ship. Then, after fettering the worthy shipmaster and putting him into a stupor with narcotic or drink, they take command of the ship. Feasting and drinking, they consume the ship's stores and make a voyage of it as might be expected from such a crew. Further, they will use such terms as master mariner, navigator, and pilot to flatter the man who has shown most cunning in persuading or forcing the captain to turn over control of the ship. The man who is innocent of such skills they will call useless. They, in turn, are innocent of any understanding that one who is a real captain must concentrate his attention on the year's round, the seasons, the sky, wind, and stars, and all the arts that make him the true master of the ship. The captain does not believe there is any art or science involved in seizing control of a ship—with or without the consent of others. Nor does he believe that the practice and mastery of this alleged art is possible to combine with the science of navigation. With such activities going on would it surprise you if the sailors running the ship would call the true captain a useless stargazer and lunatic?

It would not surprise me.

And I presume you perceive my meaning. . . . Then teach the parable to anyone who wonders why philosophers are not honored in our cities; convince him it would be the greater wonder if they were so honored.

I will teach him.

And tell him also that he is right in saying that the best philosophers are of no use to the multitude. But bid him place the blame not on those who are best of men but on those who do not know how to use their skills. For it is unnatural that a pilot should beg his sailors to give him the command—or that wise men should go to the doors of the rich. (The inventor of this last epigram was a liar, of course.) But what is natural is that the sick man, whether rich or poor, must go to the door of the physician. Everyone who needs to be governed should go to the door of the man who knows how to govern. . . .

I think everyone will agree that one perfectly possessing all the qualities of the philosophic nature we have just described is a rare phenomenon among men and will be found only in a few. Do you concur?

Emphatically.

Now consider how many and powerful are the causes at work to ruin these few.

What are they?

Most surprisingly, they include those very virtues we have praised—courage, temperance, and the others—which play their own part in the corruption of the soul that possesses them and tear it away from philosophy.

Strange.

Further, those things men call good—beauty, wealth, bodily strength, powerful family connections in the city, and similar attributes—they, too, distract and corrupt the soul. . . . Consider: we know it to be true of every growing thing, whether seedling or flesh, that when it is deprived of the food, climate, or location suitable to its growth, it will suffer the greater damage, the greater its inherent vigor. For evil is a greater enemy of the good than of the commonplace.

Of course.

So it follows that the superior nature does less well than the inferior, where conditions of nurture are unfavorable?

Yes.

e   Then, Adeimantus, must we not say the same of men's minds? The most gifted, when exposed to a bad education, turn out the worst. Great crimes and systematic wickedness are not the products of half-hearted natures but of the vigorous ones who have been corrupted by their upbringing. Mediocrity will never attain to any great thing, good or evil.

That is true.

492   Then the qualities we assumed in the philosopher's nature will necessarily thrive and mature in all excellence, provided he is properly taught. But if sowing, planting, and germination take place in the wrong environment, the contrary outcome must be anticipated—unless some god comes to the rescue. . . .

502d   What studies and activities will our constitution makers pursue before their appointment to offices in the city? What are the appropriate age levels for the various studies they will undertake?

Yes, we need to discuss these things. . . .

503e   We must see to it that candidates are trained and tested in many subjects. And we
504 must observe them closely in order to judge whether they are capable of mastering the greatest and most difficult studies, or whether they will flinch and slip, as men will sometimes do in athletic trials and contests.

That certainly seems to be the right procedure, but what do you mean by the
d   greatest studies? . . . There is something still greater than justice and the other virtues we have considered?

Yes. There are some things still greater. . . .

e   Do you think anyone is going to let you get away without asking what you mean by the greatest study and what its subject is?

Go ahead and ask. You have already heard the answer often enough. Either you have not understood it, or you have made up your mind to make trouble for me again
505 by attacking my argument. I would guess the latter. After all, you have heard often enough that the greatest of all studies concerns the idea of the good. It is the one and indispensable source of what is useful and excellent in justice and the other virtues. Now, I am almost sure you know what I was going to say and that I would add, as well, that we know too little about it—and that however much we may know about other things will avail us nothing if we do not know this. Neither would any kind of posses-
b   sion profit us if we had not possession of the good. Or do you think there is any profit in possessing everything except that which is good? Or in understanding and knowing everything, but understanding and knowing nothing about the good and the beautiful?

No, by Zeus, I don't.

You know very well that for the multitude the good is pleasure. For those who claim greater refinement, the good is knowledge.

Yes, I know.

And you also know that the latter, after failing to explain what kind of knowledge they mean, ultimately find themselves forced to say that it is knowledge of the good.
c   Absurd.

Downright comical: first they taunt us that we are ignorant of the good and then turn around and talk to us as if we knew what it was after all. On top of that they assume that we understand the word *good* the way they do.

Very true.

Well, are their thoughts any more confused than those who define the good as pleasure? Or are these not also forced into a like contradiction, having finally to admit that some pleasures are bad?

Right.

The result of all this is that both persuasions find themselves using the terms *good* and *bad* for the same things.

Yes.

With the necessary consequence of numerous and vehement disputes?   d

Of course.

Still further: we see that many prefer to seem just and honorable rather than actually to be so. But do we not see it is different with the good? Here no one is content with mere appearances. When it comes to the good, all men seek the reality, and no   e one is satisfied with less.

Quite.

The good, then, is what every man wants. For its sake he will do all that he does. He intuits what the good is, but at the same time he is baffled, for the nature of the good is something he comprehends only inadequately. Nor is he able to invest in it the same sure confidence that he does in other things. For this very reason the benefits   506 these other things might otherwise yield are lost. Now, in a matter of this kind and importance, I ask you whether we can permit such blindness and ignorance in those best of men we want to govern the city?

Those least of all.

At any rate, a man who does not understand how justice and honor are related to the good won't guard them very effectively. I believe they cannot be understood in themselves without an understanding of this larger relationship.

Your belief is well founded.

Then our constitution can achieve its definitive form only if governed by a guar-   b dian who knows these things.

Necessarily. But, Socrates, what do you yourself think the good is? Is it knowledge, or pleasure, or something else?

Ah, what a man! You have been making it clear for a long time that you will not be content with the opinions of others in such matters.

That is true, Socrates. It does not seem right to me that someone like you who has examined these matters for so long should confine yourself to recounting the convictions of others but not express your own.

On the other hand, do you think it right to speak about what one does not know as if he knew it?

Of course no. But one doesn't have to claim knowledge; one can simply express opinion and label it as opinion.

No, no. Surely you know that opinions divorced from knowledge are ugly? Even the best of opinions are blind. An opinion can be true, but those who hold it without the requisite knowledge are no different from blind men who have chosen the right direction simply by chance. Or do you think there is a difference? . . .

d   No, by Zeus. But what I do want is that you not retreat at the very moment when
we are in sight of the goal. We shall be perfectly content if you explain the good to us
in the same way you explained the nature of justice, temperance, and the other virtues.

That would content me, too, my dear friend. But I fear my powers may not be able
to reach so far; I fear that my zeal might only make me ludicrous. No, my comrades,
e   let us set aside for a time the nature of the good itself. At the present moment I believe
that it is too great a task to attain what it appears to be in my thoughts. However, I am
willing to speak of what is most nearly like the good—of what seems to me the child
of the good—if you wish. Otherwise, we can let the matter drop.

No, speak. Another time you'll pay what remains due with an account of the
father. . . .

507b   We assert the existence of many beautiful things, many good things, and many
other kinds of things, and to each we give a name.

Yes.

At the same time, we speak of beauty as a single form and of the good in the same
way. In these and all other cases, then, we refer to the same things as both many and
one. Further, we can integrate the many into a single category and so make them one
again, a unity. This unity is what we call a form, something that really is.

Yes.

And we say that the multiplicity of things can be seen but not thought, while ideas
can be thought but not seen.

c   True.

And with which of our faculties do we perceive the visible?

With our eyesight. . . .

d   One may have vision in his eyes and try to put it to use, and color may be present
e   in the landscape; but unless a third component is present, the eyes will be sightless and
color will remain invisible.

What are you talking about?

Light.

I understand. . . .

508   Which of the deities in heaven can you name as author and cause of the light that
makes possible both vision and visibility?

Why, the one you and other people as well have in mind. You are talking about the
sun.

Then what is the relation of vision to that deity?

What do you mean?

Neither sight nor the eye in which sight is lodged is the sun itself?

b   Surely not.

But together, I think, they are the most sunlike of the sense organs.

By far.

And is the sun's abundance their source of power?

Yes.

Then the sun is not vision but the cause of vision as well as being the cause of sight.

That is right.

So here is the analogy I tried to draw when I spoke about the child of the good,
c   begotten in the likeness of the good. The relation of the sun to vision and its objects

in the visible world is the same as the relation of the good to reason and the objects of reason in the world of intellect.

What do you mean? Explain further.

You know that when night shades replace the light of day, the ability of the eyes to perceive color and shape is reduced almost to the point of blindness, altogether as if   d
they were bereft of vision.

Yes.

But when the eyes gaze upon objects illuminated by the sun, they see clearly; they evidently possess vision.

Right.

Now compare the eyes with the soul. When the soul beholds the realm illuminated by the splendor of truth and reality, it knows and understands and so appears to possess reason. But when it turns its gaze to that region where darkness and light intermingle, to the transient world where all things are either quickening or dying, reason's edge is blunted. The soul becomes mired in opinion; and since opinion shifts from one direction to another, it appears that reason has vanished.

It does seem that way.   e

The idea of the good, then, imbues the objects of knowledge with truth and confers upon the knower the power to know. Because the idea of the good is the very cause of knowledge and of truth, it is also the chief objective in the pursuit of knowledge. Yet as fair as truth and knowledge are, you will be right if you think there is something   509
fairer still. In our analogy when we proposed knowledge and truth as the counterparts of vision and light, it was proper to consider the latter two as sunlike but wrong to assume they are the same as the sun. In just the same way, knowledge and truth are like the good, but it is wrong to suppose that they are the good. A still greater glory belongs to the good.

If the good is the source of knowledge and truth and at the same time surpasses them both in beauty, you must have in mind a beauty quite beyond imagination. Surely you cannot be speaking of pleasure?

Be still. Let us consider how the good manifests itself in another way.

How?   b

I assume you would agree that the sun not only confers visibility on all that can be seen but is equally the source of generation, nurture, and growth in all things, though not itself the same as generation?

I agree.

If we pursue the comparison, the objects of knowledge are not only made manifest by the presence of goodness. Goodness makes them real. Still goodness is not in itself being. It transcends being, exceeding all else in dignity and power.

Glaucon had to laugh. My god, hyperbole can go no further than that!   c

It's your fault. You pushed me to express my thoughts.

Please don't desist. At least elaborate on the metaphor of the sun if there is anything you have been omitting.

I have been omitting a lot.

Well, omit no more, not the least bit.

I imagine I shall have to exclude a good deal. Nonetheless, as far as is practical at this point, I shall not willingly leave anything out.

Please don't.

d Recall, then, that we were speaking of two entities. One is the good, governor of the intelligible order. The other is the sun, governing the world of things seen . . . . In any case, you will keep in mind the visible and the intelligible?

I will.

Let us represent them as a divided line, partitioned into two unequal segments, one to denote the visual and the other the intelligible order. Then, using the same ratio as before, subdivide each of the segments. Let the relative length of these subdivisions
e serve as indicators of the relative clarity of perception all along the line. Now, within the visible sector the first one of the two subdivisions will contain nothing but images.
510 I mean such things as shadows or the reflections we see in water or mirrored in smooth, bright, and highly polished surfaces. Do you understand?

I understand.

In the subdivision above it are physical objects—the objects casting the shadows and reflections we observed below. I mean the living creatures all about us and all the works of man and nature.

Let it be so.

Would you also agree that the ratio between subdivisions—between shadow and substance—represents the degree of reality to be found in each and that it is also the same ratio dividing opinion from knowledge?
b Yes.

Now consider how we should go about dividing the intelligible sector.

How?

First, by identifying its own two subdivisions. In the lower one the soul's perception is restrained by a method of inquiry that reduces to images those things we defined as physical objects or models in the subdivision immediately below. Moreover, it operates with the kind of assumptions that lead to conclusions and not to first principles. But in the highest subdivision the soul makes no use of images. It also begins with assumptions and hypotheses but rises to a level where it relies exclusively on forms, a level of intellection that is free from all hypothetical thinking.

I don't think I understand all of what you say.

c Let's try again. What we have just said will help you understand better as we proceed. Among those who work with geometry and arithmetic and related subjects you know that the odd and the even, the several geometrical figures, the three kinds of angles, and other things related to their inquiries are treated as givens. That is, having adopted them as assumptions, they see no purpose in giving any account of them to
d themselves or others. They perceive them as self-evident. These premises are for them the starting points of inquiries, which they then pursue in all consistency until they arrive at the conclusions they originally set out to verify.

Yes, I know.

You know as well that they make use of visible shapes and objects and subject them to analysis. At the same time, however, they consider them only as images of the originals: the square as such or the diagonal as such. In all cases the originals are their con-
e cern and not the figures they draw. But the objects they draw or construct cast shadows or reflections in water and are therefore real, yet they convert what is real into images. And all the while they seek a reality which only the mind can discover.
511 Yes.

The method of investigation I have just described certainly belongs to the realm of the intelligible, but we must recognize its limitations. First, the method is necessarily dependent upon hypotheses. Because it is unable to go beyond these hypotheses, it is also unable to attain the level of first principles and new beginnings. Second, it transforms into images things that in the visible world below are physical objects. These objects are themselves copied in the visible order, where they are deemed far brighter and more distinct than those below them.

I understand that you are discussing things that pertain to geometry and its   b
allied arts.

Then let us go on to understand intelligibility at the highest level. This is the realm that reason masters with the power of dialectic. Assumptions are not treated as first principles but as real hypotheses. That is, they are not employed as beginnings but as ladders and springboards, used in order to reach that realm that requires no hypotheses and is therefore the true starting point for the attainment of unobstructed knowledge. When reason attains that level and becomes aware of the whole intelligible order, it descends at will to the level of conclusions but without the aid of sense objects. It rea-   c
sons only by using forms. It moves from forms through forms to forms. And it completes its journey in forms.

I understand you, but not fully. I see that you are describing an enormous undertaking. What I do understand is that you mean to make a distinction between, on the one hand, the realm of reality and intelligibility accessible only to the power of the dialectic and, on the other, the realm of the arts and sciences that depend on unexamined hypotheses. It is true that those who pursue arts and sciences do so with understanding and not by means of the senses. But they do not start from the beginning by going   d
behind their assumptions and examining them; instead they take them for granted. That is why you do not call these men truly intelligent, though the subject matters they investigate would clearly be intelligible to the dialectician. And you seem to call the intellectual efforts of the geometer and those like him understanding and not reason because you consider understanding to be something between opinion and reason.

You have understood me well. And now, let us match the four divisions we have made in the line with these four kinds of cognition in the soul. The highest will be intellection or reason; the next, understanding. The third is belief, and the last, con-   e
jecture. Now they must be assigned a space proportionate to the divisions in the line in order to show that each kind of cognition exhibits clarity and precision to the same degree as its cognates manifest truth and reality.

I understand and agree. I shall arrange them according to the order you have proposed.

Book VII

Here allegory may show us best how education—or the lack of it—affects our nature.   514
Imagine men living in a cave with a long passageway stretching between them and the cave's mouth, where it opens wide to the light. Imagine further that since childhood the cave dwellers have had their legs and necks shackled so as to be confined to the   b
same spot. They are further constrained by blinders that prevent them from turning their heads; they can see only directly in front of them. Next, imagine a light from

a fire some distance behind them and burning at a higher elevation. Between the prisoners and the fire is a raised path along whose edge there is a low wall like the partition at the front of a puppet stage. The wall conceals the puppeteers while they manipulate their puppets above it.

So far I can visualize it.

Imagine, further, men behind the wall carrying all sorts of objects along its length and holding them above it. The objects include human and animal images made of stone and wood and all other material. Presumably, those who carry them sometimes speak and are sometimes silent.

You describe a strange prison and strange prisoners.

Like ourselves. Tell me, do you not think those men would see only the shadows cast by the fire on the wall of the cave? Would they have seen anything of themselves or of one another?

How could they if they couldn't move their heads their whole life long?

Could they see the objects held above the wall behind them or only the shadows cast in front?

Only the shadows.

If, then, they could talk with one another, don't you think they would impute reality to the passing shadows?

Necessarily.

Imagine an echo in their prison, bouncing off the wall toward which the prisoners were turned. Should one of those behind the wall speak, would the prisoners not think that the sound came from the shadows in front of them?

No doubt of it.

By every measure, then, reality for the prisoners would be nothing but shadows cast by artifacts.

It could be nothing else.

Imagine now how their liberation from bondage and error would come about if something like the following happened. One prisoner is freed from his shackles. He is suddenly compelled to stand up, turn around, walk, and look toward the light. He suffers pain and distress from the glare of the light. So dazzled is he that he cannot even discern the very objects whose shadows he used to be able to see. Now what do you suppose he would answer if he were told that all he had seen before was illusion but that now he was nearer reality, observing real things and therefore seeing more truly? What if someone pointed to the objects being carried above the wall, questioning him as to what each one is? Would he not be at a loss? Would he not regard those things he saw formerly as more real than the things now being shown him?

He would.

Again, let him be compelled to look directly at the light. Would his eyes not feel pain? Would he not flee, turning back to those things he was able to discern before, convinced that they are in every truth clearer and more exact than anything he has seen since?

He would.

Then let him be dragged away by force up the rough and steep incline of the cave's passageway, held fast until he is hauled out into the light of the sun. Would not such a rough passage be painful? Would he not resent the experience? And when he came out into the sunlight, would he not be dazzled once again and unable to see what he calls realities?

He could not see even one of them, at least not immediately.

Habituation, then, is evidently required in order to see things higher up. In the beginning he would most easily see shadows; next, reflections in the water of men and other objects. Then he would see the objects themselves. From there he would go on to behold the heavens and the heavenly phenomena—more easily the moon and stars b by night than the sun by day.

Yes.

Finally, I suppose, he would be able to look on the sun itself, not in reflections in the water or in fleeting images in some alien setting. He would look at the sun as it is, in its own domain, and so be able to see what it is really like.

Yes.

It is at this stage that he would be able to conclude that the sun is the cause of the seasons and of the year's turning, that it governs all the visible world and is in some c sense also the cause of all visible things.

This is surely the next step he would take.

Now, supposing he recalled where he came from. Supposing he thought of his fellow prisoners and of what passed for wisdom in the place they were inhabiting. Don't you think he would feel pity for all that and rejoice in his own change of circumstance?

He surely would.

Suppose there had been honors and citations those below bestowed upon one another. Suppose prizes were offered for the one quickest to identify the shadows as they go by and best able to remember the sequence and configurations in which they appear. All these skills, in turn, would enhance the ability to guess what would come d next. Do you think he would covet such rewards? More, would he envy and want to emulate those who hold power over the prisoners and are in turn reverenced by them? Or would he not rather hold fast to Homer's words that it is "better to be the poor servant of a poor master," better to endure anything, than to believe those things and live that way?

I think he would prefer anything to such a life. e

Consider, further, if he should go back down again into the cave and return to the place he was before, would not his eyes now go dark after so abruptly leaving the sunlight behind?

They would. 517

Suppose he should then have to compete once more in shadow watching with those who never left the cave. And this before his eyes had become accustomed to the dark and his dimmed vision still required a long period of habituation. Would he not be laughed at? Would it not be said that he had made the journey above only to come back with his eyes ruined and that it is futile even to attempt the ascent? Further, if anyone tried to release the prisoners and lead them up and they could get their hands on him and kill him, would they not kill him?

Of course.

Now, my dear Glaucon, we must apply the allegory as a whole to all that has been said so far. The prisoners' cave is the counterpart of our own visible order, and the light b of the fire betokens the power of the sun. If you liken the ascent and exploration of things above to the soul's journey through the intelligible order, you will have understood my thinking, since that is what you wanted to hear. God only knows whether it is true. But, in any case, this is the way things appear to me: in the intelligible world the last thing to be seen—and then only dimly—is the idea of the good. Once seen, c however, the conclusion becomes irresistible that it is the cause of all things right and good, that in the visible world it gives birth to light and its sovereign source, that in the intelligible world it is itself sovereign and the author of truth and reason, and that the man who will act wisely in private and public life must have seen it.

I agree, insofar as I can follow your thinking.

Come join me, then, in this further thought. Don't be surprised if those who have d attained this high vision are unwilling to be involved in the affairs of men. Their souls will ever feel the pull from above and yearn to sojourn there. Such a preference is likely enough if the assumptions of our allegory continue to be valid....

518 Nonetheless, a man with common sense would know that eyesight can be impaired in two different ways by dint of two different causes, namely, transitions from light into darkness and from darkness into light. Believing that the soul also meets with the same experience, he would not thoughtlessly laugh when he saw a soul perturbed and having difficulty in comprehending something. Instead he would try to ascertain whether the cause of its faded vision was the passage from a brighter life to unaccustomed darkness or from the deeper darkness of ignorance toward the world of light, b whose brightness then dazzled the soul's eye....

A fair statement.

If this is true, it follows that education is not what some professors say it is. They c claim they can transplant the power of knowledge into a soul that has none, as if they were engrafting vision into blind eyes.

They do claim that.

But our reasoning goes quite to the contrary. We assert that this power is already in the soul of everyone. The way each of us learns compares with what happens to the eye: it cannot be turned away from darkness to face the light without turning the whole body. So it is with our capacity to know; together with the entire soul one must turn away from the world of transient things toward the world of perpetual being, until d finally one learns to endure the sight of its most radiant manifestation. This is what we call goodness, is it not?

Yes.

Then there must be some art that would most easily and effectively turn and convert the soul in the way we have described. It would lay no claim to produce sight in the soul's eye. Instead it would assume that sight is already there but wrongly directed; wrongly the soul is not looking where it should. This condition it would be the purpose of the art to remedy.

Such an art might be possible.

Wisdom, then, seems to be of a different order than those other things that are also called virtues of the soul. They seem more akin to the attributes of the body, for when they are not there at the outset, they can be cultivated by exercise and habit. But the e ability to think is more divine. Its power is constant and never lost. It can be useful and benign or malevolent and useless, according to the purposes toward which it is 519 directed. Or have you never observed in men who are called vicious but wise how sharp-sighted the petty soul is and how quickly it can pick out those things toward which it has turned its attention?...

I have seen these things....

b Supposing, I say, he were freed from all these kinds of things that draw the soul's vision downward. If he were then turned and converted to the contemplation of real things, he would be using the very same faculties of vision and be seeing them just as keenly as he now sees their opposites.

That is likely.

And must we not draw other likely and necessary conclusions from all that has been said so far? On the one hand, men lacking education and experience in truth cannot adequately preside over a city. Without a sense of purpose or duty in life they will also be without a sense of direction to govern their public and private acts. On the other hand, those who prolong their education endlessly are also unfit to rule because   c they become incapable of action. Instead, they suffer themselves to believe that while still living they have already been transported to the Islands of the Blessed.

So our duty as founders is to compel the best natures to achieve that sovereign knowledge we described awhile ago, to scale the heights in order to reach the vision of the good. But after they have reached the summit and have seen the view, we must   d not permit what they are now allowed to do.

What is that?

Remain above, refusing to go down again among those prisoners to share their labors and their rewards, whatever their worth may be.

Must we wrong them in this way, making them live a worse life when a better is possible?

My friend, you have forgotten again that the law is concerned not with the happiness of any particular class in the city but with the happiness of the city as a whole.   e Its method is to create harmony among the citizens by persuasion and compulsion, making them share the benefits that each is able to bestow on the community. The law   520 itself produces such men in the city, not in order to let them do as they please but with the intention of using them to bind the city together.

True, I did forget.

Consider further, Glaucon, that in fact we won't be wronging the philosophers who come among us. When we require them to govern the city and be its guardians, we shall vindicate our actions. For we shall say to them that it is quite understandable that men of their quality do not participate in the public life of other cities. After all, there   b they develop autonomously without favor from the government. It is only just that self-educated men, owing nothing to others for their enlightenment, are not eager to pay anyone for it. But you have been begotten by us to be like kings and leaders in a hive of bees, governing the city for its good and yours. Your education is better and   c more complete, and you are better equipped to participate in the two ways of life. So down you must go, each in turn, to where the others live and habituate yourselves to see in the dark. Once you have adjusted, you will see ten thousand times better than those who regularly dwell there. Because you have seen the reality of beauty, justice, and goodness, you will be able to know idols and shadows for what they are. Together and wide awake, you and we will govern our city, far differently from most cities today whose inhabitants are ruled darkly as in a dream by men who will fight with each other   d over shadows and use faction in order to rule, as if that were some great good. The truth is that the city where those who rule are least eager to do so will be the best governed and the least plagued by dissension. The city with the contrary kind of rulers will be burdened with the contrary characteristics.

SELECTED BIBLIOGRAPHY

The Collected Dialogues of Plato. ed. by E. Hamilton and H. Cairns. Princeton, N.J.: Princeton University Press, 1961.

Annas, Julia. *An Introduction to Plato's Republic*. New York: Oxford University Press, 1981.

Brumbaugh, Robert S. *Plato for the Modern Age*. New York: Crowell-Collier Press, 1962.

Friedlander, Paul. *Plato*. 3 vols. Trans. Hans Meyerhoff. Princeton, N.J.: Princeton University Press, 1970.

Gosling, J.C. *Plato*. The Arguments of the Philosophers. New York: Routledge, Chapman, and Hall, 1984.

Grube, G.M.A. *Plato's Thought*. Indianapolis: Hackett, 1980.

Guthrie, W.K.C. *Socrates*. Cambridge: Cambridge University Press, 1969.

Hare, R.M. *Plato*. New York: Oxford University Press, 1982.

Melling, D.J. *Understanding Plato*. New York: Oxford University Press, 1987.

Nettleship, Richard L. *Lectures on the Republic of Plato*. London: Macmillan, 1897.

Robinson, Richard. *Plato's Earlier Dialectic*. Oxford: Oxford University Press, 1953.

Shorey, Paul. *The Unity of Plato's Thought*. Chicago: University of Chicago Press, 1903.

_____. *What Plato Said*. Chicago: University of Chicago Press, 1933.

Taylor, A.E. *Plato: The Man and His Work*. London: Methuen, 1927.

_____. *Socrates: The Man and His Thought*. New York: Appleton, 1933.

Vlastos, Gregory. *The Philosophy of Socrates: A Collection of Critical Essays*. Garden City, N.Y.: Doubleday, 1971.

_____. *Plato: A Collection of Critical Essays*. 2 vols. Garden City, N.Y.: Doubleday, 1971.

White, Nicholas P. *A Companion to Plato's Republic*. Indianapolis: Hackett, 1979.

_____. *Plato on Knowledge and Reality*. Indianapolis: Hackett, 1976.

Aristotle

Aristotle was born in the northern Greek town of Stagira in 384 B.C.E. His father served as court physician to Amyntas II, king of Macedon, a fact that probably accounts for Aristotle's fascination with natural processes and established his long-standing ties to the Macedonian court.

In 367 B.C.E., at the age of seventeen, Aristotle went to Athens, where he joined Plato's Academy. Stories passed down tell us that Aristotle became known as "the reader" at the Academy, and that Plato recognized him as "the mind of the school." At the Academy, Aristotle lectured on rhetoric and other subjects and composed a number of dialogues in the Platonic style that were highly praised for their literary quality but of which only fragments remain. The twenty years he spent at the Academy were obviously very important in Aristotle's development; the influence of Plato is pervasive in Aristotle's works, even when Aristotle is at pains to distinguish his views from the Platonic.

When Plato died in 347, leadership of the Academy passed to his nephew Speusippus. Aristotle then left the Academy. The gossip was that he was irate at having been passed over for the leadership; and indeed, Speusippus was taking the Academy in a more mathematically oriented direction than Aristotle found congenial. But the facts that Aristotle was not a native Athenian and therefore could not own land and that the recent military adventures of Philip of Macedon had stirred up anti-Macedonian feelings that Aristotle felt wise to avoid probably also contributed to his decision to leave.

Aristotle then went to Atarneus, a city in Asia Minor ruled by Hermias, whose acquaintance he had first made at the Academy. There he married Pythias, Hermias' niece, and three years later moved to Mitylene, where he worked with Theophrastus, his longtime colleague and eventual successor at the Lyceum. It is during this post-Academy period that Aristotle undertook his biological, botanical, and zoological investigations. This turn to empirical science was as great an influence on Aristotle's ultimate philosophical position as the rarified debates of the Academy.

In 343 Aristotle was summoned by Philip to become tutor to his thirteen-year-old son, Alexander, later to be the greatest conqueror the world had yet known. We know little of what Aristotle taught the young prince or how much of it Alexander absorbed, but Aristotle supposedly wrote treatises on monarchy and on colonies for Alexander, who in return later sent Aristotle interesting biological specimens discovered during his conquests. Alexander became regent in 340, and Aristotle returned to Stagira, where he continued his investigations until 335, when he returned to Athens, now a city subject to Alexander's Macedonian dominion.

There Aristotle founded his own school, the Lyceum, where for the next dozen years he taught difficult subjects each morning to a select group of dedicated students and lectured more broadly on popular topics in the afternoon. The Lyceum was more like a modern university than the Academy had been, for Aristotle began to collect systematically both books and specimens, and his pupils began to specialize in particular departments of knowledge. It is from this period that the surviving works derive.

Alexander's sudden death in 323 put an end to Aristotle's most productive period. Athens turned against Macedonia, and a trumped-up charge of impiety (the same charge that had been directed at Socrates) was handed down against Aristotle. Aristotle quickly departed, as he reportedly remarked, lest Athens sin twice against philosophy. The following year he died of a digestive problem.

The breadth and depth of Aristotle's mastery of all that was known at the time remains unsurpassed in Western history. His contributions to biology, botany, zoology, astronomy, meteorology, anatomy, psychology, ethics, politics, metaphysics, economics, rhetoric, literary theory, theology, and logic were all fundamental, his influence on later ages of monumental proportions. The Lyceum continued to operate for another five hundred years, and though Aristotle's work went into temporary eclipse after the Fall of Rome, Saint Thomas Aquinas, writing in the thirteenth century, referred to Aristotle simply as "the Philosopher." Western philosophy is simply unimaginable without its twin pillars: Plato and Aristotle.

Philosophy

The breadth of Aristotle's work makes any brief overview of his philosophy extremely difficult. He is, perhaps above all, the philosopher who reasserted the importance of materiality in the face of Plato's overweening emphasis on ideality and the forms. Plato championed the notion that there is a separable essence or Idea for each kind of thing and a distinctive realm in which these Ideas or Forms exist apart from the sensible objects that copy or participate in them. Aristotle's inability to accept the doctrine of separable Ideas or Forms was apparently the root of his disagreements with Plato. To say that Aristotle reasserted the importance of materiality is not to say that Aristotle was a materialist. Neither idealistic nor materialistic, Aristotle's metaphysics is *hylomor-phic*. (This term, essentially created just to describe Aristotle's attempt to balance the ideal and the material, derives from the Greek *hyle*, for "matter," and *morphos*, for "form.") According to Aristotle, what there is in the world, primarily, are individual substances, each of which can be analyzed (but not necessarily decomposed) into a form, which makes that object what it is, inhabiting a certain kind of matter, which matter will, in its turn, have some form. Thus human beings have a certain typical form (our *psyche*) that inhabits flesh and blood, our matter. Aristotle is still Platonic enough (and antimaterialist enough) to give pride of place to form over matter, even though the two are almost (but not entirely) interdependent.

But the static form/matter distinction gives only half the story, for Aristotle's world is dynamic, full of life, growth, and change. Plato denied that we could ever have knowledge of the changing sensible world, but Aristotle dedicated himself to constructing precisely that knowledge. His important distinction between actuality and potentiality—the fundamental concepts in his explanation of change—arose for precisely this purpose. To defend the possibility of knowing the changing, Aristotle had to be able to claim that change need not be disordered anarchy, that there must be an order within all change. Change is the actualization of preexistent potentialities, not a series of random jumps.

The order in change that Aristotle saw around him was governed not by rigid laws but rather by *purpose*. Most of the changes that occur, according to Aristotle, occur for some end. The acorn grows in order to become an oak; animals hunt in order to eat; people act in order to be happy. Purposes can be either internal or external. An external purpose is assigned to an object from outside: beds are for sleeping because people have decided that is their purpose. All artifacts have external purposes. An internal purpose belongs intrinsically to the object, regardless of anyone's designs or intentions: plants and animals feed in order to live, and living is *natural* for them. There is a natural course that events tend to follow, and it can best be understood by examining the goals that different objects in the world naturally seek. In fact, the form of any natural object is also its end, for Aristotle treats objects as in some sense striving to fulfill the ideal of their form.

These important distinctions—form versus matter, actuality versus potentiality, and the notion of a natural end or purpose—lead to Aristotle's doctrine of the four causes, or four different ways to explain what a thing is. These four causes do not compete, and each thing must have all four—a material, a formal, an efficient, and a final cause. Take, for example, a chair. Its material cause is the wood and glue out of which it is made. Its efficient cause is the woodworker who put it together. Its formal cause is the form of a chair, which it may embody more or less well. And its final cause, the end for which it exists, is to be sat on comfortably.

As fundamental to Western philosophy as Aristotle's contributions to metaphysics are, there is still ongoing debate about his precise answer to his central question: what is substance, what are the primary objects in the world? As we have seen, Aristotle, unlike Plato, thinks that the changing individual substances of the world (e.g., the horse or the human being) can be genuine objects of understanding. But what are the *ultimate* realities or substances? Are they, as the *Categories* suggests, the concrete individual substances? Or are they the forms of the individuals (their souls, in the case of human beings or horses), as the *Metaphysics* suggests? And if the forms are the ultimate realities, should we think of them as universals (as in the form of humanity) or as individualized (Socrates' form)? These are the fascinating and perplexing puzzles that Aristotle's cryptic notes on metaphysics raise and that continue to challenge us today.

Aristotle's ethics are founded on his metaphysics, for he believed that ethics, the purpose of which is to mold good men, requires understanding what the good is for man—man's own final cause. (Unfortunately, *man* is the appropriate word choice here: unlike Plato, Aristotle reflected his times in treating women as lower beings.) We all strive for happiness, but what makes one truly happy? Happiness, Aristotle concludes, is the activity of the soul in accordance with *aretê* (variously translatable as "excellence," "virtue," "goodness," or the "best form of life"). The distinctive activity of man is reasoning; reasoning in its purest form, contemplation, is therefore the highest of human activities. Reason can rule throughout one's life, in one's practical activity as well as in theorizing. In our practical lives, right living must be a matter of forming the proper *habits* conducive to living well.

Some people have questioned whether Aristotle's ethics is an ethics at all, whether it isn't merely a self-help guide to a successful, but not necessarily *moral*, life. But Aristotle would surely have held that a society of people living in accordance with his precepts would be the best possible society, and not just in the sense of practical efficiency. The good life, according to Aristotle, is necessarily a life in the *polis*, among other people. The distinction between one's good as an individual and one's good as a member of the community would strike him as superficial.

The Reading Context

Categories

This presumably early work sets the stage for much of Aristotle's other work, for it raises the question of the primary form of being, substance, and its relation to all subsidiary forms of being. The ordinary meaning of *category* that Aristotle uses is "predicate," but substances are never predicates. Aristotle seems to assume that the structure of language reflects the structure of the world, an assumption that many of his successors have shared. As you read, keep experimenting with language to see if different ways of saying things seem to point to different conclusions about the categories and their relations.

Physics

Aristotle's goal in the *Physics* is twofold. He wants to show that a science of nature is possible, which some of his predecessors denied. And he wants to lay out the fundamental terms of the theory he has developed to understand natural change. Aristotle's physics dominated the human understanding of nature for two millennia. As you read, try to construct Aristotelian explanations of a rock's falling, a tree's growing, and the change from day to night.

Metaphysics

One of the most difficult works in the Western tradition, the *Metaphysics* is usually thought to be a heterogeneous collection of treatises and notes from various periods of Aristotle's life, put together posthumously by his editors. It can therefore be difficult to see what Aristotle intends in the different sections of the book. It is important to understand the sense in which the questions asked in the *Metaphysics* go beyond those of the *Physics* and form the heart of *first philosophy*, the discipline that investigates the assumptions that even physics must make and in particular raises the question of the formal and final cause of the world. Of central importance throughout is the question of substance: what is the most real, most fundamental aspect of reality?

Nicomachean Ethics

Ethics translates into English as "matters to do with character," and, as used in this work, the word so often translated as "virtue," *aretê*, could perhaps better be translated as the more neutral "excellence." Cultivating excellence of character is therefore the topic of the *Ethics*, and it is not clear that Aristotle intends a peculiarly *moral* kind of excellence. The *Nicomachean Ethics* (named for Aristotle's son Nicomachus) is, in part, a guide for success—success as a human being. It can be read in quite different ways: either as a historical document describing what the upperclass Greeks of the era thought constituted a good life or as a prescription for a good life that still has a claim on us. Try to conjure up a vision of Aristotle's successful human, and compare that person with the models of success we find paraded before us today.

A Note on the Texts

Aristotle's works were preserved in the Lyceum for many centuries after his death, collected and edited by his followers. None of the manuscripts currently available can be traced back that far, however, and a number of spurious works have been attributed to Aristotle. Hence constructing a reliable text of Aristotle's works is a difficult task.

It is currently believed that although some of his works were written as homogenous pieces by Aristotle, others, notably the *Metaphysics*, are more likely compilations from lecture notes, either Aristotle's own or those of his pupils. His lecture notes are essentially terse discussions on which he would have expanded during actual lectures. Some passages are worked out very fully; others are particularly sketchy and obscure. Gaps in presentation occur, as do several repetitions, where slight revisions of similar material was preserved. This inconsistency of presentation makes Aristotle one of the most challenging of all philosophers to read.

Except for the *Categories*, Aristotle's work was relatively unknown in the early medieval period. The Crusaders' contact with Islamic philosophers reintroduced Aristotle to the West, and he once again became a dominant philosophical figure.

References to Aristotle have a standard form, derived from I. Bekker's 1831 edition, which is printed in two-column pages. Thus a reference like "1097b24" refers to the sentence that appears on line 24 of the second column of page 1097 in Bekker's edition. The translation used here is the revised Oxford translation published originally under the editorship of W. D. Ross and revised under that of Jonathan Barnes.

Reading Questions

Categories

1. What is it to be said of a subject? To be in a subject?
2. What does Aristotle mean by "substance"? What things does he think are substances, according to the *Categories*?
3. Is Aristotle's list of categories exhaustive?
4. Does Aristotle assume that the structure of language reflects the structure of the world?

Physics

5. Distinguish the four forms of causation. How does Aristotle's use of *cause* differ from the modern use of the term?
6. How does Aristotle argue against the view that nature operates by blind necessity without final causes?

Metaphysics

7. What is the *Metaphysics* about?
8. What are the different senses of being that Aristotle discusses? How are they all related?
9. In what sense is Aristotelian metaphysics a theology?
10. Aristotle seems to subscribe to the following theses: (a) The real (substance) is knowable. (b) Only the universal is knowable. (c) The real (substance) is the individual. How does he reconcile them?
11. Why is it wrong to say that form and matter are *parts* of a substance?
12. Could either form or matter be entirely separable from the other?

Nicomachean Ethics

13. What is the purpose of ethical reflection? What are its standards of success?
14. What does Aristotle understand by "an activity of the soul in accordance with excellence"?
15. Are all virtues means between extremes? How about honesty?
16. When is an action voluntary? Involuntary? Under what conditions are we responsible for our actions?
17. Is the Aristotelian man someone you would like as a friend? As yourself? What of the Aristotelian woman?

Categories

1. When things have only a name in common and the definition of being which 1a1 corresponds to the name is different, they are called *homonymous*. Thus, for example, both a man and a picture are animals. These have only a name in common and the definition of being which corresponds to the name is different; for if one is to say what being an animal is for each of them, one will give two distinct definitions. 5

When things have the name in common and the definition of being which corresponds to the name is the same, they are called *synonymous*. Thus, for example, both a man and an ox are animals. Each of these is called, by a common name, an animal, and the definition of being is also the same; for if one is to give the definition of 10 each—what being an animal is for each of them—one will give the same definition.

When things get their name from something, with a difference of ending, they are called *paronymous*. Thus, for example, the grammarian gets his name from grammar, the brave get theirs from bravery. 15

2. Of things that are said, some involve combination while others are said without combination. Examples of those involving combination are: man runs, man wins; and of those without combination: man, ox, runs, wins.

Of things there are: (*a*) some are *said of* a subject but are not *in* any subject. For exam- 20 ple, man is said of a subject, the individual man, but is not in any subject. (*b*) Some are in a subject but are not said of any subject. (By "in a subject" I mean what is in some- thing, not as a part, and cannot exist separately from what it is in.) For example, the 25 individual knowledge-of-grammar is in a subject, the soul, but is not said of any subject; and the individual white is in a subject, the body (for all colour is in a body), but is not said of any subject. (*c*) Some are both said of a subject and in a subject. For example, knowledge is in a subject, the soul, and is also said of a subject, knowledge-of-grammar. 1b1 (*d*) Some are neither in a subject nor said of a subject, for example, the individual man 5 or the individual horse—for nothing of this sort is either in a subject or said of a subject. Things that are individual and numerically one are, without exception, not said of any subject, but there is nothing to prevent some of them from being in a subject—the individual knowledge-of-grammar is one of the things in a subject.

3. Whenever one thing is predicated of another as of a subject, all things said of 10 what is predicated will be said of the subject also. For example, man is predicated of the individual man, and animal of man; so animal will be predicated of the individual man also—for the individual man is both a man and an animal. 15

The differentiae of genera which are different and not subordinate one to the other are themselves different in kind. For example, animal and knowledge: footed, winged, aquatic, two-footed, are differentiae of animal, but none of these is a differentia of 20 knowledge; one sort of knowledge does not differ from another by being two-footed. However, there is nothing to prevent genera subordinate one to the other from having the same differentiae. For the higher are predicated of the genera below them, so that all differentiae of the predicated genus will be differentiae of the subject also.

Translated by J.L. Ackrill. All Aristotle excerpts from Jonathan Barnes, ed., *The Complete Works of Aristotle: The Revised Oxford Translation*. Bollingen Series 71. Copyright © 1984 Jowett Copyright Trustees. Excerpts reprinted with permission of Princeton University Press.

25   4. Of things said without any combination, each signifies either substance or quantity or qualification or a relative or where or when or being-in-a-position or having or doing or being-affected. To give a rough idea, examples of substance are man, horse;

2a1   of quantity: four-foot, five-foot; of qualification: white, grammatical; of a relative: double, half, larger; of where: in the Lyceum, in the market-place; of when: yesterday, last-year; of being-in-a-position: is-lying, is-sitting; of having: has-shoes-on, has-armour-on; of doing: cutting, burning; of being-affected: being-cut, being-burned.

5   None of the above is said just by itself in any affirmation, but by the combination of these with one another an affirmation is produced. For every affirmation, it seems,

10   is either true or false; but of things said without any combination none is either true or false (e.g. man, white, runs, wins).

      5. A *substance*—that which is called a substance most strictly, primarily, and most of all—is that which is neither said of a subject nor in a subject, e.g. the individual

15   man or the individual horse. The species in which the things primarily called substances are, are called *secondary substances*, as also are the genera of these species. For example, the individual man belongs in a species, man, and animal is a genus of the species; so these—both man and animal—are called secondary substances.

      It is clear from what has been said that if something is said of a subject both its

20   name and its definition are necessarily predicated of the subject. For example, man is said of a subject, the individual man, and the name is of course predicated (since you will be predicating man of the individual man), and also the definition of man will be

25   predicated of the individual man (since the individual man is also a man). Thus both the name and the definition will be predicated of the subject. But as for things which are in a subject, in most cases neither the name nor the definition is predicated of the

30   subject. In some cases there is nothing to prevent the name from being predicated of the subject, but it is impossible for the definition to be predicated. For example, white, which is in a subject (the body), is predicated of the subject; for a body is called white. But the definition of white will never be predicated of the body.

35   All the other things are either said of the primary substances as subjects or in them as subjects. This is clear from an examination of cases. For example, animal is predicated of man and therefore also of the individual man; for were it predicated of none

2b1   of the individual men it would not be predicated of man at all. Again, colour is in body and therefore also in an individual body; for were it not in some individual body it would not be in body at all. Thus all the other things are either said of the primary

5   substances as subjects or in them as subjects. So if the primary substances did not exist it would be impossible for any of the other things to exist.

      Of the secondary substances the species is more a substance than the genus, since it is nearer to the primary substance. For if one is to say of the primary substance what it

10   is, it will be more informative and apt to give the species than the genus. For example, it would be more informative to say of the individual man that he is a man than that he is an animal (since the one is more distinctive of the individual man while the other

15   is more general); and more informative to say of the individual tree that it is a tree than that it is a plant. Further, it is because the primary substances are subjects for all the other things and all the other things are predicated of them or are in them, that they are called substances most of all. But as the primary substances stand to the other things,

20   so the species stands to the genus: the species is a subject for the genus (for the genera are predicated of the species but the species are not predicated reciprocally of the genera). Hence for this reason too the species is more a substance than the genus.

But of the species themselves—those which are not genera—one is no more a substance than another: it is no more apt to say of the individual man that he is a man than to say of the individual horse that it is a horse. And similarly of the primary substances one is no more a substance than another: the individual man is no more a substance than the individual ox. . . .   25

It is a characteristic common to every substance not to be in a subject. For a primary substance is neither said of a subject nor in a subject. And as for secondary substances, it is obvious at once that they are not in a subject. For man is said of the   3a10 individual man as subject but is not in a subject: man is not *in* the individual man. Similarly, animal also is said of the individual man as subject, but animal is not *in* the individual man. Further, while there is nothing to prevent the name of what is in a   15 subject from being sometimes predicated of the subject, it is impossible for the definition to be predicated. But the definition of the secondary substances, as well as the name, is predicated of the subject: you will predicate the definition of man of the individual man, and also that of animal. No substance, therefore, is in a subject.   20

This is not, however, peculiar to substance, since the differentia also is not in a subject. For footed and two-footed are said of man as subject but are not in a subject; neither two-footed nor footed is *in* man. Moreover, the definition of the differentia is   25 predicated of that of which the differentia is said. For example, if footed is said of man the definition of footed will also be predicated of man; for man is footed.

We need not be disturbed by any fear that we may be forced to say that the parts   30 of a substance, being in a subject (the whole substance), are not substances. For when we spoke of things *in a subject* we did not mean things belonging in something as *parts*.

It is a characteristic of substances and differentiae that all things called from them are so called synonymously. For all the predicates from them are predicated either of   35 the individuals or of the species. (For from a primary substance there is no predicate, since it is said of no subject; and as for secondary substances, the species is predicated of the individual, the genus both of the species and of the individual. Similarly, differentiae too are predicated both of the species and of the individuals.). . .   3b1

Every substance seems to signify a certain "this." As regards the primary substances,   10 it is indisputably true that each of them signifies a certain "this"; for the thing revealed is individual and numerically one. But as regards the secondary substances, though it appears from the form of the name—when one speaks of man or animal—that a secon-   15 dary substance likewise signifies a certain "this," this is not really true; rather, it signifies a certain qualification—for the subject is not, as the primary substance is, one, but man and animal are said of many things. However, it does not signify simply a certain qualification, as white does. White signifies nothing but a qualification, whereas the   20 species and the genus mark off the qualification of substance—they signify substance of a certain qualification. . . .

Another characteristic of substances is that there is nothing contrary to them. For what would be contrary to a primary substance? For example, there is nothing contrary   25 to an individual man, nor yet is there anything contrary to man or to animal. This, however, is not peculiar to substance but holds of many other things also, for example, of quantity. For there is nothing contrary to four-foot or to ten or to anything of this kind—unless someone were to say that many is contrary to few or large to small; but   30 still there is nothing contrary to any *definite* quantity.

Substance, it seems, does not admit of a more and a less. I do not mean that one substance is not more a substance than another (we have said that it is), but that any   35 given substance is not called more, or less, that which it is. For example, if this substance is a man, it will not be more a man or less a man either than itself or than another man. For one man is not more a man than another, as one pale thing is more pale than another and one beautiful thing more beautiful than another. Again, a thing is called more, or less, such-and-such than itself. . . . For a man is not called more a man now than before, nor is anything else that is a substance. Thus substance does not admit of a more and a less.

It seems most distinctive of substance that what is numerically one and the same is able to receive contraries. In no other case could one bring forward anything, numerically one, which is able to receive contraries. For example, a colour which is numerically one and the same will not be black and white, nor will numerically one and the same action be bad and good; and similarly with everything else that is not substance. A substance, however, numerically one and the same, is able to receive contraries. For example, an individual man—one and the same—becomes pale at one time and dark at another, and hot and cold, and bad and good.

Physics

Book II

1. Of things that exist, some exist by nature, some from other causes. By nature the animals and their parts exist, and the plants and the simple bodies (earth, fire, air, water)—for we say that these and the like exist by nature.

192b10

All the things mentioned plainly differ from things which are *not* constituted by nature. For each of them has within itself a principle of motion and of stationariness (in respect of place, or of growth and decrease, or by way of alteration). On the other hand, a bed and a coat and anything else of that sort, *qua* receiving these designations—i.e. in so far as they are products of art—have no innate impulse to change. But in so far as they happen to be composed of stone or of earth or of a mixture of the two, they *do* have such an impulse, and just to that extent—which seems to indicate that nature is a principle or cause of being moved and of being at rest in that to which it belongs primarily, in virtue of itself and not accidentally. . . .

Nature then is what has been stated. Things have a nature which have a principle of this kind. Each of them is a substance; for it is a subject, and nature is always in a subject.

The term "according to nature" is applied to all these things and also to the attributes which belong to them in virtue of what they are, for instance the property of fire to be carried upwards—which is not a nature nor has a nature but is by nature or according to nature.

What nature is, then, and the meaning of the terms "by nature," and "according to nature," has been stated. *That* nature exists, it would be absurd to try to prove; for it is obvious that there are many things of this kind, and to prove what is obvious by what is not is the mark of a man who is unable to distinguish what is self-evident from what is not. (This state of mind is clearly possible. A man blind from birth might reason about colours.) Presumably therefore such persons must be talking about words without any thought to correspond.

Some identify the nature or substance of a natural object with that immediate constituent of it which taken by itself is without arrangement, e.g. the wood is the nature of the bed, and the bronze the nature of the statue. . . .

But if the material of each of these objects has itself the same relation to something else, say bronze (or gold) to water, bones (or wood) to earth and so on, *that* (they say) would be their nature and substance. Consequently some assert earth, others fire or air or water or some or all of these, to be the nature of the things that are. For whatever any one of them supposed to have this character—whether one thing or more than one thing—this or these he declared to be the whole of substance, all else being its affections, states, or dispositions. Every such thing they held to be eternal (for it could not pass into anything else), but other things to come into being and cease to be times without number.

This then is one account of nature, namely that it is the primary underlying matter of things which have in themselves a principle of motion or change.

Translated by W.D. Ross.

30   Another account is that nature is the shape or form which is specified in the definition of the thing.

For the word "nature" is applied to what is according to nature and the natural in the same way as "art" is applied to what is artistic or a work of art. We should not say in the latter case that there is anything artistic about a thing, if it is a bed only poten-
35   tially, not yet having the form of a bed; nor should we call it a work of art. The same is true of natural compounds. What is potentially flesh or bone has not yet its own
193b1   nature, and does not exist by nature, until it receives the form specified in the definition, which we name in defining what flesh or bone is. Thus on the second account of nature, it would be the shape or form (not separable except in statement) of things
5   which have in themselves a principle of motion. (The combination of the two, e.g. man, is not nature but by nature.)

The form indeed is nature rather than the matter; for a thing is more properly said to be what it is when it exists in actuality than when it exists potentially. Again man is born from man but not bed from bed. That is why people say that the shape is not
10   the nature of a bed, but the wood is—if the bed sprouted, not a bed but wood would come up. But even if the shape is art, then on the same principle the shape of man is his nature. For man is born from man.

Again, nature in the sense of a coming-to-be proceeds towards nature. For it is not like doctoring, which leads not to the art of doctoring but to health. Doctoring must
15   start from the art, not lead to it. But it is not in this way that nature is related to nature. What grows qua growing grows from something into something. Into what then does it grow? Not into that from which it arose but into that to which it tends. The shape then is nature. . . .

2. We have distinguished, then, the different ways in which the term "nature" is used. . . .

Since two sorts of thing are called nature, the form and the matter, we must investigate its objects as we would the essence of snubness, that is neither independently
194a15 of matter nor in terms of matter only. Here too indeed one might raise a difficulty. Since there are two natures, with which is the student of nature concerned? Or should he investigate the combination of the two? But if the combination of the two, then also each severally. Does it belong then to the same or to different sciences to know each severally?

If we look at the ancients, natural science would seem to be concerned with the
20   matter. (It was only very slightly that Empedocles and Democritus touched on form and essence.)

But if on the other hand art imitates nature, and it is the part of the same discipline to know the form and the matter up to a point (e.g. the doctor has a knowledge of
25   health and also of bile and phlegm, in which health is realized . . . : if this is so, it would be the part of natural science also to know nature in both its senses.

Again, that for the sake of which, or the end, belongs to the same department of knowledge as the means. But the nature is the end or that for the sake of which. For
30   if a thing undergoes a continuous change toward some end, that last stage is actually that for the sake of which. . . .

For the arts make their material (some simply make it, others make it serviceable),
35   and we use everything as if it was there for our sake. (We also are in a sense an end. "That for the sake of which" may be taken in two ways, as we said in our work On

Philosophy.) The arts, therefore, which govern the matter and have knowledge are two, 194b1
namely the art which uses the product and the art which directs the production of it.
That is why the using art also is in a sense directive; but it differs in that it knows the
form, whereas the art which is directive as being concerned with production knows 5
the matter. For the helmsman knows and prescribes what sort of form a helm should
have, the other from what wood it should be made and by means of what operations.
In the products of art, however, we make the material with a view to the function,
whereas in the products of nature the matter is there all along. . . .

3. Now that we have established these distinctions, we must proceed to consider
causes, their character and number. Knowledge is the object of our inquiry, and men
do not think they know a thing till they have grasped the "why" of it (which is to grasp 20
its primary cause). So clearly we too must do this as regards both coming to be and
passing away and every kind of natural change, in order that, knowing their principles,
we may try to refer to these principles each of our problems.

In one way, then, that out of which a thing comes to be and which persists, is called
a cause, e.g. the bronze of the statue, the silver of the bowl, and the genera of which 25
the bronze and the silver are species.

In another way, the form or the archetype, i.e. the definition of the essence, and its
genera, are called causes (e.g. of the octave the relation of 2:1, and generally number),
and the parts in the definition.

Again, the primary source of the change or rest; e.g. the man who deliberated is a 30
cause, the father is cause of the child, and generally what makes of what is made and
what changes of what is changed.

Again, in the sense of end or that for the sake of which a thing is done, e.g. health
is the cause of walking about. ("Why is he walking about?" We say: "To be healthy," and,
having said that, we think we have assigned the cause.) The same is true also of all the 35
intermediate steps which are brought about through the action of something else as
means towards the end, e.g. reduction of flesh, purging, drugs, or surgical instruments
are means towards health. . . .

This then perhaps exhausts the number of ways in which the term "cause" is used.

As things are called causes in many ways, it follows that there are several causes of
the same thing (not merely accidentally), e.g. both the art of the sculptor and the 195a5
bronze are causes of the statue. These are causes of the statue *qua* statue, not in virtue
of anything else that it may be—only not in the same way, the one being the material
cause, the other the cause whence the motion comes. Some things cause each other
reciprocally, e.g. hard work causes fitness and *vice versa*, but again not in the same way,
but the one as end, the other as the principle of motion. Further the same thing is the 10
cause of contrary results. For that which by its presence brings about one result is sometimes blamed for bringing about the contrary by its absence. Thus we ascribe the wreck
of a ship to the absence of the pilot whose presence was the cause of its safety.

All the causes now mentioned fall into four familiar divisions. The letters are the 15
causes of syllables, the material of artificial products, fire and the like of bodies, the
parts of the whole, and the premisses of the conclusion, in the sense of "that from
which." Of these pairs the one set are causes in the sense of what underlies, e.g. the
parts, the other set in the sense of essence—the whole and the combination and the 20
form. But the seed and the doctor and the deliberator, and generally the maker, are all
sources whence the change or stationariness originates, which the others are causes in

the sense of the end or the good of the rest; for that for the sake of which tends to be
25   what is best and the end of the things that lead up to it. (Whether we call it good or
apparently good makes no difference.)

Such then is the number and nature of the kinds of cause.

Now the modes of causation are many, though when brought under heads they too
can be reduced in number. For things are called causes in many ways and even within
30   the same kind one may be prior to another; e.g. the doctor and the expert are causes
of health, the relation 2:1 and number of the octave, and always what is inclusive to
what is particular. Another mode of causation is the accidental and its genera, e.g. in
one way Polyclitus, in another a sculptor is the cause of a statue, because being Polycli-
35   tus and a sculptor are accidentally conjoined. Also the classes in which the accidental
attribute is included; thus a man could be said to be the cause of a statue or, generally,
195b1 a living creature. An accidental attribute too may be more or less remote, e.g. suppose
that a pale man or a musical man were said to be the cause of the statue.

All causes, both proper and accidental, may be spoken of either as potential or as
5   actual; e.g. the cause of a house being built is either a house-builder or a house-builder
building. . . .

All these various uses, however, come to six in number, under each of which again
the usage is twofold. It is either what is particular or a genus, or an accidental attribute
15   or a genus of that, and these either as a complex or each by itself; and all either as
actual or as potential. The difference is this much, that causes which are actually at
work and particular exist and cease to exist simultaneously with their effect, e.g. this
healing person with this being-healed person and that housebuilding man with that
20   being-built house; but this is not always true of potential causes—the house and the
housebuilder do not pass away simultaneously.

In investigating the cause of each thing it is always necessary to seek what is most
precise (as also in other things): thus a man builds because he is a builder, and a builder
25   builds in virtue of his art of building. This last cause then is prior; and so generally.

Further, generic effects should be assigned to generic causes, particular effects
to particular causes, e.g. statue to sculptor, this statue to this sculptor; and powers
are relative to possible effects, actually operating causes to things which are actually
being effected.

This must suffice for our account of the number of causes and the modes of
30   causation.

4. But chance and spontaneity are also reckoned among causes: many things are
said both to be and to come to be as a result of chance and spontaneity. We must
inquire therefore in what manner chance and spontaneity are present among the
35   causes enumerated, and whether they are the same or different, and generally what
chance and spontaneity are.

Some people even question whether there are such things or not. They say that
196a1 nothing happens by chance, but that everything which we ascribe to chance or spontaneity has some definite cause, e.g. coming by chance into the market and finding
5   there a man whom one wanted but did not expect to meet is due to one's wish to go
and buy in the market. Similarly, in other so-called cases of chance it is always possible, they maintain, to find something which is the cause. . . .

Certainly the early physicists found no place for chance among the causes which
they recognized—love, strife, mind, fire, or the like. . . .

There are some who actually ascribe this heavenly sphere and all the worlds to   25
spontaneity. They say that the vortex arose spontaneously, i.e. the motion that separated and arranged the universe in its present order. This statement might well cause
surprise. For they are asserting that chance is not responsible for the existence or
generation of animals and plants, nature or mind or something of the kind being the   30
cause of them (for it is not any chance thing that comes from a given seed but an olive
from one kind and a man from another); and yet at the same time they assert that the
heavenly sphere and the divinest of visible things arose spontaneously, having no such
cause as is assigned to animals and plants. . . .

Thus we must inquire what chance and spontaneity are, whether they are the same
or different, and how they fit into our division of causes.

5. First then we observe that some things always come to pass in the same way, and   196b10
others for the most part. It is clearly of neither of these that chance, or the result of
chance, is said to be the cause—neither of that which is by necessity and always, nor
of that which is for the most part. But as there is a third class of events besides these
two—events which all say are by chance—it is plain that there is such a thing as   15
chance and spontaneity. . . .

Of things that come to be, some come to be for the sake of something, others not.
Again, some of the former class are in accordance with intention, others not, but both
are in the class of things which are for the sake of something. Hence it is clear that
even among the things which are outside what is necessary and what is for the most   20
part, there are some in connexion with which the phrase "for the sake of something"
is applicable. (Things that are for the sake of something include whatever may be done
as a result of thought or of nature.) Things of this kind, then, when they come to pass
accidentally are said to be by chance. For just as a thing is something either in virtue   25
of itself or accidentally, so may it be a cause. For instance, the housebuilding faculty
is in virtue of itself a cause of a house, whereas the pale or the musical is an accidental
cause. That which is *per se* cause is determinate, but the accidental cause is indeter-
minable; for the possible attributes of an individual are innumerable. As we said, then,
when a thing of this kind comes to pass among events which are for the sake of some-   30
thing, it is said to be spontaneous or by chance. (The distinction between the two
must be made later—for the present it is sufficient if it is plain that both are in the
sphere of things done for the sake of something.)

Example: A man is engaged in collecting subscriptions for a feast. He would have
gone to such and such a place for the purpose of getting the money, if he had known.   35
He actually went there for another purpose, and it was only accidentally that he got
his money by going there; and this was not due to the fact that he went there as a rule
or necessarily, nor is the end effected (getting the money) a cause present in himself—   197a1
it belongs to the class of things that are objects of choice and the result of thought.
It is when these conditions are satisfied that the man is said to have gone by chance.
If he had chosen and gone for the sake of this—if he always or normally went there
when he was collecting payments—he would not be said to have gone by chance.   5

It is clear then that chance is an accidental cause in the sphere of those actions for
the sake of something which involve choice. Thought, then, and chance are in the
same sphere, for choice implies thought. . . .

And the causes of the man's coming and getting the money (when he did not come
for the sake of that) are innumerable. He may have wished to see somebody or been

following somebody or avoiding somebody, or may have gone to see a spectacle. Thus to say that chance is unaccountable is correct. For an account is of what holds
20   always or for the most part, whereas chance belongs to a third type of event. Hence, since causes of this kind are indefinite, chance too is indefinite. (Yet in some cases one might raise the question whether *any* chance fact might be the cause of the chance occurrence, e.g. of health the fresh air or the sun's heat may be the cause, but having had one's hair cut *cannot*; for some accidental causes are more relevant to the effect than others.). . .

Both are then, as I have said, accidental causes—both chance and spontaneity—in the sphere of things which are capable of coming to pass not simply, nor for the
35   most part and with reference to such of these as might come to pass for the sake of something.

6. They differ in that spontaneity is the wider. Every result of chance is from what is spontaneous, but not everything that is from what is spontaneous is from chance.

197b1   Chance and what results from chance are appropriate to agents that are capable of good fortune and of action generally. Therefore necessarily chance is in the sphere of
5   actions. . . . Hence what is not capable of action cannot do anything by chance. Thus an inanimate thing or a beast or a child cannot do anything by chance, because it is incapable of choice. . . .

The spontaneous on the other hand is found both in the beasts and in many inani-
15   mate objects. We say, for example, that the horse came spontaneously, because, though his coming saved him, he did not come for the sake of safety. . . .

Hence it is clear that events which belong to the general class of things that may come to pass for the sake of something, when they come to pass not for the sake of
20   what actually results, and have an external cause, may be described by the phrase "from spontaneity." These spontaneous events are said to be from chance if they have the further characteristics of being the objects of choice and happening to agents capable of choice. . . .

198a1   We have now explained what chance is and what spontaneity is, and in what they differ from each other. Both belong to the mode of causation "source of change," for either some natural or some intelligent agent is always the cause; but in this sort of causation the number of possible causes is infinite. . . .

7. Now, the causes being four, it is the business of the student of nature to know about them all, and if he refers his problems back to all of them, he will assign the "why" in the way proper to his science—the matter, the form, the mover, that for the
25   sake of which. The last three often coincide; for the what and that for the sake of which are one, while the primary source of motion is the same in species as these. For man generates man—and so too, in general, with all things which cause movement by being themselves moved; and such as are not of this kind are no longer inside the province of natural science, for they cause motion not by possessing motion or a source
30   of motion in themselves, but being themselves incapable of motion. Hence there are three branches of study, one of things which are incapable of motion, the second of things in motion, but indestructible, the third of destructible things.

The question "why," then, is answered by reference to the matter, to the form, and to the primary moving cause. For in respect of coming to be it is mostly in this last way that causes are investigated—"what comes to be after what? what was the primary
35   agent or patient?" and so at each step of the series.

Now the principles which cause motion in a natural way are two, of which one is 198b1
not natural, as it has no principle of motion in itself. Of this kind is whatever causes
movement, not being itself moved, such as that which is completely unchangeable,
the primary reality, and the essence of a thing, i.e. the form; for this is the end or that
for the sake of which. Hence since nature is for the sake of something, we must know
this cause also. We must explain the "why" in all the senses of the term, namely, that 5
from this that will necessarily result ("from this" either without qualification or for the
most part); that this must be so if that is to be so (as the conclusion presupposes the
premises); that this was the essence of the thing; and because it is better thus (not
without qualification, but with reference to the substance in each case).

8. We must explain then first why nature belongs to the class of causes which act 10
for the sake of something; and then about the necessary and its place in nature, for all
writers ascribe things to this cause, arguing that since the hot and the cold and the like
are of such and such a kind, therefore certain things *necessarily* are and come to be—
and if they mention any other cause (one friendship and strife, another mind), it is 15
only to touch on it, and then good-bye to it.

A difficulty presents itself: why should not nature work, not for the sake of something, nor because it is better so, but just as the sky rains, not in order to make the corn
grow, but of necessity? (What is drawn up must cool, and what has been cooled must
become water and descend, the result of this being that the corn grows.) Similarly if 20
a man's crop is spoiled on the threshing-floor, the rain did not fall for the sake of this—
in order that the crop might be spoiled—but that result just followed. Why then
should it not be the same with the parts in nature, e.g. that our teeth should come up 25
of necessity—the front teeth sharp, fitted for tearing, the molars broad and useful for
grinding down the food—since they did not arise for this end, but it was merely a coin-
cident result; and so with all other parts in which we suppose that there is purpose?
Wherever then all the parts came about just what they would have been if they had
come to be for an end, such things survived, being organized spontaneously in a fitting 30
way; whereas those which grew otherwise perished and continue to perish, as Empedocles says his "man-faced oxprogeny" did.

Such are the arguments (and others of the kind) which may cause difficulty on this
point. Yet it is impossible that this should be the true view. For teeth and all other
natural things either invariably or for the most part come about in a given way; but of
not one of the results of chance or spontaneity is this true. We do not ascribe to chance 199a1
or mere coincidence the frequency of rain in winter, but frequent rain in summer we
do; nor heat in summer but only if we have it in winter. If then, it is agreed that things
are either the result of coincidence or for the sake of something, and these cannot be
the result of coincidence or spontaneity, it follows that they must be for the sake of 5
something; and that such things are all due to nature even the champions of the
theory which is before us would agree. Therefore action for an end is present in things
which come to be and are by nature.

Further, where there is an end, all the preceding steps are for the sake of that. Now
surely as in action, so in nature; and as in nature, so it is in each action, if nothing 10
interferes. Now action is for the sake of an end; therefore the nature of things also is
so. Thus if a house, e.g., had been a thing made by nature, it would have been made
in the same way as it is now by art; and if things made by nature were made not only
by nature but also by art, they would come to be in the same way as by nature. The one, 15

then, is for the sake of the other; and generally art in some cases completes what nature cannot bring to a finish, and in others imitates nature. If, therefore, artificial products are for the sake of an end, so clearly also are natural products. The relation of the later to the earlier items is the same in both.

20   This is most obvious in the animals other than man: they make things neither by art nor after inquiry or deliberation. That is why people wonder whether it is by intelligence or by some other faculty that these creatures work—spiders, ants, and the like. By gradual advance in this direction we come to see clearly that in plants too that is

25   produced which is conducive to the end—leaves, e.g. grow to provide shade for the fruit. If then it is both by nature and for an end that the swallow makes its nest and the spider its web, and plants grow leaves for the sake of the fruit and send their roots

30   down (not up) for the sake of nourishment, it is plain that this kind of cause is operative in things which come to be and are by nature. And since nature is twofold, the matter and the form, of which the latter is the end, and since all the rest is for the sake of the end, the form must be the cause in the sense of that for the sake of which.

Now mistakes occur even in the operations of art: the literate man makes a mistake in writing and the doctor pours out the wrong dose. Hence clearly mistakes are

199b1   possible in the operations of nature also. If then in art there are cases in which what is rightly produced serves a purpose, and if where mistakes occur there was a purpose in what was attempted, only it was not attained, so must it be also in natural products, and monstrosities will be failures in the purposive effort. Thus in the original

5   combinations the "ox-progeny," if they failed to reach a determinate end must have arisen through the corruption of some principle, as happens now when the seed is defective. . . .

The end and the means towards it may come about by chance. We say, for instance,

20   that a stranger has come by chance, paid the ransom, and gone away, when he does so as if he had come for that purpose, though it was not for that that he came. This is

25   accidental, for chance is an accidental cause, as I remarked before. But when an event takes place always or for the most part, it is not accidental or by chance. In natural products the sequence is invariable, if there is no impediment.

It is absurd to suppose that purpose is not present because we do not observe the agent deliberating. Art does not deliberate. If the ship-building art were in the wood, it would produce the same results by nature. If, therefore, purpose is present in art, it

30   is present also in nature. The best illustration is a doctor doctoring himself: nature is like that.

It is plain then that nature is a cause, a cause that operates for a purpose.

9. As regards what is of necessity, we must ask whether the necessity is hypothetical, or simple as well. The current view places what is of necessity in the process of

200a1   production, just as if one were to suppose that the wall of a house necessarily comes to be because what is heavy is naturally carried downwards and what is light to the top, so that the stones and foundations take the lowest place, with earth above because it is lighter, and wood at the top of all as being the lightest. Whereas, though the wall

5   does not come to be *without* these, it is not *due* to these, except as its material cause: it comes to be for the sake of sheltering and guarding certain things. Similarly in all other things which involve that for the sake of which: the product cannot come to be without things which have a necessary nature, but it is not due to these (except as its material); it comes to be for an end. . . . What is necessary then, is necessary on a

hypothesis, not as an end. Necessity is in the matter, while that for the sake of which is in the definition. . . .

The necessary in nature, then, is plainly what we call by the name of matter, and the changes in it. Both causes must be stated by the student of nature, but especially the end; for that is the cause of the matter, not *vice versa*; and the end is that for the sake of which, and the principle starts from the definition or essence: as in artificial products, since a house is of such-and-such a kind, certain things must *necessarily* come to be or be there already, or since health is this, these things must necessarily come to be or be there already, so too if man is this, then these; if these, then those. Perhaps the necessary is present also in the definition. For if one defines the operation of sawing as being a certain kind of dividing, then this cannot come about unless the saw has teeth of a certain kind; and these cannot be unless it is of iron. For in the definition too there are some parts that stand as matter.

200b1

5

Metaphysics

Book I

1. All men by nature desire to know. An indication of this is the delight we take in our senses: for even apart from their usefulness they are loved for themselves; and

980a25   above all others the sense of sight. For not only with a view to action, but even when we are not going to do anything, we prefer sight to almost everything else. The reason is that this, most of all the senses, makes us know and brings to light many differences between things.

By nature animals are born with the faculty of sensation, and from sensation memory is produced in some of them, though not in others. And therefore the former are more intelligent and apt at learning than those which cannot remember: those which are incapable of hearing sounds are intelligent though they cannot be taught, e.g. the bee, and any other race of animals that may be like it; and those which besides

980b25   memory have this sense of hearing, can be taught.

The animals other than man live by appearances and memories, and have but little of connected experience; but the human race lives also by art and reasonings. And from memory experience is produced in men: for many memories of the same thing

981a1   produce finally the capacity for a single experience. Experience seems to be very similar to science and art, but really science and art come to men *through* experience; for

5   "experience made art," as Polus says, "but inexperience luck." And art arises, when from many notions gained by experience one universal judgement about similar objects is produced. For to have a judgement that when Callias was ill of this disease this did him good, and similarly in the case of Socrates and in many individual cases, is a matter

10   of experience; but to judge that it has done good to all persons of a certain constitution, marked off in one class, when they were ill of this disease, e.g. to phlegmatic or bilious people when burning with fever—this is a matter of art.

With a view to action experience seems in no respect inferior to art, and we even see men of experience succeeding more than those who have theory without

15   experience. The reason is that experience is knowledge of individuals, art of universals, and actions and productions are all concerned with the individual: for the physician does not cure a man, except in an incidental way, but Callias or Socrates or some

20   other called by some such individual name, who happens to be a man. If, then, a man has theory without experience, and knows the universal but does not know the individual included in this, he will often fail to cure; for it is the individual that is to be cured. But yet we think that *knowledge* and *understanding* belong to art rather than

25   to experience, and we suppose artists to be wiser than men of experience (which implies that wisdom depends in all cases rather on knowledge); and this because the former know the cause, but the latter do not. For men of experience know that the thing is so, but do not know why, while the others know the "why" and the cause.

30   Hence we think that the master-workers in each craft are more honourable and know

981b1   in a truer sense and are wiser than the manual workers, because they know the causes

5   of the things that are done...; thus we view them as being wiser not in virtue of

---

Translated by W. D. Ross.

being able to act, but of having the theory for themselves and knowing the causes. And in general it is a sign of the man who knows, that he can teach, and therefore we think art more truly knowledge than experience is: for artists can teach, and men of mere experience cannot.

We have said in the *Ethics* what the difference is between art and science and the other kindred faculties; but the point of our present discussion is this, that all men suppose what is called wisdom to deal with the first causes and the principles of things. This is why, as has been said before, the man of experience is thought to be wiser than the possessors of any perception whatever, the artist wiser than the men of experience, the master-worker than the mechanic, and the theoretical kinds of knowledge to be more of the nature of wisdom than the productive. Clearly then wisdom is knowledge about certain causes and principles.

2. Since we are seeking this knowledge, we must inquire of what kind are the causes and the principles, the knowledge of which is wisdom. If we were to take the notions we have about the wise man, this might perhaps make the answer more evident. We suppose first, then, that the wise man knows all things, as far as possible, although he has not knowledge of each of them individually; secondly, that he who can learn things that are difficult, and not easy for man to know, is wise (sense-perception is common to all, and therefore easy and no mark of wisdom); again, he who is more exact and more capable of teaching the causes is wiser, in every branch of knowledge; and of the sciences, also, that which is desirable on its own account and for the sake of knowing it is more of the nature of wisdom than that which is desirable on account of its results, and the superior science is more of the nature of wisdom than the ancillary: for the wise man must not be ordered but must order, and he must not obey another, but the less wise must obey *him*.

Such and so many are the notions, then, which we have about wisdom and the wise. Now of these characteristics that of knowing all things must belong to him who has in the highest degree universal knowledge: for he knows in a sense all the subordinate objects. And these things, the most universal, are on the whole the hardest for men to know: for they are furthest from the senses. And the most exact of the sciences are those which deal most with first principles: for those which involve fewer principles are more exact than those which involve additional principles, e.g. arithmetic than geometry. But the science which investigates causes is also more capable of teaching, for the people who teach are those who tell the causes of each thing. And understanding and knowledge pursued for their own sake are found most in the knowledge of that which is most knowable: for he who chooses to know for the sake of knowing will choose most readily that which is most truly knowledge, and such is the knowledge of that which is most knowable: and the first principles and the causes are most knowable; for by reason of these, and from these, all other things are known, but these are not known by means of the things subordinate to them. And the science which knows to what end each thing must be done is the most authoritative of the sciences, and more authoritative than any ancillary science: and this end is the good in each class, and in general the supreme good in the whole of nature. Judged by all the tests we have mentioned, then, the name in question falls to the same science; this must be a science that investigates the first principles and causes: for the good, i.e. that for the sake of which, is one of the causes.

That it is not a science of production is clear even from the history of the earliest philosophers. For it is owing to their wonder that men both now begin and at first

began to philosophize: they wondered originally at the obvious difficulties, then
15   advanced little by little and stated difficulties about the greater matters, e.g. about the
phenomena of the moon and those of the sun and the stars, and about the genesis of
the universe. And a man who is puzzled and wonders thinks himself ignorant (whence
even the lover of myth is in a sense a lover of wisdom, for myth is composed of
20   wonders); therefore since they philosophized in order to escape from ignorance, evidently they were pursuing science in order to know, and not for any utilitarian end.
And this is confirmed by the facts: for it was when almost all the necessities of life and
the things that make for comfort and recreation were present, that such knowledge
25   began to be sought. Evidently then we do not seek it for the sake of any other advantage; but as the man is free, we say, who exists for himself and not for another, so we
pursue this as the only free science, for it alone exists for itself.

Hence the possession of it might be justly regarded as beyond human power; for in
30   many ways human nature is in bondage, so that according to Simonides "God alone
can have this privilege," and it is unfitting that man should not be content to seek the
knowledge that is suited to him. If, then, there is something in what the poets say, and
983a1   jealousy is natural to the divine power, it would probably occur in this case above all,
and all who excelled in this knowledge would be unfortunate. But the divine power
cannot be jealous (indeed, according to the proverb, "bards tell many a lie"), nor should
any science be thought more honourable than one of this sort. For the most divine
5   science is also most honourable; and this science alone is, in two ways, most divine.
For the science which it would be most meet for God to have is a divine science, and
so is any science that deals with divine objects: and this science alone has both these
qualities: for God is thought to be among the causes of all things and to be a first prin-
10   ciple, and such a science either God alone can have, or God above all others. All the
sciences, indeed, are more necessary than this, but none is better. . . .

We have stated, then, what is the nature of the science we are searching for, and
what is the mark which our search and our whole investigation must reach. . . .

Book IV

1. There is a science which investigates being as being and the attributes which belong
to this in virtue of its own nature. Now this is not the same as any of the so-called
1003a25   special sciences: for none of these others deals generally with being as being. They cut
off a part of being and investigate the attributes of this part—this is what the mathematical sciences for instance do. Now since we are seeking the first principles and the
highest causes, clearly there must be some thing to which these belong in virtue of its
own nature. If then our predecessors who sought the elements of existing things were
30   seeking these same principles, it is necessary that the elements must be elements of
being not by accident but just because it is being. Therefore it is of being as being that
we also must grasp the first causes.

2. There are many senses in which a thing may be said to "be," but they are related
to one central point, one definite kind of thing, and are not homonymous. Everything
35   which is healthy is related to health, one thing in the sense that it preserves health,
another in the sense that it produces it, another in the sense that it is a symptom of
1003b1   health, another because it is capable of it. And that which is medical is relative to the

medical art, one thing in the sense that it possesses it, another in the sense that it is naturally adapted to it, another in the sense that it is a function of the medical art. And we shall find other words used similarly to these. So, too, there are many senses 5
in which a thing is said to be, but all refer to one starting-point; some things are said to be because they are substances, others because they are affections of substance, others because they are a process towards substance, or destructions or privations or qualities of substance, or productive or generative of substance, or of things which are relative to substance, or negations of some of these things or of substance itself. It is 10
for this reason that we say even of non-being that it *is* non-being. As, then, there is one science which deals with all healthy things, the same applies in the other cases also. For not only in the case of things which have one common notion does the investigation belong to one science, but also in the case of things which are related to one common nature; for even these in a sense have one common notion. It is clear then 15
that it is the work of one science also to study all things that are, *qua* being.—But everywhere science deals chiefly with that which is primary, and on which the other things depend, and in virtue of which they get their names. If, then, this is substance, it is of substances that the philosopher must grasp the principles and the causes.

Now for every single class of things, as there is one perception, so there is one science, as for instance grammar, being one science, investigates all articulate sounds. 20
Therefore to investigate all the species of being *qua* being, is the work of a science which is generically one, and to investigate the several species is the work of the specific parts of the science.

If, now, being and unity are the same and are one thing in the sense that they are implied in one another as principle and cause are, not in the sense that they are explained by the same formula (though it makes no difference even if we interpret 25
them similarly—in fact this would strengthen our case); for one man and a man are the same thing and existent man and a man are the same thing, and the doubling of the words in "one man" and "one existent man" does not give any new meaning (it is clear that they are not separated either in coming to be or in ceasing to be); and similarly with "one," so that it is obvious that the addition in these cases means the same thing, 30
and unity is nothing apart from being; and if, further, the essence of each thing is one in no merely accidental way, and similarly is from its very nature something that *is*:— all this being so, there must be exactly as many species of being as of unity. And to investigate the essence of these is the work of a science which is generically one—I mean, for instance, the discussion of the same and the similar and the other concepts 35
of this sort. . . .—And there are as many parts of philosophy as there are kinds of substance, so that there must necessarily be among them a first philosophy and one which follows this. For being falls immediately into genera; and therefore the sciences too 1004a5
will correspond to these genera. . . .

Now since it is the work of one science to investigate opposites, and plurality is 10
opposite to unity, and it belongs to one science to investigate the negation and the privation because in both cases we are really investigating unity, to which the negation or the privation refers. . ., the contraries of the concepts we named above, the other and the dissimilar and the unequal, and everything else which is derived either from these or from plurality and unity, must fall within the province of the science above-named.—And contrariety is one of these concepts, for contrariety is a kind of differ- 20
ence, and difference is a kind of otherness. Therefore, since there are many senses in

which a thing is said to be one, these terms also will have many senses, but yet it
belongs to one science to consider them all; for a term belongs to different sciences
25   not if it has different senses, but if its definitions neither are identical nor can be
referred to one central meaning. And since all things are referred to that which is
primary, as for instance all things which are one are referred to the primary one, we
must say that this holds good also of the same and the other and of contraries in
general; so that after distinguishing the various senses of each, we must then explain
30   by reference to what is primary in each term, saying how they are related to it; some
in the sense that they possess it, others in the sense that they produce it, and others
in other such ways.

It is evident then that it belongs to one science to be able to give an account of
these concepts as well as of substance. . . .

And it is the function of the philosopher to be able to investigate all things. For
1004b1   if it is not the function of the philosopher, who is it who will inquire whether Socrates
and Socrates seated are the same thing, or whether one thing has one contrary, or
what contrariety is, or how many meanings it has? And similarly with all other such
5   questions. Since, then, these are essential modifications of unity *qua* unity and of
being *qua* being, not *qua* numbers or lines or fire, it is clear that it belongs to this
science to investigate both the essence of these concepts and their properties. And
those who study these properties err not by leaving the sphere of philosophy, but by
10   forgetting that substance, of which they have no correct idea, is prior to these other
things. For number *qua* number has peculiar attributes, such as oddness and evenness,
commensurability and equality, excess and defect, and these belong to numbers either
in themselves or in relation to one another. And similarly the solid and the motionless
15   and that which is in motion and the weightless and that which has weight have other
peculiar properties. So too certain properties are peculiar to being as such, and it is
about these that the philosopher has to investigate the truth.

Book VII

1028a10   1. There are several senses in which a thing may be said to be. . ., for in one sense it
means what a thing is or a "this," and in another sense it means that a thing is of a certain quality or quantity or has some such predicate asserted of it. While "being" has
all these senses, obviously that which is primarily is the "what," which indicates the
15   substance of the thing. For when we say of what quality a thing is, we say that it is good
or beautiful, but not that it is three cubits long or that it is a man; but when we say
what it is, we do not say "white" or "hot" or "three cubits long," but "man" or "God." And
all other things are said to be because they are, some of them, quantities of that which
is in this primary sense, others qualities of it, others affections of it, and others some
20   other determination of it. And so one might raise the question whether "to walk" and
"to be healthy" and "to sit" signify in each case something that is, and similarly in any
other case of this sort; for none of them is either self-subsistent or capable of being
separated from substance, but rather, if anything, it is that which walks or is seated or
25   is healthy that is an existent thing. Now these are seen to be more real because there
is something definite which underlies them; and this is the substance or individual,
which is implied in such a predicate; for "good" or "sitting" are not used without this.

Clearly then it is in virtue of this category that each of the others *is*. Therefore that
which is primarily and *is* simply (not is something) must be substance.   30

Now there are several senses in which a thing is said to be primary; but substance
is primary in every sense—in formula, in order of knowledge, in time. For of the other
categories none can exist independently, but only substance. And in formula also this   35
is primary; for in the formula of each term the formula of its substance must be present.
And we think we know each thing most fully, when we know what it is, e.g. what man   1028b1
is or what fire is, rather than when we know its quality, its quantity, or where it is; since
we know each of these things also, only when we know *what* the quantity or the
quality *is*.

And indeed the question which, both now and of old, has always been raised, and
always been the subject of doubt, viz. what being is, is just the question, what is substance? For it is this that some assert to be one, others more than one, and that some   5
assert to be limited in number, others unlimited. And so we also must consider chiefly
and primarily and almost exclusively what that is which *is* in this sense. . . .

3. The word "substance" is applied, if not in more senses, still at least to four main
objects; for both the essence and the universal and the genus are thought to be the
substance of each thing, and fourthly the substratum. Now the substratum is that of   35
which other things are predicated, while it is itself not predicated of anything else.
And so we must first determine the nature of this; for that which underlies a thing
primarily is thought to be in the truest sense its substance. And in one sense matter   1029a1
is said to be of the nature of substratum, in another, shape, and in a third sense, the
compound of these. By the matter I mean, for instance, the bronze, by the shape the
plan of its form, and by the compound of these (the concrete thing) the statue. There-   5
fore if the form is prior to the matter and more real, it will be prior to the compound
also for the same reason.

We have now outlined the nature of substance, showing that it is that which is not
predicated of a subject, but of which all else is predicated. But we must not merely
state the matter thus; for this is not enough. The statement itself is obscure, and further, on this view, *matter* becomes substance. For if this is not substance, it is beyond   10
us to say what else is. When all else is taken away evidently nothing but matter
remains. For of the other elements some are affections, products, and capacities of
bodies, while length, breadth, and depth are quantities and not substances. . . . But   15
when length and breadth and depth are taken away we see nothing left except that
which is bounded by these, whatever it be; so that to those who consider the question
thus matter alone must seem to be substance. By matter I mean that which in itself is   20
neither a particular thing nor of a certain quantity nor assigned to any other of the
categories by which being is determined. For there is something of which each of these
is predicated, so that its being is different from that of each of the predicates; for the
predicates other than substance are predicated of substance, while substance is predicated of matter. Therefore the ultimate substratum is of itself neither a particular thing
nor of a particular quantity nor otherwise positively characterized; nor yet negatively,   25
for negations also will belong to it only by accident.

For those who adopt this point of view, then, it follows that matter is substance. But
this is impossible; for both separability and individuality are thought to belong chiefly
to substance. And so form and the compound of form and matter would be thought
to be substance, rather than matter. The substance compounded of both, i.e. of matter   30

and shape, may be dismissed; for it is posterior and its nature is obvious. And matter also is in a sense manifest. But we must inquire into the third kind of substance; for this is the most difficult. . . .

1029b10   4. Since at the start we distinguished the various marks by which we determine substance, and one of these was thought to be the essence, we must investigate this. And first let us say something about it in the abstract. The essence of each thing is what it is said to be in virtue of itself. For being you is not being musical; for you are not musical in virtue of yourself. What, then, you are in virtue of yourself is your essence.

But not the whole of this is the essence of a thing; not that which something is in virtue of itself in the way in which a surface is white, because being a surface is not being white. But again the combination of both—being a white surface—is not the essence of surface. Why? Because "surface" itself is repeated. The formula, therefore, in which the term itself is not present but its meaning is expressed, this is the formula of the essence of each thing. Therefore if to be a white surface is to be a smooth surface, to be white and to be smooth are one and the same.

But since there are compounds of substance with the other categories (for there is a substrate for each category, e.g. for quality, quantity, time, place, and motion), we must inquire whether there is a formula of the essence of each of them, i.e. whether to these compounds also there belongs an essence, e.g. to white man. . . . Probably not. For the essence is what something is; but when one thing is said of another, that is not what a "this" is, e.g. white man is not what a "this" is since being a "this" belongs only to substances. Therefore there is an essence only of those things whose formula is a definition. But we have a definition not where we have a word and a formula identical in meaning (for in that case all formulae would be definitions; for there will be some name for any formula whatever, so that even the *Iliad* would be a definition), but where there is a formula of something primary; and primary things are those which do not involve one thing's being said of another. Nothing, then, which is not a species of a genus will have an *essence*—only species will have it, for in these the subject is not thought to participate in the attribute and to have it as an affection, nor to have it by accident; but for everything else as well, if it has a name, there will be a formula of its meaning—viz. that this attribute belongs to this subject; or instead of a simple formula we shall be able to give a more accurate one; but there will be no definition nor essence.

But after all, "definition," like "what a thing is," has several meanings; "what a thing is" in one sense means substance and a "this," in another one or other of the predicates, quantity, quality, and the like. For as "is" is predicable of all things, not however in the same sense, but of one sort of thing primarily and of others in a secondary way, so too the "what" belongs simply to substance, but in a limited sense to the other categories. For even of a quality we might ask what it is, so that a quality also is a "what"—not simply, however, but just as, in the case of that which is not, some say, in the abstract, that that which is not *is*—not *is* simply, but *is* non-existent. So too with a quality. . . .

5. It is a difficult question, if one denies that a formula with an addition is a definition, whether any of the things that are not simple but coupled will be definable. For we *must* explain them by an addition. E.g. there is the nose, and concavity, and snubness, which is compounded out of the two by the presence of the one in the other, and it is not by accident that the nose has the attribute either of concavity or of snubness, but in virtue of its nature; nor do they attach to it as whiteness does to Callias, or to man (because Callias, who happens to be a man, is white), but rather as "male"

attaches to animal and "equal" to quantity, and as everything else which is said of something in its own right. And such attributes are those in which is involved either the *formula* or the *name* of the subject of the particular attribute, and which cannot be explained without this; e.g. white can be explained apart from man, but not female 25 apart from animal. Therefore there is either no essence and definition of any of these things, or if there is, it is in another sense, as we have said.

But there is also a second difficulty about them. For if snub nose and concave nose are the same thing, snub and concave will be the same thing; but if snub and concave are not the same (because it is impossible to speak of snubness apart from the 30 thing of which, in its own right, it is an attribute, for snubness is concavity *in the nose*), either it is impossible properly to say "snub nose" or the same thing will have been said twice, concave nose nose; for snub nose will be concave nose nose. And so it is absurd that such things should have an essence; if they have, there will be an infinite regress; for in snub nose yet another nose will be involved.

Clearly then only substance is definable. For if the other categories also are defin- 1031a1 able, it must be by addition, e.g. the qualitative is defined thus, and so is the odd, for it cannot be defined apart from number; nor can female be defined apart from animal. (When I say "by addition" I mean the expressions in which we have to say the same thing twice, as in these instances.) And if this is true, coupled terms also, like "odd 5 number," will not be definable (but this escapes our notice because our formulae are not accurate). But if these also are definable, either it is in some other way or, as we said, definition and essence must be said to have more than one sense. Therefore in 10 one sense nothing will have a definition and nothing will have an essence, except sub- stances, but in another sense other things will have them. Clearly, then, definition is the formula of the essence, and essence must belong to substances either alone or chiefly and primarily and in the unqualified sense.

6. We must inquire whether each thing and its essence are the same or differ- 15 ent. This is of some use for the inquiry concerning substance; for each thing is thought to be not different from its substance, and the essence is said to be the sub- stance of each thing.

Now in the case of things with accidental attributes the two would be generally thought to be different, e.g. white man would be thought to be different from the 20 essence of white man. For if they are the same, the essence of man and that of white man are also the same; for a man and a white man are the same, as people say, so that the essence of white man and that of man would be also the same. But probably it is 25 not necessary that things with accidental attributes should be the same. For the extreme terms are not in the same way the same.—Perhaps *this* might be thought to fol- low, that the extreme terms, the accidents, should turn out to be the same, e.g. the essence of white and that of musical; but this is not actually thought to be the case.

But in the case of so-called self-subsistent things, is a thing necessarily the same as its essence? E.g. if there are some substances which have no other substances nor enti- ties prior to them—substances such as some assert the Ideas to be? If the essence of 30 good is to be different from the Idea of good, and the essence of animal from the Idea of animal, and the essence of being from the Idea of being, there will, firstly, be other 1031b1 substances and entities and Ideas besides those which are asserted, and, secondly, these others will be prior substances if the essence is substance. And if the posterior substances are severed from one another, there will be no knowledge of the ones and

5   the others will have no being. (By "severed" I mean, if the Idea of good has not the
essence of good, and the latter has not the property of being good.) For there is
knowledge of each thing only when we know its essence. And the case is the same for
other things as for the good; so that if the essence of good is not good, neither will the
10 essence of being be, nor the essence of unity be one. And all essences alike exist or
none of them does; so that if the essence of being is not, neither will any of the others
be. Again, that which has not the property of being good is not good. The good, then,
must be one with the essence of good, and the beautiful with the essence of beauty,
and so with all things which do not depend on something else but are self-subsistent
15 and primary. For it is enough if they are this, even if there are no Forms; and perhaps
all the more if there are Forms.—At the same time it is clear that if there are Ideas such
as some people say there are, the substratum of them will not be substance; for these
must be substances, and not predicable of a substratum; for if they were they would
exist only by being participated in.—Each thing then and its essence are one and the
same in no merely accidental way, as is evident both from the preceding arguments and
20 because to *know* each thing, at least, is to know its essence, so that even by the exhibi-
tion of instances it becomes clear that both must be one.

(But of an accidental term, e.g. "the musical" or "the white," since it has two meanings, it is not true to say that it itself is identical with its essence; for both that to
25 which the accidental quality belongs, and the accidental quality, are white, so that in
a sense the accident and its essence are the same, and in a sense they are not; for the
essence of white is not the same as the man or the white man, but it is the same as
the attribute white.)

The absurdity of the separation would appear also if one were to assign a name to
each of the essences; for there would be another essence besides the original one, e.g.
30 to the essence of horse there will belong a second essence. Yet why should not some
things be their essences from the start, since essence is substance? But not only are a
1032a1 thing and its essence one, but the formula of them is also the same, as is clear even
from what has been said; for it is not by accident that the essence of one, and the one,
are one. Further, if they were different, the process would go on to infinity; for we
should have the essence of one, and the one, so that in their case also the same infinite
regress would be found. Clearly, then, each primary and self-subsistent thing is one
5   and the same as its essence. . . .
1034b20   10. Since a definition is a formula, and every formula has parts, and as the formula
is to the thing, so is the part of the formula to the part of the thing, we are already
faced by the question whether the formula of the parts must be present in the formula
of the whole or not. For in some cases the formulae of the parts are seen to be present,
25 and in some not. The formula of the circle does not include that of the segments, but
that of the syllable includes that of the letters; yet the circle is divided into segments
as the syllable is into letters.—And further if the parts are prior to the whole, and the
acute angle is a part of the right angle and the finger a part of the animal, the acute
30 angle will be prior to the right angle and the finger to the man. But the latter are
thought to be prior; for in formula the parts are explained by reference to them, and
in virtue also of their power of existing apart from the parts the wholes are prior.

Perhaps we should rather say that "part" is used in several senses. One of these is
"that which measures another thing in respect of quantity." But let this sense be set
aside; let us inquire about the parts of which *substance* consists. If then matter is one

thing, form another, the compound of these a third, and both the matter and the form 1035a1
and the compound are substance, even the matter is in a sense called part of a thing,
while in a sense *it* is not, but only the elements of which the formula of the form consists. E.g. flesh (for this is the matter in which it is produced) is not a part of concavity, 5
but of snubness it is a part; and the bronze is a part of the particular statue, but not of
the statue as form. (For each thing must be referred to by naming its form, and as having form, but never by naming its material aspect as such.)...

The truth has really now been stated, but still let us state it yet more clearly, taking
up the question again. The parts of the formula, into which the formula is divided, are 1035b5
prior to it, either all or some of them. The formula of the right angle, however, does
not include the formula of the acute, but the formula of the acute includes that of the
right angle; for he who defines the acute uses the right angle; for the acute is less than
a right angle. The circle and the semicircle also are in a like relation; for the semicircle
is defined by the circle; and so is the finger by the whole body, for a finger is such and 10
such a part of a man. Therefore the parts which are of the nature of matter and into
which as its matter a thing is divided, are posterior; but those which are parts of the
formula, and of the substance according to its formula, are prior, either all or some of
them. And since the soul of animals (for this is the substance of living beings) is their 15
substance according to the formula, i.e. the form and the essence of a body of a certain
kind (at least we shall define each part, if we define it well, not without reference to
its function, and this cannot belong to it without perception), therefore the parts of
soul are prior, either all or some of them, to the concrete animal, and similarly in each
case of a concrete whole; and the body and its parts are posterior to this its substance, 20
and it is not the substance but the concrete thing that is divided into these parts
as its matter. To the concrete thing these are in a sense prior, but in a sense they
are not. For they cannot even exist if severed from the whole; for it is not a finger
in *any* state that is the finger of a living thing, but the dead finger is a finger only 25
homonymously....

When any one asks whether the right angle and the circle and the animal are prior
to that into which they are divided and of which they consist, i.e. the parts, we must 1036a15
meet the inquiry by saying that the question cannot be answered simply. For if the soul
is the animal or the living thing, or the soul of each individual is the individual itself,
and being a circle is the circle, and being a right angle and the essence of the right
angle is the right angle, then the whole in one sense must be called posterior to the
part in one sense, i.e. to the parts included in the formula and to the parts of the
individual right angle (for both the material right angle which is made of bronze, and 20
that which is formed by individual lines, are posterior to their parts); while the
immaterial right angle is posterior to the parts included in the formula, but prior to
those included in the particular instance. But the question must not be answered simply. If, however, the soul is something different and is not identical with the animal,
even so some parts must be called prior and others must not, as has been said. 25

11. The question is naturally raised, what sort of parts belong to the form and what
sort not to the form, but to the concrete thing. Yet if this is not plain it is not possible
to define anything; for definition is of the universal and of the form. If then it is not
evident which of the parts are of the nature of matter and which are not, neither will
the formula of the thing be evident. In the case of things which are found to occur in 30
specifically different materials, as a circle may exist in bronze or stone or wood, it

seems plain that these, the bronze or the stone, are no part of the essence of the circle, since it is found apart from them. Of things which are *not* seen to exist apart, there is no reason why the same may not be true, e.g. even if all circles that had ever been seen were of bronze (for none the less the bronze would be no part of the form); but it is hard to effect this severance in thought. E.g. the form of man is always found in flesh and bones and parts of this kind; are these then also parts of the form and the formula? No, they are matter; but because man is not found also in other matters we are unable to effect the severance. . . .

Now we have stated that the question of definitions contains some difficulty, and why this is so. Therefore to bring all things thus to Forms and to eliminate the matter is useless labour; for some things surely are a particular form in a particular matter, or particular things in a particular state. And the comparison which Socrates the younger used to make in the case of animal is not good; for it leads away from the truth, and makes one suppose that man can possibly exist without his parts, as the circle can without the bronze. But the case is not similar; for an animal is something perceptible, and it is not possible to define it without reference to movement—nor, therefore, without reference to the parts and to their being in a certain state. For it is not a hand in *any* state that is a part of man, but the hand which can fulfil its work, which therefore must be alive; if it is not alive it is not a part.

Regarding the objects of mathematics, why are the formulae of the parts not parts of the formulae of the wholes, e.g. why are not the formulae of the semicircles parts of the formula of the circle? It cannot be said, "because these parts are perceptible things"; for they are not. But perhaps this makes no difference; for even some things which are not perceptible must have matter; for there is some matter in everything which is not an essence and a bare form but a "this." The semicircles, then, will be parts, not of the universal circle, but of the individual circles, as has been said before; for while one kind of matter is perceptible, there is another which is intelligible.

It is clear also that the soul is the primary substance and the body is matter, and man or animal is the compound of both taken universally; and Socrates or Coriscus, if even the soul of Socrates is Socrates, is taken in two ways (for some mean by such a term the soul, and others mean the concrete thing), but if he is simply this particular soul and this particular body, the individual is analogous to the universal. . . .

12. Now let us treat first of definition. . . . I mean this problem:—wherein consists the unity of that, the formula of which we call a definition, as for instance in the case of man, two-footed animal; for let this be the formula of man. Why, then, is this one, and not many, viz. animal *and* two-footed? For in the case of "man" and "white" there is a plurality when one term does not belong to the other, but a unity when it does belong and the subject, man, has a certain attribute; for then a unity is produced and we have the white man. In the present case, on the other hand, one does not share in the other; the genus is not thought to share in its differentiae; for then the same thing would share in contraries; for the differentiae by which the genus is divided are contrary. And even if the genus does share in them, the same argument applies, since the differentiae present in man are many, e.g. endowed with feet, two-footed, featherless. Why are these one and not many? Not because they are present in one thing; for on this principle a unity can be made out of any set of attributes. But surely all the attributes in the definition *must* be one; for the definition is a single formula and a formula of substance, so that it must be a formula of some one thing; for substance means a "one" and a "this," as we maintain.

We must first inquire about definitions arising out of divisions. There is nothing in the definition except the first-named genus and the differentiae. The other genera are the first genus and along with this the differentiae that are taken with it, e.g. the first may be animal, the next animal which is two-footed, and again animal which is two-footed and featherless, and similarly if the definition includes more terms. And in general it makes no difference whether it includes many or few terms—nor, therefore, whether it includes few or simply two; and of the two the one is differentia and the other genus, e.g. in "two-footed animal" "animal" is genus, and the other is differentia. If then the genus absolutely does not exist apart from the species which it as genus includes, or if it exists but exists as matter (for the voice is genus and matter, but its differentiae make the species, i.e. the letters, out of it), clearly the definition is the formula which comprises the differentiae.

But it is also necessary in division to take the differentia of the differentia; e.g. endowed with feet is a differentia of animal; again we must know the differentia of animal endowed with feet *qua* endowed with feet. Therefore we must not say, if we are to speak rightly, that of that which is endowed with feet one part has feathers and one is featherless; if we say this we say it through incapacity; we must divide it into cloven-footed or not-cloven; for these are differentiae in the foot; cloven-footedness is a form of footedness. And we always want to go on so till we come to the species that contain no differences. And then there will be as many kinds of foot as there are differentiae, and the kinds of animals endowed with feet will be equal in number to the differentiae. If then this is so, clearly the *last* differentia will be the substance of the thing and its definition, since it is not right to state the same things more than once in our definitions; for it is superfluous. And this does happen; for when we say "animal which is endowed with feet, and two-footed" we have said nothing other than "animal having feet, having two feet"; and if we divide this by the proper division, we shall be saying the same thing many times—as many times as there are differentiae.

If then a differentia of a differentia be taken at each step, one differentia—the last—will be the form and the substance; but if we divide according to accidental qualities, e.g. if we were to divide that which is endowed with feet into the white and the black, there will be as many differentiae as there are processes of division. Therefore it is plain that the definition is the formula which contains the differentiae, or, according to the right method, the last of these. This would be evident, if we were to change the order of such definitions, e.g. that of man, saying "animal which is two-footed and endowed with feet"; for "endowed with feet" is superfluous when "two-footed" has been said. But order is no part of the substance; for how are we to think the one element posterior and the other prior? Regarding the definitions, then, which arise out of divisions, let this much be taken as stated in the first place as to their nature.

13. Let us again return to the subject of our inquiry, which is substance. As the substrate and the essence and the compound of these are called substance, so also is the universal. About two of these we have spoken; about the essence and about the substrate, of which we have said that it underlies in two senses, either being a "this"—which is the way in which an animal underlies its attributes—or as the matter underlies the complete reality. The universal also is thought by some to be in the fullest sense a cause, and a principle; therefore let us attack the discussion of this point also. For it seems impossible that any universal term should be the name of a substance. For primary substance is that kid of substance which is peculiar to an individual, which does not belong to anything else; but the universal is common, since that is called

30

1038a1

5

10

15

20

25

30

35

1038b1

5

10

universal which naturally belongs to more than one thing. Of which individual then will this be the substance? Either of all or of none. But it cannot be the substance of all; and if it is to be the substance of one, this one will be the others also; for things whose substance is one and whose essence is one are themselves also one.

15   Further, substance means that which is not predicable of a subject, but the universal is predicable of some subject always.

But perhaps the universal, while it cannot be substance in the way in which the essence is so, can be present in this, e.g. animal can be present in man and horse. Then clearly there is a formula of the universal. And it makes no difference even if there is
20   not a formula of everything that is in the substance; for none the less the universal will be the substance of something. Man is the substance of the individual man in whom it is present; therefore the same will happen again, for a substance, e.g. animal, must be the substance of that in which it is present as something peculiar to it. And further
25   it is impossible and absurd that the "this," i.e. the substance, if it consists of parts, should not consist of substances nor of what is a "this," but of quality; for that which is not substance, i.e. the quality, will then be prior to substance and to the "this." Which is impossible; for neither in formula nor in time nor in coming to be can the affections be prior to the substance; for then they would be separable from it. Further,
30   in Socrates there will be a substance in a substance, so that he will be the substance of two things. And in general it follows, if man and such things are substances, that none of the elements in their formulae is the substance of anything, nor does it exist apart from the species or in anything else; I mean, for instance, that no animal exists apart from the particular animals, nor does any other of the elements present in formulae exist apart.

If, then, we view the matter from these standpoints, it is plain that no universal
1039a1 attribute is a substance, and this is plain also from the fact that no common predicate indicates a "this," but rather a "such." If not, many difficulties follow and especially the "third man.". . .

1039b20   15. Since substance is of two kinds, the concrete thing and the formula (I mean that one kind of substance is the formula taken with the matter, while another kind is the formula in its generality), substances in the former sense are capable of destruction (for they are capable also of generation), but there is no destruction of the formula in the sense that it is ever in course of being destroyed; for there is no generation of
25   it (the being of house is not generated, but only the being of *this* house), but without generation and destruction formulae are and are not; for it has been shown that no one produces nor makes these. For this reason, also, there is neither definition nor demonstration of sensible individual substances, because they have matter whose nature is
30   such that they are capable both of being and of not being; for which reason all the individual instances of them are destructible. If then demonstration is of necessary truths and definition involves knowledge, and if, just as knowledge cannot be sometimes knowledge and sometimes ignorance, but the state which varies thus is opinion,
1040a1 so too demonstration and definition cannot vary thus, but it is opinion that deals with that which can be otherwise than as it is, clearly there can neither be definition nor demonstration of sensible individuals. For perishing things are obscure to those who have knowledge of them, when they have passed from our perception; and though the
5   formulae remain in the soul unchanged, there will no longer be either definition or demonstration. Therefore when one of those who aim at definition defines any

individual, he must recognize that his definition may always be overthrown; for it is not possible to define such things.

Nor is it possible to define any Idea. For the Idea is, as its supporters say, an individual, and can exist apart; and the formula must consist of words; and he who defines must not invent a word (for it would be unknown), but the established words are common to each of a number of things; these then must apply to something besides the thing defined; e.g. if one were defining you, he would say "an animal which is lean" or "white," or something else which will apply also to some one other than you. If any one were to say that perhaps all the attributes taken apart may belong to many subjects, but together they belong only to this one, we must reply firstly that they belong also to both the elements, e.g. two-footed animal belongs to animal and to the two-footed. And where the elements are eternal this is even necessary, since the elements are prior to and parts of the compound; what is more, they can also exist apart, if "man" can exist apart. For either neither or both can. If, then, neither can, the genus will not exist apart from the species; but if it does, the differentia will also. Secondly, we must reply that they are prior in being; and things which are prior to others are not destroyed when the others are. . . .

17. We should say what, and what sort of thing, substance is, taking another starting-point; for perhaps from this we shall get a clear view also of that substance which exists apart from sensible substances. Since, then, substance is a principle and a cause, let us attack it from this standpoint. The "why" is always sought in this form—"why does one thing attach to another?" For to inquire why the musical man is a musical man, is either to inquire—as we have said—why the man is musical, or it is something else. Now "why a thing is itself" is doubtless a meaningless inquiry; for the fact or the existence of the thing must already be evident (e.g. that the moon is eclipsed), but the fact that a thing is itself is the single formula and the single cause to all such questions as why the man is man, or the musical musical, unless one were to say that each thing is inseparable from itself; and its being one just meant this. This, however, is common to all things and is a short and easy way with the question. But we *can* inquire why man is an animal of such and such a nature. Here, then, we are evidently not inquiring why he who is a man is a man. We are inquiring, then, why something is predicable of something; that it is predicable must be clear; for if not, the inquiry is an inquiry into nothing. E.g. why does it thunder?—why is sound produced in the clouds? Thus the inquiry is about the predication of one thing of another. And why are certain things, i.e. stones and bricks, a house? Plainly we are seeking the cause. And this is the essence (to speak abstractly), which in some cases is that for the sake of which, e.g. perhaps in the case of a house or a bed, and in some cases is the first mover; for this also is a cause. But while the efficient cause is sought in the case of genesis and destruction, the final cause is sought in the case of being also.

The object of the inquiry is most overlooked where one term is not expressly predicated of another (e.g. when we inquire why man is), because we do not distinguish and do not say definitely "why do these parts form this whole?" But we must distinguish the elements before we begin to inquire; if not, it is not clear whether the inquiry is significant or unmeaning. Since we must know the existence of the thing and it must be given, clearly the question is *why* the matter is some individual thing, e.g. why are these materials a house? Because that which was the essence of a house is present. And why is this individual thing, or this body in this state, a man? Therefore what we seek

10

15

20

1041a10

15

20

25

30

1041b1

5

is the cause, i.e. the form, by reason of which the matter is some definite thing; and this is the substance of the thing. Evidently, then, in the case of simple things no
10 inquiry nor teaching is possible; but we must inquire into them in a different way.

As regards that which is compounded out of something so that the whole is one—not like a heap, however, but like a syllable—the syllable is not its elements, *ba* is not the same as *b* and *a*, nor is flesh fire and earth; for when they are dissolved the wholes,
15 i.e. the flesh and the syllable, no longer exist, but the elements of the syllable exist, and so do fire and earth. The syllable, then, is something—not only its elements (the vowel and the consonant) but also something else; and the flesh is not only fire and earth or the hot and the cold, but also something else. Since, then, that something
20 must be either an element or composed of elements, if it is an element the same argument will again apply; for flesh will consist of this and fire and earth and something still further, so that the process will go on to infinity; while if it is a compound, clearly it will be a compound not of one but of many (or else it will itself be that one), so that
25 again in this case we can use the same argument as in the case of flesh or of the syllable. But it would seem that this is something, and not an element, and that it is the cause which makes *this* thing flesh and *that* a syllable. And similarly in all other cases. And this is the substance of each thing; for this is the primary cause of its being; and
30 since, while some things are not substances, as many as are substances are formed naturally and by nature, their substance would seem to be this nature, which is not an element but a principle. An *element* is that into which a thing is divided and which is present in it as matter, e.g. *a* and *b* are the elements of the syllable.

Book XII

1. Substance is the subject of our inquiry; for the principles and the causes we are seeking are those of substances. For if the universe is of the nature of a whole, substance
1069a20 is its first part; and if it coheres by virtue of succession, on this view also substance is first, and is succeeded by quality, and then by quantity. . . .
30 There are three kinds of substance—one that is sensible (of which one subdivision is eternal and another is perishable, and which all recognize, as comprising e.g. plants and animals)—of this we must grasp the elements, whether one or many; and another that is immovable, and this certain thinkers assert to be capable of existing apart, some dividing it into two, others combining the Forms and the objects of mathematics into
35 one class, and others believing only in the mathematical part of this class. The former
1069b1 two kinds of substance are the subject of natural science (for they imply movement); but the third kind belongs to another science, if there is no principle common to it and to the other kinds. . . .

6. Since there were three kinds of substance, two of them natural and one unmovable, regarding the latter we must assert that it is necessary that there should be an eter-
1071b5 nal unmovable substance. For substances are the first of existing things, and if they are all destructible, all things are destructible. But it is impossible that movement should either come into being or cease to be; for it must always have existed. Nor can time come into being or cease to be; for there could not be a before and an after if time did not exist. Movement also is continuous, then, in the sense in which time is; for time
10 is either the same thing as movement or an attribute of movement. And there is no

continuous movement except movement in place, and of this only that which is circular is continuous.

But if there is something which is capable of moving things or acting on them, but is not actually doing so, there will not be movement; for that which has a capacity need not exercise it. Nothing, then, is gained even if we suppose eternal substances, as the believers in the Forms do, unless there is to be in them some principle which   15
can cause movement; and even this is not enough, nor is another substance besides the Forms enough; for if it does not *act*, there will be no movement. Further, even if it acts, this will not be enough, if its substance is potentiality; for there will not be *eternal* movement; for that which is potentially may possibly not be. There must, then, be   20
such a principle, whose very substance is actuality. Further, then, these substances must be without matter; for they must be eternal, at least if anything else is eternal. Therefore they must be actuality.

Yet there is a difficulty; for it is thought that everything that acts is able to act, but that not everything that is able to act acts, so that the potentiality is prior. But if this is so, nothing at all will exist; for it is possible for things to be capable of existing but   25
not yet to exist. Yet if we follow the mythologists who generate the world from night, or the natural philosophers who say that all things were together, the same impossible result ensues. For how will there be movement, if there is no actual cause? Matter will surely not move itself—the carpenter's art must act on it; nor will the menstrual fluids   30
nor the earth set themselves in motion, but the seeds and the semen must act on them.

This is why some suppose eternal actuality—e.g. Leucippus and Plato; for they say there is always movement. But why and what this movement is they do not say, nor, if the world moves in this way or that, do they tell us the cause of its doing so. Now nothing is moved at random, but there must always be something present, e.g. as a   35
matter of fact a thing moves in one way by nature, and in another by force or through the influence of thought or something else. Further, what sort of movement is primary? This makes a vast difference. But again Plato, at least, cannot even say what   1072a1
it is that he sometimes supposes to be the source of movement—that which moves itself; for the *soul* is later, and simultaneous with the heavens, according to his account. To suppose potentiality prior to actuality, then, is in a sense right, and in a sense not; and we have specified these senses. . . .

Therefore chaos or night did not exist for any infinite time, but the same things have always existed (either passing through a cycle of changes or in some other way), since actuality is prior to potentiality. If, then, there is a constant cycle, something must always remain, acting in the same way. And if there is to be generation and des-   10
truction, there must be something else which is always acting in different ways. This must, then, act in one way in virtue of itself, and in another in virtue of something else—either of a third agent, therefore, or of the first. But it must be in virtue of the first. For otherwise this again causes the motion both of the third agent and of the   15
second. Therefore it is better to say the first. For it was the cause of eternal movement; and something else is the cause of variety, and evidently both together are the cause of eternal variety. This, accordingly, is the character which the motions actually exhibit. What need then is there to seek for other principles?

7. Since this is a possible account of the matter, and if it were not true, the world would have proceeded out of night and "all things together" and out of non-being,   20
these difficulties may be taken as solved. There is, then, something which is always

moved with an unceasing motion, which is motion in a circle; and this is plain not in theory only but in fact. Therefore the first heavens must be eternal. There is there-
25   fore also something which moves them. And since that which is moved and moves is intermediate, there is a mover which moves without being moved, being eternal, sub-stance, and actuality. And the object of desire and the object of thought move in this way; they move without being moved. The primary objects of desire and of thought are the same. For the apparent good is the object of appetite, and the real good is the primary object of wish. But desire is consequent on opinion rather than opinion on
30   desire; for the thinking is the starting-point. And thought is moved by the object of thought, and one side of the list of opposites is in itself the object of thought; and in this, substance is first, and in substance, that which is simple and exists actually. . . .

1072b1   That that for the sake of which is found among the unmovables is shown by making a distinction; for that for the sake of which is both that *for* which and that *towards* which, and of these the one is unmovable and the other is not. Thus it produces motion by being loved, and it moves the other moving things. Now if something is
5   moved it is capable of being otherwise than as it is. Therefore if the actuality of the heavens is primary motion, then in so far as they are in motion, in *this* respect they are capable of being otherwise—in place, even if not in substance. But since there is some-thing which moves while itself unmoved, existing actually, this can in no way be otherwise than as it is. For motion in space is the first of the kinds of change, and
10   motion in a circle the first kind of spatial motion; and this the first mover *produces*. The first mover, then, of necessity exists; and in so far as it is necessary, it is good, and in this sense a first principle. For the necessary has all these senses—that which is necessary perforce because it is contrary to impulse, that without which the good is impossible, and that which cannot be otherwise but is *absolutely* necessary.

On such a principle, then, depend the heavens and the world of nature. And its life
15   is such as the best which we enjoy, and enjoy for but a short time. For it is ever in this state (which we cannot be), since its actuality is also pleasure. (And therefore waking, perception, and thinking are most pleasant, and hopes and memories are so because of their reference to these.) And thought in itself deals with that which is best in itself, and that which is thought in the fullest sense with that which is best in the fullest
20   sense. And thought thinks itself because it shares the nature of the object of thought; for it becomes an object of thought in coming into contact with and thinking its objects, so that thought and object of thought are the same. For that which is *capable* of receiving the object of thought, i.e. the substance, is thought. And it is *active* when it *possesses* this object. Therefore the latter rather than the former is the divine ele-ment which thought seems to contain, and the act of contemplation is what is most
25   pleasant and best. If, then, God is always in that good state in which we sometimes are, this compels our wonder; and if in a better this compels it yet more. And God *is* in a better state. And life also belongs to God; for the actuality of thought is life, and God is that actuality; and God's essential actuality is life most good and eternal. We say therefore that God is a living being, eternal, most good, so that life and duration
30   continuous and eternal belong to God; for this *is* God. . . .

It is clear then from what has been said that there is a substance which is eternal
1073a5   and unmovable and separate from sensible things. It has been shown also that this sub-stance cannot have any magnitude, but is without parts and indivisible. For it produces movement through infinite time, but nothing finite has infinite power. And, while

every magnitude is either infinite or finite, it cannot, for the above reason, have finite magnitude, and it cannot have infinite magnitude because there is no infinite magnitude at all. But it is also clear that it is impassive and unalterable; for all the other changes are posterior to change of place. It is clear, then, why the first mover has these attributes.

8. We must not ignore the question whether we have to suppose one such substance or more than one, and if the latter, how many; we must also mention, regarding the opinions expressed by others, that they have said nothing that can even be clearly stated about the number of the substances. . . .

We however must discuss the subject, starting from the presuppositions and distinctions we have mentioned. The first principle or primary being is not movable either in itself or accidentally, but produces the primary eternal and single movement. And since that which is moved must be moved by something, and the first mover must be in itself unmovable, and eternal movement must be produced by something eternal and a single movement by a single thing, and since we see that besides the simple spatial movement of the universe, which we say the first and unmovable substance produces, there are other spatial movements—those of the planets—which are eternal (for the body which moves in a circle is eternal and unresting; we have proved these points in the *Physics*), each of *these* movements also must be caused by a substance unmovable in itself and eternal. For the nature of the stars is eternal, being a kind of substance, and the mover is eternal and prior to the moved, and that which is prior to a substance must be a substance. Evidently, then, there must be substances which are of the same number as the movements of the stars, and in their nature eternal, and in themselves unmovable, and without magnitude, for the reason before mentioned. . . .

9. The nature of the divine thought involves certain problems; for while thought is held to be the most divine of phenomena, the question what it must be in order to have that character involves difficulties. For if it thinks nothing, what is there here of dignity? It is just like one who sleeps. And if it thinks, but this depends on something else, then (as that which is its substance is not the act of thinking, but a capacity) it cannot be the best substance; for it is through thinking that its value belongs to it. Further, whether its substance is the faculty of thought or the act of thinking, what does it think? Either itself or something else; and if something else, either the same always or something different. Does it matter, then, or not, whether it thinks the good or any chance thing? Are there not some things about which it is incredible that it should think? Evidently, then, it thinks that which is most divine and precious, and it does not change; for change would be change for the worse, and this would be already a movement. First, then, if it is not the act of thinking but a capacity, it would be reasonable to suppose that the continuity of its thinking is wearisome to it. Secondly, there would evidently be something else more precious than thought, viz. that which is thought. For both thinking and the act of thought will belong even to one who has the worst of thoughts. Therefore if this ought to be avoided (and it ought, for there are even some things which it is better not to see than to see), the act of thinking cannot be the best of things. Therefore it must be itself that thought thinks (since it is the most excellent of things), and its thinking is a thinking on thinking.

But evidently knowledge and perception and opinion and understanding have always something else as their object, and themselves only by the way. Further, if thinking and being thought are different, in respect of which does goodness belong to

10

15

25

30

35

1073b1
1074b15

20

25

30

35

thought? For being an act of thinking and being an object of thought are not the same.
1075a1   We answer that in some cases the knowledge is the object. In the productive sciences
(if we abstract from the matter) the substance in the sense of essence, and in the theoretical sciences the formula or the act of thinking, *is* the object. As, then, thought and
the object of thought are not different in the case of things that have not matter, they
will be the same, i.e. the thinking will be one with the object of its thought.

5   A further question is left—whether the object of the thought is composite; for if it
were, thought would change in passing from part to part of the whole. We answer that
everything which has not matter is indivisible. As human thought, or rather the
thought of composite objects, is in a certain period of time (for it does not possess the
good at this moment or at that, but its best, being something *different* from it, is
attained only in a whole period of time), so throughout eternity is the thought which
10   has *itself* for its object.

Nicomachean Ethics

Book I

1. Every art and every inquiry, and similarly every action and choice, is thought to aim   1094a1
at some good; and for this reason the good has rightly been declared to be that at
which all things aim. But a certain difference is found among ends: some are activities,
others are products apart from the activities that produce them. Where there are ends
apart from the actions, it is the nature of the products to be better than the activities.   5
Now, as there are many actions, arts, and sciences, their ends also are many; the end
of the medical art is health, that of shipbuilding a vessel, that of strategy victory, that
of economics wealth. But where such arts fall under a single capacity—as bridle-   10
making and the other arts concerned with the equipment of horses fall under the art
of riding, and this and every military action under strategy, in the same way other arts
fall under yet others—in all of these the ends of the master arts are to be preferred to   15
all the subordinate ends; for it is for the sake of the former that the latter are pursued.
It makes no difference whether the activities themselves are the ends of the actions,
or something else apart from the activities, as in the case of the sciences just mentioned.

2. If, then, there is some end of the things we do, which we desire for its own sake
(everything else being desired for the sake of this), and if we do not choose everything
for the sake of something else (for at that rate the process would go on to infinity, so   20
that our desire would be empty and vain), clearly this must be the good and the chief
good. Will not the knowledge of it, then, have a great influence on life? Shall we not,
like archers who have a mark to aim at, be more likely to hit upon what we should?
If so, we must try, in outline at least, to determine what it is, and of which of the   25
sciences or capacities it is the object. It would seem to belong to the most authoritative art and that which is most truly the master art. And politics appears to be of this   1094b1
nature; for it is this that ordains which of the sciences should be studied in a state, and
which each class of citizens should learn and up to what point they should learn them;
and we see even the most highly esteemed of capacities to fall under this, e.g. strategy,
economics, rhetoric; now, since politics uses the rest of the sciences, and since, again,   5
it legislates as to what we are to do and what we are to abstain from, the end of this
science must include those of the others, so that this end must be the good for man.
For even if the end is the same for a single man and for a state, that of the state seems
at all events something greater and more complete both to attain and to preserve; for
though it is worth while to attain the end merely for one man, it is finer and more god-   10
like to attain it for a nation or for city-states. These, then, are the ends at which our
inquiry, being concerned with politics, aims.

Our discussion will be adequate if it has as much clearness as the subject-matter
admits of; for precision is not to be sought for alike in all discussions, any more than
in all the products of the crafts. Now fine and just actions, which political science
investigates, exhibit much variety and fluctuation, so that they may be thought   15
to exist only by convention, and not by nature. And goods also exhibit a similar

Translated by W. D. Ross; revised by J. O. Urmson.

fluctuation because they bring harm to many people; for before now men have been
undone by reason of their wealth, and others by reason of their courage. We must be
20 content, then, in speaking of such subjects and with such premises to indicate the
truth roughly and in outline, and in speaking about things which are only for the most
part true and with premises of the same kind to reach conclusions that are no better.
In the same spirit, therefore, should each of our statements be *received*; for it is the
25 mark of an educated man to look for precision in each class of things just so far as the
nature of the subject admits: it is evidently equally foolish to accept probable reasoning from a mathematician and to demand from a rhetorician demonstrative proofs.

Now each man judges well the things he knows, and of these he is a good judge.
And so the man who has been educated in a subject is a good judge of that subject,
1095a1 and the man who has received an all-round education is a good judge in general.
Hence a young man is not a proper hearer of lectures on political science; for he is
inexperienced in the actions that occur in life, but its discussions start from these and
are about these; and, further, since he tends to follow his passions, his study will be
5 vain and unprofitable, because the end aimed at is not knowledge but action. And it
makes no difference whether he is young in years or youthful in character; the defect
does not depend on time, but on his living and pursuing each successive object as
passion directs. For to such persons, as to the incontinent, knowledge brings no profit;
10 but to those who desire and act in accordance with a rational principle knowledge
about such matters will be of great benefit.

These remarks about the student, the way in which our statements should be
received, and the purpose of the inquiry, may be taken as our preface.

Let us resume our inquiry and state, in view of the fact that all knowledge and
15 choice aims at some good, what it is that we say political science aims at and what is
the highest of all goods achievable by action. Verbally there is very general agreement;
for both the general run of men and people of superior refinement say that it is happi-
20 ness, and identify living well and faring well with being happy; but with regard to what
happiness is they differ, and the many do not give the same account as the wise. For
the former think it is some plain and obvious thing, like pleasure, wealth, or honour;
they differ, however, from one another—and often even the same man identifies it with
different things, with health when he is ill, with wealth when he is poor; but, con-
25 scious of their ignorance, they admire those who proclaim some great thing that is
above their comprehension. Now some thought that apart from these many goods
there is another which is good in itself and causes the goodness of all these as well. To
examine all the opinions that have been held would no doubt be somewhat fruitless:
it is enough to examine those that are most prevalent or that seem to have some reason
30 in their favour. . . .

5. To judge from the lives that men lead, most men, and men of the most vulgar
1095b15 type, seem (not without some reason) to identify the good, or happiness, with pleasure;
which is the reason why they love the life of enjoyment. For there are, we may say, three
prominent types of life—that just mentioned, the political, and thirdly the contemplative life. Now the mass of mankind are evidently quite slavish in their tastes, preferring
20 a life suitable to beasts, but they get some reason for their view from the fact that many
of those in high places share the tastes of Sardanapallus. But people of superior refinement and of active disposition identify happiness with honour; for this is, roughly
speaking, the end of the political life. But it seems too superficial to be what we are

looking for, since it is thought to depend on those who bestow honour rather than on 25
him who receives it, but the good we divine to be something of one's own and not easily taken from one. Further, men seem to pursue honour in order that they may be
assured of their merit; at least it is by men of practical wisdom that they seek to be
honoured, and among those who know them, and on the ground of their excellence;
clearly, then, according to them, at any rate, excellence is better. And perhaps one 30
might even suppose this to be, rather than honour, the end of the political life. But
even this appears somewhat incomplete; for possession of excellence seems actually
compatible with being asleep, or with lifelong inactivity, and, further, with the
greatest sufferings and misfortunes; but a man who was living so no one would call 1096a1
happy, unless he were maintaining a thesis at all costs. But enough of this; for the
subject has been sufficiently treated even in ordinary discussion. Third comes the contemplative life, which we shall consider later. . . . 5

6. We had perhaps better consider the universal good and discuss thoroughly what
is meant by it, although such an inquiry is made an uphill one by the fact that the
Forms have been introduced by friends of our own. Yet it would perhaps be thought to
be better, indeed to be our duty, for the sake of maintaining the truth even to destroy 15
what touches us closely, especially as we are philosophers; for, while both are dear,
piety requires us to honour truth above our friends.

The men who introduced this doctrine did not posit Ideas of classes within which
they recognized priority and posteriority (which is the reason why they did not maintain the existence of an Idea embracing all numbers); but things are called good both 20
in the category of substance and in that of quality and in that of relation, and that
which is *per se*, i.e. substance, is prior in nature to the relative (for the latter is like an
offshoot and accident of what is); so that there could not be a common Idea set over
all these goods. Further, since things are said to be good in as many ways as they are
said to be (for things are called good both in the category of substance, as God and 25
reason, and in quality, e.g. the virtues, and in quantity, e.g. that which is moderate,
and in relation, e.g. the useful, and in time, e.g. the right opportunity, and in place,
e.g. the right locality and the like), clearly the good cannot be something universally
present in all cases and single; for then it would not have been predicated in all the
categories but in one only. Further, since of the things answering to one Idea there is 30
one science, there would have been one science of all the goods; but as it is there are
many sciences even of the things that fall under one category, e.g. of opportunity (for
opportunity in war is studied by strategy and in disease by medicine), and the moderate
in food is studied by medicine and in exercise by the science of gymnastics. . . .

But let us discuss these matters elsewhere; an objection to what we have said,
however, may be discerned in the fact that the Platonists have not been speaking
about *all* goods, and that the goods that are pursued and loved for themselves are called 1096b10
good by reference to a single Form, while those which tend to produce or to preserve
these somehow or to prevent their contraries are called so by reference to these, and
in a different sense. Clearly, then, goods must be spoken of in two ways, and some must
be good in themselves, the others by reason of these. Let us separate, then, things good
in themselves from things useful, and consider whether the former are called good by 15
reference to a single Idea. What sort of goods would one call good in themselves? Is
it those that are pursued even when isolated from others, such as intelligence, sight,
and certain pleasures and honours? Certainly, if we pursue these also for the sake of

20   something else, yet one would place them among things good in themselves. Or is nothing other than the Idea good in itself? In that case the Form will be empty. But if the things we have named are also things good in themselves, the account of the good will have to appear as something identical in them all, as that of whiteness is identical in snow and in white lead. But of honour, wisdom, and pleasure, just in

25   respect of their goodness, the accounts are distinct and diverse. The good, therefore, is not something common answering to one Idea. . . .

1097a15   7. Let us again return to the good we are seeking, and ask what it can be. It seems different in different actions and arts; it is different in medicine, in strategy, and in the other arts likewise. What then is the good of each? Surely that for whose sake every-thing else is done. In medicine this is health, in strategy victory, in architecture a

20   house, in any other sphere something else, and in every action and choice the end; for it is for the sake of this that all men do whatever else they do. Therefore, if there is an end for all that we do, this will be the good achievable by action, and if there are more than one, these will be the goods achievable by action.

So the argument has by a different course reached the same point; but we must try

25   to state this even more clearly. Since there are evidently more than one end, and we choose some of these (e.g. wealth, flutes, and in general instruments) for the sake of something else, clearly not all ends are complete ends; but the chief good is evidently something complete. Therefore, if there is only one complete end, this will be what we are seeking, and if there are more than one, the most complete of these will be what

30   we are seeking. Now we call that which is in itself worthy of pursuit more complete than that which is worthy of pursuit for the sake of something else, and that which is never desirable for the sake of something else more complete than the things that are desirable both in themselves and for the sake of that other thing, and therefore we call complete without qualification that which is always desirable in itself and never for the sake of something else.

Now such a thing happiness, above all else, is held to be; for this we choose always

1097b1   for itself and never for the sake of something else, but honour, pleasure, reason, and every excellence we choose indeed for themselves (for if nothing resulted from them we should still choose each of them), but we choose them also for the sake of happi-

5   ness, judging that through them we shall be happy. Happiness, on the other hand, no one chooses for the sake of these, nor, in general, for anything other than itself.

From the point of view of self-sufficiency the same result seems to follow; for the

15   complete good is thought to be self-sufficient. . . . The self-sufficient we now define as that which when isolated makes life desirable and lacking in nothing; and such we think happiness to be; and further we think it most desirable of all things, without being counted as one good thing among others—if it were so counted it would clearly be made more desirable by the addition of even the least of goods; for that which is

20   added becomes an excess of goods, and of goods the greater is always more desirable. Happiness, then, is something complete and self-sufficient, and is the end of action.

Presumably, however, to say that happiness is the chief good seems a platitude, and a clearer account of what it is is still desired. This might perhaps be given, if we could

25   first ascertain the function of man. For just as for a flute-player, a sculptor, or any artist, and, in general, for all things that have a function or activity, the good and the "well" is thought to reside in the function, so would it seem to be for man, if he has a func-tion. Have the carpenter, then, and the tanner certain functions or activities, and has

man none? Is he naturally functionless? Or as eye, hand, foot, and in general each of the 30
parts evidently has a function, may one lay it down that man similarly has a function
apart from all these? What then can this be? Life seems to be common even to plants,
but we are seeking what is peculiar to man. Let us exclude, therefore, the life of nutrition 1098a1
and growth. Next there would be a life of perception, but *it* also seems to be common
even to the horse, the ox, and every animal. There remains, then, an active life of the
element that has a rational principle (of this, one part has such a principle in the sense
of being obedient to one, the other in the sense of possessing one and exercising thought);
and as this too can be taken in two ways, we must state that life in the sense of activity 5
is what we mean; for this seems to be the more proper sense of the term. Now if the function of man is an activity of soul in accordance with, or not without, rational principle,
and if we say a so-and-so and a good so-and-so have a function which is the same in kind,
e.g. a lyre-player and a good lyre-player, and so without qualification in all cases, emi- 10
nence in respect of excellence being added to the function (for the function of a lyre-
player is to play the lyre, and that of a good lyre-player is to do so well): if this is the case,
and we state the function of man to be a certain kind of life, and this to be an activity
or actions of the soul implying a rational principle, and the function of a good man to
be the good and noble performance of these, and if any action is well performed when
it is performed in accordance with the appropriate excellence: if this is the case, human 15
good turns out to be activity of soul in conformity with excellence, and if there are more
than one excellence, in conformity with the best and most complete.

But we must add in a "complete life." For one swallow does not make a summer, nor
does one day; and so too one day, or a short time, does not make a man blessed
and happy. . . .

With those who identify happiness with excellence or some one excellence our 1098b30
account is in harmony; for to excellence belongs activity in accordance with excellence. But it makes, perhaps, no small difference whether we place the chief good in
possession or in use, in state or in activity. For the state may exist without producing
any good result, as in a man who is asleep or in some other way quite inactive, but the 1099a1
activity cannot; for one who has the activity will of necessity be acting, and acting
well. And as in the Olympic Games it is not the most beautiful and the strongest that
are crowned but those who compete (for it is some of these that are victorious), so 5
those who act rightly win the noble and good things in life.

Their life is also in itself pleasant. For pleasure is a state of soul, and to each man
that which he is said to be a lover of is pleasant; e.g. not only is a horse pleasant to
the lover of horses, and a spectacle to the lover of sights, but also in the same way just 10
acts are pleasant to the lover of justice and in general excellent acts to the lover of
excellence. Now for most men their pleasures are in conflict with one another because
these are not by nature pleasant, but the lovers of what is noble find pleasant the
things that are by nature pleasant; and excellent actions are such, so that these are
pleasant for such men as well as in their own nature. Their life, therefore, has no further need of pleasure as a sort of adventitious charm, but has its pleasure in itself. For, 15
besides what we have said, the man who does not rejoice in noble actions is not even
good; since no one would call a man just who did not enjoy acting justly, nor any man
liberal who did not enjoy liberal actions; and similarly in all other cases. If this is so, 20
excellent actions must be in themselves pleasant. But they are also *good* and *noble*, and
have each of these attributes in the highest degree. . . .

Yet evidently, as we said, it needs the external goods as well; for it is impossible, or not easy, to do noble acts without the proper equipment. In many actions we use
1099b1 friends and riches and political power as instruments; and there are some things the lack of which takes the lustre from blessedness, as good birth, satisfactory children, beauty; for the man who is very ugly in appearance or ill-born or solitary and childless
5 is hardly happy, and perhaps a man would be still less so if he had thoroughly bad children or friends or had lost good children or friends by death. As we said, then, happiness seems to need this sort of prosperity in addition; for which reason some identify happiness with good fortune, though others identify it with excellence. . . .

1100a10   10. Must no one at all, then, be called happy while he lives; must we, as Solon says, see the end? Even if we are to lay down this doctrine, is it also the case that a man is happy when he is *dead*? Or is not this quite absurd, especially for us who say that happi-
15 ness is an activity? But if we do not call the dead man happy, and if Solon does not mean this, but that one can then safely *call* a man blessed as being at last beyond evils and misfortunes, this also affords matter for discussion; for both evil and good are thought to exist for a dead man, as much as for one who is alive but not aware of them;
20 e.g. honours and dishonours and the good or bad fortunes of children and in general of descendants. And this also presents a problem; for though a man has lived blessedly
25 up to old age and has had a death worthy of his life, many reverses may befall his descendants. . . . It would be odd, then, if the dead man were to share in these changes and become at one time happy, at another wretched; while it would also be
30 odd if the fortunes of the descendants did not for *some* time have *some* effect on the happiness of their ancestors.

But we must return to our first difficulty; for perhaps by a consideration of it our present problem might be solved. Now if we must see the end and only then call a man blessed, not as being blessed but as having been so before, surely it is odd that when he is happy the attribute that belongs to him is not to be truly predicated of him
1100b1 because we do not wish to call men happy, on account of the changes that may befall them, and because we have assumed happiness to be something permanent and by no means easily changed, while a single man may suffer many turns of fortune's wheel. . . . Or is this following his fortunes quite wrong? Success or failure in life does not depend on these, but human life, as we said, needs these as well, while excellent
10 activities or their opposites are what determine happiness or the reverse.

The question we have now discussed confirms our definition. For no function of man has so much permanence as excellent activities (these are thought to be more
15 durable even than knowledge), and of these themselves the most valuable are more durable because those who are blessed spend their life most readily and most continuously in these: for this seems to be the reason why we do not forget them. The attribute in question, then, will belong to the happy man, and he will be happy throughout his life; for always, or by preference to everything else, he will do and contemplate what
20 is excellent, and he will bear the chances of life most nobly and altogether decorously, if he is "truly good" and "foursquare beyond reproach." . . .

If activities are, as we said, what determines the character of life, no blessed man can become miserable; for he will never do the acts that are hateful and mean. For the
1101a1 man who is truly good and wise, we think, bears all the chances of life becomingly and always makes the best of circumstances, as a good general makes the best military use
5 of the army at his command and a shoemaker makes the best shoes out of the hides

that are given him; and so with all other craftsmen. And if this is the case, the happy man can never become miserable—though he will not reach *blessedness*, if he meet with fortunes like those of Priam. . . .

Why then should we not say that he is happy who is active in conformity with complete excellence and is sufficiently equipped with external goods, not for some chance period but throughout a complete life? Or must we add "and who is destined to live thus and die as befits his life"? Certainly the future is obscure to us, while happiness, we claim, is an end and something in every way final. If so, we shall call blessed those among living men in whom these conditions are, and are to be, fulfilled—but blessed *men*. So much for these questions. . . .

13. Since happiness is an activity of soul in accordance with complete excellence, we must consider the nature of excellence; for perhaps we shall thus see better the nature of happiness. The true student of politics, too, is thought to have studied this above all things; for he wishes to make his fellow citizens good and obedient to the laws. As an example of this we have the lawgivers of the Cretans and the Spartans, and any others of the kind that there may have been. And if this inquiry belongs to political science, clearly the pursuit of it will be in accordance with our original plan. But clearly the excellence we must study is human excellence; for the good we were seeking was human good and the happiness human happiness. By human excellence we mean not that of the body but that of the soul; and happiness also we call an activity of soul. But if this is so, clearly the student of politics must know somehow the facts about soul, as the man who is to heal the eyes must know about the whole body also; and all the more since politics is more prized and better than medicine; but even among doctors the best educated spend much labour on acquiring knowledge of the body. The student of politics, then, must study the soul, and must study it with these objects in view, and do so just to the extent which is sufficient for the questions we are discussing; for further precision is perhaps something more laborious than our purposes require.

Some things are said about it, adequately enough, even in the discussions outside our school, and we must use these; e.g. that one element in the soul is irrational and one has a rational principle. . . .

Of the irrational element one division seems to be widely distributed, and vegetative in its nature, I mean that which causes nutrition and growth; for it is this kind of power of the soul that one must assign to all nurslings and to embryos, and this same power to full-grown creatures; this is more reasonable than to assign some different power to them. Now the excellence of this seems to be common to all and not specifically human; for this part or faculty seems to function most in sleep, while goodness and badness are least manifest in sleep (whence comes the saying that the happy are not better off than the wretched for half their lives; and this happens naturally enough, since sleep is an inactivity of the soul in that respect in which it is called good or bad), unless perhaps to a small extent some of the movements actually penetrate, and in this respect the dreams of good men are better than those of ordinary people. Enough of this subject, however; let us leave the nutritive faculty alone, since it has by its nature no share in human excellence.

There seems to be also another irrational element in the soul—one which in a sense, however, shares in a rational principle. For we praise the reason of the continent man and of the incontinent, and the part of their soul that has reason, since it urges

them aright and towards the best objects; but there is found in them also another natural element beside reason, which fights against and resists it . . . . No doubt . . . we must . . . suppose that in the soul too there is something beside reason, resisting and
25   opposing it. In what sense it is distinct from the other elements does not concern us. Now even this seems to have a share in reason, as we said; at any rate in the continent man it obeys reason—and presumably in the temperate and brave man it is still more obedient; for in them it speaks, on all matters, with the same voice as reason.

Therefore the irrational element also appears to be two-fold. For the vegetative
30   element in no way shares in reason, but the appetitive and in general the desiring element in a sense shares in it, in so far as it listens to and obeys it . . . . That the irrational element is in some sense persuaded by reason is indicated also by the giving of advice
1103a1   and by all reproof and exhortation. And if this element also must be said to have reason, that which has reason also will be twofold, one subdivision having it in the strict sense and in itself, and the other having a tendency to obey as one does one's father.

Excellence too is distinguished into kinds in accordance with this difference; for we
5   say that some excellences are intellectual and others moral,[1] philosophic wisdom and understanding and practical wisdom being intellectual, liberality and temperance moral. For in speaking about a man's character we do not say that he is wise or has understanding but that he is good-tempered or temperate; yet we praise the wise man
10   also with respect to his state; and of states we call those which merit praise excellences.

Book II

1. Excellence, then, being of two kinds, intellectual and moral, intellectual excellence
15   in the main owes both its birth and its growth to teaching (for which reason it requires experience and time), while moral excellence comes about as a result of habit . . . .
20   From this it is also plain that none of the moral excellences arises in us by nature; for nothing that exists by nature can form a habit contrary to its nature. For instance the stone which by nature moves downwards cannot be habituated to move upwards, not even if one tries to train it by throwing it up ten thousand times; nor can fire be habituated to move downwards, nor can anything else that by nature behaves in one way be trained to behave in another. Neither by nature, then, nor contrary to nature do excel-
25   lences arise in us; rather we are adapted by nature to receive them, and are made perfect by habit.

Again, of all the things that come to us by nature we first acquire the potentiality and later exhibit the activity (this is plain in the case of the senses; for it was not by often seeing or often hearing that we got these senses, but on the contrary we had
30   them before we used them, and did not come to have them by using them); but excellences we get by first exercising them, as also happens in the case of the arts as well. For the things we have to learn before we can do, we learn by doing, e.g. men become
1103b1   builders by building and lyre-players by playing the lyre; so too we become just by doing just acts, temperate by doing temperate acts, brave by doing brave acts.

This is confirmed by what happens in states; for legislators make the citizens good by forming habits in them, and this is the wish of every legislator; and those who do

---

1. *Moral*, here and hereafter, is used in the archaic sense of "pertaining to character or *mores*." [Trans. note]

not effect it miss their mark, and it is in this that a good constitution differs from   5
a bad one.

Again, it is from the same causes and by the same means that every excellence is
both produced and destroyed, and similarly every art: for it is from playing the lyre that
both good and bad lyre-players are produced. . . . For if this were not so, there would
have been no need of a teacher, but all men would have been born good or bad at their
craft. This, then, is the case with the excellences also; by doing the acts that we do
in our transactions with other men we become just or unjust, and by doing the acts   15
that we do in the presence of danger, and being habituated to feel fear or confidence,
we become brave or cowardly. The same is true of appetites and feelings of anger; some
men become temperate and good-tempered, others self-indulgent and irascible, by
behaving in one way or the other in the appropriate circumstances. Thus, in one word,   20
states arise out of like activities. This is why the activities we exhibit must be of a certain kind; it is because the states correspond to the differences between these. It makes
no small difference, then, whether we form habits of one kind or of another from our
very youth; it makes a very great difference, or rather *all* the difference.   25

2. Since, then, the present inquiry does not aim at theoretical knowledge like the
others (for we are inquiring not in order to know what excellence is, but in order to
become good, since otherwise our inquiry would have been of no use), we must examine the nature of actions, namely how we ought to do them; for these determine also   30
the nature of the states that are produced, as we have said. . . . The whole account of   1104a1
matters of conduct must be given in outline and not precisely, as we said at the very
beginning that the accounts we demand must be in accordance with the subject-
matter; matters concerned with conduct and questions of what is good for us have no
fixity, any more than matters of health. The general account being of this nature, the   5
account of particular cases is yet more lacking in exactness; for they do not fall under
any art or set of precepts, but the agents themselves must in each case consider what
is appropriate to the occasion, as happens also in the art of medicine or of navigation.

But though our present account is of this nature we must give what help we can.   10
First, then, let us consider this, that it is the nature of such things to be destroyed by
defect and excess, as we see in the case of strength and of health (for to gain light on
things imperceptible we must use the evidence of sensible things); both excessive and
defective exercise destroys the strength, and similarly drink or food which is above or   15
below a certain amount destroys the health, while that which is proportionate both
produces and increases and preserves it. So too is it, then, in the case of temperance
and courage and the other excellences. For the man who flies from and fears every-   20
thing and does not stand his ground against anything becomes a coward, and the
man who fears nothing at all but goes to meet every danger becomes rash; and similarly the man who indulges in every pleasure and abstains from none becomes self-
indulgent, while the man who shuns every pleasure, as boors do, becomes in a way   25
insensible; temperance and courage, then, are destroyed by excess and defect, and
preserved by the mean.

But not only are the sources and causes of their origination and growth the same
as those of their destruction, but also the sphere of their activity will be the same; for
this is also true of the things which are more evident to sense, e.g. of strength; it is   30
produced by taking much food and undergoing much exertion, and it is the strong
man that will be most able to do these things. So too is it with the excellences; by

1104b1 abstaining from pleasures we become temperate, and it is when we have become so that we are most able to abstain from them; and similarly too in the case of courage; for by being habituated to despise things that are terrible and to stand our ground against them we become brave, and it is when we have become so that we shall be most able to stand our ground against them.

5 3. We must take as a sign of states the pleasure or pain that supervenes on acts; for the man who abstains from bodily pleasures and delights in this very fact is temperate, while the man who is annoyed at it is self-indulgent, and he who stands his ground against things that are terrible and delights in this or at least is not pained is brave, while the man who is pained is a coward. For moral excellence is concerned with 10 pleasures and pains; it is on account of pleasure that we do bad things, and on account of pain that we abstain from noble ones. Hence we ought to have been brought up in a particular way from our very youth, as Plato says, so as both to delight in and to be pained by the things that we ought; for this is the right education.

Again, if the excellences are concerned with actions and passions, and every passion and every action is accompanied by pleasure and pain, for this reason also excel-15 lence will be concerned with pleasures and pains. This is indicated also by the fact that punishment is inflicted by these means; for it is a kind of cure, and it is the nature of cures to be effected by contraries. . . .

The following facts also may show us that they are concerned with these same 30 things. There being three objects of choice and three of avoidance, the noble, the advantageous, the pleasant, and their contraries, the base, the injurious, the painful, about all of these the good man tends to go right and the bad man to go wrong, and especially about pleasure; for this is common to the animals, and also it accompanies 1105a1 all objects of choice; for even the noble and the advantageous appear pleasant.

Again, it has grown up with us all from our infancy; this is why it is difficult to rub off this passion, engrained as it is in our life. And we measure even our actions, some 5 of us more and others less, by pleasure and pain. For this reason, then, our whole inquiry must be about these; for to feel delight and pain rightly or wrongly has no small effect on our actions. . . .

That excellence, then, is concerned with pleasures and pains, and that by the acts 15 from which it arises it is both increased and, if they are done differently, destroyed, and that the acts from which it arose are those in which it actualizes itself—let this be taken as said.

4. The question might be asked, what we mean by saying that we must become just by doing just acts, and temperate by doing temperate acts; for if men do just and tem-20 perate acts, they are already just and temperate, exactly as, if they do what is grammatical or musical they are proficient in grammar and music.

Or is this not true even of the arts? It is possible to do something grammatical either by chance or under the guidance of another. A man will be proficient in grammar, then, only when he has both done something grammatical and done it grammatically; and 25 this means doing it in accordance with the grammatical knowledge in himself.

Again, the case of the arts and that of the excellences are not similar; for the products of the arts have their goodness in themselves, so that it is enough that they should have a certain character, but if the acts that are in accordance with the excel-30 lences have themselves a certain character it does not follow that they are done justly or temperately. The agent also must be in a certain condition when he does them; in the first place he must have knowledge, secondly he must choose the acts, and choose them for their own sakes, and thirdly his action must proceed from a firm and 1105b1 unchangeable character. These are not reckoned in as conditions of the possession of the arts, except the bare knowledge; but as a condition of the possession of the excellences, knowledge has little or no weight, while the other conditions count not for a little but for everything, i.e. the very conditions which result from often doing just and temperate acts.

Actions, then, are called just and temperate when they are such as the just or the 5 temperate man would do; but it is not the man who does these that is just and temperate, but the man who also does them *as* just and temperate men do them. It is well said, then, that it is by doing just acts that the just man is produced, and by doing temperate acts the temperate man; without doing these no one would have even a prospect of 10 becoming good.

But most people do not do these, but take refuge in theory and think they are being philosophers and will become good in this way, behaving somewhat like patients who listen attentively to their doctors, but do none of the things they are ordered to do. As 15 the latter will not be made well in body by such a course of treatment, the former will not be made well in soul by such a course of philosophy.

5. Next we must consider what excellence is. Since things that are found in the soul are of three kinds—passions, faculties, states—excellence must be one of these. By 20 passions I mean appetite, anger, fear, confidence, envy, joy, love, hatred, longing, emulation, pity, and in general the feelings that are accompanied by pleasure or pain; by faculties the things in virtue of which we are said to be capable of feeling these, e.g. of becoming angry or being pained or feeling pity; by states the things in virtue of 25 which we stand well or badly with reference to the passions, e.g. with reference to anger we stand badly if we feel it violently or too weakly, and well if we feel it moderately; and similarly with references to the other passions.

Now neither the excellences nor the vices are *passions*, because we are not called good or bad on the ground of our passions, but are so called on the ground of our excel- 30 lences and our vices, and because we are neither praised nor blamed for our passions (for the man who feels fear or anger is not praised, nor is the man who simply feels anger blamed, but the man who feels it in a certain way), but for our excellences and 1106a1 our vices we *are* praised or blamed.

Again, we feel anger and fear without choice, but the excellences are choices or involve choice. Further, in respect of the passions we are said to be moved, but in respect of the excellences and the vices we are said not to be moved but to be disposed 5 in a particular way.

For these reasons also they are not *faculties*; for we are neither called good nor bad, nor praised nor blamed, for the simple capacity of feeling the passions; again, we have the faculties by nature, but we are not made good or bad by nature; we have spoken of 10 this before.

If, then, the excellences are neither passions nor faculties, all that remains is that they should be *states*.

Thus we have stated what excellence is in respect of its genus.

6. We must, however, not only describe it as a state, but also say what sort of state it is. We may remark, then, that every excellence both brings into good condition the 15 thing of which it is the excellence and makes the work of that thing be done well;

e.g. the excellence of the eye makes both the eye and its work good; for it is by the excellence of the eye that we see well. . . . Therefore, if this is true in every case, the excellence of man also will be the state which makes a man good and which makes him do his own work well.

How this is to happen we have stated already, but it will be made plain also by the following consideration of the nature of excellence. In everything that is continuous and divisible it is possible to take more, less, or an equal amount, and that either in terms of the thing itself or relatively to us; and the equal is an intermediate between excess and defect. By the intermediate in the object I mean that which is equidistant from each of the extremes, which is one and the same for all men; by the intermediate relatively to us that which is neither too much nor too little—and this is not one, nor the same for all. For instance, if ten is many and two is few, six is intermediate, taken in terms of the object; for it exceeds and is exceeded by an equal amount; this is intermediate according to arithmetical proportion. But the intermediate relatively to us is not to be taken so; if ten pounds are too much for a particular person to eat and two too little, it does not follow that the trainer will order six pounds; for this also is perhaps too much for the person who is to take it, or too little—too little for Milo, too much for the beginner in athletic exercises. The same is true of running and wrestling. Thus a master of any art avoids excess and defect, but seeks the intermediate and chooses this—the intermediate not in the object but relatively to us.

If it is thus, then, that every art does its work well—by looking to the intermediate and judging its works by this standard (so that we often say of good works of the art that it is not possible either to take away or to add anything, implying that excess and defect destroy the goodness of works of art, while the mean preserves it; and good artists, as we say, look to this in their work), and if, further, excellence is more exact and better than any art, as nature also is, then it must have the quality of aiming at the intermediate. I mean moral excellence; for it is this that is concerned with passions and actions, and in these there is excess, defect, and the intermediate. For instance, both fear and confidence and appetite and anger and pity and in general pleasure and pain may be felt both too much and too little, and in both cases not well; but to feel them at the right times, with reference to the right objects, towards the right people, with the right aim, and in the right way, is what is both intermediate and best, and this is characteristic of excellence. Similarly with regard to actions also there is excess, defect, and the intermediate. Now excellence is concerned with passions and actions, in which excess is a form of failure, and so is defect, while the intermediate is praised and is a form of success; and both these things are characteristics of excellence. Therefore excellence is a kind of mean, since it aims at what is intermediate. . . .

Excellence, then, is a state concerned with choice, lying in a mean relative to us, this being determined by reason and in the way in which the man of practical wisdom would determine it. Now it is a mean between two vices, that which depends on excess and that which depends on defect; and again it is a mean because the vices respectively fall short of or exceed what is right in both passions and actions, while excellence both finds and chooses that which is intermediate. Hence in respect of its substance and the account which states its essence it is a mean, with regard to what is best and right it is an extreme. . . .

7. We must, however, not only make this general statement, but also apply it to the individual facts. For among statements about conduct those which are general apply

more widely, but those which are particular are more true, since conduct has to do with individual cases, and our statements must harmonize with the facts in these cases. We may take these cases from the diagram. With regard to feelings of fear and confidence courage is the mean; of the people who exceed, he who exceeds in fearlessness has no 1107b1 name (many of the states have no name), while the man who exceeds in confidence is rash, and he who exceeds in fear and falls short in confidence is a coward. With regard to pleasures and pains—not all of them, and not so much with regard to the 5 pains—the mean is temperance, the excess self-indulgence. Persons deficient with regard to the pleasures are not often found; hence such persons also have received no name. But let us call them "insensible."

With regard to giving and taking of money the mean is liberality, the excess and the 10 defect prodigality and meanness. . . . With regard to honour and dishonour the mean is proper pride, the excess is known as a sort of empty vanity, and the deficiency is undue humility. . . . With regard to truth, then, the intermediate is a truthful sort of person and the mean may be called truthfulness, while the pretence which exaggerates 1108a20 is boastfulness and the person characterized by it a boaster, and that which understates is mock modesty and the person characterized by it mock-modest. With regard to pleasantness in the giving of amusement the intermediate person is ready-witted and the disposition ready wit, the excess is buffoonery and the person characterized by it 25 a buffoon, while the man who falls short is a sort of boor and his state is boorishness. With regard to the remaining kind of pleasantness, that which is exhibited in life in general, the man who is pleasant in the right way is friendly and the mean is friendliness, while the man who exceeds is an obsequious person if he has no end in view, a flatterer if he is aiming at his own advantage, and the man who falls short and is unpleasant in all circumstances is a quarrelsome and surly sort of person. 30

There are also means in the passions and concerned with the passions; since shame is not an excellence, and yet praise is extended to the modest man. For even in these matters one man is said to be intermediate, and another to exceed, as for instance the bashful man who is ashamed of everything; while he who falls short or is not ashamed of anything at all is shameless, and the intermediate person is modest. . . . 1108b1

8. There are three kinds of disposition, then, two of them vices, involving excess and deficiency and one an excellence, viz. the mean, and all are in a sense opposed to all; for the extreme states are contrary both to the intermediate state and to each other, and the intermediate to the extremes. . . . 15

To the mean in some cases the deficiency, in some the excess is more opposed; e.g. 1109a1 it is not rashness, which is an excess, but cowardice, which is a deficiency, that is more opposed to courage, and not insensibility, which is a deficiency, but self-indulgence, which is an excess, that is more opposed to temperance. This happens from two rea- 5 sons, one being drawn from the thing itself; for because one extreme is nearer and liker to the intermediate, we oppose not this but rather its contrary to the intermediate. E.g., since rashness is thought liker and nearer to courage, and cowardice more unlike, 10 we oppose rather the latter to courage; for things that are further from the intermediate are thought more contrary to it. This, then, is one cause, drawn from the thing itself; another is drawn from ourselves; for the thing to which we ourselves more naturally tend seem more contrary to the intermediate. For instance, we ourselves tend more 15 naturally to pleasures, and hence are more easily carried away towards self-indulgence than toward propriety. We describe as contrary to the mean, then, the states into which we are more inclined to lapse; and therefore self-indulgence, which is an excess, is the more contrary to temperance.

20   9. That moral excellence is a mean, then, and in what sense it is so, and that it is a mean between two vices, the one involving excess, the other deficiency, and that it is such because its character is to aim at what is intermediate in passions and in actions, has been sufficiently stated. Hence also it is no easy task to be

25   good. For in everything it is no easy task to find the middle, e.g. to find the middle of a circle is not for every one but for him who knows; so, too, any one can get angry— that is easy—or give or spend money; but to do this to the right person, to the right extent, at the right time, with the right aim, and in the right way, *that* is not for every one, nor is it easy; that is why goodness is both rare and laudable and noble.

30   Hence he who aims at the intermediate must first depart from what is the more contrary to it, as Calypso advises—

Hold the ship out beyond that surf and spray.[2]

For of the extremes one is more erroneous, one less so; therefore, since to hit the mean is hard in the extreme, we must as a second best, as people say, take the least of the

1109b1 evils; and this be done best in the way we describe.

But we must consider the things towards which we ourselves also are easily carried away; for some of us tend to one thing, some to another; and this will be recognizable from the pleasure and the pain we feel. We must drag ourselves away to the contrary

5   extreme; for we shall get into the intermediate state by drawing well away from error, as people do in straightening sticks that are bent.

Now in everything the pleasant or pleasure is most to be guarded against; for we do not judge it impartially. We ought, then, to feel towards pleasure as the elders of the

10   people felt towards Helen, and in all circumstances repeat their saying; for if we dismiss pleasure thus we are less likely to go astray. It is by doing this, then, (to sum the matter up) that we shall best be able to hit the mean.

But this is no doubt difficult, and especially in individual cases; for it is not

15   easy to determine both how and with whom and on what provocation and how long one should be angry; for we too sometimes praise those who fall short and call them good-tempered, but sometimes we praise those who get angry and call them manly. The man, however who deviates little from goodness is not blamed, whether he do so in the direction of the more or of the less, but only the man

20   who deviates more widely; for *he* does not fail to be noticed. But up to what point and to what extent a man must deviate before he becomes blameworthy it is not easy to determine by reasoning, any more than anything else that is perceived by the senses; such things depend on particular facts, and the decision rests with perception. So much, then, makes it plain that the intermediate state is in all

25   things to be praised, but that we must incline sometimes towards the excess, sometimes towards the deficiency; for so shall we most easily hit the mean and what is right.

---

2. *Odyssey* 12:219.

Book III

1. Since excellence is concerned with passions and actions, and on voluntary passions 30
and actions praise and blame are bestowed, on those that are involuntary forgiveness,
and sometimes also pity, to distinguish the voluntary and the involuntary is presumably necessary for those who are studying excellence and useful also for legislators with
a view to the assigning both of honours and of punishments.

Those things, then, are thought involuntary, which take place under compulsion
or owing to ignorance; and that is compulsory of which the moving principle is out- 1110a1
side, being a principle in which nothing is contributed by the person who acts or is
acted upon, e.g. if he were to be carried somewhere by a wind, or by men who had him
in their power.

But with regard to the things that are done from fear of greater evils or for some
noble object (e.g. if a tyrant were to order one to do something base, having one's 5
parents and children in his power, and if one did the action they were to be saved, but
otherwise would be put to death), it may be debated whether such actions are involuntary or voluntary. Something of the sort happens also with regard to the throwing of
goods overboard in a storm; for in the abstract no one throws goods away voluntarily,
but on condition of its securing the safety of himself and his crew any sensible man 10
does so. Such actions, then, are mixed, but are more like voluntary actions; for they
are worthy of choice at the time when they are done, and the end of an action is relative to the occasion. Both the terms, then, "voluntary" and "involuntary," must be used
with reference to the moment of action. Now the man acts voluntarily; for the princi- 15
ple that moves the instrumental parts of the body in such actions is in him, and the
things of which the moving principle is in a man himself are in his power to do or not
to do. Such actions, therefore, are voluntary, but in the abstract perhaps involuntary;
for no one would choose any such act in itself.

For such actions men are sometimes even praised, when they endure something 20
base or painful in return for great and noble objects gained; in the opposite case they
are blamed, since to endure the greatest indignities for no noble end or for a trifling
end is the mark of an inferior person. On some actions praise indeed is not bestowed,
but forgiveness is, when one does what he ought not under pressure which overstrains
human nature and which no one could withstand. But some acts, perhaps, we cannot 25
be forced to do, but ought rather to face death after the most fearful sufferings; for the
things that forced Euripides' Alcmaeon to slay his mother seem absurd. . . .

What sort of acts, then, should be called compulsory? We answer that without 1110b1
qualification actions are so when the cause is in the external circumstances and the
agent contributes nothing. . . .

But if some one were to say that pleasant and noble objects have a compelling power,
forcing us from without, all acts would be for him compulsory; for it is for these objects 10
that all men do everything they do. And those who act under compulsion and unwillingly act with pain, but those who do acts for their pleasantness and nobility do them
with pleasure; it is absurd to make external circumstances responsible, and not oneself,
as being easily caught by such attractions, and to make oneself responsible for noble acts
but the pleasant objects responsible for base acts. The compulsory, then, seems to be 15
that whose moving principle is outside, the person compelled contributing nothing.

Everything that is done by reason of ignorance is *non*-voluntary; it is only what produces pain and regret that is *in*voluntary. For the man who has done something
20   owing to ignorance, and feels not the least vexation at his action, has not acted voluntarily, since he did not know what he was doing, nor yet involuntarily, since he is not pained. Of people, then, who act by reason of ignorance he who regrets is thought an involuntary agent, and the man who does not regret may, since he is different, be called a non-voluntary agent; for, since he differs from the other, it is better that he should have a name of his own.
25   Acting by reason of ignorance seems also to be different from acting *in* ignorance; for the man who is drunk or in a rage is thought to act as a result not of ignorance but of one of the causes mentioned, yet not knowingly but in ignorance.

Now every wicked man is ignorant of what he ought to do and what he ought to abstain from, and error of this kind makes men unjust and in general bad; but the term
30   "involuntary" tends to be used not if a man is ignorant of what is to his advantage—for it is not ignorance in choice that makes action involuntary (it makes men wicked), nor ignorance of the universal (for *that* men are *blamed*), but ignorance of particular cir-
1111a1   cumstances of the action and the objects with which it is concerned. For it is on these that both pity and forgiveness depend, since the person who is ignorant of any of these acts involuntarily.

Perhaps it is just as well, therefore, to determine their nature and number. A man may be ignorant, then, of who he is, what he is doing, what or whom he is acting on, and sometimes also what (e.g. what instrument) he is doing it with, and to what end
5   (e.g. for safety), and how he is doing it (e.g. whether gently or violently). Now of all of these no one could be ignorant unless he were mad, and evidently also he could not be ignorant of the agent; for how could he not know himself? But of what he is doing a man might be ignorant, as for instance people say "it slipped out of their mouths as
10   they were speaking," or "they did not know it was a secret," as Aeschylus said of the mysteries, or a man might say he "let it go off when he merely wanted to show its working," as the man did with the catapult. Again, one might think one's son was an enemy, as Merope did, or that a pointed spear had a button on it, or that a stone was pumice-stone; or one might give a man a draught to save him, and really kill him; or one might
15   want to touch a man, as people do in sparring, and really strike him. The ignorance may relate, then, to any of these things, i.e. of the circumstances of the action, and the man who was ignorant of any of these is thought to have acted involuntarily, and especially if he was ignorant on the most important points; and these are thought to be
20   what he is doing and with what aim. Further, the doing of an act that is called involuntary in virtue of ignorance of this sort must be painful and involve regret.

Since that which is done under compulsion or by reason of ignorance is involuntary, the voluntary would seem to be that of which the moving principle is in the agent himself, he being aware of the particular circumstances of the action. Presumably acts
25   done by reason of anger or appetite are not rightly called involuntary. For in the first place, on that showing none of the other animals will act voluntarily, nor will children; and secondly, is it meant that we do not do voluntarily *any* of the acts that are due to appetite or anger, or that we do the noble acts voluntarily and the base acts involuntarily? Is not this absurd, when one and the same thing is the cause? But it
30   would surely be odd to describe as involuntary the things one ought to desire; and we ought both to be angry at certain things and to have an appetite for certain things, e.g.

for health and for learning. Also what is involuntary is thought to be painful, but what is in accordance with appetite is thought to be pleasant. Again, what is the difference in respect of involuntariness between errors committed upon calculation and those committed in anger? Both are to be avoided, but the irrational passions are thought 1111b1 not less human than reason is, and therefore also the actions which proceed from anger or appetite are the man's actions. It would be odd, then, to treat them as involuntary.

2. Both the voluntary and the involuntary having been delimited, we must next discuss choice; for it is thought to be most closely bound up with excellence and to 5 discriminate characters better than actions do.

Choice, then, seems to be voluntary, but not the same thing as the voluntary; the latter extends more widely. For both children and the other animals share in voluntary action, but not in choice, and acts done on the spur of the moment we describe as voluntary, but not as chosen. 10

Those who say it is appetite or anger or wish or a kind of opinion do not seem to be right. For choice is not common to irrational creatures as well, but appetite and anger are. Again, the incontinent man acts with appetite, but not with choice; while the continent man on the contrary acts with choice, but not with appetite. Again, appetite is contrary to choice, but not appetite to appetite. Again, appetite relates to 15 the pleasant and the painful, choice neither to the painful nor to the pleasant.

Still less is it anger; for acts due to anger are thought to be less than any other objects of choice.

But neither is it wish, though it seems near to it; for choice cannot relate to impos- 20 sibles, and if any one said he chose them he would be thought silly; but there may be a wish even for impossibles, e.g. for immortality. And wish may relate to things that could in no way be brought about by one's own efforts, e.g. that a particular actor or athlete should win in a competition; but no one chooses such things, but only the things that he thinks could be brought about by his own efforts. Again, wish relates 25 rather to the end, choice to what contributes to the end; for instance, we wish to be healthy, but we choose the acts which will make us healthy, and we wish to be happy and say we do, but we cannot well say we choose to be so; for, in general, choice seems to relate to the things that are in our own power. 30

For this reason, too, it cannot be opinion; for opinion is thought to relate to all kinds of things, no less to eternal things and impossible things than to things in our own power; and it is distinguished by its falsity or truth, not by its badness or goodness, while choice is distinguished rather by these. . . .

What, then, or what kind of thing is it, since it is none of the things we have mentioned? It seems to be voluntary, but not all that is voluntary to be an object of choice. Is it, then, what has been decided on by previous deliberation? For choice 1112a15 involves reason and thought. Even the name seems to suggest that it is what is chosen before other things.

3. Do we deliberate about everything, and is everything a possible subject of deliberation, or is deliberation impossible about some things? We ought presumably to call not what a fool or a madman would deliberate about, but what a sensible man 20 would deliberate about, a subject of deliberation. Now about eternal things no one deliberates, e.g. about the universe or the incommensurability of the diagonal and the side of a square. But no more do we deliberate about the things that involve movement

but always happen in the same way, whether of necessity or by nature or from any other
cause, e.g. the solstices and the risings of the stars; nor about things that happen now
in one way, now in another, e.g. droughts and rains; nor about chance events, like the
finding of treasure. But we do not deliberate even about all human affairs; for instance,
no Spartan deliberates about the best constitution for the Scythians. For none of these
things can be brought about by our own efforts.

We deliberate about things that are in our power and can be done; and these are
in fact what is left. For nature, necessity, and chance are thought to be causes, and also
thought and everything that depends on man. Now every class of men deliberates
about the things that can be done by their own efforts. And in the case of exact and
self-contained sciences there is no deliberation, e.g. about the letters of the alphabet
(for we have no doubt how they should be written); but the things that are brought
about by our own efforts, but not always in the same way, are the things about which
we deliberate, e.g. questions of medical treatment or of money-making. And we do so
more in the case of the art of navigation than in that of gymnastics, inasmuch as it has
been less exactly worked out, and again about other things in the same ratio, and more
also in the case of the arts than in that of the sciences; for we have more doubt about
the former. Deliberation is concerned with things that happen in a certain way for the
most part, but in which the event is obscure, and with things in which it is indeterminate. We call in others to aid us in deliberation on important questions, distrusting
ourselves as not being equal to deciding.

We deliberate not about ends but about what contributes to ends. For a doctor does
not deliberate whether he shall heal, nor an orator whether he shall convince nor a
statesman whether he shall produce law and order, nor does any one else deliberate
about his end. Having set the end they consider how and by what means it is to be
attained; and if it seems to be produced by several means they consider by which it is
most easily and best produced, while if it is achieved by one only they consider how
it will be achieved by this and by what means *this* will be achieved, till they come to
the first cause, which in the order of discovery is last. . . . It seems, then, as has been
said, that man is a moving principle of actions; now deliberation is about the things
to be done by the agent himself, and actions are for the sake of things other than themselves. For the end cannot be a subject of deliberation, but only what contributes to
the ends; nor indeed can the particular facts be a subject of it, as whether this is bread
or has been baked as it should; for these are matters of perception. If we are to be always
deliberating, we shall have to go on to infinity.

The same thing is deliberated upon and is chosen, except that the object of choice
is already determinate, since it is that which has been decided upon as a result of
deliberation that is the object of choice. For every one ceases to inquire how he is to
act when he has brought the moving principle back to himself and to the ruling part
of himself; for this is what chooses. . . . The object of choice being one of the things
in our own power which is desired after deliberation, choice will be deliberate desire
of things in our own power; for when we have decided as a result of deliberation, we
desire in accordance with our deliberation.

We may take it, then, that we have described choice in outline, and stated the nature
of its objects and the fact that it is concerned with what contributes to the ends. . . .

5. The end, then, being what we wish for, the things contributing to the end what
we deliberate about and choose, actions concerning the latter must be according to

choice and voluntary. Now the exercise of the excellences is concerned with these.   1113b5
Therefore excellence also is in our own power, and so too vice. For where it is in our
power to act it is also in our power not to act, and *vice versa*; so that, if to act, where
this is noble, is in our power, not to act, which will be base, will also be in our power,
and if not to act, where this is noble, is in our power, to act, which will be base, will   10
also be in our power. Now if it is in our power to do noble or base acts, and likewise
in our power not to do them, and this was what being good or bad meant, then it is
in our power to be virtuous or vicious.

The saying that "no one is voluntarily wicked nor involuntarily blessed" seems to   15
be partly false and partly true; for no one is involuntarily blessed, but wickedness *is*
voluntary. Or else we shall have to dispute what has just been said, at any rate, and
deny that man is a moving principle or begetter of his actions as of children. But if
these facts are evident and we cannot refer actions to moving principles other than   20
those in ourselves, the acts whose moving principles are in us must themselves also be
in our power and voluntary.

Witness seems to be borne to this both by individuals in their private capacity and
by legislators themselves; for these punish and take vengeance on those who do
wicked acts (unless they have acted under compulsion or as a result of ignorance for
which they are not themselves responsible), while they honour those who do noble   25
acts, as though they meant to encourage the latter and deter the former. But no one
is encouraged to do the things that are neither in our power nor voluntary; it is
assumed that there is no gain in being persuaded not to be hot or in pain or hungry
or the like, since we shall experience these feelings none the less. Indeed, we punish
a man for his very ignorance, if he is thought responsible for the ignorance, as when   30
penalties are doubled in the case of drunkenness; for the moving principle is in the
man himself, since he had the power of not getting drunk and his getting drunk was
the cause of his ignorance. And we punish those who are ignorant of anything in the
laws that they ought to know and that is not difficult, and so too in the case of any-   1114a1
thing else that they are thought to be ignorant of through carelessness; we assume that
it is in their power not to be ignorant, since they have the power of taking care.

But perhaps a man is the kind of man not to take care. Still they are themselves by
their slack lives responsible for becoming men of that kind, and men are themselves
responsible for being unjust or self-indulgent, in that they cheat or spend their time   5
in drinking bouts and the like; for it is activities exercised on particular objects that
make the corresponding character. . . .

Now some one may say that all men aim at the apparent good, but have no control
over how things appear to him; but the end appears to each man in a form answering   1114b1
to his character. We reply that if each man is somehow responsible for the state he is
in, he will also be himself somehow responsible for how things appear; but if not, no
one is responsible for his own evildoing, but everyone does evil acts through ignorance
of the end, thinking that by these he will get what is best, and the aiming at the end   5
is not self-chosen but one must be born with an eye, as it were, by which to judge
rightly and choose what is truly good, and he is well endowed by nature who is well
endowed with this. For it is what is greatest and most noble, and what we cannot get   10
or learn from another, but must have just such as it was when given us at birth, and
to be well and nobly endowed with this will be complete and true natural endowment.
If this is true, then, how will excellence be more voluntary than vice? To both men

15   alike, the good and the bad, the end appears and is fixed by nature or however it may
be, and it is by referring everything else to this that men do whatever they do.

Whether, then, it is not by nature that the end appears to each man such as it does
appear, but something also depends on him, or the end is natural but because the good
man does the rest voluntarily excellence is voluntary, vice also will be none the less
20   voluntary; for in the case of the bad man there is equally present that which depends
on himself in his actions even if not in his end. If, then, as is asserted, the excellences
are voluntary (for we are ourselves somehow part-causes of our states of character, and
25   it is by being persons of a certain kind that we assume the end to be so and so), the
vices also will be voluntary; for the same is true of them.

With regard to the excellences in *general* we have stated their genus in outline, viz.
that they are means and that they are states, and that they tend by their own nature to
the doing of the acts by which they are produced, and that they are in our power and
30   voluntary, and act as right reason prescribes. But actions and states are not voluntary in
the same way; for we are masters of our actions from the beginning right to the end, if
1115a1   we know the particular facts, but though we control the beginning of our states the
gradual progress is not obvious, any more than it is in illnesses; because it was in our
power, however, to act in this way or not in this way, therefore the states are voluntary.

Let us take up the several excellences, however, and say which they are and what
sort of things they are concerned with and how they are concerned with them; at the
5   same time it will become plain how many they are. And first let us speak of courage.

6. That it is a mean with regard to fear and confidence has already been made evident; and plainly the things we fear are terrible things, and these are, to speak without
10   qualification, evils; for which reason people even define fear as expectation of evil.
Now we fear all evils, e.g. disgrace, poverty, disease, friendlessness, death, but the brave
man is not thought to be concerned with all; for to fear some things is even right and
noble, and it is base not to fear them—e.g. disgrace; he who fears this is good and
15   modest, and he who does not is shameless. He is, however, by some people called
brave, by an extension of the word; for he has in him something which is like the brave
man, since the brave man also is a fearless person. . . . With what sort of terrible
25   things, then, is the brave man concerned? Surely with the greatest; for no one is more
likely than he to stand his ground against what is dreadful. Now death is the most terrible of all things; for it is the end, and nothing is thought to be any longer either good
or bad for the dead. But the brave man would not seem to be concerned even with
death in *all* circumstances, e.g. at sea or in disease. In what circumstances, then? Surely
30   in the noblest. Now such deaths are those in battle; for these take place in the greatest
and noblest danger. And this agrees with the ways in which honours are bestowed in
city-states and at the courts of monarchs. Properly, then, he will be called brave who
is fearless in face of a noble death, and of all emergencies that involve death; and the
emergencies of war are in the highest degree of this kind. Yet at sea also, and in disease,
1115b1   the brave man is fearless, but not in the same way as the seamen; for he has given up
hope for safety, and is disliking the thought of death in this shape, while they are hopeful because of their experience. At the same time, we show courage in situations where
there is the opportunity of showing prowess or where death is noble; but in these forms
5   of death neither of these conditions is fulfilled.

7. What is terrible is not the same for all men; but we say there are things terrible
even beyond human strength. These, then, are terrible to every one—at least to every

sensible man; but the terrible things that are *not* beyond human strength differ in magnitude and degree, and so too do the things that inspire confidence. Now the brave   10
man is as dauntless as man may be. Therefore, while he will fear even the things that
are not beyond human strength, he will fear them as he ought and as reason directs,
and he will face them for the sake of what is noble; for this is the end of excellence.
But it is possible to fear these more, or less, and again to fear things that are not terrible   15
as if they were. Of the faults that are committed one consists in fearing what one
should not, another in fearing as we should not, another in fearing when we should
not, and so on; and so too with respect to the things that inspire confidence. The man,
then, who faces and who fears the right things and with the right aim, in the right way
and at the right time, and who feels confidence under the corresponding conditions,
is brave; for the brave man feels and acts according to the merits of the case and in
whatever way reason directs.   20

Book X

6. What remains is to discuss in outline the nature of happiness, since this is what we
state the end of human nature to be. Our discussion will be the more concise if we first
sum up what we have said already. We said, then, that it is not a state; for if it were it
might belong to some one who was asleep throughout his life, living the life of a plant,
or, again, to some one who was suffering the greatest misfortunes. If these implications
are unacceptable, and we must rather class happiness as an activity, as we have said
before, and if some activities are necessary and desirable for the sake of something else,   1176b1
while others are so in themselves, evidently happiness must be placed among those
desirable in themselves, not among those desirable for the sake of something else; for
happiness does not lack anything, but is self-sufficient. Now those activities are desir-   5
able in themselves from which nothing is sought beyond the activity. And of this
nature excellent actions are thought to be; for to do noble and good deeds is a thing
desirable for its own sake.

  Pleasant amusements also are thought to be of this nature; we choose them not for
the sake of other things; for we are injured rather than benefited by them, since we are   10
led to neglect our bodies and our property. But most of the people who are deemed
happy take refuge in such pastimes, which is the reason why those who are ready-witted
at them are highly esteemed at the courts of tyrants; they make themselves pleasant
companions in the tyrant's favourite pursuits, and that is the sort of man they want. . . .   15
Now, as we have often maintained, those things are both valuable and pleasant which   25
are such to the good man; and to each man the activity in accordance with his own state
is most desirable, and, therefore, to the good man that which is in accordance with
excellence. Happiness, therefore, does not lie in amusement; it would, indeed, be
strange if the end were amusement, and one were to take trouble and suffer hardship all   30
one's life in order to amuse oneself. For, in a word, everything that we choose we choose
for the sake of something else—except happiness, which is an end. Now to exert oneself
and work for the sake of amusement seems silly and utterly childish. But to amuse oneself in order that one may exert oneself, as Anacharsis puts it, seems right; for amusement is a sort of relaxation, and we need relaxation because we cannot work continuously. Relaxation, then, is not an end; for it is taken for the sake of activity.   1177a1

The happy life is thought to be one of excellence; now an excellent life requires exertion, and does not consist in amusement. And we say that serious things are better than laughable things and those connected with amusement, and that the activity of
5   the better of any two things—whether it be two parts or two men—is the better; but the activity of the better is *ipso facto* superior and more of the nature of happiness. And any chance person—even a slave—can enjoy the bodily pleasures no less than the best man; but no one assigns to a slave a share in happiness—unless he assigns to him also
10   a share in human life. For happiness does not lie in such occupations, but, as we have said before, in excellent activities.

7. If happiness is activity in accordance with excellence, it is reasonable that it should be in accordance with the highest excellence; and this will be that of the best thing in us. Whether it be intellect or something else that is this element which is
15   thought to be our natural ruler and guide and to take thought of things noble and divine, whether it be itself also divine or only the most divine element in us, the activity of this in accordance with its proper excellence will be complete happiness. . . .

Now this would seem to be in agreement both with what we said before and with
20   the truth. For this activity is the best (since not only is intellect the best thing in us, but the objects of intellect are the best of knowable objects); and, secondly, it is the most continuous, since we can contemplate truth more continuously than we can *do* anything. And we think happiness has pleasure mingled with it, but the activity of wisdom is admittedly the pleasantest of excellent activities; at all events philosophy is thought
25   to offer pleasures marvellous for their purity and their enduringness, and it is to be expected that those who know will pass their time more pleasantly than those who inquire. And the self-sufficiency that is spoken of must belong most to the contemplative activity. For while a wise man, as well as a just man and the rest, needs the neces-
30   saries of life, when they are sufficiently equipped with things of that sort the just man needs people towards whom and with whom he shall act justly, and the temperate man, the brave man, and each of the others is in the same case, but the wise man, even when by himself, can contemplate truth, and the better the wiser he is; he can perhaps do so
1177b1 better if he has fellow-workers, but still he is the most self-sufficient. And this activity alone would seem to be loved for its own sake; for nothing arises from it apart from the contemplating, while from practical activities we gain more or less apart from the action. And happiness is thought to depend on leisure; for we are busy that we may have
5   leisure, and make war that we may live in peace. Now the activity of the practical excellences is exhibited in political or military affairs, but the actions concerned with
15   these seem to be unleisurely. . . . So if among excellent actions political and military actions are distinguished by nobility and greatness, and these are unleisurely and aim at an end and are not desirable for their own sake, but the activity of intellect, which is
20   contemplative, seems both to be superior in worth and to aim at no end beyond itself, and to have its pleasure proper to itself (and this augments the activity), and the self-sufficiency, leisureliness, unweariedness (so far as this is possible for man), and all the other attributes ascribed to the blessed man are evidently those connected with this
25   activity, it follows that this will be the complete happiness of man, if it be allowed a complete term of life (for none of the attributes of happiness is *in*complete).

But such a life would be too high for man; for it is not in so far as he is man that he will live so, but in so far as something divine is present in him; and by so much as this is superior to our composite nature is its activity superior to that which is the exer-

cise of the other kind of excellence. If intellect is divine, then, in comparison with   30
man, the life according to it is divine in comparison with human life. But we must not
follow those who advise us, being men, to think of human things, and, being mortal,
of mortal things, but must, so far as we can, make ourselves immortal, and strain every
nerve to live in accordance with the best thing in us; for even if it be small in bulk,
much more does it in power and worth surpass everything. This would seem, too, to   1178a1
be each man himself, since it is the authoritative and better part of him. It would be
strange, then, if he were to choose not the life of himself but that of something else.
And what we said before will apply now; that which is proper to each thing is by   5
nature best and most pleasant for each thing; for man, therefore, the life according to
intellect is best and pleasantest, since intellect more than anything else *is* man. This
life therefore is also the happiest.

   8. But in a secondary degree the life in accordance with the other kind of excellence is happy; for the activities in accordance with this befit our human estate. Just   10
and brave acts, and other excellent acts, we do in relation to each other, observing
what is proper to each with regard to contracts and services and all manner of actions
and with regard to passions; and all of these seem to be human. Some of them seem
even to arise from the body, and excellence of character to be in many ways bound up
with the passions. Practical wisdom, too, is linked to excellence of character, and this   15
to practical wisdom, since the principles of practical wisdom are in accordance with
the moral excellences and rightness in the moral excellences is in accordance with
practical wisdom. Being connected with the passions also, the moral excellences must   20
belong to our composite nature; and the excellences of our composite nature are
human; so, therefore, are the life and the happiness which correspond to these. The
excellence of the intellect is a thing apart; we must be content to say this much about
it, for to describe it precisely is a task greater than our purpose requires. It would seem,
however, also to need external equipment but little, or less than moral excellence   25
does. . . . It is debated, too, whether the choice or the deed is more essential to excellence, which is assumed to involve both; it is surely clear that its completion involves
both; but for deeds many things are needed, and more, the greater and nobler the   1178b1
deeds are. But the man who is contemplating the truth needs no such thing, at least
with a view to the exercise of his activity; indeed they are, one may say, even hin-   5
drances, at all events to his contemplation; but in so far as he is a man and lives with
a number of people, he chooses to do excellent acts; he will therefore need such aids
to living a human life.

   But that complete happiness is a contemplative activity will appear from the following consideration as well. We assume the gods to be above all other beings blessed
and happy; but what sort of actions must we assign to them? . . . If we were to run   10
through them all, the circumstances of action would be found trivial and unworthy of
gods. Still, every one supposes that they *live* and therefore that they are active; we
cannot suppose them to sleep like Endymion. Now if you take away from a living being   20
action, and still more production, what is left but contemplation? Therefore the
activity of God, which surpasses all others in blessedness, must be contemplative; and
of human activities, therefore, that which is most akin to this must be most of the
nature of happiness.

   This is indicated, too, by the fact that the other animals have no share in happiness, being completely deprived of such activity. For while the whole life of the gods   25

is blessed, and that of men too in so far as some likeness of such activity belongs to them, none of the other animals is happy, since they in no way share in contemplation. Happiness extends, then, just so far as contemplation does, and those to whom

30   contemplation more fully belongs are more truly happy, not accidentally, but in virtue of the contemplation; for this is in itself precious. Happiness, therefore, must be some form of contemplation.

But, being a man, one will also need external prosperity; for our nature is not self-sufficient for the purpose of contemplation, but our body also must be healthy and must have food and other attention. Still, we must not think that the man who is to

1179a1   be happy will need many things or great things, merely because he cannot be blessed without external goods; for self-sufficiency and action do not depend on excess, and we can do noble acts without ruling earth and sea; for even with moderate advantages

5   one can act excellently (this is manifest enough; for private persons are thought to do worthy acts no less than despots—indeed even more); and it is enough that we should have so much as that; for the life of the man who is active in accordance with excellence will be happy. . . .

9. If these matters and the excellences, and also friendship and pleasure, have been dealt with sufficiently in outline, we are to suppose that our programme has reached its end? Surely, as is said, where there are things to be done the end is not to survey

1179b1   and recognize the various things, but rather to do them; with regard to excellence, then, it is not enough to know, but we must try to have and use it, or try any other way

5   there may be of becoming good. Now if arguments were in themselves enough to make men good, they would justly, as Theognis says, have won very great rewards, and such rewards should have been provided; but as things are, while they seem to have power to encourage and stimulate the generous-minded among the young, and to make a character which is gently born, and a true lover of what is noble, ready to be possessed

10   by excellence, they are not able to encourage the many to nobility and goodness. For these do not by nature obey the sense of shame, but only fear, and do not abstain from bad acts because of their baseness but through fear of punishment; living by passion they pursue their own pleasures and the means to them, and avoid the opposite pains,

15   and have not even a conception of what is noble and truly pleasant, since they have never tasted it. What argument would remould such people? It is hard, if not impossible, to remove by argument the traits that have long since been incorporated in the character; and perhaps we must be content if, when all the influences by which we are thought to become good are present, we get some tincture of excellence.

20   Now some think that we are made good by nature, others by habituation, others by teaching. Nature's part evidently does not depend on us, but as a result of some divine causes is present in those who are truly fortunate; while argument and teaching, we may suspect, are not powerful with all men, but the soul of the student must first have

25   been cultivated by means of habits for noble joy and noble hatred, like earth which is to nourish the seed. For he who lives as passion directs will not hear argument that dissuades him, nor understand it if he does; and how can we persuade one in such a state to change his ways? And in general passion seems to yield not to argument but

30   to force. The character, then, must somehow be there already with a kinship to excellence, loving what is noble and hating what is base.

But it is difficult to get from youth up a right training for excellence if one has not been brought up under right laws; for to live temperately and hardily is not pleasant to most people, especially when they are young. For this reason their nurture and occupations should be fixed by law; for they will not be painful when they have become customary. But it is surely not enough that when they are young they should get the right nurture and attention; since they must, even when they are grown up, practise and be habituated to them, we shall need laws for this as well, and generally speaking to cover the whole of life; for most people obey necessity rather than argument, and punishments rather than what is noble. . . . 1180a1 5

However that may be, if (as we have said) the man who is to be good must be well trained and habituated, and go on to spend his time in worthy occupations and neither willingly nor unwillingly do bad actions, and if this can be brought about if men live in accordance with a sort of intellect and right order, provided this has force—if this be so, the paternal command indeed has not the required force or compulsive power (nor in general has the command of one man, unless he be a king or something similar), but the law *has* compulsive power, while it is at the same time an account proceeding from a sort of practical wisdom and intellect. And while people hate *men* who oppose their impulses, even if they oppose them rightly, the law in its ordaining of what is good is not burdensome. . . . 15 20

It would seem from what has been said that he can do this better if he makes himself capable of legislating. For public care is plainly effected by laws, and good care by good laws; whether written or unwritten would seem to make no difference, nor whether they are laws providing for the education of individuals or of groups—any more than it does in the case of music or gymnastics and other such pursuits. For as in cities laws and character have force, so in households do the injunctions and the habits of the father, and these have even more because of the tie of blood and the benefits he confers; for the children start with a natural affection and disposition to obey. Further, individual education has an advantage over education in common, as individual medical treatment has; for while in general rest and abstinence from food are good for a man in a fever, for a particular man they may not be; and a boxer presumably does not prescribe the same style of fighting to all his pupils. It would seem, then, that the detail is worked out with more precision if the care is particular to individuals; for each person is more likely to get what suits his case. 1180b1 5 10

But individuals can be best cared for by a doctor or gymnastic instructor or any one else who has the universal knowledge of what is good for every one or for people of a certain kind (for the sciences both are said to be, and are, concerned with what is common). . . . 15

And surely he who wants to make men, whether many or few, better by his care must try to become capable of legislating, if it is through laws that we can become good. For to get anyone whatever—anyone who is put before us—into the right condition is not for the first chance comer; if anyone can do it, it is the man who knows, just as in medicine and all other matters which give scope for care and practical wisdom. 25

SELECTED BIBLIOGRAPHY

Aristotle. *The Complete Works of Aristotle: The Revised Oxford Translation*. Ed. Jonathan Barnes. Princeton, N.J.: Princeton University Press, 1984.

_____. *A New Aristotle Reader*. Ed. J.L. Ackrill. Princeton, N.J.: Princeton University Press, 1987.

Ackrill, J.L. *Aristotle the Philosopher*. New York: Oxford University Press, 1981.

Allan, D.J. *The Philosophy of Aristotle*. New York: Oxford University Press, 1970.

Barnes, Jonathan. *Aristotle*. New York: Oxford University Press, 1982.

Brentano, Franz. *Aristotle and His World View*. Berkeley: University of California Press, 1978.

Lear, Jonathan. *Aristotle: The Desire to Understand*. Cambridge: Cambridge University Press, 1988.

Lloyd, Geoffrey E. *Aristotle: Growth and Structure of His Thought*. Cambridge: Cambridge University Press, 1968.

Mure, G.R.G. *Aristotle*. New York: Oxford University Press, 1932.

Ross, W.D. *Aristotle*. Cleveland: Meridian Books, 1959.

Taylor, A.E. *Aristotle*. New York: Dover, 1919.

MEDIEVAL
PHILOSOPHY

There are two large gaps in this anthology. The first occurs between Aristotle and Saint Augustine, a period of some seven hundred years; the second is between Saint Augustine and Saint Thomas Aquinas, a gap of almost nine hundred years. These gaps can easily be misread: it is certainly not the case that philosophy disappeared in those intervals, despite the lull in intellectual life after the Fall of Rome from about 450 until around 1000.

Plato's Academy and Aristotle's Lyceum continued to operate for hundreds of years after the deaths of their founders (in 347 B.C.E. and 322 B.C.E., respectively). Although Athens long remained the hub of philosophic activity, great centers of learning also arose at Alexandria, Rome, and elsewhere. Yet despite the somewhat high level of philosophical activity in the period, no giants of philosophy emerged. Philosophers organized into fairly cohesive schools of thought, many of which traced their lineage to one revered founder, but the cohesiveness of these schools seems to have dampened the originality that marks philosophic greatness. Besides the Academy and the Lyceum, the schools of the Stoics, the Epicureans, and the Skeptics were prominent.

Between the first century B.C.E. and the third century C.E., there was a neoclassical revival, in which interest focused on the originators of the various schools, especially Plato and Aristotle. One of these movements gained ascendency and remained a dominant force in intellectual circles for several more centuries: Neoplatonism, whose most prominent advocate was Plotinus (c. 204–270). It is through Neoplatonism that Plato exercised his influence on medieval Christian thought, for only a few of Plato's writings were available to Latin-speaking thinkers. The Neoplatonists preserved and even heightened Plato's doctrine that truth is immaterial, nonsensible, and entirely spiritual. The Neoplatonists sought to instill a clearer and more unified structure into the intelligible, spiritual realm. For Plotinus the principle of all things is God, the One and the Good, whose nature is ineffable and incomprehensible. No predicate can capture the nature of the One in its fullness, and all other things are seen as *emanations* from the One. *Nous*, mind or intelligence, is the first emanation, still entirely immaterial and spiritual, and from it in turn emanates the world-soul. The Neoplatonic emphasis on spirituality and transcendence of the material and sensible, as well as the fact that there are three stages of purely spiritual emanation before the emanation of the finite spirits, played nicely into the hands of Christian thinkers. Though much of Neoplatonism was adaptable to Christian theology, a good deal conflicted strongly with Christian doctrine—for example, the fact that the emanations are thoroughly *necessary* and not a free, creative act of divine will.

Medieval philosophy differs most significantly from its predecessors in that it is always in the service of religion. Significant contributions were made by Islamic philosophers, such as al-Farabi (c. 870–950), Avicenna (Ibn-Sina, 980–1037), and Averroës (Ibn-Rushd, 1126–1198), and by Jewish philosophers, such as Maimonides (1135–1204) and Crescas (d. c. 1412). Indeed, it was the Islamic and Jewish philosophers who did the most to keep alive the traditions of Greek philosophy during the Dark Ages. Without their efforts the Greek tradition would have been lost entirely. But they did much more than preserve the ancients; they sought to forge a new vision of the world that unified the knowledge of the Greeks with the tenets of their faiths. This project also dominated thought in Europe, where the Christian faith formed the bedrock and foundation for all further philosophical reflection, and all speculation was ultimately in the service of the faith. Medieval philosophy might even be seen as a series of explorations of how the rational, discursive methods of philosophy can best be made to agree with and support a religious faith founded on Scripture.

Conforming to the doctrines of the Church colored every aspect of medieval philosophic speculation. Any theory of knowledge had to account for the ability to know both the doctrines of faith and the differences between faith and other kinds of knowledge, either purely rational or sensible. The fundamental metaphysical questions of the era concerned the relation between the infinite, omnipotent God and his finite creatures. Can God's existence be proved by reason? Does God's foreknowledge of our actions entail that we are not free beings? The rigors of medieval life—a time when life, if not, as Thomas Hobbes said later, "solitary, poor, nasty, brutish, and short," was nonetheless a harsh and constant struggle—turned thoughts of the good life into thoughts of the salvation of one's soul.

Augustine (354–430) stands on the border of the classical and medieval worlds. The Roman Empire, long thought eternal, was crumbling around him. A new order—at first a disorder—was forming. As the temporal powers of the empire declined, the spiritual order of the Church gained ascendency. The tremendous social, economic, and political upheavals that accompanied the disintegration of the Roman Empire made the study of philosophy extremely difficult. Monasteries, the sole surviving centers of knowledge, struggled to maintain and transmit what culture and learning they commanded; the fostering of new and original thought was out of the question.

By the time of Aquinas (1225–1274), the Dark Ages had given way to a new stability in which culture and learning could again flourish. No longer wracked by invasions from the east and the north, European trade was on the rise and reaching out to increasingly distant lands. The Crusades to regain the holy lands also played a major role in the broadening of European culture. Universities grew out of the older cathedral schools and enabled the best minds of the age to devote themselves to learning. The works of Aristotle, long unknown to Europe (only Aristotle's logical works had been passed down), were reintroduced through contact with Islamic philosophers, and still later the works of Plato were regained.

Medieval thought flourished most strongly in the thirteenth century. In the fourteenth and fifteenth centuries the delicate balances of reason and faith that earlier thinkers had achieved seemed increasingly remote. The estrangement of faith and reason pushed many toward either a nonrational mysticism or a rationalistic skepticism about faith itself. The Church now also had to contend with increasingly powerful secular authorities, and in its massive wealth it had grown corrupt. Poverty, chastity, and humility were no longer practiced by the papal bureaucracy. These struggles were reflected in medieval philosophy, driving it ever further into a relatively sterile scholasticism and eclecticism from which only the bold new thinkers of the early modern era could awaken it.

SELECTED BIBLIOGRAPHY

McKeon, Richard, ed. *Selections from Medieval Philosophers.* 2 vols. New York: Scribner, 1929.

Shapiro, Herman, ed. *Medieval Philosophy.* New York: Modern Library, 1964.

Walsh, J.J., and A. Hyman eds. *Philosophy in the Middle Ages.* Indianapolis: Hackett, 1983.

Armstrong, A.H. *The Cambridge History of Later Greek and Early Medieval Philosophy.* Cambridge: Cambridge University Press, 1967.

Copleston, Frederick. *Medieval Philosophy.* New York: Harper & Row, 1961.

DeWulf, Maurice. *An Introduction to Scholastic Philosophy.* New York: Dover, 1956.

Gilson, Étienne. *A History of Christian Philosophy in the Middle Ages.* London: Sheed & Ward, 1953.

_____. *Reason and Revelation in the Middle Ages.* New York: Scribner, 1938.

Henry, D.P. *Medieval Logic and Metaphysics.* London: Hutchinson, 1972.

Knowles, David. *The Evolution of Medieval Thought.* New York: Random House, 1962.

Kretzmann, N., et al. *The Cambridge History of Later Medieval Philosophy.* Cambridge: Cambridge University Press, 1982.

Leff, Gordon. *Medieval Thought: St. Augustine to Ockham.* Harmondsworth, England: Penguin, 1958.

Marebon, John. *Early Medieval Philosophy: An Introduction.* London: Routledge & Kegan Paul, 1983.

Pott, Timothy, ed. *Conscience in Medieval Philosophy.* Cambridge: Cambridge University Press, 1980.

Sirat, Colette. *A History of Jewish Philosophy in the Middle Ages.* Cambridge: Cambridge University Press, 1985.

Vignaux, Paul. *Philosophy in the Middle Ages: An Introduction.* Trans. E.C. Hall. New York: Meridian, 1959.

Saint Augustine

Aurelius Augustinus was born in 354 at Tagaste, Africa (now Souq Ahras, Algeria). Patricius, his father, was a mid-level Roman administrator and not a Christian, although the Roman emperors had been Christians since Constantine, forty years earlier. His mother, Monica, was a Christian, but Augustine was not baptized as a child. His father apparently wanted a standard Roman upbringing for the child, and his mother, hoping that he would eventually be led to Christianity, did not fight Patricius' plans. Both of them wanted a good education for their son—training in classical literature and rhetoric—but Augustine admits that he did not devote a great deal of energy to his studies. In his sixteenth year, having completed a course of study at nearby Madaurus, Augustine returned home and in idleness fell into a life of dissipation and sin—or so he tells us much later in his *Confessions*, one of the classics of medieval literature.

A year later Augustine went to Carthage to continue his studies, continuing as well, at first, his shallow and dissolute life. His son, Adeodatus, was born in Carthage when Augustine was eighteen. A book of Cicero's (now unfortunately lost) awakened the love of wisdom in Augustine, and he began to throw himself into his studies. He also turned his attention to the Christian scriptures, initially finding them too lowly, too common for his tastes. He eventually adopted Manichaeism—a heretical Christian sect that took the world to be the product of two equal forces, one good and one evil.

Augustine, now himself a teacher of rhetoric, remained Manichaean for a number of years. At the age of twenty-nine he began to doubt the doctrine of the Manichaeans, and when his travels took him to Italy, he came under the influence of Saint Ambrose. Though Ambrose's preaching ultimately led him away from Manichaeism, Augustine's first reaction was one of deep skepticism. Turning to the Neoplatonists for a resolution of this problem, he found that the Scriptures, especially St. Paul, relieved his doubt. Only his lust for pleasures of the flesh seemed to stand between him and Christianity. In his thirty-second year Augustine heard "a childlike voice" telling him to "take up the book" and read, and when he opened the Scripture at a random place, he encountered an admonition against sexual desire. Soon after, to his mother's great joy, he was baptized a Christian.

Augustine then abandoned his teaching of rhetoric and began writing to defend his faith against heretics and to unveil it to the ignorant. He returned to Africa and established a monastery where he might live his faith in peace and contemplation, but he was soon persuaded to take ordination as a priest in order to assist the bishop of Hippo. Four years later, in 395, Augustine was himself the bishop of Hippo, working tirelessly for his Church. Amid his administrative and pastoral duties, Augustine wrote prolifically, mostly tracts against various heresies, such as those of the Donatists and the Pelagians, but also such major works as *The City of God*.

Augustine was led to his Christian faith through the writings of the Neoplatonic philosophers, and his early writings reflect the belief that although philosophy cannot bring one all the way to faith, it can prepare the soul to receive God's grace. As he grew older and more entrenched in his faith, and with pastoral concerns weighing more heavily than philosophical abstractions, Augustine increasingly emphasized Scripture rather than reason as the proper path for the soul seeking salvation.

Augustine died in 430, in the third month of the siege of Hippo by the Vandals, a marauding Germanic tribe that wreaked havoc throughout the empire.

Philosophy

Augustine's life was a search for wisdom, and his writings are testimonies—often deeply personal and moving—to the faith he discovered. As explorations and defenses of his faith, his writings were not intended as pieces of pure philosophy and cannot be read as if they were.

Augustine is a crucial figure in medieval philosophy, in part because of his understanding of the relation between faith and reason. He does not believe that humanity's natural, rational faculties alone can achieve wisdom or beatitude: the gift of God's grace is necessary to lift humanity from its fallen state and restore to it the clarity essential to wisdom and blessedness. His insistence on the necessity of divine grace, however, does not preclude the importance of understanding or reason. The search for understanding can itself be a path to faith, as it was for Augustine himself. Even more important, faith itself, though the key to wisdom, is still only a beginning: faith provides the foundation for the full understanding that is wisdom. "Believe in order that you may understand; unless you believe, you shall not understand."[1]

This attitude pervades Augustine's metaphysics, heavily influenced as well by Neoplatonic speculation. The world is a divine creation and therefore full of traces of

---

1. *Letter 120.*

God's presence. Our task is to be able to see this divine presence in all things and value them as his work, for in themselves there is nothing of worth.

Augustine's philosophy focuses on a single, essentially moral concern—attaining beatitude, that is, achieving the happiness and peace that result from a faithful understanding of and obedience to God. This is the universal human task, and there are numerous natural impediments. As fallen creatures, we must battle our material, sensible, lustful natures in order to restore the harmony present before the fall. Our "loves," or desires, must be brought into harmony, not just with each other but also with the divine order. Virtue is the achievement of such a "rightly ordered love."

Augustine agrees with his Greek predecessors that humans are naturally social, but the machinery of state—coercive authorities and government—is an evil made necessary by the fall of mankind, a punishment for our sins. Whereas earlier Christian thinkers had seen the Roman Empire as an instrument of God's purpose, Augustine, witness to the collapse of the supposedly eternal empire around him, relegated it to a merely historical position. The true, eternal city of God, composed of all the faithful, exists wherever the faithful exist; the role of the state is to secure the temporal order necessary to acceptable human life. The concern of the state is with public order; the concern of faith and religion is with the inner order that goes beyond any external arrangement and prepares one's soul for eternity.

The Reading Context

Augustine's work marks a historical watershed. Rome, the eternal empire, was collapsing under invasions from the north; the uncertainty, even futility, of worldly endeavors was starkly evident. Augustine found in the Christian faith the strength to endure and the hope of enjoying eternal beatitude. Yet the Christian faith was not at that time the dominant creed of the West; it was challenged and threatened from many sides. In reading Augustine, keep in mind that answering specific philosophical questions was decidedly secondary in his mind to testifying to and defending his faith. The reader's accepting his reasoning is not as important to Augustine as the reader's understanding and accepting the Christian faith. For each reader the question arises whether Augustine's reasoned arguments are even the right kind of medium in which to convey the evangelical message.

A Note on the Texts

Letter 120 was written about 410 in reply to an earlier letter from Consentium; its principal topic is the nature of the Trinity and our knowledge of it. *On the Morals of the Catholic Church* is one of Augustine's earliest tracts against heretics, written in Rome in 388. Augustine describes the origin of *The City of God* as follows: "Rome having been stormed and sacked by the Goths under Alaric their king [in 410], the worshippers of false gods, or pagans, as we commonly call them, made an attempt to attribute this calamity to the Christian religion, and began to blaspheme the true God with even more than their wonted bitterness and acerbity. It was this which kindled my zeal for the house of God, and prompted me to undertake the defence of the city of God against the charges and misrepresentations of its assailants." Begun in 413, *The City of God* was issued in installments until completed in 426.

Reading Questions

1. Why does Augustine believe that faith should precede reason? How could it, if this principle is itself subject to rational defense?
2. In what way does Augustine think we "see" the nature of the Trinity? How does this "seeing" compare with seeing material objects?
3. How and why does Augustine avoid having to decide whether a person is a body, a soul, or a combination of the two?
4. Is it possible for someone to love God with heart, soul, and mind—and yet be a bad or immoral person?
5. Is the city of man related to the city of God as the real to the ideal?
6. Augustine integrally connects peace and being well ordered. But how can we distinguish what is well ordered?
7. What is the proper relation between church and state, according to Augustine?

Letter 120

God forbid that He should hate in us that faculty by which He made us superior to all other living beings. Therefore, we must refuse so to believe as not to receive or seek a reason for our belief, since we could not believe at all if we did not have rational souls. So, then, in some points that bear on the doctrine of salvation, which we are not yet able to grasp by reason—but we shall be able to sometime—let faith precede reason, and let the heart be cleansed by faith so as to receive and bear the great light of reason; this is indeed reasonable. Therefore the Prophet said with reason: "If you will not believe, you will not understand" (Isa. 7:9); thereby he undoubtedly made a distinction between these two things and advised us to believe first so as to be able to understand whatever we believe. It is, then, a reasonable requirement that faith precede reason, for, if this requirement is not reasonable, then it is contrary to reason, which God forbid. But, if it is reasonable that faith precede a certain great reason which cannot yet be grasped, there is no doubt that, however slight the reason which proves this, it does precede faith.

That is why the Apostle warns us that we ought to be ready to give an answer to anyone who asks us a reason for our faith and hope, since if an unbeliever asks me a reason for my faith and hope, and I see that he cannot accept it until he believes, I give him that very reason, so that he may see how absurd it is for him to ask a reason for things which he cannot grasp until he believes. But if a believer asks a reason that he may understand what he believes, his mental ability is to be considered, and then, when the reason for his faith has been given according to it, he may draw as much understanding as he can, more if he is capable of more, less if he is less capable, but with the provision that, to the extent that he attains to the fullness and perfection of knowledge, he does not withdraw from the way of faith. . . . If, then, we are faithful now, we shall attain to the way of faith, and if we do not leave it, we shall unfailingly come not only to a great understanding of incorporeal and unchanging things, such as cannot be reached by all in this life, but even to the height of contemplation, which the Apostle calls "face to face." For some have very little knowledge, yet by walking with great perseverance in the way of faith they attain to that most blessed contemplation; whereas others, although they know even now what the invisible, unchanging, and incorporeal nature is and what way leads to the abode of such happiness, cannot attain to it because the way, which is Christ crucified, seems foolish to them, and they refuse to withdraw to the innermost chamber of that repose by whose light their mind is stunned as by a far-shining radiance. . . .

I should like to say these things to rouse your faith to a love of understanding to which true reason leads the mind and for which faith prepares it. For that reasoning which argues about the Trinity, which is God, that the Son is not co-eternal with the Father, or that He is of another substance, and that the Holy Spirit is unlike Him in some way and therefore inferior, and that reasoning which claims that the Father and the Son are of one and the same substance, but that the Holy Spirit is of another, are to be avoided and detested, not because they are reasoning but because they are false

From *Fathers of the Church* (vol. 18): *St. Augustine: Letters*, trans. Sister Wilfred Parsons (Washington, D.C.: Catholic University of America Press, 1953), pp. 47–52, by permission of the Catholic University of America Press.

reasoning; for if the reasoning were true, it would surely not go wrong. Therefore, just as you ought not to give up all speech because there is false speech, so you ought not to turn against all reasoning because there is false reasoning. I would say the same of wisdom: that wisdom is not to be avoided because there is also false wisdom, to which Christ crucified is foolishness, though He is "the power of God and the wisdom of God.". . .

Therefore, should we not listen in vain to what is true, unless faith which clothes us with piety had preceded reason, through whose outward argument, together with the light of truth within us, we are roused to perceive that these idols are false? Thus, when faith acts in its own sphere, reason following after finds something of what faith was seeking, and true reason is to be preferred to false reason because it makes us understand what we believe, but faith in things not yet understood is undoubtedly even more to be preferred. It is better to believe in something true but not yet seen than to take the false thing one sees for true. For faith has its own eyes with which it sees, so to speak, that what it does not yet see is true, and with which it most certainly sees that it does not yet see what it believes. . . .

As a matter of fact, we hold things visible but past by faith alone, since there is no hope of seeing again what has slipped away with time. They are regarded as finished and gone by, as it is expressed in the words: "Christ died once for our sins, and rose again and dieth now no more: death shall no more have dominion over him" (I Pet. 3:18). The things which are not yet in existence but are to come, such as the resurrection of our spiritual bodies, are believed in such wise that we hope to see them, but they cannot be experienced now. And of the things which are such that they are neither past nor future, but remain forever, some are invisible, like justice and wisdom, and some are visible, like the Body of Christ, now immortal. But, "the invisible things are clearly seen, being understood" (Rom. 1:20), and in that way they are also seen in a special and appropriate manner. And when they are seen, they are much more certain than the objects of the bodily sense, but they are said to be visible because they cannot, in any way, be seen by these mortal eyes. On the other hand, those living things which are visible and perpetual can be seen even by these mortal eyes, if they are made manifest; as the Lord showed Himself to the disciples after His Resurrection, and even after His Ascension, to the Apostle Paul and to the Deacon Stephen.

Therefore, we believe in those visible and perpetual things in such wise that even if they are not manifested to us, we hope we shall see them some day, and we do not make an effort to understand them by reasoning and thought, except that we make a distinction in our thought between these visible things and invisible ones, and we imagine to ourselves in thought what they are like, although we know quite well that they are not known to us. Thus, I think in one way of Antioch, a city unknown to me, and in another way of Carthage, which I do know; my mind makes an image of the former but recalls the latter. There is, however, no doubt in my mind that my belief about the former is based on the evidence of numerous witnesses; but about the latter, on my own sense-impressions. Nevertheless, we do not form an image of justice and wisdom or anything else of this sort in any other way, but we see them differently; we behold these invisible qualities by a simple intellectual attention of the mind and reason, without any forms or physical bulk, without any features or appearance of parts, without any locality, whether limited or of unbounded space. The light itself by which we distinguish all this, by which we are made aware of what we believe without knowing it, that we hold as objects of knowledge, what physical shape we recall, what one we imagine, what the sense-organ perceives, what the mind imagines in the likeness of a body, what is present to the intellect as certain yet totally unlike any physical object, this light by which all these mental acts are differentiated is not diffused in any special place, like the brilliance of this sun or of any physical light, and does not illumine our mind as if it were a visible brightness, but it shines invisibly and indescribably, yet intelligibly, and it is as certain a fact itself as are the realities which we see as certain by means of it.

We have, then, three classes of objects which are seen: the first, of material things, such as heaven and earth and everything the physical sense-organ perceives or experiences in them; the second, of representations of material things, such as those we picture to ourselves in thought by means of our imagination, whether we behold them inwardly as remembered or as imagined objects. In this class are visions, such as occur either in sleep or in some state of ecstasy and are presented in these spatial dimensions. The third class is different from both the former and consists of things which are not corporeal and have no corporeal representation: for example, wisdom, which is perceived by the understanding and by whose light all these other things are correctly estimated. But, in which class are we to believe that the Trinity, which we wish to know about, is included? Obviously, in some one of them or in none. If in some one, it must be the one which is superior to the other two, namely, the one in which wisdom is included. . . .

But if the Trinity is not to be included in any of those classes, and if it is so far invisible that it is not seen by the mind, we have no reason at all to believe that it is not seen by the mind, we have no reason at all to believe that it is like either material objects or the representations of material objects. It is not in the beauty of its shape nor in its immensity that it surpasses material things but in the difference and complete dissimilarity of its nature. It is also remote from any comparison with our spiritual goods, such as wisdom, justice, charity, chastity, and other like qualities, which we certainly do not value for their physical size, nor do we endow them in our thoughts with bodily shapes, but when we understand them properly, we behold them by the light of our mind without bodily attributes or any likeness of bodily attributes. How much more, then, must we refrain from any comparison of physical qualities and dimensions in thinking of the Trinity!

On the Morals of the Catholic Church

Chapter 3

Happiness is in the enjoyment of man's chief good.
Two conditions of the chief good: 1st, nothing is better than it;
2d, it cannot be lost against the will

How then, according to reason, ought man to live? We all certainly desire to live happily; and there is no human being but assents to this statement almost before it is made. But the title happy cannot, in my opinion, belong either to him who has not what he loves, whatever it may be, or to him who has what he loves if it is hurtful, or to him who does not love what he has, although it is good in perfection. For one who seeks what he cannot obtain suffers torture, and one who has got what is not desirable is cheated, and one who does not seek for what is worth seeking for is diseased. Now in all these cases the mind cannot but be unhappy, and happiness and unhappiness cannot reside at the same time in one man; so in none of these cases can the man be happy. I find, then, a fourth case, where the happy life exists—when that which is man's chief good is both loved and possessed. For what do we call enjoyment but having at hand the objects of love? And no one can be happy who does not enjoy what is man's chief good, nor is there any one who enjoys this who is not happy. We must then have at hand our chief good, if we think of living happily.

We must now inquire what is man's chief good, which of course cannot be anything inferior to man himself. For whoever follows after what is inferior to himself, becomes himself inferior. But every man is bound to follow what is best. Wherefore man's chief good is not inferior to man. Is it then something similar to man himself? It must be so, if there is nothing above man which he is capable of enjoying. But if we find something which is both superior to man, and can be possessed by the man who loves it, who can doubt that in seeking for happiness man should endeavor to reach that which is more excellent than the being who makes the endeavor. For if happiness consists in the enjoyment of a good than which there is nothing better, which we call the chief good, how can a man be properly called happy who has not yet attained to his chief good? or how can that be the chief good beyond which something better remains for us to arrive at? Such, then, being the chief good, it must be something which cannot be lost against the will. For no one can feel confident regarding a good which he knows can be taken from him, although he wishes to keep and cherish it. But if a man feels no confidence regarding the good which he enjoys, how can he be happy while in such fear of losing it?

From *A Select Library of the Nicene and Post-Nicene Fathers of the Christian Church* (vol. 4), ed. Philip Schaff, trans. Richard Stothert (New York: Scribner's, 1887), pp. 320–343.

Chapter 4

Man—what?

Let us then see what is better than man. This must necessarily be hard to find, unless we first ask and examine what man is. I am not now called upon to give a definition of man. The question here seems to me to be—since almost all agree . . . that we are made up of soul and body—What is man? Is he both of these? or is he the body only, or the soul only? For although the things are two, soul and body, and although neither without the other could be called man (for the body would not be man without the soul, nor again would the soul be man if there were not a body animated by it), still it is possible that one of these may be held to be man, and may be called so. What then do we call man? Is he soul and body, as in a double harness, or like a centaur? Or do we mean the body only, as being in the service of the soul which rules it, as the word lamp denotes not the light and the case together, but only the case, yet it is on account of the light that it is so called? Or do we mean only the mind, and that on account of the body which it rules, as horseman means not the man and the horse, but the man only, and that as employed in ruling the horse? . . . Whether the name man belongs to both, or only to the soul, the chief good of man is not the chief good of the body; but what is the chief good either of both soul and body, or of the soul only, that is man's chief good.

Chapter 5

Man's chief good is not the chief good of the body only, but the chief good of the soul

Now if we ask what is the chief good of the body, reason obliges us to admit that it is that by means of which the body comes to be in its best state. But of all the things which invigorate the body, there is nothing better or greater than the soul. The chief good of the body, then, is not bodily pleasure, not absence of pain, not strength, not beauty, not swiftness, or whatever else is usually reckoned among the goods of the body, but simply the soul. For all the things mentioned the soul supplies to the body by its presence, and, what is above them all, life. . . . According to reason, the chief good of the body is that which is better than the body, and from which the body receives vigor and life, so whether the soul itself is man, or soul and body both, we must discover whether there is anything which goes before the soul itself, in following which the soul comes to the perfection of good of which it is capable in its own kind. If such a thing can be found, all uncertainty must be at an end, and we must pronounce this to be really and truly the chief good of man. . . .

When we speak of attaining to virtue, the question does not regard the body. But if it follows, as it does, that the body which is ruled over by a soul possessed of virtue is ruled both better and more honorably, and is in its greatest perfection in consequence of the perfection of the soul which rightfully governs it, that which gives perfection to the soul will be man's chief good. . . . So the question seems to me to be not, whether soul and body is man, or the soul only, or the body only, but what gives perfection to the soul; for when this is obtained, a man cannot but be either perfect, or at least much better than in the absence of this one thing.

Chapter 6

Virtue gives perfection to the soul; the soul obtains virtue by following God; following God is the happy life

No one will question that virtue gives perfection to the soul. But it is a very proper subject of inquiry whether this virtue can exist by itself or only in the soul. . . . In either case, whether virtue can exist by itself without the soul, or can exist only in the soul, undoubtedly in the pursuit of virtue the soul follows after something, and this must be either the soul itself, or virtue, or something else. But if the soul follows after itself in the pursuit of virtue, it follows after a foolish thing; for before obtaining virtue it is foolish. . . . But if it follows after virtue in the desire to reach it, how can it follow what does not exist? or how can it desire to reach what it already possesses? Either, therefore, virtue exists beyond the soul, or if we are not allowed to give the name of virtue except to the habit and disposition of the wise soul, which can exist only in the soul, we must allow that the soul follows after something else in order that virtue may be produced in itself. . . .

This something else then, by following after which the soul becomes possessed of virtue and wisdom, is either a wise man or God. But we have said already that it must be something that we cannot lose against our will. No one can think it necessary to ask whether a wise man, supposing we are content to follow after him, can be taken from us in spite of our unwillingness or our persistence. God then remains, in following after whom we live well, and in reaching whom we live both well and happily. If any deny God's existence, why should I consider the method of dealing with them, when it is doubtful whether they ought to be dealt with at all? At any rate, it would require a different starting-point, a different plan, a different investigation from what we are now engaged in. . . .

Chapter 7

The knowledge of God to be obtained from the Scripture. The plan and principal mysteries of the divine scheme of redemption

But how can we follow after Him whom we do not see? or how can we see Him, we who are not only men, but also men of weak understanding? For though God is seen not with the eyes but with the mind, where can such a mind be found as shall, while obscured by foolishness, succeed or even attempt to drink in that light? We must therefore have recourse to the instructions of those whom we have reason to think wise. Thus far argument brings us. For in human things reasoning is employed, not as of greater certainty, but as easier from use. But when we come to divine things, this faculty turns away; it cannot behold; it pants, and gasps, and burns with desire; it falls back from the light of truth, and turns again to its wonted obscurity, not from choice, but from exhaustion.... So, when we are hasting to retire into darkness, it will be well that by the appointment of adorable Wisdom we should be met by the friendly shade of authority, and should be attracted by the wonderful character of its contents, and by the utterances of its pages, which, like shadows, typify and attemper the truth.

What more could have been done for our salvation? What can be more gracious and bountiful than divine providence, which, when man had fallen from its laws, and, in just retribution for his coveting mortal things, had brought forth a mortal offspring, still did not wholly abandon him?...

Chapter 8

God is the chief good, whom we are to seek after with supreme affection

...Let us hear, O Christ, what chief end Thou dost prescribe to us; and that is evidently the chief end after which we are told to strive with supreme affection. "Thou shalt love," He says, "the Lord thy God." Tell me also, I pray Thee, what must be the measure of love; for I fear lest the desire enkindled in my heart should either exceed or come short in fervor. "With all thy heart," He says. Nor is that enough. "With all thy soul." Nor is it enough yet. "With all thy mind" (Matt. 22:37).... We have heard, then, what and how much we must love; this we must strive after, and to this we must refer all our plans. The perfection of all our good things and our perfect good is God. We must neither come short of this nor go beyond it: the one is dangerous, the other impossible.

Chapter 11

God is the one object of love; therefore he is man's chief good.
Nothing is better than God. God cannot be lost against our will

Following after God is the desire of happiness; to reach God is happiness itself. We follow after God by loving Him; we reach Him, not by becoming entirely what He is, but in nearness to Him, and in wonderful and immaterial contact with Him, and in being inwardly illuminated and occupied by His truth and holiness.... If, then, to those who love God all things issue in good, and if, as no one doubts, the chief or perfect good is not only to be loved, but to be loved so that nothing shall be loved better, as is expressed in the words, "With all thy soul, with all thy heart, and with all thy mind," who, I ask, will not at once conclude, when these things are all settled and most surely believed, that our chief good which we must hasten to arrive at in preference to all other things is nothing else than God?...

Chapter 15

The Christian definition of the four virtues

As to virtue leading us to a happy life, I hold virtue to be nothing else than perfect love of God. For the fourfold division of virtue I regard as taken from four forms of love. For these four virtues (would that all felt their influence in their minds as they have their names in their mouths!), I should have no hesitation in defining them: that temperance is love giving itself entirely to that which is loved; fortitude is love readily bearing all things for the sake of the loved object; justice is love serving only the loved object, and therefore ruling rightly; prudence is love distinguishing with sagacity between what hinders it and what helps it. The object of this love is not anything, but only God, the chief good, the highest wisdom, the perfect harmony. So we may express the definition thus: that temperance is love keeping itself entire and incorrupt for God; fortitude is love bearing everything readily for the sake of God; justice is love serving God only, and therefore ruling well all else, as subject to man; prudence is love making a right distinction between what helps it towards God and what might hinder it.

Chapter 25

Four moral duties regarding the love of God, of which love the reward is eternal life and the knowledge of the truth

I need say no more about right conduct. For if God is man's chief good, which you cannot deny, it clearly follows, since to seek the chief good is to live well, that to live well is nothing else but to love God with all the heart, with all the soul, with all the mind; and, as arising from this, that this love must be preserved entire and incorrupt, which is the part of temperance; that it give way before no troubles, which is the part of fortitude; that it serve no other, which is the part of justice; that it be watchful in its inspection of things lest craft or fraud steal in, which is the part of prudence. This is the one perfection of man, by which alone he can succeed in attaining to the purity of truth. . . .

Let us then, as many as have in view to reach eternal life, love God with all the heart, with all the soul, with all the mind. For eternal life contains the whole reward in the promise of which we rejoice; nor can the reward precede desert, nor be given to a man before he is worthy of it. What can be more unjust than this, and what is more just than God? We should not then demand the reward before we deserve to get it. Here, perhaps, it is not out of place to ask what is eternal life; or rather let us hear the Bestower of it: "This," He says, "is life eternal, that they should know Thee, the true God, and Jesus Christ whom thou hast sent" (John 17:3). So eternal life is the knowledge of the truth. . . . What else, then, have we to do but first to love with full affection Him whom we desire to know? (*Retract*. 1:7,4). Hence arises that principle on which we have all along insisted, that there is nothing more wholesome in the Catholic Church than using authority before argument.

Chapter 26

Love of ourselves and of our neighbor

To proceed to what remains. It may be thought that there is nothing here about man himself, the lover. But to think this, shows a want of clear perception. For it is impossible for one who loves God not to love himself. For he alone has a proper love for himself who aims diligently at the attainment of the chief and true good; and if this is nothing else but God, as has been shown, what is to prevent one who loves God from loving himself? And then, among men should there be no bond of mutual love? Yea, verily; so that we can think of no surer step towards the love of God than the love of man to man.

. . . Now you love yourself suitably when you love God better than yourself. What, then, you aim at in yourself you must aim at in your neighbor, namely, that he may love God with a perfect affection. For you do not love him as yourself, unless you try to draw him to that good which you are yourself pursuing. For this is the one good which has room for all to pursue it along with thee. From this precept proceed the duties of human society, in which it is hard to keep from error. But the first thing to aim at is, that we should be benevolent, that is, that we cherish no malice and no evil design against another. For man is the nearest neighbor of man.

The City of God

Book XIV

Chapter 28

Accordingly, two cities have been formed by two loves: the earthly by the love of self, even to the contempt of God; the heavenly by the love of God, even to the contempt of self. The former, in a word, glories in itself, the latter in the Lord. For the one seeks glory from men; but the greatest glory of the other is God, the witness of conscience. . . . In the one, the princes and the nations it subdues are ruled by the love of ruling; in the other, the princes and the subjects serve one another in love, the latter obeying, while the former take thought for all. The one delights in its own strength, represented in the persons of its rulers; the other says to its God, "I will love Thee, O Lord my strength" (Ps. 18:1). And therefore the wise men of the one city, living according to man, have sought for profit to their own bodies or souls, or both, and those who have known God "glorified Him not as God, neither were thankful, but became vain in their imaginations, and their foolish heart was darkened; professing themselves to be wise"—that is, glorying in their own wisdom, and being possessed by pride. . . . But in the other city there is no human wisdom, but only godliness, which offers due worship to the true God, and looks for its reward in the society of the saints, of holy angels as well as holy men, "that God may be all in all" (I Cor. 15:28).

Book XV

Chapter 1

. . . We have distributed [the human race] into two parts, the one consisting of those who live according to man, the other of those who live according to God. And these we also call mystically the two cities, or the two communities of men. . . . It seems suitable to attempt an account of their career, from the time when our two first parents began to propagate the race until all human generation shall cease. For this whole time or world-age, in which the dying give place and those who are born succeed, is the career of these two cities concerning which we treat.

Of these two first parents of the human race, then, Cain was the first-born and belonged to the city of men; after him was born Abel, who belonged to the city of God. For as in the individual the truth of the apostle's statement is discerned, "that is not first which is spiritual, but that which is natural, and afterward that which is spiritual" (I Cor. 15:46), whence it comes to pass that each man, being derived from a condemned stock, is first of all born of Adam evil and carnal and becomes good and spiritual only afterwards by regeneration through Christ: so was it in the human race as a whole. . . . For in each individual, as I have already said, there is first of all that

From *The Works of Aurelius Augustine, Bishop of Hippo: A New Translation* (vols. 1, 2), ed. Reverend Marcus Dods (Edinburgh: T. & T. Clark, 1871).

which is reprobate, that from which we must begin, but in which we need not necessarily remain. . . . Not, indeed, that every wicked man shall be good, but that no one
will be good who was not first of all wicked. . . .

Book XIX

Chapter 4

If, then, we be asked what the city of God has to say . . . regarding the supreme good
and evil, it will reply that life eternal is the supreme good, death eternal the supreme
evil, and that to obtain the one and escape the other we must live rightly. And thus
it is written, "The just lives by faith," for we do not as yet see our good and must therefore live by faith; neither have we in ourselves power to live rightly; we can do so only
if He who has given us faith to believe in His help does help us when we believe and
pray. As for those who have supposed that the sovereign good and evil are to be found
in this life and have placed it either in the soul or the body, or in both, or, to speak more
explicitly, either in pleasure or in virtue, or in both; in repose or in virtue, or in both;
in pleasure and repose, or in virtue, or in all combined—all these have, with a marvellous shallowness, sought to find their blessedness in this life and in themselves. . . .

For what flood of eloquence can suffice to detail the miseries of this life? . . . For
when, where, how in this life can these primary objects of nature be possessed so that
they may not be assailed by unforeseen accident? Is the body of the wise man exempt
from any pain which may dispel pleasure, from any disquietude which may banish
repose? . . . What shall I say of the fundamental blessings of the soul, sense and intellect,
of which the one is given for the perception, and the other for the comprehension of
truth? . . . Where are reason and intellect when disease makes a man delirious? . . .

Virtue itself . . . though it holds the highest place among human good things, what
is its occupation save to wage perpetual war with vices—not those that are outside of
us, but within; not other men's, but our own—a war which is waged especially by that
virtue which the Greeks call σωφροσύνη [*sophrosyne*], and we temperance, and
which bridles carnal lusts, and prevents them from winning the consent of the spirit
to wicked deeds? . . .

What shall I say of that virtue which is called prudence? Is not all its vigilance
spent in the discernment of good from evil things, so that no mistake may be admitted
about what we should desire and what avoid? And thus it is itself a proof that we are
in the midst of evils, or that evils are in us. . . . And justice, whose office it is to render
to every man his due . . . does not this virtue demonstrate that it is as yet rather labor-
ing towards its end than resting in its finished work? . . . Then that virtue which goes
by the name of fortitude is the plainest proof of the ills of life, for it is these ills which
it is compelled to bear patiently. . . .

Chapter 5

We give a much more unlimited approval to their idea that the life of the wise man
must be social. For how could the city of God . . . either take a beginning or be developed, or attain its proper destiny, if the life of the saints were not a social life? But who

can enumerate all the great grievances with which human society abounds in the misery of this mortal state?... On all hands we experience these slights, suspicions, quarrels, war, all of which are undoubted evils; while, on the other hand, peace is a doubtful good, because we do not know the heart of our friend, and though we did know it today, we should be as ignorant of what it might be tomorrow....

Chapter 7

After the state or city comes the world, the third circle of human society—the first being the house and the second the city. And the world, as it is larger, so it is fuller of dangers, as the greater sea is the more dangerous.... But, say they, the wise man will wage just wars. As if he would not at all then rather lament the necessity of just wars, if he remembers that he is a man; for if they were not just he would not wage them and would therefore be delivered from all wars. For it is the wrong-doing of the opposing party which compels the wise man to wage just wars; and this wrong-doing, even though it gave rise to no war, would still be a matter of grief to man because it is man's wrong-doing. Let every one, then, who thinks with pain on all these great evils, so horrible, so ruthless, acknowledge that this is misery....

Chapter 12

Whoever gives even moderate attention to human affairs and to our common nature, will recognize that if there is no man who does not wish to be joyful, neither is there any one who does not wish to have peace. For even they who make war desire nothing but victory—desire, that is to say, to attain to peace with glory. For what else is victory than the conquest of those who resist us? and when this is done there is peace. It is, therefore, with the desire for peace that wars are waged, even by those who take pleasure in exercising their warlike nature in command and battle. And hence it is obvious that peace is the end sought for by war. For every man seeks peace by waging war, but no man seeks war by making peace. For even they who intentionally interrupt the peace in which they are living have no hatred of peace but only wish it changed into a peace that suits them better. They do not, therefore, wish to have no peace but only one more to their mind....

Chapter 13

The peace of the body then consists in the duly proportioned arrangement of its parts. The peace of the irrational soul is the harmonious repose of the appetites; and that of the rational soul, the harmony of knowledge and action. The peace of body and soul is the well-ordered and harmonious life and health of the living creature. Peace between man and God is the well-ordered obedience of faith to eternal law. Peace between man and man is well-ordered concord. Domestic peace is the well-ordered concord between those of the family who rule and those who obey. Civil peace is a similar concord among the citizens. The peace of the celestial city is the perfectly ordered and harmonious enjoyment of God and of one another in God. The peace of all things is the tranquillity of order. Order is the distribution which allots things equal and unequal, each to its own place. And hence, though the miserable, in so far as they are such, do certainly not enjoy peace but are severed from the tranquillity of order in which there is no disturbance. Nevertheless, inasmuch as they are deservedly and unjustly miserable, they are by their very misery connected with order. They are not, indeed, conjoined with the blessed, but they are disjoined from them by the law of order. And though they are disquieted, their circumstances are notwithstanding adjusted to them, and consequently they have some tranquillity of order and therefore some peace. . . . As, then, there may be life without pain, while there cannot be pain without some kind of life, so there may be peace without war, but there cannot be war without some kind of peace, because war supposes the existence of some natures to wage it, and these natures cannot exist without peace of one kind or other.

And therefore there is a nature in which evil does not or even cannot exist; but there cannot be a nature in which there is no good. Hence not even the nature of the devil himself is evil, in so far as it is nature, but it was made evil by being perverted. . . .

God, then, . . . imparted to men some good things adapted to this life, to wit, temporal peace, such as we can enjoy in this life from health and safety and human fellowship, and all things needful for the preservation and recovery of this peace, such as the objects which are accommodated to our outward senses, light, night, the air, and waters suitable for us, and everything the body requires to sustain, shelter, heal, or beautify it: and all under this most equitable condition, that every man who made a good use of these advantages suited to the peace of his mortal condition, should receive ampler and better blessings, namely, the peace of immortality, accompanied by glory and honor in an endless life made fit for the enjoyment of God and of one another in God; but that he who used the present blessings badly should both lose them and should not receive the others.

Chapter 14

The whole use, then, of things temporal has a reference to this result of earthly peace in the earthly community, while in the city of God it is connected with eternal peace. And therefore, if we were irrational animals, we should desire nothing beyond the proper arrangement of the parts of the body and the satisfaction of the appetites— nothing, therefore, but bodily comfort and abundance of pleasures, that the peace of the body might contribute to the peace of the soul. . . . But, as man has a rational soul, he subordinates all this which he has in common with the beasts to the peace of his rational soul, that his intellect may have free play and may regulate his actions, and that he may thus enjoy the well-ordered harmony of knowledge and action which constitutes, as we have said, the peace of the rational soul. . . . But, owing to the liability of the human mind to fall into mistakes, this very pursuit of knowledge may be a snare to him unless he has a divine Master, whom he may obey without misgiving, and who may at the same time give him such help as to preserve his own freedom. And because, so long as he is in this mortal body, he is a stranger to God, he walks by faith, not by sight; and he therefore refers all peace, bodily or spiritual or both, to that peace which mortal man has with the immortal God, so that he exhibits the well-ordered obedience of faith to eternal law. But as this divine Master inculcates two precepts— the love of God and the love of our neighbor—and as in these precepts a man finds three things he has to love—God, himself, and his neighbor—and that he who loves God loves himself thereby, it follows that he must endeavor to get his neighbor to love God, since he is ordered to love his neighbor as himself. . . .

Chapter 15

This is prescribed by the order of nature: it is thus that God created man. . . . He did not intend that His rational creature, who was made in His image, should have dominion over anything but the irrational creation—not man over man but man over the beasts. And hence the righteous men in primitive times were made shepherds of cattle rather than kings of men, God intending thus to teach us what the relative position of the creatures is and what the desert of sin; for it is with justice, we believe, that the condition of slavery is the result of sin. . . . And these circumstances could never have arisen save through sin. For even when we wage a just war, our adversaries must be sinning; and every victory, even though gained by wicked men, is a result of the first judgment of God, who humbles the vanquished either for the sake of removing or of punishing their sins. . . . And beyond question it is a happier thing to be the slave of a man than of a lust; for even this very lust of ruling, to mention no others, lays waste men's hearts with the most ruthless dominion. Moreover, when men are subjected to one another in a peaceful order, the lowly position does as much good to the servant as the proud position does harm to the master. But by nature, as God first created us, no one is the slave either of man or of sin. . . .

Chapter 17

. . . The earthly city, which does not live by faith, seeks an earthly peace, and the end it proposes, in the well-ordered concord of civil obedience and rule, is the combination of men's wills to attain the things which are helpful to this life. The heavenly city, or rather the part of it which sojourns on earth and lives by faith, makes use of this peace only because it must, until this mortal condition which necessitates it shall pass away. Consequently, so long as it lives like a captive and a stranger in the earthly city, though it has already received the promise of redemption and the gift of the Spirit as the earnest of it, it makes no scruple to obey the laws of the earthly city, whereby the things necessary for the maintenance of this mortal life are administered; and thus, as this life is common to both cities, so there is a harmony between them in regard to what belongs to it. . . . This heavenly city, then, while it sojourns on earth, calls citizens out of all nations and gathers together a society of pilgrims of all languages, not scrupling about diversities in the manners, laws, and institutions whereby earthly peace is secured and maintained but recognizing that, however various these are, they all tend to one and the same end of earthly peace. It, therefore, is so far from rescinding and abolishing these diversities that it even preserves and adapts them, so long only as no hindrance to the worship of the one supreme and true God is thus introduced. . . .

SELECTED BIBLIOGRAPHY

Bourke, Vernon J., ed. *The Essential Augustine*. Indianapolis: Hackett, 1974.

Mourant, John A., ed. *Introduction to the Philosophy of St. Augustine: Selected Readings and Commentaries*. University Park: Pennsylvania State University Press, 1964.

Oates, Whitney J., ed. *Basic Writings of Saint Augustine*. 2 vols. New York: Random House, 1948.

Brown, Peter. *Augustine of Hippo*. Berkeley: University of California Press, 1967.

Chadwick, Henry. *Augustine*. New York: Oxford University Press, 1986.

O'Donnell, James J. *Augustine*. Boston: Twayne, 1985.

Gilson, Étienne. *The Christian Philosophy of St. Augustine*. New York: Random House, 1960.

Markus, R.A. *Augustine: A Collection of Critical Essays*. Garden City, N.Y.: Doubleday, 1972.

Meagher, Robert. *An Introduction to St. Augustine*. New York: New York University Press, 1978.

Montgomery, W. *St. Augustine: Aspects of His Life and Thought*. London, New York: Hodder and Stoughton, 1914.

West, Rebecca. *St. Augustine*. New York: Appleton, 1933.

Smith, W. Thomas. *Augustine: His Life and Thought*. Westminster, England: John Knox, 1980.

Saint Thomas Aquinas

Born in 1225 in the family castle at Rocca Secca, about midway between Rome and Naples, Thommaso d'Aquino was sent at the age of five to the Benedictine abbey at nearby Monte Cassino to begin his formal education. In 1239 he went off to continue his studies at the University of Naples, a decision prompted in part by the friction between the pope and Emperor Frederick II that had made the outlying regions around Naples, including Monte Cassino, fairly dangerous. The University of Naples, founded in 1224 by Frederick II, was open to a wide range of influences, including Jewish and Islamic thought, which must have left a mark on the young scholar. During this period (1243 or 1244), Aquinas made the decision to join the Dominicans, a relatively new monastic order dedicated to preaching. His family, however, was unhappy with this decision, and when the Dominicans sent Aquinas north to Paris, his brothers kidnapped and held him in the family stronghold. Only after being convinced that they could not dissuade him from his course did they set him free.

Aquinas then completed his journey to Paris, but little is known of him between 1245 and 1248. It is supposed that he spent that period studying in Paris. From 1248 to 1252, Aquinas studied in Cologne under Albertus Magnus (Albert the Great), one of the most gifted and learned men of the time. He returned to Paris for further study in 1252 and was awarded a master of theology degree in 1257. (The *magister* was then the terminal degree, equivalent to our doctorate.) He taught theology at the University of Paris from 1256 until 1259, at which point he was sent to Italy.

From 1259 to 1268, Aquinas was a roving preacher general, centered first in Anagni, south of Rome; then in Orvieto and Santa Sabina in Rome; and finally in Viterbo. He also visited a number of other Italian cities to give classes. During much of this time Aquinas was near the papal court, where his former teacher Albertus Magnus was in residence and where he undoubtedly encountered the Flemish Dominican William of Moerbeke. William undertook the daunting task of translating Aristotle's works, newly rediscovered in the West, directly and more accurately from the Greek. Legend has it that William undertook this labor at Aquinas's request, but in any event Aquinas used William's translations to write commentaries on Aristotle's principal works. Aquinas had already begun his prodigious literary efforts back in Paris, and it is during this middle Italian period that many of his best-known works were composed or begun. The *Summa Contra Gentiles*, from which the selections are drawn, was written during this period, and the *Summa Theologiae* was begun.

Aquinas was recalled to Paris to teach theology from 1269 to 1272. Regent masters standardly taught a three-year cycle of classes and then moved on to another assignment, so it was a singular honor to serve a second term as regent in Paris, the leading center of theology. This was a period of growing controversy over the reception of Aristotle into Christian thought. The power and cogency of Aristotle's thought was undeniable (and 1,500 years had given it a patina of respectability), but Aristotelian and Christian doctrines were not always consistent. Aquinas attempted to tread a fine line between brazen acceptance of Aristotle despite Church dogma and complete rejection of Aristotle in favor of established doctrine. His strategy was twofold. First, he maintained that a careful interpretation of Aristotle's text reveals less disagreement with Church doctrine than had been thought, and second, he carefully separated the realms in which reason and faith operate.

In 1272, Aquinas was again sent south to Naples to set up a house of studies connected to the University of Naples. But he then ceased to write and teach, remarking to his secretary, Reginald of Piperno, that after the things he had seen, everything he had written now seemed to him as so much straw. Aquinas had apparently experienced several visions, direct experiences of the truth, after which his necessarily earthbound attempts to explain and understand the faith no longer seemed adequate. Called to a general council of the Church to be held in Lyon, France, in 1274, Aquinas was stricken ill on the road and died at the Cistercian monastery at Fossanova, Italy.

Though now considered among the very greatest of Catholic theologians, Aquinas's thought was originally quite controversial. Many of his contemporaries believed that he was too Aristotelian and that his views would lead to the adoption of Averroism, a set of doctrines espoused by several philosophers of the era who treated philosophy as a discipline independent of theology with truths that did not agree with doctrine. In 1277, Averroist doctrines were condemned in Paris and Oxford, and several characteristically Thomist doctrines were among the condemned propositions. Despite this initial setback, Aquinas was canonized in 1325, and the condemnation of his propositions was lifted. His teachings remained essential to the Dominican order, but their influence spread slowly through the other orders within the Church. His special position in Catholic theology was not officially recognized until the nineteenth century.

Philosophy

Aquinas has become the official theologian of the Catholic church, someone with whose thought every Catholic theologian is assumed to be familiar. But he is much more than the leading ideologist of a widespread and powerful religious body. Though all his writings—and his life itself—were dedicated to the service of his faith, Saint Thomas Aquinas was also a profoundly philosophical scholar whose keen insight and careful exposition reward study.

Aquinas is known as the Christian theologian who was most able to appropriate the philosophy of Aristotle without betraying the fundamental tenets of his faith. But Aquinas's talent for synthesis extended beyond Aristotelian philosophy. He digested a tremendous amount of his predecessors' writings and successfully formulated a unitary and coherent position out of the many strands of medieval thought.

The keystone in Aquinas's synthesis of philosophy and theology is his careful demarcation between reason and faith. Reason and faith are not in the least at odds, he believes; reason supplements faith, and it is clear that Aquinas always used his reason in the service of his faith. Reason is the careful construction of knowledge, beginning from the sensible world, working up toward universal truths. Reason is a complement to faith in this regard, for the world, as God's creation, bears God's mark on it, and the careful user of reason can discover that mark and be led to God. Reason leads from the finite and imperfect to the infinite and perfect, just as in the arguments for God's existence (the Five Ways) contained in the selection excerpted here. There are essential limitations on just how much reason can accomplish, however, and where reason confronts equally plausible but incompatible arguments, it must reserve judgment and accept the teaching of faith. It is, furthermore, reasonable that there be faith, for reason can demonstrate the propriety of accepting divine revelation.

Natural human knowledge is essentially tied to the senses; we can escape the sensible realm altogether only through divine revelation. Just as full comprehension is possible only through divine intercession, full virtue is also beyond our natural (fallen) condition. Aquinas holds that all human action is for some end, directed toward some goal, and there is but one ultimate goal that all human action subserves, namely, the contemplation of God. Though there are natural virtues, such as prudence, God's grace is necessary for the achievement of the ultimate end and the possession of the highest virtues—faith, hope, and love.

The Reading Context

Besides Aquinas's argumentative subtlety, one must be immediately struck by the orderliness of his writing and the vision of the world that informs it. When Aquinas wrote, the horizons of the world were beginning to expand explosively and, to many minds, threateningly. Much of the power of Aquinas's system comes from the fact that it seems to have a place for everything and exhibits an underlying order that enables us to make sense of the world. But this means that any one small piece of Aquinas's writing is never as powerful and engaging on its own as it is within the entire structure. It also means that doubts about any one aspect of his thought might be expected to raise questions elsewhere as well.

A Note on the Text

Tradition tells us that the *Summa Contra Gentiles* was written at the request of Raymond of Peñafort, who resigned after a short two years as master general of the Dominican order so that he might evangelize in Barcelona. The *Summa Contra Gentiles* was intended to provide the missionaries with arguments they could use in their efforts to convert Jews and Moslems. The first of Saint Thomas Aquinas's great summaries of Catholic doctrine, the *Summa Contra Gentiles* was not originally intended for classroom use. It was begun in Paris and completed in Italy before 1265.

Reading Questions

1. Would Aquinas say that faith precedes reason? How does he believe reason operates? Would he say that one must believe in order to understand?
2. What does Aquinas count as a demonstration of God's existence? Why does he discount all a priori arguments for God's existence?
3. How many demonstrations of God's existence does Aquinas recognize? How many rely on an outmoded conception of causation?
4. Does Aquinas believe that earthquakes serve some purpose? What are the characteristics of an agent?
5. If all things are directed to one end—namely, God—how could sin or evil be possible?
6. To what extent are we capable of understanding God? Since Aquinas limits our ability to understand God and thinks nothing can serve an impossible end, how can the end of the intellect be the understanding of God?
7. Is there any intrinsic connection, according to Aquinas, between leading a virtuous life and being happy?

Summa Contra Gentiles

Book I

Chapter 3

On the way in which divine truth is to be made known

. . . There is a twofold mode of truth in what we profess about God. Some truths about God exceed all the ability of the human reason. Such is the truth that God is triune. But there are some truths which the natural reason also is able to reach. Such are that God exists, that He is one, and the like. In fact, such truths about God have been proved demonstratively by the philosophers, guided by the light of the natural reason.

That there are certain truths about God that totally surpass man's ability appears with the greatest evidence. Since, indeed, the principle of all knowledge that the reason perceives about some thing is the understanding of the very substance of that being (for according to Aristotle "what a thing is" is the principle of demonstration), it is necessary that the way in which we understand the substance of a thing determines the way in which we know what belongs to it. Hence, if the human intellect comprehends the substance of some thing, for example, that of a stone or of a triangle, no intelligible characteristic belonging to that thing surpasses the grasp of the human reason. But this does not happen to us in the case of God. For the human intellect is not able to reach a comprehension of the divine substance through its natural power. For, according to its manner of knowing in the present life, the intellect depends on the sense for the origin of knowledge; and so those things that do not fall under the senses cannot be grasped by the human intellect except in so far as the knowledge of them is gathered from sensible things. Now, sensible things cannot lead the human intellect to the point of seeing in them the nature of the divine substance, for sensible things are effects that fall short of the power of their cause. Yet, beginning with sensible things, our intellect is led to the point of knowing about God that He exists, and other such characteristics that must be attributed to the First Principle. There are, consequently, some intelligible truths about God that are open to the human reason; but there are others that absolutely surpass its power. . . .

The same thing, moreover, appears quite clearly from the defect that we experience every day in our knowledge of things. We do not know a great many of the properties of sensible things, and in most cases we are not able to discover fully the natures of those properties that we apprehend by the sense. Much more is it the case, therefore, that the human reason is not equal to the task of investigating all the intelligible characteristics of that most excellent substance. . . .

We should not, therefore, immediately reject as false, following the opinion of the Manicheans and many unbelievers, everything that is said about God even though it cannot be investigated by reason.

From Saint Thomas Aquinas, *Summa Contra Gentiles* (*On the Truth of the Catholic Faith*), trans. Anton C. Pegis (Garden City, N.Y.: Doubleday, 1955), pp. 63–86, translation copyright © 1955 by Doubleday, Dell Publishing Group, Inc. Used by permission of the publisher.

Chapter 4

That the truth about God to which the natural reason reaches
is fittingly proposed to men for belief

Since, therefore, there exists a twofold truth concerning the divine being, one to which the inquiry of the reason can reach, the other which surpasses the whole ability of the human reason, it is fitting that both of these truths be proposed to man divinely for belief. This point must first be shown concerning the truth that is open to the inquiry of the reason; otherwise, it might perhaps seem to someone that, since such a truth can be known by the reason, it was uselessly given to men through a supernatural inspiration as an object of belief.

Yet, if this truth were left solely as a matter of inquiry for the human reason, three awkward consequences would follow.

The first is that few men would possess the knowledge of God. For there are three reasons why most men are cut off from the fruit of diligent inquiry which is the discovery of truth. Some do not have the physical disposition for such work. . . . Others are cut off from pursuing this truth by the necessities imposed upon them by their daily lives. For some men must devote themselves to taking care of temporal matters. . . . Finally, there are some who are cut off by indolence. In order to know the things that the reason can investigate concerning God, a knowledge of many things must already be possessed. . . . This means that we are able to arrive at the inquiry concerning the aforementioned truth only on the basis of a great deal of labor spent in study. Now, those who wish to undergo such a labor for the mere love of knowledge are few, even though God has inserted into the minds of men a natural appetite for knowledge.

The second awkward effect is that those who would come to discover the above-mentioned truth would barely reach it after a great deal of time. The reasons are several. There is the profundity of this truth, which the human intellect is made capable of grasping by natural inquiry only after a long training. Then, there are many things that must be presupposed, as we have said. There is also the fact that, in youth, when the soul is swayed by the various movements of the passions, it is not in a suitable state for the knowledge of such lofty truth. . . . The result is this. If the only way open to us for the knowledge of God were solely that of the reason, the human race would remain in the blackest shadows of ignorance. For then the knowledge of God, which especially renders men perfect and good, would come to be possessed only by a few, and these few would require a great deal of time in order to reach it.

The third awkward effect is this. The investigation of the human reason for the most part has falsity present within it, and this is due partly to the weakness of our intellect in judgment, and partly to the admixture of images. The result is that many, remaining ignorant of the power of demonstration, would hold in doubt those things that have been most truly demonstrated. . . . That is why it was necessary that the unshakeable certitude and pure truth concerning divine things should be presented to men by way of faith. . . .

Chapter 5

*That the truths the human reason is not able to investigate
are fittingly proposed to men for belief*

Now, perhaps some will think that men should not be asked to believe what the reason is not adequate to investigate, since the divine Wisdom provides in the case of each thing according to the mode of its nature. We must therefore prove that it is necessary for man to receive from God as objects of belief even those truths that are above the human reason.

No one tends with desire and zeal towards something that is not already known to him. But, as we shall examine later on in this work, men are ordained by the divine Providence towards a higher good than human fragility can experience in the present life.[1] That is why it was necessary for the human mind to be called to something higher than the human reason here and now can reach, so that it would thus learn to desire something and with zeal tend towards something that surpasses the whole state of the present life. This belongs especially to the Christian religion, which in a unique way promises spiritual and eternal goods. And so there are many things proposed to men in it that transcend human sense. . . .

It is also necessary that such truth be proposed to men for belief so that they may have a truer knowledge of God. For then only do we know God truly when we believe Him to be above everything that it is possible for man to think about Him. . . .

Another benefit that comes from the revelation to men of truths that exceed the reason is the curbing of presumption, which is the mother of error. For there are some who have such a presumptuous opinion of their own ability that they deem themselves able to measure the nature of everything. . . .

Chapter 6

*That to give assent to the truths of faith is not foolishness
even though they are above reason*

Those who place their faith in this truth, however, "for which the human reason offers no experimental evidence," do not believe foolishly, as though "following artificial fables" (II Pet. 1:16). For these "secrets of divine Wisdom" (Job 11:6) the divine Wisdom itself, which knows all things to the full, has deigned to reveal to men. It reveals its own presence, as well as the truth of its teaching and inspiration, by fitting arguments; and in order to confirm those truths that exceed natural knowledge, it gives visible manifestation to works that surpass the ability of all nature. Thus, there are the wonderful cures of illnesses, there is the raising of the dead, and the wonderful immutation in the heavenly bodies; and what is more wonderful, there is the inspiration given to human minds, so that simple and untutored persons, filled with the gift of the Holy Spirit, come to possess instantaneously the highest wisdom and the readiest eloquence. . . . Now, for the minds of mortal men to assent to these things is the greatest of miracles, just as it is a manifest work of divine inspiration that, spurning visible things, men should seek only what is invisible. Now, that this has happened neither without preparation nor by chance, but as a result of the disposition of God, is clear

---

1. 3:48. [All notes in this selection are the translator's.]

from the fact that through many pronouncements of the ancient prophets God had foretold that He would do this. . . .

This wonderful conversion of the world to the Christian faith is the clearest witness of the signs given in the past; so that it is not necessary that they should be further repeated, since they appear most clearly in their effect. For it would be truly more wonderful than all signs if the world had been led by simple and humble men to believe such lofty truths, to accomplish such difficult actions, and to have such high hopes. . . .

Chapter 7

That the truth of reason is not opposed to the truth of the Christian faith

Now, although the truth of the Christian faith which we have discussed surpasses the capacity of the reason, nevertheless that truth that the human reason is naturally endowed to know cannot be opposed to the truth of the Christian faith. For that with which the human reason is naturally endowed is clearly most true; so much so, that it is impossible for us to think of such truths as false. Nor is it permissible to believe as false that which we hold by faith, since this is confirmed in a way that is so clearly divine. Since, therefore, only the false is opposed to the true, as is clearly evident from an examination of their definitions, it is impossible that the truth of faith should be opposed to those principles that the human reason knows naturally.

Furthermore, that which is introduced into the soul of the student by the teacher is contained in the knowledge of the teacher—unless his teaching is fictitious, which it is improper to say of God. Now, the knowledge of the principles that are known to us naturally has been implanted in us by God; for God is the Author of our nature. These principles, therefore, are also contained by the divine Wisdom. . . .

Again. In the presence of contrary arguments our intellect is chained, so that it cannot proceed to the knowledge of the truth. If, therefore, contrary knowledges were implanted in us by God, our intellect would be hindered from knowing truth by this very fact. Now, such an effect cannot come from God. . . .

From this we evidently gather the following conclusion: whatever arguments are brought forward against the doctrines of faith are conclusions incorrectly derived from the first and self-evident principles imbedded in nature. Such conclusions do not have the force of demonstration; they are arguments that are either probable or sophistical. And so, there exists the possibility to answer them.

Chapter 8

How the human reason is related to the truth of faith

There is also a further consideration. Sensible things, from which the human reason takes the origin of its knowledge, retain within themselves some sort of trace of a likeness to God. This is so imperfect, however, that it is absolutely inadequate to manifest the substance of God. For effects bear within themselves, in their own way, the likeness of their causes, since an agent produces its like; yet an effect does not always reach to the full likeness of its cause. Now, the human reason is related to the knowledge of the truth of faith (a truth which can be most evident only to those who see the divine substance) in such a way that it can gather certain likenesses of it, which are yet not sufficient so that the truth of faith may be comprehended as being understood demonstratively or through itself. . . .

Chapter 10

The opinion of those who say that the existence of God,
being self-evident, cannot be demonstrated

There are some persons to whom the inquiry seeking to demonstrate that God exists may perhaps appear superfluous. These are the persons who assert that the existence of God is self-evident, in such wise that its contrary cannot be entertained in the mind. It thus appears that the existence of God cannot be demonstrated, as may be seen from the following arguments.

Those propositions are said to be self-evident that are known immediately upon the knowledge of their terms. Thus, as soon as you know the nature of a *whole* and the nature of a *part*, you know immediately that every whole is greater than its part. The proposition God *exists* is of this sort. For by the name *God* we understand something than which a greater cannot be thought. This notion is formed in the intellect by one who hears and understands the name *God*. As a result, God must exist already at least in the intellect. But He cannot exist solely in the intellect, since that which exists both in the intellect and in reality is greater than that which exists in the intellect alone. Now, as the very definition of the name points out, nothing can be greater than God. Consequently, the proposition that God exists is self-evident, as being evident from the very meaning of the name God.

Again, it is possible to think that something exists whose non-existence cannot be thought. Clearly, such a being is greater than the being whose non-existence can be thought. Consequently, if God Himself could be thought not to be, then something greater than God could be thought. This, however, is contrary to the definition of the name God. Hence, the proposition that God exists is self-evident. . . .

Chapter 11

A refutation of the abovementioned opinion and a solution of the arguments

In part, the above opinion arises from the custom by which from their earliest days people are brought up to hear and to call upon the name of God. Custom, and especially custom in a child, comes to have the force of nature. As a result, what the mind is steeped in from childhood it clings to very firmly, as something known naturally and self-evidently.

In part, however, the above opinion comes about because of a failure to distinguish between that which is self-evident in an absolute sense and that which is self-evident in relation to us. For assuredly that God exists is, absolutely speaking, self-evident, since what God is is His own being. Yet, because we are not able to conceive in our minds that which God is, that God exists remains unknown in relation to us. So, too, that every whole is greater than its part is, absolutely speaking, self-evident; but it would perforce be unknown to one who could not conceive the nature of a whole. . . .

And, contrary to the point made by the *first* argument, it does not follow immediately that, as soon as we know the meaning of the name *God*, the existence of God is known. It does not follow first because it is not known to all, even including those who admit that God exists, that God is that than which a greater cannot be thought. After all, many ancients said that this world itself was God. . . . What is more, granted that everyone should understand by the name *God* something than which a greater cannot be thought, it will still not be necessary that there exist in reality something than which a greater cannot be thought. For a thing and the definition of a name are posited in the same way. Now, from the fact that that which is indicated by the name *God* is conceived by the mind, it does not follow that God exists save only in the intellect. Hence, that than which a greater cannot be thought will likewise not have to exist save only in the intellect. From this it does not follow that there exists in reality something than which a greater cannot be thought. No difficulty, consequently, befalls anyone who posits that God does not exist. For that something greater can be thought than anything given in reality or in the intellect is a difficulty only to him who admits that there is something than which a greater cannot be thought in reality.

Nor, again, is it necessary, as the *second* argument advanced, that something greater than God can be thought if God can be thought not to be. For that He can be thought not to be does not arise either from the imperfection or the uncertainty of His own being, since this is in itself most manifest. It arises, rather, from the weakness of our intellect, which cannot behold God Himself except through His effects and which is thus led to know His existence through reasoning. . . .

Chapter 12

The opinion of those who say that the existence of God cannot be demonstrated but is held by faith alone

There are others who hold a certain opinion, contrary to the position mentioned above, through which the efforts of those seeking to prove the existence of God would likewise be rendered futile. For they say that we cannot arrive at the existence of God through the reason; it is received by way of faith and revelation alone. . . .

Nevertheless, the present error might erroneously find support in its behalf in the words of some philosophers who show that in God essence and being are identical, that is, that that which answers to the question *what is it?* is identical with that which answers to the question *is it?* Now, following the way of the reason we cannot arrive at a knowledge of what God is. Hence, it seems likewise impossible to demonstrate by the reason that God exists. . . .

Again, if, as is shown in the *Posterior Analytics*, the knowledge of the principles of demonstration takes its origin from sense, whatever transcends all sense and sensibles seems to be indemonstrable. That God exists appears to be a proposition of this sort and is therefore indemonstrable.

The falsity of this opinion is shown to us, first, from the art of demonstration which teaches us to arrive at causes from their effects. Then, it is shown to us from the order of the sciences. For, as it is said in the *Metaphysics*,[2] if there is no knowable substance

---

2. Aristotle, *Metaphysics* 4:3 (1005a18).

higher than sensible substance, there will be no science higher than physics. It is shown, thirdly, from the pursuit of the philosophers, who have striven to demonstrate that God exists. Finally, it is shown to us by the truth in the words of the Apostle Paul: "For the invisible things of God . . . are clearly seen, being understood by the things that are made" (Rom. 1:20).

Nor, contrary to the *first* argument, is there any problem in the fact that in God essence and being are identical. For this is understood of the being by which God subsists in Himself. But we do not know of what sort this being is, just as we do not know the divine essence. The reference is not to the being that signifies the composition of intellect. For thus the existence of God does fall under demonstration; this happens when our mind is led from demonstrative arguments to form such a proposition of God whereby it expresses that He exists. . . .

It is thereby likewise evident that, although God transcends all sensible things and the sense itself, His effects, on which the demonstration proving His existence is based, are nevertheless sensible things. And thus, the origin of our knowledge in the sense applies also to those things that transcend the sense.

Chapter 13

Arguments in proof of the existence of God

We have now shown that the effort to demonstrate the existence of God is not a vain one. We shall therefore proceed to set forth the arguments by which both philosophers and Catholic teachers have proved that God exists.

We shall first set forth the arguments by which Aristotle proceeds to prove that God exists. The aim of Aristotle is to do this in two ways, beginning with motion.

Of these ways the first is as follows. Everything that is moved is moved by another. That some things are in motion—for example, the sun—is evident from sense. Therefore, it is moved by something else that moves it. This mover is itself either moved or not moved. If it is not, we have reached our conclusion—namely, that we must posit some unmoved mover. This we call God. If it is moved, it is moved by another mover. We must, consequently, either proceed to infinity, or we must arrive at some unmoved mover. Now, it is not possible to proceed to infinity. Hence, we must posit some prime unmoved mover.

In this proof, there are two propositions that need to be proved, namely, that *everything that is moved is moved by another*, and that *in movers and things moved one cannot proceed to infinity*.

The first of these propositions Aristotle proves in [several] ways. The *first* way is as follows. If something moves itself, it must have within itself the principle of its own motion; otherwise, it is clearly moved by another. Furthermore, it must be primarily moved. This means that it must be moved by reason of itself, and not by reason of a part of itself, as happens when an animal is moved by the motion of its foot. For, in this sense, a whole would not be moved by itself, but a part, and one part would be moved by another. . . .

On the basis of these suppositions Aristotle argues as follows. That which is held to be moved by itself is primarily moved. For if, while one part was at rest, another part in it were moved, then the whole itself would not be primarily moved; it would be that part in it which is moved while another part is at rest. But nothing that is at rest because something else is at rest is moved by itself; for that being whose rest follows upon the rest of another must have its motion follow upon the motion of another. It is thus not moved by itself. Therefore, that which was posited as being moved by itself is not moved by itself. Consequently, everything that is moved must be moved by another.

. . . The force of Aristotle's argument lies in this: *if* something moves itself primarily and through itself, rather than through its parts, that it is moved cannot depend on another. But the moving of the divisible itself, like its being, depends on its parts; it cannot therefore move itself primarily and through itself. Hence, for the truth of the inferred conclusion it is not necessary to assume as an absolute truth that a part of a being moving itself is at rest. What must rather be true is this conditional proposition: *if the part were at rest, the whole would be at rest.* Now, this proposition would be true even though its antecedent be impossible. In the same way, the following conditional proposition is true: *if man is an ass, he is irrational.*

In the *second* way, Aristotle proves the proposition by induction. Whatever is moved by accident is not moved by itself, since it is moved upon the motion of another. So, too, as is evident, what is moved by violence is not moved by itself. Nor are those beings moved by themselves that are moved by their nature as being moved from within; such is the case with animals, which evidently are moved by the soul. Nor, again, is this true of those beings, such as heavy and light bodies, which are moved through nature. For such beings are moved by the generating cause and the cause removing impediments. Now, whatever is moved is moved through itself or by accident. If it is moved through itself, then it is moved either violently or by nature; if by nature, then either through itself, as the animal, or not through itself, as heavy and light bodies. Therefore, everything that is moved is moved by another. . . .

The second proposition, namely, *that there is no procession to infinity among movers and things moved*, Aristotle proves in three ways.

The *first* is as follows. If among movers and things moved we proceed to infinity, all these infinite beings must be bodies. For whatever is moved is divisible and a body, as is proved in the *Physics*. But every body that moves some thing moved is itself moved while moving it. Therefore, all these infinites are moved together while one of them is moved. But one of them, being finite, is moved in a finite time. Therefore, all those infinites are moved in a finite time. This, however, is impossible. It is, therefore, impossible that among movers and things moved one can proceed to infinity. . . .

The *second* argument proving the same conclusion is the following. In an ordered series of movers and things moved (this is a series in which one is moved by another according to an order), it is necessarily the fact that, when the first mover is removed or ceases to move, no other mover will move or be moved. For the first mover is the cause of motion for all the others. But, if there are movers and things moved following an order to infinity, there will be no first mover, but all would be as intermediate movers. Therefore, none of the others will be able to be moved, and thus nothing in the world will be moved.

The *third* proof comes to the same conclusion, except that, by beginning with the superior, it has a reversed order. It is as follows. That which moves as an instrumental cause cannot move unless there be a principal moving cause. But, if we proceed to infinity among movers and things moved, all movers will be as instrumental causes, because they will be moved movers and there will be nothing as a principal mover. Therefore, nothing will be moved. . . .

[Aristotle's second demonstration is this.] If every mover is moved, this proposition is true either by itself or by accident. If by accident, then it is not necessary, since what is true by accident is not necessary. It is something possible, therefore, that no mover is moved. But, if a mover is not moved, it does not move: as the adversary says. It is therefore possible that nothing is moved. For, if nothing moves, nothing is moved. This, however, Aristotle considers to be impossible—namely, that at any time there be no motion. Therefore, the first proposition was not possible, since from a false possible, a false impossible does not follow. Hence, this proposition, *every mover is moved by another*, was not true by accident. . . .

It remains, therefore, that we must posit *some first mover that is not moved by any exterior moving cause*.

Granted this conclusion—namely, that there is a first mover that is not moved by an exterior moving cause—it yet does not follow that this mover is absolutely unmoved. That is why Aristotle goes on to say that the condition of the first mover may be twofold. The first mover can be absolutely unmoved. If so, we have the conclusion we are seeking: there is a first unmoved mover. On the other hand, the first mover can be self-moved. This may be argued, because that which is through itself is prior to what is through another. Hence, among things moved as well, it seems reasonable that the first moved is moved through itself and not by another.

But, on this basis, the same conclusion again follows. For it cannot be said that, when a mover moves himself, the whole is moved by the whole. Otherwise, the same difficulties would follow as before. . . . It would also follow that a being would be both in potency and in act; for a mover is, as such, in act, whereas the thing moved is in potency. Consequently, one part of the self-moved mover is solely moving, and the other part solely moved. We thus reach the same conclusion as before: there exists an unmoved mover. . . .

Now, God is not part of any self-moving mover. In his *Metaphysics*, therefore, Aristotle goes on from the mover who is a part of the self-moved mover to seek another mover—God—who is absolutely separate.[3] For, since everything moving itself is moved through appetite, the mover who is part of the self-moving being moves because of the appetite of some appetible object. This object is higher, in the order of motion, than the mover desiring it; for the one desiring is in a manner a moved mover, whereas an appetible object is an absolutely unmoved mover. There must, therefore, be an absolutely unmoved separate first mover. This is God. . . .

In *Metaphysics* II Aristotle also uses another argument to show that there is no infinite regress in efficient causes and that we must reach one first cause—God. This way is as follows. In all ordered efficient causes, the first is the cause of the intermediate cause, whether one or many, and this is the cause of the last cause. But, when you suppress a cause, you suppress its effect. Therefore, if you suppress the first cause, the intermediate cause cannot be a cause. Now, if there were an infinite regress among efficient causes, no cause would be first. Therefore, all the other causes, which are intermediate, will be suppressed. But this is manifestly false. We must, therefore, posit that there exists a first efficient cause. This is God.

---

3. Aristotle, *Metaphysics* 12:7 (1072a23).

Another argument may also be gathered from the words of Aristotle. In *Metaphysics II* he shows that what is most true is also most a being. But in *Metaphysics IV* he shows the existence of something supremely true from the observed fact that of two false things one is more false than the other, which means that one is more true than the other. This comparison is based on the nearness to that which is absolutely and supremely true. From these Aristotelian texts we may further infer that there is something that is supremely being. This we call God.

Damascene proposes another argument for the same conclusion taken from the government of the world. Averroës likewise hints at it. The argument runs thus. Contrary and discordant things cannot, always or for the most part, be parts of one order except under someone's government, which enables all and each to tend to a definite end. But in the world we find that things of diverse natures come together under one order, and this not rarely or by chance, but always or for the most part. There must therefore be some being by whose providence the world is governed. This we call God. . . .

Book II

Chapter 6

That it is proper to God to be the source of the being of other things

Presupposing the things already demonstrated in Book I, let us now show that it belongs to God to be the principle and cause of being to other things.

For in Book I of this work it was shown, by means of Aristotle's demonstration, that there is a first efficient cause, which we call God.[4] But an efficient cause brings its effects into being. Therefore, God is the cause of being to other things.

Also, it was shown in Book I, by the argument of the same author, that there is a first immovable mover, which we call God.[5] But the first mover in any order of movements is the cause of all the movements in that order. Since, then, many things are brought into existence by the movements of the heaven, and since God has been shown to be the first mover in the order of those movements, it follows necessarily that God is the cause of being to many things. . . .

Moreover, the more perfect is the principle of a thing's action, to so many more and more remote things can it extend its action: thus, fire, if weak, heats only things nearby; if strong, it heats even distant things. But pure act, which God is, is more perfect than act mingled with potentiality, as it is in us. But act is the principle of action. Since, then, by the act which is in us we can proceed not only to actions abiding in us, such as understanding and willing, but also to actions which terminate in things outside of us, and through which certain things are made by us, much more can God, because He is in act, not only understand and will, but also produce an effect. And thus He can be the cause of being to other things. . . .

---

4. 1:13.
5. 1:13.

Book III

Chapter 2

That every agent acts for an end

. . . Every agent, by its action, intends an end.

For in those things which clearly act for an end, we declare the end to be that towards which the movement of the agent tends: for when this is reached, the end is said to be reached, and to fail in this is to fail in the end intended. This may be seen in the physician who aims at health, and in a man who runs towards an appointed goal. Nor does it matter, as to this, whether that which tends to an end be endowed with knowledge or not: for just as the target is the end of the archer, so is it the end of the arrow's flight. Now the movement of every agent tends to something determinate, since it is not from any force that any action proceeds, but heating proceeds from heat, and cooling from cold: and therefore actions are differentiated by their active principles. Action sometimes terminates in something made, as for instance building terminates in a house, and healing in health: while sometimes it does not so terminate, as for instance, in the case of understanding and sensation. And if action terminates in something made, the movement of the agent tends by that action towards the thing made; while if it does not terminate in something made, the movement of the agent tends to the action itself. It follows therefore that every agent intends an end while acting, which end is sometimes the action itself, sometimes a thing made by the action.

Again. In all things that act for an end, that is said to be the last end beyond which the agent seeks nothing further: and thus the physician's action goes as far as health, and when this is attained, his efforts cease. But in the action of every agent, a point can be reached beyond which the agent does not desire to go: or else actions would tend to infinity, which is impossible, for since *it is not possible to pass through an infinite medium*, the agent would never begin to act, because nothing moves towards what it cannot reach. Therefore every agent acts for an end. . . .

If, however, the result of such actions be not something made, the order of these actions must be either according to the order of active powers (for instance, if a man feels that he may imagine, and imagines that he may understand, and understands that he may will), or according to the order of objects (for instance, I consider the body that I may consider the soul, which I consider in order to consider a separate substance, which again I consider so that I may consider God). Now it is not possible to proceed to infinity, either in active powers (as neither is this possible in the forms of things, as is proved in *Metaphysics II*, since the form is the principle of activity), or in objects (as neither is this possible in beings, since there is one first being, as we have proved above).[6] Therefore it is not possible for agents to proceed to infinity, and consequently there must be something, upon whose attainment the efforts of the agent cease. Therefore every agent acts for an end. . . .

Again. Every agent acts either by nature or by intellect. Now there can be no doubt that those which act by intellect act for an end, since they act *with* an intellectual

---

6. 1:42.

preconception of what they attain by their action, and they act *through* such a preconception; for this is to act by intellect. Now just as in the preconceiving intellect there exists the entire likeness of the effect that is attained by the action of the intellectual being, so in the natural agent there pre-exists the likeness of the natural effect, by virtue of which the action is determined to the appointed effect; for fire begets fire, and an olive produces an olive. Therefore, even as that which acts by intellect tends by its action to a definite end, so also does that which acts by nature. Therefore every agent acts for an end.

Moreover. Fault is not found save in those things which are for an end, for we do not find fault with one who fails in that to which he is not appointed; and thus we find fault with a physician if he fail to heal, but not with a builder or a grammarian. But we find fault in things done according to art, as when a grammarian fails to speak correctly, and in things that are ruled by nature, as in the case of monstrosities. Therefore every agent, whether according to nature, or according to art, or acting of set purpose, acts for an end. . . .

There are, however, certain actions which would seem not to be for an end, such as playful and contemplative actions, and those which are done without attention, such as scratching one's beard, and the like. . . . But we must observe that contemplative actions are not for another end, but are themselves an end. Playful actions are sometimes an end, when one plays for the mere pleasure of play; and sometimes they are for an end, as when we play that afterwards we may study better. Actions done without attention do not proceed from the intellect, but from some sudden act of the imagination, or some natural principle. . . . Hereby is excluded the error of certain natural philosophers of old, who maintained that all things happen by the necessity of matter, thus utterly banishing the final cause from things.[7]

Chapter 3

That every agent acts for a good

Hence we must go on to prove that every agent acts for a good.

For that every agent acts for an end clearly follows from the fact that every agent tends to something definite. Now that to which an agent tends definitely must needs be befitting to that agent, since the agent would not tend to it save because of some fittingness thereto. But that which is befitting to a thing is good for it. Therefore every agent acts for a good.

Further. The end is that wherein the appetite of the agent or mover comes to rest, as also the appetite of that which is moved. Now it is the very notion of good to be the term of appetite, since *good is the object of every appetite.*[8] Therefore all action and movement is for a good.

Again. All action and movement would seem to be directed in some way to being, either for the preservation of being in the species or in the individual, or for the acquisition of being. Now this itself, namely, being, is a good; and for this reason all things desire being. Therefore all action and movement is for a good. . . .

---

7. Cf. Aristotle, *Physics* 2:8 (198b12).
8. Aristotle, *Ethics* 1:1 (1094a1).

Moreover. The intellectual agent acts for an end, as determining for itself its end; whereas the natural agent,... does not determine its end for itself, since it knows not the nature of end, but is moved to the end determined for it by another. Now an intellectual agent does not determine the end for itself except under the aspect of good; for the intelligible object does not move except it be considered as a good, which is the object of the will. Therefore the natural agent also is not moved, nor does it act for an end, except in so far as this end is a good, since the end is determined for the natural agent by some appetite. Therefore every agent acts for a good....

Chapter 17

That all things are directed to one end, which is God

From the foregoing it is clear that all things are directed to one good as their last end.

For if nothing tends to something as its end, except in so far as this is good, it follows that good, as such, is an end. Consequently that which is the supreme good is supremely the end of all. Now there is but one supreme good, namely God, as we have shown in the First Book.[9] Therefore all things are directed to the highest good, namely God, as their end.

Again. *That which is supreme in any genus is the cause of everything in that genus.* Thus fire which is supremely hot is the cause of heat in other bodies. Therefore the supreme good, namely God, is the cause of goodness in all things good. Therefore He is the cause of every end being an end, since whatever is an end is such in so far as it is good. Now *the cause that a thing is so is itself more so.* Therefore God is supremely the end of all things....

Moreover. In all ordered ends the last must needs be the end of each preceding end. Thus if a potion be mixed to be given to a sick man, and is given to him that he may be purged, and he be purged that he may be lowered, and lowered that he may be healed, it follows that health is the end of the lowering, and of the purging, and of those that precede. Now all things are ordered in various degrees of goodness to the one supreme good, which is the cause of all goodness; and so, since good has the nature of an end, all things are ordered under God as preceding ends under the last end. Therefore God must be the end of all.

Furthermore. The particular good is directed to the common good as its end, for the being of the part is for the sake of the being of the whole. So it is that *the good of the nation is more godlike than the good of one man.*[10] Now the supreme good, namely God, is the common good, since the good of all things depends on Him; and the good, whereby each thing is good, is the particular good of that thing, and of those that depend thereon. Therefore all things are directed to one good, namely God, as their end....

---

9. 1:42.
10. Aristotle, *Ethics* 1:2 (1094b9).

Chapter 18

How God is the end of things

It remains to ask how God is the end of all things. This will be made clear from what has been said.

For He is the end of all things, yet so as to precede all in being.[11] Now there is an end which, though it holds the first place in causing in so far as it is in the intention, is nevertheless last in execution. This applies to any end which the agent establishes by his action. Thus the physician by his action establishes health in the sick man, which is nevertheless his end. There is also an end which, just as it precedes in causing, so also does it precede in being. Thus, that which one intends to acquire by one's motion or action is said to be one's end. For instance, fire seeks to reach a higher place by its movement, and the king seeks to take a city by fighting. Accordingly, God is the end of things as something to be obtained by each thing in its own way. . . .

Further. If a thing act for the sake of something already in existence, and if by its action some result ensue, then something through the agent's action must accrue to the thing for the sake of which it acts; and thus soldiers fight for the cause of their captain, to whom victory accrues, which the soldiers bring about by their actions. Now nothing can accrue to God from the action of anything whatever, since His goodness is perfect in every way, as we proved in the First Book.[12] It follows, then, that God is the end of things, not as something made or effected by them, nor as though He obtained something from things, but in this way alone, that He is obtained by them.

Moreover. The effect must tend to the end in the same way as the agent acts for the end. Now God, who is the first agent of all things, does not act as though He gained something by His action, but as bestowing something thereby; since He is not in potentiality so that He can acquire something, but solely in perfect actuality, whereby He is able to bestow. Things therefore are not ordered to God as to an end to which something will be added; they are ordered to Him to obtain God Himself from Him according to their measure, since He is their end.

Chapter 25

That to know God is the end of every intellectual substance

Now, seeing that all creatures, even those that are devoid of reason, are directed to God as their last end, and that all reach this end in so far as they have some share of a likeness to Him, the intellectual creature attains to Him in a special way, namely, through its proper operation, by understanding Him. Consequently this must be the end of the intellectual creature, namely, to understand God.

For, as we have shown above,[13] God is the end of each thing, and hence, as far as it is possible to it, each thing intends to be united to God as its last end. Now a thing is more closely united to God by reaching in a way to the very substance of God; which

---

11. 1:13.
12. 1:37ff.
13. 3:17.

happens when it knows something of the divine substance, rather than when it reaches to a divine likeness. Therefore the intellectual substance tends to the knowledge of God as its last end.

Again. The operation proper to a thing is its end, for it is its second perfection; so that when a thing is well conditioned for its proper operation it is said to be fit and good. Now understanding is the proper operation of the intellectual substance, and consequently is its end. Therefore, whatever is most perfect in this operation is its last end; and especially in those operations which are not directed to some product, such as understanding and sensation. And since operations of this kind take their species from their objects, by which also they are known, it follows that the more perfect the object of any such operation, the more perfect is the operation. Consequently to understand the most perfect intelligible, namely God, is the most perfect in the genus of the operation which consists in understanding. Therefore to know God by an act of understanding is the last end of every intellectual substance. . . .

Again. That which is lovable only because of another is for the sake of that which is lovable for its own sake alone; because we cannot go on indefinitely in the appetite of nature, since then nature's desire would be in vain, for it is impossible to pass through an infinite number of things. Now all practical sciences, arts and powers are lovable only for the sake of something else, since their end is not knowledge, but work. But speculative sciences are lovable for their own sake, for their end is knowledge itself. Nor can we find any action in human life that is not directed to some other end, with the exception of speculative consideration. For even playful actions, which seem to be done without any purpose, have some end due to them, namely that the mind may be relaxed, and that thereby we may afterwards become more fit for studious occupations; or otherwise we should always have to be playing, if play were desirable for its own sake, and this is unreasonable. Accordingly, the practical arts are directed to the speculative arts, and again every human operation, to intellectual speculation, as its end. Now, in all sciences and arts that are mutually ordered, the last end seems to belong to the one from which others take their rules and principles. Thus the art of sailing, to which belongs the ship's purpose, namely its use, provides rules and principles to the art of ship-building. And such is the relation of first philosophy to other speculative sciences, for all others depend thereon, since they derive their principles from it, and are directed by it in defending those principles; and moreover first philosophy is wholly directed to the knowledge of God as its last end, and is consequently called the *divine science*.[14] Therefore the knowledge of God is the last end of all human knowledge and activity. . . .

Chapter 27

That human happiness does not consist in carnal pleasures

From what has been said it is clearly impossible that human happiness consist in pleasures of the body, the chief of which are pleasures of the table and of sex.

---

14. Aristotle, *Metaphysics* 1:2 (983a6).

It has been shown that according to nature's order pleasure is for the sake of operation, and not conversely.[15] Therefore, if an operation be not the ultimate end, the consequent pleasure can neither be the ultimate end, nor accompany the ultimate end. Now it is manifest that the operations which are followed by the pleasures mentioned above are not the last end; for they are directed to certain manifest ends: eating, for instance, to the preservation of the body, and carnal intercourse to the begetting of children. Therefore the aforesaid pleasures are not the last end, nor do they accompany the last end. Therefore happiness does not consist in them. . . .

Moreover. Happiness is a good proper to man, for it is an abuse of terms to speak of brute animals as being happy. Now these pleasures are common to man and brute. Therefore we must not assign happiness to them.

The last end is the most noble of things belonging to a reality, for it has the nature of that which is best. But the aforementioned pleasures do not befit man according to what is most noble in him, namely, the intellect, but according to the sense. Therefore happiness is not to be located in such pleasures.

Besides. The highest perfection of man cannot consist in his being united to things lower than himself, but consists in his being united to something above him; for the end is better than that which tends to the end. Now the above pleasures consist in man's being united through his senses to things beneath him, namely, certain sensible things. Therefore we must not assign happiness to such pleasures.

Further. That which is not good unless it be moderate is not good in itself, but receives its goodness from its moderator. Now the use of the aforesaid pleasures is not good for man unless it be moderate; for otherwise they would frustrate one another. Therefore these pleasures are not in themselves man's good. But the highest good is good of itself, because that which is good of itself is better than what is good through another. Therefore such pleasures are not man's highest good, which is happiness. . . .

Chapter 30

That man's happiness does not consist in wealth

Hence it is evident that neither is wealth man's highest good. For wealth is not sought except for the sake of something else, because of itself it brings us no good, but only when we use it, whether for the support of the body or for some similar purpose. Now the highest good is sought for its own, and not for another's sake. Therefore wealth is not man's highest good.

Again. Man's highest good cannot consist in the possession or preservation of things whose chief advantage for man consists in their being spent. Now the chief advantage of wealth is in its being spent, for this is its use. Therefore the possession of wealth cannot be man's highest good. . . .

Further. Man's highest good is not subject to fortune. For things that are fortuitous escape the forethought of reason, whereas man has to attain his own end by means of his reason. But fortune occupies the greatest place in the attaining of wealth. Therefore human happiness does not consist in wealth. . . .

---

15. 3:26.

Chapter 31

That happiness does not consist in worldly power

In like manner, neither can worldly power be man's highest happiness, since in the achievement thereof chance can effect much. Again, it is unstable, and not subject to man's will; and it is often obtained by evil men. These are incompatible with the highest good, as was already stated.[16]

Again. Man is said to be good especially according as he approaches the highest good. But in respect to his having power, he is not said to be either good or evil, since not everyone who can do good deeds is good, nor is a person evil because he can do evil deeds. Therefore the highest good does not consist in being powerful. . . .

Chapter 34

That man's ultimate happiness does not consist in acts of the moral virtues

It is clear that man's ultimate happiness does not consist in moral activities.

For human happiness, if ultimate, cannot be directed to a further end. But all moral activities can be directed to something else. This is clear from a consideration of the principal among them. Because deeds of fortitude in time of war are directed to victory and peace; for it were foolish to go to war merely for its own sake. Again, deeds of justice are directed to keeping peace among men, for each man possesses with contentment what is his own. The same applies to all the other virtues. Therefore man's ultimate happiness is not in moral deeds.

Again. The purpose of the moral virtues is that through them we may observe the mean in the passions within us, and in things outside us. Now it is impossible that the moderation of passions or of external things be the ultimate end of man's life, since both passions and external things can be directed to something less. Therefore it is not possible that the practice of moral virtue be man's final happiness.

Further. Since man is man through the possession of reason, his proper good, which is happiness, must needs be in accordance with that which is proper to reason. Now that which reason has in itself is more proper to reason than what it effects in something else. Seeing, then, that the good of moral virtue is a good established by reason in something other than itself, it cannot be the greatest good of man which happiness is; rather this good must be a good that is in reason itself.

Moreover. We have already proved that the last end of all things is to become like God.[17] Therefore that in which man chiefly becomes like God will be his happiness. Now this is not in terms of moral actions, since such actions cannot be ascribed to God, except metaphorically; for it is not befitting to God to have passions, or the like, with which moral virtue is concerned. Therefore man's ultimate happiness, which is his last end, does not consist in moral actions.

Furthermore. Happiness is man's proper good. Therefore that good, which of all goods is most proper to man in comparison with other animals, is the one in which we must seek his ultimate happiness. Now this is not the practice of moral virtue, for

---

16. 3:28ff.
17. 3:19.

animals share somewhat either in liberality or in fortitude, whereas no animal has a share in intellectual activity. Therefore man's ultimate happiness does not consist in moral acts.

Chapter 35

That ultimate happiness does not consist in the act of prudence

It is also evident from the foregoing that neither does man's happiness consist in the act of prudence.

For acts of prudence are solely about matters of moral virtue. But human happiness does not consist in the practice of moral virtue.[18] Neither therefore does it consist in the practice of prudence.

Again. Man's ultimate happiness consists in man's most excellent operation. Now man's most excellent operation, in terms of what is proper to man, is in relation to most perfect objects. But the act of prudence is not concerned with the most perfect objects of intellect or reason; for it is not about necessary things, but about contingent practical matters.[19] Therefore its act is not man's ultimate happiness. . . .

Chapter 37

That man's ultimate happiness consists in contemplating God

Accordingly, if man's ultimate happiness does not consist in external things, which are called goods of fortune; nor in goods of the body; nor in goods of the soul, as regards the sensitive part; nor as regards the intellectual part, in terms of the life of moral virtue; nor in terms of the intellectual virtues which are concerned with action, namely, art and prudence:—it remains for us to conclude that man's ultimate happiness consists in the contemplation of truth.

For this operation alone is proper to man, and it is in it that none of the other animals communicates.

Again. This is not directed to anything further as to its end, since the contemplation of the truth is sought for its own sake.

Again. By this operation man is united to beings above him, by becoming like them; because of all human actions this alone is both in God and in the separate substances. Also, by this operation man comes into contact with those higher beings, through knowing them in any way whatever. . . .

Further. All other human operations seem to be ordered to this as to their end. For perfect contemplation requires that the body should be disencumbered, and to this effect are directed all the products of art that are necessary for life. Moreover, it requires freedom from the disturbance caused by the passions, which is achieved by means of the moral virtues and of prudence; and freedom from external disturbance, to which the whole governance of the civil life is directed. So that, if we consider the matter rightly, we shall see that all human occupations appear to serve those who contemplate the truth.

---

18. 3:34.
19. Aristotle, *Ethics* 6:5 (1104a35).

Now, it is not possible that man's ultimate happiness consist in contemplation based on the understanding of first principles; for this is most imperfect, as being most universal, containing potentially the knowledge of things. Moreover, it is the beginning and not the end of human inquiry, and comes to us from nature, and not through the pursuit of the truth. Nor does it consist in contemplation based on the sciences that have the lowest things for their object, since happiness must consist in an operation of the intellect in relation to the most noble intelligible objects. It follows then that man's ultimate happiness consists in wisdom, based on the consideration of divine things.

It is therefore evident also by way of induction that man's ultimate happiness consists solely in the contemplation of God, which conclusion was proved above by arguments.

Chapter 48

That man's ultimate happiness is not in this life

Seeing, then, that man's ultimate happiness does not consist in that knowledge of God whereby He is known by all or many in a vague kind of opinion, nor again in that knowledge of God whereby He is known in the speculative sciences through demonstration, nor in that knowledge whereby He is known through faith, as we have proved above;[20] and seeing that it is not possible in this life to arrive at a higher knowledge of God in His essence, or at least so that we understand other separate substances, and thus know God through that which is nearest to Him, so to say, as we have proved;[21] and since we must place our ultimate happiness in some kind of knowledge of God, as we have shown:[22]—it is impossible for man's happiness to be in this life.

Again. Man's last end is the term of his natural appetite, so that when he has obtained it, he desires nothing more; because if he still has a movement towards something, he has not yet reached an end wherein to be at rest. Now this cannot happen in this life, since the more man understands, the more is the desire to understand increased in him (for this is natural to man), unless perhaps there be someone who understands all things. Now in this life this never did nor can happen to anyone that was a mere man, seeing that in this life we are unable to know separate substances which in themselves are most intelligible, as we have proved.[23] Therefore man's ultimate happiness cannot possibly be in this life.

Besides. Whatever is in motion towards an end has a natural desire to be established and at rest therein. Hence a body does not move away from the place towards which it has a natural movement, except by a violent movement which is contrary to that appetite. Now happiness is the last end which man naturally desires. Therefore it is his natural desire to be established in happiness. Consequently, unless together with happiness he acquires a state of immobility, he is not yet happy, since his natural desire is not yet at rest. When, therefore, a man acquires happiness, he also acquires stability and rest; so that all agree in conceiving stability as a necessary condition of

---

20. 3:38ff.
21. 3:45.
22. 3:37.
23. 3:45.

happiness. Hence the Philosopher says: *We do not look upon the happy man as a kind of chameleon.* Now in this life there is no sure stability, since, however happy a man may be, sickness and misfortune may come upon him, so that he is hindered in the operation, whatever it be, in which happiness consists. Therefore man's ultimate happiness cannot be in this life. . . .

Again. Man naturally shuns death, and is sad about it, not only shunning it at the moment when he feels its presence, but also when he thinks about it. But man, in this life, cannot obtain not to die. Therefore it is not possible for man to be happy in this life. . . .

But someone might say that, since happiness is a good of the intellectual nature, perfect and true happiness is for those in whom the intellectual nature is perfect, namely, in separate substances, and that in man it is imperfect, and by a kind of participation. For man can arrive at a full understanding of the truth only by a sort of movement of inquiry; and he fails entirely to understand things that are by nature most intelligible, as we have proved. Therefore neither is happiness, in its perfect nature, possible to man; but he has a certain participation of it, even in this life. This seems to have been Aristotle's opinion about happiness. Hence, inquiring whether misfortunes destroy happiness, he shows that happiness seems especially to consist in deeds of virtue, which seem to be most stable in this life, and concludes that those who in this life attain to this perfection are happy *as men*, as though not attaining to happiness absolutely, but in a human way.[24]

We must now show that this explanation does not remove the foregoing arguments. For although man is below the separate substances according to the order of nature, he is above irrational creatures, and so he attains his ultimate end in a more perfect way than they. Now these attain their last end so perfectly that they seek nothing further. Thus a heavy body rests when it is in its own proper place, and when an animal enjoys sensible pleasure, its natural desire is at rest. Much more, therefore, when man has obtained his last end, must his natural desire be at rest. But this cannot happen in this life. Therefore in this life man does not obtain happiness considered as his proper end, as we have proved. Therefore he must obtain it after this life.

Again. Natural desire cannot be empty, since *nature does nothing in vain.* But nature's desire would be empty if it could never be fulfilled. Therefore man's natural desire can be fulfilled. But not in this life, as we have shown. Therefore it must be fulfilled after this life. Therefore man's ultimate happiness is after this life. . . .

---

24. Aristotle, *Ethics* 1:10 (1101a18).

SELECTED BIBLIOGRAPHY

Bourke, Vernon J., ed. *The Pocket Aquinas*. New York: Washington Square Press, 1960.

_____. *Basic Writings of Saint Thomas Aquinas*. 2 vols. New York: Random House, 1945.

Chesterton, G.K. *Saint Thomas Aquinas*. Garden City, N.Y.: Doubleday, 1974.

Copleston, F.C. *Aquinas*. Harmondsworth, England: Penguin, 1956.

Gilson, Étienne. *The Christian Philosophy of St. Thomas Aquinas*. New York: Random House, 1956.

_____. *Wisdom and Love in Saint Thomas Aquinas*. Milwaukee: Marquette University Press, 1951.

Kenny, Anthony. *Aquinas*. New York: Oxford University Press, 1980.

_____. *The Five Ways: St. Thomas Aquinas' Proofs of God's Existence*. South Bend, Ind.: University of Notre Dame Press, 1980.

McInerny, Ralph. *Ethica Thomistica: The Moral Philosophy of Thomas Aquinas*. Washington, D.C.: Catholic University Press, 1982.

_____. *St. Thomas Aquinas*. South Bend, Ind.: University of Notre Dame Press, 1982.

Pegis, Anton C. *St. Thomas and Philosophy*. Milwaukee: Marquette University Press, 1964.

_____. *Saint Thomas and the Greeks*. Milwaukee: Marquette University Press, 1939.

Pieper, Josef. *Guide to Thomas Aquinas*. South Bend, Ind.: University of Notre Dame Press, 1987.

EARLY MODERN PHILOSOPHY

Modern philosophy emerged in the seventeenth century, and René Descartes is most commonly cited as its father. (Very recent philosophy—roughly since the beginning of the twentieth century—is referred to as "contemporary philosophy.") The classical period of modern philosophy, often called "early modern," lasted through Immanuel Kant, until the end of the eighteenth century. The nineteenth century is usually treated as a philosophical period in its own right.

The seventeenth and eighteenth centuries, the period from Descartes through Kant, was filled with philosophical ferment. At the time of Descartes, philosophy as it was taught in the universities was highly scholastic and out of touch with the exciting new developments abroad in the world: the growth of science, the discovery of the New World, the breakdown of feudal society, and the Reformation. So philosophy moved out of the universities: from Descartes until Kant, none of the leading philosophers was on a university faculty. Philosophy has never been more vibrant, more entwined with the progressive thought of the day than during this period.

The trait most typical of modern philosophy is its epistemological focus; that is, modern philosophers are generally less quick to turn their attention to metaphysics and the description of the true nature of reality than their predecessors were. Rather, modern philosophers first concern themselves with discovering the nature and boundaries of our knowledge. They are then willing to pronounce about the nature of reality only to the degree their prior investigation of knowledge legitimates such an enterprise.

The major philosophers of the modern era shared a common framework, which John Locke called "the new way of ideas," for discussing their problems, the central notion of which is that the elements of our thought and perceptions are *ideas*. Our ideas are supposed to form an atomistic, compositional, internal representational system that constitutes the sole cognitive medium for our confrontation with the world. The system of ideas is *atomistic* because basic (simple) ideas were conceived of as discrete, independent, and capable of molecular combinations. This internal or mental system is *compositional* because the meanings of the complex, molecular combinations of ideas were supposedly determined solely by the meanings of the atomistic ideas composing them and the way they are combined. Everyone agreed that complex ideas derive their meanings from their simple components, but there was great disagreement about which ideas were simple and how the simple ideas got their meanings.

The deepest controversy evolved over the notion that ideas constitute our sole cognitive contact with the world. If all thought and perception consist in having ideas, then it seems that we have access only to our ideas—and that means that the world remains beyond our reach. The notion that we can know only our ideas and not the material world external to our minds was, perhaps, the dominant philosophical problem of the period and the key to its epistemological tenor.

The two major schools of thought in the period—rationalism (which emphasized the role of reason and logic in knowledge) and empiricism (which emphasized the role of sensory perception in knowledge)—rose out of the new science in the late sixteenth and seventeenth centuries. Up until the late medieval period there was little or no empirical challenge to ancient beliefs about the world, nor was there thought to be any reason to question the received doctrines. Physicians still relied on Galen's (c. 120–200) ancient texts, astronomers still accepted Ptolemy's (second-century) geocentric theory of the heavens, and Aristotle was the final authority in matters scientific. In the sixteenth century, however, this blind reliance on ancient authority finally broke, as curious investigators began turning to observation and experiment. Vesalius (1514–1564) corrected Galen's old mistakes by carefully dissecting cadavers and recording his observations in faithful drawings. Though Copernicus' (1473–1543) heliocentric astronomy was proposed for essentially mathematical reasons, Tycho Brahe (1546–1601) greatly improved the accuracy of astronomical observations, providing the data essential for Johannes Kepler's (1571–1630) discovery of the true paths of the planets around the sun. Galileo Galilei (1564–1642), perhaps the most oustanding early figure in the sudden growth of scientific knowledge, united a keen experimental mind with the conviction that the proper language for describing nature was mathematical. Galileo's discovery of the moons of Jupiter, his defense of the heliocentric astronomy (for which Roman Catholic Church authorities imposed eleven years of house arrest), and especially his laws of terrestrial motion established the model for virtually all subsequent scientific work.

The use of quantitative, mathematical representations of the subject investigated and the reliance on experimental methods for gathering data and testing theories were two important elements in the new science. Philosophical theories of the time, trying to understand how the new results in the sciences fit into a larger picture of the world, tended to emphasize one of these aspects over the other, leading to a great divide in early modern philosophy. The rationalists (chronologically the earlier writers, for the most part, and practicing scientists of no mean accomplishment in some cases) emphasized the mathematical, purely rational aspect of scientific thought, while the empiricists emphasized the importance of observation and experience in our knowledge.

The rationalists—among them René Descartes, Baruch Spinoza, Gottfried Wilhelm Leibniz, and Nicolas de Malebranche—generalized several features of mathematics. The model of how mathematics should be done was Euclid's geometry, which presented for them the ideal formulation of knowledge: self-evident axioms from which a wealth of detailed knowledge could be deduced by perfectly clear rules of reason. The task of science was to find the correct simple elements (abstract, general terms corresponding to Euclid's simple terms *point, line, straight*) and laws (Euclid's axioms) that together define other domains for knowledge. These fundamental principles of knowledge were thought to be *innate*: since they were the foundation of all our knowledge, they are necessary for being able to learn. Nevertheless, the rationalists recognized that there was a problem in justifying the belief that our simple, innate ideas do truthfully capture the nature of reality. In their thinking, God assures that our knowledge can reach beyond ideas to the material world around us and even further to God himself and our immortal souls. The rationalists thus claimed far-reaching insight into the nature of reality.

The empiricists—among whom are Thomas Hobbes, John Locke, George Berkeley, David Hume, and John Stuart Mill—took as their model of knowledge not the deductive proof of a Euclidean theorem but the simple perception of some physical object. Convinced that all ideas arise from experience, the empiricists denied that there are any innate ideas. The simple ideas out of which our knowledge is compounded are not, according to them, highly general, abstract ideas like *point* and *line, substance* and *cause*, but particular sensory experiences or sequences of sensory experiences. If all our knowledge arises out of sensory experience, it follows that our knowledge cannot go beyond experience. If our sensory experience cannot answer questions about God or the soul, then such questions cannot be answered at all. Not surprisingly, it became difficult for the empiricists to show that there were any interesting philosophical questions that could be answered satisfactorily, including whether we can know anything beyond our own ideas.

This division of the pre-Kantians into two opposing camps is a heuristic oversimplification: individual thinkers balanced the views of these two schools in different ways. Using this classification as a reference point, however, is helpful in differentiating among these thinkers and in understanding their relation to Kant, who tried to preserve what was right in each school while avoiding the weaknesses.

In reflections on the good life, the most salient change in modern philosophy is the rise of the individual. The assumption that individual humans exist to serve the *polis* (state) or community was supplanted by the notion that the state or society exists to serve the ends of individual humans.

These changes in the relation between the individual and society stem most directly from the Reformation. According to Roman Catholic orthodoxy, the Church is the necessary intermediary between humans and God; people took their places in the universal order of the world by submitting to the Church. Martin Luther (1483–1546) rejected that position, maintaining that each person has to face God on his or her own. The Church can aid and succor the individual, but it cannot replace or supersede the individual's personal relation to the deity. Freeing the individual from the authority of the Church played an important role both in the rise of the new science and in reassessing the individual's role in society. No longer were people assumed to be mere receptacles for social authority; instead, they possess their own direct relations to God to which they must hold true, despite society's dictates. The autonomous person accepts religious and social authority not out of inner or natural necessity but out of free choice because it furthers his or her own ends.

It was hence no longer clear that governments were instituted among people by God or that God intended to set one person over others as a monarch. The fundamental principles governing human interaction needed to be rethought. Why would intrinsically independent humans unite to form a society, and what internal structures would make that cooperative enterprise most successful? If being good is not just a matter of following God's laws, then what is it to be good, and why would we bother?

The reflections of Hobbes, Locke, Hume, and Kant have deeply influenced contemporary understanding of the nature and goals of human beings and our social institutions. These early modern philosophers laid the conceptual foundations of constitutional government. We understand ourselves better by studying them.

SELECTED BIBLIOGRAPHY

Beck, Lewis White. *Early German Philosophy*. Cambridge, Mass.: Harvard University Press, 1969.

Burtt, E.A. *The Metaphysical Foundations of Modern Science*. Garden City, N.Y.: Anchor/Doubleday, 1954.

Cassirer, Ernst. *The Philosophy of the Enlightenment*. Trans. Fritz Koelln and James Pettegrove. Princeton, N.J.: Princeton University Press, 1951.

Gay, Peter. *The Enlightenment: An Interpretation*. New York: Knopf, 1976.

Gilson, Étienne, and Thomas Langan. *Modern Philosophy: Descartes to Kant*. New York: Random House, 1963.

Kenney, Anthony. *Rationalism, Empiricism, and Idealism*. New York: Oxford University Press, 1986.

Kuhn, Thomas S. *The Copernican Revolution*. Cambridge, Mass.: Harvard University Press, 1957.

Loeb, Louis. *From Descartes to Hume: Continental Metaphysics and the Development of Modern Philosophy*. Ithaca, N.Y.: Cornell University Press, 1981.

Schacht, Richard. *Classical Modern Philosophers: Descartes to Kant*. London: Routledge, Chapman & Hall, 1984.

Scruton, Roger. *From Descartes to Wittgenstein: A Short History of Modern Philosophy*. New York: Harper & Row, 1981.

Yolton, John. *Perceptual Acquaintance from Descartes to Reid*. Minneapolis: University of Minnesota Press, 1984.

René Descartes

René Descartes (1596–1650), like Galileo, Kepler, Huygens, Boyle, and Newton, was a major figure in the birth of the new science, abandoning the traditional nonempirical, qualitative, and teleological (attributing intrinsic goals to objects) approach to explaining natural interactions typical of medieval Aristotelianism and turning to clearly testable, empirical theories expressed in mathematical terms. Born in La Haye, Touraine, France, Descartes attended the Jesuit college of La Flèche. Though he admired his teachers, he found little substance in the traditional scholastic program; only in mathematics was his thirst for clarity and certainty satisfied. After leaving La Flèche, he spent a number of years traveling in Europe, sometimes as a soldier, making the acquaintance of many of the learned people across the continent.

In 1618 Descartes met Isaac Beeckman, eight years his senior, who together with Descartes dreamed of achieving in physics the kind of knowledge they had up to then found only in mathematics. One year later, during a day of quiet contemplation, Descartes had a vision of a new foundation for the sciences on which he was to build for the rest of his life. (It was probably a vision of the mathematization of physics, which we now take for granted, but he never described the dream in detail.) The *Meditations* re-creates the kind of contemplative situation in which Descartes formulated his most profound and daring ideas.

In 1628 Descartes settled in the Netherlands to develop his science and philosophy more systematically. By 1634 he had completed *Le Monde* ("The World"), which he suppressed before publication on hearing of the Church's condemnation and punishment of Galileo for teaching the Copernican system. Thereafter, Descartes was careful to avoid confrontation with the Church whenever possible. His next work, which contained treatises on geometry, optics, and astronomy, was a pioneering effort in several ways. Most memorably, it lays out the basis for the algebraic treatment of geometry we now know as Cartesian geometry.

In 1641 *Le Monde* was followed by the more purely philosophical *Meditations on First Philosophy*, reprinted here, which was originally published together with several sets of objections by well-known intellectuals (including Pierre Gassendi, Thomas Hobbes, and Antoine Arnauld) and Descartes' replies to the objections. This small but exquisitely written work is a concise statement of Descartes' philosophy. His *Principles of Philosophy* was published shortly afterward, in 1644, and *The Passions of the Soul* in 1649. In that year he also left the Netherlands to join the coterie of intellectuals assembling around Queen Christina of Sweden. Long used to late mornings, his tutoring sessions with the Queen at 5:00 A.M. did not agree with him, and he died of pneumonia soon after beginning in her service.

Besides revolutionizing philosophy, Descartes left behind him major advances in mathematics, and his work in physics, though not as successful as his mathematics, set the agenda for many of his successors and ultimately paved the way for Newton. He also contributed notably and originally in astronomy, anatomy (he discovered the pineal gland at the base of the brain), and countless other disciplines to which he turned his attention. His work shows a constant reliance on human reason and a conviction that the methods that proved so successful in his mathematical efforts would prove equally fruitful in other fields.

Philosophy

Descartes' title as the father of modern philosophy does not so much rest on his specific philosophical doctrines as on the underlying assumptions guiding his inquiries. Though he pays lip service to the Church, there is no room in his philosophy for special revelation. The firm foundation for the sciences sought by Descartes is available in principle to all people without special intervention from the deity. There is no need to consult Scripture; our own faculties, if we but use them properly, suffice for adequate knowledge of the world and ourselves, even of the general nature of the deity itself.

Descartes does not separate himself just from religious dogmatism; he seeks equally to rebut skepticism about our knowledge. His efforts to establish a firm foundation for the sciences address both aims: Descartes claims that scientific procedure, by which he means rational analysis and reconstruction of ideas, is both the *necessary* and *sufficient* condition of knowledge—*necessary* because dogmatism cannot justify its own claims and *sufficient* because once the foundation and justificational structure of scientific knowledge are revealed, skepticism can be forever laid to rest.

Descartes believed it crucial to establish our right to claim to know, and he thus pushed epistemology to the forefront in philosophy. Descartes' vision of how that right is to be established and the resulting philosophical agenda have captured the philosophical imagination ever since. In the first meditation, Descartes himself rehearses the most common skeptical arguments, slowly and carefully leading his reader into the "coal-pit of skepticism." In the second meditation, he finds a stopping point for the slide into skepticism: his knowledge of his own thoughts and of his own existence. Whatever else doubt may assail, these remain impervious and certain. It is the clarity and distinctness of these ideas that forces conviction in them, so Descartes takes clarity and distinctness to be the mark of truth. When he attempts to climb back out of the skeptical hole he has dug himself, Descartes turns his attention to whether anything other than himself exists. He argues that there must be a beneficent God in order to explain facts already incontrovertibly established: that he has the idea of God and he, Descartes, exists. A beneficent God plays a crucial role in Descartes' philosophy, providing the key to the justification of our knowledge of everything else in the world. It would be inconsistent with the nature of a good and truthful creator if our faculties do not provide us with a generally accurate understanding of the world around us. Sensory knowledge can never possess the surety of pure rational knowledge, but neither is it negligible.

Besides this epistemological strategy, Descartes also makes important claims here about the nature of the world and of human beings. There are two kinds of created substance, according to Descartes: extended substance, which occupies space, is divisible, and is thoroughly passive, and thinking substance, which is not spatially localizable, is indivisible, and is constantly active. Every extended substance operates solely on mechanical principles. Even animals, according to Descartes, are nothing but very complex machines. Human beings, however, are different, for though our bodies are also complex machines, they are conjoined with a soul, a thinking substance, which can influence their behavior. A human being is a team of body and mind, with the mind the dominant partner. This doctrine of a two-part person, known as Cartesian dualism, has become the default belief in Western culture over the past 350 years. The *Meditations* is rich with insights about the structure of our minds, the nature of thought, and the relation between thought and reality.

The Reading Context

The *Meditations* is very concise and extremely well written. Descartes sets modern philosophy a seldom-matched standard with this work. As you read, keep in mind that every sentence serves a purpose. You have understood Descartes fully only when you understand the role each sentence plays in the whole.

The *Meditations* invites the reader to meditate along, to participate in the process, and it sometimes seduces the reader to acquiesce to inferences or principles he or she would not normally accept. Meditating with Descartes, questioning his moves and testing them against your own instincts, is a good way to begin confronting this text.

The *Meditations* is also an excellent work on which to practice the analysis of arguments, for almost every paragraph contains an identifiable argument.

Descartes begins by challenging most of the beliefs he formerly accepted without question. This methodical doubt, he hopes, will find the ultimate and certain bedrock of our knowledge. Does his slide into the "coal-pit of skepticism" take him to the ultimate foundation of knowledge, and does he go far enough into that pit? Is he able, in the course of *Meditations* 2–6, to escape from the pit he has dug himself?

A Note on the Text

Descartes' *Meditations* was originally written as a summary of his philosophy and accompanied by a dedication to the theologians at the University of Paris, the leading center of theology. More important for later scholars, however, is the fact that Descartes also sent the manuscript to a number of respected thinkers and invited their criticisms. Among those who responded were some of the leading minds of the era: Thomas Hobbes, Antoine Arnauld, Pierre Gassendi. These objections and Descartes' replies were published together with the *Meditations*. The *Meditations* was originally written in Latin, but it was soon translated into French by Clerselier, a close associate of Descartes. Apparently Descartes himself made some changes and additions in the French version, which are now commonly included in the text.

Reading Questions

1. Since much of a philosopher's position is implicit in the distinctions he or she recognizes, try to define the contrasts among clear, distinct, and confused ideas; sensation, imagination, and intellection; and between formal reality and objective reality; essence and existence; simple and complex; the mental and the material; and finally, finite and infinite.
2. In the first meditation we meet a series of arguments, each leading deeper into skepticism. Are the arguments all so good that we must follow him into the depths of skepticism?
3. Does Descartes have the right to an inference of the form "I think, therefore, I am"? How does he know the premise? What principle licenses the inference, and how does he know that principle?
4. Descartes gives us a criterion of truth—clarity and distinctness. When we clearly and distinctly perceive, we know. But how do we know that we clearly and distinctly perceive?
5. How many proofs of God's existence are there in the third meditation?
6. Having introduced clarity and distinctness as the criterion of truth, Descartes goes on to establish the existence of God. But he then asserts that God's veracity guarantees the truth of clear and distinct ideas. Is this a vicious circle at the heart of Descartes' philosophy?
7. What arguments does Descartes give for the real distinction between the mind and the body? How good are they?
8. Are Descartes' efforts to regain the material, external world in meditation 6 sufficient to overcome the skeptical doubts of the first meditation?

Meditations on First Philosophy

Synopsis of the Six Following Meditations

In the first meditation I set forth the grounds on which all things, and especially
material things, can be doubted—so long, that is to say, as we have no other foundations for the sciences than those on which we have hitherto relied. Although the utility of a doubt so general may not, on first suggestion, be apparent, it is none the less
very great. It frees us from all prejudices; it opens to us the easiest way of detaching the
mind from the senses; and lastly, it secures us against further doubting of what we shall
conclude to be true.

In the second meditation the mind, on making use of the freedom proper to it,
finds that it can suppose to be non-existent all those things the existence of which can
in any wise be doubted, but while so doing it has perforce to recognise that it must
itself exist. This is a point of the greatest importance; it is in this way that the mind
is enabled to distinguish easily between the things which pertain to itself, that is, to
its intellectual nature, and the things which pertain to the body. Some may, perhaps,
be led to expect to find at this stage in my argument a statement of grounds in proof
of the immortality of the soul, and I therefore think it proper to give warning that,
since it has been my endeavour to write in this treatise nothing of which I cannot give
exact demonstration, I have found myself obliged to adopt an order similar to that used
by geometers, viz. to state all the premises on which the proposition in question
depends, before coming to any conclusion regarding it. Now the first and chief prerequisite for knowledge of the immortality of the soul is our being able to form as perspicuous an apprehension of it as possible, an apprehension completely distinct from all
apprehension of body; and this is what has been done in this second meditation. In
addition we have to be assured (1) that all the things we judge clearly and distinctly
are true in that very mode in which we are judging them, and this could not be proved
at any point prior to the fourth meditation; (2) that we have a distinct apprehension
of the corporeal, and this I give partly in the second and partly in the fifth and sixth
meditations; and (3) that on these grounds we have to conclude that whatever things
are clearly and distinctly apprehended as being diverse substances, as are mind and
body, are indeed distinct each from the other, a conclusion drawn in the sixth meditation. This is further confirmed in that same meditation, where it is pointed out that
we cannot apprehend body save as divisible, nor, on the other hand, the mind save as
indivisible. For we cannot think of the half of a mind as we can of the half of any body,
however small; so that, as we thus see, not only are their natures diverse but also in
some measure contraries. I have not, however, pursued the matter further in this
present treatise, not only for the reason that these considerations suffice to show that
the extinction of the mind does not follow from the corruption of the body, thus
affording men the hope of a life after death, but also because the premises which enable us to infer the immortality of the mind call for an exposition of the whole science
of physics. We should have to establish (1) that all substances whatsoever, all things

From *Descartes' Philosophical Writings*, trans. Norman Kemp Smith (London: Macmillan, 1952), pp. 192–265.
Used with permission of Macmillan, London and Basingstoke.

that is to say, which owe their existence to God's creation of them, are by their very nature incorruptible, and that they can never cease to be, unless through God's withdrawing from them His concurrence they are thereby reduced to nothing; (2) that whereas body, taken generally [i.e. taking body collectively, as meaning matter], is a substance, and therefore can never perish, the human body, in so far as it differs from other bodies [i.e. taking "bodies" in the plural, thereby meaning material things], is composed entirely of a certain configuration of members, and other similar accidents, while the human mind is not constituted of accidents of any kind whatever, but is a pure substance. For though all the accidents of the mind suffer change, though, for instance, it thinks of other things, wills others, and senses others, it is yet always the same mind. The human body, on the contrary, is no longer the same, if a change takes place in the structure of some of its parts. Thus it follows, that while the body may, indeed, easily enough perish, the mind is in its own nature immortal.

In the third meditation I have, as it seems to me, developed at sufficient length my chief argument in proof of the existence of God. None the less, being anxious to withdraw the minds of my readers from the senses, I was unwilling to make use in that section of any comparisons drawn from corporeal things, and there may perhaps have remained many obscurities which, as I hope, may later be entirely removed by my replies to objections. . . .

In the fourth meditation it is shown that whatever we judge clearly and distinctly is true; and also at the same time it is explained in what the nature of error consists. Knowledge of these conclusions is required not only for the confirming of the preceding truths but also for the understanding of those that follow. (In passing, I may remark that I do not here treat of sin, that is, of error committed in the pursuit of good and evil, but solely of that which arises in deciding between the true and the false. Nor do I dwell on matters bearing on faith or on the conduct of life, but only on those speculative truths which can be known by way of the natural light.)

In the fifth meditation, in addition to a general account of corporeal nature, a new proof is given of the existence of God, a proof not perhaps free any more than the former from certain difficulties. The countering of these difficulties has again to await my reply to objections. I further show in what sense it is true that the certainty even of geometrical demonstrations is dependent on our knowledge of there being a God.

Finally, in the sixth meditation I distinguish the action of the understanding from that of the imagination; their distinguishing characters are described; the mind is proved to be really distinct from the body, and yet to be so closely conjoined with it as to form with it one single thing. All the errors which are wont to originate in the senses are then brought under review, and the manner of avoiding them indicated. Then in conclusion I give an account of all the grounds enabling us to be assured of the existence of material things; not that I consider them to be of great utility in establishing what they prove, viz. that a world does indeed exist, that men have bodies and the like, things which no one of sound mind has ever doubted; but because, on viewing them closely, we come to discern that they are neither so strong nor so evident as those through which we gain knowledge of our mind and of God, so that these latter are, of all the things which can be known through our human powers, the most certain and the most evident. The establishing of this conclusion has been my prime aim in these meditations; and that is why, in this synopsis, I have omitted mention of the many other issues on which I have dwelt only incidentally.

Meditation 1

Concerning the Things of which we may doubt

It is now several years since I first became aware how many false opinions I had from my childhood been admitting as true, and how doubtful was everything I have subsequently based on them. Accordingly I have ever since been convinced that if I am to establish anything firm and lasting in the sciences, I must once for all, and by a deliberate effort, rid myself of all those opinions to which I have hitherto given credence, starting entirely anew, and building from the foundations up. But as this enterprise was evidently one of great magnitude, I waited until I had attained an age so mature that I could no longer expect that I should at any later date be better able to execute my design. This is what has made me delay so long; and I should now be failing in my duty, were I to continue consuming in deliberation such time for action as still remains to me.

Today, then, as I have suitably freed my mind from all cares, and have secured for myself an assured leisure in peaceful solitude, I shall at last apply myself earnestly and freely to the general overthrow of all my former opinions. In doing so, it will not be necessary for me to show that they are one and all false; that is perhaps more than can be done. But since reason has already persuaded me that I ought to withhold belief no less carefully from things not entirely certain and indubitable than from those which appear to me manifestly false, I shall be justified in setting all of them aside, if in each case I can find any ground whatsoever for regarding them as dubitable. Nor in so doing shall I be investigating each belief separately—that, like inquiry into their falsity, would be an endless labour. The withdrawal of foundations involves the downfall of whatever rests on these foundations, and what I shall therefore begin by examining are the principles on which my former beliefs rested.

Whatever, up to the present, I have accepted as possessed of the highest truth and certainty I have learned either from the senses or through the senses. Now these senses I have sometimes found to be deceptive; and it is only prudent never to place complete confidence in that by which we have even once been deceived.

But, it may be said, although the senses sometimes deceive us regarding minute objects, or such as are at a great distance from us, there are yet many other things which, though known by way of sense, are too evident to be doubted; as, for instance, that I am in this place, seated by the fire, attired in a dressing-gown, having this paper in my hands, and other similar seeming certainties. Can I deny that these hands and this body are mine, save perhaps by comparing myself to those who are insane, and whose brains are so disturbed and clouded by dark bilious vapours that they persist in assuring us that they are kings, when in fact they are in extreme poverty; or that they are clothed in gold and purple when they are in fact destitute of any covering; or that their head is made of clay and their body of glass, or that they are pumpkins. They are mad; and I should be no less insane were I to follow examples so extravagant.

None the less I must bear in mind that I am a man, and am therefore in the habit of sleeping, and that what the insane represent to themselves in their waking moments I represent to myself, with other things even less probable, in my dreams. How often, indeed, have I dreamt of myself being in this place, dressed and seated by the fire, whilst all the time I was lying undressed in bed! At the present moment it certainly seems that in looking at this paper I do so with open eyes, that the head which I move is not asleep, that it is deliberately and of set purpose that I extend this hand, and that I am sensing the hand. The things which happen to the sleeper are not so clear nor so distinct as all of these are. I cannot, however, but remind myself that on many occasions I have in sleep been deceived by similar illusions; and on more careful study of them I see that there are no certain marks distinguishing waking from sleep; and I see this so manifestly that, lost in amazement, I am almost persuaded that I am now dreaming.

Let us, then, suppose ourselves to be asleep, and that all these particulars—namely, that we open our eyes, move the head, extend the hands—are false and illusory; and let us reflect that our hands perhaps, and the whole body, are not what we see them as being. Nevertheless we must at least agree that the things seen by us in sleep are as it were like painted images, and cannot have been formed save in the likeness of what is real and true. The types of things depicted, eyes, head, hands, etc.—these at least are not imaginary, but true and existent. For in truth when painters endeavour with all possible artifice to represent sirens and satyrs by forms the most fantastic and unusual, they cannot assign them natures which are entirely new, but only make a certain selection of limbs from different animals. Even should they excogitate something so novel that nothing similar has ever before been seen, and that their work represents to us a thing entirely fictitious and false, the colours used in depicting them cannot be similarly fictitious; they at least must truly exist. And by this same reasoning, even should those general things, viz. a body, eyes, a head, hands and such like, be imaginary, we are yet bound to admit that there are things simpler and more universal which are real existents and by the intermixture of which, as in the case of the colours, all the images of things of which we have any awareness, be they true and real or false and fantastic, are formed. To this class of things belong corporeal nature in general and its extension, the shape of extended things, their quantity or magnitude, and their number, as also the location in which they are, the time through which they endure, and other similar things.

This, perhaps, is why we not unreasonably conclude that physics, astronomy, medicine, and all other disciplines treating of composite things are of doubtful character, and that arithmetic, geometry, etc., treating only of the simplest and most general things and but little concerned as to whether or not they are actual existents, have a content that is certain and indubitable. For whether I am awake or dreaming, 2 and 3 are 5, a square has no more than four sides; and it does not seem possible that truths so evident can ever be suspected of falsity.

Yet even these truths can be questioned. That God exists, that He is all-powerful and has created me such as I am, has long been my settled opinion. How, then, do I know that He has not arranged that there be no Earth, no heavens, no extended thing, no shape, no magnitude, no location, while at the same time securing that all these things appear to me to exist precisely as they now do? Others, as I sometimes think, deceive themselves in the things which they believe they know best. How do I know that I am not myself deceived every time I add 2 and 3, or count the sides of a square, or judge of things yet simpler, if anything simpler can be suggested? But perhaps God has not been willing that I should be thus deceived, for He is said to be supremely good. If, however, it be repugnant to the goodness of God to have created me such that I am constantly subject to deception, it would also appear to be contrary to His goodness to permit me to be sometimes deceived, and that He does permit this is not in doubt.

There may be those who might prefer to deny the existence of a God so powerful, rather than to believe that all other things are uncertain. Let us, for the present, not oppose them; let us allow, in the manner of their view, that all which has been said regarding God is a fable. Even so we shall not have met and answered the doubts suggested above regarding the reliability of our mental faculties; instead we shall have given added force to them. For in whatever way it be supposed that I have come to be what I am, whether by fate or by chance, or by a continual succession and connection of things, or by some other means, since to be deceived and to err is an imperfection, the likelihood of my being so imperfect as to be the constant victim of deception will be increased in proportion as the power to which they assign my origin is lessened. To such argument I have assuredly nothing to reply; and thus at last I am constrained to confess that there is no one of all my former opinions which is not open to doubt, and this not merely owing to want of thought on my part, or through levity, but from cogent and maturely considered reasons. Henceforth, therefore, should I desire to discover something certain, I ought to refrain from assenting to these opinions no less scrupulously than in respect of what is manifestly false.

But it is not sufficient to have taken note of these conclusions; we must also be careful to keep them in mind. For long-established customary opinions perpetually recur in thought, long and familiar usage having given them the right to occupy my mind, even almost against my will, and to be masters of my belief. Nor shall I ever lose this habit of assenting to and of confiding in them, not at least so long as I consider them as in truth they are, namely, as opinions which, though in some fashion doubtful (as I have just shown), are still, none the less, highly probable and such as it is much more reasonable to believe than to deny. This is why I shall, as I think, be acting prudently if, taking a directly contrary line, I of set purpose employ every available device for the deceiving of myself, feigning that all these opinions are entirely false and imaginary. Then, in due course, having so balanced my old-time prejudices by this new prejudice that I cease to incline to one side more than to another, my judgment, no longer dominated by misleading usages, will not be hindered by them in the apprehension of things. In this course there can, I am convinced, be neither danger nor error. What I have under consideration is a question solely of knowledge, not of action, so that I cannot for the present be at fault as being over-ready to adopt a questioning attitude.

Accordingly I shall now suppose, not that a true God, who as such must be supremely good and the fountain of truth, but that some malignant genius exceedingly powerful and cunning has devoted all his powers in the deceiving of me; I shall suppose that the sky, the earth, colours, shapes, sounds and all external things are illusions and impostures of which this evil genius has availed himself for the abuse of my credulity; I shall consider myself as having no hands, no eyes, no flesh, no blood, nor any senses, but as falsely opining myself to possess all these things. Further, I shall obstinately persist in this way of thinking; and even if, while so doing, it may not be within my power to arrive at the knowledge of any truth, there is one thing I have it in me to do, viz. to suspend judgment, refusing assent to what is false. Thereby, thanks to this resolved firmness of mind, I shall be effectively guarding myself against being imposed upon by this deceiver, no matter how powerful or how craftily deceptive he may be.

This undertaking is, however, irksome and laborious, and a certain indolence drags me back into the course of my customary life. Just as a captive who has been enjoying in sleep an imaginary liberty, should he begin to suspect that his liberty is a dream, dreads awakening, and conspires with the agreeable illusions for the prolonging of the deception, so in similar fashion I gladly lapse back into my accustomed opinions. I dread to be awakened, in fear lest the wakefulness may have to be laboriously spent, not in the tranquilising light of truth, but in the extreme darkness of the above suggested questionings.

Meditation 2

Concerning the Nature of the Human Mind, and how it is more easily known than the Body

So disquieting are the doubts in which yesterday's meditation has involved me that it is no longer in my power to forget them. Nor do I yet see how they are to be resolved. It is as if I had all of a sudden fallen into very deep water, and am so disconcerted that I can neither plant my feet securely on the bottom nor maintain myself by swimming on the surface. I shall, however, brace myself for a great effort, entering anew on the path which I was yesterday exploring; that is, I shall proceed by setting aside all that admits even of the very slightest doubt, just as if I had convicted it of being absolutely false; and I shall persist in following this path, until I have come upon something certain, or, failing in that, until at least I know, and know with certainty, that in the world there is nothing certain.

Archimedes, that he might displace the whole earth, required only that there might be some one point, fixed and immovable, to serve in leverage; so likewise I shall be entitled to entertain high hopes if I am fortunate enough to find some one thing that is certain and indubitable.

I am supposing, then, that all the things I see are false; that of all the happenings my memory has ever suggested to me, none has ever so existed; that I have no senses; that body, shape, extension, movement and location are but mental fictions. What is there, then, which can be esteemed true? Perhaps this only, that nothing whatsoever is certain.

But how do I know that there is not something different from all the things I have thus far enumerated and in regard to which there is not the least occasion for doubt? Is there not some God, or other being by whatever name we call Him, who puts these thoughts into my mind? Yet why suppose such a being? May it not be that I am myself capable of being their author? Am I not myself at least a something? But already I have denied that I have a body and senses. This indeed raises awkward questions. But what is it that thereupon follows? Am I so dependent on the body and senses that without them I cannot exist? Having persuaded myself that outside me there is nothing, that there is no heaven, no Earth, that there are no minds, no bodies, am I thereby committed to the view that I also do not exist? By no means. If I am persuading myself of something, in so doing I assuredly do exist. But what if, unknown to me, there be some deceiver, very powerful and very cunning, who is constantly employing his ingenuity in deceiving me? Again, as before, without doubt, if he is deceiving me, I exist. Let him deceive me as much as he will, he can never cause me to be nothing so long as I shall be thinking that I am something. And thus, having reflected well, and carefully examined all things, we have finally to conclude that this declaration, *Ego sum, ego existo*, is necessarily true every time I propound it or mentally apprehend it.

But I do not yet know in any adequate manner what I am, I who am certain that I am; and I must be careful not to substitute some thing in place of myself, and so go astray in this knowledge which I am holding to be the most certain and evident of all that is knowable by me. This is why I shall now meditate anew on what, prior to my venturing on these questionings, I believed myself to be. I shall withdraw those beliefs which can, even in the least degree, be invalidated by the reasons cited, in order that at length, of all my previous beliefs, there may remain only what is certain and indubitable.

What then did I formerly believe myself to be? Undoubtedly I thought myself to be a man. But what is a man? Shall I say a rational animal? No, for then I should have to inquire what is "animal," what "rational"; and thus from the one question I should be drawn on into several others yet more difficult. I have not, at present, the leisure for any such subtle inquiries. Instead, I prefer to meditate on the thoughts which of themselves sprang up in my mind on my applying myself to the consideration of what I am, considerations suggested by my own proper nature. I thought that I possessed a face, hands, arms, and that whole structure to which I was giving the title "body," composed as it is of the limbs discernible in a corpse. In addition, I took notice that I was nourished, that I walked, that I sensed, that I thought, all of which actions I ascribed to the soul. But what the soul might be I did not stop to consider; or if I did, I imaged it as being something extremely rare and subtle, like a wind, a flame or an aether, and as diffused throughout my grosser parts. As to the nature of "body," no doubts whatsoever disturbed me. I had, as I thought, quite distinct knowledge of it; and had I been called upon to explain the manner in which I then conceived it, I should have explained myself somewhat thus: by body I understand whatever can be determined by a certain shape, and comprised in a certain location, whatever so fills a certain space as to exclude from it every other body, whatever can be apprehended by touch, sight, hearing, taste or smell, and whatever can be moved in various ways, not indeed of itself but by something foreign to it by which it is touched and impressed. For I nowise conceived the power of self-movement, of sensing or knowing, as pertaining to the nature of body: on the contrary I was somewhat astonished on finding in certain bodies faculties such as these.

But what am I now to say that I am, now that I am supposing that there exists a very powerful, and if I may so speak, malignant being, who employs all his powers and skill in deceiving me? Can I affirm that I possess any one of those things which I have been speaking of as pertaining to the nature of body? On stopping to consider them with closer attention, and on reviewing all of them, I find none of which I can say that it belongs to me; to enumerate them again would be idle and tedious. What then, of those things which I have been attributing not to body, but to the soul? What of nutrition or of walking? If it be that I have no body, it cannot be that I take nourishment or that I walk. Sensing? There can be no sensing in the absence of body; and besides I have seemed during sleep to apprehend things which, as I afterwards noted, had not been sensed. Thinking? Here I find what does belong to me: it alone cannot be separated from me. *I am, I exist.* This is certain. How often? As often as I think. For it might indeed be that if I entirely ceased to think, I should thereupon altogether cease to exist. I am not at present admitting anything which is not necessarily true; and, accurately speaking, I am therefore [taking myself to be] only a thinking thing, that is to say, a mind, an understanding or reason—terms the significance of which has hitherto been unknown to me. I am, then, a real thing, and really existent. What thing? I have said it, a thinking thing.

And what more am I? I look for aid to the imagination. [But how mistakenly!] I am not that assemblage of limbs we call the human body; I am not a subtle penetrating air distributed throughout all these members; I am not a wind, a fire, a vapour, a breath or anything at all that I can image. I am supposing all these things to be nothing. Yet I find, while so doing, that I am still assured that I am a something.

But may it not be that those very things which, not being known to me, I have been supposing non-existent, are not really different from the self that I know? As to that I cannot say, and am not now discussing it. I can judge only of things that are known to me. Having come to know that I exist, I am inquiring as to what I am, this I that I thus know to exist. Now quite certainly this knowledge, taken in the precise manner as above, is not dependent on things the existence of which is not yet known to me; consequently and still more evidently it does not depend on any of the things which are feigned by the imagination. Indeed this word *feigning* warns me of my error; for I should in truth be feigning were I to image myself to be a something; since imaging is in no respect distinguishable from the contemplating of the shape or image of a cor-poreal thing. Already I know with certainty that I exist, and that all these imaged things, and in general whatever relates to the nature of body, may possibly be dreams merely or deceptions. Accordingly, I see clearly that it is no more reasonable to say, "I will resort to my imagination in order to learn more distinctly what I am," than if I were to say, "I am awake and apprehend something that is real, true; but as I do not yet apprehend it sufficiently well, I will of express purpose go to sleep, that my dreams may represent it to me with greater truth and evidence." I know therefore that nothing of all I can comprehend by way of the imagination pertains to this knowledge I [already] have of myself, and that if the mind is to determine the nature of the self with perfect distinctness, I must be careful to restrain it, diverting it from all such imaginative modes of apprehension.

What then is it that I am? A thinking thing. What is a thinking thing? It is a thing that doubts, understands, affirms, denies, wills, abstains from willing, that also can be aware of images and sensations.

Assuredly if all these things pertain to me, I am indeed a something. And how could it be they should not pertain to me? Am I not that very being who doubts of almost everything, who none the less also apprehends certain things, who affirms that one thing only is true, while denying all the rest, who yet desires to know more, who is averse to being deceived, who images many things, sometimes even despite his will, and who likewise apprehends many things which seem to come by way of the senses? Even though I should be always dreaming, and though he who has created me employs all his ingenuity in deceiving me, is there any one of the above assertions which is not as true as that I am and that I exist? Any one of them which can be distinguished from my thinking? Any one of them which can be said to be separate from the self? So manifest is it that it is I who doubt, I who apprehend, I who desire, that there is here no need to add anything by way of rendering it more evident. It is no less certain that

I can apprehend images. For although it may happen (as I have been supposing) that none of the things imaged are true, the imaging, *qua* active power, is none the less really in me, as forming part of my thinking. Again, I am the being who senses, that is to say, who apprehends corporeal things, as if by the organs of sense, since I do in truth see light, hear noise, feel heat. These things, it will be said, are false, and I am only dreaming. Even so, it is none the less certain that it seems to me that I see, that I hear, and that I am warmed. This is what in me is rightly called sensing, and as used in this precise manner is nowise other than thinking.

From all this I begin to know what I am somewhat better than heretofore. But it still seems to me—for I am unable to prevent myself continuing in this way of thinking—that corporeal things, which are reconnoitred by the senses, and whose images inform thought, are known with much greater distinctness than that part of myself (whatever it be) which is not imageable—strange though it may be to be thus saying that I know and comprehend more distinctly those things which I am supposing to be doubtful and unknown, and as not belonging to me, than others which are known to me, which appertain to my proper nature and of the truth of which I am convinced—in short are known more distinctly than I know myself. But I can see how this comes about: my mind delights to wander and will not yet suffer itself to be restrained within the limits of truth.

Let us, therefore, once again allow the mind the freest reign, so that when afterwards we bring it, more opportunely, under due constraint, it may be the more easily controlled. Let us begin by considering the things which are commonly thought to be the most distinctly known, viz. the bodies which we touch and see; not, indeed, bodies in general, for such general notions are usually somewhat confused, but one particular body. Take, for example, this piece of wax; it has been but recently taken from the hive; it has not yet lost the sweetness of the honey it contained; it still retains something of the odour of the flowers from which it has been gathered; its colour, its shape, its size, are manifest to us; it is hard, cold, easily handled, and when struck upon with the finger emits a sound. In short, all that is required to make a body known with the greatest possible distinctness is present in the one now before us. But behold! While I am speaking let it be moved towards the fire. What remains of the taste exhales, the odour evaporates, the colour changes, the shape is destroyed, its size increases, it becomes liquid, it becomes hot and can no longer be handled, and when struck upon emits no sound. Does the wax, notwithstanding these changes, still remain the same wax? We must admit that it does; no one doubts that it does, no one judges otherwise. What, then, was it I comprehended so distinctly in knowing the piece of wax? Certainly, it could be nothing of all that I was aware of by way of the senses, since all the things that came by way of taste, smell, sight, touch and hearing, are changed, and the wax none the less remains.

Perhaps it has all along been as I am now thinking, viz. that the wax was not that sweetness of honey, nor that pleasing scent of flowers, nor that whiteness, that shape, that sound, but a body which a little while ago appeared to me decked out with those modes, and now appears decked out with others. But what precisely is it that I am here imaging? Let us attentively consider the wax, withdrawing from it all that does not belong to it, that we may see what remains. As we find, what then alone remains is a something extended, flexible and movable. But what is this "flexible," this "movable"? What am I then imaging? That the piece of wax from being round in shape can become square, or from being square can become triangular? Assuredly not. For I am apprehending that it admits of an infinity of similar shapes, and am not able to compass this infinity by way of images. Consequently this comprehension of it cannot be the product of the faculty of imagination.

What, we may next ask, is its extension? Is it also not known [by way of the imagination]? It becomes greater when the wax is melted, greater when the wax is made to boil, and ever greater as the heat increases; and I should not be apprehending what the wax truly is, if I did not think that this piece of wax we are considering allows of a greater variety of extensions than I have ever imaged. I must, therefore, admit that I cannot by way of images comprehend what this wax is, and that it is by the mind alone that I [adequately] apprehend it. I say this particular wax, for as to wax in general that is yet more evident. Now what is this wax which cannot be [adequately] apprehended save by the mind? Certainly the same that I see, touch, image, and in short, the very body that from the start I have been supposing it to be. And what has especially to be noted is that our [adequate] apprehension of it is not a seeing, nor a touching, nor an imaging, and has never been such, although it may formerly have seemed so, but is solely an inspection of the mind which may be imperfect and confused, as it formerly was, or clear and distinct, as it now is, according as my attention is directed less or more to the constituents composing the body.

I am indeed amazed when I consider how weak my mind is and how prone to error. For although I can, dispensing with words, [directly] apprehend all this in myself, none the less words have a hampering hold upon me, and the accepted usages of ordinary speech tend to mislead me. Thus when the wax is before us we say that we see it to be the same wax as that previously seen, and not that we judge it to be the same from its retaining the same colour and shape. From this I should straightway conclude that the wax is known by ocular vision, independently of a strictly mental inspection, were it not that perchance I recall how when looking from a window at beings passing by on the street below, I similarly say that it is men I am seeing, just as I say that I am seeing the wax. What do I see from the window beyond hats and cloaks, which might cover automatic machines? Yet I judge those to be men. In analogous fashion, what I have been supposing myself to see with the eyes I am comprehending solely with the faculty of judgment, a faculty proper not to my eyes but to my mind.

But aiming as I do at knowledge superior to the common, I should be ashamed to draw grounds for doubt from the forms and terms of ordinary speech. I prefer therefore to pass on, and to ask whether I apprehended the wax on my first seeing it, and while I was still believing that I knew it by way of the external senses, or at least by the *sensus communis*, as they call it, that is to say by the imaginative faculty, more perfectly and more evidently than I now apprehend it after having examined with greater care what it is and in what way it can be known. It would indeed be foolish to have doubts as to the answer to this question. Was there anything in that first apprehension which was distinct? What did I apprehend that any animal might not have seen? When, however, I distinguish the wax from its external forms; when stripped as it were of its vestments I consider it in complete nakedness, it is certain that though there may still be error in my judgment, I could not be thus apprehending it without a mind that is human.

What now shall I say of the mind itself, i.e. of myself? For as yet I do not admit in myself anything but mind. What am I to say in regard to this I which seems to apprehend this piece of wax so distinctly? Do I not know myself much more truly and much more certainly, and also much more distinctly and evidently, than I do the wax? For if I judge that the wax is or exists because I see it, evidently it follows, with yet greater evidence that I myself am or exist, inasmuch as I am thus seeing it. For though it may be that what I see is not in truth wax, and that I do not even possess eyes with which to see anything, yet assuredly when I see, or (for I no longer allow the distinction) when I think I see, it cannot be that I myself who think am not a something. So likewise, if I judge that the wax exists because I touch it, it will follow that I am; and if I judge that the imagination, or some other cause whatever it be, persuades me that the wax exists, the same conclusion follows [viz. that I am *thinking* by way of an image and *thinking* what I thus image to be independently existing]. And what I have here said regarding the piece of wax may be said in respect of all other things which are external to me.

And yet a further point: if the apprehension of the wax has seemed to me more determinate and distinct when sight and touch, and many causes besides, have rendered it manifest to me, how much more evidently and distinctly must I now know myself, since all the reasons which can aid in the apprehension of wax, or of any body whatsoever, afford yet better evidence of the nature of my mind. Besides, in the mind itself there are so many more things which can contribute to the more distinct knowledge of it, that those which come to it by way of the body scarcely merit being taken into account.

Thus, then, I have been brought step by step to the conclusion I set out to establish. For I now know that, properly speaking, bodies are cognised not by the senses or by the imagination, but by the understanding alone. They are not thus cognised because seen or touched, but only in so far as they are apprehended understandingly. Thus, as I now recognise, nothing is more easily or more evidently apprehended by me than my mind. Difficult, however, as it is to rid oneself of a way of thinking to which the mind has been so long accustomed, it is well that I should halt for some time at this point, that by prolonged meditation I may more deeply impress upon myself this new knowledge.

Meditation 3

Concerning God: that He exists

I shall now close my eyes, stop my ears, withdraw all my senses, I shall even efface from my thinking all images of corporeal things; or since that can hardly be done, I shall at least view them as empty and false. In this manner, holding converse only with myself and closely examining my nature, I shall endeavour to obtain, little by little, better and more familiar knowledge of myself. I am a thinking thing, i.e. a thing that doubts, affirms, denies, knows some few things, is ignorant of many, that loves, that hates, that wills, that refuses, that images also and senses. For as I before remarked, although the things which I sense or image are perhaps, apart from me, nothing at all, I am nevertheless certain that those ways of thinking, which I call sensings and imagings, in so far as they are no more than ways of thinking, pertain to me. In those few words I have summed up all that I truly know, or at least all that I have thus far been aware of knowing.

I shall now endeavour to discover whether, on closer attention, there may not perhaps pertain to me other things which I have not yet considered. I am certain that I am a thinking thing. But do I thereby know also what is required to render me thus certain of anything? In this first knowledge there is indeed nothing save the clear and distinct apprehension of what I am affirming; yet this would not suffice to render me certain of its truth, if it could ever happen that anything which I apprehend thus clearly and distinctly should yet prove false; and accordingly I would now seem to be able to adopt as a general rule that everything I apprehend in a genuinely clear and distinct manner is true.

I have, however, been receiving and admitting as altogether certain and manifest several other things which yet I have afterwards found to be altogether doubtful. What were those things? They were the Earth, the sky, the stars, and all the other things I was apprehending by way of the senses. But what was there that I clearly apprehended in them? Nothing save that the ideas or thoughts of such things presented themselves to my mind. And even now I do not deny that those ideas are to be met with in me. There was, however, another thing which I was affirming, and which, being habituated to belief in it, I supposed myself to be apprehending clearly, although in truth I was not so apprehending it, namely that there were things outside me, from which these proceed and to which they are altogether similar. It was in this that I was mistaken; or if I was perhaps judging correctly, assuredly this was not due to any knowledge conveyed to me by way of direct apprehension.

But when I considered something very simple and easy, bearing on arithmetic or geometry, for instance that 2 and 3 together make 5, and other things of this sort, was I not, then at least, intuiting them sufficiently perspicuously to justify me in affirming their truth? If afterwards I entertained doubts regarding them, this was indeed for no other reason than that it occurred to me that a God might perhaps have endowed me with a nature such that I may be deceived even in respect of the things which seem to me the most manifest of all. For whenever this supposition of God's omnipotence comes up in my mind, I cannot but confess that it is easy for Him, if He so wishes, to cause me to err, even in those matters which I regard myself as intuiting with the eyes of the mind in the most evident manner. None the less, when I direct my attention to the things which I believe myself to be apprehending quite clearly, I am so persuaded of their truth that I cannot but break into protestations such as these: Let who will deceive me, he will never be able to bring it about that in the very time during which I shall be thinking that I am a something, I shall yet be nothing; or that, at some future time, it will be true that I have never been, it now being true to say that I am; or that 2 and 3 could make more or less than 5; or that any other such things which I clearly see, cannot be other than I apprehend them as being. And certainly since I have no reason to believe that there is a God who is a deceiver (and indeed have not yet even considered the grounds for supposing that a God of any kind exists), the ground of my doubts, entirely dependent as it is on this supposition, is but slight, and so to speak metaphysical. But to be able to eliminate it, I must at the earliest possible opportunity inquire whether there is indeed a God; and should I find there is a God, I must also inquire whether He can be a deceiver. For without the knowledge of these two truths I do not see how I can be certain of anything.

Now in order that I may be enabled to conduct this inquiry without interrupting the order of meditation I have proposed to myself—namely to pass step by step from the first notions I discover in my mind to those which I can afterwards find to be there—I must here divide all my thoughts into certain kinds, and consider in which of these kinds truth and error, in the strict sense, are to be found. Some of my thoughts are, as it were, images of things; and to them alone strictly belongs the title "idea," e.g. when I represent to myself a man, or a chimera, or the sky, or an angel, or even God. Other thoughts have in addition other forms; for instance when I will, fear, affirm, deny, while in so doing I am always indeed apprehending something as the subject of my thought, I am also embracing in thought something more than the similitude of this thing; and of the thoughts of this kind some are called volitions or affections, whereas others are called judgments. If ideas are considered only in themselves, and not as referred to some other thing, they cannot, strictly speaking, be false. For whether I image a goat or a chimera, that I am imaging the latter is no less true than that I am imaging the former. Nor need I fear there may be falsity in the will or in the affections. For though I am able to desire things that are evil, or even what has never existed, it is yet none the less true that I so desire them. There thus remain only our judgments; and it is in respect of them that I must take diligent heed lest I be deceived. And assuredly the chief and most usual error to be met with in them consists in judging that the ideas which are in me are similar to, conformed to, the things which are outside me; if I considered them as being only certain modes or ways in which I think, without referring them to anything beyond, they would hardly afford any material for error.

To consider now the ideas [that are strictly so called], some appear to me to be innate, others to be adventitious, that is to say foreign to me and coming from without, and others to be made or invented by me. When I apprehend what a thing is, what a truth is, or what a thought is, I would seem to be holding the power of so doing from no other source than my own nature. On the other hand, when I hear a sound, see the Sun, or sense fire, I have hitherto judged these to proceed from certain things situated outside me. Lastly it appears to me that sirens, hippogriffs and other similar chimeras are my own mental inventions. But perhaps I may yet come to hold that all of these ideas are of the kind I call adventitious, coming to me from without, or that they are all innate, or are all made by me; for I have not yet clearly discerned their true origin.

Here my chief task must be to inquire, in respect of those ideas which seem to me to come from things existing outside me, what grounds there are obliging me to believe they are similar to the outside things. The first of those grounds is that I seem to be so taught by nature; and the second, that I experience in myself that these ideas are not in any wise dependent on my will, nor therefore on myself. Often they present themselves to me in spite of myself, as, for instance, at the present moment, whether I will or not, I feel heat; and because of this I am persuaded that this sensation or idea is produced in me by a thing that is different from me, viz. by the heat of the fire near which I am sitting. And as it has seemed to me, nothing is more obvious than that I may therefore judge that what this external thing is impressing on me is not anything different from itself, but its similitude.

Next, I must consider whether these grounds are sufficiently strong and convincing. When I here say that I am so taught by nature I understand by the word nature only a certain spontaneous impulse which constrains me to this belief, and not a natural light enabling me to know that the belief is true. These two things are widely different; for what the natural light shows me to be true (e.g. that inasmuch as I doubt, it follows that I am, and the like), I cannot anywise call in doubt, since I have in me no other faculty or power whereby to distinguish the true from the false, none as trust-worthy as the natural light, and none that can teach me the falsity of what the natural light shows me to be true. As I have often observed, when this question relates to the choice between right and wrong in action, the natural impulses have frequently misled me; and I do not see that I have any better ground for following them in questions of truth and error.

As to the other ground, that these ideas, as not being dependent on my will, must necessarily proceed from things situated outside me, I do not find it any more convinc-ing than that of which I have been speaking. For just as the natural impulses, notwith-standing the fact that they are not always in accordance with my will, are none the less in me, so likewise it may be that I have in me, though indeed unknown to me, some faculty or power capable of producing the ideas, and of doing so without the aid of any external things. That, as I have hitherto thought, is precisely what I am doing when I dream.

And lastly, even should the ideas proceed from things other than myself, it does not therefore follow that they must be similar to those things. On the contrary, I have observed in a number of instances how greatly a thing can differ from our ideas of it. For example, I find present to me two completely diverse ideas of the Sun; the one in which the Sun appears to me as extremely small is, it would seem, derived from the senses, and to be counted as belonging to the class of adventitious ideas; the other, in which the Sun is taken by me to be many times larger than the whole Earth, has been arrived at by way of astronomical reasonings, that is to say, elicited from certain notions innate in me, or formed by me in some other manner. Certainly, these two ideas of the Sun cannot both resemble the same Sun; and reason constrains me to believe that the one which seems to have emanated from it in a direct manner is the more unlike.

These various considerations convince me that hitherto it has not been by any assured judgment, but only from a sort of blind impulse, that I have believed in the existence of things outside me and different from me, things which by way of the sense-organs or by whatever means they employ, have conveyed to me their ideas or images, and have thus impressed on me their similitudes.

But there is yet another way of inquiring whether any of those things, the ideas of which are in me, exist outside me. If ideas are taken in so far only as they are certain ways of thinking, I recognise among them no differences or inequality; they all appear to me to proceed from me in the same manner. When, however, they are viewed as images, of which one represents one thing and another some other thing, it is evident that they differ greatly one from another. Those which represent substances are without doubt something more, and contain in themselves, so to speak, more objective reality (that is to say participate by representation in a higher degree of being or of perfection) than those which represent only modes or accidents; and again, the idea by which I appre-hend a supreme God, eternal, infinite, immutable, omniscient, omnipotent, and the creator of all things which are in addition to Himself, has certainly in it more objective reality than those ideas by which finite substances are represented.

Now it is manifest by the natural light that there must be at least as much reality in the efficient and total cause as in its effect. For whence can the effect draw its reality if not from its cause? How could this cause communicate to it this reality if it did not itself have it? And hence it follows, not only that something cannot proceed from nothing; but also that what is more perfect, i.e. contains more reality, cannot proceed from what is less perfect. And this is not only evidently true of those effects the reality of which philosophers term actual or formal, but also of the ideas the reality of which is viewed only as being what they term objective [i.e. representational]. Thus, for example, a stone which has not yet existed cannot now begin to be unless it be produced by some thing which possesses in itself, either formally or eminently, all that enters into the composition of the stone (i.e. which contains in itself the same things or others more excellent than those which are in the stone). Thus heat cannot be produced in a subject previously devoid of it save by a cause of an order or degree or kind at least as perfect as the heat, and so in all other cases. But neither can the idea of the heat or of the stone exist in me unless it too has been placed in me by a cause which contains in itself at least as much reality as I am ascribing to the heat or the stone. For although this cause may not communicate to the idea anything of its formal, i.e. of its actual reality, we ought not on that account to view this cause as less real. As we have to recognise, it is the very nature of an idea to require for itself no other formal [i.e. actual] reality save that which it receives and borrows from the thought or mind of which it is a mode, i.e. a manner or way of thinking. But nevertheless, if an idea is to contain one [particular] objective reality rather than some other, it must undoubtedly derive it from some cause in which there is to be found at least as much formal [i.e. actual] reality as in the idea there is objective [i.e. representational] reality. For if anything [of that kind] be allowed as being met with in the idea and yet not in the cause of the idea, it must have derived its origin from nothing. But however imperfect that mode of being—the mode of being objectively in the understanding by way of representation through its idea—we certainly cannot, for all that, declare it to be in itself nothing, nor consequently that the idea owes its origin to nothing.

Nor may I, on the ground that the reality which I ascribe to my ideas is only objective [i.e. representational], suspect it of not being also formally [i.e. actually] present in their causes, and so hold it to be sufficient if in them also it exists only objectively. Just as the objective mode of existence belongs to ideas by their very nature, so the formal mode of existence appertains to the causes of these ideas, at least to the first and chief of their causes, by the very nature of those causes. For although, it may be, one idea gives birth to another, the series of the ideas cannot be carried back *in infinitum*; we must in the end reach a first idea, the cause of which is, as it were, the archetype in which all the reality or perfection that is in the idea only objectively, by way of representation, is contained formally [i.e. actually]. In this way the natural light makes it evident to me that the ideas are in me in the manner of images, which may indeed fall short of the perfection of the things from which they have been derived, but can never contain anything greater or more perfect.

The longer and more carefully I examine all these things, the more clearly and distinctly do I recognise their truth. What then am I to conclude from it all? This, namely, that if the objective reality of any one of my ideas be so great that I am certain it cannot be in me either formally or eminently, and that consequently I cannot myself be the cause of it, it necessarily follows that I am not alone in the world and that there is likewise existing some other thing, which is the cause of this idea. Were no idea of this kind to be met with in me, I should have no argument sufficient to render me certain of the existence of anything different from me. For after careful inquiry in every possible quarter, I have up to the present failed to discover any other.

Now among my ideas in addition to the idea which exhibits me to myself—an idea as to which there can here be no difficulty—there is another which represents God, others representing corporeal and inanimate things, others representing angels, others representing animals, and again others representing to me men similar to myself. As regards the ideas which represent other men, or animals, or angels, I can easily understand that they may have been compounded from those which I have of myself, of corporeal things, and of God, even although there may be, outside myself, neither men, animals nor angels. As regards the ideas of corporeal things, there is nothing in them so great or so excellent that it might not possibly have proceeded from myself, and on considering them closely and examining each separately in the way in which I yesterday examined the idea of wax, I find that there is but little in them which is clearly and distinctly apprehended, viz. magnitude or extension in length, breadth and depth, shape which results from the limitation of extension, the location which bodies have in relation to one another, and motion or change of location, to which may be added substance, duration and number. As to other things such as light and the colours, sounds, odours, tastes, heat and cold and the other tactual qualities, they present themselves to me so confusedly and obscurely that I cannot tell whether they are true or false, i.e. whether the ideas I have of them are ideas of real things or whether they present only chimerical beings which are incapable of [independent] existence. For though, as I have before remarked, it is only in judgments that formal falsity, falsity properly so called, can be met with, there can yet in ideas be a certain material falsity, namely when the ideas represent what is nothing as if it were something. For example, so far are the ideas I have of heat and cold from being clear and distinct, that I cannot learn from them whether cold is only a privation of heat or heat a privation of cold, or indeed whether either or neither is a real quality. And inasmuch as ideas are taken as being images [i.e. as standing for something], there cannot be any that do not seem to us to represent something; and accordingly, if it be indeed true that cold is nothing but a privation of heat, the idea which represents it to me as something real and positive may quite properly be termed false; and so in other cases. Ideas of this kind I need not indeed assign to any author other than myself. For, if they are false, i.e. if they represent what is not a thing, then by the light of reason it is known to me that they proceed from nothing, i.e. that they are in me only because of some lack of perfection in my nature. On the other hand, even supposing them to be true, if what they exhibit to me has such little reality—so little that I cannot even distinguish the thing thus represented from not-being—I do not see why they may not have been produced by myself.

As to the clear and distinct ideas I have of corporeal things, there are some which, as it seems to me, I can have obtained from the idea [i.e. the immediate awareness] I have of myself, e.g. those of substance, duration, number and the like. For when I think a stone to be a substance or to be a thing capable of existing by itself, and in like manner think myself to be a substance, though I am then indeed apprehending myself to be a thinking non-extended thing, and the stone, on the contrary, to be an extended non-thinking thing, and though there is accordingly a notable difference between the two, none the less they appear to agree in this, that they represent substances. In the same way, when I apprehend myself as now existing and recollect that I have existed at other times, and when I have thoughts of which I apprehend the number, I acquire the ideas of duration and number, which I can thereafter freely transfer to other things. As to the other qualities composing the ideas of corporeal things, extension, shape, location and motion, it is true that they are not indeed formally [i.e. actually] in me, since I am nothing other than a thinking thing; but as they are merely certain modes of substance—and as it were the vestments under which corporeal substance appears to us—whereas I am myself a substance, it would seem that they may be contained in me eminently.

The only idea that remains for consideration, therefore, is the idea of God. Is there in that idea anything which cannot be regarded as proceeding from myself? By the name God I mean a substance that is infinite, immutable, independent, all-knowing, all-powerful, and by which I myself and everything else, if any such other things there be, have been created. All those attributes are so great and so eminent, that the more attentively I consider them the less does it seem possible that they can have proceeded from myself alone; and thus, in the light of all that has been said, we have no option save to conclude that God exists. For though the idea of substance may be in me in so far as I am myself a substance, yet, being as I am a finite entity, it would not be the idea of an *infinite* substance; it can be this only as having proceeded from some sub-stance which is in itself infinite.

The argument cannot be met by supposing that I apprehend the infinite not through a true idea but only by negation of that which is finite, in the manner in which I apprehend rest and darkness by the negation of motion and light. On the con-trary there is manifestly more reality in the infinite substance than in the finite sub-stance, and my awareness of the infinite must therefore be in some way prior to my awareness of the finite, that is to say, my awareness of God must be prior to that of myself. For how could I know that I doubt and desire, i.e. know that something is lack-ing to me and that I am not wholly perfect, save by having in me the idea of a being more perfect than myself, by comparison with which I may recognise my deficiencies. Nor can our argument be evaded by declaring that this idea of God is perhaps materi-ally false, and that consequently, as in the already mentioned ideas of heat and cold, it may have nothing as its source, i.e. that its existence may be due to my imperfection. On the contrary, since this idea is completely clear and distinct, and contains within itself more objective reality than any other, there can be none which is of itself more true or less open to the suspicion of falsity. . . . This holds true, even though it be that I do not comprehend the infinite, and that in God there is an infinitude of things which I cannot comprehend, or even reach in any way by thought. For it is of the nature of the infinite that I, finite as I am and limited, cannot comprehend it. It suffices that I understand this, and that I judge that whatever I apprehend clearly, and which I know to purport some perfection, and perchance also an infinitude of yet other perfections of which I am ignorant, is in God formally or eminently. Conse-quently, the idea I have of Him is the most completely true, the most completely clear and distinct, of all the ideas that are in me.

But perhaps I am something more than I am supposing myself to be; perhaps all those perfections which I am attributing to God are in some fashion potentially in me, although they do not yet show themselves or issue in action. Indeed I am already aware that my knowledge increases, perfecting itself little by little; and I see nothing to prevent its thus increasing more and more *in infinitum*, nor any reason why on its being thus increased and perfected I may not in this way be able to acquire all the other perfections of the Divine nature, nor finally, why the power I have of acquiring these perfections, if the power be indeed thus already in me, may not suffice to provide the idea of them.

But on closer examination I recognise that this cannot be allowed. For, in the first place, even should it be true that my knowledge, little by little, daily increases, and that many things potentially mine are not yet actual, none the less these powers do not pertain to, or make the least approach to, the idea I have of God in whom nothing is merely potential, and all is actual and operative. There can indeed be no more convincing evidence of the imperfection of my knowledge than that it gradually increases. Again, although my knowledge can be ever more and more increased, I may not, for this reason, suppose that it can ever be actually infinite; for it can never be so increased as not still to allow of yet further increase. But when I judge God to be actually infinite, I do so as judging that nothing can be added to His sovereign perfection. And lastly, I comprehend that what is objective in an idea cannot be produced by a being that exists potentially only—which properly speaking is nothing—but only by a being that is formal, that is to say, actual. . . .

Here, therefore, there can be no further question in their regard, and from this alone, viz. that I exist, and have in me the idea of a Being sovereignly perfect, that is to say, God, I have forthwith to conclude that His existence is demonstrated in the most evident manner.

It only remains to me to examine how I have obtained this idea. I have not acquired it through the senses, and it is never presented to me unexpectedly, as sensible things are wont to be, when these act, or seem to act, on the external sense-organs. Nor is it a product or fiction of my mind; for it is not in my power to take from or add anything to it. Consequently the only alternative is to allow that it is innate in me, just as is the idea of myself.

Certainly I ought not to find it strange that God, in creating me, has placed this in me, to be, as it were, the mark of the workman imprinted on his work. Nor need the mark be something different from the work itself. From this alone, that God has created me, it is highly likely that He has in some fashion made me in His image and similitude, and that I apprehend this similitude by means of the same faculty by which I apprehend myself—that is to say, when my mind is attentively directed upon myself, not only do I know that I am a thing imperfect, incomplete and dependent on what is other than myself, ever aspiring after something better and greater than myself, but I also know that He on whom I depend possesses in Himself all the great things to which I aspire, and this not indefinitely or potentially only, but really, i.e. actually and infinitely, and that He is thus God. The whole force of this argument, as thus used to prove the existence of God, consists in this, that I recognise that it is not possible that my nature should be what it is, viz. that I should have in me the idea of God, if God did not veritably exist—a God, I say, the idea of whom is in me, who possesses all those high perfections which, however they may transcend my powers of comprehension, I am yet in some fashion able to reach in thought, and who is subject to no defects. And from all this it is sufficiently evident that He cannot be a deceiver, it being manifest by the natural light that all fraud and deception proceed from defect.

But before I examine this conclusion with more care, and before passing to the consideration of other truths which can be obtained by way of it, it seems to me right to linger for a while on the contemplation of this all-perfect God, to ponder at leisure His marvellous attributes, to intuit, to admire, to adore, the incomparable beauty of this inexhaustible light, so far at least as the powers of my mind may permit, dazzled as they are by what they are endeavouring to see. For just as by faith we believe that the supreme felicity of the life to come consists in the contemplation of the Divine majesty, so do we now experience that a similar meditation, though one so much less perfect, can enable us to enjoy the highest contentment of which we are capable in this present life.

Meditation 4

Concerning the True and the False

In these past days I have become so accustomed to detaching my mind from the senses, and have so convincingly noted how very little we can apprehend with certainty regarding things corporeal, how we can know much more regarding the human mind, and even more regarding God, that I shall no longer have difficulty in diverting my thought from things imageable to what, in distinction from all that is material, is purely intelligible. Certainly the idea I have of the human mind, in so far as it is a thinking thing, not extended in length, breadth or depth, and not characterised by anything that appertains to body, is incomparably more distinct than the idea of any corporeal thing. And when I consider that I doubt, that is to say that I am an incomplete and dependent thing, the idea of a being complete and independent, that is to say, of God, then presents itself to my mind with such clearness and distinctness that I can be confident that nothing more evident or more certain can be known by way of our human faculties. I am so confident, owing to this alone, that the idea of God is in me, i.e. that I exist and have the idea, that I can conclude with certainty that God exists, and that my existence depends entirely on Him at every moment of my life. Already, therefore, I here seem to find a path that will lead us from this contemplation of the true God, in whom all the treasures of the sciences and of wisdom are contained, to the knowledge of the other things in the universe.

For, in the first place, I recognise that it is impossible that He should ever deceive me, since in all fraud and deception there is some element of imperfection. The power of deception may indeed seem to be evidence of subtlety or power; yet unquestionably the will to deceive testifies to malice and feebleness, and accordingly cannot be found in God.

Further, I experience in myself a certain power of judging, which undoubtedly I have received from God along with all the other things I possess; and since He does not will to deceive me, it is certain that this God-given faculty cannot, if I use it aright, ever lead me astray.

As to this, no question would remain, did it not seem to follow that I can never err. For if I hold from God all that I possess, and if He has given me no faculty which is deceitful, it seems that I can never be betrayed into error. It is indeed true that when I think only of God, I am aware of nothing which can cause error or falsity. But on reverting to myself, experience at once shows that I am indeed subject to an infinity of errors, and on examining the cause of these more closely, I note that in addition to the real and positive idea of God, that is, of a Being of sovereign perfection, there is also present to me a certain negative idea, so to speak, of nothing, i.e. of what is infinitely far removed from every kind of perfection, and that I am a something intermediate between God and nothingness, that is to say, placed between sovereign Being and not-being in such fashion that while there is in truth nothing in me, in so far as I have been created by sovereign Being, which can deceive me or lead me into error, yet none the less, in so far as I likewise participate in nothingness, i.e. in not-being, in other words, in so far as I am not myself the sovereign Being, I find myself subject to innumerable imperfections, and ought not therefore to be surprised that I should be liable to error. Thus also I come to know that error, in so far as it is error, is not something real depending on God, but only a defect. To incur an error I have therefore no need of any special power assigned me by God, enabling me to do so. I fall into error because the power which God has given me of distinguishing the true from the false is not in me an infinite power.

This does not, however, entirely satisfy me. Error is not a pure negation; it is a privation, i.e. the absence of some knowledge that I ought to possess; and on considering the nature of God, it does not seem possible that He should have given me any faculty which is not perfect of its kind, that is to say which is anywise wanting in the perfection proper to it. For if it be true that the more skilled the artisan the more perfectly accomplished is the work of his hands, how can we allow that anything produced by this sovereign Creator of all things can be other than absolutely perfect in all respects. Certainly God could have created me such that I could never be liable to error; and no less certain is it that He invariably wills what is best. Is it then better that I should be liable to error than that I should not?

On considering this more closely, what first occurs to me is that I need not be surprised if I fail to understand why God acts as He does. Nor may I doubt His existence because of my perhaps finding that there are several other things respecting which I can understand neither for what reason nor how He has created them. Already knowing, as I do, that my nature is extremely weak and limited, and that the nature of God is immense, incomprehensible and infinite, I have no difficulty in recognising that there is an infinity of things in His power, the causes of which transcend my powers of understanding. This consideration is alone sufficient to convince me that the species of cause which we term final is not applicable in respect of physical things; for, as it seems to me, we cannot without foolhardiness inquire into and profess to discover God's inscrutable ends.

I also bethink myself that in inquiring as to whether the works of God are perfect, we should not consider any one creature separately, but the universe of things as a whole. For what, regarded by itself, might perhaps with some semblance of reason appear to be very imperfect, may none the less, when regarded as but a part of the universe, prove to be quite perfect in nature. Thus far, since my resolve has been to doubt of all things, I have as yet known with certainty only my own existence and that of God. But having also thereby come to know the infinite power of God, I am in no position to deny that He may have produced many other things, or at least that He has the power of producing them, so that the existence He has assigned me is no more than that of being a part only in the totality of things.

Consequently, on regarding myself more closely, and on examining what are my errors (for they alone testify to there being imperfection in me), I find that they depend on two concurrent causes, on my power of knowing and on the power of choice, that is, of free will—in other words, on the co-operation of the understanding and the will. For by the understanding alone, I neither affirm nor deny anything, but merely apprehend the ideas of things I can affirm or deny. Viewing the understanding thus precisely, we can say that no error is ever to be found in it. And although there may be an infinity of things in the world of which I have in my understanding no ideas, we cannot on this account say that it is deprived of those ideas as of something which its nature requires, but only that it does not have them, there being indeed no sufficient proof that God ought to have given me a greater power of knowing than He has given me. However skilled an artificer I represent Him to be, I have no reason to think of Him as bound to place in each of His works all the perfections which He can place in some of them. Nor again can I complain that God has not given me a will ample and perfect, that is, a free will. I am conscious of a will so extended as to be subject to no limits. What here, as it seems to me, is truly noteworthy, is that of all the other things which are in me, no one is so perfect and so extensive that I do not recognise it as allowing of being yet greater and more perfect. To take, for example, my faculty of understanding, I at once recognise it as being in me of small extent and extremely limited; and at the same time I frame the idea of another faculty, much more extended and even infinite; and from this alone, that I can represent the latter idea in this way [i.e. as being a faculty that is infinite], I have no difficulty in likewise recognising that it pertains to the nature of God. If in the same way I examine my memory, my imagination, or any other of my faculties, I do not find any which is not in me small and circumscribed, and in God infinite. Free will alone, that is liberty of choice, do I find to be so great in me that I can entertain no idea of any such power possibly greater, so that it is chiefly my will which enables me to know that I bear a certain image and similitude of God. The power of will is indeed incomparably greater in God than in man; the knowledge and the potency which in God are conjoined with it, render it more constant and more efficacious, and in respect of its object extend it to a greater number of things; nevertheless it does not seem to be greater, considered formally and precisely in itself [i.e. as a faculty]. The power of will consists solely in this, that we have the power to do a thing or not to do it (that is to say, to affirm or to deny, to pursue or to shun it), or rather in this alone, that in affirming or denying, pursuing or shunning, what is proposed to us by the understanding, we so act that we have no feeling of being constrained to it by any external force. For in order to be free it is not necessary that I should be indifferent in the choice between alternatives; on the contrary, the more I am inclined towards one of them, whether because I approve it as evidently good and true, or because God in this inward manner determines my inward thinking, the more freely do I choose and embrace it. Divine grace and natural knowledge, so far from diminishing liberty, augment and confirm it. The indifference of which I am aware when for want of a reason I am not carried to one side rather than to another, is the lowest grade of liberty, testifying to a lack of knowledge, i.e. to a certain negation, not to a perfection in the will. Were the true and the good always clear to me, I should never need to deliberate as to what I ought to judge or choose, and I should thus be entirely free, without ever being indifferent.

All this enables me to recognise that the power of will which I have received from God is not of itself the cause of my errors; in its kind it is altogether ample and perfect. Nor is the cause of my errors traceable to my power of understanding or thinking; for since I understand nothing save by the power of understanding which God has given me, undoubtedly all that I apprehend I apprehend rightly, and it is impossible that I should be deceived regarding it. What then is the source of my errors? This alone, that the will is of wider range than the understanding, and that I do not restrain it within

the same limits as the understanding, but extend it to things which I do not understand; and as the will is of itself, in respect of such things, indifferent, it is easily
deflected from the true and the good, and readily falls into error and sin, choosing the
evil in place of the good, or the false in place of the true. . . .

Now if I abstain from all judging of a thing which I do not apprehend sufficiently
clearly and distinctly, it is evident that I am acting rightly and am not deceived.
Should I, on the other hand, decide to deny or affirm, I am not in that case making
a right use of my free will, and should I in so deciding choose the wrong alternative,
it is evident that I am deceived. Even should I decide for what is true, it is by chance
only that I shall be doing so, and still shall not be free from the fault of misusing my
freedom. The natural light teaches us that knowledge, by way of the understanding,
ought always to precede the determination of the will; and it is in the failure to do so
that the privation, which constitutes the form of error, consists. Privation is then, I
say, there in the act, in so far as it proceeds from me; it is not to be found in the faculty
as I have it from God, nor even in the act in so far as it depends on Him [through His
continued upholding of me in existence].

Nor have I any ground for complaint that God has not given me a greater power
of understanding or a natural light stronger than that which He has actually given,
since it is of the very nature of a finite understanding not to apprehend all things, and
of a created understanding to be finite. Having every reason to render thanks to God
who owes me nothing, and who has yet given me all the perfections I possess, I should
be far from thinking Him to have been unjust in depriving me of, or in keeping back,
the other perfections which He has not given me.

Nor have I ground to complain in that He has given me a will more ample than my
understanding. Since the will consists entire in one single thing, and is, so to speak,
indivisible, it would appear that its nature is such that nothing can be taken from it
without destroying it; and certainly the more ample it is, the more reason I have to be
grateful.

Nor, finally, ought I to complain that God concurs with me in framing those
[wrongful] acts of the will, that is to say, the judgments in which I suffer deception. In
so far as they depend on God they are entirely true and good and my ability to form
them is, in its own way, a greater perfection in me than if I were unable to do so. The
privation in which alone the formal [i.e. actual] reason of error or sin consists has no
need of concurrence from God since it is not a thing; and if referred to God as to its
cause, it ought (in conformity with the usage of the Schools) to be entitled negation,
not privation. For it is not in truth an imperfection in God that He has given me the
freedom of assenting or not assenting to things of which He has not placed a clear and
distinct knowledge in my understanding. On the other hand, unquestionably, it is an
imperfection in me that I do not use this freedom aright, rashly passing judgment on
things which I apprehend only obscurely and confusedly. I recognise, indeed, that God
could easily have so created me that, while still remaining free and while still with
only limited knowledge, I should yet not err, viz. by endowing my understanding with
a clear and distinct knowledge of all the things upon which I shall ever have to deliberate, or simply by so deeply engraving on my memory the resolution never to pass judgment on anything of which I have no clear and distinct understanding, that I shall
never lose hold on that resolution. And I easily understand that in so far as I consider
myself alone, as if in the world there were only myself, I should have been much more

perfect than I now am, had God created me in that fashion. But this does not justify me in refusing to recognise that in respect of the universe as a whole it is a greater perfection that certain of its parts should not be exempt from defect than that they should all be exactly alike. And I have, therefore, no right to complain because God, in placing me in the world, has not willed to assign me the nobler, more perfect role. If He has not done so by the first of the means above noted, that which would depend on my having a clear and evident knowledge of all the things upon which I may have to deliberate, at least He has left within my power the other means, viz. that of firmly adhering to the resolution never to pass judgment on things not clearly known to me. For although I am aware of a certain weakness in my nature which prevents me from continuously concentrating my mind on any one thought, I can yet by attentive and oft-repeated meditation so imprint it on my memory that I shall never fail to recall it as often as I have need of it, and so can acquire the habit of not erring.

Inasmuch as it is in this habit that the highest and chief perfection of man consists, I have, I consider, gained not a little by this day's meditation, discovering, as I have done, the cause of error and falsity. Certainly there can be no other cause than that which I have now explained; for so long as I so restrain my will within the limits of my knowledge that it frames no judgment save on things which are clearly and distinctly apprehended by the understanding, I can never be deceived. Since all clear and distinct awareness is undoubtedly something, it cannot owe its origin to nothing, and must of necessity have God as its author—God, I say, who being supremely perfect, cannot be the cause of any error. Consequently, as we have to conclude, all such awareness is true. Nor have I today learned merely what, to escape error, I should avoid, but also what I must do to arrive at knowledge of the truth. Such knowledge is assured to me provided I direct my attention sufficiently to those things which I perfectly understand, separating them from those which I apprehend only confusedly and obscurely. To this task I shall, from now on, give diligent heed.

Meditation 5

Concerning the Essence of Material Things; and again, concerning God, that He exists

Many other questions respecting the attributes of God, and respecting my own proper nature, that is to say, respecting my mind, remain for investigation; and perhaps, on some future occasion, I shall return to them. Meanwhile, having discovered what must be done, and what avoided, in order to arrive at the knowledge of truth, what I have now chiefly to do is to endeavour to emerge from the state of doubt into which I fell in the preceding days respecting material things, and to determine whether, with certainty, anything can be known of them.

But before inquiring as to whether any material things exist outside me, I have first to examine the ideas of them in so far as these are in my thought, and to determine which of them are distinct and which confused.

Beyond question, I image distinctly that quantity which philosophers commonly term continuous, the extension in length, breadth and depth that is in this quantity, or rather in the quantified thing to which it is attributed. Further, I can number in it many diverse parts, and attribute to each of them all sorts of sizes, shapes, locations and local motions, and to each of these motions all degrees of duration.

Not only do I know these things distinctly when considering them in general, I can also, on giving attention to them, apprehend innumerable particulars respecting shapes, number, motion and other such things, which are so evidently true and so accordant with my nature, that on beginning to discover them it does not seem to me that I am learning something new, but rather that I am recollecting what I already knew, i.e. that I am for the first time taking note of things that were already in my mind but to which I had not hitherto directed my attention.

What here seems to me especially noteworthy is that I find in my mind innumerable ideas of things which, even if they do not perhaps exist anywhere outside my thought, yet cannot be said to be in themselves nothing. Though it may be in my power to think or not to think them, they are not framed by me, and possess true and immutable natures of their own. For instance, when I image a triangle, although there is not perhaps and never has been anywhere in the world apart from my thought any such shape, it has yet a certain determinate nature or essence or form which is immutable and eternal, not framed by me, and in no wise dependent on my mind, as appears from the fact that diverse properties can be demonstrated as belonging to the triangle, viz. that its three angles are equal to two right angles, that its greatest side is subtended by its greatest angle and the like, which, whether I will or not, I now clearly recognise as proper to it, although I had no thought whatsoever of them when for the first time I imaged a triangle. It cannot, therefore, be said that they have been framed and invented by me.

Nor does the objection hold that perhaps this idea of the triangle has come into my mind from external things by way of the sense-organs, through my having seen bodies triangularly shaped. I am in a position to think of innumerable other shapes which cannot be suspected of ever having been objects of sense, and of which, no less than of the triangle, I can demonstrate diverse properties, all of them clearly apprehended and therefore assuredly true. Each of these shapes is therefore a something, not a mere nothing; for it is evident that everything true is something; and as I have already shown, all those things which I know clearly and distinctly are true. And even if I had not proved this to be so, the nature of my mind is such that I cannot but assent to what I clearly apprehend, at least while I am so apprehending it. Always, as I recall, even while my mind was chiefly preoccupied with the objects of sense, I recognised as being the most certain of all truths those which relate to shapes and numbers, and all else that pertains to arithmetic and geometry, and in general to pure and abstract mathematics.

Now if, directly on my being able to find an idea of something in my thought, it at once follows that whatever I clearly and distinctly apprehend as pertaining to the thing does in truth belong to it, may I not derive from this an argument for the existence of God? Certainly the idea of God, that is of a being sovereignly perfect, is no less present to me than is that of any shape or number; and I know that an actual and external existence pertains to His nature no less clearly and distinctly than I know that whatever is demonstrable of a shape or number belongs to the nature of the shape or number. Even, therefore, were it the case that not all of what I have been meditating in these preceding days is true, this at least holds that the existence of God ought not to have for me a lesser degree of certainty than I have hitherto been ascribing to mathematical truths.

This, on first hearing, is not immediately evident, seeming to be a sophism. Being accustomed in all other things to distinguish between existence and essence, I readily believe that existence can also be disjoined from the essence of God, and that God can therefore be conceived as not actually existing. But on closer study, it becomes manifest to me that it is no more possible to separate existence from the essence of God than the equality of its three angles to two right angles from the essence of a triangle or the idea of a mountain from that of a valley; so that to think of God (that is, of a being completely perfect) as without existence (that is, as lacking a certain perfection) is as impossible as to think of a mountain without a valley.

Though I cannot think of God save as existing, any more than I can think of a mountain without a valley, yet just as it does not follow that because I cannot think a mountain without a valley, a mountain exists anywhere in the world, so likewise it does not follow that because I think of God as existing that He does in fact exist. My thinking imposes no necessity on things. I can image a winged horse, though there is no existing horse that has wings. May I not in similar fashion be attributing existence to God although there is no God who is existent?

This objection rests on a fallacy. Because I cannot think of a mountain without a valley, it does not indeed follow that there is any mountain or valley in existence, but only that mountain and valley, be they existent or non-existent, are inseparably conjoined each with the other. In the case of God, however, I cannot think Him save as existing; and it therefore follows that existence is inseparable from Him, and that He therefore really exists. It is not that this necessity is brought about by my thought, or that my thought is imposing any necessity on things; on the contrary, the necessity which lies in the thing itself, that is the necessity of God's existence, determines me to think in this way. It is not in my power to think God as lacking existence (i.e. to think of this sovereignly perfect being as devoid of complete perfection) in the manner in which I am free to image a horse with wings or without wings. . . .

Thus, whatever proof or mode of argument I may adopt, it always comes back to this, that it is only the things I apprehend clearly and distinctly which have the power to convince me. And although among the things which I apprehend in this manner some are indeed obvious to everyone, others are manifest only to those who consider them more closely, scrutinising them earnestly. Once they have been discovered, they are, however, not esteemed any less certain than those others. To take, as an example, the right-angled triangle: that the square of the base is equal to the squares of the other two sides is not at first as manifest to us as that the base lies opposite the greatest angle; yet once it has been apprehended we are not less certain of its truth. As regards God, if my mind were not overlaid by so many prejudices, and beset on all sides by the images of sensible things, I should know nothing prior to knowing Him and nothing more easily. For is there anything more evident than that there is a God, that is to say, a sovereign being, and that of all beings He alone has existence as appertaining to His essence? For a proper grasp of this truth close attention has indeed been required. Now, however, I am as completely assured of it as of all that I hold most certain; and now also I have come to recognise that so absolutely dependent on it are all those other certainties, that save through knowledge of it nothing whatsoever can be perfectly known.

But while my nature is such that I cannot but accept as true all that I apprehend in a really clear and distinct manner, it is also such that I am unable to keep my mind always fixed on one and the same object. Often I have occasion to recall having judged a thing to be true without at the same time being aware of the reasons that determined me in so doing; and it may happen meanwhile that other reasons are presented to me—such as would readily cause me to change my opinion, were I ignorant that there is a God. I should then have no true and certain knowledge of anything; but only vague and vacillating opinions. When for instance I consider the nature of the triangle, instructed, as I have been, in the principles of geometry, it is quite evident to me that its three angles are equal to two right angles; and so long as I attend to the demonstrations I cannot but believe this to be true. None the less, as soon as I cease to attend to the demonstration, and although I may still recollect having had a clear comprehension of it, I may readily come to doubt its truth, if I do not know that there is a God. For I can then persuade myself of being so constituted by nature as to be easily deceived even in those things which I believe myself to apprehend in the most evident manner, especially when I recollect that frequently I have held to be true and certain what afterwards other reasons have constrained me to reckon as false.

But once I have recognised that there is a God, and that all things depend on Him and that He is not a deceiver, and from this, in turn, have inferred that all things which I clearly and distinctly apprehend are of necessity true, then, even although I may no longer be attending to the reasons on account of which I have judged this to be so (provided only I bear in mind that I once recognised them clearly and distinctly), no contrary reason can be brought forward sufficient to lead me to doubt it; and the knowledge I have of it is thus true and certain.

Thus, in this evident manner, I see that the certainty and truth of all knowledge depends on knowledge of the true God, and that before I knew Him I could have no perfect knowledge of any other thing. And now that I know Him, I have the means of acquiring a perfect knowledge of innumerable things, not only in respect of God Himself and other intelligible things, but also in respect of that corporeal nature which is the object of pure mathematics.

Meditation 6

Concerning the Existence of Material Things and the Real Distinction between the Mind and Body of Man

There now remains only the inquiry as to whether material things exist. This at least I already know, that in so far as they are dealt with by pure mathematics, they are possible existents, since, as there treated, they are apprehended clearly and distinctly. Indubitably God possesses the power of producing everything that I am capable of apprehending distinctly; and I have never considered anything to be impossible to Him save what I found to be impossible of distinct apprehension. Further, the faculty of imagination, of which, as experience tells me, I make use when I apply myself to the consideration of material things, is able to persuade me of their existence; for when I attentively consider what imagination is, I find that it is nothing but a certain application of the cognitive faculty to a body which is immediately present to it and therefore existent.

To make this plain, I shall first dwell on the difference there is between the imagination and pure intellection. For instance, when I image a triangle I not only apprehend it to be a shape bounded by three lines, but also by concentrating my attention on these three lines I intuit them as present, this being what I term imaging. When, however, I wish to think of a chiliagon, I do indeed apprehend it to be a shape composed of a thousand sides, and do so just as easily as in apprehending a triangle to be composed of three sides only. I cannot, however, image the thousand sides of a chiliagon as I do the three sides of a triangle, nor intuit them as present, as it were, with the eyes of the mind. And although in accordance with the habit I have of always imaging something when I think of corporeal things, it may happen that I confusedly represent to myself some shape, it is yet evident that this shape is not a chiliagon, since it in no wise differs from what I represent to myself when I think of a myriagon or any other shape of many sides, nor would it be of any use in determining the properties distinguishing a chiliagon from those other polygons. If, however, it be a pentagon which is under question, while I can indeed, as in the case of the chiliagon, apprehend its shape without the aid of the imagination, I am able also to image it, applying my mind attentively to each of its five sides and the area they enclose. Now in thus imaging its shape, I am plainly aware of having to make a certain special effort of the mind, an effort not required in merely thinking of it; and this special effort of the mind makes clear to me the difference there is between imagination and pure intellection.

Therewith I also note that this power of imaging which is in me, in so far as it differs from the power of understanding, is nowise necessary to my essential being, that is to say, to the essence of my mind. For even if I did not have it, I should undoubtedly none the less remain the same as I now am; and from this, it seems, we may conclude that my power of imaging depends on something different from me, i.e. from my mind. And I easily understand that if there exist some body to which the mind is so united that it is able, when it pleases, to apply itself to it, i.e. as it were, to contemplate it, it may in this way be able to image corporeal things. If this be so, this mode of thinking differs from pure intellection solely in this, that the mind, in intellection, is turning in some way in upon itself, taking note of some one of the ideas which it possesses in itself, whereas when imaging it is turning itself towards the body and is intuiting in it something conformed to the idea which it has formed for itself or has apprehended by way of the senses. Now if it be the case that body exists, I can, I say, easily understand that the imaging may be carried out in this manner. There is indeed no other way equally convincing of accounting for it; and for this reason I conjecture that body probably does exist. The conjecture [as thus arrived at] is, however, probable only. For however careful and comprehensive my inquiries may be, I nevertheless do not find that even from what is distinct in the idea I have of corporeal nature by way of these imagings, any argument can be obtained which justifies my concluding, in a necessary manner, the existence of any body.

Now I am accustomed to image many other things besides that corporeal nature which is the object of pure mathematics, viz. colours, sounds, tastes, pain and the like, though none of them so distinctly. And inasmuch as I apprehend them much better by way of the senses (by the mediation of which and of memory they seem to have reached the imagination), it is proper that, for the more convenient examination of them, I should likewise examine the nature of sense and inquire whether from those ideas which are apprehended by this mode of thinking—the mode which I entitle sensing—I can obtain any certain proof of the existence of corporeal things.

First, I shall recall to mind the things which, as having been sensed, I have hitherto held to be true, and what my grounds were for so regarding them. Secondly, I shall then examine the reasons which afterwards led me to doubt of them. And finally, I shall consider what I ought now to believe in regard to them.

From the start, then, I have sensed myself as having a head, hands, feet and the other members of which this body—a body I considered to be part of myself, and possibly even the whole of myself—is composed. I also sensed this body as being located among other bodies by which it could be affected in many ways, beneficial or harmful, being made aware of what was beneficial by a certain sensation of pleasure and of what was harmful by a sensation of pain. In addition to pleasure and pain, I was aware in myself of hunger, thirst, and other such appetites, as also of certain corporeal inclinations to joy, sorrow, anger, and other such affections. On the other hand, as foreign to myself, I sensed, besides the extension, shapes and movements of bodies, also their hardness, heat and other tactual qualities, and in addition, light, colours, odours, tastes and sounds, the variety of which enabled me to distinguish from one another the sky, the Earth, the sea, and all the other bodies.

Assuredly, since the ideas of all these qualities were claiming my attention, and since it was they alone that I properly and immediately sensed, it was not without reason that I thought I was sensing certain things plainly different from my thinking, namely, bodies from which those ideas proceeded. For as experience showed me, they presented themselves to me without my consent being required, and in such fashion that I could not sense any object, however I might wish to do so, save on its being present to the sense-organ, and was unable not to sense it when it was present.

Further, since the ideas I received by way of the senses were much more lively, better defined, and even in their way more distinct, than any of those which I could deliberately and knowingly frame for myself, it seemed impossible that they could have proceeded from myself; and it followed, therefore, that they must have been caused in me by other things. Having no information regarding these things beyond what these same ideas gave me, the only supposition that could then commend itself to me was that they resemble the ideas. And because I likewise recalled that formerly I had relied more on the senses than on reason, and had observed that the ideas which I framed for myself were not so well defined as those which I apprehended by way of sense, and were for the most part composed of parts of those latter, I was readily persuaded that I had not in my understanding any idea not previously sensed.

Nor was it without reason that I regarded the body, which by a certain special right I called my own, as belonging to me more closely than any other. I could never, indeed, be separated from it as from other bodies; I felt in it, and on account of it, all my passions and all my affections; I was aware of pain and the titillation of pleasure in its parts, and not in the parts of the other bodies located outside it.

When, however, I inquired why from some—I know not what—sensing of pain a certain sadness of mind follows, and a certain joy on the sensing of pleasure, or why that strange twitching of the stomach which I call hunger should put me in mind of taking food, and dryness of throat of drinking, I could, as in other experiences of this kind, give no reason, save that I am so taught by nature. For assuredly there is no affinity, none at least that I can understand, between this twitching of the stomach and the desire to eat, any more than between the sensing of a thing which causes pain and the thought of sadness which springs from this sensing. And in the same way, it seemed to me, all the other judgments which I was accustomed to pass on the objects of sense had been taught me by nature. For I observed that they were formed in me before I had the leisure to weigh and consider any reasons which might oblige me to make them.

In due course, however, numerous experiences by degrees sapped the faith I had thus reposed in the senses. As I from time to time observed, towers which from afar seemed round on closer view appeared square, colossal statutes erected on the summits of these towers appeared small when similarly viewed from below. In innumerable other instances I similarly found the judgments which concerned the things of the external senses to be erroneous: nor indeed only those based on the external senses, but those also which are based on the internal senses. What can be more internal than pain? Yet I have been assured by men whose arm or leg has been amputated, that it still seemed to them that they occasionally felt pain in the limb they had lost—thus giving me ground to think that I could not be quite certain that a pain I endured was indeed due to the limb in which I seemed to feel it.

To these grounds of doubt I have lately added two others of the widest generality. The first of these was that there is nothing of all that I believed myself to be sensing when awake which I cannot think of as being also sometimes sensed during sleep; and since I do not believe that the things I seem to sense in dreams come to me from things located outside me, I no longer found any ground for believing this of the things I seem to sense while awake. Secondly, since I was still ignorant of the Author of my being, or rather was feigning myself to be so, I saw nothing to prevent my being so constituted by nature that I might be deceived even in those things which appeared to me to be unquestionably true.

As to the grounds on which I had before been persuaded of the truth of these things, I had no difficulty in countering them. For inasmuch as I seem to be inclined by nature to many things from which reason was dissuading me, I considered that I ought not to place much confidence in its teaching; and though my sensuous apprehensions do not depend on my will, I did not think that I ought on this ground to conclude that they proceed from things other than myself. There can perhaps exist in me some faculty hitherto unknown to me, which produces them.

Now that I begin to know myself better and to discover the Author of my being, I do not in truth think that I ought rashly to admit all the things which the senses may seem to teach; but neither do I think that they should all be called in doubt.

In the first place, since I know that all the things I clearly and distinctly apprehend can be created by God exactly as I apprehend them, my being able to apprehend one thing apart from another is, in itself, sufficient to make me certain that the one is different from the other, or at least that it is within God's power to posit them separately; and even though I do not comprehend by what power this separation comes about, I shall have no option but to view them as different. Accordingly, simply from knowing that I exist, and that, meantime, I do not observe any other thing as evidently pertaining to my nature, i.e. to my essence, except this only, that I am a thinking thing, I rightly conclude that my essence consists in this alone, that I am a thinking thing (i.e. a substance, the whole nature or essence of which consists in thinking). And although possibly (or rather certainly, as I shall shortly be declaring) I have a body with which I am very closely conjoined, yet since on the one hand I have a clear and distinct idea of myself, in so far as I am only a thinking unextended thing, and on the other hand a distinct idea of the body, in so far as it is only an extended unthinking thing, it is certain that I am truly distinct from my body, and can exist without it.

I further find in myself faculties of thinking which are quite special modes of thinking, distinct from myself, viz. the faculties of imaging and sensing; I can clearly and distinctly apprehend myself as complete without them, but not them without the self, i.e. without an intelligent substance in which they reside. For in the notion we have of them, or (to use the terms of the Schools) in their formal concept, they include some sort of intellection, and I am thereby enabled to recognise that they are at once related to, and distinguished from, the self, as being its modes (just as shapes, movements, and the other modes and accidents of bodies are in respect of the bodies which uphold them).

I am also aware in me of certain faculties, such as the power of changing location, of assuming diverse postures, and the like, which cannot be thought, and cannot therefore exist, any more than can the preceding, apart from some substance in which they reside. But evidently, since the clear and distinct apprehension of these faculties involves the feature of extension, but not any intellection, they must, if they indeed exist, belong to some substance which is corporeal, i.e. extended and unthinking. Now there is, indeed, a certain passive faculty of sense, i.e. of receiving and knowing the ideas of sensible things, but this would be useless to me if there did not also exist in me, or in some other being, an active faculty capable of producing or effecting these ideas. This active faculty cannot, however, be in me—not at least in so far as I am only a thinking thing—since it does not presuppose intellection, and since the ideas present themselves to me without my contributing in any way to their so doing, and often even against my will. This faculty must therefore exist in some substance different from me—a substance that, as already noted, contains, either formally or eminently, all the reality which is objectively [i.e. by way of representation] in the ideas produced by the faculty, and this substance is either body, i.e. corporeal nature, in which there is contained formally, i.e. actually, all that is objectively, i.e. by representation, in those ideas; or it is God Himself, or some creature nobler than body, in which all of it is eminently contained.

But since God is no deceiver, it is evident that He does not of Himself, and immediately, communicate those ideas to me. Nor does He do so by way of some creature in which their objective reality is not contained formally [i.e. actually], but only eminently. For as He has given me no faculty whereby I could discover this to be the case, but on the contrary a very strong inclination to believe that those ideas are conveyed to me by corporeal things, I do not see how He could be defended against the charge of deception, were the ideas produced otherwise than by corporeal things. We have, therefore, no option save to conclude that corporeal things do indeed exist.

Yet they are not perhaps exactly such as we apprehend by way of the senses; in many instances they are apprehended only obscurely and confusedly. But we must at least admit that whatever I there clearly and distinctly apprehend, i.e. generally speaking, everything comprised in the object of pure mathematics, is to be found in them. As regards those other things which are only particular, such as that the Sun is of this or that magnitude and shape, and the like, or as regards those things which are apprehended less clearly, such as light, sound, pain and the like, however dubious and uncertain all of these may be, yet inasmuch as God is no deceiver and that there cannot therefore, in the opinions I form, be any falsity for the correction of which He has not given me some faculty sufficient thereto, I may, I believe, confidently conclude that in regard to these things also the means of avoiding error are at my disposal.

Thus there can be no question that all those things in which I am instructed by nature contain some truth; for by nature, considered in general, I now understand no other than either God Himself or the order of created things as instituted by Him, and by my nature in particular I understand the totality of all those things which God has given me.

Now there is nothing which nature teaches me more expressly, or more sensibly, than that I have a body which is adversely affected when I sense pain, and stands in need of food and drink when I suffer hunger or thirst, etc.; and consequently I ought not to doubt there being some truth in all this.

Nature also teaches me by these sensings of pain, hunger, thirst, etc., that I am not lodged in my body merely as a pilot in a ship, but so intimately conjoined, and as it were intermingled with it, that with it I form a unitary whole. Were not this the case, I should not sense pain when my body is hurt, being, as I should then be, merely a thinking thing, but should apprehend the wound in a purely cognitive manner, just as a sailor apprehends by sight any damage to his ship; and when my body has need of food and drink I should apprehend this expressly, and not be made aware of it by confused sensings of hunger, thirst, pain, etc. For these sensings of hunger, thirst, pain, etc., are in truth merely confused modes of thinking, arising from and dependent on the union, and, as it were, the intermingling of mind and body. . . .

Many other things, however, that may seem to have been taught me by nature, are not learned from her, but have gained a footing in my mind only through a certain habit I have of judging inconsiderately. Consequently, as easily happens, the judgments I pass are erroneous: for example in the judgment that all space in which there is nothing capable of affecting my senses is a vacuum, that in a hot body there is something similar to the idea of heat which is in my mind, that in a white or green body there is the very whiteness or greenness which I am sensing, that in a bitter or sweet body there are these very tastes, and so in other like instances; that the stars, towers and other distant objects are of the sizes and shapes they exhibit to my eyes, etc.

In order, however, that there may in this regard be no lack of distinctness of apprehension, I must define more accurately what I ought to mean, when I speak of being taught by nature. Nature I am here taking in a more restricted sense than when it signifies the totality of all that God has given me. Many things included in that totality belong to the mind alone, e.g. the notion I have of the truth that what has once taken place can no longer not have taken place, and all those other truths which are known by the natural light, without the aid of the body; of these latter I am not here speaking. The term nature likewise extends to many things which pertain only to body, such as its having weight, and the like, and with these also I am not here dealing, but only with what God has given me as a being composed of body as well as of mind. Nature, taken in this special [restricted] sense, does indeed teach me to shun whatever causes me to sense pain, or to pursue what causes me to sense pleasure, and other things of that sort; but I do not find that it teaches me, by way of sensory apprehensions, that we should, without previous careful and mature mental examination of them, likewise draw conclusions regarding things located in the world outside us; for, as would seem, it is the task of the mind alone, not of the composite mind-body, to discern truth in questions of this kind.

Thus, although the impression a star makes on my eye is no larger than that made by the flame of a small candle, there is yet in me no real or positive power determining me to believe that the star is no larger than the flame; it is merely that, without reason, I have so judged from my earliest years. And though on approaching fire I sense heat, and on approaching it too closely I sense pain, this is no ground for concluding that something resembling the heat is in the fire and also something resembling the pain, but only that in it there is something, whatever it be, which produces in me these sensations of heat and pain.

So also, although there are spaces in which I find nothing to affect my senses, it does not follow that in them there is no body, for in this, as in many other matters, I have been accustomed to pervert the order of nature. These sensuous apprehensions have been given me by nature only as testifying to my mind what things are beneficial or harmful to the composite whole of which it is a part. For this they are indeed sufficiently clear and distinct. But what I have done is to use them as rules sufficiently reliable to be employed in the immediate determination of the essence of bodies external to me; and, as so employed, their testimony cannot be other than obscure and confused.

I have already sufficiently examined how it happens that, notwithstanding the sovereign goodness of God, falsity has to be recognised as occurring in judgments of this kind. . . .

And certainly, this consideration is of the greatest help in enabling me not only to recognise all the errors to which my nature is subject, but also in making it easier for me to avoid or to amend them. For in knowing that in respect of those things which concern the well-being of the body, all my senses more frequently indicate the true than the false, and being able almost always to avail myself of more than one sense in the examining of any one thing, and being able also to make use of my memory for the connecting of the present with the past, and of my understanding for the reviewing (as already done) of all the causes of error, I ought no longer to fear that the things ordinarily exhibited to me by sense are false. I ought indeed to reject as hyperbolical and ridiculous all the doubts of these past days, more especially that regarding sleep, as being indistinguishable from the waking state. How marked, I now find, is the difference between them! Our memory can never connect our dreams with one another and with the whole course of our lives, in the manner in which we are wont to connect the things which happen to us while awake. If, while I am awake, someone should all of a sudden appear to me, and as suddenly disappear, as happens in dreams, and in such fashion that I could not know whence he came or whither he went, quite certainly it would not be unreasonable to esteem it a spectre, that is, a phantom formed in my brain, rather than a real man. When, on the other hand, in apprehending things, I know the place whence they have come, and that in which they are, and the time at which they present themselves to me, and while doing so can connect them, uninterruptedly, with the course of my life as a whole, I am completely certain that what I thus experience is taking place while I am awake, and not in dreams. And if after having summoned to my aid all my senses, my memory and my understanding, in scrutiny of these occurrences, I find that none of them presents me with what is at variance with any other, I ought no longer to entertain the least doubt as to their truth. God being no deceiver, it cannot be that I am here being misled.

But since the necessities of active living do not always allow of the delay required for so accurate a scrutiny, it must be confessed that the life of man is, in respect of this and that particular, frequently subject to error, and that we have thus to acknowledge the weakness of our nature.

SELECTED BIBLIOGRAPHY

Descartes, René. *The Philosophical Writings of Descartes.* 2 vols. Trans. John Cottingham, Robert Stoothoff, and Dugald Murdoch. Cambridge: Cambridge University Press, 1984–85.

Beck, L.J. *The Metaphysics of Descartes: A Study of the "Meditations."* New York: Oxford University Press, 1965.

Caton, Hiram. *The Origin of Subjectivity: An Essay on Descartes.* New Haven, Conn.: Yale University Press, 1973.

Cottingham, John. *Descartes.* New York: Basil Blackwell, 1986.

Curley, E.M. *Descartes against the Skeptics.* Cambridge, Mass.: Harvard University Press, 1978.

Doney, Willis. *Descartes: A Collection of Critical Essays.* Garden City, N.Y.: Doubleday, 1967.

Frankfurt, Harry. *Demons, Dreamers, and Madmen: The Defense of Reason in Descartes's Meditations.* Indianapolis: Bobbs-Merrill, 1970.

Gibson, A. Boyce. *The Philosophy of Descartes.* New York: Russell & Russell, 1967.

Grene, Marjorie. *Descartes.* Minneapolis: University of Minnesota Press, 1985.

Kenny, Anthony. *Descartes: A Study of His Philosophy.* New York: Random House, 1968.

Ree, Jonathan. *Descartes.* New York: Pica Press, 1974.

Smith, Norman Kemp. *New Studies in the Philosophy of Descartes.* London: Macmillan, 1952.

_____. *Studies in the Cartesian Philosophy.* London: Macmillan, 1902.

Sorell, Tom. *Descartes.* New York: Oxford University Press, 1987.

Williams, Bernard. *Descartes: The Project of Pure Inquiry.* Harmondsworth, England: Penguin, 1978.

Wilson, Margaret D. *Descartes.* London: Routledge, Chapman and Hall, 1978.

Thomas Hobbes

Thomas Hobbes (1588–1679) is one of the *enfants terribles* of modern philosophy, vilified for several centuries as a wicked, blasphemous atheist. But though his vision of human affairs is not particularly pretty, the simplicity, honesty, and power of his depiction of human nature cannot be denied.

Hobbes was born in Malmesbury, England. Fear was his constant companion, owing, he claimed, to his mother's fright over the approach of the Spanish Armada. Nevertheless, he lived a long and productive life. After completing a degree in classical studies at Magdalen College, Oxford, he entered the service of the Cavendishes, earls of Devonshire, with whom he was to spend a total of fifty-seven years in three different periods. He also served as secretary to Sir Francis Bacon and published a translation of Thucydides' *Peloponnesian War* during the early period of his life.

In 1629, during his second trip to the Continent, Hobbes discovered geometry. Aubrey's well-known account of it captures the flavor best:

> He was forty yeares old before he looked on Geometry; which happened accidentally. Being in a Gentleman's Library, Euclid's Elements lay open, and 'twas the 47 El. libri L. He read the Proposition. "By G—," sayd he (he would now and then sweare an emphaticall Oath by way of emphasis) "*this is impossible.*" So he reads the demonstration of it, which referred him back to such a Proposition;

which proposition he read. That referred him back to another, which he also read. *Et sic deincips* [and so on] that at last he was demonstratively convinced of that trueth. This made him in love with Geometry.[1]

A few years later, on his third trip to the Continent, Hobbes became well acquainted with many of the leading proponents of the new science of motion and undertook a special trip to meet Galileo. It is during this fertile period that Hobbes conceived of applying the methods of the new sciences to law and politics, the first result of which was "The Elements of Law Natural and Politic," published in 1640. His doctrines, never popular, drove against the antiroyalist winds prevailing in England at the time, so he fled to France, where he continued elaborating his philosophy in several different works as well as pursuing his scientific and mathematical investigations and serving as mathematics tutor to Charles II. His political reflections were given particular urgency by the destructive civil war in England, for which Hobbes hoped his doctrines would provide a resolution. *Leviathan* was published in 1651, and though his doctrine had not changed substantially, it incurred the wrath of the exiled royalists and the French government as well, so Hobbes returned to England. There, too, *Leviathan* was banned from further publication, for virtually everyone thought it a dangerous book.

Hobbes continued writing on diverse subjects until his death, at the age of ninety-one. Though he has often been attacked as godless, for holding the lowest possible view of humanity, and for espousing absolute monarchy, Hobbes set the parameters of modern political theory.

Philosophy

Thomas Hobbes shares with his contemporary Descartes the belief that proper method is absolutely fundamental to achievement in philosophy. Also like Descartes, his model of proper method came from mathematics, particularly geometry. Through his acquaintance with scientists at the university in Padua (among whom was Galileo), he interpreted this as the method of resolution and composition: to understand any complex phenomenon, one needs to resolve it into its simplest, most elemental factors and then show how it is composed out of those elements.

Hobbes believed that the new mathematical science of motion being elaborated by Galileo, Descartes, and others had isolated the elements and laws of the world. All things being more or less complex bodies acting in accordance with the universal laws of motion, there is no need to postulate any immaterial substances. Human behavior at every level, Hobbes believed, is as susceptible to the scientific method of resolution and composition as any other phenomenon, and Hobbes devoted several works to laying out his theory of the nature of human action and interaction.

Life is a form of self-sustaining internal motion. Sentient beings, humans in particular, have the springs of their external motion in complex internal motions—the imagination and thought. The elements of human behavior are our appetites and aversions, some of which are inborn and some acquired. Our primary instinct is survival—but

---

1. Aubrey, *Brief Lives.*

Hobbes does not establish once and for all what the inborn appetites and aversions of humanity are, and debate has long raged about whether Hobbes thinks we are necessarily egoists, always selfish in our motivations, or we can, at least sometimes, act out of regard for others. Everyone, however, desires power, for power is simply the ability to get what one wants.

Hobbes calls human interaction abstracted from all historical and contingent ties between people "the state of nature." In such a state we are all roughly equal in power. Nor is there anything in the human condition itself to bind anyone to any particular course of action; therefore, apart from any bonds we have ourselves assumed, individuals each have the right to provide for themselves as they see fit. However, three human characteristics make conflict inevitable: competitiveness, diffidence (distrust of other people), and glory (the pleasure of feeling one's own power). Without an external authority regulating human interaction, Hobbes claims, we would find ourselves in a war of all against all, a miserable condition in which life itself is "solitary, poor, nasty, brutish, and short."

It is obviously not in people's interest to perpetuate the war of all against all. It is in their own rational self-interest to contract with one another, resigning their rights of self-protection against one another. This contract, however, would be worthless were not an authority capable of enforcing it established at the same time. This authority, to whom all people have surrendered their rights and who is charged with protecting its subjects, is the sovereign, the absolute power, who, as enforcer of the contract, is not itself subject to the contract.

In accordance with his method of resolution and composition, Hobbes wants to show how social structures and patterns of social activity emerge spontaneously out of the natural interactions of individual people. In setting this as a goal, however, Hobbes instituted a revolution in social and political thought. For it had been the common assumption since antiquity that the natural condition of the human race was *social*, that is, as Aristotle had insisted, that we are political animals. Hobbes rejected the prevailing idea that society and its structure are either natural or divine institutions. Instead, he attempted to derive all legitimate political structures from a rational agreement among rational, self-interested humans unencumbered by prior social allegiances—humans in a "state of nature." Hobbes claimed that the result of such an agreement would be an absolute monarchy in which the monarch serves not by the will of God but rather by the will of his or her subjects.

Demonstrating the rationality of social cooperation without justifying tyranny has remained a problem to this day. But Hobbes's work was a watershed in political and social theory, for the source of the legitimacy of government could no longer be God but the people themselves, the governed.

The Reading Context

Hobbes is the first great analyst to examine the conditions under which peace can be obtained in a bourgeois, free-market society. This assures his continued relevance. Few commentators, however, have been comfortable with Hobbes's solution to this problem. Despite the clarity and directness of his analysis, his conclusions are not the only ones available. As you read Hobbes, try to identify assumptions that should be challenged.

His assumptions about the natural behavioral patterns of his fellow humans often seem particularly pessimistic. Hobbes wrote during a period of great social upheaval —the English Civil War. Even if Hobbes's picture of humanity seems overdrawn in comparison with our own peacetime experience, is it perhaps an accurate depiction of humanity in time of war?

A Note on the Text

The most recent complete edition of Hobbes's English writings was published in 1839, edited by W. Molesworth. This edition has become the standard and serves as the text here. Molesworth's pagination is indicated in the margins. Molesworth modernized Hobbes's seventeenth-century English to nineteenth-century standards, and these modernizations have been allowed to stand. The publishing history of *Leviathan*, however, stands in further need of clarification, for several pirated editions of the work were also published, and it is quite possible that Molesworth's edition is not based on the most reliable text. For further notes on the state of the texts of *Leviathan*, see C.B. Macpherson's edition.

Reading Questions

1. What does Hobbes think a mind is? What does he think having a sensation or a thought is? How would Hobbes distinguish humans from other animals?
2. Hobbes believed that the world is a deterministic mechanism, yet he also believed that there is ample room for human freedom. How does Hobbes reconcile freedom and determinism?
3. What are the governing motives of humanity, according to Hobbes? Is a Hobbesian person purely egocentric, acting always for his or her own interests?
4. Why does Hobbes believe that left to themselves, humans will inevitably end up fighting? Why is the state of nature a state of war?
5. Would denying that humans have ever lived in a "state of nature" damage the very foundations of Hobbes's political theory?
6. Hobbes says that no laws are binding unless there is some coercive force to ensure obedience, yet he also names a number of "natural laws"; how could these have any force in the state of nature?
7. Consider Locke's question: "Are men so foolish that they take care to avoid what mischiefs may be done them by polecats or foxes, but are content, nay think it safety, to be devoured by lions?"[2] If Hobbes's reason for instituting a powerful sovereign is to provide protection from the depredations of random individuals in the state of nature, none of whom is particularly strong, why would he invest a monarch with so much power and authority that protection from his whims would be impossible?
8. What limitations does Hobbes believe restrict the power of a government?

---

2. John Locke, *Second Treatise on Government*, sec. 93.

9. Must a Hobbesian subject do *whatever* the sovereign commands? Could Hobbes countenance a right of revolt?
10. Hobbes justifies governmental structures and laws by reference to *prudential* considerations. Does this make these structures and laws *morally* binding on us?

Leviathan

Or the Matter, Form, and Power of a
Commonwealth Ecclesiastical and Civil

Introduction

Nature, the art whereby God hath made and governs the world, is by the *art* of man, as in many other things, so in this also imitated, that it can make an artificial animal. For seeing life is but a motion of limbs, the beginning whereof is in some principal part within; why may we not say, that all *automata* (engines that move themselves by springs and wheels as doth a watch) have an artificial life: For what is the *heart*, but a *spring*; and the *nerves*, but so many *strings*; and the *joints*, but so many *wheels*, giving motion to the whole body, such as was intended by the artificer? *Art* goes yet further, imitating that rational and most excellent work of nature, *man*. For by art is created that great LEVIATHAN called a COMMONWEALTH, or STATE, in Latin CIVITAS, which is but an artificial man; though of greater stature and strength than the natural, for whose protection and defence it was intended. . . .

Part I
Of Man

Chapter 1

Of sense

Concerning the thoughts of man, I will consider them first singly, and afterwards in   1
train, or dependence upon one another. Singly, they are every one a *representation* or *appearance*, of some quality, or other accident of a body without us, which is commonly called an *object*. Which object worketh on the eyes, ears, and other parts of a man's body; and by diversity of working, produceth diversity of appearances.

    The original of them all, is that which we call SENSE, for there is no conception in a man's mind, which hath not at first, totally, or by parts, been begotten upon the organs of sense. The rest are derived from that original. . . .

    The cause of sense, is the external body, or object, which presseth the organ proper   2
to each sense, either immediately, as in the taste and touch; or mediately, as in seeing, hearing, and smelling; which pressure, by the mediation of the nerves, and other strings and membranes of the body, continued inwards to the brain and heart, causeth there a resistance, or counter-pressure, or endeavour of the heart to deliver itself, which endeavour, because *outward*, seemeth to be some matter without. And this *seeming*, or *fancy*, is that which men call sense. . . . Which qualities, called *sensible*, are in the object, that causeth them, but so many several motions of the matter, by which it presseth our organs diversely. Neither in us that are pressed, are they any thing else, but divers motions; for motion produceth nothing but motion. But their appearance to us is fancy, the same waking, that dreaming. . . . And though at some certain dis-

---

From Thomas Hobbes, *English Works* (vol. 3), ed. Sir W. Molesworth (London: J. Bohn, 1840).

tance, the real and very object seem invested with the fancy it begets in us; yet still the
3   object is one thing, the image or fancy is another. . . .

Chapter 2

Of imagination

4   . . . When a body is once in motion, it moveth, unless something else hinder it, eternally; and whatsoever hindreth it, cannot in an instant, but in time, and by degrees,
quite extinguish it. . . . After the object is removed, or the eye shut, we still retain an
image of the thing seen, though more obscure than when we see it. . . . IMAGINATION
5   therefore is nothing but *decaying sense*; and is found in men, and many other living
creatures, as well sleeping, as waking.

The decay of sense in men waking, is not the decay of the motion made in sense;
but an obscuring of it, in such manner as the light of the sun obscureth the light of
the stars. . . . Any object being removed from our eyes, though the impression it made
in us remain, yet other objects more present succeeding, and working on us, the imagination of the past is obscured, and made weak, as the voice of a man is in the noise
of the day. From whence it followeth, that the longer the time is, after the sight or
sense of any object, the weaker is the imagination. . . . This *decaying sense*, when we
would express the thing itself, I mean *fancy* itself, we call *imagination*, as I said before:
6   but when we would express the decay, and signify that the sense is fading, old, and
past, it is called *memory*. So that imagination and memory are but one thing, which
for divers considerations hath divers names.

Much memory, or memory of many things, is called *experience*. Again, imagination
being only of those things which have been formerly perceived by sense, either all
at once, or by parts at several times; the former, which is the imagining the whole object
as it was presented to the sense, is *simple* imagination, as when one imagineth a man,
or horse, which he hath seen before. The other is *compounded*; as when, from the sight
of a man at one time, and of a horse at another, we conceive in our mind a Centaur. . . .
11   The imagination that is raised in man, or any other creature indued with the faculty
of imagining, by words, or other voluntary signs, is that we generally call *understanding*;
and is common to man and beast. For a dog by custom will understand the call, or the
rating of his master; and so will many other beasts. That understanding which is peculiar to man, is the understanding not only his will, but his conceptions and thoughts,
by the sequel and contexture of the names of things into affirmations, negations, and
other forms of speech; and of this kind of understanding I shall speak hereafter.

Chapter 3

Of the consequence or train of imaginations

By *Consequence*, or TRAIN of thoughts, I understand that succession of one thought to
another, which is called, to distinguish it from discourse in words, *mental discourse*.

When a man thinketh on any thing whatsoever, his next thought after, is not
altogether so casual as it seems to be. Not every thought to every thought succeeds
indifferently. But as we have no imagination, whereof we have not formerly had sense,
in whole, or in parts; so we have no transition from one imagination to another,
whereof we never had the like before in our senses. The reason whereof is this. All

fancies are motions within us, relics of those made in the sense: and those motions
that immediately succeeded one another in the sense, continue also together after
sense: insomuch as the former coming again to take place, and be predominant, the
latter followeth, by coherence of the matter moved, in such manner, as water upon a
plane table is drawn which way any one part of it is guided by the finger. But because
in sense, to one and the same thing perceived, sometimes one thing, sometimes
another succeedeth, it comes to pass in time, that in the imagining of any thing, there
is no certainty what we shall imagine next; only this is certain, it shall be something
that succeeded the same before, at one time or another.   **12**

This train of thoughts, or mental discourse, is of two sorts. The first is *unguided,
without design*, and inconstant; wherein there is no passionate thought, to govern and
direct those that follow, to itself, as the end and scope of some desire, or other passion:
in which case the thoughts are said to wander, and seem impertinent one to another,
as in a dream....

The second is more constant; as being *regulated* by some desire, and design....   **13**

The train of regulated thoughts is of two kinds: one, when of an effect imagined we
seek the causes, or means that produce it: and this is common to man and beast. The
other is, when imagining any thing whatsoever, we seek all the possible effects, that
can by it be produced; that is to say, we imagine what we can do with it, when we have
it.... In sum, the discourse of the mind, when it is governed by design, is nothing but   **14**
seeking, or the faculty of invention,... a hunting out of the causes, of some effect,
present or past; or of the effects, of some present or past cause....

A *sign* is the evident antecedent of the consequent; and contrarily, the consequent   **15**
of the antecedent, when the like consequences have been observed, before: and the
oftener they have been observed, the less uncertain is the sign. And therefore he that
has most experience in any kind of business, has most signs, whereby to guess at the
future time; and consequently is the most prudent: and so much more prudent than he
that is new in that kind of business, as not to be equalled by any advantage of natural   **16**
and extemporary wit: though perhaps many young men think the contrary....

Whatsoever we imagine is *finite*. Therefore there is no idea, or conception of any   **17**
thing we call *infinite*. No man can have in his mind an image of infinite magnitude;
nor conceive infinite swiftness, infinite time, or infinite force, or infinite power. When
we say any thing is infinite, we signify only, that we are not able to conceive the ends,
and bounds of the things named; having no conception of the thing, but of our own
inability. And therefore the name of God is used, not to make us conceive him, for he
is incomprehensible; and his greatness, and power are unconceivable; but that we may
honour him. Also because, whatsoever, as I said before, we conceive, has been perceived first by sense, either all at once, or by parts; a man can have no thought,
representing any thing, not subject to sense. No man therefore can conceive any
thing, but he must conceive it in some place; and indued with some determinate magnitude; and which may be divided into parts....

Chapter 4

Of speech

The invention of *printing*, though ingenious, compared with the invention of *letters*,   **18**
is no great matter. But who was the first that found the use of letters, is not known....
But the most noble and profitable invention of all other, was that of SPEECH, consist-

ing of *names* or *appellations*, and their connexion; whereby men register their thoughts; recall them when they are past; and also declare them one to another for mutual utility and conversation; without which, there had been amongst men, neither commonwealth, nor society, nor contract, nor peace, no more than amongst lions, bears, and wolves. The first author of *speech* was God himself, that instructed Adam how to name such creatures as he presented to his sight. . . .

19   The general use of speech, is to transfer our mental discourse, into verbal; or the train of our thoughts, into a train of words: and that for two commodities, whereof one is the registering of the consequences of our thoughts; which being apt to slip out of our memory, and put us to a new labour, may again be recalled, by such words as they were marked by. So that the first use of names is to serve for *marks*, or *notes* of remembrance. Another is, when many use the same words, to signify, by their connexion and

20   order, one to another, what they conceive, or think of each matter; and also what they desire, fear, or have any other passion for. And for this use they are called *signs*. Special uses of speech are these; first, to register, what by cogitation, we find to be the cause of any thing, present or past; and what we find things present or past may produce, or effect; which in sum, is acquiring of arts. Secondly, to show to others that knowledge which we have attained, which is, to counsel and teach one another. Thirdly, to make known to others our wills and purposes, that we may have the mutual help of one another. Fourthly, to please and delight ourselves and others, by playing with our words, for pleasure or ornament, innocently.

To these uses, there are also four correspondent abuses. First, when men register their thoughts wrong, by the inconstancy of the signification of their words; by which they register for their conception, that which they never conceived, and so deceive themselves. Secondly, when they use words metaphorically; that is, in other sense than that they are ordained for; and thereby deceive others. Thirdly, by words, when they declare that to be their will, which is not. Fourthly, when they use them to grieve one another; for seeing nature hath armed living creatures, some with teeth, some with horns, and some with hands, to grieve an enemy, it is but an abuse of speech, to grieve him with the tongue, unless it be one whom we are obliged to govern; and then it is not to grieve, but to correct and amend.

The manner how speech serveth to the remembrance of the consequence of causes

21   and effects, consisteth in the imposing of *names*, and the *connexion* of them.

Of names, some are *proper*, and singular to one only thing, as *Peter*, *John*, *this man*, *this tree*; and some are *common* to many things, *man*, *horse*, *tree*; every of which, though but one name, is nevertheless the name of divers particular things; in respect of all which together, it is called an universal; there being nothing in the world universal but names; for the things named are every one of them individual and singular. . . .

And of names universal, some are of more, and some of less extent; the larger comprehending the less large; and some again of equal extent, comprehending each other reciprocally. As for example: the name *body* is of larger signification than the word *man*, and comprehendeth it; and the names *man* and *rational*, are of equal extent, comprehending mutually one another. But here we must take notice, that by a name is not always understood, as in grammar, one only word; but sometimes, by circumlocution, many words together. For all these words, *he that in his actions observeth the laws of his country*, make but one name, equivalent to this one word, *just*.

By this imposition of names, some of larger, some of stricter signification, we turn the reckoning of the consequences of things imagined in the mind, into a reckoning

of the consequences of appellations. For example: a man that hath no use of speech 22
at all, such as is born and remains perfectly deaf and dumb, if he set before his eyes a
triangle, and by it two right angles, such as are the corners of a square figure, he may,
by meditation, compare and find, that the three angles of that triangle, are equal to
those two right angles that stand by it. But if another triangle be shown him, different
in shape from the former, he cannot know, without a new labour, whether the three
angles of that also be equal to the same. But he that hath the use of words, when he
observes, that such equality was consequent, not to the length of the sides, nor to any
other particular thing in his triangle; but only to this, that the sides were straight, and
the angles three; and that that was all, for which he named it a triangle; will boldly
conclude universally, that such equality of angles is in all triangles whatsoever; and
register his invention in these general terms, *every triangle hath its three angles equal to
two right angles*. And thus the consequence found in one particular, comes to be
registered and remembered, as a universal rule, and discharges our mental reckoning,
of time and place, and delivers us from all labour of the mind, saving the first, and
makes that which was found true *here*, and *now*, to be true in *all times* and *places*. . . .

When two names are joined together into a consequence, or affirmation, as thus, 23
a man is a living creature; or thus, *if he be a man, he is a living creature*; if the latter name,
living creature, signify all that the former name *man* signifieth, then the affirmation,
or consequence, is *true*; otherwise *false*. For *true* and *false* are attributes of speech, not
of things. And where speech is not, there is neither *truth* nor *falsehood*; *error* there may
be, as when we expect that which shall not be, or suspect what has not been; but in
neither case can a man be charged with untruth.

Seeing then that truth consisteth in the right ordering of names in our affirmations,
a man that seeketh precise truth had need to remember what every name he uses stands
for, and to place it accordingly, or else he will find himself entangled in words, as a bird
in lime twigs, the more he struggles the more belimed. And therefore in geometry,
which is the only science that it hath pleased God hitherto to bestow on mankind, men 24
begin at settling the significations of their words; which settling of significations they
call *definitions*, and place them in the beginning of their reckoning. . . .

. . . Nor is it possible without letters for any man to become either excellently wise, 25
or, unless his memory be hurt by disease or ill constitution of organs, excellently foolish. For words are wise men's counters, they do but reckon by them; but they are the
money of fools. . . .

When a man, upon the hearing of any speech, hath those thoughts which the words 28
of that speech and their connexion were ordained and constituted to signify, then he is
said to understand it; *understanding* being nothing else but conception caused by speech.
And therefore if speech be peculiar to man, as for aught I know it is, then is understanding peculiar to him also. And therefore of absurd and false affirmations, in case they be
universal, there can be no understanding; though many think they understand then,
when they do but repeat the words softly, or con them in their mind. . . .

The names of such things as affect us, that is, which please and displease us,
because all men be not alike affected with the same thing, nor the same man at all
times, are in the common discourses of men of *inconstant* signification. For seeing all
names are imposed to signify our conceptions, and all our affections are but conceptions, when we conceive the same things differently, we can hardly avoid different
naming of them. . . . And therefore in reasoning a man must take heed of words;
which besides the signification of what we imagine of their nature, have a signification 29

also of the nature, disposition, and interest of the speaker; such as are the names of virtues and vices; for one man calleth *wisdom*, what another calleth *fear*; and one *cruelty*, what another *justice*. . . .

Chapter 5

Of reason and science

When a man *reasoneth*, he does nothing else but conceive a sum total, from *addition* of parcels; or conceive a remainder, from *subtraction* of one sum from another; which, if it be done by words, is conceiving of the consequence of the names of all the parts, to the name of the whole; or from the names of the whole and one part, to the name of the other part. . . . These operations are not incident to numbers only, but to all manner of things that can be added together, and taken one out of another. For as
30 arithmeticians teach to add and subtract in *numbers*; so the geometricians teach the same in *lines, figures,* solid and superficial, *angles, proportions, times,* degrees of *swiftness, force, power,* and the like; the logicians teach the same in *consequences of words*; adding together two *names* to make an *affirmation*, and two *affirmations* to make a *syllogism*; and *many syllogisms* to make a *demonstration*; and from the *sum*, or *conclusion* of a *syllogism*, they subtract one *proposition* to find the other. Writers of politics add together *pactions* [agreements, contracts] to find men's *duties*; and lawyers, *laws* and *facts*, to find what is *right* and *wrong* in the actions of private men. In sum, in what matter soever there is place for *addition* and *subtraction*, there also is place for *reason*; and where these have no place, there *reason* has nothing at all to do.

Out of all which we may define, that is to say determine, what that is, which is meant by this word *reason*, when we reckon it amongst the faculties of the mind. For REASON, in this sense, is nothing but *reckoning*, that is adding and subtracting, of the consequences of general names agreed upon for the *marking* and *signifying* of our thoughts; I say *marking* them when we reckon by ourselves, and *signifying*, when we demonstrate or approve our reckonings to other men.

And, as in arithmetic, unpractised men must, and professors themselves may often, err, and cast up false; so also in any other subject of reasoning, the ablest, most attentive, and most practised men may deceive themselves, and infer false conclusions; not but that reason itself is always right reason, as well as arithmetic is a certain and infalli-
31 ble art: but no one man's reason, nor the reason of any one number of men, makes the certainty. . . . And therefore, as when there is a controversy in an account, the parties must by their own accord, set up, for right reason, the reason of some arbitrator, or judge, to whose sentence they will both stand. . . .
32   . . . When we reason in words of general signification, and fall upon a general inference which is false, though it be commonly called *error*, it is indeed an *absurdity*, or senseless speech. For error is but a deception, in presuming that somewhat is past, or to come; of which, though it were not past, or not to come, yet there was no impossibility discoverable. But when we make a general assertion, unless it be a true one, the possibility of it is inconceivable. And words whereby we conceive nothing but the sound, are those we call *absurd, insignificant,* and *nonsense*. And therefore if a man should talk to me of a *round quadrangle*; or, *accidents of bread in cheese*; or, *immaterial*
33 *substances*; or of a *free subject*; *a free will*; or any *free*, but free from being hindered by

opposition, I should not say he were in an error, but that his words were without meaning, that is to say, absurd.

I have said before, in the second chapter, that a man did excel all other animals in this faculty, that when he conceived any thing whatsoever, he was apt to inquire the consequences of it, and what effects he could do with it. And now I add this other degree of the same excellence, that he can by words reduce the consequences he finds to general rules, called *theorems*, or *aphorisms*; that is, he can reason, or reckon, not only in number, but in all other things, whereof one may be added unto, or subtracted from another.

But this privilege is allayed by another; and that is, by the privilege of absurdity; to which no living creature is subject, but man only. And of men, those are of all most subject to it, that profess philosophy. For it is most true that Cicero saith of them somewhere; that there can be nothing so absurd, but may be found in the books of philosophers. And the reason is manifest. For there is not one of them that begins his ratiocination from the definitions, or explications of the names they are to use; which is a method that hath been used only in geometry; whose conclusions have thereby been made indisputable.

I. The first cause of absurd conclusions I ascribe to the want of method: in that they begin not their ratiocination from definitions; that is, from settled significations of their words: as if they could cast account, without knowing the value of the numeral words, *one*, *two*, and *three*. . . .

II. The second cause of absurd assertions, I ascribe to the giving of names of *bodies* to *accidents*; or of *accidents* to *bodies*; as they do, that say, *faith is infused*, or *inspired*; when nothing can be *poured*, or *breathed* into anything, but body; and that, *extension is body*; that *phantasms* are *spirits*, &c.

III. The third I ascribe to the giving of the names of the *accidents* of *bodies without us*, to the *accidents* of our *own bodies*; as they do that say, the *colour is in the body*; the *sound is in the air*, &c.

IV. The fourth, to the giving of the names of *bodies* to *names*, or *speeches*; as they do that say, that *there be things universal*; that *a living creature is genus*, or *a general thing*, &c.

V. The fifth, to the giving of the names of *accidents* to *names* and *speeches*; as they do that say, *the nature of a thing is its definition*; *a man's command is his will*; and the like.

VI. The sixth, to the use of metaphors, tropes, and other rhetorical figures, instead of words proper. For though it be lawful to say, for example, in common speech, *the way goeth*, *or leadeth hither, or thither*; *the proverb says this or that*, whereas ways cannot go, nor proverbs speak; yet in reckoning, and seeking of truth, such speeches are not to be admitted.

VII. The seventh, to names that signify nothing; but are taken up, and learned by rote from the schools, as *hypostatical*, *transubstantiate*, *consubstantiate*, *eternal-now*, and the like canting of schoolmen. . . .

By this it appears that reason is not, as sense and memory, born with us; nor gotten by experience only, as prudence is; but attained by industry; first in apt imposing of names; and secondly by getting a good and orderly method in proceeding from the elements, which are names, to assertions made by connexion of one of them to another; and so to syllogisms, which are the connexions of one assertion to another, till we come to a knowledge of all the consequences of names appertaining to the subject in

34

35

hand; and that is it, men call SCIENCE. And whereas sense and memory are but knowledge of fact, which is a thing past and irrevocable. *Science* is the knowledge of consequences, and dependance of one fact upon another. . . .

36   Children therefore are not endued with reason at all, till they have attained the use of speech; but are called reasonable creatures, for the possibility apparent of having the use of reason in time to come. . . .

Chapter 13

Of the natural condition of mankind as concerning their felicity, and misery

110   Nature hath made men so equal, in the faculties of the body, and mind; as that though there be found one man sometimes manifestly stronger in body, or of quicker mind than another; yet when all is reckoned together, the difference between man, and man, is not so considerable, as that one man can thereupon claim to himself any benefit, to which another may not pretend, as well as he. For as to the strength of body, the weakest has strength enough to kill the strongest, either by secret machination, or by confederacy with others, that are in the same danger with himself.

And as to the faculties of the mind, setting aside the arts grounded upon words, and especially that skill of proceeding upon general, and infallible rules, called science; . . . I find yet a greater equality amongst men, than that of strength. For prudence, is but experience; which equal time, equally bestows on all men, in those things they
111   equally apply themselves unto. . . . For such is the nature of men, that howsoever they may acknowledge many others to be more witty, or more eloquent, or more learned; yet they will hardly believe there be many so wise as themselves. . . . But this proveth rather that men are in that point equal, than unequal. For there is not ordinarily a greater sign of the equal distribution of any thing, than that every man is contented with his share.

From this equality of ability, ariseth equality of hope in the attaining of our ends. And therefore if any two men desire the same thing, which nevertheless they cannot both enjoy, they become enemies; and in the way to their end, which is principally their own conservation, and sometimes their delectation only, endeavour to destroy, or subdue one another. . . .

And from this diffidence of one another, there is no way for any man to secure himself, so reasonable, as anticipation; that is, by force, or wiles, to master the persons of all men he can, so long, till he see no other power great enough to endanger him: and this is no more than his own conservation requireth, and is generally allowed. . . .

112   Again, men have no pleasure, but on the contrary a great deal of grief, in keeping company, where there is no power able to over-awe them all. For every man looketh that his companion should value him, at the same rate he sets upon himself: and upon all signs of contempt, or undervaluing, naturally endeavours, as far as he dares, (which amongst them that have no common power to keep them in quiet, is far enough to make them destroy each other), to extort a greater value from his contemners, by damage; and from others, by the example.

So that in the nature of man, we find three principal causes of quarrel. First, competition; secondly, diffidence; thirdly, glory.

The first, maketh men invade for gain; the second, for safety; and the third, for reputation. The first use violence, to make themselves masters of other men's persons, wives, children, and cattle; the second, to defend them; the third, for trifles, as a word, a smile, a different opinion, and any other sign of undervalue. . . .

Hereby it is manifest, that during the time men live without a common power to   113
keep them all in awe, they are in that condition which is called war; and such a war, as is of every man, against every man. For WAR, consisteth not in battle only, or the act of fighting; but in a tract of time, wherein the will to contend by battle is sufficiently known: and therefore the notion of *time*, is to be considered in the nature of war. . . . All other time is PEACE.

Whatsoever therefore is consequent to a time of war, where every man is enemy to every man; the same is consequent to the time, wherein men live without other security, than what their own strength, and their own invention shall furnish them withal. In such condition, there is no place for industry; because the fruit thereof is uncertain: and consequently no culture of the earth; no navigation, nor use of the commodities that may be imported by sea; no commodious building; no instruments of moving, and removing, such things as require much force; no knowledge of the face of the earth; no account of time; no arts; no letters; no society; and which is worst of all, continual fear, and danger of violent death; and the life of man, solitary, poor, nasty, brutish, and short. . . .

To this war of every man, against every man, this also is consequent; that nothing   115
can be unjust. The notions of right and wrong, justice and injustice have there no place. Where there is no common power, there is no law: where no law, no injustice. Force, and fraud, are in war the two cardinal virtues. Justice, and injustice . . . are qualities, that relate to men in society, not in solitude. It is consequent also to the same condition, that there be no propriety, no dominion, no *mine* and *thine* distinct; but only that to be every man's, that he can get; and for so long, as he can keep it. . . .

The passions that incline men to peace, are fear of death; desire of such things as   116
are necessary to commodious living; and a hope by their industry to obtain them. And reason suggesteth convenient articles of peace, upon which men may be drawn to agreement. These articles, are they, which otherwise are called the Laws of Nature: whereof I shall speak more particularly, in the two following chapters.

Chapter 14

Of the first and second natural laws, and of contracts

The RIGHT OF NATURE, which writers commonly call *jus naturale*, is the liberty each man hath, to use his own power, as he will himself, for the preservation of his own nature; that is to say, of his own life; and consequently, of doing any thing, which in his own judgment, and reason, he shall conceive to be the aptest means thereunto.

By LIBERTY, is understood, according to the proper signification of the word, the absence of external impediments: which impediments, may oft take away part of a man's power to do what he would; but cannot hinder him from using the power left him, according as his judgment, and reason shall dictate to him.

A LAW OF NATURE, *lex naturalis*, is a precept or general rule, found out by reason, by which a man is forbidden to do that, which is destructive of his life, or taketh away   117
the means of preserving the same; and to omit that, by which he thinketh it may be best preserved. . . .

And because the condition of man, as hath been declared in the precedent chapter, is a condition of war of every one against every one: in which case every one is governed by his own reason; and there is nothing he can make use of, that may not be a help unto him, in preserving his life against his enemies; it followeth, that in such a condition, every man has a right to every thing; even to one another's body. And therefore, as long as this natural right of every man to every thing endureth, there can be no security to any man, how strong or wise soever he be, of living out the time, which nature ordinarily alloweth men to live. And consequently it is a precept, or general rule of reason, *that every man, ought to endeavour peace, as far as he has hope of obtaining it; and when he cannot obtain it, that he may seek, and use, all helps, and advantages of war.* The first branch of which rule, containeth the first, and fundamental law of nature; which is, *to seek peace, and follow it.* The second, the sum of the right of nature; which is, *by all means we can, to defend ourselves.*

118   From this fundamental law of nature, by which men are commanded to endeavour peace, is derived this second law; *that a man be willing, when others are so too, as far-forth, as for peace, and defence of himself he shall think it necessary, to lay down this right to all things; and be contented with so much liberty against other men, as he would allow other men against himself.* For as long as every man holdeth this right, of doing any thing he liketh; so long are all men in the condition of war. But if other men will not lay down their right, as well as he; then there is no reason for any one, to divest himself of his: for that were to expose himself to prey, which no man is bound to, rather than to dispose himself to peace. This is that law of the Gospel; *whatsoever you require that others should do to you, that do ye to them.* . . .

To *lay down* a man's *right* to any thing, is to *divest* himself of the *liberty*, of hindering another of the benefit of his own right to the same. . . .

119   Right is laid aside, either by simply renouncing it; or by transferring it to another. . . . And when a man hath in either manner abandoned, or granted away his right; then is he said to be OBLIGED, or BOUND, not to hinder those, to whom such right is granted, or abandoned, from the benefit of it: and that he *ought*, and it is his DUTY, not to make void that voluntary act of his own: and that such hindrance is INJUSTICE, and INJURY, as being *sine jure*; the right being before renounced, or transferred. So that *injury*, or *injustice*, in the controversies of the world, is somewhat like to that, which in the disputations of scholars is called *absurdity*. For as it is there called an absurdity, to contradict what one maintained in the beginning: so in the world, it is called injustice, and injury, voluntarily to undo that, which from the beginning he had voluntarily done. The way by which a man either simply renounceth, or transferreth his right, is a declaration, or signification, by some voluntary and sufficient sign, or signs, that he doth so renounce, or transfer. . . . And these signs are either words only, or actions only; or, as it happeneth most often, both words, and actions. . . .

120   Whensoever a man transferreth his right, or renounceth it; it is either in consideration of some right reciprocally transferred to himself; or for some other good he hopeth for thereby. For it is a voluntary act: and of the voluntary acts of every man, the object is some *good to himself.* And therefore there be some rights, which no man can be understood by any words, or other signs, to have abandoned, or transferred. As first a man cannot lay down the right of resisting them, that assault him by force,

to take away his life; because he cannot be understood to aim thereby, at any good to himself. . . .

Chapter 15

Of other laws of nature

From that law of nature, by which we are obliged to transfer to another, such rights, as being retained, hinder the peace of mankind, there followeth a third; which is this, *that men perform their covenants made*: without which, covenants are in vain, and but empty words; and the right of all men to all things remaining, we are still in the condition of war.   130

And in this law of nature, consisteth the fountain and original of JUSTICE. For where no covenant hath preceded, there hath no right been transferred, and every man has right to every thing; and consequently, no action can be unjust. But when a covenant is made, then to break it is *unjust*: and the definition of INJUSTICE, is no other than *the not performance of covenant*. And whatsoever is not unjust, is *just*.   131

But because covenants of mutual trust, where there is a fear of not performance on either part, as hath been said in the former chapter, are invalid; though the original of justice be the making of covenants; yet injustice actually there can be none, till the cause of such fear be taken away; which while men are in the natural condition of war, cannot be done. Therefore before the names of just, and unjust can have place, there must be some coercive power, to compel men equally to the performance of their covenants, by the terror of some punishment, greater than the benefit they expect by the breach of their covenant; and to make good that propriety, which by mutual contract men acquire, in recompense of the universal right they abandon: and such power there is none before the erection of a commonwealth. And this is also to be gathered out of the ordinary definition of justice in the Schools: for they say, that *justice is the constant will of giving to every man his own*. And therefore where there is no *own*, that is no propriety, there is no injustice; and where there is no coercive power erected, that is, where there is no commonwealth, there is no propriety; all men having right to all things: therefore where there is no commonwealth, there nothing is unjust. So that the nature of justice, consisteth in keeping of valid covenants: but the validity of covenants begins not but with the constitution of a civil power, sufficient to compel men to keep them: and then it is also that propriety begins. . . .

As justice dependeth on antecedent covenant; so does GRATITUDE depend on antecedent grace; that is to say, antecedent free gift: and is the fourth law of nature; which may be conceived in this form, *that a man which receiveth benefit from another of mere grace, endeavour that he which giveth it, have no reasonable cause to repent him of his good will*. For no man giveth, but with intention of good to himself; because gift is voluntary; and of all voluntary acts, the object is to every man his own good; of which if men see they shall be frustrated, there will be no beginning of benevolence, or trust; nor consequently of mutual help; nor of reconciliation of one man to another; and therefore they are to remain still in the condition of *war*; which is contrary to the first and fundamental law of nature, which commandeth men to *seek peace*. The breach of this law, is called *ingratitude*; and hath the same relation to grace, that injustice hath to obligation by covenant.   138

A fifth law of nature, is COMPLAISANCE; that is to say, *that every man strive to accom-*
139   *modate himself to the rest.* For the understanding whereof, we may consider, that there
is in men's aptness to society, a diversity of nature, rising from their diversity
of affections; not unlike to that we see in stones brought together for building of
an edifice. . . .

A sixth law of nature, is this, *that upon caution of the future time, a man ought to*
pardon the offences past of them that repenting, desire it. For PARDON, is nothing but granting of peace; which though granted to them that persevere in their hostility, be not
peace, but fear; yet not granted to them that give caution of the future time, is sign of
an aversion to peace; and therefore contrary to the law of nature.

140   A seventh is, *that in revenges,* that is, retribution of evil for evil, *men look not*
at the greatness of the evil past, but the greatness of the good to follow. Whereby we
are forbidden to inflict punishment with any other design, than for correction of
the offender, or direction of others. For this law is consequent to the next before it,
that commandeth pardon, upon security of the future time. Besides, revenge without
respect to the example, and profit to come, is a triumph, or glorying in the hurt of
another, tending to no end. . . .

And because all signs of hatred, or contempt, provoke to fight; insomuch as most
men choose rather to hazard their life, than not to be revenged; we may in the eighth
place, for a law of nature, set down this precept, *that no man by deed, word, countenance,*
or gesture, declare hatred, or contempt of another. The breach of which law, is commonly
called *contumely.*

The question who is the better man, has no place in the condition of mere nature;
where, as has been shewn before, all men are equal. The inequality that now is, has
141   been introduced by the laws civil. . . . If nature therefore have made men equal, that
equality is to be acknowledged: or if nature have made men unequal; yet because men
that think themselves equal, will not enter into conditions of peace, but upon equal
terms, such equality must be admitted. And therefore for the ninth law of nature, I put
this, *that every man acknowledge another for his equal by nature.* The breach of this
precept is *pride.*

On this law, dependeth another, *that at the entrance into conditions of peace, no man*
require to reserve to himself any right, which he is not content should be reserved to every one
of the rest. As it is necessary for all men that seek peace, to lay down certain rights of
nature; that is to say, not to have liberty to do all they list: so is it necessary for man's
life, to retain some; as right to govern their own bodies; enjoy air, water, motion, ways
to go from place to place; and all things else, without which a man cannot live, or not
live well. . . .

142   Also if *a man be trusted to judge between man and man,* it is a precept of the law of
nature, *that he deal equally between them.* For without that, the controversies of men
cannot be determined but by war. He therefore that is partial in judgment, doth what
in him lies, to deter men from the use of judges, and arbitrators; and consequently,
against the fundamental law of nature, is the cause of war. . . .

And from this followeth another law, *that such things as cannot be divided, be enjoyed*
in common, if it can be; and if the quantity of the thing permit, without stint; otherwise
proportionably to the number of them that have right. For otherwise the distribution is
unequal, and contrary to equity. . . .

Part II
Of Commonwealth

Chapter 17

Of the causes, generation, and definition of a commonwealth

The final cause, end, or design of men, who naturally love liberty, and dominion over   153
others, in the introduction of that restraint upon themselves, in which we see them
live in commonwealths, is the foresight of their own preservation, and of a more contented life thereby; that is to say, of getting themselves out from that miserable condition of war, which is necessarily consequent . . . to the natural passions of men, when
there is no visible power to keep them in awe, and tie them by fear of punishment to
the performance of their covenants, and observation of the laws of nature. . . .

For the laws of nature, as *justice, equity, modesty, mercy*, and, in sum, *doing to others,
as we would be done to*, of themselves, without the terror of some power, to cause them
to be observed, are contrary to our natural passions, that carry us to partiality, pride,   154
revenge, and the like. And covenants, without the sword, are but words, and of no
strength to secure a man at all. Therefore notwithstanding the laws of nature, which
every one hath then kept, when he has the will to keep them, when he can do it safely,
if there be no power erected, or not great enough for our security; every man will, and
may lawfully rely on his own strength and art, for caution against all other men. . . .

Nor is it the joining together of a small number of men, that gives them this security; because in small numbers, small additions on the one side or the other, make the
advantage of strength so great, as is sufficient to carry the victory; and therefore gives
encouragement to an invasion. The multitude sufficient to confide in for our security,
is not determined by any certain number, but by comparison with the enemy we fear;   155
and is then sufficient, when the odds of the enemy is not of so visible and conspicuous
moment, to determine the event of war, as to move him to attempt.

And be there never so great a multitude; yet if their actions be directed according
to their particular judgments, and particular appetites, they can expect thereby no
defence, nor protection, neither against a common enemy, nor against the injuries of
one another. For being distracted in opinions concerning the best use and application
of their strength, they do not help but hinder one another; and reduce their strength
by mutual opposition to nothing. . . .

The only way to erect such a common power, as may be able to defend them from   157
the invasion of foreigners, and the injuries of one another, and thereby to secure them
in such sort, as that by their own industry, and by the fruits of the earth, they may
nourish themselves and live contentedly; is, to confer all their power and strength
upon one man, or upon one assembly of men, that may reduce all their wills, by plurality of voices, unto one will: which is as much as to say, to appoint one man, or assembly of men, to bear their person; and every one to own, and acknowledge himself to
be author of whatsoever he that so beareth their person, shall act, or cause to be acted,   158
in those things which concern the common peace and safety; and therein to submit
their wills, every one to his will, and their judgments, to his judgment. This is more
than consent, or concord; it is a real unity of them all, in one and the same person,

made by covenant of every man with every man, in such manner, as if every man should say to every man, *I authorise and give up my right of governing myself, to this man, or to this assembly of men, on this condition, that thou give up thy right to him, and authorize all his actions in like manner.* This done, the multitude so united in one person, is called a COMMONWEALTH, in latin CIVITAS. This is the generation of that great LEVIATHAN, or rather, to speak more reverently, of that *mortal god*, to which we owe under the *immortal* God, our peace and defence. For by this authority, given him by every particular man in the commonwealth, he hath the use of so much power and strength conferred on him, that by terror thereof, he is enabled to perform the wills of them all, to peace at home, and mutual aid against their enemies abroad. And in him consisteth the essence of the commonwealth; which, to define it, is *one person, of whose acts a great multitude, by mutual covenants one with another, have made themselves every one the author, to the end he may use the strength and means of them all, as he shall think expedient, for their peace and common defence.*

And he that carrieth this person, is called SOVEREIGN, and said to have *sovereign power*; and every one besides, his SUBJECT.

159   The attaining to this sovereign power, is by two ways. One, by natural force; as when a man maketh his children, to submit themselves, and their children to his government, as being able to destroy them if they refuse; or by war subdueth his enemies to his will, giving them their lives on that condition. The other, is when men agree amongst themselves, to submit to some man, or assembly of men, voluntarily, on confidence to be protected by him against all others. This latter, may be called a political commonwealth, or commonwealth by *institution*; and the former, a commonwealth by *acquisition*. And first, I shall speak of a commonwealth by institution.

Chapter 18

Of the rights of sovereigns by institution

A *commonwealth* is said to be *instituted*, when a *multitude* of men do agree, and *covenant, every one, with every one,* that to whatsoever *man,* or *assembly of men,* shall be given by the major part, the *right* to *present* the person of them all, that is to say, to be their *representative*: every one, as well he that *voted for it,* as he that *voted against it,* shall *authorize* all the actions and judgments, of that man, or assembly of men, in the same manner, as if they were his own, to the end, to live peaceably amongst themselves, and be protected against other men.

From this institution of a commonwealth are derived all the *rights,* and *faculties* of him, or them, on whom sovereign power is conferred by the consent of the people assembled.

160   First, because they covenant, it is to be understood, they are not obliged by former covenant to anything repugnant hereunto. And consequently they that have already instituted a commonwealth, being thereby bound by covenant, to own the actions, and judgments of one, cannot lawfully make a new covenant, amongst themselves, to be obedient to any other, in any thing whatsoever, without his permission. And therefore, they that are subjects to a monarch, cannot without his leave cast off monarchy, and return to the confusion of a disunited multitude; nor transfer their person from him that beareth it, to another man, or other assembly of men: for they are bound, every man to every man, to own, and be reputed author of all, that he that already is

their sovereign, shall do, and judge fit to be done: so that any one man dissenting, all the rest should break their covenant made to that man, which is injustice: and they have also every man given the sovereignty to him that beareth their person; and therefore if they depose him, they take from him that which is his own, and so again it is injustice. Besides, if he that attempteth to depose his sovereign, be killed, or punished by him for such attempt, he is author of his own punishment, as being by the institution, author of all his sovereign shall do: and because it is injustice for a man to do anything, for which he may be punished by his own authority, he is also upon that title, unjust. And whereas some men have pretended for their disobedience to their sovereign, a new covenant, made, not with men, but with God; this also is unjust: for there is no covenant with God, but by meditation of somebody that representeth God's person; which none doth but God's lieutenant, who hath the sovereignty under God. But this pretence of covenant with God, is so evident a lie, even in the pretenders' own consciences, that it is not only an act of an unjust, but also of a vile, and unmanly disposition. 161

Secondly, because the right of bearing the person of them all, is given to him they make sovereign, by covenant only of one to another, and not of him to any of them; there can happen no breach of covenant on the part of the sovereign; and consequently none of his subjects, by any pretence of forfeiture, can be freed from his subjection. That he which is made sovereign maketh no covenant with his subjects beforehand, is manifest; because either he must make it with the whole multitude, as one party to the covenant; or he must make a several covenant with every man. With the whole, as one party, it is impossible; because as yet they are not one person: and if he make so many several covenants as there be men, those covenants after he hath the sovereignty are void; because what act soever can be pretended by any one of them for breach thereof, is the act both of himself, and of all the rest, because done in the person, and by the right of every one of them in particular. Besides, if any one, or more of them, pretend a breach of the covenant made by the sovereign at his institution; and others, or one other of his subjects, or himself alone, pretend there was no such breach, there is in this case, no judge to decide the controversy; it returns therefore to the sword again; and every man recovereth the right of protecting himself by his own strength, contrary to the design they had in the institution. It is therefore in vain to 162 grant sovereignty by way of precedent covenant. The opinion that any monarch receiveth his power by covenant, that is to say, on condition, proceedeth from want of understanding this easy truth, that covenants being but words and breath, have no force to oblige, contain, constrain, or protect any man, but what it has from the public sword; that is, from the untied hands of that man, or assembly of men that hath the sovereignty, and whose actions are avouched by them all, and performed by the strength of them all, in him united. . . .

Thirdly, because the major part hath by consenting voices declared a sovereign; he that dissented must now consent with the rest; that is, be contented to avow all the actions he shall do, or else justly be destroyed by the rest. For if he voluntarily entered into the congregation of them that were assembled, he sufficiently declared thereby his will, and therefore tacitly covenanted, to stand to what the major part should ordain. . . .

Fourthly, because every subject is by this institution author of all the actions, and 163 judgments of the sovereign instituted; it follows, that whatsoever he doth, it can be no injury to any of his subjects; nor ought he to be by any of them accused of injustice.

For he that doth anything by authority from another, doth therein no injury to him by whose authority he acteth: but by this institution of a commonwealth, every particular man is author of all the sovereign doth: and consequently he that complaineth of injury from his sovereign, complaineth of that whereof he himself is author; and therefore ought not to accuse any man but himself; no nor himself of injury: because to do injury to one's self, is impossible. It is true that they that have sovereign power may commit iniquity; but not injustice, or injury in the proper signification.

Fifthly, and consequently to that which was said last, no man that hath sovereign power can justly be put to death, or otherwise in any manner by his subjects punished. For seeing every subject is author of the actions of his sovereign; he punisheth another for the actions committed by himself. . . .

164   Sixthly, it is annexed to the sovereignty, to be judge of what opinions and doctrines are averse, and what conducing to peace; and consequently, on what occasions, how far, and what men are to be trusted withal, in speaking to multitudes of people; and who shall examine the doctrines of all books before they be published. For the actions of men proceed from their opinions; and in the well-governing of opinions, consisteth the well-governing of men's actions, in order to their peace, and concord. . . .

165   Seventhly, is annexed to the sovereignty, the whole power of prescribing the rules, whereby every man may know, what goods he may enjoy, and what actions he may do, without being molested by any of his fellow-subjects; and this is it men call *propriety*. . . . These rules of propriety, or *meum* and *tuum*, and of *good, evil, lawful*, and *unlawful* in the actions of subjects, are the civil laws: that is to say, the laws of each commonwealth in particular. . . .

Eighthly, is annexed to the sovereignty, the right of judicature; that is to say, of hearing and deciding all controversies, which may arise concerning law, either civil, or natural; or concerning fact. For without the decision of controversies, there is no protection of one subject, against the injuries of another. . . .

166   Ninthly, is annexed to the sovereignty, the right of making war and peace with other nations, and commonwealths; that is to say, of judging when it is for the public good, and how great forces are to be assembled, armed, and paid for that end; and to levy money upon the subjects, to defray the expenses thereof. For the power by which the people are to be defended, consisteth in their armies; and the strength of an army, in the union of their strength under one command. . . .

167   These are the rights, which make the essence of sovereignty; and which are the marks, whereby a man may discern in what man, or assembly of men, the sovereign power is placed, and resideth. For these are incommunicable, and inseparable. The power to coin money; to dispose of the estate and persons of infant heirs; to have praeemption in markets; and all other statute prerogatives, may be transferred by the sovereign; and yet the power to protect his subjects be retained. But if he transfer the *militia*, he retains the judicature in vain, for want of execution of the laws: or if he grant
168   away the power of raising money; the *militia* is in vain: or if he give away the government of doctrines, men will be frighted into rebellion with the fear of spirits. And so if we consider any one of the said rights, we shall presently see, that the holding of all the rest will produce no effect, in the conservation of peace and justice, the end for which all commonwealths are instituted. And this division is it, whereof it is said, *a kingdom divided in itself cannot stand*: for unless this division precede, division into opposite armies can never happen. . . .

Chapter 19

Of the several kinds of commonwealth by Institution,
and of succession to the sovereign power

The difference of commonwealths, consisteth in the difference of the sovereign, or the 171
person representative of all and every one of the multitude. And because the
sovereignty is either in one man, or in an assembly of more than one; and into that
assembly either every man hath right to enter, or not every one; but certain men distinguished from the rest; it is manifest, there can be but three kinds of commonwealth.
For the representative must needs be one man, or more: and if more, then it is the
assembly of all, or but of a part. When the representative is one man, then is the commonwealth a MONARCHY: when an assembly of all that will come together, then it is
a DEMOCRACY, or popular commonwealth: when an assembly of a part only, then it is
called an ARISTOCRACY. . . .

The difference between these three kinds of commonwealth, consisteth not in the 173
difference of power; but in the difference of convenience, or aptitude to produce the
peace, and security of the people; for which end they were instituted. And to compare
monarchy with the other two, we may observe; first, that whosoever beareth the person
of the people, or is one of that assembly that bears it, beareth also his own natural person. And though he be careful in his politic person to procure the common interest; yet
he is more, or no less careful to procure the private good of himself, his family, kindred
and friends; and for the most part, if the public interest chance to cross the private, he
prefers the private: for the passions of men, are commonly more potent than their reason. From whence it follows, that where the public and private interest are most closely
united, there is the public most advanced. Now in monarchy, the private interest is the 174
same with the public. The riches, power, and honour of a monarch arise only from the
riches, strength and reputation of his subjects. . . . In a democracy, or aristocracy, the
public prosperity confers not so much to the private fortune of one that is corrupt, or
ambitious, as doth many times a perfidious advice, a treacherous action, or a civil war.

Secondly, that a monarch receiveth counsel of whom, when, and where he pleaseth;
and consequently may hear the opinion of men versed in the matter about which he
deliberates, of what rank or quality soever, and as long before the time of action, and
with as much secrecy, as he will. But when a sovereign assembly has need of counsel,
none are admitted but such as have a right thereto from the beginning; which for the
most part are of those who have been versed more in the acquisition of wealth than of
knowledge; and are to give their advice in long discourses, which may, and do commonly excite men to action, but not govern them in it. For the *understanding* is by the
flame of the passions, never enlightened, but dazzled. Nor is there any place, or time,
wherein an assembly can receive counsel with secrecy, because of their own multitude.

Thirdly, that the resolutions of a monarch, are subject to no other inconstancy, than
that of human nature; but in assemblies, besides that of nature, there ariseth an incon- 175
stancy from the number. . . .

Fourthly, that a monarch cannot disagree with himself, out of envy, or interest; but
an assembly may; and that to such a height, as may produce a civil war.

Fifthly, that in monarchy there is this inconvenience; that any subject, by the power
of one man, for the enriching of a favourite or flatterer, may be deprived of all he posses-
seth; which I confess is a great and inevitable inconvenience. But the same may as well

happen, where the sovereign power is in an assembly: for their power is the same; and they are as subject to evil counsel, and to be seduced by orators, as a monarch by flatterers; and becoming one another's flatterers, serve one another's covetousness and ambition by turns. . . .

Chapter 21

Of the liberty of subjects

196 LIBERTY, or FREEDOM, signifieth, properly, the absence of opposition; by opposition, I mean external impediments of motion; and may be applied no less to irrational, and inanimate creatures, than to rational. For whatsoever is so tied, or environed, as it cannot move but within a certain space, which space is determined by the opposition of some external body, we say it hath not liberty to go further. And so of all living creatures, whilst they are imprisoned, or restrained, with walls, or chains; and of the water whilst it is kept in by banks, or vessels, that otherwise would spread itself into a larger space, we use to say, they are not at liberty, to move in such manner, as without those external impediments they would. But when the impediment of motion, is in the constitution of the thing itself, we use not to say; it wants the liberty; but the power to move; as when a stone lieth still, or a man is fastened to his bed by sickness.

And according to this proper, and generally received meaning of the word, a FREE-MAN, *is he, that in those things, which by his strength and wit he is able to do, is not hindered*
197 *to do what he has a will to.* But when the words *free*, and *liberty*, are applied to any thing but *bodies*, they are abused; for that which is not subject to motion, is not subject to impediment. . . . From the use of the word *free-will*, no liberty can be inferred of the will, desire, or inclination, but the liberty of the man; which consisteth in this, that he finds no stop, in doing what he has the will, desire, or inclination to do.

Fear and liberty are consistent; as when a man throweth his goods into the sea for *fear* the ship should sink, he doth it nevertheless very willingly, and may refuse to do it if he will: it is therefore the action of one that was *free*. . . . And generally all actions which men do in commonwealths, for *fear* of the law, are actions, which the doers had *liberty* to omit.

Liberty, and *necessity* are consistent: as in the water, that hath not only *liberty*, but *a necessity* of descending by the channel; so likewise in the actions which men voluntarily do: which, because they proceed from their will, proceed from *liberty*; and yet,
198 because every act of man's will, and every desire, and inclination proceedeth from some cause, and that from another cause, in a continual chain, whose first link is in the hand of God the first of all causes, proceed from *necessity*. So that to him that could see the connexion of those causes, the *necessity* of all men's voluntary actions, would appear manifest. . . .

But as men, for the attaining of peace, and conservation of themselves thereby, have made an artificial man, which we call a commonwealth; so also have they made artificial chains, called *civil laws*, which they themselves, by mutual covenants, have fastened at one end, to the lips of that man, or assembly, to whom they have given the sovereign power; and at the other end to their own ears. These bonds, in their own nature but weak, may nevertheless be made to hold, by the danger, though not by the difficulty of breaking them.

199 In relation to these bonds only it is, that I am to speak now, of the *liberty* of *subjects*. For seeing there is no commonwealth in the world, wherein there be rules enough set

down, for the regulating of all the actions, and words of men; as being a thing impossible: it followeth necessarily, that in all kinds of actions by the laws praetermitted, men have the liberty, of doing what their own reasons shall suggest, for the most profitable to themselves. . . .

To come now to the particulars of the true liberty of a subject; that is to say, what are the things, which though commanded by the sovereign, he may nevertheless, without injustice, refuse to do. . . .   203

First . . . , seeing sovereignty by institution, is by covenant of every one to every one; and sovereignty by acquisition, by covenants of the vanquished to the victor, or child to the parent; it is manifest, that every subject has liberty in all those things, the right whereof cannot by covenant be transferred. I have shewn before . . . that covenants, not to defend a man's own body, are void. Therefore,   204

If the sovereign command a man, though justly condemned, to kill, wound, or maim himself; or not to resist those that assault him; or to abstain from the use of food, air, medicine, or any other thing, without which he cannot live; yet hath that man the liberty to disobey.

If a man be interrogated by the sovereign, or his authority, concerning a crime done by himself, he is not bound, without assurance of pardon, to confess it; because no man, as I have shown in the same chapter, can be obliged by covenant to accuse himself. . . .

To resist the sword of the commonwealth, in defence of another man, guilty, or innocent, no man hath liberty: because such liberty, takes away from the sovereign, the means of protecting us: and is therefore destructive of the very essence of government. But in case a great many men together, have already resisted the sovereign power unjustly, or committed some capital crime, for which every one of them expecteth death, whether have they not the liberty then to join together, and assist, and defend one another? Certainly they have: for they but defend their lives, which the guilty man may as well do, as the innocent. There was indeed injustice in the first breach of their duty; their bearing of arms subsequent to it, though it be to maintain what they have done, is no new unjust act. And if it be only to defend their persons, it is not unjust at all. But the offer of pardon taketh from them, to whom it is offered, the plea of self-defence, and maketh their perseverance in assisting, or defending the rest, unlawful.   205   206

As for other liberties, they depend on the silence of the law. In cases where the sovereign has prescribed no rule, there the subject hath the liberty to do, or forbear, according to his own discretion. And therefore such liberty is in some places more, and in some less; and in some times more, in other times less, according as they that have the sovereignty shall think most convenient. . . .

The obligation of subjects to the sovereign, is understood to last as long, and no longer, than the power lasteth, by which he is able to protect them. For the right men have by nature to protect themselves, when none else can protect them, can by no covenant be relinquished. The sovereignty is the soul of the commonwealth; which once departed from the body, the members do no more receive their motion from it. The end of obedience is protection; which, wheresoever a man seeth it, either in his own, or in another's sword, nature applieth his obedience to it, and his endeavour to maintain it. And though sovereignty, in the intention of them that make it, be immortal; yet is it in its own nature, not only subject to violent death, by foreign war; but also through the ignorance, and passions of men, it hath in it, from the very institution, many seeds of a natural mortality, by intestine discord. . . .   208

SELECTED BIBLIOGRAPHY

Hobbes, Thomas. *English Works*. Ed. Sir W. Molesworth. 11 vols. London: J. Bohn, 1839–1845.

_____. *Hobbes Selections*. Ed. F.J.E. Woodbridge. New York: Scribner, 1930.

_____. *Leviathan*. Ed. C.B. Macpherson. Harmondsworth, England: Penguin, 1968.

Baumrin, Bernard H. *Hobbes's Leviathan: Interpretation and Criticism*. Belmont, Calif.: Wadsworth, 1969.

Gauthier, David. *The Logic of Leviathan: The Moral and Political Theory of Thomas Hobbes*. New York: Oxford University Press, 1969.

Goldsmith, M.M. *Hobbes' Science of Politics*. New York: Columbia University Press, 1966.

Hinnant, Charles H. *Thomas Hobbes*. Boston: Twayne, 1977.

Hood, F.C. *The Divine Politics of Thomas Hobbes: An Interpretation of "Leviathan."* New York: Oxford University Press, 1964.

Jessop, T.E. *Thomas Hobbes*. London: British Book, 1960.

Kavka, Gregory. *Hobbesian Moral and Political Theory*. Princeton, N.J.: Princeton University Press, 1986.

Lemos, Ramon. *Hobbes and Locke: Power and Consent*. Athens: University of Georgia Press, 1978.

MacPherson, C.B. *The Political Theory of Possessive Individualism: Hobbes to Locke*. New York: Oxford University Press, 1962.

McNeilly, F.S. *The Anatomy of Leviathan*. New York: St. Martin's Press, 1968.

Mintz, S.I. *The Hunting of Leviathan*. Cambridge: Cambridge University Press, 1962.

Peters, R.S. *Hobbes*. Harmondsworth, England: Penguin, 1956.

Taylor, A.E. *Thomas Hobbes*. London: Oxford University Press, 1908.

Tuck, Richard. *Hobbes*. New York: Oxford University Press, 1989.

Warrender, H. *The Political Philosophy of Hobbes: His Theory of Obligation*. New York: Oxford University Press, 1957.

Watkins, J.W.N. *Hobbes's System of Ideas: A Study in the Political Significance of Philosophical Theories*. New York: Hillary House, 1965.

John Locke

John Locke (1632–1704) was born the son of a Puritan lawyer. Sent at fifteen to Westminster School in London, he heartily disliked the conservative curriculum and the unruly interactions among the boys. He performed well, however, and won a scholarship in 1652 to Christ Church, Oxford, where the curriculum was again quite conservative: metaphysics, logic, rhetoric, and classical languages. Locke did well in his studies, and after taking his B.A. in 1665, remained at Oxford to take the M.A. and then to become a Fellow of Christ Church (1658), Reader in Greek (1660), Reader in Rhetoric (1662), and Censor of Moral Philosophy (1664). During his undergraduate career Locke developed a fascination for the experimental sciences and spent increasing amounts of time on science, especially after making the acquaintance of Robert Boyle, the ground-breaking chemist. Locke's interest in science led him to take a degree in medicine in 1674.

Locke interrupted his academic career to become secretary to a diplomatic mission to the German principality of Brandenburg in 1665, but that assignment ended without success. The following year, however, Locke met Anthony Ashley Cooper, later Lord Shaftesbury, who engaged him as his personal physician and political secretary. In Shaftesbury's service Locke devoted much of his time to scientific and philosophical investigations, becoming a Fellow of the Royal Society in 1668. During the many discussions of moral and religious issues at Shaftesbury's house, Locke decided that all such questions had to await a thorough general assessment of the nature and extent of human knowledge, which task he then undertook. This was the beginning of his *Essay concerning Human Understanding*, perhaps the single most influential piece of philosophy ever written in English.

From 1675 to 1679 Locke was in France for his health (he suffered from asthma and bronchitis in the damp English air), where he contacted Pierre Gassendi and other leading scientists on the Continent and apparently made his first acquaintance with the works of Descartes. In the meantime, though, Locke's patron, Lord Shaftesbury, fell in and out of favor with the British Crown. In 1681 Shaftesbury was charged with high treason and acquitted but thought it nonetheless advisable to leave the country. Locke joined him in Holland soon after, where because of his association with Shaftesbury Locke had to live for a time under the alias Dr. van der Linden to prevent extradition to England. In Holland, Locke devoted himself to his writing, working on the *Essay* and the *Letter concerning Toleration*, among other things.

After the Glorious Revolution of 1688, in which the Catholic James II was replaced in a bloodless revolt by the Protestant William and Mary, previously rulers of Holland, Locke returned to England and published his *Two Treatises of Civil Government* anonymously. The first edition of the *Essay* also appeared. Locke finally felt free to publish the pieces he had been working on for some twenty years. In 1691, unable to tolerate the air in London, Locke took up residence at Oates in Essex, the country house of Sir Francis and Lady Masham, where he remained until his death. At Oates, Locke devoted himself to new writing, including *The Reasonableness of Christianity*, revised the *Essay* (which went through four editions during Locke's lifetime), and defended himself against his critics. Throughout much of his life Locke held various public positions (including Commissioner of Appeals and Commissioner of the Board of Trade and Plantations), corresponded voluminously, and wrote almost constantly. The *Essay* made him one of Europe's most celebrated figures, yet Locke never lost his humility or his conviction that the sole worthy motive for his investigations was truth.

Philosophy

Despite his self-characterization as an underlaborer clearing the way for great scientists such as Boyle and Isaac Newton, Locke was one of the most influential thinkers of the modern age. He was less impressed with the accomplishments of pure mathematics than his immediate philosophical predecessors and correspondingly more impressed with the methods, results, and possibilities of the experimental sciences. Locke's rejection of innate knowledge in favor of the doctrine that all our knowledge is derived from experience marks him as a founder of empiricism. In investigating "the original, certainty, and extent of human knowledge, together with the grounds and degrees of belief, opinion and assent" (1:1.2), Locke always sought to show how we construct our knowledge from our experiences.

The fundamental building blocks of Locke's analysis of human understanding are *ideas*, which he says are "whatsoever is the object of the understanding when a man thinks." Locke was not particularly careful in his use of this term, but having insisted that all our ideas come from experience, he is concerned to understand what kinds of ideas we have within us, what psychological abilities we possess for manipulating these ideas, and what we can consequently infer about the relations among our ideas and between our ideas and reality itself. He therefore devotes many pages to analyzing our ideas of power, substance, identity, and so forth, trying to show whence they arise and with what right we can use them. The positions he staked out became virtually the received opinion for the next century; he helped shape today's commonsense understanding of the world.

His conclusion that we can have intuitive knowledge of our own existence, demonstrative knowledge of God's existence, and sensitive knowledge of particular things has been attacked from all sides, both for allowing too much knowledge and for allowing too little. Locke's beliefs about the extent of our knowledge, however, are less interesting in the long run than his speculations about the nature of the thinking activities necessary to any knowing mind.

Locke's *Second Treatise of Government* was written in part to justify the Glorious Revolution of 1688, in part to answer political writer Sir Robert Filmer's defense of the divine and inheritable right of monarchs to rule, and in part to answer Thomas Hobbes's nonreligious defense of absolute monarchy. Locke's state of nature is far less miserable than Hobbes's, for Locke believed that humans would be more able in such a state to recognize the universal natural rights of others to life, liberty, and so on, and to govern themselves accordingly. Nonetheless, in the state of nature, all act principally for themselves, which makes unavailable the benefits of social coordination. We undertake (actively or tacitly) a social contract in order to secure these benefits to ourselves. For Locke a major advantage of instituting a government is the recognition and stabilization of private property rights, founded on the idea that one acquires a property interest in anything in which one has mixed one's labor. The *Second Treatise* was influential on the framers of the U.S. Constitution.

Reading Context

Locke's *Essay* and the *Second Treatise* are difficult for twentieth-century English speakers; their language is antiquated and often verbose. Locke himself said that the *Essay* should be abridged. Although abridging the text, as has been done here, reduces the verbosity, it also makes the text denser and eliminates some of the rambling examples and illustrations that occasionally aid the reader's comprehension. Locke's writing is that of an explorer: his views shift as he attempts to make sense out of his world and as he comes into contact with new influences and ideas. In this he is remarkably nondoctrinaire.

Though generally considered the founder of British empiricism, Locke still possessed strong rationalist tendencies. One of the changes he introduced was that he conceived of simple ideas as individual sensations, not as universal concepts, as the rationalists did. But if none of our ideas is innate, as Locke claims, then all our ideas must ultimately stem from our simple ideas of sensation and reflection. Keep this requirement firmly in mind as you read Locke's *Essay*, and challenge not only Locke's accounts of the concepts he discusses explicitly but also his *methodological* concepts—the concepts he *uses* in his discussion, without necessarily discussing those very concepts. How can he account for them in his empirical philosophy? Is a strict empiricism possible?

A Note on the Texts

An Essay concerning Human Understanding was begun while Locke was in the service of Lord Shaftesbury in the 1660s. According to Locke's own testimony, the *Essay* began during a discussion among friends about some quite different matter. Finding themselves unable to resolve the issue, Locke turned to question the abilities and proper objects of the human mind. It was not until twenty years later, in 1689, that the *Essay* first saw the light of day, shortly after his *Two Treatises of Government*, on which he had worked for a full decade, appeared. Locke revised the *Essay* several more times before his death. This abridgment is based on the critical edition by P. H. Nidditch. The abridgment of the *Second Treatise* is based on Peter Laslett's critical edition. Locke's seventeenth-century spelling and punctuation have been modernized throughout. Standard references to passages in Locke consist of book, chapter, and section number.

Reading Questions

An Essay concerning Human Understanding

1. What arguments for a belief in innate ideas does Locke report? What are his arguments against such a belief?
2. What is the distinction between ideas of sensation and ideas of reflection? Give an example of each. Is this an exhaustive classification?
3. How does Locke distinguish primary and secondary qualities? Why does he think the ideas of primary qualities resemble the qualities in bodies?
4. What operations does Locke attribute to our minds? How do we come by them?
5. How do complex ideas originate? What kinds of complex ideas are there?
6. Where do we get our idea of power? What is this idea?
7. What is Locke's position on *free will*? How does he define *free will, liberty, voluntary* and *involuntary, deliberation*?
8. What is Locke's criterion for *identity*? How does it compare with our standard usage of the term?
9. What is Locke's theory of personal identity? What does it mean to say that *person* is a forensic term?
10. According to Locke, how do I know that I exist? That other things exist? That God exists?

The Second Treatise of Government

11. Does Locke, like Hobbes, envision the state of nature as a war of all against all? Explain.
12. Why, according to Locke, are governments instituted among humans?
13. How adequate is Locke's concept of property? Is your body your property? Do you have a claim to own anything you've worked on?
14. Does Locke recognize a right of a people to revolt against a sovereign? Under what conditions?

An Essay concerning Human Understanding

Book I

Chapter 1

Introduction

1. An inquiry into the understanding pleasant and useful. Since it is the *understanding* that sets man above the rest of sensible beings, and gives him all the advantage and dominion which he has over them; it is certainly a subject, even for its nobleness, worth our labor to inquire into. The understanding, like the eye, while it makes us see and perceive all other things, takes no notice of itself; and it requires art and pains to set it at a distance, and make it its own object. But whatever be the difficulties that lie in the way of this inquiry, whatever it be that keeps us so much in the dark to ourselves, sure I am that all the light we can let in upon our own minds, all the acquaintance we can make with our own understandings, will not only be very pleasant, but bring us great advantage, in directing our thoughts in the search of other things.

2. Design. This, therefore, being my *purpose*—to inquire into the original, certainty, and extent of human knowledge, together with the grounds and degrees of belief, opinion, and assent—I shall not at present meddle with the physical consideration of the mind or trouble myself to examine wherein its essence consists or by what motions of our spirits or alterations of our bodies we come to have any sensation by our organs or any *ideas* in our understandings and whether those *ideas* do in their formation, any, or all of them, depend on matter, or not. These are speculations, which however curious and entertaining, I shall decline as lying out of my way in the design I am now upon. It shall suffice to my present purpose to consider the discerning faculties of a man as they are employed about the objects which they have to do with. And I shall imagine I have not wholly misemployed myself in the thoughts I shall have on this occasion, if, in this historical, plain method I can give any account of the ways whereby our understandings come to attain those notions of things we have, and can set down any measures of the certainty of our knowledge, or the grounds of those persuasions which are to be found among men so various, different, and wholly contradictory. . . .

3. Method. It is therefore worthwhile to search out the *bounds* between opinion and knowledge and examine by what measures in things, whereof we have no certain knowledge, we ought to regulate our assent and moderate our persuasions. In order whereunto I shall pursue this following method.

First, I shall inquire into the *original* of those *ideas*, notions, or whatever else you please to call them, which a man observes and is conscious to himself he has in his mind, and the ways whereby the understanding comes to be furnished with them.

Secondly, I shall endeavor to show what *knowledge* the understanding hath by those *ideas*, and the certainty, evidence, and extent of it.

From John Locke, *An Essay concerning Human Understanding*, ed. P.H. Nidditch (New York: Oxford University Press, 1975). Reprinted by permission of Oxford University Press.

Thirdly, I shall make some inquiry into the nature and grounds of *faith* or *opinion,* whereby I mean that assent which we give to any proposition as true, of whose truth yet we have no certain knowledge. And here we shall have occasion to examine the reasons and degrees of *assent.*

4. *Useful to know the extent of our comprehension.*   If by this inquiry into the nature of the understanding I can discover the powers thereof, *how far* they reach, to what things they are in any degree proportionate, and where they fail us, I suppose it may be of use to prevail with the busy mind of man to be more cautious in meddling with things exceeding its comprehension, to stop when it is at the utmost extent of its tether, and to sit down in a quiet ignorance of those things which upon examination are found to be beyond the reach of our capacities. . . .

6. *Knowledge of our capacity a cure of skepticism and idleness.*   When we know our own *strength,* we shall the better know what to undertake with hopes of success, and when we have well surveyed the *powers* of our own minds and made some estimate what we may expect from them, we shall not be inclined either to sit still and not set our thoughts on work at all, in despair of knowing anything, nor on the other side question everything and disclaim all knowledge because some things are not to be understood. . . . Our business here is not to know all things but those which concern our conduct. If we can find out those measures, whereby a rational creature put in that state which man is in in this world may and ought to govern his opinions and actions depending thereon, we need not be troubled that some other things escape our knowledge. . . .

8. *What idea stands for.*   This much I thought necessary to say concerning the occasion of this inquiry into human understanding. But before I proceed on to what I have thought on this subject, I must here in the entrance beg pardon of my reader, for the frequent use of the word *idea,* which he will find in the following treatise. It being that term which, I think, serves best to stand for whatsoever is the object of the understanding when a man thinks, I have used it to express whatever is meant by *phantasm, notion, species,* or whatever it is, which the mind can be employed about in thinking; and I could not avoid frequently using it.

I presume it will be easily granted me that there are such *ideas* in men's minds; everyone is conscious of them in himself, and men's words and actions will satisfy him that they are in others.

Our first inquiry then shall be how they come into the mind.

Chapter 2

No Innate Principles in the Mind

1. *The way shown how we come by any knowledge, sufficient to prove it not innate.*   It is an established opinion among some men that there are in the understanding certain *innate principles,* some primary notions, Κοιναι ἔννοιαι, characters, as it were stamped upon the mind of man, which the soul receives in its very first being and brings into the world with it. It would be sufficient to convince unprejudiced readers of the false-

ness of this supposition, if I should only show (as I hope I shall in the following parts of this discourse) how men, barely by the use of their natural faculties, may attain to all the knowledge they have, without the help of any innate impressions, and may arrive at certainty, without any such original notions or principles. . . .

2. General assent the great argument.   There is nothing more commonly taken for granted than that there are certain principles both *speculative* and *practical* (for they speak of both) universally agreed upon by all mankind, which therefore they argue must needs be the constant impressions, which the souls of men receive in their first beings and which they bring into the world with them, as necessarily and really as they do any of their inherent faculties.

3. Universal consent proves nothing innate.   This argument, drawn from *universal consent*, has this misfortune in it that if it were true in matter of fact, that there were certain truths wherein all mankind agreed, it would not prove them innate if there can be any other way shown how men may come to that universal agreement in the things they do consent in, which I presume may be done.

4. What is, is; and It is impossible for the same thing to be and not to be, not universally assented to.   But, which is worse, this argument of universal consent, which is made use of to prove innate principles, seems to me a demonstration that there are none such, because there are none to which all mankind gives a universal assent. I shall begin with the speculative, and instance in those magnified principles of demonstration, *Whatsoever is, is*; and *It is impossible for the same thing to be and not to be*, which of all others I think have the most allowed title to innate. These have so settled a reputation of maxims universally received that it will no doubt be thought strange if anyone should seem to question it. But yet I take liberty to say that these propositions are so far from having a universal assent that there is a great part of mankind to whom they are not so much as known.

5. Not on the mind naturally imprinted, because not known to children, idiots, etc.   For first it is evident that all *children* and *idiots* have not the least apprehension or thought of them, and the want of that is enough to destroy that universal assent, which must needs be the necessary concomitant of all innate truths, it seeming to me near a contradiction to say that there are truths imprinted on the soul which it perceives or understands not. . . . For to imprint anything on the mind without the mind's perceiving it seems to me hardly intelligible. If therefore children and *idiots* have souls, have minds, with those impressions upon them, they must unavoidably perceive them and necessarily know and assent to these truths; since they do not, it is evident that there are no such impressions. . . . No proposition can be said to be in the mind, which it never yet knew, which it was never yet conscious of. For if any one may, then by the same reason all propositions that are true, and the mind is capable ever of assenting to, may be said to be in the mind and to be imprinted, since if any one can be said to be in the mind, which it never yet knew, it must be only because it is capable of knowing it; and so the mind is of all truths it ever shall know. . . . If truths can be imprinted on the understanding without being perceived, I can see no difference there can be between any truths the mind is capable of knowing in respect of their original, they must all be innate, or all adventitious. In vain shall a man go about to distinguish them. . . .

6. *That men know them when they come to the use of reason, answered.*   To avoid this, it is usually answered that all men know and *assent* to them *when they come to the use of reason*, and this is enough to prove them innate. . . .

7. . . . This answer . . . must signify one of these two things: either that as soon as men come to the use of reason, these supposed native inscriptions come to be known and observed by them, or else that the use and exercise of men's reasons assists them in the discovery of these principles and certainly makes them known to them.

8. *If reason discovered them, that would not prove them innate.*   If they mean that by the *use of reason* men may discover these principles and that this is sufficient to prove them innate, their way of arguing will stand thus (*viz.*): that whatever truths reason can certainly discover to us and make us firmly assent to, those are all naturally imprinted on the mind; . . . and by this means there will be no difference between the maxims of the mathematicians and theorems they deduce from them: All must be equally allowed innate. . . .

9. *It is false that reason discovers them.*   But how can these men think the *use of reason* necessary to discover principles that are supposed innate when reason (if we may believe them) is nothing else but the faculty of deducing unknown truths from principles or propositions that are already known? That certainly can never be thought innate, which we have need of reason to discover, unless as I have said, we will have all the certain truths that reason ever teaches us to be innate. . . .

12. *The coming to the use of reason, not the time we come to know these maxims.*   If by knowing and assenting to them *when we come to the use of reason* be meant that this is the time when they come to be taken notice of by the mind and that as soon as children come to the use of reason, they come also to know and assent to these maxims, this also is false and frivolous. *First*, it is false because it is evident these maxims are not in the mind so early as the use of reason. . . . [This] is so because till after they come to the use of reason, those general abstract *ideas* are not framed in the mind, about which those general maxims are, which are mistaken for innate principles but are indeed discoveries made and verities introduced and brought into the mind by the same way and discovered by the same steps as several other propositions, which nobody was ever so extravagant as to suppose innate. . . .

14. *If coming to the use of reason were the time of their discovery, it would not prove them innate.*   But *secondly*, were it true that the precise time of their being known and assented to were when men come to the *use of reason*, neither would that prove them innate. This way of arguing is as frivolous as the supposition of itself is false. For by what kind of logic will it appear that any notion is originally by nature imprinted in the mind in its first constitution because it comes first to be observed and assented to when a faculty of the mind, which has quite a distinct province, begins to exert itself? . . .

15. The steps by which the mind attains several truths. The senses at first let in particu-lar *ideas* and furnish the yet empty cabinet. And the mind by degrees growing familiar with some of them, they are lodged in the memory, and names got to them. Afterwards the mind, proceeding farther, abstracts them and by degrees learns the use of general names. In this manner the mind comes to be furnished with *ideas* and language, the materials about which to exercise its discursive faculty. And the use of reason becomes daily more visible, as these materials that give it employment increase. But though the having of general *ideas* and the use of general words and reason usually grow together, I see not how this any way proves them innate. The knowledge of some truths, I con-fess, is very early in the mind, but in a way that shows them not to be innate. For if we will observe, we shall find it still to be about *ideas* not innate but acquired: It being about those first, which are imprinted by external things, with which infants have earliest to do and which make the most frequent impressions on their senses. In *ideas* thus got, the mind discovers that some agree and others differ probably as soon as it has any use of memory, as soon as it is able to retain and receive distinct *ideas*. But whether it be then or not, this is certain, it does so long before it has the use of words or comes to that which we commonly call the *use of reason*. For a child knows as cer-tainly before it can speak the difference between the *ideas* of sweet and bitter (*i.e.*, that sweet is not bitter) as it knows afterwards (when it comes to speak) that wormwood and sugarplums are not the same thing. . . .

Book II

Chapter 1

Of Ideas in General and Their Original

1. Idea is the object of thinking. Every man being conscious to himself that he thinks and that which his mind is employed about while thinking being the *ideas* that are there, it is past doubt that men have in their minds several *ideas*, such as are those expressed by the words *whiteness, hardness, sweetness, thinking, motion, man, elephant, army, drunkenness*, and others: It is in the first place then to be inquired how he comes by them? I know it is a received doctrine, that men have native *ideas* and original characters stamped upon their minds in their very first being. This opinion I have at large examined already, and I suppose what I have said in the foregoing book will be much more easily admitted when I have shown whence the understanding may get all the *ideas* it has and by what ways and degrees they may come into the mind, for which I shall appeal to everyone's own observation and experience.

2. All ideas come from sensation or reflection. Let us then suppose the mind to be, as we say, white paper, void of all characters, without any *ideas*. How comes it to be fur-nished? Whence comes it by that vast store which the busy and boundless fancy of man has painted on it with an almost endless variety? Whence has it all the materials of reason and knowledge? To this I answer, in one word, from *experience*, in that all our knowledge is founded and from that it ultimately derives itself. Our observation employed either about *external, sensible objects or about the internal operations of our minds, perceived and reflected on by ourselves, is that which supplies our understandings with all the materials of thinking.* These two are the fountains of knowledge, from whence all the *ideas* we have, or can naturally have, do spring.

3. *The objects of sensation one source of ideas.*   First, *our senses,* conversant about particular sensible objects, do *convey into the mind* several distinct *perceptions* of things, according to those various ways wherein those objects do affect them. And thus we come by those *ideas* we have of *yellow, white, heat, cold, soft, hard, bitter, sweet,* and all those which we call sensible qualities.... This great source of most of the *ideas* we have depending wholly upon our senses and derived by them to the understanding, I call *sensation.*

4. *The operations of our minds, the other source of them.*   Secondly, the other fountain from which experience furnishes the understanding with *ideas* is the *perception of the operations of our own minds* within us, as it is employed about the *ideas* it has got, which operations, when the soul comes to reflect on and consider, do furnish the understanding with another set of *ideas* which could not be had from things without, and such are *perception, thinking, doubting, believing, reasoning, knowing, willing,* and all the different actings of our own minds which we being conscious of and observing in ourselves do from these receive into our understandings as distinct *ideas,* as we do from bodies affecting our senses. This source of *ideas* every man has wholly in himself, and though it be not sense, as having nothing to do with external objects, yet it is very like it and might properly enough be called internal sense. But as I call the other *sensation,* so I call this *reflection,* the *ideas* it affords being such only as the mind gets by reflecting on its own operations within itself....

5. *All our ideas are of the one or the other of these.*   The understanding seems to me not to have the least glimmering of any *ideas* which it doth not receive from one of these two. *External objects furnish the mind with the* ideas *of sensible qualities,* which are all those different perceptions they produce in us. And the *mind furnishes the understanding with* ideas *of its own operations....*

6. *Observable in children.*   He that attentively considers the state of a *child* at his first coming into the world will have little reason to think him stored with plenty of *ideas* that are to be the matter of his future knowledge. It is by degrees he comes to be furnished with them. And though the *ideas* of obvious and familiar qualities imprint themselves before the memory begins to keep a register of time and order, yet it is often so late before some unusual qualities come in the way that there are few men that cannot recollect the beginning of their acquaintance with them. And if it were worthwhile, no doubt a child might be so ordered as to have but a very few even of the ordinary *ideas* till he were grown up to a man.... If a child were kept in a place where he never saw any other but black and white till he were a man, he would have no more *ideas* of scarlet or green than he that from his childhood never tasted an oyster or a pineapple has of those particular relishes....

9. *The soul begins to have ideas when it begins to perceive.*   To ask *at what time a man has first any ideas* is to ask when he begins to perceive, having *ideas* and perception being

the same thing. I know it is an opinion that the soul always thinks and that it has the actual perception of *ideas* in itself constantly, as long as it exists, and that actual thinking is as inseparable from the soul as actual extension is from the body, which, if true, to inquire after the beginning of a man's *ideas* is the same as to inquire after the beginning of his soul. For by this account, soul and its *ideas*, like body and its extension, will begin to exist both at the same time.

10. *The soul thinks not always, for this wants proofs.*   But whether the soul be supposed to exist antecedent to or coeval with or sometime after the first rudiments of organization or the beginnings of life in the body I leave to be disputed by those who have better thought of that matter. I confess myself to have one of those dull souls that does not perceive itself always to contemplate *ideas* nor can conceive it any more necessary for the *soul always to think* than for the body always to move, the perception of *ideas* being (as I conceive) to the soul what motion is to the body—not its essence but one of its operations. . . .

18. *How does anyone know that the soul always thinks? For if it is not a self-evident proposition, it needs proof.*   I would be glad also to learn from these men who so confidently pronounce that the human soul, or, which is all one, that a man always thinks, how they come to know it, nay, *how they come to know that they themselves think when they themselves do not perceive it*. This, I am afraid, is to be sure without proofs and to know without perceiving. . . .

19. *That a man should be busy in thinking and yet not retain it the next moment, very improbable.*   To suppose the soul to think and the man not to perceive it is to make two persons in one man. And if one considers well these men's way of speaking, one should be led into a suspicion that they do so. For they who tell us that the soul always thinks do never, that I remember, say that a man always thinks. Can the soul think and not the man? Or a man think and not be conscious of it? This, perhaps, would be suspected of *jargon* in others. . . . They who talk thus may, with as much reason, if it be necessary to their hypothesis, say that a man is always hungry but that he does not always feel it, whereas hunger consists of that very sensation, as thinking consists of being conscious that one thinks. If they say that a man is always conscious to himself of thinking, I ask, How do they know it? Consciousness is the perception of what passes in a man's own mind. Can another man perceive that I am conscious of anything when I perceive it not myself? . . . They must needs have a penetrating sight, who can certainly see that I think, when I cannot perceive it myself and when I declare that I do not, and yet can see that dogs or elephants do not think, when they give all the demonstration of it imaginable, except only telling us that they do so. . . .

Chapter 2

Of Simple Ideas

1. *Uncompounded appearances.*   The better to understand the nature, manner, and extent of our knowledge, one thing is carefully to be observed concerning the *ideas* we have, and that is that *some* of them are *simple* and *some complex.*

Though the qualities that affect our senses are, in the things themselves, so united and blended that there is no separation, no distance between them, yet it is plain the *ideas* they produce in the mind enter by the senses simple and unmixed. For though the sight and touch often take in from the same object, at the same time, different *ideas*, as a man sees at once motion and color, the hand feels softness and warmth in the same piece of wax. Yet the simple *ideas* thus united in the same subject are as perfectly distinct as those that come in by different senses. The coldness and hardness which a man feels in a piece of *ice*, being as distinct *ideas* in the mind as the smell and whiteness of a lily,. . .and there is nothing can be plainer to a man than the clear and distinct perception he has of those simple *ideas*, which being each in itself uncompounded contains in it nothing but *one uniform appearance*, or conception in the mind, and is not distinguishable into different *ideas*.

2. The mind can neither make nor destroy them.   These simple *ideas*, the materials of all our knowledge, are suggested and furnished to the mind only by those two ways above mentioned, *viz., sensation* and *reflection*. When the understanding is once stored with these simple *ideas*, it has the power to repeat, compare, and unite them even to an almost infinite variety, and so can make at pleasure new complex *ideas*. But it is not in the power of the most exalted wit, or enlarged understanding, by any quickness or variety of thought, to *invent or frame one new simple idea* in the mind not taken in by the ways before mentioned, nor can any force of the understanding *destroy* those that are there. . . .

3. This is the reason why. . . it is *not possible* for anyone *to imagine* any other *qualities* in bodies, howsoever constituted, whereby they can be taken notice of besides sounds, tastes, smells, visible and tangible qualities. And had mankind been made with but four senses, the qualities then which are the object of the fifth sense would have been as far from our notice, imagination, and conception as now any *belonging to a sixth, seventh, or eighth sense* can possibly be. . . .

Chapter 3

Of Ideas of One Sense

1. Division of simple ideas.   The better to conceive the *ideas* we receive from sensation, it may not be amiss for us to consider them in reference to the different ways whereby they make their approaches to our minds and make themselves perceivable by us.

First then, there are some which come into our minds *by one sense* only.

Secondly, there are others that convey themselves into the mind *by more senses than one.*

Thirdly, others that are had from *reflection* only.

Fourthly, there are some that make themselves way and are suggested to the mind *by all the ways of sensation and reflection.*

We shall consider them apart under these several heads.

Ideas of one sense.   First there are *some* ideas *which have admittance only through one sense*, which is peculiarly adapted to receive them. Thus light and colors, as white, red, yellow, blue, with their several degrees or shades, and mixtures, as green, scarlet, purple, sea-green, and the rest, come in only by the eyes, all kinds of noises, sounds, and tones only by the ears, the several tastes and smells by the nose and palate. . . .

2. Few simple ideas have names.   I think it will be needless to enumerate all the particular *simple ideas* belonging to each sense. Nor indeed is it possible if we would, there being a great many *more* of them belonging to most of the senses *than we have names for.* . . . I shall therefore in the account of simple *ideas* I am here giving content myself to set down only such as are most material to our present purpose or are in themselves less apt to be taken notice of, though they are very frequently the ingredients of our complex *ideas*, among which I think I may well account solidity, which therefore I shall treat of in the next chapter.

Chapter 4

Of Solidity

1. We receive this idea from touch.   The *idea* of *solidity* we receive by our touch, and it arises from the resistance which we find in body to the entrance of any other body into the place it possesses till it has left it. There is no *idea* which we receive more constantly from sensation than *solidity*. Whether we move or rest in what posture soever we are, we always feel something under us that supports us and hinders our farther sinking downwards. . . . That which thus hinders the approach of two bodies when they are moving one towards another, I call *solidity*. . ., but if any one think it better to call it *impenetrability*, he has my consent. . . . This of all other seems the *idea* most intimately connected with and essential to body, so as nowhere else to be found or imagined but only in matter, and though our senses take no notice of it but in masses of matter of a bulk sufficient to cause a sensation in us, yet the mind, having once got this *idea* from such grosser sensible bodies, traces it farther and considers it as well as figure, in the minutest particle of matter that can exist and finds it inseparably inherent in body, wherever or however modified.

2. Solidity fills space.   This is the *idea* belongs to body, whereby we conceive it *to fill space.* The *idea* of which filling of space is that where we imagine any space taken up by a solid substance, we conceive it so to possess it, that it excludes all other solid substances. . . .

3. Distinct from space.   This resistance, whereby it keeps other bodies out of the space which it possesses, is so great that no force, how great soever, can surmount it. All the bodies in the world, pressing a drop of water on all sides, will never be able to overcome the resistance which it will make, as soft as it is, to their approaching one another, till it be removed out of their way, whereby our *idea of solidity* is *distinguished from pure space.* . . .

4. From hardness.   *Solidity* is hereby also *differenced from hardness* in that solidity consists in repletion and so an utter exclusion of other bodies out of the space it possesses, but hardness in a firm cohesion of the parts of matter making up masses of a sensible bulk, so that the whole does not easily change its figure. . . .

Chapter 6

Of Simple Ideas of Reflection

1. Are the operations of the mind about its other ideas?   The mind receiving the *ideas* mentioned in the foregoing chapters from without, when it turns its view inward upon itself and observes its own actions about those *ideas* it has takes from thence other *ideas*, which are as capable to be the objects of its contemplation as any of those it received from foreign things.

2. The idea of perception and idea of willing we have from reflection.   The two great and principal actions of the mind which are most frequently considered and which are so frequent that everyone that pleases may take notice of them in himself are these two:

> *Perception*, or *thinking*, and
> *Volition*, or *willing*.

The power of thinking is called the *understanding*, and the power of volition is called the *will*, and these two powers or abilities in the mind are denominated *faculties*. Of some of the modes of these simple *ideas* of reflection, such as are *remembrance, discerning, reasoning, judging, knowledge, faith*, etc., I shall have occasion to speak hereafter.

Chapter 7

Of Simple Ideas of Both Sensation and Reflection

1. Pleasure and pain.   There be other simple *ideas* which convey themselves into the mind by all the ways of sensation and reflection, *viz.*

> *Pleasure*, or *delight*, and its opposite.
> *Pain*, or *uneasiness*.
> *Power*.
> *Existence*.
> *Unity*.

2. Delight, or *uneasiness*, one or other of them join themselves to almost all our *ideas*, both of sensation and reflection, and there is scarce any affection of our senses from without, any retired thought of our mind within, which is not able to produce in us *pleasure* or *pain*. By *pleasure* and *pain* I would be understood to signify whatsoever delights or molests us, whether it arises from the thoughts of our minds or anything operating on our bodies. . . .

7. Existence and unity.   *Existence* and *unity* are two other *ideas* that are suggested to the understanding by every object without and every *idea* within. When *ideas* are in our minds, we consider them as being actually there, as well as we consider things to be actually without us—that is, that they exist or have *existence*. And whatever we can consider as one thing, whether a real being or *idea*, suggests to the understanding the *idea of unity*.

8. *Power.*   *Power* also is another of those simple *ideas* which we receive from *sensation and reflection.* For observing in ourselves that we can, at pleasure, move several parts of our bodies which were at rest, [and] the effects also that natural bodies are able to produce in one another occurring every moment to our senses, we both these ways get the *idea* of *power.*

9. *Succession.*   Besides these, there is another *idea* which, though suggested by our senses, yet is more constantly offered us by what passes in our own minds; and that is the *idea* of *succession.* For if we look immediately into ourselves and reflect on what is observable there, we shall find our *ideas* always, while we are awake or have any thought, passing in train, one going and another coming, without intermission. . . .

Chapter 8

Some Further Considerations Concerning Our Simple Ideas

7. *Ideas in the mind, qualities in bodies.*   To discover the nature of our *ideas* the better, and to discourse of them intelligibly, it will be convenient to distinguish them, as they are *ideas* or perceptions in our minds and as they are modifications of matter in the bodies that cause such perceptions in us—that so we *may not* think (as perhaps usually is done) that they are exactly the images and *resemblances* of something inherent in the subject, most of those of sensation being in the mind no more the likeness of something existing without us than the names that stand for them are the likeness of our *ideas* which yet upon hearing they are apt to excite in us.

8. Whatsoever the mind perceives in itself or is the immediate object of perception, thought, or understanding, that I call *idea*; and the power to produce any *idea* in our mind, I call *quality* of the subject wherein that power is. Thus a snowball having the power to produce in us the *ideas* of *white, cold,* and *round,* the powers to produce those *ideas* in us, as they are in the snowball, I call *qualities*; and as they are sensations, or perceptions, in our understandings, I call them *ideas*, which *ideas*, if I speak of sometimes as in the things themselves, I would be understood to mean those qualities in the objects which produce them in us.

9. *Primary and secondary qualities.*   Qualities thus considered in bodies are, first, such as are utterly inseparable from the body, in what state soever it be, such as in all the alterations and changes it suffers, all the force can be used upon it, it constantly keeps and such as sense constantly finds in every particle of matter which has bulk enough to be perceived and the mind finds inseparable from every particle of matter, though less than to make itself singly be perceived by our senses; *v.g.,* take a grain of wheat, divide it into two parts, [and] each part has still *solidity, extension, figure,* and *mobility*; divide it again, and it retains still the same qualities; and so divide it on, till the parts become insensible, they must retain still each of them all those qualities. . . . These I call *original* or *primary qualities* of body, which I think we may observe to produce simple *ideas* in us, *viz.* solidity, extension, figure, motion, or rest, and number.

10. Secondly, such *qualities*, which in truth are nothing in the objects themselves but powers to produce various sensations in us by their *primary qualities*, i.e., by the bulk, figure, texture, and motion of their insensible parts, as colors, sounds, tastes, *etc.* These I call *secondary qualities*. To these might be added a third sort which are allowed to be barely powers though they are as much real qualities in the subject, as those which I to comply with the common way of speaking call *qualities*, but for distinction *secondary qualities*. For the power in fire to produce a new color, or consistency in wax or clay by its primary qualities, is as much a quality in fire as the power it has to produce in me a new *idea* or sensation of warmth or burning, which I felt not before, by the same primary qualities, *viz.*, the bulk, texture, and motion of its insensible parts.

11. How primary qualities produce their ideas. The next thing to be considered is how *bodies* produce *ideas* in us, and that is manifestly *by impulse*, the only way which we can conceive bodies operate in.

12. If then external objects be not united to our minds when they produce *ideas* in it and yet we perceive *these original qualities* in such of them as singly fall under our senses, it is evident that some motion must be thence continued by our nerves, or animal spirits, by some parts of our bodies, to the brains or the seat of sensation, there to *produce in our minds the particular ideas we have of them. . . .*

13. How secondary. After the same manner that the *ideas* of these original qualities are produced in us, we may conceive that the *ideas of secondary qualities* are also *produced, viz., by the operation of insensible particles on our senses. . . .*

15. Ideas of primary qualities are resemblances; of secondary, not. From whence I think it is easy to draw this observation: that the *ideas of primary qualities* of bodies *are resemblances* of them, and their patterns do really exist in the bodies themselves; but the *ideas*, *produced* in us by these *secondary qualities have no resemblance* of them at all. There is nothing like our *ideas* existing in the bodies themselves. They are in the bodies we denominate from them only a power to produce those sensations in us, and what is sweet, blue, or warm in *idea* is but the certain bulk, figure, and motion of the insensible parts in the bodies themselves, which we call so. . . .

23. Three sorts of qualities in bodies. The *qualities* then that are in *bodies* rightly considered are of *three sorts.*

First, the *bulk, figure, number, situation*, and *motion, or rest* of their solid parts; those are in them, whether we perceive them or not; and when they are of that size that we can discover them, we have by these an *idea* of the thing as it is in itself, as is plain in artificial things. These I call *primary qualities*.

Secondly, the *power* that is in any body, *by* reason of *its* insensible *primary qualities*, to operate after a peculiar manner on any of our senses and thereby *produce in us* the *different ideas* of several colors, sounds, smells, tastes, *etc.* These are usually called sensible qualities.

Thirdly, the *power* that is in any body, *by* reason of the particular constitution of *its primary qualities, to* make such a *change in the bulk, figure, texture, and motion of another body*, as to make it operate on our senses differently from what it did before. Thus the sun has a power to make wax white and fire to make lead fluid. These are usually called powers.

The first of these, as has been said, I think, may be properly called *real original*, or *primary qualities*, because they are in the things themselves, whether they are perceived or not, and upon their different modifications it is that the secondary qualities depend.

The other two are only powers to act differently upon other things, which powers result from the different modifications of those primary qualities. . . .

Chapter 9

Of Perception

1. It is the first simple idea of reflection. Perception, as it is the first faculty of the mind exercised about our *ideas*, so it is the first and simplest *idea* we have from reflection and is by some called thinking in general. Though thinking, in the propriety of the *English* tongue, signifies that sort of operation of the mind about its *ideas* wherein the mind is active, where it with some degree of voluntary attention considers any thing. For in bare naked *perception*, the mind is, for the most part, only passive, and what it perceives, it cannot avoid perceiving.

2. Perception is only when the mind receives the impression. What perception is, everyone will know better by reflecting on what he does himself when he sees, hears, feels, *etc.*, or thinks than by any discourse of mine. Whoever reflects on what passes in his own mind cannot miss it, and if he does not reflect, all the words in the world cannot make him have any notion of it.

3. This is certain: that whatever alterations are made in the body, if they reach not the mind, whatever impressions are made on the outward parts, if they are not taken notice of within, there is no perception. Fire may burn our bodies with no other effect than it does a billet unless the motion be continued to the brain and there the sense of heat, or *idea* of pain, be produced in the mind, wherein consists *actual perception*.

4. How often may a man observe in himself that while his mind is intently employed in the contemplation of some objects and curiously surveying some *ideas* that are there, it takes no notice of impressions of sounding bodies made upon the organ of hearing with the same alteration that uses to be for the producing the *idea* of a sound? A sufficient impulse there may be on the organ, but it not reaching the observation of the mind, there follows no perception. . . . *So wherever there is sense, or perception, there some idea is actually produced, and present in the understanding.* . . .

8. Ideas of sensation often changed by the judgment. We are further to consider concerning perception that the *ideas we receive by sensation are often* in grown people *altered by the judgment* without our taking notice of it. When we set before our eyes a round globe, of any uniform color, *v.g.*, gold, alabaster, or jet, it is certain that the *idea* thereby imprinted in our mind is of a flat circle variously shadowed, with several degrees of light and brightness coming to our eyes. But we having by use been accustomed to perceive what kind of appearance convex bodies are wont to make in us, what alterations are made in the reflections of light by the difference of the sensible figures of bodies, the judgment presently, by a habitual custom, alters the appearances into their causes, so that from that which truly is variety of shadow or color, collecting the figure, it makes it pass for a mark of figure and frames to itself the perception of a convex figure, and a uniform color when the *idea* we receive from thence is only a plain variously colored, as is evident in painting. To which purpose I shall here insert a problem of that very ingenious and studious promoter of real knowledge, the learned and worthy Mr. *Molineux*, which he was pleased to send me in a letter some months since; and it is this: *Suppose a man born blind and now adult and taught by his touch to distinguish between a cube and a sphere of the same metal and nearly of the same bigness so as to tell when he felt one and the other which is the cube and which the sphere. Suppose then the cube and sphere placed on a table and the blind man is made to see. Question: Whether by his sight, before he touched them, he could now distinguish and tell which is the globe and which the cube.* To which the acute and judicious proposer answers: *No. For though he has obtained the experience of how a globe and how a cube affects his touch, yet he has not yet attained the experience that what affects his touch so or so must affect his sight so or so or that a protuberant angle in the cube that pressed his hand unequally shall appear to his eye as it does in the cube.* I agree with this thinking gent, whom I am proud to call my friend, in his answer to this his problem and am of opinion that the blind man, at first sight, would not be able with certainty to say which was the globe and which the cube while he only saw them, though he could unerringly name them by his touch and certainly distinguish them by the difference of their figures felt. . . .

11. *Perception puts the difference between animals and inferior beings.* This faculty of *perception* seems to me to be that which *puts the distinction betwixt the animal kingdom and the inferior parts of nature.* For however vegetables have, many of them, some degrees of motion, and upon the different application of other bodies to them do very briskly alter their figures and motions and so have obtained the name of sensitive plants from a motion which has some resemblance to that which in animals follows upon sensation, yet, I suppose, it is all bare mechanism, and no otherwise produced than the turning of a wild oat-beard by the insinuation of the particles of moisture or the shortening of a rope by the affusion of water, all which is done without any sensation in the subject or the having or receiving of any *ideas*. . . .

15. *Perception the inlet of knowledge.* Perception then being *the first step and degree towards knowledge and the inlet of all the materials of it,* the fewer senses any man, as well as any other creature, has and the fewer and duller the impressions are that are made by them and the duller the faculties are that are employed about them, the more remote are they from that knowledge which is to be found in some men. . . .

Chapter 10

Of Retention

1. *Contemplation.* The next faculty of the mind, whereby it makes a further progress towards knowledge, is that which I call *retention*, or the keeping of those simple *ideas*

which from sensation or reflection it has received. This is done two ways: first, by keeping the *idea*, which is brought into it, for some time actually in view, which is called *contemplation*.

2. Memory. The other way of retention is the power to revive again in our minds those *ideas* which after imprinting have disappeared or have been, as it were, laid aside out of sight. And thus we do when we conceive heat or light, yellow or sweet, the object being removed. This is *memory*, which is, as it were, the storehouse of our *ideas*. For the narrow mind of man, not being capable of having many *ideas* under view and consideration at once, it was necessary to have a repository to lay up those *ideas* which at another time it might have use of. But our *ideas* being nothing but actual perceptions in the mind which cease to be anything when there is no perception of them, this *laying up* of our *ideas* in the repository of the memory signifies no more but this: that the mind has a power, in many cases, to revive perceptions which it has once had, with this additional perception annexed to them, that it has had them before. And in this sense it is that our *ideas* are said to be in our memories when indeed they are actually nowhere, but only there is an ability in the mind, when it will, to revive them again and, as it were, paint them anew on itself, though some with more, some with less difficulty; some more lively, and others more obscurely. . . .

5. Ideas fade in the memory. . . . The memory in some men, it is true, is very tenacious, even to a miracle. But yet there seems to be a constant decay of all our *ideas*, even of those which are struck deepest, and in minds the most retentive, so that if they be not sometimes renewed by repeated exercise of the senses or reflection on those kind of objects which at first occasioned them, the print wears out, and at last there remains nothing to be seen. . . .

Chapter 11

Of Discerning and Other Operations of the Mind

1. No knowledge without it. Another faculty we may take notice of in our minds is that of *discerning* and distinguishing between the several *ideas* it has. It is not enough to have a confused perception of something in general. Unless the mind had a distinct perception of different objects and their qualities, it would be capable of very little knowledge; though the bodies that affect us were as busy about us as they are now and the mind were continually employed in thinking. On this faculty of distinguishing one thing from another depends the *evidence and certainty* of several even very general propositions which have passed for innate truths because men, overlooking the true cause why those propositions find universal assent, impute it wholly to native uniform impressions, whereas it in truth *depends upon this clear discerning faculty* of the mind whereby it perceives two *ideas* to be the same or different. . . .

3. Clearness alone hinders confusion. To the well distinguishing our *ideas*, it chiefly contributes that they be *clear and determinate*, and when they are so, it *will not breed any confusion* or mistake about them, though the senses should (as sometimes they do) convey them from the same object differently, on different occasions, and so seem to err. For though a man in a fever should from sugar have a bitter taste, which at another time would produce a sweet one, yet the *idea* of bitter in that man's mind would be as clear and distinct from the *idea* of sweet as if he had tasted only gall. . . .

4. *Comparing.* The *comparing* them one with another, in respect of extent, degrees, time, place, or any other circumstances, is another operation of the mind about its *ideas* and is that upon which depends all that large tribe of *ideas* comprehended under *relation*, which of how vast an extent it is I shall have occasion to consider hereafter.

5. *Brutes compare, but imperfectly.* How far brutes partake in this faculty is not easy to determine; I imagine they have it not in any great degree. For though they probably have several *ideas* distinct enough, yet it seems to me to be the prerogative of human understanding, when it has sufficiently distinguished any *ideas*, so as to perceive them to be perfectly different and so consequently two, to cast about and consider in what circumstances they are capable to be compared. . . .

6. *Compounding.* The next operation we may observe in the mind about its *ideas* is *composition*, whereby it puts together several of those simple ones it has received from sensation and reflection and combines them into complex ones. . . .

7. *Brutes compound but little.* In this also, I suppose, *brutes* come far short of men. For though they take in and retain together several combinations of simple *ideas*, as possibly the shape, smell, and voice of his master make up the complex *idea* a dog has of him, or rather are so many distinct marks whereby he knows him, yet I *do not* think they do of themselves ever compound them and *make complex ideas*. . . .

8. *Naming.* When children have, by repeated sensations, got *ideas* fixed in their memories, they begin, by degrees, to learn the use of signs. And when they have got the skill to apply the organs of speech to the framing of articulate sounds, they begin to make *use of words* to signify their *ideas* to others. . . .

9. *Abstraction.* The use of words then being to stand as outward marks of our internal *ideas*, and those *ideas* being taken from particular things, if every particular *idea* that we take in should have a distinct name, names must be endless. To prevent this, the mind makes the particular *ideas* received from particular objects to become general, which is done by considering them as they are in the mind such appearances separate from all other existences and the circumstances of real existence, as time, place, or any other concomitant *ideas*. This is called *abstraction*, whereby *ideas* taken from particular beings become general representatives of all of the same kind, and their names general names, applicable to whatever exists conformable to such abstract *ideas*. Such precise, naked appearances in the mind, without considering how, whence, or with what others they came there, the understanding lays up (with names commonly annexed to them) as the standards to rank real existences into sorts, as they agree with these patterns, and to *denominate* them accordingly. Thus the same color being observed today in chalk or snow, which the mind yesterday received from milk, it considers that appearance alone, makes it a representative of all of that kind, and having given it the name *whiteness*, it by that sound signifies the same quality wheresoever to be imagined or met with; and thus universals, whether *ideas* or terms, are made.

10. Brutes abstract not. If it may be doubted whether *beasts* compound and enlarge their *ideas* that way to any degree, this, I think, I may be positive in: that the power of *abstracting* is not at all in them and that the having of general *ideas* is that which puts a perfect distinction betwixt man and brutes and is an excellency which the faculties of brutes do by no means attain to. For it is evident, we observe no footsteps in them of making use of general signs for universal *ideas*, from which we have reason to imagine that they have not the faculty of abstracting, or making general *ideas*, since they have no use of words, or any other general signs. . . .

17. Dark room. I pretend not to teach but to inquire and therefore cannot but confess here again that external and internal sensation are the only passages that I can find of knowledge to the understanding. These alone, as far as I can discover, are the windows by which light is let into this *dark room*. For, methinks, the *understanding* is not much unlike a closet wholly shut from light, with only some little openings left to let in external visible resemblances, or *ideas* of things without; would the pictures coming into such a dark room but stay there and lie so orderly as to be found upon occasion, it would very much resemble the understanding of a man, in reference to all objects of sight, and the *ideas* of them. . . .

Chapter 12

Of Complex Ideas

1. Made by the mind out of simple ones. We have hitherto considered those *ideas* in the reception whereof the mind is only passive, which are those simple ones received from *sensation* and *reflection* before-mentioned, whereof the Mind cannot make any one to itself nor have any *idea* which does not wholly consist of them. But as the mind is wholly passive in the reception of all its simple *ideas*, so it exerts several acts of its own, whereby out of its simple *ideas*, as the materials and foundations of the rest, the other are framed. The acts of the mind wherein it exerts its power over its simple *ideas* are chiefly these three: 1. Combining several simple *ideas* into one compound one, and thus all complex *ideas* are made. 2. The 2d is bringing two *ideas*, whether simple or complex, together and setting them by one another so as to take a view of them at once without uniting them into one, by which way it gets all its *ideas* of relations. 3. The 3d is separating them from all other *ideas* that accompany them in their real existence; this is called *abstraction*. And thus all its general *ideas* are made. This shows man's power and its way of operation to be much the same in the material and intellectual world. For the materials in both being such as he has no power over, either to make or destroy, all that man can do is either to unite them together or to set them by one another or wholly separate them. I shall here begin with the first of these in the consideration of complex *ideas* and come to the other two in their due places. . . .

2. Made voluntarily. In this faculty of repeating and joining together its *ideas*, the mind has great power in varying and multiplying the objects of its thoughts, infinitely beyond what *sensation* or *reflection* furnished it with. . . .

3. Are either modes, substances, or relations. *Complex ideas*, however compounded and decompounded, though their number be infinite and the variety endless, wherewith they fill and entertain the thoughts of men, yet, I think, they may be all reduced under these three heads:

1. *Modes*
2. *Substances*
3. *Relations*

4. *Modes.* First, *modes* I call such complex *ideas* which however compounded contain not in them the supposition of subsisting by themselves but are considered as dependences on or affections of substances; such are the *ideas* signified by the words *triangle, gratitude, murder,* etc. . . .

5. *Simple and mixed modes.* Of these *modes* there are two sorts, which deserve distinct consideration. First, there are some which are only variations or different combinations of the same simple *idea,* without the mixture of any other, as a dozen or score, which are nothing but the *ideas* of so many distinct units added together, and these I call *simple modes,* as being contained within the bounds of one simple *idea.* Secondly, there are others compounded of simple *ideas* of several kinds, put together to make one complex one, *v.g., beauty,* consisting of a certain composition of color and figure, causing delight in the beholder; *theft,* which being the concealed change of the possession of any thing, without the consent of the proprietor, contains, as is visible, a combination of several *ideas* of several kinds; and these I call *mixed modes.*

6. *Substances single or collective.* Secondly, the *ideas* of *substances* are such combinations of simple *ideas* as are taken to represent distinct particular things subsisting by themselves, in which the supposed or confused *idea* of substance, such as it is, is always the first and chief. Thus if to substance be joined the simple *idea* of a certain dull whitish color, with certain degrees of weight, hardness, ductility, and fusibility, we have the *idea* of *lead*; and a combination of the *ideas* of a certain sort of figure with the powers of motion, thought, and reasoning, joined to substance, make the ordinary *idea of a man.* . . .

7. *Relation.* Thirdly, the last sort of complex *ideas* is that we call *relation,* which consists in the consideration and comparing one *idea* with another. . . .

Chapter 21

Of Power

1. *This idea how got.* The mind, being every day informed by the senses of the alteration of those simple *ideas* it observes in things without, and taking notice how one comes to an end and ceases to be and another begins to exist which was not before, reflecting also on what passes within itself and observing a constant change of its *ideas,* sometimes by the impression of outward objects on the senses and sometimes by the determination of its own choice, and concluding from what it has so constantly observed to have been that the like changes will for the future be made in the same things by like agents and by the like ways considers in one thing the possibility of

having any of its simple *ideas* changed and in another the possibility of making that change, and so comes by that *idea* which we call *power*. Thus we say fire has a *power* to melt gold, *i.e.*, to destroy the consistency of its insensible parts, and consequently its hardness, and make it fluid; and gold has a *power* to be melted; that the sun has a *power* to blanch wax, and wax a *power* to be blanched by the sun, whereby the yellowness is destroyed and whiteness made to exist in its room. In which, and the like cases, the *power* we consider is in reference to the change of perceivable *ideas*. For we cannot observe any alteration to be made in or operation upon any thing but by the observable change of its sensible *ideas*, nor conceive any alteration to be made but by conceiving a change of some of its *ideas*.

2. *Power active and passive.*   *Power* thus considered is twofold, *viz.*, as able to make or able to receive any change: The one may be called *active*, and the other *passive power*. Whether matter be not wholly destitute of *active power*, as its author God is truly above all *passive power*, and whether the intermediate state of created spirits be not that alone which is capable of both *active* and *passive power* may be worth consideration. I shall not now enter into that inquiry, my present business being not to search into the original of power but how we come by the *idea* of it. But since *active powers* make so great a part of our complex *ideas* of natural substances (as we shall see hereafter), and I mention them as such, according to common apprehension, yet they being not, perhaps, so truly *active powers* as our hasty thoughts are apt to represent them, I judge it not amiss, by this intimation, to direct our minds to the consideration of God and spirits for the clearest *idea* of *active power*.

3. *Power includes relation.*   I confess *power includes in it some kind of relation* (a relation to action or change)—as indeed which of our *ideas*, of what kind soever, when attentively considered, does not?. . . . Our *idea* therefore of *power*, I think, may well have a place among other simple *ideas* and be considered as one of them, being one of those that make a principal ingredient in our complex *ideas* of substances, as we shall hereafter have occasion to observe.

4. *The clearest idea of active power had from spirit.*   We are abundantly furnished with the *idea* of *passive power* by almost all sorts of sensible things. In most of them we cannot avoid observing their sensible qualities, nay their very substances, to be in a continual flux. And therefore with reason we look on them as liable still to the same change. Nor have we of *active power* (which is the more proper signification of the word *power*) fewer instances. Since whatever change is observed, the mind must collect a power somewhere able to make that change, as well as a possibility in the thing itself to receive it. But yet if we will consider it attentively, bodies, by our senses, do not afford us so clear and distinct an *idea* of *active power* as we have from reflection on the operations of our minds. For all *power* relating to action, and there being but two sorts of action whereof we have any *idea*, *viz.*, thinking and motion, let us consider whence we have the clearest *ideas* of the *powers* which produce these actions. 1. Of thinking, body affords us no *idea* at all, it is only from reflection that we have that. 2. Neither have we from body any *idea* of the beginning of motion. A body at rest affords us no *idea* of any *active power* to move; and when it is set in motion itself, that

motion is rather a passion than an action in it. For when the ball obeys the stroke of a billiard stick, it is not any action of the ball but bare passion, . . .which gives us but a very obscure *idea* of an *active power* of moving in body, while we observe it only to transfer but not produce any motion. . . . The *idea* of the beginning of motion we have only from reflection on what passes in ourselves, where we find by experience that barely by willing it, barely by a thought of the mind, we can move the parts of our bodies which were before at rest. So that it seems to me, we have from the observation of the operation of bodies by our senses but a very imperfect obscure *idea* of *active power*, since they afford us not any *idea* in themselves of the *power* to begin any action, either motion or thought. . . .

5. *Will and understanding: two powers.* This at least I think evident: that we find in ourselves a *power* to begin or forbear, continue or end several actions of our minds and motions of our bodies barely by a thought or preference of the mind ordering or, as it were, commanding the doing or not doing such or such a particular action. This *power* which the mind has thus to order the consideration of any *idea* or the forbearing to consider it or to prefer the motion of any part of the body to its rest, and *vice versa* in any particular instance is that which we call the *will*. The actual exercise of that power, by directing any particular action, or its forbearance is that which we call *volition* or *willing*. The forbearance or performance of that action, consequent to such order or command of the mind, is called *voluntary*. And whatsoever action is performed without such a thought of the mind is called *involuntary*. . . .

7. *Whence the ideas of liberty and necessity.* Everyone, I think, finds in himself a *power* to begin or forbear, continue or put an end to several actions in himself. From the consideration of the extent of this power of the mind over the actions of the man, which everyone finds in himself, arise the *ideas* of *liberty* and *necessity*.

8. *Liberty what.* All the actions that we have any *idea* of, reducing themselves, as has been said, to these two, *viz.*, thinking and motion, so far as a man has a power to think or not to think, to move or not to move, according to the preference or direction of his own mind, so far is a man *free*. Wherever any performance or forbearance are not equally in a man's power, wherever doing or not doing will not equally follow upon the preference of his mind directing it, there he is not *free*, though perhaps the action may be voluntary. So that the *idea* of *liberty* is the *idea* of a power in any agent to do or forbear any particular action, according to the determination or thought of the mind, whereby either of them is preferred to the other; where either of them is not in the power of the agent to be produced by him according to his *volition*, there he is not at *liberty*, that agent is under *necessity*. So that *liberty* cannot be where there is no thought, no volition, no will; but there may be thought, there may be will, there may be volition where there is no *liberty*. A little consideration of an obvious instance or two may make this clear. . . .

10. *Belongs not to volition.* . . . Suppose a man be carried while fast asleep into a room where is a person he longs to see and speak with and be there locked fast in, beyond his power to get out; he awakes and is glad to find himself in so desirable company,

which he stays willingly in, *i.e.*, prefers his stay to going away. I ask, is not this stay voluntary? I think nobody will doubt it; and yet being locked fast in, it is evident he is not at liberty not to stay, he has not freedom to be gone. So that *liberty is not an idea belonging to volition*, or preferring, but to the person having the power of doing, or forbearing to do, according as the mind shall choose or direct. . . .

11. *Voluntary opposed to involuntary, not to necessary.* We have instances enough, and often more than enough, in our own bodies. A man's heart beats, and the blood circulates, which it is not in his power by any thought or volition to stop; and therefore in respect of these motions, where rest depends not on his choice nor would follow the determination of his mind, if it should prefer it, he is not a *free agent.* . . . There is want of *freedom*, though the sitting still even of a paralytic, while he prefers it to a removal, is truly voluntary. *Voluntary* then *is not opposed to necessary but to involuntary.* For a man may prefer what he can do to what he cannot do, the state he is in to its absence or change, though necessity has made it in itself unalterable.

12. *Liberty what.* As it is in the motions of the body, so it is in the thoughts of our minds; where any one is such that we have power to take it up or lay it by, according to the preference of the mind, there we are *at liberty.* A waking man being under the necessity of having some *ideas* constantly in his mind is not at *liberty* to think or not to think, no more than he is at *liberty* whether his body shall touch any other or not. But whether he will remove his contemplation from one *idea* to another is many times in his choice; and then he is in respect of his *ideas* as much at *liberty* as he is in respect of bodies he rests on: He can at pleasure remove himself from one to another. But yet some *ideas* to the mind, like some motions to the body are such as in certain circumstances it cannot avoid nor obtain their absence by the utmost effort it can use. A man on the rack is not at *liberty* to lay by the *idea* of pain and divert himself with other contemplations. . . .

14. *Liberty belongs not to the will.* If this be so (as I imagine it is), I leave it to be considered whether it may not help to put an end to that long agitated and, I think, unreasonable, because unintelligible, question, *viz.*, *whether man's will be free or not.* For if I mistake not, it follows from what I have said that the question itself is altogether improper, and it is as insignificant to ask whether man's *will* be free as to ask whether his sleep be swift or his virtue square, *liberty* being as little applicable to the *will* as swiftness of motion is to sleep or squareness to virtue. . . .

16. *Powers belong to agents.* It is plain, then, that the *will* is nothing but one power or ability and *freedom* another power or ability, so that to ask whether the *will has freedom* is to ask whether one power has another power, one ability another ability—a question at first sight too grossly absurd to make a dispute or need an answer. . . .

21. *But to the agent or man.* To return, then, to the inquiry about liberty, I think *the question is not proper whether the will be free but whether a man be free.* Thus I think,
    1. That so far as anyone can, by the direction or choice of his mind, preferring the existence of any action, to the nonexistence of that action and, *vice versa*, make it to exist or not exist, so far he is *free.* . . .

23.   2. That *willing* or *volition* being an action and freedom consisting in a power of acting or not acting, *a man in respect of willing, or the act of volition, when any action in his power is once proposed to his thoughts as presently to be done cannot be free.* The reason whereof is very manifest: For it being unavoidable that the action depending on his *will* should exist or not exist, and its existence or not existence following perfectly the determination and preference of his will, he cannot avoid willing the existence or not existence of that action; it is absolutely necessary that he *will* the one or the other, *i.e.*, *prefer* the one to the other, since one of them must necessarily follow; and that which does follow, follows by the choice and determination of his mind, that is, by his *willing* it, for if he did not *will* it, it would not be. . . .

30. Will and desire must not be confounded.   . . . He that shall turn his thoughts inwards upon what passes in his mind when he *wills* shall see that the *will* or power of *volition* is conversant about nothing but our own actions, terminates there, and reaches no farther, and that *volition* is nothing but that particular determination of the mind whereby barely by a thought the mind endeavors to give rise, continuation, or stop to any action which it takes to be in its power. This well-considered plainly shows that the *will* is perfectly distinguished from *desire*, which in the very same action may have a quite contrary tendency from that which our *wills* sets us upon. A man whom I cannot deny may oblige me to use persuasions to another, which at the same time I am speaking I may wish may not prevail on him. In this case, it is plain the *will* and *desire* run counter. I will the action that tends one way, while my desire tends another, and that the direct contrary. . . . Whence it is evident that *desiring* and *willing* are two distinct acts of the mind, and consequently that the *will*, which is but the power of *volition*, is much more distinct from *desire*.

31. Uneasiness determines the will.   To return, then, to the inquiry, *what is it that determines the will in regard to our actions?* And that upon second thoughts I am apt to imagine is not, as is generally supposed, the greater good in view, but some (and for the most part the most pressing) *uneasiness* a man is at present under. This is that which successively determines the *will* and sets us upon those actions we perform. This *uneasiness* we may call, as it is, *desire*, which is an *uneasiness* of the mind for want of some absent good. . . .

47. The power to suspend the prosecution of any desire makes way for consideration. There being in us a great many *uneasinesses* always soliciting and ready to determine the *will*, it is natural, as I have said, that the greatest and most pressing should determine the *will* to the next action; and so it does for the most part, but not always. For the mind having in most cases, as is evident in experience, a power to *suspend* the execution and satisfaction of any of its desires, and so all, one after another, is at liberty to consider the objects of them, examine them on all sides, and weigh them with others. In this lies the liberty man has; and from the not using of it right comes all that variety of mistakes, errors, and faults which we run into in the conduct of our lives and our endeavors after happiness, while we precipitate the determination of our *wills* and engage too soon before due *examination.* To prevent this we have a power to *suspend* the prosecution of this or that desire, as everyone daily may experiment in himself. This seems to me the source of all liberty; in this seems to consist that which is (as I think improperly) called *free will*. For during this *suspension* of any desire, before the *will* be determined to action and the action (which follows that determination) done, we have opportunity to examine, view, and judge of the good or evil of what we are going to do, and when, upon due *examination*, we have judged we have done our duty, all that we can or ought to do in pursuit of our happiness, and it is not a fault but a perfection of our nature to desire, will, and act according to the last result of a fair *examination*. . . .

56. *How men come to choose ill.* These things duly weighed will give us, as I think, a clear view into the state of human liberty. Liberty, it is plain, consists in a power to do or not to do; to do or forbear doing as we *will*. This cannot be denied. But this seeming to comprehend only the actions of a man consecutive to volition, it is further inquired whether he be at liberty to *will* or not? And to this it has been answered that in most cases a man is not at liberty to forbear the act of volition; he must exert an act of his *will*, whereby the action proposed is made to exist or not to exist. But yet there is a case wherein a man is at liberty in respect of *willing*, and that is the choosing of a remote good as an end to be pursued. Here a man may suspend the act of his choice from being determined for or against the thing proposed till he has examined whether it be really of a nature in itself and consequences to make him happy or not. For when he has once chosen it, and thereby it is become a part of his happiness, it raises desire, and that proportionably gives him *uneasiness*, which determines his *will* and sets him at work in pursuit of his choice on all occasions that offer. . . .

Chapter 22

Of Mixed Modes

1. *Mixed modes what.* Having treated of *simple modes* in the foregoing chapters and given several instances of some of the most considerable of them to show what they are and how we come by them, we are now in the next place to consider those we call *mixed modes*, such are the complex *ideas* we mark by the names *obligation, drunkenness, a lie*, etc. . . . These mixed modes being also such combinations of simple *ideas* as are not looked upon to be the characteristic marks of any real beings that have a steady existence, but scattered and independent *ideas* put together by the mind are thereby distinguished from the complex *ideas* of substances.

2. *Made by the mind.* That the mind, in respect of its simple *ideas*, is wholly passive and receives them all from the existence and operations of things, such as sensation or reflection offers them, without being able to make any one *idea*, experience shows us. But if we attentively consider these *ideas* I call *mixed modes* we are now speaking of, we shall find their original quite different. *The mind often exercises an active power in the making these* several *combinations*. For it being once furnished with simple *ideas*, it can put them together in several compositions and so make variety of complex *ideas* without examining whether they exist so together in nature. . . .

3. *Sometimes got by the explication of their names.* Indeed, now that languages are made and abound with words standing for such combinations, *a usual way of getting*

these complex ideas is by the explication of those terms that stand for them. For consisting of a company of simple *ideas* combined, they may by words standing for those simple *ideas* be represented to the mind of one who understands those words, though that complex combination of simple *ideas* were never offered to his mind by the real existence of things. . . .

4. *The name ties the parts of the mixed modes into one idea.* Every *mixed mode* consisting of many distinct simple *ideas*, it seems reasonable to inquire *whence it has its unity* and how such a precise multitude comes to make but one *idea*, since that combination does not always exist together in nature. To which I answer it is plain, it has its unity from an act of the mind combining those several simple *ideas* together and considering them as one complex one consisting of those parts; and the mark of this union, or that which is looked on generally to complete it, is one name given to that combination. For it is by their names that men commonly regulate their account of their distinct species of mixed modes, seldom allowing or considering any number of simple *ideas* to make one complex one but such collections as there be names for. Thus though the killing of an old man be as fit in nature to be united into one complex *idea* as the killing a man's father, yet there being no name standing precisely for the one, as there is the name of *parricide* to mark the other, it is not taken for a particular complex *idea* nor a distinct species of actions from that of killing a young man or any other man.

5. *The cause of making mixed modes.* If we should inquire a little further to see *what it is that occasions men to make several combinations of simple ideas* into distinct and, as it were, settled *modes,* . . . we shall find . . . they usually make such collections of *ideas* into complex modes and affix names to them, as they have frequent use of in their way of living and conversation, leaving others, which they have but seldom an occasion to mention, loose and without names that tie them together. . . .

9. *How we get the ideas of mixed modes.* There are therefore *three ways whereby we get the complex ideas of mixed modes.* 1. By experience and *observation* of things themselves. Thus by seeing two men wrestle or fence, we get the *idea* of wrestling or fencing. 2. By *invention*, or voluntary putting together of several simple *ideas* in our own minds. So he that first invented printing, or etching, had an *idea* of it in his mind before it ever existed. 3. Which is the most usual way, by *explaining the names* of actions we never saw or notions we cannot see and by enumerating and thereby, as it were, setting before our imaginations all those *ideas* which go to the making them up and are the constituent parts of them. . . .

Chapter 23

Of Our Complex Ideas of Substances

1. *Ideas of substances how made.* The Mind being, as I have declared, furnished with a great number of the simple *ideas* conveyed in by the *senses*, as they are found in exterior things, or by *reflection* on its own operations, takes notice also that a certain number of these simple *ideas* go constantly together, which being presumed to belong to one thing, and words being suited to common apprehensions and made use of for

quick dispatch, are called so united in one subject by one name, which by inadvertency we are apt afterward to talk of and consider as one simple *idea*, which indeed is a complication of many *ideas* together, because, as I have said, not imagining how these simple *ideas* can subsist by themselves, we accustom ourselves to suppose some *substratum* wherein they do subsist and from which they do result, which therefore we call *substance*.

2. Our idea of substance in general.   So that if anyone will examine himself concerning his *notion of pure substance in general*, he will find he has no other *idea* of it at all, but only a supposition of he knows not what support of such qualities which are capable of producing simple *ideas* in us, which qualities are commonly called accidents. If anyone should be asked what is the subject wherein color or weight inheres, he would have nothing to say but the solid extended parts; and if he were demanded what is it that that solidity and extension inhere in, he would not be in a much better case than the *Indian* . . . who, saying that the world was supported by a great elephant, was asked what the elephant rested on, to which his answer was a great tortoise. But being again pressed to know what gave support to the broad-backed tortoise, he replied something, he knew not what. . . .

3. Of the sorts of substances.   An obscure and relative *idea* of substance in general being thus made, we come to have the *ideas of particular sorts of substances* by collecting such combinations of simple *ideas* as are by experience and observation of men's senses taken notice of to exist together and are therefore supposed to flow from the particular internal constitution or unknown essence of that substance. Thus we come to have the *ideas* of a man, horse, gold, water, *etc*. . . . Only we must take notice that our complex *ideas* of substances, besides all these simple *ideas* they are made up of, have always the confused *idea* of *something* to which they belong and in which they subsist, and therefore when we speak of any sort of substance, we say it is a *thing* having such or such qualities, as body is a *thing* that is extended, figured, and capable of motion [and] a spirit a *thing* capable of thinking. . . . These and the like fashions of speaking intimate that the substance is supposed always *something* besides the extension, figure, solidity, motion, thinking, or other observable *ideas*, though we know not what it is. . . .

5. As clear an idea of spirit as body. . . . *We have as clear a notion of the substance of spirit as we have of body*, the one being supposed to be (without knowing what it is) the *substratum* to those simple *ideas* we have from without, and the other supposed (with a like ignorance of what it is) to be the *substratum* to those operations which we experiment in ourselves within. . . .

11. The now secondary qualities of bodies would disappear if we could discover the primary ones of their minute parts.   Had we senses acute enough to discern the minute particles of bodies and the real constitution on which their sensible qualities depend, I doubt not but they would produce quite different *ideas* in us and that which is now the yellow color of gold would then disappear and instead of it we should see an admirable texture of parts of a certain size and figure. This microscopes plainly discover to us, for what to our naked eyes produces a certain color is by thus augmenting the acuteness of our senses discovered to be quite a different thing. . . .

22. *Idea of soul and body compared.*   Let us *compare*, then, our complex *idea* of an immaterial spirit with our complex *idea* of body and see whether there be any more obscurity in one than in the other, and in which most. Our *idea* of body, as I think, is an extended solid substance capable of communicating motion by impulse; and our *idea* of our soul, as an immaterial spirit, is of a substance that thinks and has a power of exciting motion in body by will or thought. These, I think, are *our complex ideas of soul and body, as contradistinguished*; and now let us examine which has most obscurity in it and difficulty to be apprehended. . . .

23. *Cohesion of solid parts in body, as hard to be conceived as thinking in a soul.*   If anyone says he knows not what thinks in him, he means he knows not what the substance is of that thinking thing—no more, say I, knows he what the substance is of that solid thing. Further, if he says he knows not how he thinks, I answer, neither knows he how he is extended, how the solid parts of body are united or cohere together to make extension. . . .

32. *We know nothing beyond our simple ideas*. . . . *We have as much reason to be satisfied with our notion of immaterial spirit as with our notion of body and the existence of the one as well as the other.* For it being no more a contradiction that thinking should exist separate and independent from solidity than it is a contradiction that solidity should exist separate and independent from thinking, they being both but simple *ideas* independent one from another; and having as clear and distinct *ideas* in us of thinking, as of solidity, I know not why we may not as well allow a thinking thing without solidity, i.e., *immaterial*, to exist as a solid thing without thinking, i.e., *matter*, to exist, especially since it is no harder to conceive how thinking should exist without matter than how matter should think. For whensoever we would proceed beyond these simple *ideas* we have from sensation and reflection and dive further into the nature of things, we fall presently into darkness and obscurity, perplexedness and difficulties and can discover nothing further but our own blindness and ignorance. . . .

33. *Idea of God.*   For if we examine the *idea* we have of the incomprehensible supreme being, we shall find that we come by it the same way and that the complex *ideas* we have both of God and separate Spirits are made up of the simple *ideas* we receive from *reflections*, v.g., having from what we experiment in ourselves got the *ideas* of existence and duration, of knowledge and power, of pleasure and happiness, and of several other qualities and powers which it is better to have than to be without; when we would frame an *idea* the most suitable we can to the supreme being, we enlarge every one of these with our *idea* of infinity and so putting them together make our complex *idea of God.* For that the mind has such a power of enlarging some of its Ideas received from sensation and reflection has been already shown. . . .

37. *Recapitulation.*   And thus we have seen *what kind of ideas we have of substances of all kinds*, wherein they consist, and how we come by them. From whence, I think, it is very evident.

First, that all our *ideas* of the several sorts of substances are nothing but collections of simple *ideas* with a supposition of something to which they belong and in which they subsist, though of this supposed something we have no clear distinct *idea* at all.

Secondly, that all the simple *ideas* that thus united in one common *substratum* make up our complex *ideas* of the several sorts of substances are no other but such as we have received from *sensation* or *reflection*. So that even in those which we think we are most intimately acquainted with and come nearest the comprehension of, our most enlarged conceptions cannot reach beyond those simple *ideas*. And even in those which seem most remote from all we have to do with and do infinitely surpass anything we can perceive in ourselves by *reflection* or discover by *sensation* in other things, we can attain to nothing but those simple *ideas* which we originally received from *sensation* or *reflection*, as is evident in the complex *ideas* we have of angels and particularly of God himself.

Thirdly, that most of the simple *ideas* that make up our complex *ideas* of substances, when truly considered, are only powers, however we are apt to take them for positive qualities; *v.g.*, the greatest part of the *ideas* that make our complex *idea* of gold are yellowness, great weight, ductility, fusibility, and solubility in *aqua regia*, etc., all united together in an unknown *substratum*, all which *ideas* are nothing else but so many relations to other substances and are not really in the gold, considered barely in itself, though they depend on those real and primary qualities of its internal constitution, whereby it has a fitness, differently to operate and be operated on by several other substances.

Chapter 27

Of Identity and Diversity

1. Wherein identity consists.   Another occasion the mind often takes of comparing is the very being of things; when considering anything as existing at any determined time and place, we compare it with itself existing at another time and thereon form the *ideas* of *identity* and *diversity*. When we see anything to be in any place in any instant of time, we are sure (be it what it will) that it is that very thing and not another which at that same time exists in another place, how like and undistinguishable soever it may be in all other respects. And in this consists *identity*, when the *ideas* it is attributed to vary not at all from what they were that moment wherein we consider their former existence and to which we compare the present. For we never finding nor conceiving it possible that two things of the same kind should exist in the same place at the same time, we rightly conclude that whatever exists anywhere at any time excludes all of the same kind and is there itself alone. When therefore we demand whether anything be the same or not, it refers always to something that existed such a time in such a place, which it was certain at that instant was the same with itself and no other, from whence it follows that one thing cannot have two beginnings of existence, nor two things one beginning, it being impossible for two things of the same kind to be or exist in the same instant in the very same place or one and the same thing in different places. . . .

2. Identity of substances.   We have the *ideas* but of three sorts of substances: 1. God. 2. Finite intelligences. 3. *Bodies*. First, God is without beginning, eternal, unalterable, and everywhere; and therefore concerning his Identity, there can be no doubt. Secondly, finite spirits having had each its determinate time and place of beginning to exist, the relation to that time and place will always determine to each of them its identity as long as it exists.

Thirdly, the same will hold of every particle of matter, to which no addition or sub-traction of matter being made, it is the same. For though these three sorts of sub-stances, as we term them, do not exclude one another out of the same place, yet we cannot conceive but that they must necessarily each of them exclude any of the same kind out of the same place, or else the notions and names of identity and diversity would be in vain, and there could be no such distinction of substances or anything else one from another. . . .

3. Principium individuationis. From what has been said, it is easy to discover what is so much inquired after, the *principium individuationis*, and that it is plain is existence itself, which determines a being of any sort to a particular time and place incom-municable to two beings of the same kind. . . . Let us suppose an atom, *i.e.*, a con-tinued body under one immutable superficies, existing in a determined time and place. It is evident that, considered in any instant of its existence, it is in that instant the same with itself. . . . In like manner, if two or more atoms be joined together into the same mass, every one of those atoms will be the same, by the foregoing rule. And while they exist united together, the mass, consisting of the same atoms, must be the same mass or the same body, let the parts be never so differently jumbled. But if one of these atoms be taken away or one new one added, it is no longer the same mass or the same body. In the state of living creatures, their identity depends not on a mass of the same particles but on something else. For in them the variation of great parcels of matter alters not the identity. An oak, growing from a plant to a great tree and then lopped is still the same oak. . . . The reason whereof is that in these . . . cases of a mass of matter and a living body, *identity* is not applied to the same thing.

4. Identity of vegetables. We must therefore consider wherein an oak differs from a mass of matter, and that seems to me to be in this: that the one is only the cohesion of particles of matter anyhow united, the other such a disposition of them as consti-tutes the parts of an oak and such an organization of those parts as is fit to receive and distribute nourishment so as to continue and frame the wood, bark, and leaves, *etc.*, of an oak in which consists the vegetable life. That being then one plant, which has such an organization of parts in one coherent body, partaking of one common life, it continues to be the same plant as long as it partakes of the same life, though that life be communicated to new particles of matter vitally united to the living plant in a like continued organization conformable to that sort of plants. . . .

5. Identity of animals. The case is not so much different in *brutes* but that anyone may hence see what makes an animal and continues it the same. Something we have like this in machines and may serve to illustrate it. For example, what is a watch? It is plain it is nothing but a fit organization or construction of parts to a certain end, which, when a sufficient force is added to it, it is capable to attain. If we would suppose this machine one continued body, all whose organized parts were repaired, increased, or diminished by a constant addition or separation of insensible parts with one common life, we should have something very much like the body of an animal, with this difference: that in an animal the fitness of the organization and the motion wherein life consists begin together, the motion coming from within; but in machines the force, coming sensibly from without, is often away, when the organ is in order and well fitted to receive it.

6. *Identity of man.* This also shows wherein the identity of the same *man* consists, *viz.*, in nothing but a participation of the same continued life by constantly fleeting particles of matter in succession vitally united to the same organized body. He that shall place the *identity* of man in anything else but like that of other animals in one fitly organized body taken in any one instant and from thence continued under one organization of life in several successively fleeting particles of matter, united to it, will find it hard to make an *embryo* [and] one of years, mad, and sober, the same man by any supposition that will not make it possible for *Seth, Ishmael, Socrates, Pilate, St. Austin,* and *Caesar Borgia* to be the same man. For if the *identity* of soul alone makes the same man and there be nothing in the nature of matter why the same individual spirit may not be united to different bodies, it will be possible that those men, living in distant ages and of different tempers, may have been the same man—which way of speaking must be from a very strange use of the word *man,* applied to an *idea* out of which body and shape is excluded. . . .

7. *Identity suited to the idea.* It is not therefore unity of substance that comprehends all sorts of *identity* or will determine it in every case. But to conceive, and judge of it aright, we must consider what *idea* the word it is applied to stands for, it being one thing to be the same *substance,* another the same *man,* and a third the same *person.* . . .

9. *Personal identity.* This being premised, to find wherein *personal identity* consists, we must consider what *person* stands for, which, I think, is a thinking intelligent being that has reason and reflection and can consider itself as itself, the same thinking thing in different times and places, which it does only by that consciousness which is inseparable from thinking and as it seems to me essential to it, it being impossible for anyone to perceive without perceiving that he does perceive. When we see, hear, smell, taste, feel, meditate, or will anything, we know that we do so. Thus it is always as to our present sensations and perceptions. And by this everyone is to himself, that which he calls *self,* it not being considered in this case whether the same *self* be continued in the same or divers substances. For since consciousness always accompanies thinking, and it is that that makes everyone to be what he calls *self* and thereby distinguishes himself from all other thinking things, in this alone consists *personal identity,* *i.e.,* the sameness of a rational being. And as far as this consciousness can be extended backwards to any past action or thought, so far reaches the identity of that *person;* it is the same *self* now it was then, and it is by the same *self* with this present one that now reflects on it that that action was done.

10. *Consciousness makes personal identity.* But it is further inquired whether it be the same identical substance. This few would think they had reason to doubt of, if these

perceptions, with their consciousness, always remained present in the mind, whereby the same thinking thing would be always consciously present and, as would be thought, evidently the same to itself. But that which seems to make the difficulty is this: that . . . our consciousness being interrupted and we losing the sight of our past *selves*, doubts are raised whether we are the same thinking thing, *i.e.*, the same substance or not—which, however reasonable or unreasonable, concerns not *personal identity* at all, the question being what makes the same *person* and not whether it be the same identical substance which always thinks in the same person. . . . For it being the same consciousness that makes a man be himself to himself, *personal identity* depends on that only, whether it be annexed only to one individual substance or can be continued in a succession of several substances. For as far as any intelligent being can repeat the *idea* of any past action with the same consciousness it had of it at first and with the same consciousness it has of any present action, so far it is the same *personal self*. For it is by the consciousness it has of its present thoughts and actions that it is *self* to itself now and so will be the same *self* as far as the same consciousness can extend to actions past or to come. . . .

18. *Object of reward and punishment.* In this *personal identity* is founded all the right and justice of reward and punishment, happiness and misery, being that for which every one is concerned for *himself*, not mattering what becomes of any substance not joined to or affected with that consciousness. . . .

26. *Person a forensic term.* *Person*, as I take it, is the name for this *self*. Wherever a man finds what he calls *himself*, there I think another may say is the same *person*. It is a forensic term appropriating actions and their merit and so belongs only to intelligent agents capable of a law and happiness and misery. This personality extends *itself* beyond present existence to what is past only by consciousness, whereby it becomes concerned and accountable, owns, and imputes to *itself* past actions just upon the same ground and for the same reason that it does the present. All which is founded in a concern for happiness the unavoidable concomitant of consciousness, that which is conscious of pleasure and pain, desiring, that that *self* that is conscious should be happy. And therefore whatever past actions it cannot reconcile or appropriate to that present *self* by consciousness, it can be no more concerned in than if they had never been done. And to receive pleasure or pain, *i.e.*, reward or punishment, on the account of any such action, is all one as to be made happy or miserable in its first being, without any demerit at all. . . .

Book IV

Chapter 1

Of Knowledge in General

1. *Our knowledge conversant about our ideas.* Since *the mind*, in all its thoughts and reasonings, has no other immediate object but its own *ideas*, which it alone does or can contemplate, it is evident that our knowledge is only conversant about them.

2. Knowledge is the perception of the agreement or disagreement of two ideas. Knowledge, then, seems to me to be nothing but *the perception of the connection and agreement, or disagreement and repugnancy, of any of our ideas.* In this alone it consists. Where this perception is, there is knowledge, and where it is not, there, though we may fancy, guess, or believe, yet we always come short of knowledge. For when we know that *white is not black,* what do we else but perceive that these two *ideas* do not agree? When we possess ourselves with the utmost security of the demonstration that *the three angles of a triangle are equal to two right ones,* what do we more but perceive that equality to two right ones does necessarily agree to and is inseparable from the three angles of a triangle?

3. This agreement fourfold. But to understand a little more distinctly wherein this agreement or disagreement consists, I think we may reduce it all to these four sorts:

1. Identity, or *diversity*
2. *Relation*
3. Coexistence, or *necessary connection*
4. *Real existence*

4. First, of identity or diversity. First, as to the first sort of agreement or disagreement, viz., *identity,* or *diversity.* It is the first act of the mind, when it has any sentiments or *ideas* at all, to perceive its *ideas* and, so far as it perceives them, to know each what it is and thereby also to perceive their difference and that one is not another. This is so absolutely necessary that without it there could be no knowledge, no reasoning, no imagination, no distinct thoughts at all. By this the mind clearly and infallibly perceives each *idea* to agree with itself and to be what it is and all distinct *ideas* to disagree, i.e., the one not to be the other. And this it does without any pains, labor, or deduction but, at first view, by its natural power of perception and distinction. . . . And if there ever happen any doubt about it, it will always be found to be about the names and not the *ideas* themselves, whose identity and diversity will always be perceived as soon and as clearly as the *ideas* themselves are, nor can it possibly be otherwise.

5. Secondly, relative. Secondly, the next sort of agreement or disagreement the mind perceives in any of its *ideas* may, I think, be called *relative* and is nothing but *the perception of the relation between any two ideas,* of what kind soever, whether substances, modes, or any other. For since all distinct *ideas* must eternally be known not to be the same and so be universally and constantly denied one of another, there could be no room for any positive knowledge at all if we could not perceive any relation between our *ideas* and find out the agreement or disagreement they have one with another in several ways the mind takes of comparing them.

6. Thirdly, of coexistence. Thirdly, the third sort of agreement or disagreement to be found in our *ideas* which the perception of the mind is employed about is *coexistence* or *noncoexistence* in the same subject, and this belongs particularly to substances. Thus when we pronounce concerning *gold* that it is fixed, our knowledge of this truth amounts to no more but this: that fixedness, or a power to remain in the fire unconsumed, is an *idea* that always accompanies and is joined with that particular sort of yellowness, weight, fusibility, malleableness, and solubility in *aqua regia* which make our complex *idea* signified by the word *gold*.

7. *Fourthly, of real existence.*   Fourthly, the fourth and last sort is that of *actual real existence* agreeing to any *idea*. Within these four sorts of agreement or disagreement is, I suppose, contained all the knowledge we have or are capable of. . . . I should now proceed to examine the several degrees of our knowledge but that it is necessary first to consider the different acceptations of the word *knowledge*.

8. *Knowledge actual or habitual.*   There are several ways wherein the mind is possessed of truth, each of which is called *knowledge*.
    1. There is *actual knowledge*, which is the present view the mind has of the agreement or disagreement of any of its *ideas* or of the relation they have one to another.
    2. A man is said to know any proposition which, having been once laid before his thoughts, he evidently perceived the agreement or disagreement of the *ideas* whereof it consists and so lodged it in his memory that whenever that proposition comes again to be reflected on, he, without doubt or hesitation, embraces the right side, assents to, and is certain of the truth of it. This, I think, one may call *habitual knowledge*. . . .

9. *Habitual knowledge twofold.*   Of habitual knowledge there are also, vulgarly speaking, two degrees:
    First, the one is of *such truths laid up in the memory as whenever they occur to the mind, it actually perceives the relation is between those ideas.* And this is in all those truths whereof we have an *intuitive knowledge*, where the *ideas* themselves, by an immediate view, discover their agreement or disagreement one with another.
    Secondly, the other is of *such truths whereof the mind having been convinced, it retains the memory of the conviction without the proofs.* Thus a man that remembers certainly that he once perceived the demonstration that the three angles of a triangle are equal to two right ones is certain that he knows it because he cannot doubt of the truth of it. . . . This way of entertaining a truth seemed formerly to me like something between opinion and knowledge, a sort of assurance which exceeds bare belief, for that relies on the testimony of another; yet upon a due examination I find it comes not short of perfect certainty and is in effect true knowledge. . . . If then the perception that the same *ideas* will eternally have the same habitudes and relations be not a sufficient ground of knowledge, there could be no knowledge of general propositions in mathematics, for no mathematical demonstration would be any other than particular. . . .

Chapter 2

Of the Degrees of Our Knowledge

1. *Intuitive.*   All our knowledge consisting, as I have said, in the view the mind has of its own *ideas*, which is the utmost light and greatest certainty, we with our faculties and in our way of knowledge are capable of, it may not be amiss to consider a little the degrees of its evidence. The different clearness of our knowledge seems to me to lie in the different way of perception the mind has of the agreement or disagreement of any

of its *ideas*. For if we will reflect on our own ways of thinking, we shall find that some-times the mind perceives the agreement or disagreement of two *ideas* immediately by themselves, without the intervention of any other, and this, I think, we may call *intuitive knowledge*. For in this, the mind is at no pains of proving or examining but per-ceives the truth, as the eye does light, only by being directed toward it. Thus the mind perceives that *white* is not *black*, that a *circle* is not a *triangle*, that *three* are more than *two* and equal to *one* and *two*. . . . It is on this *intuition* that depends all the certainty and evidence of all our knowledge, which certainty everyone finds to be so great that he cannot imagine and therefore not require a greater. . . .

2. *Demonstrative.* The next degree of knowledge is where the mind perceives the agreement or disagreement of any *ideas*, but not immediately. . . .

3. *Depends on proofs.* Those intervening *ideas* which serve to show the agreement of any two others are called *proofs*, and where the agreement or disagreement is by this means plainly and clearly perceived, it is called *demonstration*, it being *shown* to the understanding, and the mind made see that it is so. . . .

4. *But not so easy.* This knowledge by intervening *proofs*, though it be certain, yet the evidence of it is *not* altogether *so clear* and bright, nor the assent so ready, *as in intuitive* knowledge. For though in *demonstration* the mind does at last perceive the agreement or disagreement of the *ideas* it considers, yet it is not without pains and attention. There must be more than one transient view to find it. . . .

7. *Each step must have intuitive evidence.* Now, *in every step reason makes in demonstra-tive knowledge, there is an intuitive knowledge* of that agreement or disagreement it seeks with the next intermediate *idea*, which it uses as a proof, for if it were not so, that yet would need a proof. . . . By which it is plain that every step in reasoning that produces knowledge, has intuitive certainty; which when the mind perceives, there is no more required but to remember it to make the agreement or disagreement of the *ideas*, con-cerning which we inquire, visible and certain. . . .

14. *Sensitive knowledge of particular existence.* . . . Intuition and demonstration are the degrees of our knowledge; whatever comes short of one of these, with what assurance soever embraced, is but faith or opinion but not knowledge, at least in all general truths. There is, indeed, another *perception* of the mind employed about *the particular existence of finite beings* without us, which, going beyond bare probability and yet not reaching perfectly to either of the foregoing degrees of certainty, passes under the name of knowledge. There can be nothing more certain than that the *idea* we receive from an external object is in our minds; this is intuitive knowledge. But whether there be anything more than barely that *idea* in our minds, whether we can thence certainly infer the existence of anything without us which corresponds to that *idea*, is that whereof some men think there may be a question made, because men may have such *ideas* in their minds when no such thing exists, no such object affects their senses. But yet here, I think, we are provided with an evidence that puts us past doubting, for I ask anyone, whether he be not invincibly conscious to himself of a different perception,

when he looks on the sun by day and thinks on it by night. . . . We as plainly find the difference there is between any *idea* revived in our minds by our own memory and actually coming into our minds by our senses as we do between any two distinct *ideas*. If anyone say a dream may do the same thing and all these *ideas* may be produced in us without any external objects, he may please to dream that I make him this answer: 1. That it is no great matter whether I remove his scruple or not: Where all is but dream, reasoning and arguments are of no use, truth and knowledge nothing. 2. That I believe he will allow a very manifest difference between dreaming of being in the fire and being actually in it. . . . So that, I think, we may add to the two former sorts of *knowledge* this also, of the existence of particular external objects by that perception and consciousness we have of the actual entrance of *ideas* from them, and allow these *three degrees of knowledge*, viz., *intuitive, demonstrative, and sensitive*, in each of which there are different degrees and ways of evidence and certainty. . . .

Chapter 3

Of the Extent of Human Knowledge

1. Knowledge, as has been said, lying in the perception of the agreement or disagreement of any of our *ideas*, it follows from hence that,

First, no farther than we have ideas.   First, we can have *knowledge* no farther than we have *ideas*.

2. Secondly, no farther than we can perceive their agreement or disagreement.   Secondly, that we can have no *knowledge* farther than we can have perception of that agreement or disagreement, which perception being either (1) *by intuition*, or the immediate comparing any two *ideas*; or (2) by *reason*, examining the agreement or disagreement of two *ideas* by the intervention of some others; or (3) by *sensation*, perceiving the existence of particular things. Hence it also follows,

3. Thirdly, intuitive knowledge extends itself not to all the relations of all our ideas. *Thirdly*, that we cannot have an *intuitive knowledge* that shall extend itself to all our *ideas* and all that we would know about them, because we cannot examine and perceive all the relations they have one to another by juxtaposition, or an immediate comparison one with another. . . .

4. Fourthly, nor demonstrative knowledge.   *Fourthly*, it follows also from what is above observed that our *rational knowledge* cannot reach to the whole extent of our *ideas*. Because between two different *ideas* we would examine, we cannot always find such *mediums* as we can connect one to another with an intuitive knowledge in all the parts of the deduction, and wherever that fails, we come short of knowledge and demonstration.

5. Fifthly, sensitive knowledge narrower than either.   *Fifthly, sensitive knowledge* reaching no farther than the existence of things actually present to our senses is yet much narrower than either of the former.

6. *Sixthly, our knowledge therefore narrower than our ideas.* From all which it is evident that *the extent of our knowledge* comes not only short of the reality of things but even of the extent of our own *ideas.* . . . Nevertheless, I do not question, but that human knowledge, under the present circumstances of our beings and constitutions, may be carried much farther than it hitherto has been if men would sincerely and with freedom of mind employ all that industry and labor of thought in improving the means of discovering truth which they do for the coloring or support of falsehood to maintain a system, interest, or party they are once engaged in. . . .

7. *How far our knowledge reaches.* The affirmations or negations we make concerning the *ideas* we have may, as I have before intimated in general, be reduced to these four sorts, *viz.*, identity, coexistence, relation, and real existence. I shall examine how far our knowledge extends in each of these.

8. *First, our knowledge of identity and diversity.* First, *as to identity and diversity*, in this way of the agreement or disagreement of our *ideas, our intuitive knowledge is as far extended as our ideas* themselves, and there can be no *idea* in the mind which it does not presently, by an intuitive knowledge, perceive to be what it is and to be different from any other.

9. *Secondly, of coexistence a very little way.* Secondly, *as to* the second sort, which is the *agreement or disagreement* of our *ideas in coexistence*, in this our knowledge is very short, though in this consists the greatest and most material part of our knowledge concerning substances. For our *ideas* of the species of substances being, as I have shown, nothing but certain collections of simple *ideas* united in one subject and so coexisting together. . . . When we would know anything farther concerning these or any other sort of substances, what do we inquire but what other qualities or powers these substances have or have not? which is nothing else but to know what other simple *ideas* do or do not coexist with those that make up that complex *idea*.

10. *Because the connection between most simple ideas is unknown.* This, how weighty and considerable a part soever of human science, is yet very narrow, and scarce any at all. The reason whereof is that the simple *ideas* whereof our complex *ideas* of substances are made up are for the most part such as carry with them, in their own nature, no visible necessary connection or inconsistency with any other simple *ideas*, whose *coexistence* with them we would inform ourselves about. . . .

14. *Especially of secondary qualities, because all connection between any secondary and primary qualities is undiscoverable.* . . . So that let our complex *idea* of any species of substances be what it will, we can hardly, from the simple *ideas* contained in it, certainly determine the *necessary coexistence* of any other quality whatsoever. Our knowledge in all these inquiries reaches very little farther than our experience. . . .

18. *Thirdly, of other relations it is not easy to say how far.* As to the third sort of our knowledge, *viz.*, the *agreement or disagreement of any of our ideas in any other relation*: This, as it is the largest field of our knowledge, so it is hard to determine how far it may extend, because the advances that are made in this part of knowledge depending on

our sagacity in finding intermediate *ideas* that may show the *relations* and *habitudes* of *ideas* whose coexistence is not considered, it is a hard matter to tell when we are at an end of such discoveries and when reason has all the helps it is capable of for the finding of proofs or examining the agreement or disagreement of remote *ideas*....

[18, cont.] *Morality capable of demonstration.* The *idea* of a supreme being, infinite in power, goodness, and wisdom, whose workmanship we are and on whom we depend, and the *idea* of ourselves as understanding, rational beings being such as are clear in us would, I suppose, if duly considered and pursued, afford such foundations of our duty and rules of action as might place *morality among the sciences capable of demonstration*, wherein I doubt not but from self-evident propositions, by necessary consequences as incontestable as those in mathematics, the measures of right and wrong might be made out to anyone that will apply himself with the same indifference and attention to the one as he does to the other of these sciences.... *Where there is no property, there is no injustice* is a proposition as certain as any demonstration in *Euclid*, for the *idea* of *property* being a right to anything and the *idea* to which the name *injustice* is given being the invasion or violation of that right, it is evident that these *ideas* being thus established and these names annexed to them, I can as certainly know this proposition to be true as that a triangle has three angles equal to two right ones....

21. *Fourthly, of real existence we have an intuitive knowledge of our own, demonstrative of God's, sensible of some few other things.* As to the fourth sort of our knowledge, *viz.*, of the *real, actual existence* of things, we have an intuitive knowledge of our own *existence*, a demonstrative knowledge of the *existence* of a God; of the *existence* of anything else we have no other but a sensitive knowledge, which extends not beyond the objects present to our senses....

Chapter 9

Of Our Knowledge of Existence

1. *General certain propositions concern not existence.* Hitherto we have only considered the essences of things, which being only abstract *ideas* and thereby removed in our thoughts from particular existence (that being the proper operation of the mind, in abstraction, to consider an *idea* under no other existence but what it has in the understanding), gives us no knowledge of real existence at all....

2. *A threefold knowledge of existence....* Let us proceed now to inquire concerning our knowledge of the *existence* of things and how we come by it. I say, then, that we have the knowledge of *our own existence* by intuition, of the *existence of God* by demonstration, and of other things by sensation.

3. *Our knowledge of our own existence is intuitive.* As for *our own existence*, we perceive it so plainly and so certainly that it neither needs nor is capable of any proof. For nothing can be more evident to us than our own existence. *I think, I reason, I feel pleasure and pain*; can any of these be more evident to me than my own existence? If I doubt of all other things, that very doubt makes me perceive my own *existence* and will not

suffer me to doubt of that. For if I know *I feel pain*, it is evident I have as certain a perception of my own existence, as of the existence of the pain I feel. Or if I know *I doubt*, I have as certain a perception of the existence of the thing doubting as of that thought which I call *doubt*. Experience then convinces us that *we have an intuitive knowledge of our own existence* and an internal infallible perception that we are. In every act of sensation, reasoning, or thinking, we are conscious to ourselves of our own being and in this matter come not short of the highest degree of *certainty*.

Chapter 10

Of Our Knowledge of the Existence of a God

1. We are capable of knowing certainly that there is a God. . . . To show . . . that we are capable of *knowing, i.e., being certain that there is a God*, and how we may come by this certainty, I think we need go no farther than ourselves and that undoubted knowledge we have of our own existence. . . .

3. He knows also that nothing cannot produce a being, therefore something external. . . . Man knows by an intuitive certainty that bare *nothing can no more produce any real being than it can be equal to two right angles*. . . . If therefore we know there is some real being and that nonentity cannot produce any real being, it is an evident demonstration that from eternity there has been something, since what was not from eternity had a beginning, and what had a beginning must be produced by something else.

4. That eternal being must be most powerful. Next, it is evident that what had its being and beginning from another must also have all that which is in and belongs to its being from another too. All the powers it has must be owing to and received from the same source. This eternal source, then, of all being must also be the source and original of all power; and so *this eternal being must be also the most powerful*.

5. And most knowing. Again, a man finds in himself *perception* and *knowledge*. We have then got one step farther, and we are certain now that there is not only some being but some knowing intelligent being in the world.

There was a time, then, when there was no knowing being and when knowledge began to be, or else there has been also *a knowing being from eternity*. If it be said there was a time when no being had any knowledge, when that eternal being was void of all understanding, I reply that then it was impossible there should ever have been any knowledge. It being as impossible that things wholly void of knowledge and operating blindly and without any perception should produce a knowing being, as it is impossible, that a triangle should make itself three angles bigger than two right ones. . . .

6. And therefore God. Thus from the consideration of ourselves and what we infallibly find in our own constitutions, our reason leads us to the knowledge of this certain and evident truth: that *there is an eternal, most powerful, and most knowing being*, which whether anyone will please to call *God* it matters not. . . .

Chapter 11

Of Our Knowledge of the Existence of Other Things

1. *Is to be had only by sensation.* The knowledge of our own being we have by intuition. The existence of a God reason clearly makes known to us, as has been shown.

The *knowledge of the existence* of any other thing we can have only by *sensation*, for there being no necessary connection of *real existence* with any *idea* a man has in his memory, nor of any other existence but that of God with the existence of any particular man, no particular man can know the *existence* of any other being but only when by actual operating upon him it makes itself perceived by him. For the having the *idea* of anything in our mind no more proves the existence of that thing than the picture of a man evidences his being in the world or the visions of a dream make thereby a true history.

2. *Instance whiteness of this paper.* It is therefore the actual receiving of *ideas* from without that gives us notice of the *existence* of other things and makes us know that something does exist at that time without us which causes that *idea* in us, though perhaps we neither know nor consider how it does it, for it takes not from the certainty of our senses and the *ideas* we receive by them that we know not the manner wherein they are produced. . . .

3. *This though not so certain as demonstration, yet may be called knowledge and proves the existence of things without us.* The notice we have by our senses of the existing of things without us, though it be not altogether so certain as our intuitive knowledge or the deductions of our reason employed about the clear abstract *ideas* of our own minds, yet it is an assurance that *deserves the name of knowledge*. If we persuade ourselves that our faculties act and inform us right concerning the existence of those objects that affect them, it cannot pass for an ill-grounded confidence, for I think nobody can in earnest be so skeptical as to be uncertain of the existence of those things which he sees and feels. At least, he that can doubt so far (whatever he may have with his own thoughts) will never have any controversy with me, since he can never be sure I say anything contrary to his opinion. . . . But besides the assurance we have from our senses themselves, that they do not err in the information they give us of the existence of things without us when they are affected by them, we are farther confirmed in this assurance by other concurrent reasons.

4. *First, because we cannot have them but by the inlet of the senses.* First, it is plain those perceptions are produced in us by exterior causes affecting our senses, because *those that want the organs of any sense never can have the ideas belonging to that sense* produced in their minds. . . .

5. *Because an idea from actual sensation and another from memory are very distinct perceptions.* Secondly, because *sometimes I find that I cannot avoid the having those ideas produced in my mind.* . . . If I turn my eyes at noon towards the sun, I cannot avoid the *ideas* which the light or sun then produces in me, so that there is a manifest difference between the *ideas* laid up in my memory (over which, if they were there only, I should

have constantly the same power to dispose of them and lay them by at pleasure) and those which force themselves upon me and I cannot avoid having. And therefore it must needs be some exterior cause, and the brisk acting of some objects without me, whose efficacy I cannot resist, that produces those *ideas* in my mind, whether I will or not. . . .

6. *Thirdly, pleasure or pain, which accompanies actual sensation, accompanies not the returning of those ideas without the external objects.* Thirdly, add to this that many of those ideas are produced in us with pain, which afterwards we remember without the least offense. Thus the pain of heat or cold, when the *idea* of it is revived in our minds, gives us no disturbance, which, when felt, was very troublesome and is again when actually repeated. . . .

7. *Fourthly, our senses assist one anothers testimony of the existence of outward things.* Fourthly, our *senses* in many cases bear *witness* to the truth of each other's report concerning the existence of sensible things without us. He that sees a *fire* may, if he doubt whether it be anything more than a bare fancy, feel it too and be convinced by putting his hand in it. . . .

8. *This certainty is as great as our condition needs.* But yet, if after all this, anyone will be so skeptical as to distrust his senses and to affirm that all we see and hear, feel and taste, think and do during our whole being is but the series and deluding appearances of a long dream, . . . I must desire him to consider that if all be a dream, then he doth but dream that he makes the question, and so it is not much matter that a waking man should answer him. But yet, if he pleases, he may dream that I make him this answer, that *the certainty of* things existing *in rerum natura*, when we have *the testimony of our senses* for it, is not only *as great* as our frame can attain to but *as our condition needs.* . . .

The Second Treatise of Government

An Essay concerning the True Original, Extent, and End of Civil Government

Book II

Chapter 1

3. *Political power*, then, I take to be a *right* of making laws with penalties of death, and consequently all less penalties, for the regulating and preserving of property, and of employing the force of the community in the execution of such laws and in the defense of the commonwealth from foreign injury; and all this only for the public good.

Chapter 2

Of the State of Nature

4. To understand political power right and derive it from its original, we must consider what state all men are naturally in, and that is a *state of perfect freedom* to order their actions and dispose of their possessions and persons as they think fit, within the bounds of the law of nature, without asking leave or depending upon the will of any other man.

A *state* also *of equality*, wherein all the power and jurisdiction is reciprocal, no one having more than another, there being nothing more evident than that creatures of the same species and rank, promiscuously born to all the same advantages of nature and the use of the same faculties, should also be equal one among another without subordination or subjection. . . .

6. But though this be a *state of liberty*, yet it is *not a state of license*; though man in that state has an uncontrollable liberty to dispose of his person or possessions, yet he has not liberty to destroy himself, or so much as any creature in his possession, but where some nobler use than its bare preservation calls for it. The *state of nature* has a law of nature to govern it which obliges everyone, and reason, which is that law, teaches all mankind who will but consult it that being all equal and independent, no one ought to harm another in his life, health, liberty, or possessions. For men being all the workmanship of one omnipotent and infinitely wise Maker, all the servants of one sovereign Master, sent into the world by His order and about His business, they are His property, whose workmanship they are, made to last during His, not one another's, pleasure. And being furnished with like faculties, sharing all in one community of nature, there cannot be supposed any such *subordination* among us that may authorize us to destroy one another as if we were made for one another's uses, as the inferior ranks of creatures are for ours. Everyone, as he is *bound to preserve himself* and

From John Locke, *Two Treatises concerning Government*, ed. Peter Laslett (Cambridge: Cambridge University Press, 1960). Reprinted by permission of Cambridge University Press.

not to quit his station willfully, so by the like reason when his own preservation comes not in competition, ought he, as much as he can, *to preserve the rest of mankind* and may not, unless it be to do justice on an offender, take away or impair the life or what tends to the preservation of the life, liberty, health, limb, or goods of another.

7. And that all men may be restrained from invading others' rights and from doing hurt to one another and the law of nature be observed which wills the peace and *preservation of all mankind*, the *execution* of the law of nature is in that state put into every man's hands, whereby everyone has a right to punish the transgressors of that law to such a degree as may hinder its violation. For the *law of nature* would, as all other laws that concern men in this world, be in vain if there were nobody that in the state of nature had a *power to execute* that law; and if anyone in the state of nature may punish another for any evil he has done, everyone may do so. For in that *state of perfect equality*, where naturally there is no superiority or jurisdiction of one over another, what any may do in prosecution of that law, everyone must needs have a right to do.

8. And thus in the state of nature *one man comes by a power over another*, but yet no absolute or arbitrary power to use a criminal, when he has got him in his hands, according to the passionate heats or boundless extravagance of his own will, but only to retribute to him, so far as calm reason and conscience dictates, what is proportionate to his transgression, which is so much as may serve for *reparation* and *restraint*. For these two are the only reasons why one man may lawfully do harm to another, which is that we call *punishment*. . . .

10. Besides the crime which consists in violating the law and varying from the right rule of reason, . . . there is commonly *injury* done to some person or other, and some other man receives damage by his transgression, in which case he who has received any damage has, besides the right of punishment common to him with other men, a particular right to seek *reparation* from him that has done it. And any other person who finds it just may also join with him that is injured and assist him in recovering from the offender so much as may make satisfaction for the harm he has suffered . . . .

12. . . . Each transgression may be *punished* to that degree and with so much *severity* as will suffice to make it an ill bargain to the offender, give him cause to repent, and terrify others from doing the like. . . .

13. To this strange doctrine, *viz.*, that *in the state of nature everyone has the executive power* of the law of nature, I doubt not but it will be objected that it is unreasonable for men to be judges in their own cases, that self-love will make men partial to themselves and their friends. And on the other side, that ill nature, passion, and revenge will carry them too far in punishing others. And hence nothing but confusion and disorder will follow, and that therefore God has certainly appointed government to restrain the partiality and violence of men. I easily grant that *civil government* is the proper remedy for the inconveniences of the state of nature, which must certainly be great, where men may be judges in their own case, since it is easily to be imagined that he who was so unjust as to do his brother an injury will scarce be so just as to condemn himself for it. But I shall desire those who make this objection to remember that *absolute monarchs* are but men, and if government is to be the remedy of those evils which necessarily follow from men being judges in their own cases, and the state of nature is therefore not to be endured, I desire to know what kind of government that is and how much better it is than the state of nature, where one man commanding a multitude has the liberty to be judge in his own case and may do to all his subjects whatever

he pleases without the least liberty to anyone to question or control those who execute
his pleasure. . . .

Chapter 3

Of the State of War

16. The *state of war* is a state of enmity and destruction, and therefore declaring
by word or action not a passionate and hasty but a sedate settled design upon another
man's life *puts him in a state of war* with him against whom he has declared such an
intention and so has exposed his life to the other's power to be taken away by him or
anyone that joins with him in his defense and espouses his quarrel; it being reasonable
and just I should have a right to destroy that which threatens me with destruction. For
by the fundamental law of nature, man being to be preserved, as much as possible, when
all cannot be preserved, the safety of the innocent is to be preferred. . . .

17. And hence it is that he who attempts to get another man into his absolute
power does thereby *put himself into a state of war* with him, it being understood as a
declaration of a design upon his life. For I have reason to conclude that he who would
get me into his power without my consent would use me as he pleased when he had
got me there and destroy me too when he had a fancy to it. . . . To be free from such
force is the only security of my preservation, and reason bids me look on him as an
enemy to my preservation who would take away that *freedom* which is the fence to
it. . . . He that in the state of nature *would take away the freedom* that belongs to anyone in that state must necessarily be supposed to have a design to take away everything
else, that *freedom* being the foundation of all the rest, as he that in the state of society
would take away the *freedom* belonging to those of that society or commonwealth must
be supposed to design to take away from them everything else and so be looked on as
in a state of war. . . .

19. And here we have the plain *difference between the state of nature and the state of
war*, which, however some men have confounded, are as distant as a state of peace,
good will, mutual assistance, and preservation and a state of enmity, malice, violence,
and mutual destruction are one from another. Men living together according to reason, without a common superior on earth with authority to judge between them, is
properly the state of nature. But force or a declared design of force upon the person of
another, where there is no common superior on earth to appeal to for relief, *is the state
of war*. . . . *Want of a common judge with authority puts all men in a state of nature; force
without right upon a man's person makes a state of war*, both where there is and is not a
common judge. . . .

21. To avoid this state of war. . . is one great *reason of men's putting themselves into
society* and quitting the state of nature. For where there is an authority, a power on
earth, from which relief can be had by appeal, there the continuance of the state of
war is excluded, and the controversy is decided by that power. . . .

Chapter 4

Of Slavery

22. The *natural liberty* of man is to be free from any superior power on earth and
not to be under the will or legislative authority of man but to have only the law of

nature for his rule. The *liberty of man in society* is to be under no other legislative power but that established by consent in the commonwealth, nor under the dominion of any will or restraint of any law but what the legislative shall enact according to the trust put in it. *Freedom*, then, is not . . . *for everyone to do what he lists, to live as he pleases, and not to be tied by any laws*, but *freedom of men under government* is to have a standing rule to live by, common to everyone of that society and made by the legislative power erected in it, a liberty to follow my own will in all things where the rule prescribes not, and not to be subject to the inconstant, uncertain, unknown, arbitrary will of another man. . . .

23. This *freedom* from absolute, arbitrary power is so necessary to and closely joined with a man's preservation that he cannot part with it but by what forfeits his preservation and life together. . . .

Chapter 5

Of Property

25. . . . I shall endeavor to show how men might come to have a *property* in several parts of that which God gave to mankind in common, and that without any express compact of all commoners. . . .

27. Though the earth and all inferior creatures be common to all men, yet every man has a *property* in his own *person*. This nobody has any right to but himself. The *labor* of his body and the *work* of his hands, we may say, are properly his. Whatsoever then he removes out of the state that nature has provided and left it in, he has mixed his labor with and joined to it something that is his own and thereby makes it his *property*. It being by him removed from the common state nature placed it in, has by this *labor* something annexed to it that excludes the common right of other men. For this *labor* being the unquestionable property of the laborer, no man but he can have a right to what that is once joined to, at least where there is enough and as good left in common for others.

28. He that is nourished by the acorns he picked up under an oak or the apples he gathered from the trees in the wood has certainly appropriated them to himself. Nobody can deny but the nourishment is his. I ask, then, when did they begin to be his? When he digested? Or when he ate? Or when he boiled? Or when he brought them home? Or when he picked them up? And it is plain, if the first gathering made them not his, nothing else could. That *labor* put a distinction between them and common. That added something to them more than nature, the common mother of all, had done; and so they became his private right. And will anyone say he had no right to those acorns or apples he thus appropriated because he had not the consent of all mankind to make them his? Was it a robbery thus to assume to himself what belonged to all in common? If such a consent as that was necessary, man had starved, notwithstanding the plenty God had given him. . . .

31. It will perhaps be objected to this, that if gathering the acorns or other fruits of the earth, etc., makes a right to them, then any one may *engross* as much as he will. To which I answer, Not so. The same law of nature that does by this means give us property does also *bound* that *property* too. . . . As much as anyone can make use of to any advantage of life before it spoils, so much he may by his labor fix a property in. Whatever is beyond this is more than his share and belongs to others. . . .

32. But the *chief matter of property* being now not the fruits of the earth and the beasts that subsist on it but the *earth itself*, as that which takes in and carries with it all the rest, I think it is plain that *property* in that too is acquired as the former. *As much land* as a man tills, plants, improves, cultivates, and can use the product of, so much is his *property*. He by his labor does, as it were, enclose it from the common. . . .

35. It is true in *land* that is *common* in *England* or any other country where there is plenty of people under government who have money and commerce, no one can enclose or appropriate any part without the consent of all his fellow commoners, because this is left common by compact, *i.e.*, by the law of the land, which is not to be violated. And though it be common in respect of some men, it is not so to all mankind, but is the joint property of this country or this parish. . . .

36. . . . This I dare boldly affirm: that the same *rule of propriety* (*viz.*) that every man should have as much as he could make use of would hold still in the world without straitening anybody, since there is land enough in the world to suffice double the inhabitants had not the *invention of money* and the tacit agreement of men to put a value on it introduced (by consent) larger possessions and a right to them, which how it has done I shall by and by show more at large. . . .

45. Thus *labor*, in the beginning, *gave a right of property*, wherever anyone was pleased to employ it, upon what was common, which remained a long while the far greater part and is yet more than mankind makes use of. Men at first for the most part contented themselves with what unassisted nature offered to their necessities, and though afterwards, in some parts of the world (where the increase of people and stock, with the *use of money* had made land scarce and so of some value), the several *communities* settled the bounds of their distinct territories and by laws within themselves regulated the properties of the private men of their society and so, *by compact* and agreement, *settled the property* which labor and industry began; and the leagues that have been made between several states and kingdoms either expressly or tacitly disowning all claim and right to the land in the others' possession have, by common consent, given up their pretences to their natural common right, which originally they had to those countries, and so have, by *positive agreement, settled a property* among themselves in distinct parts and parcels of the earth. . . .

46. The greatest part of *things really useful* to the life of man, and such as the necessity of subsisting made the first commoners of the world look after, as it does the *Americans* now, *are* generally things *of short duration*, such as, if they are not consumed by use, will decay and perish of themselves. Gold, silver, and diamonds are things that fancy or agreement has put the value on, more than real use and the necessary support of life. . . . He that *gathered* a hundred bushels of acorns or apples had thereby a *property* in them; they were his goods as soon as gathered. He was only to look that he used them before they spoiled; else he took more than his share and robbed others. . . . And if he. . . bartered away plums that would have rotted in a week for nuts that would last good for his eating a whole year, he did no injury; he wasted not the common stock, destroyed no part of the portion of goods that belonged to others, so long as nothing perished uselessly in his hands. Again, if he would give us nuts for a piece of metal . . . or wool for a sparkling pebble or a diamond and keep those by him all his life, he invaded not the right of others, [and] he might heap up as much of these durable things as he pleased; the *exceeding of the bounds of his just property* not lying in the largeness of his possession but the perishing of anything uselessly in it.

47. And thus *came in the use of money*, some lasting thing that men might keep without spoiling and that by mutual consent men would take in exchange for the truly useful but perishable supports of life.

48. And as different degrees of industry were apt to give men possessions in different proportions, so this *invention of money* gave them the opportunity to continue to enlarge them. For supposing an island separated from all possible commerce with the rest of the world, wherein there were but a hundred families but there were sheep, horses, and cows, with other useful animals, wholesome fruits, and land enough for corn for a hundred thousand times as many but nothing in the island, either because of its commonness or perishableness, fit to supply the place of *money*, what reason could anyone have there to enlarge his possessions beyond the use of his family. . .? Where there is not something both lasting and scarce, and so valuable to be hoarded up, there men will not be apt to enlarge their *possessions of land*, were it never so rich, never so free for them to take. . . .

50. But since gold and silver, being little useful to the life of man in proportion to food, raiment, and carriage, has its *value* only from the consent of men, whereof labor yet makes in great part *the measure*, it is plain that men have agreed to disproportionate and unequal possession of the earth, they having by a tacit and voluntary consent found out a way how a man may fairly possess more land than he himself can use the product of, by receiving in exchange for the overplus, gold and silver, which may be hoarded up without injury to anyone, these metals not spoiling or decaying in the hands of the possessor. This partage of things, in an inequality of private possessions, men have made practicable out of the bounds of society and without compact, only by putting a value on gold and silver and tacitly agreeing in the use of money. . . .

Chapter 7

Of Political or Civil Society

77. God, having made man such a creature that in his own judgment it was not good for him to be alone, put him under strong obligations of necessity, convenience, and inclination to drive him into *society*, as well as fitted him with understanding and language to continue and enjoy it. The *first society* was between man and wife, which gave beginning to that between parents and children; to which, in time, that between master and servant came to be added. And though all these might, and commonly did, meet together and make up but one family, wherein the master or mistress of it had some sort of rule proper to a family, each of these, or all together, came short of *political society*, as we shall see, if we consider the different ends, ties, and bounds of each of these.

78. *Conjugal society* is made by a voluntary compact between man and woman. And though it consist chiefly in such a communion and right in one another's bodies as is necessary to its chief end, procreation, yet it draws with it mutual support and assistance, and a communion of interest too, as necessary not only to unite their care and affection but also necessary to their common offspring, who have a right to be nourished and maintained by them till they are able to provide for themselves.

79. For the end of *conjunction between male and female*, being not barely procreation but the continuation of the species, this conjunction betwixt male and female

ought to last, even after procreation, so long as is necessary to the nourishment and support of the young ones, who are to be sustained by those that got them till they are able to shift and provide for themselves. . . .

80. And herein I think lies the chief, if not the only, reason *why the male and female in mankind are tied to a longer conjunction* than other creatures, *viz.*, because the female is capable of conceiving and *de facto* is commonly with child again and brings forth too a new birth long before the former is out of a dependency for support on his parents' help and able to shift for himself and has all the assistance is due to him from his parents, whereby the father, who is bound to take care for those he has begotten, is under an obligation to continue in conjugal society with the same woman longer than other creatures, whose young being able to subsist of themselves before the time of procreation returns again, the conjugal bond dissolves of itself. . . .

87. Man being born, as has been proved, with a title to perfect freedom and an uncontrolled enjoyment of all the rights and privileges of the law of nature equally with any other man or number of men in the world, has by nature a power not only to preserve his property, that is, his life, liberty, and estate, against the injuries and attempts of other men, but to judge of and punish the breaches of that law in others as he is persuaded the offense deserves, even with death itself, in crimes where the heinousness of the fact, in his opinion, requires it. But because no *political society* can be nor subsist without having in itself the power to preserve the property, and in order thereunto punish the offenses of all those of that society, there and there only is *political society*, where every one of the members has quitted this natural power [and] resigned it up into the hands of the community in all cases that exclude him not from appealing for protection to the law established by it. And thus all private judgment of every particular member being excluded, the community comes to be umpire, by settled standing rules, indifferent and the same to all parties, and by men having authority from the community for the execution of those rules decides all the differences that may happen between any members of that society concerning any matter of right and punishes those offenses which any member has committed against the society with such penalties as the law has established—whereby it is easy to discern who are and who are not in *political society* together. Those who are united into one body and have a common established law and judicature to appeal to, with authority to decide controversies between them and punish offenders *are in civil society* one with another, but those who have no such common appeal, I mean on earth, are still in the state of nature, each being, where there is no other, judge for himself and executioner—which is, as I have before shown it, the perfect *state of nature*.

88. And thus the commonwealth comes by a power to set down what punishment shall belong to the several transgressions which they think worthy of it, committed among the members of that society (which is the *power of making laws*), as well as it has the power to punish any injury done unto any of its members by anyone that is not of it (which is the *power of war and peace*), and all this for the preservation of the property of all the members of that society as far as is possible. . . . And herein we have the original of the *legislative* and *executive power* of civil society. . . .

90. Hence it is evident that *absolute monarchy*, which by some men is counted the only government in the world, is indeed *inconsistent with civil society* and so can be no form of civil government at all. For the *end of civil society* being to avoid and remedy those inconveniencies of the state of nature which necessarily follow from every man's being judge in his own case by setting up a known authority to which everyone of that

society may appeal upon any injury received or controversy that may arise and which everyone of the society ought to obey, wherever any persons are who have not such an authority to appeal to for the decision of any difference between them, there those persons are still *in the state of nature*. And so is every *absolute prince* in respect of those who are under his *dominion*.

91. For he being supposed to have all, both legislative and executive power in himself alone, there is no judge to be found, no appeal lies open to anyone who may fairly and indifferently and with authority decide and from whose decision relief and redress may be expected of any injury or inconvenience that may be suffered from the prince or by his order, so that such a man, however titled, *czar* or *grand signior* or how you please, is as much *in the state of nature* with all under his dominion as he is with the rest of mankind. . . .

SELECTED BIBLIOGRAPHY

Locke, John. *An Essay concerning Human Understanding.* Ed. P.H. Nidditch. New York: Oxford University Press, 1975.

————. *Letter concerning Toleration.* Ed. J. Tully. Indianapolis: Hackett, 1983.

————. *Two Treatises concerning Government.* Ed. Peter Laslett. Cambridge: Cambridge University Press, 1960.

Aaron, Richard I. *John Locke,* 3d ed. New York: Oxford University Press, 1971.

Colman, John. *John Locke's Moral Philosophy.* Edinburgh: Edinburgh University Press, 1983.

Cranston, Maurice. *John Locke: A Biography.* New York: Oxford University Press, 1957.

Dunn, John. *Locke.* New York: Oxford University Press, 1984.

Jenkins, J.J. *Understanding Locke.* New York: Columbia University Press, 1983.

Jolley, Nicholas. *Leibnitz and Locke: A Study of the New Essays in Human Understanding.* New York: Oxford University Press, 1984.

Leibniz, Gottfried Wilhelm. *New Essays on the Human Understanding.* Trans. Peter Remnant and Jonathan Bennett. Cambridge: Cambridge University Press, 1981.

Squadrito, Kathleen. *John Locke.* Boston: Twayne, 1979.

Tipton, I.C. *Locke on Human Understanding.* New York: Oxford University Press, 1977.

Woolhouse, R.S. *Locke.* Minneapolis: University of Minnesota Press, 1983.

Yolton, J.W. *John Locke: An Introduction.* Oxford: Basil Blackwell, 1985.

————. *Locke and the Compass of Human Understanding.* Cambridge: Cambridge University Press, 1970.

Gottfried Wilhelm Leibniz

Gottfried Wilhelm Leibniz (1646–1716) was born in Leipzig, Germany. His father was a professor of philosophy at the university, and his mother was the daughter of a professor. Although his father died when Leibniz was only six, Leibniz used his father's library and was quickly recognized as a precocious learner. He took his bachelor's degree at Leipzig in 1663 and then studied law there, but the university refused to grant him his doctorate in 1666 because he was still too young. Leibniz then quickly transferred to Altdorf, where he graduated the following year and was offered a professorship. He declined this academic post, choosing instead to enter the service of the German nobility.

Leibniz rapidly made connections and landed a post with the elector of Mainz. As a Protestant in a Catholic court, however, his position was not assured, so when the opportunity presented itself in 1672 to travel to Paris, Leibniz grabbed at it. His mission—to encourage the French Crown to direct its imperialist tendencies against Egypt and therefore away from Germany—failed, but Leibniz used this time to make the acquaintance of the leading figures in Western philosophy and science.

Descartes' followers dominated the philosophical arena at that time, and Leibniz met many of them, including Antoine Arnauld, Nicholas de Malebranche, and Baruch Spinoza, whom Leibniz visited in the Netherlands in 1675. The new sciences were in great ferment: Galileo and Descartes were gone, but Robert Boyle was still young, Isaac Newton only beginning. Leibniz was soon taken under the wing of the great Dutch mathematician-physicist Christiaan Huygens, and he also established correspondences with numerous other leading scientists. In 1673 a political mission took Leibniz to London, where he exhibited to the Royal Society a calculating machine of his own design that improved on Pascal's earlier invention. He was elected a member of the Royal Society later that year. It was also during this period that, with Huygens's help, Leibniz began to devote himself intensively to higher mathematics. He soon outstripped his master, however, for his investigations, sparked perhaps by claims about Newton's work, led to his development—quite independently of Newton's own work—of differential and integral calculus.

During this period Leibniz also transferred from the service of the Elector of Mainz to that of Johann Friedrich, the duke of Brunswick-Lüneburg, ruler of a sizable principality in northern Germany, where he remained for forty years as a counselor in charge of historical, cultural, and scientific affairs. His duties ranged from attempting to justify various rights and claims for the dukes to superintending the mint and writing the history of the house of Brunswick. With respect to the latter project, Leibniz was one of the first historians to collect primary sources systematically in order to research his subject. In 1690 he became ducal librarian in Wolfenbüttel. Among his other projects, Leibniz attempted to compile a code of international law and to argue for its adoption. He also worked tirelessly to promote learning in all its forms, especially by founding academies modeled after those in London and Paris.

In 1679 Ernst August succeeded Johann Friedrich and began an ambitious series of alliances, including his marriage to Sophia, the daughter of the Elector Palatine and granddaughter of James I of England, which elevated the house of Brunswick-Lüneburg, now seated in Hanover, to the position of elector of the imperial diet. Sophie Charlotte, Ernst August's daughter, to whom Leibniz was very close, became Queen of Prussia, and Leibniz visited her often in Berlin, where he helped found the Prussian Royal Academy, for which he served as lifelong president. George Louis, Ernst August's son and heir, great-grandson of James I of England, succeeded to the British Crown in 1714 as George I.

Leibniz was eager to move to London, a more worldly stage than little Hanover, but a rancorous dispute had developed between Leibniz and Newton's followers over the invention of calculus and the status of space and time, and feelings against Leibniz ran too high for him to join the court in England. Careful investigation has since shown that Newton and Leibniz developed calculus independently, Newton perhaps a few years earlier, but Leibniz in a more general form and with a more powerful notation. In 1716 Leibniz died, neglected, in Hanover, now a minor city of a more glorious realm.

Leibniz published little of his philosophical work. Most of the works by which we now know him were published posthumously as they were discovered among his voluminous papers at Hanover by various scholars. He always hoped that he would be able to provide a philosophy that could unite Protestants and Catholics and furnish a foundation for a lasting European peace. The breadth of his interests and accomplishments is astounding. He made key contributions in philosophy, logic, mathematics, law, technology, physics, theology, politics, and history.

Philosophy

Leibniz shares with other rationalists the conviction that pure and unaided human reason is capable of ascertaining the fundamental features of the world. Leibniz dreams of a *characteristica universalis*, or universal symbolism, in which every meaningful proposition can be expressed, and expressed as a relation among absolutely simple, primitive elements. With such a language, Leibniz hopes, all reasoning could be reduced to calculation from given primitives. Leibniz holds that these primitives are innate, not derived from or justified by reference to sensory experience.

As the last of the great rationalists, Leibniz also had to contend with the rising force of empiricism, and his *New Essays on Human Understanding* were a direct reply in commentary form to Locke's tremendously influential *Essay concerning Human Understanding.* Locke died before Leibniz finished his *New Essays,* and Leibniz did not think it fair to publish a criticism of someone who was not able to defend himself, so the *New Essays* remained unpublished until 1765. In it Leibniz defends the innateness of the fundamental concepts and principles of reason.

In line with his belief that the greatest single requirement for progress in all intellectual enterprises was the development of a more adequate symbolic system, Leibniz drew many conclusions from his own analysis of the logical form of judgment. Leibniz held that the fundamental form of all judgment is subject-predicate and, picking up on a theme familiar since Aristotle, that names of substances can serve only as subjects, never as predicates, in judgments, because substances are what possess properties. Since Leibniz also held that true judgments report an intrinsic relation between the subject and the predicate, he concluded that the concept of any substance must include all the predicates it ever has. Such a complete individual substance Leibniz calls a *monad.*

It follows from this position that all truths are analytically true—in every truth the predicate concept is contained within the concept of the subject. Thus every truth is grounded in the nature of things themselves: for every truth there is sufficient reason. This doctrine would seem to make all truths necessary truths, but Leibniz argues that we need to distinguish between *finitely* analytic propositions (judgments that are either explicitly identical, for example, "An orange ball is a ball," or can be reduced to such an identical judgment in a finite number of steps) and *infinitely* analytic judgments (which require an infinite number of steps to reduce to an identical proposition). Finitely analytic judgments are *necessary* truths; infinitely analytic judgments, which God alone can know independently of sensory experience, are *contingent* truths.

Building on this basic insight, Leibniz attempted to explain the fundamental structure of reality and knowledge. The true substances of the world are nonextended monads, each of which represents with greater or lesser clarity the states of all the others, even though there is no causal influence between them. Space, time, and the causal interactions that seem so familiar to us from our sensory experience of the world are really *phenomena bene fundata*, appearances reflecting an essentially different underlying reality.

Leibniz hoped that his system would provide answers to a number of philosophical problems, such as the nature of human freedom and the proper relation between God and humanity. The one book Leibniz published during his lifetime, the *Theodicy*, was an attempt to justify the ways of God to humans, to show, using Leibniz's philosophical system, that God created the best of all possible worlds in which free human souls can strive for salvation.

The Reading Context

It was Leibniz's dream to be a great reconciliator, forging a permanent European peace, reuniting the Christian faiths, reconciling humanity to its world. He once remarked that in everything that has been written there is some truth. (Leibniz's assurance that such reconciliation is possible—that this is the best of all possible worlds—was devastatingly mocked in Voltaire's character Dr. Pangloss in *Candide*.)

In reading Leibniz's philosophy, it is important to see how his logic and metaphysics support and are supported by his larger reconciliationist goal and to recognize that his version of reconciliation is not a bland and homogenous sameness but, like his metaphysics, a harmony of independent units. Look for the ways in which he tries to give something to each of his opponents so that no one comes out simply *wrong*. Is he capable, for instance, of reconciling the opposing views about the existence of innate ideas?

A Note on the Texts

Leibniz wrote his *New Essays on Human Understanding* as a commentary on and reply to Locke's *Essay*. Unfortunately, Locke died before Leibniz could bring it to publication, and Leibniz thought it unfair to publish a criticism of someone who could not reply. The *New Essays* remained unpublished until 1765, when it appeared in time to influence Immanuel Kant. Other than the *Theodicy* and a smattering of articles, Leibniz published little in his lifetime. Most of his writings were published posthumously, found among his papers by later scholars.

"Necessary and Contingent Truths" was written in about 1686, and the "Principles of Nature and Grace" was written in about 1714 for Prince Eugen of Savoy. Both were published after Leibniz's death.

Reading Questions

1. According to Leibniz, what truths cannot be derived from experience? What is an innate idea?
2. How does Leibniz argue that there are states of mind that are not conscious states? What explanatory role do insensible perceptions serve?
3. What answer does Leibniz give to the question "Can matter think?"
4. How does Leibniz define *substance*? If a monad has no parts, how can it represent something complex?

5. What role does the notion of preestablished harmony play in Leibniz's philosophy?
6. What are the levels of mentality, and how do they differ? How do animals differ from inorganic beings? From humans?
7. Is there sufficient reason for the principle of sufficient reason? Why is there something and not nothing?
8. What does Leibniz mean when he claims that this is the most perfect world possible?

New Essays on Human Understanding

Introduction

As the *Essay on the Understanding*, by an illustrious Englishman, is one of the best and most highly esteemed works of the present time, I have resolved to make some remarks upon it, because, having for a long time given considerable attention to the same subject and to most of the matters with which the essay deals, I have thought that this would be a good occasion for publishing some of my opinions under the title of *New Essays on the Understanding*, in the hope that my thoughts will obtain a favourable reception through appearing in such good company. . . .

In fact, although the author of the *Essay* says a thousand fine things of which I cordially approve, our systems greatly differ. His has more relation to Aristotle and mine to Plato, although in many things both of us have departed from the doctrine of these two ancient writers. He is more popular, and I for my part am sometimes compelled to be a little more *acroamatic*[1] and abstract, which is not of advantage to me, especially when a living language is used. . . .

The differences between us have regard to subjects of some importance. There is the question whether the soul, in itself, is entirely empty, like a writing-tablet on which nothing has yet been written (*tabula rasa*), (which is the opinion of Aristotle and of the author of the *Essay*), and whether everything that is inscribed upon it comes solely from the senses and experience; or whether the soul originally contains the principles of several notions and doctrines, which are merely roused on certain occasions by external objects, as I hold along with Plato and even with the Schoolmen. . . . The Stoics called these principles *prolepses*, that is, fundamental assumptions or what we take for granted beforehand. Mathematicians call them *common notions*. . . . Hence there arises another question, whether all truths are dependent on experience, that is, on induction and instances; or whether there are some which have yet another foundation. For if some events can be foreseen before we have made any trial of them, it is manifest that we contribute to them something of our own. The senses, although they are necessary for all our actual acquiring of knowledge, are by no means sufficient to give us the whole of our knowledge, since the senses never give anything but instances, that is to say particular or individual truths. Now all the instances which confirm a general truth, however numerous they may be, are not sufficient to establish the universal necessity of this same truth; for it does not at all follow that what has happened will happen in the same way. . . . Whence it seems that necessary truths, such as we find in pure mathematics and especially in arithmetic and geometry, must have principles whose proof does not depend upon instances nor, consequently, upon the witness of the senses, although without the senses it would never have come into our heads to think of them. This is a point which should be carefully

From Gottfried Wilhelm Leibniz, *The Monadology and Other Philosophical Writings*, trans. Robert Latta (Oxford: Oxford University Press, 1898), pp. 357–402.

1. Esoteric.

noted, and it is one which Euclid so well understood that he often proves by reason that which is evident enough through experience and through sense-images. Logic also, along with metaphysics and ethics [la morale], of which the one forms natural theology and the other natural jurisprudence, are full of such truths; and consequently their demonstration can come only from the inner principles which are called innate. It is true we must not imagine that we can read these eternal laws of reason in the soul as in an open book. . .; but it is enough that we can discover these laws in ourselves by means of attention, for which opportunities are furnished by the senses; and the success of experiments serves also as a confirmation of reason, somewhat as in arithmetic "proofs" are useful in helping us to avoid errors of calculation when the process is a long one. In this also lies the difference between human knowledge and that of the lower animals. The lower animals are purely empirical and direct themselves by particular instances alone; for, so far as we can judge, they never succeed in forming necessary propositions; while men, on the other hand, have the capacity for demonstrative science. It is also on this account that the power of making *concatenations* [of ideas] which the lower animals possess is something inferior to the reason which is in men. The concatenations [of ideas] made by the lower animals are simply like those of mere empirics, who maintain that what has sometimes happened will happen again in a case which resembles the former in characteristics which strike them, although they are incapable of judging whether or not the same reasons hold good in both cases. That is why it is so simple a matter for men to entrap animals, and so easy for mere empirics to make mistakes. . . . The concatenations [of ideas] in the lower animals are only a shadow of reasoning, that is to say they are only connexions of imagination and passings from one image to another, because in new circumstances which seem to resemble others which have occurred before we expect anew what we at other times found along with them, as if things were actually connected together because their images are connected in memory. It is true that reason also leads us to expect, as a rule, that there will occur in the future what is in harmony with a long experience of the past, but this is, nevertheless, not a necessary and infallible truth; and our forecast may fail when we least expect it, because the reasons which have hitherto justified it no longer operate. And on this account the wisest people do not trust altogether to experience, but try, so far as possible, to get some hold of the reason of what happens, in order to decide when exceptions must be made. . . .

Perhaps our able author may not entirely differ from me in opinion. For after having devoted the whole of his first book to the rejection of innate knowledge [lumières], understood in a certain sense, he nevertheless admits, at the beginning of the second book and in those which follow, that the ideas which do not originate in sensation come from reflexion. Now reflexion is nothing but an attention to that which is in us, and the senses do not give us what we already bring with us. That being so, can it be denied that there is much that is innate in our mind [esprit], since we are, so to speak, innate to ourselves, and since in ourselves there are being, unity, substance, duration, change, activity [action], perception, pleasure and a thousand other objects of our intellectual ideas? And as these objects are immediate objects of our understanding and are always present (although they cannot always be consciously perceived [aperçus] because of our distractions and wants), why should it be surprising that we say that these ideas, along with all that depends on them, are innate in us?. . . Ideas and truths are innate in us, as natural inclinations, dispositions, habits or powers [virtualités], and not as activities [actions], although these powers [virtualités] are always accompanied by some activities [actions], often imperceptible, which correspond to them.

Our able author seems to maintain that there is in us nothing virtual, and even nothing of which we are not always actually conscious. But this cannot be understood in a strict sense; otherwise his opinion would be too paradoxical, since, for instance, we are not always conscious of acquired habits and of the things stored in our memory, and, indeed, they do not always come to our aid when we require them, although we often bring them back easily into our mind on some slight occasion which recalls them to us, as we need only the beginning of a song in order to remember it. Our author also limits his thesis in other places, saying that there is in us nothing of which we have not at least been conscious [aperçus] formerly. . . . I say . . . why must every-thing be acquired by us through apperception of external things, and why should it be impossible to unearth anything in ourselves? Is our soul, then, so empty that, beyond images borrowed from outside, it is nothing? . . . Why, then, should not we also be able to provide ourselves with some sort of thought out of our own inner being, when we deliberately try to penetrate its depths? Thus I am led to believe that his opinion on this point is not fundamentally different from mine, or rather from the common opin-ion, inasmuch as he recognizes two sources of our knowledge, the senses and reflexion.

I do not know that it will be so easy to reconcile him with us and with the Carte-sians, when he maintains that the mind does not always think, and especially that it is without perception when we sleep without dreaming; and he holds that, since bod-ies can exist without motion, souls might also quite well exist without thinking. . . .

There are countless indications which lead us to think that there is at every moment an infinity of perceptions within us, but without apperception and without reflexion; that is to say, changes in the soul itself of which we are not conscious [s'aper-cevoir], because the impressions are either too small and too numerous or too closely combined [trop unies], so that each is not distinctive enough by itself, but nevertheless in combination with others each has its effect and makes itself felt, at least confusedly, in the whole. Thus it is that, through being accustomed to it, we take no notice of the motion of a mill or a waterfall when we have for some time lived quite near them. Not that this motion does not continually affect our organs, nor that something does not pass into the soul, which responds to it because of the harmony of the soul and the body, but these impressions which are in the soul and in the body, having lost the attractions of novelty, are not strong enough to attract our attention and our memory, busied with more engrossing objects. For all attention requires memory, and often when we are not, so to speak, admonished and warned to take notice of some of our present perceptions, we let them pass without reflexion and even without observing them; but if some one directs our attention to them immediately afterwards, and for instance bids us notice some sound that has just been heard, we remember it, and we are conscious that we had some feeling of it at the time. Thus there were perceptions of which we were not immediately conscious [s'apercevoir], apperception arising in this case only from our attention being directed to them after some interval, however small. And for an even better understanding of the petites perceptions which we cannot individually distinguish in the crowd, I am wont to employ the illustration of the moaning or sound of the sea, which we notice when we are on the shore. In order to hear this sound as we do, we must hear the parts of which the whole sound is made up, that is to say the sounds which come from each wave, although each of these little sounds makes itself known only in the confused combination of all the sounds taken together, that is to say, in the moaning of the sea, and no one of the sounds would be observed if the wave which makes it were alone. For we must be affected a little by the motion of this wave, and we must have some perception of each of these sounds, however little they may be; otherwise we should not have the perception of a hundred thousand waves, for a hundred thousand nothings cannot make something. We never sleep so profoundly as not to have some feeble and confused feeling, and we should never be wakened by the greatest noise in the world if we had not some perception of its beginning which is small. . . .

These *petites perceptions* have thus through their consequences an influence greater than people think. It is they that form this something I know not what, these tastes, these images of sense-qualities, clear in combination but confused in the parts, these impressions which surrounding bodies make upon us, who contain infinity, this connexion which each being has with all the rest of the universe. It may even be said that in consequence of these *petites perceptions* the present is big with the future and laden with the past, that there is a conspiration of all things (σύμπνοια πάντα [sympnoia panta], as Hippocrates said), and that in the least of substances eyes as penetrating as those of God might read the whole succession of the things of the universe,

> *Quae sint, quae fuerint, quae mox futura trahantur?*[2]

These unconscious [*insensible*] perceptions also indicate and constitute the identity of the individual, who is characterized by the traces or expressions of his previous states which these unconscious perceptions preserve, as they connect his previous states with his present state; and these unconscious perceptions may be known by a higher mind [*esprit*], although the individual himself may not be conscious of them, that is to say, though he may no longer have a definite recollection of them. But they [these perceptions] furnish also the means of recovering this recollection, when it is needed, through periodic developments which may some day occur. That is why death, owing to these perceptions, can only be a sleep, and cannot even last as a sleep, for in animals perceptions merely cease to be distinct [*distingué*] enough, and are reduced to a state of confusion, in which consciousness [*aperception*] is suspended, but which cannot last for ever, not to speak here of man who must have great privileges in this regard in order to keep his personality.

Further, the unconscious [*insensible*] perceptions explain that wonderful pre-established harmony of body and soul, and indeed of all Monads or simple substances, which takes the place of the untenable theory of the influence of one upon another. . . . After this I should add little, if I were to say that it is these *petites perceptions* which *determine* us on many occasions without our thinking it, and which deceive people by the appearance of an *indifference of equilibrium*, as if, for instance, we were completely indifferent whether to turn to the right or to the left. It is also unnecessary for me to point out here . . . that they cause that *uneasiness* which I show to consist in something which differs from pain only as the small from the great, and which nevertheless often constitutes our desire and even our pleasure, giving to it a

---

2. "What things are, what things have been, and what future things may soon be brought forth." Virgil, *Georgics*, 4:393.

kind of stimulating relish. It is also due to these unconscious [*insensible*] parts of our conscious [*sensible*] perceptions that there is a relation between these perceptions of colour, heat, and other sensible qualities, and the motions in bodies which correspond to them; while the Cartesians, along with our author, in spite of all his penetration, regard the perceptions we have of these qualities as arbitrary, that is to say, as if God had given them to the soul according to His good pleasure, without regard to any essential relation between the perceptions and their objects. . . .

In a word, *unconscious* [*insensible*] *perceptions* are of as great use in pneumatics[3] as imperceptible [*insensible*] corpuscles are in physics; and it is as unreasonable to reject the one as the other on the ground that they are beyond the reach of our senses. Nothing takes place all at once, and it is one of my great maxims, one among the most completely verified of maxims, that *nature never makes leaps*; which I [have] called the *law of continuity*. . . ; and the use of this law in physics is very considerable: it is to the effect that we always pass from small to great, and *vice versa*, through that which is intermediate in degrees as in parts. . . . And all this leads us to think that *noticeable perceptions* also come by degrees from those which are too small to be noticed. To think otherwise is to know little of the illimitable fineness [*subtilité*] of things, which always and everywhere contains [*enveloppe*] an actual infinity.

I have also noticed that, in virtue of imperceptible [*insensible*] variations, two individual things cannot be perfectly alike, and that they must always differ more than *numero*. This makes an end of "the empty tablets of the soul," "a soul without thought," "a substance without activity" [*action*], "the void in space," "atoms," and even particles not actually divided in matter, "absolute rest," "complete uniformity in one part of time, place or matter," . . . and a thousand other fictions of philosophers, which come from their incomplete notions and which the nature of things does not admit of, and which are made passable by our ignorance and the slight attention we give to the imperceptible [*insensible*]. . . . Otherwise, if we seriously meant this, namely that the things of which we are not conscious [*s'apercevoir*] are neither in the soul nor in the body, we should err in philosophy as is done in statecraft [*politique*], when no account is taken of τό μικρόν [the micron], imperceptible [*insensible*] progressions; but on the other hand an abstraction is not an error, provided we know that what we ignore is actually there. So mathematicians make use of abstractions when they speak of the perfect lines which they ask us to consider, the uniform motions and other regular effects, although *matter* (that is to say, the intermingling of the effects of the surrounding infinite) always makes some exception. We proceed thus in order to discriminate conditions [*considérations*] from one another and in order to reduce effects to their grounds [*raisons*], as far as possible, and to foresee some of their consequences: for the more we are careful to neglect none of the conditions which we can control, the more does practice correspond to theory. But it belongs only to the supreme reason, which nothing escapes, to comprehend distinctly all the infinite and to see all grounds [*raisons*] and all consequences. All that we can do as regards infinities is to recognize them confusedly, and to know at least distinctly that they are there; otherwise we have a very poor idea of the beauty and greatness of the universe, and also we cannot have

---

3. A name for the philosophy of mind or spirit, derived from the New Testament use of πνευμα [pneuma]. [Trans. note]

a sound physics, which explains the nature of bodies in general, and still less a sound pneumatics, which includes the knowledge of God, of souls, and of simple substances in general.

This knowledge of unconscious [*insensible*] perceptions serves also to explain why and how no two souls, human or other, of one and the same kind, ever come perfectly alike from the hands of the Creator, and each has always from the first a reference to the point of view it will have in the universe. But this indeed follows already from what I observed regarding two individuals, namely, that their *difference* is always *more than a numerical one*. There is also another important point, as to which I must differ, not only from the opinions of our author, but also from those of the majority of modern writers. I believe, with the majority of the ancients, that all superhuman spirits [*genies*], all souls, all created simple substances are always combined with a body, and that there never are souls entirely separated [from body]. I have *a priori* reasons for this, but it will also be found that the doctrine is of advantage in this respect, that it solves all the philosophical difficulties about the state of souls, about their perpetual preservation, about their immortality and about their working; for the difference between one state of the soul and another never is and never has been anything but a difference between the more and the less conscious [*sensible*], the more and the less perfect, or vice versa, and thus the past or the future state of the soul is as explicable as its present state. . . . I have already said that no sleep can last for ever; and it will last for the shortest time or almost not at all in the case of rational souls, which are destined always to preserve the personal character [*personnage*] which has been given them in the City of God, and consequently to retain memory; and this is so, in order that they may be more susceptible of punishments and rewards. And I add further that no derangement of its visible organs is capable of reducing things to complete confusion in an animal, or of destroying all its organs and depriving the soul of the whole of its organic body and of the ineffaceable remains of all its former impressions. . . .

I cannot but praise the modest piety of our celebrated author, who recognizes that God can do beyond what we can understand, and that thus there may be inconceivable mysteries in the articles of faith; but I would rather that we were not compelled to have recourse to miracle in the ordinary course of nature and to admit absolutely inexplicable powers and operations. Otherwise too great a licence will be given to bad philosophers on the strength of what God can do; and if we admit those *centripetal powers* [*vertus*] or those *immediate attractions* from a distance, without its being possible to make them intelligible, I see nothing to hinder our Scholastics from saying that everything happens merely through their "faculties," and from maintaining their "intentional species," which go from objects to us and find it possible to enter even into our souls. . . . [Locke] raises difficulties about the operations of *souls* when the question is merely whether that which is not *perceptible* [*sensible*] is to be admitted; and here we have him giving to *bodies* that which is not even *intelligible*, attributing to them powers and activities which surpass all that a created spirit can, in my opinion, do or understand, for he attributes to them attraction, and that at great distances without any limit to the sphere of its activity; and he does this in order to support an opinion which seems to me no less inexplicable, namely, the possibility that within the order of nature matter may think.

The question which he discusses with the distinguished prelate who had attacked him is *whether matter can think*; and, as it is an important point, even for the present work, I cannot avoid entering into it a little and examining their controversy. . . . The late Bishop of Worcester, . . . having done justice to this excellent author, in recognizing that he thinks the existence of the mind [esprit] as certain as that of the body, although the one of these substances is as little known as the other, . . . [asks] how reflexion can assure us of the existence of the mind [esprit] if God can give to matter the faculty of thinking, according to the opinion of our author,[4] since thus the way of ideas, which should enable us to discriminate what may be proper to the soul and what to the body, would become useless, while yet it was said in the second book of the *Essay on the Understanding*,[5] that the operations of the soul furnish us with the idea of the mind [esprit], and that the understanding along with the will makes this idea as intelligible to us as the nature of body is made intelligible to us by solidity and impulse. This is how our author replies in his first letter: "I think I have proved that there is a spiritual substance in us, for we experiment in ourselves thinking. The idea of this action or mode of thinking is inconsistent with the idea of self-subsistence, and therefore has a necessary connexion with a support or subject of inhesion: the idea of that support is what we call substance. . . . For *the general idea of substance being the same everywhere*,[6] the modification of thinking, or the power of thinking joined to it, makes it a spirit, without considering what other modification it has, as whether it has the modification of solidity or no. As on the other side, substance that has the modification of solidity is matter, whether it has the modification of thinking or no. And therefore if your lordship means by a spiritual an immaterial substance, I grant I have not proved, nor upon my principles can it be proved (your lordship meaning, as I think you do, demonstratively proved) that there is an immaterial substance in us that thinks."[7]

It is certain that matter is as little capable of producing feeling [sentiment] mechanically, as it is of producing reason, as our author admits; and that I most certainly recognize that it is not allowable to deny what one does not understand, but I add that we have a right to deny (at least in the order of nature) that which is absolutely neither intelligible nor explicable. I maintain also that substances (material or immaterial) cannot be conceived in their bare essence without any activity, that activity is of the essence of substance in general; and that the conceptions of created beings are not the measure of the power of God, but that their conceptivity, or ability [force] to conceive, is the measure of the power of nature: for all that is in accordance with the order of nature can be conceived or understood by some created being.

Those who will think out my system will see that I cannot wholly agree with either of these excellent authors, whose controversy, however, is very instructive. But, to explain myself distinctly, it is before all things to be considered that the modifications which can naturally or without miracle belong to a subject [sujet] must arise from the limitations or variations of a real genus or an original nature which is constant and absolute. For it is thus that among philosophers the modes of an absolute being are distinguished from the being itself: for instance, we know that size, figure and motion are manifestly limitations and variations of the bodily nature. For it is clear how an exten-

---

4. Locke, *Essay on Human Understanding* 4:3.

5. 2:23.15, 27, 28.

6. Leibniz's italics.

7. Locke, *Works* (1823), vol. 4, pp. 32ff.

sion when limited gives figures, and that the change which takes place in it is nothing but motion. And whenever we find any quality in a subject [*sujet*], we should believe that if we understood the nature of the subject [*sujet*] and of the quality, we should understand [*concevoir*] how the quality can be a result of it. Thus in the order of nature (setting aside miracles), God is not arbitrarily free to give to substances one set of qualities or another indifferently: and He will never give them any but those which are natural to them, that is to say, which can be derived from their nature, as explicable modifications of it. Thus we may hold that matter will not by nature have the attraction mentioned above, and will not of itself go in a curved line, because it is not possible to conceive how that can happen, that is to say to explain it mechanically; while that which is according to nature [*naturel*] ought to be capable of becoming distinctly conceivable, if we were admitted into the secrets of things. This distinction, between that which is natural and explicable and that which is inexplicable and miraculous, removes all difficulties. . . . That God should usually perform miracles would certainly be without rhyme or reason. Accordingly this lazy hypothesis would equally destroy our philosophy, which seeks reasons, and the Divine wisdom which furnishes them.

Now as to thinking it is certain, and our author more than once allows it, that it cannot be a modification of matter that is intelligible or can be comprehended and explained by matter: that is to say, a feeling or thinking being is not a mechanical thing, like a watch or a mill, so that one might conceive sizes, figures and motions, the mechanical combination of which could produce something thinking and even feeling in a quantity of matter in which there was nothing of this kind—which thinking and feeling would also come to an end in the same way when the mechanism falls into disorder. Accordingly it is not a natural thing for matter to feel and to think, and this can take place in it only in two ways, one of which is, that God should unite with it a substance to which it is natural to think, and the other is, that God should miraculously impart thinking to it. In this matter, then, I am entirely of the opinion of the Cartesians, except that I extend it even to the lower animals, and hold that they have feeling [*sentiment*], and that their souls are immaterial (properly speaking) and no more perishable than are atoms according to Democritus or Gassendi. . . . And it is enough that we cannot maintain that matter thinks, unless there is attributed to it an imperishable soul or rather a miracle, and that thus the immortality of our souls follows from that which is natural: since we cannot maintain that they are extinguished, unless it be by a miracle, consisting either in the exaltation of matter or in the annihilation of the soul. For we know, of course, that the power of God could make our souls mortal, although they may be quite immaterial (or immortal by nature), since He can annihilate them.

Now this truth of the immateriality of the soul is undoubtedly of importance. For it is infinitely more helpful to religion and morality, especially at the present day (when many people have very little regard for revelation by itself and for miracles), to show that souls are naturally immortal and that it would be a miracle if they were not, than to maintain that our souls would die in the course of nature, and that it is in virtue of a miraculous grace, founded on nothing but the promise of God, that they do not die. Besides it has for some time been generally known that those who have tried to destroy natural religion and to reduce all to revealed religion, as if reason taught us nothing about it, have been counted suspect, and not always without reason. . . .

Principles of Nature and of Grace, Founded on Reason

1. *Substance* is a being capable of action. It is simple or compound. *Simple substance* is that which has no parts. *Compound substance* is the combination of simple substances or *Monads*. *Monas* is a Greek word, which means unity, or that which is one. Compounds or bodies are pluralities [*multitudes*]; and simple substances, lives, souls, spirits, are unities. And everywhere there must be simple substances, for without simple substances there would not be compounds; and consequently all nature is full of life.

2. The Monads, having no parts, can neither be made [*formées*] nor unmade. They can neither come into being nor come to an end by natural means, and consequently they last as long as the universe, which will be changed, but which will not be destroyed. They can have no shape [*figure*]; otherwise they would have parts. Consequently any one Monad in itself and at a particular moment can be distinguished from any other only by internal qualities and activities [*actions*], which cannot be other than its *perceptions* (that is to say, the representations of the compound, or of that which is outside, in the simple) and its *appetitions* (that is to say, its tendencies to pass from one perception to another), which are the principles of change. For the simplicity of substance is by no means inconsistent with the multiplicity of the modifications which are to be found together in that same simple substance, and these modifications must consist in variety of relations to the things which are outside. It is as in the case of a *centre* or point, in which, although it is perfectly simple, there is an infinite number of angles formed by the lines which meet in it.

3. All nature is a *plenum*. There are simple substances everywhere, which are actually separated from one another by activities of their own, and which continually change their relations; and each specially important [*distinguée*] simple substance or Monad, which forms the centre of a compound substance (e.g. of an animal) and the principle of its oneness, is surrounded by a *mass* composed of an infinity of other Monads, which constitute the particular body of this central Monad, and according to the affections of its body the Monad represents, as in a kind of *centre*, the things which are outside of it. This *body* is *organic*, though it forms a kind of automaton or natural machine, which is a machine not only as a whole, but also in the smallest parts of it that can come into observation. Since the world is a *plenum* all things are connected together and each body acts upon every other, more or less, according to their distance, and each, through reaction, is affected by every other. Hence it follows that each Monad is a living mirror, or a mirror endowed with inner activity, representative of the universe, according to its point of view, and as subject to rule as is the universe itself. And the perceptions in the Monad are produced one from another according to the laws of desires [*appétits*] or of the *final causes of good and evil*, which consist in observable perceptions, regular or irregular, as, on the other hand, the changes of bodies and external phenomena are produced one from another according to the laws of *efficient causes*, that is to say, of motions. Thus there is a perfect *harmony* between the perceptions of the Monad and the motions of bodies, a harmony pre-established from the beginning between the system of efficient causes and that of final causes.

From Gottfried Wilhelm Leibniz, *The Monadology and Other Philosophical Writings*, trans. Robert Latta (Oxford: Oxford University Press, 1898), pp. 406–417.

And it is in this way that soul and body are in agreement and are physically united while it is not possible for the one to change the laws of the other.

4. Each Monad, with a particular body, forms a living substance. Thus not only is there everywhere life, accompanied with members or organs, but there is also an infinity of degrees in the Monads, one dominating more or less over another. But when the Monad has organs so arranged that they give prominence and sharpness [*du relief et du distingué*] to the impressions they receive, and consequently to the perceptions which represent these (as, for instance, when, by means of the form of the eye's humours, the rays of light are concentrated and act with more force), this may lead to *feeling* [*sentiment*], that is to say, to a perception accompanied by *memory*, in other words, a perception of which a certain echo long remains, so as to make itself heard on occasion. Such a living being is called an *animal*, as its Monad is called a *soul*. And when this soul is raised to *reason*, it is something more sublime and is reckoned among spirits [*esprits*], as will presently be explained.... Thus it is well to make distinction between *perception*, which is the inner state of the Monad representing outer things, and *apperception*, which is *consciousness* or the reflective knowledge of this inner state, and which is not given to all souls nor to the same soul at all times....

5. There is a connexion among the perceptions of animals which has some likeness to reason; but it is based only on the memory of *facts* or effects, and not at all on the knowledge of *causes*. Thus a dog avoids the stick with which it has been beaten, because memory represents to it the pain which this stick has caused it. And men, in so far as they are empirics, that is to say in three-fourths of their actions, do not act otherwise than the lower animals.... But *genuine reasoning* depends upon necessary or eternal truths, such as those of logic, of number, of geometry, which produce an indubitable connexion of ideas and infallible inferences. The animals in which these inferences do not appear are called the *lower animals* [*bêtes*]; but those which know these necessary truths are properly those which are called *rational animals*, and their souls are called *minds* [*esprits*]. These souls have the power to perform acts of reflexion and to observe that which is called ego, substance, soul, mind [*esprit*], in a word, immaterial things and truths. And this it is which makes science or demonstrative knowledge possible to us....

7. Thus far we have spoken merely as pure *physicists*: now we must rise to *metaphysics*, making use of the *great principle*, usually little employed, which affirms that *nothing takes place without sufficient reason*, that is to say, that nothing happens without its being possible for one who should know things sufficiently, to give a reason which is sufficient to determine why things are so and not otherwise. This principle being laid down, the first question we are entitled to put will be—*Why does something exist rather than nothing?* For "nothing" is simpler and easier than "something." Further, granting that things must exist, we must be able to give a reason *why they should exist thus* and not otherwise.

8. Now this sufficient reason of the existence of the universe cannot be found in the sequence of contingent things, that is to say, of bodies and their representations in souls: because, matter being in itself indifferent to motion and to rest and to one or another particular motion, we cannot find in it the reason of motion and still less the reason of one particular motion. And although the motion which is at present in matter comes from the preceding motion, and that again from another preceding motion, we are no farther forward, however far we go; for the same question always

remains. Thus the sufficient reason, which has no need of any other reason, must needs be outside of this sequence of contingent things and must be in a substance which is the cause of this sequence, or which is a necessary being, bearing in itself the reason of its own existence, otherwise we should not yet have a sufficient reason with which we could stop. And this ultimate reason of things is called *God*. . . .

10. It follows from the supreme perfection of God that in producing the universe He has chosen the best possible plan, in which there is the greatest variety along with the greatest order; ground, place, time being as well arranged as possible; the greatest effect produced by the simplest ways; the most power, knowledge, happiness and goodness in created things that the universe allowed. For as all possible things in the understanding of God claim existence in proportion to their perfections, the result of all these claims must be the most perfect actual world that is possible. And apart from this it would not be possible to give a reason why things have gone thus rather than otherwise. . . .

Necessary and Contingent Truths

An affirmative truth is one whose predicate is in the subject; and so in every true affirmative proposition, necessary or contingent, universal or particular, the notion of the predicate is in some way contained in the notion of the subject, in such a way that if anyone were to understand perfectly each of the two notions just as God understands it, he would by that very fact perceive that the predicate is in the subject. From this it follows that all the knowledge of propositions which is in God, whether this is of the simple intelligence, concerning the essence of things, or of vision, concerning the existence of things, or mediate knowledge concerning conditioned existences, results immediately from the perfect understanding of each term which can be the subject or predicate of any proposition. That is, the *a priori* knowledge of complexes arises from the understanding of that which is not complex.

An *absolutely necessary* proposition is one which can be resolved into identical propositions, or, whose opposite implies a contradiction. . . . This type of necessity, therefore, I call metaphysical or geometrical. That which lacks such necessity I call contingent, but that which implies a contradiction, or whose opposite is necessary, is called *impossible*. The rest are called *possible*.

In the case of a contingent truth, even though the predicate is really in the subject, yet one never arrives at a demonstration or an identity, even though the resolution of each term is continued indefinitely. In such cases it is only God, who comprehends the infinite at once, who can see how the one is in the other, and can understand *a priori* the perfect reason for contingency; in creatures this is supplied *a posteriori*, by experience. So the relation of contingent to necessary truths is somewhat like the relation of surd ratios (namely, the ratios of incommensurable numbers) to the expressible ratios of commensurable numbers. . . . I did not understand how a predicate could be in a subject, and yet the proposition would not be a necessary one. But the knowledge of geometry and the analysis of the infinite lit this light in me, so that I might understand that notions too can be resolved to infinity.

From this we learn that there are some propositions which pertain to the essences, and others to the existences of things. Propositions of essence are those which can be demonstrated by the resolution of terms; these are necessary, or virtually identical, and so their opposite is impossible, or virtually contradictory. The truth of these is eternal; not only will they hold whilst the world remains, but they would have held even if God had created the world in another way. Existential or contingent propositions differ entirely from these. Their truth is understood *a priori* by the infinite mind alone, and cannot be demonstrated by any resolution. These propositions are such as are true at a certain time; they express, not only what pertains to the possibility of things, but also what actually exists, or would exist contingently if certain things were granted—for example, that I am now alive, or that the sun is shining. . . . In each individual substance, God perceives the truth of all its accidents from its very notion, without calling in anything extrinsic; for each one in its way involves all others, and the whole universe. So all propositions into which existence and time enter have as an ingre-

From G.H.R. Parkinson, ed., *Leibniz: Philosophical Writings*, trans. Mary Morris and G.H.R. Parkinson (London: Dent, 1973), pp. 96–101. Reprinted by permission of J.M. Dent & Sons Ltd. Publishers.

dient the whole series of things, nor can "now" or "here" be understood except in relation to other things. Consequently, such propositions do not admit of demonstrations,
i.e. of a terminable resolution by which their truth may appear. The same applies to
all the accidents of individual created substances. Indeed, even if some one could
know the whole series of the universe, even then he could not give a reason for it,
unless he compared it with all other possibles. From this it is evident why no demonstration of a contingent proposition can be found, however far the resolution of
notions is continued. . . .

   This will now help us to distinguish free substances from others. The accidents of
every individual substance, if predicated of it, make a contingent proposition, which
does not have metaphysical necessity. That this stone tends downwards when its support has been removed is not a necessary but a contingent proposition, nor can such
an event be demonstrated from the notion of this stone by the help of the universal
notions which enter into it, and so God alone perceives this perfectly. For he alone
knows whether he will suspend by a miracle that subordinate law of nature by which
heavy things are driven downwards; for others neither understand the absolutely
universal laws involved, nor can they perform the infinite analysis which is necessary
to connect the notion of this stone with the notion of the whole universe, or with
absolutely universal laws. But at any rate it can be known in advance from subordinate
laws of nature that unless the law of gravity is suspended by a miracle, a descent follows. But free or intelligent substances possess something greater and more marvellous, in a kind of imitation of God. For they are not bound by any certain subordinate
laws of the universe, but act as it were by a private miracle, on the sole initiative of
their own power, and by looking towards a final cause they interrupt the connexion
and the course of the efficient causes that act on their will. So it is true that there is
no creature "which knows the heart" which could predict with certainty how some
mind will choose in accordance with the laws of nature; as it could be predicted (at any
rate by an angel) how some body will act, provided that the course of nature is not
interrupted. For just as the course of the universe is changed by the free will of God,
so the course of the mind's thoughts is changed by its free will; so that, in the case of
minds, no subordinate universal laws can be established (as is possible in the case of
bodies) which are sufficient for predicting a mind's choice. But this does not prevent
the fact that the future actions of the mind are evident to God, just as his own future
actions are. For he knows perfectly the import of the series of things which he chooses,
and so also of his own decree; and at the same time he also understands what is contained in the notion of this mind, which he himself has admitted into the number of
things which are to exist, inasmuch as this notion involves the series of things itself
and its absolutely universal laws. . . .

SELECTED BIBLIOGRAPHY

Leibniz, Gottfried Wilhelm. *New Essays on Human Understanding.* Trans. P. Remnant and J. Bennett. Cambridge: Cambridge University Press, 1981.

_____. *Philosophical Essays.* Trans. R. Ariew and D. Garber. Indianapolis: Hackett, 1989.

_____. *Philosophical Papers and Letters.* Trans. L. Loemker. Boston: Reidel, 1969.

Broad, C.D. *Leibniz: An Introduction.* Cambridge: Cambridge University Press, 1975.

Brown, Stuart. *Leibniz.* Minneapolis: University of Minnesota Press, 1985.

Carr, H.W. *Leibniz.* New York: Dover, 1960.

Frankfurt, Harry G. *Leibniz: A Collection of Critical Essays.* Garden City, N.Y.: Doubleday, 1972.

Joseph, H.W.B. *Lectures on the Philosophy of Leibniz.* Ed. J.L. Austin. Oxford: Clarendon Press, 1949.

Loemker, Leroy. *Struggle for Synthesis: The Seventeenth Century Background of Leibniz's Synthesis of Order and Freedom.* Cambridge, Mass.: Harvard University Press, 1972.

McRae, Robert. *Leibniz: Perception, Apperception and Thought.* Toronto: University of Toronto Press, 1976.

Martin, Gottfried. *Leibniz: Logic and Metaphysics.* Trans. P.G. Lucas and K.J. Northcott. Manchester: University of Machester Press, 1964.

Mates, Benson. *The Philosophy of Leibniz: Metaphysics and Language.* New York: Oxford University Press, 1986.

Parkinson, G.H.R. *Logic and Reality in Leibniz's Metaphysics.* New York: Oxford University Press, 1967.

Rescher, Nicholas. *Leibniz: An Introduction to His Philosophy.* 2d ed. Totowa, N.J.: Rowman and Littlefield, 1979.

Ross, George M. *Leibniz.* New York: Oxford University Press, 1984.

Russell, Bertrand. *A Critical Exposition of the Philosophy of Leibniz.* 2d ed. London: George Allen & Unwin, 1937.

Saw, Ruth L. *Leibniz.* Harmondsworth, England: Penguin, 1954.

Woolhouse, R.S., ed. *Leibniz: Metaphysics and Philosophy of Science.* New York: Oxford University Press, 1981.

David Hume

David Hume's own summary of his life (1711–1776) conveys the man better than any third-person account, for all the evidence indicates him to have been an exemplary student of Socrates' injunction, "Know thyself"!

"My Own Life" by David Hume (abridged)

This Narrative shall contain little more than the History of my Writings; as indeed, almost all my Life has been spent in literary Pursuits and Occupations.

I was born the 26 of April 1711, O.S. at Edinburgh. I was of a good Family both by Father and Mother. My Father's Family is a Branch of the Earl of Home's or Hume's; my Mother was Daughter of Sir David Falconar, President of the College of Justice.

My Family, however, was not rich; and being myself a younger Brother, my Patrimony, according to the Mode of my Country, was of course very slender. . . . I passed through the ordinary Course of Education with Success; and was seized very early with a passion for Literature which has been the ruling Passion of my Life, and the great Source of my Enjoyments. My studious Disposition, my Sobriety, and my Industry gave my Family a Notion that the Law was a proper Profession for me: But I found an unsurmountable Aversion to every thing but the pursuits of Philosophy and general Learning.

My very slender Fortune, however, being unsuitable to this plan of Life, and my Health being a little broken by my ardent Application, I was tempted or rather forced to make a very feeble Trial for entering into a more active Scene of Life. In 1734, I went to Bristol with some Recommendations to eminent Merchants; but in a few Months found that Scene totally unsuitable to me. I went over to France, with a View to prosecuting my Studies in a Country Retreat; and I there laid that Plan of Life, which I have steddily and successfully pursued: I resolved to make a very rigid Frugality supply my Deficiency of Fortune, to maintain unimpaired my Independency, and to regard every object as contemptible, except the Improvement of my Talents in Literature.

During my Retreat in France I composed my *Treatise of human Nature*. After passing three Years very agreeably in that Countrey, I came over to London in 1737. In the End of 1738, I published my Treatise.

Never literary Attempt was more unfortunate than my Treatise of human Nature. It fell *dead-born from the Press*; without reaching such distinction as even to excite a Murmur among the Zealots. But being naturally of a cheerful and sanguine Temper, I very soon recovered the Blow, and prosecuted with great Ardour my Studies in the Country. In 1742, I printed at Edinburgh the first part of my Essays: the work was favourably received, and soon made me entirely forget my former Disappointment. . . .

In spring 1775, I was struck with a Disorder in my Bowels, which at first gave me no Alarm, but has since, as I apprehend it, become mortal and incurable. I now reckon upon a speedy Dissolution. I have suffered very little pain from my Disorder; and what is more strange, have, notwithstanding the great Decline of my Person, never suffered a Moments Abatement of my Spirits: Insomuch, that were I to name the Period of my Life which I shoud most choose to pass over again I might be tempted to Point to this later Period. I possess the same Ardor as ever in Study, and the same Gaiety in Company. I consider besides, that a Man of sixty five, by dying, cuts off only a few Years of Infirmities: And though I see many Symptoms of my literary Reputation's breaking out at last with additional Lustre, I know, that I had but few Years to enjoy it. It is difficult to be more detached from Life than I am at present.

To conclude historically with my own Character—I am, or rather was (for that is the Style, I must now use in speaking of myself; which emboldens me the more to speak my Sentiments) I was, I say, a man of mild Dispositions, of Command of Temper, of an open, social, and cheerful Humour, capable of Attachment, but little susceptible of Enmity, and of great Moderation in all my Passions. Even my Love of literary Fame, my ruling Passion, never soured my humour, notwithstanding my frequent Disappointments. My Company was not unacceptable to the young and careless, as well as to the Studious and literary: And as I took a particular Pleasure in the Company of modest women, I had no reason to be displeased with the Reception I met with from them. In a word, though most men any wise eminent, have found reason to complain of Calumny, I never was touched, or even attacked by her baleful Tooth: and though I wantonly exposed myself to the Rage of both Civil and religious Factions, they seemed to be disarmed in my behalf of their wonted Fury: My Friends never had occasion to vindicate any one Circumstance of my Character and

Conduct. I cannot say, there is no Vanity in making this funeral Oration of myself; but I hope it is not a misplac'd one; and this is a Matter of Fact which is easily clear'd and ascertained.[1]

Philosophy

Hume is possibly the greatest philosopher ever to have written in English. His work marks the most thorough and consistent development of the archetypical school of English-language philosophy: empiricism. In fact, Hume's development of empiricism is so thorough that it has often been accused of collapsing under its own weight—even Hume confesses despair at some of the positions his principles drive him to adopt.

Hume sets out the fundamental elements of his philosophy—impressions and their fainter derivatives, ideas—and holds to the fundamental tenet of his empiricism—that every idea must be derived from some set of original impressions—with greater clarity and consistency than Locke. Hume's approach to a philosophical problem (e.g., whether we have knowledge of things external to our minds, what it means to assert a causal relation between two things, or wherein lies personal identity) is to search out the original atomic impressions from which those ideas (existence external to the mind, causation, personal identity) derive. This then tells us what those ideas must amount to, for what right have we to assume or posit anything not derived from our impressions?

Hume's major contribution to philosophical analysis is a dramatic clarification of the difference between *logical* relations among ideas and impressions and other, non-logical (or natural) relations among them, particularly causal relations. "If John has a brother, then John has a sibling" is true because of a logical relation between our ideas of being a brother and being a sibling. "If the sun rises, then the cock will crow" is also true—but not because of a logical relation between the sun's rising and the cock's crowing. We can conceive of crowless dawns and predawn or postdawn crowings, whereas we can't conceive of a siblingless brother. The relation between dawn and the cock's crow is a *causal* relation. No matter how thoroughly we analyze the concepts of dawn (the appearance of the sun over the horizon) or a cock's crowing (the emission of a loud and raucous verbal cry by a male chicken), there is no way to discover any intrinsic connection. That there is a connection between dawn and cocks crowing can be discovered only through experience, by noting that they are repeatedly associated.

For Hume, then, all judgments fall into two categories: relations of ideas (such as "Brothers are male siblings"), whose truth is logically demonstrable, and matters of fact (such as "Roosters crow at dawn"), which experience alone can justify.

Hume devoted particular care to his analysis of causality, a concept that had played a large role in the arguments of his predecessors. Submitting that concept to his rigorous scrutiny, Hume detected in its common use four elements: (1) a cause must be immediately contiguous to its effect, (2) a cause must precede its effect, (3) a cause must be constantly conjoined with its effect, and (4) a cause must *necessitate* its effect,

---

1. Ernest Campbell Mossner, *The Life of David Hume*, 2d ed. (New York: Oxford University Press, 1980), pp. 611–615. Reprinted by permission of Oxford University Press.

according to many thinkers. However, because this fourth component, unlike the first three, corresponds to nothing in our impressions, Hume rules out the idea that causes and effects must be necessarily connected. Therefore, judgments about cause-effect relations can be justified solely by appeal to experience; they are not logically demonstrable. Since the causal relation forms the foundation of all our reasoning about matters of fact, no matters of fact are logically demonstrable either.

To sharpen the issue even more, Hume points out that any nondemonstrative method that attempts to go beyond our experiential base and draw inferences about what is usually, always, or universally the case cannot be defended by any sound demonstrative reasoning and that any other form of defense would be question-begging. There is no purely rational support for our use of induction, he claims. Though neither Hume nor anyone else has doubted our need to employ inductive methods, their justification is still a live issue in philosophy.

The bombshell Hume dropped on the philosophical world (though not fully appreciated until Kant) was that many of our beliefs—and especially all philosophically interesting judgments (e.g., there are bodies external to the mind, every event has a cause)—are not relations of ideas, are not logically demonstrable, and are not self-evident either. Furthermore, they go beyond the boundaries of anyone's experience in the generalities they assert and thus also make claims that reason alone cannot defend.

Hume's attack on the vaunted power of reason continued in his ethical speculations as well. It had often been thought that moral principles were a priori—that is, knowable independently of experience—and capable of demonstration, that morals could be made a science much like geometry. According to Hume, however, reason is and ought to be the "slave of the passions." Reason can help us find the best means to a given end, but the ends we have are not themselves matters of purely rational choice: our ends arise out of our natural passions and sentiments. Morality is grounded in certain natural human sentiments, not in pure reason or in divine commands.

Because of the power of his critical arguments, Hume has often been treated as a deep skeptic, the kind of skeptic it is every philosopher's job to refute (at least this seems to have been the prevalent attitude in the nineteenth century). But however skeptical the conclusions to which his premises drove him, Hume intended no such result. Rather, he wanted to reveal to us the true, natural basis of our beliefs and actions. Reason, Hume thought, had been overvalued, made both the sole distinguishing trait of humanity and its single explanatory principle. Hume thought a far greater role was played by our natural proclivities to associate ideas and to respond emotionally to others and to our surroundings: "'Tis not, therefore, reason, which is the guide of life, but custom." These natural tendencies are not themselves under the control of reason, but they suffice to allow us to lead productive and valuable lives. And like Locke, Hume believed that we can understand nothing clearly until we have understood ourselves.

The Reading Context

Hume is a pleasure to read, for his sentences are lucid and smooth. But the rhythm of his writing extracts a toll: he is often cavalier with his terms, and the flow of his style can mask dangerous unclarities and ambiguities. Particularly vexing is Hume's tendency to shift between treating impressions and ideas as subjective states referring to objective things and treating them as the only things we have any access to at all. Technically, Hume has to insist that impressions and ideas are the only objects there are.

A close reading of Hume reveals both his immensely powerful skeptical critiques of many classic philosophical assumptions and his own positive contributions. Whenever Hume demonstrates that philosophers have hitherto been mistaken about something, ask what Hume thinks is the correct answer. The *Treatise* is a good place to practice argument analysis, for Hume had a very well-developed sense of argument and lays out his argument fairly clearly. Still, Hume is seldom doctrinaire. As John Passmore points out, "No one could be a Humean, in the sense in which he could be a Hegelian; to be a Humean, precisely, is to take no system as final, nothing as ultimate except the spirit of enquiry."[2]

A Note on the Text

David Hume wrote his *Treatise of Human Nature* while recuperating in France from overzealous study. He was an ambitious young man of twenty-eight when it was published, or in his words "fell dead-born from the Press." He subsequently recast his philosophy in a slightly more accessible and popular form in his two works *An Enquiry concerning Human Understanding* and *An Enquiry concerning the Principles of Morals*. The *Treatise* remains, however, unsurpassed as a statement of Humean empiricism. Hume manages to write not only some of the best philosophy originally written in English, but also some of the best English written in the field of philosophy. This abridgment is based on the standard edition of Hume by L.A. Selby-Bigge, revised by P.H. Nidditch. Hume wrote an admirable summary of his major arguments in "An Abstract of a Book lately Published; entitled a Treatise of Human Nature, &c. wherein the Chief Argument of that Book is farther Illustrated and Explained," which he published in 1740 in a vain attempt to draw attention to the *Treatise*. The abridgment of the *Treatise* here uses these summary passages from the "Abstract," which is included in the standard edition of the *Treatise*. The page numbers for the Selby-Bigge edition are noted in the margin.

Reading Questions

1. What exactly is the distinction between impressions and ideas? Do you find Hume's way of drawing that distinction convincing? What is the distinction between impressions of sensation and impressions of reflection? Between ideas of memory and ideas of imagination?
2. What are the three natural relations between ideas that account for their association? How do they differ from philosophical relations?
3. Hume claims that all ideas are conceived as existent. Does this mean we must believe that everything we have ideas of (e.g., a unicorn) exists, even though we know perfectly well some don't?

---

2. John Passmore, *Hume's Intentions*, rev. ed. (New York: Basic Books, 1968), p. 159.

4. Analyze Hume's argument that since perceptions are the only thing present to our minds, all we can ever form an idea of is a perception, and we cannot form an idea of anything that is not an impression or idea except insofar as we form the idea of something responsible for or relative to our perceptions.

5. Hume makes the cause-effect relation the principle of all our nontrivial knowledge. Is this correct? Hume's principle that to justify our having an idea, we must show the impressions from which this idea originates forces him to look for the impressions from which we get our idea of causation. What is his argument that causation is not a particular quality in an idea? What is his analysis of causation?

6. How can the principle of the uniformity of nature be justified?

7. Hume gives two definitions of cause. Are they synonymous? Are they equivalent?

8. How does Hume explain the fact that different perceptions that occur at separate times nonetheless cause us to believe in the continued existence of an identical object distinct from our perceptions? That is, (a) in what does the identity of an object consist? (b) Why does resemblance induce us to believe in the identity of an object? (c) Why do we unite broken appearances by reference to a continuous existent? (d) Why is this conception so forceful that we believe it?

9. Do you have an idea of self? Does Hume think you do?

10. Hume claims that he can prove (a) that reason alone can never be a motive to any action of the will and (b) that reason can never oppose passion in our ultimate choices. What arguments does Hume give to support these contentions?

11. Hume maintains that moral truths are truths about how we feel. This leaves open the objection that we should then be able to assign moral predicates to (have moral feelings about) anything whatsoever. How does Hume answer this?

A Treatise of Human Nature

Book I
Of the Understanding

Part 1
Of Ideas, Their Origin, Composition, Connexion, Abstraction, &c.

Section 1
Of the origin of our ideas

1 All the perceptions of the human mind resolve themselves into two distinct kinds, which I shall call IMPRESSIONS and IDEAS. The difference betwixt these consists in the degrees of force and liveliness, with which they strike upon the mind, and make their way into our thought or consciousness. Those perceptions, which enter with most force and violence, we may name *impressions*; and under this name I comprehend all our sensations, passions and emotions, as they make their first appearance in the soul. By *ideas* I mean the faint images of these in thinking and reasoning; such as, for instance, are all the perceptions excited by the present discourse, excepting only, those which arise from the sight and touch, and excepting the immediate pleasure or uneasiness it may occasion. I believe it will not be very necessary to employ many words in
2 explaining this distinction. Every one of himself will readily perceive the difference betwixt feeling and thinking. The common degrees of these are easily distinguished; tho' it is not impossible but in particular instances they may very nearly approach to each other. . . . [1]

There is another division of our perceptions, which it will be convenient to observe, and which extends itself both to our impressions and ideas. This division is into SIMPLE and COMPLEX. Simple perceptions or impressions and ideas are such as admit of no distinction nor separation. The complex are the contrary to these, and may be distinguished into parts. Tho' a particular colour, taste, and smell are qualities all united together in this apple, 'tis easy to perceive they are not the same, but are at least distinguishable from each other. . . .

The first circumstance, that strikes my eye, is the great resemblance betwixt our impressions and ideas in every other particular, except their degree of force and vivacity. The one seem to be in a manner the reflexion of the other; so that all the percep-
3 tions of the mind are double, and appear both as impressions and ideas. . . . Ideas and impressions appear always to correspond to each other. . . .

Upon a more accurate survey I find I have been carried away too far by the first appearance, and that I must make use of the distinction of perceptions into *simple and complex*, to limit this general decision, *that all our ideas and impressions are resem-*

From David Hume, *A Treatise of Human Nature* (2d ed.), ed. L.A. Selby-Bigge, rev. P.H. Nidditch (New York: Oxford University Press, 1978). Reprinted by permission of Oxford University Press.

1. I here make use of these terms, *impression* and *idea*, in a sense different from what is usual, and I hope this liberty will be allowed me. Perhaps I rather restore the word, idea, to its original sense, from which Mr. *Locke* had perverted it, in making it stand for all our perceptions. By the term of impression I would not be understood to express the manner, in which our lively perceptions are produced in the soul, but merely the perceptions themselves; for which there is no particular name either in the *English* or any other language, that I know of. [Hume's note.]

bling. I observe, that many of our complex ideas never had impressions, that corresponded to them, and that many of our complex impressions never are exactly copied in ideas. . . .

After the most accurate examination, of which I am capable, I venture to affirm . . . that every simple idea has a simple impression, which resembles it; and every simple impression a correspondent idea. . . . If any one should deny this universal resemblance, I know no way of convincing him, but by desiring him to shew a simple impression, that has not a correspondent idea, or a simple idea, that has not a correspondent impression. . . .   4

We shall here content ourselves with establishing one general proposition, *That all our simple ideas in their first appearance are deriv'd from simple impressions, which are correspondent to them, and which they exactly represent.*

In seeking for phaenomena to prove this proposition, I find only those of two kinds; but in each kind the phaenomena are obvious, numerous, and conclusive. . . . Every simple impression is attended with a correspondent idea, and every simple idea with a correspondent impression. From this constant conjunction of resembling perceptions I immediately conclude, that there is a great connexion betwixt our correspondent impressions and ideas, and that the existence of the one has a considerable influence upon that of the other. Such a constant conjunction, in such an infinite number of instances, can never arise from chance; but clearly proves a dependence of the impressions on the ideas, or of the ideas on the impressions. That I may know on   5 which side this dependence lies, I consider the order of their *first appearance*; and find by constant experience, that the simple impressions always take the precedence of their correspondent ideas, but never appear in the contrary order. To give a child an idea of scarlet or orange, of sweet or bitter, I present the objects, or in other words, convey to him these impressions; but proceed not so absurdly, as to endeavour to produce the impressions by exciting the ideas. . . . The constant conjunction of our resembling perceptions, is a convincing proof, that the one are the causes of the other; and this priority of the impressions is an equal proof, that our impressions are the causes of our ideas, not our ideas of our impressions.

To confirm this I consider another plain and convincing phaenomenon; which is, that where-ever by any accident the faculties, which give rise to any impressions, are obstructed in their operations, as when one is born blind or deaf; not only the impressions are lost, but also their correspondent ideas; . . . likewise where they have never been put in action to produce a particular impression. We cannot form to ourselves a just idea of the taste of a pine-apple, without having actually tasted it.

There is however one contradictory phaenomenon, which may prove, that 'tis not absolutely impossible for ideas to go before their correspondent impressions. I believe it will readily be allow'd, that the several distinct ideas of colours, which enter by the eyes, or those of sounds, which are convey'd by the hearing, are really different from   6 each other, tho' at the same time resembling. Now if this be true of different colours, it must be no less so of the different shades of the same colour, that each of them produces a distinct idea, independent of the rest. . . . Suppose therefore a person to have enjoyed his sight for thirty years, and to have become perfectly well acquainted with colours of all kinds, excepting one particular shade of blue, for instance, which it never has been his fortune to meet with. Let all the different shades of that colour, except that single one, be plac'd before him, descending gradually from the deepest to the lightest; 'tis plain, that he will perceive a blank, where that shade is wanting, and will be sensible, that there is a greater distance in that place betwixt the contiguous colours, than in any other. Now I ask, whether 'tis possible for him, from his own imagination, to supply this deficiency, and raise up to himself the idea of that particular shade, tho' it had never been conveyed to him by his senses? I believe there are few but will be of opinion that he can; and this may serve as a proof, that the simple ideas are not always derived from the correspondent impressions; tho' the instance is so particular and singular, that 'tis scarce worth our observing, and does not merit that for it alone we should alter our general maxim. . . .

7   'Tis remarkable, that the present question concerning the precedency of our impressions or ideas, is the same with what has made so much noise in other terms, when it has been disputed whether there be any *innate ideas*, or whether all ideas be derived from sensation and reflexion. . . . Now if we carefully examine these arguments, we shall find that they prove nothing but that ideas are preceded by other more lively perceptions, from which they are derived, and which they represent. I hope this clear stating of the question will remove all disputes concerning it, and will render this principle of more use in our reasonings, than it seems hitherto to have been.

Section 2

Division of the subject

Since it appears, that our simple impressions are prior to their correspondent ideas, and that the exceptions are very rare, method seems to require we should examine our impressions, before we consider our ideas. Impressions may be divided into two kinds, those of SENSATION and those of REFLEXION. The first kind arises in the soul originally, from unknown causes. The second is derived in a great measure from our ideas, 8   and that in the following order. An impression first strikes upon the senses, and makes us perceive heat or cold, thirst or hunger, pleasure or pain of some kind or other. Of this impression there is a copy taken by the mind, which remains after the impression ceases; and this we call an idea. This idea of pleasure or pain, when it returns upon the soul, produces the new impressions of desire and aversion, hope and fear, which may properly be called impressions of reflexion, because derived from it. These again are copied by the memory and imagination, and become ideas; which perhaps in their turn give rise to other impressions and ideas. . . . The examination of our sensations belongs more to anatomists and natural philosophers than to moral; and therefore shall not at present be enter'd upon. And as the impressions of reflexion, *viz.* passions, desires, and emotions, which principally deserve our attention, arise mostly from ideas, 'twill be necessary to reverse that method, which at first sight seems most natural; and in order to explain the nature and principles of the human mind, give a particular account of ideas, before we proceed to impressions. For this reason I have here chosen to begin with ideas.

Section 3

Of the ideas of the memory and imagination

We find by experience, that when any impression has been present with the mind, it again makes its appearance there as an idea; and this it may do after two different ways: either when in its new appearance it retains a considerable degree of its first vivacity,

and is somewhat intermediate betwixt an impression and an idea; or when it intirely loses that vivacity, and is a perfect idea. The faculty, by which we repeat our impressions in the first manner, is called the MEMORY, and the other the IMAGINATION. 'Tis   9
evident at first sight, that the ideas of the memory are much more lively and strong than those of the imagination. . . .

There is another difference betwixt these two kinds of ideas, which is no less evident, namely that . . . the imagination is not restrain'd to the same order and form with the original impressions; while the memory is in a manner ty'd down in that respect, without any power of variation. . . . The chief exercise of the memory is not to preserve the simple ideas, but their order and position. . . .

The same evidence follows us in our second principle, *of the liberty of the imagination*   10
to transpose and change its ideas. The fables we meet with in poems and romances put this entirely out of question. . . . Nor will this liberty of the fancy appear strange, when we consider, that all our ideas are copy'd from our impressions, and that there are not any two impressions which are perfectly inseparable. . . . Where-ever the imagination perceives a difference among ideas, it can easily produce a separation.

Section 4
Of the connexion or association of ideas

As all simple ideas may be separated by the imagination, and may be united again in what form it pleases, nothing wou'd be more unaccountable than the operations of that faculty, were it not guided by some universal principles, which render it, in some measure, uniform with itself in all times and places. Were ideas entirely loose and unconnected, chance alone wou'd join them; and 'tis impossible the same simple ideas should fall regularly into complex ones (as they commonly do) without some bond of union among them, some associating quality, by which one idea naturally introduces another. This uniting principle among ideas is not to be consider'd as an inseparable connexion; for that has been already excluded from the imagination: nor yet are we to conclude, that without it the mind cannot join two ideas; for nothing is more free than that faculty: but we are only to regard it as a gentle force. . . . The qualities, from   11
which this association arises, and by which the mind is after this manner convey'd from one idea to another, are three, *viz.* RESEMBLANCE, CONTIGUITY in time or place, and CAUSE AND EFFECT.

I believe it will not be very necessary to prove, that these qualities produce an association among ideas, and upon the appearance of one idea naturally introduce another. . . .

That we may understand the full extent of these relations, we must consider, that two objects are connected together in the imagination, not only when the one is immediately resembling, contiguous to, or the cause of the other, but also when there is interposed betwixt them a third object, which bears to both of them any of these relations. . . .

These are therefore the principles of union or cohesion among our simple ideas,   12
and in the imagination supply the place of that inseparable connexion, by which they are united in our memory. Here is a kind of ATTRACTION, which in the mental world will be found to have as extraordinary effects as in the natural, and to shew itself in as   13
many and as various forms. Its effects are every where conspicuous; but as to its causes,

they are mostly unknown, and must be resolv'd into *original* qualities of human nature, which I pretend not to explain. . . .

Amongst the effects of this union or association of ideas, there are none more remarkable, than those complex ideas, which are the common subjects of our thoughts and reasoning, and generally arise from some principle of union among our simple ideas. These complex ideas may be divided into *Relations, Modes,* and *Substances.* . . .

Section 5

Of relations

The word RELATION is commonly used in two senses considerably different from each other. Either for that quality, by which two ideas are connected together in the imagination, and the one naturally introduces the other, after the manner above-explained; or for that particular circumstance, in which, even upon the arbitrary union of two ideas in the fancy, we may think proper to compare them. In common language the former is always the sense, in which we use the word, relation; and 'tis only in philosophy, that we extend it to mean any particular subject of comparison, without a connecting principle. . . .

It may perhaps be esteemed an endless task to enumerate all those qualities, which make objects admit of comparison, and by which the ideas of *philosophical* relation are produced. But if we diligently consider them, we shall find that without difficulty they may be compriz'd under seven general heads, which may be considered as the sources of all *philosophical* relation.

1. The first is *resemblance*: And this is a relation, without which no philosophical relation can exist; since no objects will admit of comparison, but what have some degree of resemblance. . . .

2. *Identity* may be esteem'd a second species of relation. This relation I here consider as apply'd in its strictest sense to constant and unchangeable objects. . . .

3. After identity the most universal and comprehensive relations are those of *Space* and *Time.* . . .

4. All those objects, which admit of *quantity*, or *number*, may be compar'd in that particular. . . .

5. When any two objects possess the same *quality* in common, the *degrees*, in which they possess it, form a fifth species of relation. . . .

6. The relation of *contrariety* may at first sight be regarded as an exception to the rule, *that no relation of any kind can subsist without some degree of resemblance.* But let us consider, that no two ideas are in themselves contrary, except those of existence and non-existence, which are plainly resembling, as implying both of them an idea of the object. . . .

7. All other objects, such as fire and water, heat, and cold, are only found to be contrary from experience, and from the contrariety of their *causes* or *effects*; which relation of cause and effect is a seventh philosophical relation, as well as a natural one. . . .

Section 6

Of modes and substances

I wou'd fain ask those philosophers, who found so much of their reasonings on the distinction of substance and accident, and imagine we have clear ideas of each,

whether the idea of *substance* be deriv'd from the impressions of sensation or reflexion?   16
If it be convey'd to us by our senses, I ask, which of them; and after what manner? If
it be perceiv'd by the eyes, it must be a colour; if by the ears, a sound; . . .and so of the
other senses. But I believe none will assert, that substance is either a colour, or a
sound, or a taste. The idea of substance must therefore be deriv'd from an impression
of reflexion, if it really exist. But the impressions of reflexion resolve themselves into
our passions and emotions; none of which can possibly represent a substance. We have
therefore no idea of substance, distinct from that of a collection of particular qualities,
nor have we any other meaning when we either talk or reason concerning it.

The idea of a substance as well as that of a mode, is nothing but a collection of
simple ideas, that are united by the imagination, and have a particular name assigned
them, by which we are able to recall, either to ourselves or others, that collection. But
the difference betwixt these ideas consists in this, that the particular qualities, which
form a substance, are commonly refer'd to an unknown *something*, in which they are
supposed to inhere. . . .

Part 2
Of the Ideas of Space and Time

Section 6
Of the idea of existence, and of external existence

. . . There is no impression nor idea of any kind, of which we have any consciousness   66
or memory, that is not conceiv'd as existent; and 'tis evident, that from this consciousness the most perfect idea and assurance of *being* is deriv'd. From hence we may form
a dilemma, the most clear and conclusive that can be imagin'd, *viz.* that since we never
remember any idea or impression without attributing existence to it, the idea of existence must either be deriv'd from a distinct impression, conjoin'd with every perception or object of our thought, or must be the very same with the idea of the perception
or object.

As this dilemma is an evident consequence of the principle, that every idea arises
from a similar impression, so our decision betwixt the propositions of the dilemma is
no more doubtful. So far from there being any distinct impression, attending every
impression and every idea, that I do not think there are any two distinct impressions,
which are inseparably conjoin'd. . . . And thus, . . . the idea of existence is not deriv'd
from any particular impression.

The idea of existence, then, is the very same with the idea of what we conceive to
be existent. To reflect on any thing simply, and to reflect on it as existent, are nothing
different from each other. That idea, when conjoin'd with the idea of an object, makes   67
no addition to it. . . .

A like reasoning will account for the idea of *external existence*. We may observe, that
'tis universally allow'd by philosophers, and is besides pretty obvious of itself, that
nothing is ever really present with the mind but its perceptions or impressions and
ideas, and that external objects become known to us only by those perceptions they
occasion. . . .

Now since nothing is ever present to the mind but perceptions, and since all ideas
are deriv'd from something antecedently present to the mind; it follows, that 'tis
impossible for us so much as to conceive or form an idea of any thing specifically differ-

ent from ideas and impressions. Let us fix our attention out of ourselves as much as possible: Let us chace our imagination to the heavens, or to the utmost limits of the universe; we never really advance a step beyond ourselves, nor can conceive any kind of existence, but those perceptions, which have appear'd in that narrow compass. This is the universe of the imagination, nor have we any idea but what is there produc'd. . . .

68

Part 3
Of Knowledge and Probability

Section 1
Of knowledge

69   There are seven different kinds of philosophical relation, *viz. resemblance, identity, relations of time and place, proportion in quantity or number, degrees in any quality, contrariety, and causation.*[2] These relations may be divided into two classes; into such as depend entirely on the ideas, which we compare together, and such as may be chang'd without any change in the ideas. 'Tis from the idea of a triangle, that we discover the relation of equality, which its three angles bear to two right ones; and this relation is invariable, as long as our idea remains the same. On the contrary, the relations of *contiguity* and *distance* betwixt two objects may be chang'd merely by an alteration of their place, without any change on the objects themselves or on their ideas. . . . 'Tis the same case with *identity* and *causation.* . . .

70   It appears, therefore, that of these seven philosophical relations, there remain only four, which depending solely upon ideas, can be the objects of knowledge and certainty. These four are *resemblance, contrariety, degrees in quality, and proportions in quantity or number.* Three of these relations are discoverable at first sight, and fall more properly under the province of intuition than demonstration. When any objects *resemble* each other, the resemblance will at first strike the eye, or rather the mind; and seldom requires a second examination. The case is the same with *contrariety,* and with the *degrees* of any *quality.* . . .

Section 2
Of probability; and of the idea of cause and effect

73   This is all I think necessary to observe concerning those four relations, which are the foundation of science; but as to the other three, which depend not upon the idea, and may be absent or present even while *that* remains the same, 'twill be proper to explain them more particularly. These three relations are *identity, the situations in time and place, and causation.*

All kinds of reasoning consist in nothing but a *comparison,* and a discovery of those relations, either constant or inconstant, which two or more objects bear to each other. This comparison we may make, either when both the objects are present to the senses, or when neither of them is present, or when only one. When both the objects are present to the senses along with the relation, we call *this* perception rather than reasoning. . . . According to this way of thinking, we ought not to receive as reasoning any of

---

2. 1:1.5.

the observations we may make concerning *identity*, and the *relations* of *time* and *place*; since in none of them the mind can go beyond what is immediately present to the senses, either to discover the real existence or the relations of objects. 'Tis only *causation*, which produces such a connexion, as to give us assurance from the existence or action of one object, that 'twas follow'd or preceded by any other existence or action.... 74

Here then it appears, that of those three relations, which depend not upon the mere ideas, the only one, that can be trac'd beyond our senses, and informs us of existences and objects, which we do not see or feel, is *causation*. This relation, therefore, we shall endeavour to explain fully before we leave the subject of the understanding....

'Tis evident, that all reasonings concerning *matter of fact* are founded on the relation   649[3] of cause and effect, and that we can never infer the existence of one object from another, unless they be connected together, either mediately or immediately. In order therefore to understand these reasonings, we must be perfectly acquainted with the idea of a cause; and in order to that, must look about us to find something that is the cause of another.

Here is a billiard-ball lying on the table, and another ball moving towards it with rapidity. They strike; and the ball, which was formerly at rest, now acquires a motion. This is as perfect an instance of the relation of cause and effect as any which we know, either by sensation or reflection. Let us therefore examine it. 'Tis evident, that the two balls touched one another before the motion was communicated, and that there was no interval betwixt the shock and the motion. *Contiguity* in time and place is therefore a requisite circumstance to the operation of all causes. 'Tis evident likewise, that the motion, which was the cause, is prior to the motion, which was the effect. *Priority* in time, is therefore another requisite circumstance in every cause. But this is not all. Let us try any other balls of the same kind in a like situation, and we shall always find, that the impulse of the one produces motion in the other: Here therefore is a *third* circumstance, *viz.* that of a *constant conjunction* betwixt the cause and effect. Every object like the cause, produces always some object like the effect. Beyond these three cir- cumstances of contiguity, priority, and constant conjunction, I can discover noth-   650 ing in this cause. The first ball is in motion; touches the second; immediately the second is in motion: and when I try the experiment with the same or like balls, in the same or like circumstances, I find, that upon the motion and touch of the one ball, motion always follows in the other. In whatever shape I turn this matter, and however I examine it, I can find nothing farther.

This is the case when both the cause and effect are present to the senses. Let us now see upon what our inference is founded, when we conclude from the one that the other has existed or will exist. Suppose I see a ball moving in a streight line towards another, I immediately conclude, that they will shock, and that the second will be in motion. This is the inference from cause to effect; and of this nature are all our reasonings in the conduct of life: on this is founded all our belief in history: and from hence is derived all philosophy, excepting only geometry and arithmetic. If we can explain the inference from the shock of two balls, we shall be able to account for this operation of the mind in all instances.

---

3. The passage indicated by the marginal numbers 649–657 is from Hume's "Abstract" of the *Treatise*.

Were a man, such as *Adam*, created in the full vigour of understanding, without experience, he would never be able to infer motion in the second ball from the motion and impulse of the first. It is not any thing that reason sees in the cause, which make us *infer* the effect. Such an inference, were it possible, would amount to a demonstration, as being founded merely on the comparison of ideas. But no inference from cause to effect amounts to a demonstration. Of which there is this evident proof. The mind can always *conceive* any effect to follow from any cause, and indeed any event to follow upon another: whatever we *conceive* is possible, at least in a metaphysical sense: but wherever a demonstration takes place, the contrary is impossible, and implies a contradiction. There is no demonstration, therefore, for any conjunction of cause and effect. And this
651   is a principle, which is generally allowed by philosophers.

It would have been necessary, therefore, for *Adam* (if he was not inspired) to have had *experience* of the effect, which followed upon the impulse of these two balls. He must have seen, in several instances, that when the one ball struck upon the other, the second always acquired motion. If he had seen a sufficient number of instances of this kind, whenever he saw the one ball moving towards the other, he would always conclude without hesitation, that the second would acquire motion. His understanding would anticipate his sight, and form a conclusion suitable to his past experience.

It follows, then, that all reasonings concerning cause and effect, are founded on experience, and that all reasonings from experience are founded on the supposition, that the course of nature will continue uniformly the same. We conclude, that like causes, in like circumstances, will always produce like effects. It may now be worth while to consider, what determines us to form a conclusion of such infinite consequence.

'Tis evident, that *Adam* with all his science, would never have been able to *demonstrate*, that the course of nature must continue uniformly the same, and that the future must be conformable to the past. What is possible can never be demonstrated to be false; and 'tis possible the course of nature may change, since we can conceive such a change. Nay, I will go farther, and assert, that he could not so much as prove by any *probable* arguments, that the future must be conformable to the past. All probable arguments are built on the supposition, that there is this conformity betwixt the future and the past, and therefore can never prove it. This conformity is a *matter of fact*, and if it must be proved, will admit of no proof but from experience. But our experience
652   in the past can be a proof of nothing for the future, but upon a supposition, that there is a resemblance betwixt them. This therefore is a point, which can admit of no proof at all, and which we take for granted without any proof.

We are determined by CUSTOM alone to suppose the future conformable to the past. When I see a billiard-ball moving towards another, my mind is immediately carry'd by habit to the usual effect, and anticipates my sight by conceiving the second ball in motion. There is nothing in these objects, abstractly considered, and independent of experience, which leads me to form any such conclusion: and even after I have had experience of many repeated effects of this kind, there is no argument, which determines me to suppose, that the effect will be conformable to past experience. The powers, by which bodies operate, are entirely unknown. We perceive only their sensible qualities: and what *reason* have we to think, that the same powers will always be conjoined with the same sensible qualities?

'Tis not, therefore, reason, which is the guide of life, but custom. That alone determines the mind, in all instances, to suppose the future conformable to the past. However easy this step may seem, reason would never, to all eternity, be able to make it.

This is a very curious discovery, but leads us to others, that are still more curious. *When I see a billiard-ball moving towards another, my mind is immediately carried by habit to the usual effect, and anticipates my sight by conceiving the second ball in motion.* But is this all? Do I nothing but CONCEIVE the motion of the second ball? No surely. I also BELIEVE that it will move. What then is this *belief*? And how does it differ from the simple conception of any thing? Here is a new question unthought of by philosophers.

When a demonstration convinces me of any proposition, it not only makes me conceive the proposition, but also makes me sensible, that 'tis impossible to conceive any thing contrary. What is demonstratively false implies a contradiction; and what implies a contradiction cannot be conceived. But with regard to any matter of fact, however strong the proof may be from experience, I can always conceive the contrary, tho' I cannot always believe it. The belief, therefore, makes some difference betwixt the conception to which we assent, and that to which we do not assent.

To account for this, there are only two hypotheses. It may be said, that belief joins some new idea to those which we may conceive without assenting to them. But this hypothesis is false. For *first*, no such idea can be produced. When we simply conceive an object, we conceive it in all its parts. We conceive it as it might exist, tho' we do not believe it to exist. Our belief of it would discover no new qualities. We may paint out the entire object in imagination without believing it. We may set it, in a manner, before our eyes, with every circumstance of time and place. 'Tis the very object conceived as it might exist; and when we believe it, we can do no more.

Secondly, The mind has a faculty of joining all ideas together, which involve not a contradiction; and therefore if belief consisted in some idea, which we add to the simple conception, it would be in a man's power, by adding this idea to it, to believe any thing, which he can conceive.

Since therefore belief implies a conception, and yet is something more; and since it adds no new idea to the conception; it follows, that it is a different MANNER of conceiving an object; *something* that is distinguishable to the feeling, and depends not upon our will, as all our ideas do. My mind runs by habit from the visible object of one ball moving towards another, to the usual effect of motion in the second ball. It not only conceives that motion, but *feels* something different in the conception of it from a mere reverie of the imagination. The presence of this visible object, and the constant conjunction of that particular effect, render the idea different to the *feeling* from those loose ideas, which come into the mind without any introduction. This conclusion seems a little surprizing; but we are led into it by a chain of propositions, which admit of no doubt. To ease the reader's memory I shall briefly resume them. No matter of fact can be proved but from its cause or its effect. Nothing can be known to be the cause of another but by experience. We can give no reason for extending to the future our experience in the past; but are entirely determined by custom, when we conceive an effect to follow from its usual cause. But we also believe an effect to follow, as well as conceive it. This belief joins no new idea to the conception. It only varies the manner of conceiving, and makes a difference to the feeling or sentiment. Belief, therefore, in all matters of fact arises only from custom, and is an idea conceived in a peculiar *manner*.

Our author proceeds to explain the manner or feeling, which renders belief different from a loose conception. He seems sensible, that 'tis impossible by words to

653

654

describe this feeling, which every one must be conscious of in his own breast. He calls it sometimes a *stronger* conception, sometimes a more *lively*, a more *vivid*, a *firmer*, or a more *intense* conception. And indeed, whatever name we may give to this feeling, which constitutes belief, our author thinks it evident, that it has a more forcible effect on the mind than fiction and mere conception. This he proves by its influence on the passions and on the imagination; which are only moved by truth or what is taken for such. Poetry, with all its art, can never cause a passion, like one in real life. It fails in the original conception of its objects, which never *feel* in the same manner as those which command our belief and opinion.

655   Our author presuming, that he had sufficiently proved, that the ideas we assent to are different to the feeling from the other ideas, and that this feeling is more firm and lively than our common conception, endeavours in the next place to explain the cause of this lively feeling by an analogy with other acts of the mind. His reasoning seems to be curious; but could scarce be rendered intelligible, or at least probable to the reader, without a long detail, which would exceed the compass I have prescribed to myself.

I have likewise omitted many arguments, which he adduces to prove that belief consists merely in a peculiar feeling or sentiment. I shall only mention one. Our past experience is not always uniform. Sometimes one effect follows from a cause, sometimes another: In which case we always believe, that that will exist which is most common. I see a billiard-ball moving towards another. I cannot distinguish whether it moves upon its axis, or was struck so as to skim along the table. In the first case, I know it will not stop after the shock. In the second it may stop. The first is most common, and therefore I lay my account with that effect. But I also conceive the other effect, and conceive it as possible, and as connected with the cause. Were not the one conception different in the feeling or sentiment from the other, there would be no difference betwixt them.

We have confin'd ourselves in this whole reasoning to the relation of cause and effect, as discovered in the motions and operations of matter. But the same reasoning extends to the operations of the mind. Whether we consider the influence of the will in moving our body, or in governing our thought, it may safely be affirmed, that we could never foretel the effect, merely from the consideration of the cause, without 656   experience. And even after we have experience of these effects, 'tis custom alone, not reason, which determines us to make it the standard of our future judgments. When the cause is presented, the mind, from habit, immediately passes to the conception and belief of the usual effect. This belief is something different from the conception. It does not, however, join any new idea to it. It only makes it be felt differently, and renders it stronger and more lively.

Having dispatcht this material point concerning the nature of the inference from cause and effect, our author returns upon his footsteps, and examines anew the idea of that relation. In the considering of motion communicated from one ball to another, we could find nothing but contiguity, priority in the cause, and constant conjunction. But, beside these circumstances, 'tis commonly suppos'd, that there is a necessary connexion betwixt the cause and effect, and that the cause possesses something, which we call a *power*, or *force*, or *energy*. The question is, what idea is annex'd to these terms? If all our ideas or thoughts be derived from our impressions, this power must either discover itself to our senses, or to our internal feeling. But so little does any *power* discover itself to the senses in the operations of matter, that the *Cartesians* have made no scruple to assert, that matter is utterly deprived of energy, and that all its operations are perform'd merely by the energy of the supreme Being. But the question still recurs, *What idea have we of energy or power even in the supreme Being?* All our idea of a Deity (according to those who deny innate ideas) is nothing but a composition of those ideas, which we acquire from reflecting on the operations of our own minds. Now our own minds afford us no more notion of energy than matter does. When we consider our will or volition *a priori*, abstracting from experience, we are never able to infer any effect from it. And when we take the assistance of experience, it only shows us objects contiguous, successive, and   657 constantly conjoined. Upon the whole, then, either we have no idea at all of force and energy, and these words are altogether insignificant, or they can mean nothing but that determination of the thought, acquir'd by habit, to pass from the cause to its usual effect. But who-ever would thoroughly understand this must consult the author himself. 'Tis sufficient, if I can make the learned world apprehend, that there is some difficulty in the case, and that who-ever solves the difficulty must say some thing very new and extraordinary; as new as the difficulty itself.

Section 3
Why a cause is always necessary

. . . 'Tis a general maxim in philosophy, that *whatever begins to exist, must have a cause*   78 of existence. This is commonly taken for granted in all reasonings, without any proof   79 given or demanded. 'Tis suppos'd to be founded on intuition, and to be one of those maxims, which tho' they may be deny'd with the lips, 'tis impossible for men in their hearts really to doubt of. But if we examine this maxim by the idea of knowledge above-explain'd, we shall discover in it no mark of any such intuitive certainty; but on the contrary shall find, that 'tis of a nature quite foreign to that species of conviction. . . .

But here is an argument, which proves at once, that the foregoing proposition is neither intuitively nor demonstrably certain. We can never demonstrate the necessity of a cause to every new existence, or new modification of existence, without shewing at the same time the impossibility there is, that any thing can ever begin to exist without some productive principle; and where the latter proposition cannot be prov'd, we must despair of ever being able to prove the former. Now that the latter proposition is utterly incapable of a demonstrative proof, we may satisfy ourselves by considering, that as all distinct ideas are inseparable from each other, and as the ideas of cause and effect are evidently distinct, 'twill be easy for us to conceive any object to be non-existent this moment, and existent the next, without conjoining to it the distinct idea of a cause or productive principle. The separation, therefore, of the idea of a cause   80 from that of a beginning of existence, is plainly possible for the imagination; and consequently the actual separation of these objects is so far possible, that it implies no contradiction nor absurdity; and is therefore incapable of being refuted by any reasoning from mere ideas; without which 'tis impossible to demonstrate the necessity of a cause.

Accordingly we shall find upon examination, that every demonstration, which has been produc'd for the necessity of a cause, is fallacious and sophistical. . . .

Every thing, 'tis said,[4] must have a cause; for if any thing wanted a cause, *it* wou'd produce *itself*; that is, exist before it existed; which is impossible. But this reasoning is plainly unconclusive; because it supposes, that in our denial of a cause we still grant what we expressly deny, *viz.* that there must be a cause; which therefore is taken to be the object itself; and *that*, no doubt, is an evident contradiction. But to say that any thing is produc'd, or to express myself more properly, comes into existence, without a cause, is not to affirm, that 'tis itself its own cause; but on the contrary in excluding all external causes, excludes *a fortiori* the thing itself, which is created.

'Tis exactly the same case with the [next] argument,[5] which has been employ'd to demonstrate the necessity of a cause. Whatever is produc'd without any cause, is produc'd by *nothing*; or in other words, has nothing for its cause. But nothing can never be a cause, no more than it can be something, or equal to two right angles. By the same intuition, that we perceive nothing not to be equal to two right angles, or not to be something, we perceive, that it can never be a cause; and consequently must perceive, that every object has a real cause of its existence.

I believe it will not be necessary to employ many words in shewing the weakness of this argument, after what I have said of the foregoing. . . . 'Tis sufficient only to observe, that when we exclude all causes we really do exclude them, and neither suppose nothing nor the object itself to be the causes of the existence; and consequently can draw no argument from the absurdity of these suppositions to prove the absurdity of that exclusion. If every thing must have a cause, it follows, that upon the exclusion of other causes we must accept of the object itself or of nothing as causes. But 'tis the very point in question, whether every thing must have a cause or not; and therefore, according to all just reasoning, it ought never to be taken for granted.

They are still more frivolous, who say, that every effect must have a cause, because 'tis imply'd in the very idea of effect. Every effect necessarily pre-supposes a cause; effect being a relative term, of which cause is the correlative. But this does not prove, that every being must be preceded by a cause; no more than it follows, because every husband must have a wife, that therefore every man must be marry'd. . . .

Section 14

Of the idea of necessary connexion

. . . 'Tis now time to collect all the different parts of this reasoning, and by joining them together form an exact definition of the relation of cause and effect, which makes the subject of the present enquiry. . . .

There may two definitions be given of this relation, which are only different, by their presenting a different view of the same object, and making us consider it either as a *philosophical* or as a *natural* relation; either as a comparison of two ideas, or as an association betwixt them. We may define a CAUSE to be "An object precedent and contiguous to another, and where all the objects resembling the former are plac'd in like relations of precedency and contiguity to those objects, that resemble the latter." If this definition be esteem'd defective, because drawn from objects foreign to the cause, we

---

4. Dr. *Clarke* and others. [Ed. note]

5. Mr. *Locke*. [Ed. note]

may substitute this other definition in its place, *viz.* "A CAUSE is an object precedent and contiguous to another, and so united with it, that the idea of the one determines the mind to form the idea of the other, and the impression of the one to form a more lively idea of the other." Shou'd this definition also be rejected for the same reason, I know no other remedy, than that the persons, who express this delicacy, should substitute a juster definition in its place. But for my part I must own my incapacity for such an undertaking. . . .

We may now be able fully to overcome all that repugnance, which 'tis so natural for us to entertain against the foregoing reasoning, by which we endeavour'd to prove, that the necessity of a cause to every beginning of existence is not founded on any arguments either demonstrative or intuitive. . . . If we define a cause to be *an object precedent and contiguous to another, and where all the objects resembling the former are plac'd in a like relation of priority and contiguity to those objects, that resemble the latter*; we may easily conceive, that there is no absolute nor metaphysical necessity, that every beginning of existence shou'd be attended with such an object. If we define a cause to be, *An object precedent and contiguous to another, and so united with it in the imagination, that the idea of the one determines the mind to form the idea of the other, and the impression of the one to form a more lively idea of the other*; we shall make still less difficulty of assenting to this opinion. Such an influence on the mind is in itself perfectly extraordinary and incomprehensible; nor can we be certain of its reality, but from experience and observation. . . .

172

Part 4
Of the Sceptical and Other Systems of Philosophy

Section 1
Of scepticism with regard to reason

In all demonstrative sciences the rules are certain and infallible; but when we apply them, our fallible and uncertain faculties are very apt to depart from them, and fall into error. We must, therefore, in every reasoning form a new judgment, as a check or controul on our first judgment or belief; and must enlarge our view to comprehend a kind of history of all the instances, wherein our understanding has deceiv'd us, compar'd with those, wherein its testimony was just and true. Our reason must be consider'd as a kind of cause, of which truth is the natural effect; but such-a-one as by the irruption of other causes, and by the inconstancy of our mental powers, may frequently be prevented. By this means all knowledge degenerates into probability; and this probability is greater or less, according to our experience of the veracity or deceitfulness of our understanding, and according to the simplicity or intricacy of the question. . . .

180

In every judgment, which we can form concerning probability, as well as concerning knowledge, we ought always to correct the first judgment, deriv'd from the nature of the object, by another judgment, deriv'd from the nature of the understanding. . . . Here then arises a new species of probability to correct and regulate the first, and fix its just standard and proportion. As demonstration is subject to the controul of probability, so is probability liable to a new correction by a reflex act of the mind, wherein the nature of our understanding, and our reasoning from the first probability become our objects.

181
182

Having thus found in every probability, beside the original uncertainty inherent in the subject, a new uncertainty deriv'd from the weakness of that faculty, which judges, and having adjusted these two together, we are oblig'd by our reason to add a new doubt deriv'd from the possibility of error in the estimation we make of the truth and fidelity of our faculties. This is a doubt, which immediately occurs to us, and of which, if we wou'd closely pursue our reason, we cannot avoid giving a decision. But this decision, tho' it shou'd be favourable to our preceeding judgment, being founded only on proba-bility, must weaken still further our first evidence, and must itself be weaken'd by a fourth doubt of the same kind, and so on in infinitum; till at last there remain nothing of the original probability, however great we may suppose it to have been, and however small the diminution by every new uncertainty. No finite object can subsist under a decrease repeated in infinitum; and even the vastest quantity, which can enter into

183   human imagination, must in this manner be reduc'd to nothing. Let our first belief be never so strong, it must infallibly perish by passing thro' so many new examinations, of which each diminishes somewhat of its force and vigour. . . .

My intention then in displaying so carefully the arguments of that fantastic sect, is only to make the reader sensible of the truth of my hypothesis, *that all our reasonings concerning causes and effects are deriv'd from nothing but custom; and that belief is more properly an act of the sensitive, than of the cogitative part of our natures* . . . .

657[6]   By all that has been said the reader will easily perceive, that the philosophy contain'd in this book is very sceptical, and tends to give us a notion of the imperfections and narrow limits of human understanding. Almost all reasoning is there reduced to experience; and the belief, which attends experience, is explained to be nothing but a peculiar sentiment, or lively conception produced by habit. Nor is this all, when we believe any thing of *external* existence, or suppose an object to exist a moment after it is no longer perceived, this belief is nothing but a sentiment of the same kind. Our author insists upon several other sceptical topics; and upon the whole concludes, that we assent to our faculties, and employ our reason only because we cannot help it. Philosophy wou'd render us entirely *Pyrrhonian*, were not nature too strong for it.

[I shall conclude with an account of an opinion which seems peculiar, as indeed are most of these opinions.] The soul, as far as we can conceive it, is nothing but a sys-tem or train of different perceptions, those of heat and cold, love and anger, thoughts and sensations; all united together, but without any perfect simplicity or identity. *Descartes* maintained that thought was the essence of the mind; not this thought or

658   that thought, but thought in general. This seems to be absolutely unintelligible, since every thing, that exists, is particular: And therefore it must be our several particular perceptions, that compose the mind. I say, *compose* the mind, not *belong* to it. The mind is not a substance, in which the perceptions inhere. That notion is as unintelligi-ble as the *Cartesian*, that thought or perception in general is the essence of the mind. We have no idea of substance of any kind, since we have no idea but what is derived from some impression, and we have no impression of any substance either material or spiritual. We know nothing but particular qualities and perceptions. As our idea of any body, a peach, for instance, is only that of a particular taste, colour, figure, size,

---

6. The passages with marginal numbers 657 and 658 are from Hume's "Abstract."

consistence, &c. So our idea of any mind is only that of particular perceptions, without the notion of any thing we call substance, either simple or compound. . . .

Section 4
Of personal identity

. . . The mind is a kind of theatre, where several perceptions successively make their appearance; pass, re-pass, glide away, and mingle in an infinite variety of postures and situations. There is properly no *simplicity* in it at one time, nor *identity* in different; whatever natural propension we may have to imagine that simplicity and identity. The comparison of the theatre must not mislead us. They are the successive perceptions only, that constitute the mind; nor have we the most distant notion of the place, where these scenes are represented, or of the materials, of which it is compos'd. . . . 253

Section 7
Conclusion of this book

But before I launch out into those immense depths of philosophy, which lie before me, I find myself inclin'd to stop a moment in my present station, and to ponder that voyage, which I have undertaken, and which undoubtedly requires the utmost art and industry to be brought to a happy conclusion. Methinks I am like a man, who having struck on many shoals, and having narrowly escap'd ship-wreck in passing a small frith, has yet the temerity to put out to sea in the same leaky weather-beaten vessel, and even carries his ambition so far as to think of compassing the globe under these disadvantageous circumstances. My memory of past errors and perplexities, makes me diffident for the future. The wretched condition, weakness, and disorder of the faculties, I must employ in my enquiries, encrease my apprehensions. And the impossibility of amending or correcting these faculties, reduces me almost to despair, and makes me resolve to perish on the barren rock, on which I am at present, rather than venture myself upon that boundless ocean, which runs out into immensity. This sudden view of my danger strikes me with melancholy; and as 'tis usual for that passion, above all others, to indulge itself; I cannot forbear feeding my despair, with all those desponding reflections, which the present subject furnishes me with in such abundance. . . . 263 264

When we trace up the human understanding to its first principles, we find it to lead us into such sentiments, as seem to turn into ridicule all our past pains and industry, and to discourage us from future enquiries. Nothing is more curiously enquir'd after by the mind of man, than the causes of every phaenomenon; nor are we content with knowing the immediate causes, but push on our enquiries, till we arrive at the original and ultimate principle. We wou'd not willingly stop before we are acquainted with that energy in the cause, by which it operates on its effect; that tie, which connects them together; and that efficacious quality, on which the tie depends. This is our aim in all our studies and reflections: And how must we be disappointed, when we learn, that this connexion, tie, or energy lies merely in ourselves, and is nothing but that determination of the mind, which is acquir'd by custom, and causes us to make a transition from an object to its usual attendant, and from the impression of one to the lively idea of the other? Such a discovery not only cuts off all hope of ever attaining 266 267 satisfaction, but even prevents our very wishes; since it appears, that when we say we desire to know the ultimate and operating principle, as something, which resides in the external object, we either contradict ourselves, or talk without a meaning. . . .

268   The *intense* view of these manifold contradictions and imperfections in human reason has so wrought upon me, and heated my brain, that I am ready to reject all belief and reasoning, and can look upon no opinion even as more probable or likely

269 than another. Where am I, or what? From what causes do I derive my existence, and to what condition shall I return? Whose favour shall I court, and whose anger must I dread? What beings surround me? and on whom have I any influence, or who have any influence on me? I am confounded with all these questions, and begin to fancy myself in the most deplorable condition imaginable, inviron'd with the deepest darkness, and utterly depriv'd of the use of every member and faculty.

Most fortunately it happens, that since reason is incapable of dispelling these clouds, nature herself suffices to that purpose, and cures me of this philosophical melancholy and delirium, either by relaxing this bent of mind, or by some avocation, and lively impression of my senses, which obliterate all these chimeras. I dine, I play a game of back-gammon, I converse, and am merry with my friends; and when after three or four hour's amusement, I wou'd return to these speculations, they appear so cold, and strain'd, and ridiculous, that I cannot find in my heart to enter into them any farther.

Here then I find myself absolutely and necessarily determin'd to live, and talk, and act like other people in the common affairs of life. But notwithstanding that my natural propensity, and the course of my animal spirits and passions reduce me to this indolent belief in the general maxims of the world, I still feel such remains of my former disposition, that I am ready to throw all my books and papers into the fire, and resolve never more to renounce the pleasures of life for the sake of reasoning and philosophy. . . .

270   These are the sentiments of my spleen and indolence; and indeed I must confess, that philosophy has nothing to oppose to them, and expects a victory more from the returns of a serious good-humour'd disposition, than from the force of reason and conviction. In all the incidents of life we ought still to preserve our scepticism. If we believe, that fire warms, or water refreshes, 'tis only because it costs us too much pains to think otherwise. Nay if we are philosophers, it ought only to be upon sceptical principles, and from an inclination, which we feel to the employing ourselves after that manner. Where reason is lively, and mixes itself with some propensity, it ought to be assented to. Where it does not, it never can have any title to operate upon us.

At the time, therefore, that I am tir'd with amusement and company, and have indulg'd a *reverie* in my chamber, or in a solitary walk by a river-side, I feel my mind all collected within itself, and am naturally *inclin'd* to carry my view into all those subjects, about which I have met with so many disputes in the course of my reading and

271 conversation. I cannot forbear having a curiosity to be acquainted with the principles of moral good and evil, the nature and foundation of government, and the cause of those several passions and inclinations, which actuate and govern me. I am uneasy to think I approve of one object, and disapprove of another; call one thing beautiful, and another deform'd; decide concerning truth and falshood, reason and folly, without knowing upon what principles I proceed. I am concern'd for the condition of the learned world, which lies under such a deplorable ignorance in all these particulars.

I feel an ambition to arise in me of contributing to the instruction of mankind, and of acquiring a name by my inventions and discoveries. These sentiments spring up naturally in my present disposition; and shou'd I endeavour to banish them, by attaching myself to any other business or diversion, I *feel* I shou'd be a loser in point of pleasure; and this is the origin of my philosophy. . . .

Book II
Of the Passions

Part 3
Of the Will and Direct Passions

Section 1
Of liberty and necessity

We must now proceed to give some account . . . of the PASSIONS. 'Tis of more easy   659[7]
comprehension than the first; but contains opinions, that are altogether as new and extraordinary. The author begins with *pride* and *humility*. He observes, that the objects which excite these passions, are very numerous, and seemingly very different from each other. Pride or self-esteem may arise from the qualities of the mind; wit, good-   660
sense, learning, courage, integrity: from those of the body; beauty, strength, agility, good mein, address in dancing, riding, fencing: from external advantages; country, family, children, relations, riches, houses, gardens, horses, dogs, cloaths. He afterwards proceeds to find out that common circumstance, in which all these objects agree, and which causes them to operate on the passions. His theory likewise extends to love and hatred, and other affections. As these questions, tho' curious, could not be rendered intelligible without a long discourse, we shall here omit them.

It may perhaps be more acceptable to the reader to be informed of what our author says concerning *free-will.* . . .

Of all the immediate effects of pain and pleasure, there is none more remarkable than   399
the WILL; and tho', properly speaking, it be not comprehended among the passions, yet as the full understanding of its nature and properties, is necessary to the explanation of them, we shall here make it the subject of our enquiry. I desire it may be observ'd, that by the *will*, I mean nothing but *the internal impression we feel and are conscious of, when we knowingly give rise to any new motion of our body, or new perception of our mind.* This impression, like the preceding ones of pride and humility, love and hatred, 'tis impossible to define, and needless to describe any farther. . . .

He has laid the foundation of his doctrine in what he said concerning cause and   660
effect, as above explained. "'Tis universally acknowledged, that the operations of external bodies are necessary, and that in the communication of their motion, in their attraction and mutual cohesion, there are not the least traces of indifference or liberty. . . . Whatever therefore is in this respect on the same footing with matter, must be acknowledged to be necessary. That we may know whether this be the case with the actions of the mind, we may examine matter, and consider on what the idea

---

7. The passages with marginal numbers 659–661 are from Hume's "Abstract."

of a necessity in its operations are founded, and why we conclude one body or action to be the infallible cause of another.

"It has been observed already, that in no single instance the ultimate connexion of any object is discoverable either by our senses or reason, and that we can never penetrate so far into the essence and construction of bodies, as to perceive the principle on which their mutual influence is founded. 'Tis their constant union alone, with which we are acquainted; and 'tis from the constant union the necessity arises, when the mind is determined to pass from one object to its usual attendant, and infer the exis-

661   tence of one from that of the other. Here then are two particulars, which we are to regard as essential to *necessity*, *viz.* the constant *union* and the *inference* of the mind, and wherever we discover these we must acknowledge a necessity." Now nothing is more evident than the constant union of particular actions with particular motives. If all actions be not constantly united with their proper motives, this uncertainty is no more than what may be observed every day in the actions of matter, where by reason of the mixture and uncertainty of causes, the effect is often variable and uncertain. Thirty grains of opium will kill any man that is not accustomed to it; tho' thirty grains of rhubarb will not always purge him. In like manner the fear of death will always make a man go twenty paces out of his road; tho' it will not always make him do a bad action.

And as there is often a constant conjunction of the actions of the will with their motives, so the inference from the one to the other is often as certain as any reasoning concerning bodies: and there is always an inference proportioned to the constancy of the conjunction. On this is founded our belief in witnesses, our credit in history, and indeed all kinds of moral evidence, and almost the whole conduct of life.

Our author pretends, that this reasoning puts the whole controversy in a new light, by giving a new definition of necessity. And, indeed, the most zealous advocates for free-will must allow this union and inference with regard to human actions. They will only deny, that this makes the whole of necessity. But then they must shew, that we have an idea of something else in the actions of matter; which, according to the foregoing reasoning, is impossible. . . .

Section 2

The same subject continued

410   . . .This kind of necessity is so essential to religion and morality, that without it there must ensue an absolute subversion of both, and that every other supposition is entirely destructive to all laws both *divine* and *human*. 'Tis indeed certain, that as all human laws are founded on rewards and punishments, 'tis suppos'd as a fundamental principle, that these motives have an influence on the mind, and both produce the good and prevent the evil actions. We may give to this influence what name we please; but as 'tis usually conjoin'd with the action, common sense requires it shou'd be esteem'd a cause, and be look'd upon as an instance of that necessity, which I wou'd establish. This reasoning is equally solid, when apply'd to *divine* laws, so far as the deity is consider'd as a legislator, and is suppos'd to inflict punishment and bestow rewards with a design to produce obedience. . . .

411   Actions are by their very nature temporary and perishing; and where they proceed not from some cause in the characters and disposition of the person, who perform'd

them, they infix not themselves upon him, and can neither redound to his honour, if good, nor infamy, if evil. The action itself may be blameable; it may be contrary to all the rules of morality and religion: But the person is not responsible for it; and as it proceeded from nothing in him, that is durable or constant, and leaves nothing of that nature behind it, 'tis impossible he can, upon its account, become the object of punishment or vengeance. According to the hypothesis of liberty, therefore, a man is as pure and untainted, after having committed the most horrid crimes, as at the first moment of his birth, nor is his character any way concern'd in his actions. . . . 'Tis only upon the principles of necessity, that a person acquires any merit or demerit from his actions, however the common opinion may incline to the contrary. . . .

Section 3
Of the influencing motives of the will

Nothing is more usual in philosophy, and even in common life, than to talk of the   413
combat of passion and reason, to give the preference to reason, and to assert that men are only so far virtuous as they conform themselves to its dictates. Every rational creature, 'tis said, is oblig'd to regulate his actions by reason; and if any other motive or principle challenge the direction of his conduct, he ought to oppose it, 'till it be entirely subdu'd, or at least brought to a conformity with that superior principle. On this method of thinking the greatest part of moral philosophy, antient and modern, seems to be founded. . . . In order to shew the fallacy of all this philosophy, I shall endeavour to prove *first*, that reason alone can never be a motive to any action of the will; and *secondly*, that it can never oppose passion in the direction of the will.

The understanding exerts itself after two different ways, as it judges from demonstration or probability; as it regards the abstract relations of our ideas, or those relations of objects, of which experience only gives us information. I believe it scarce will be asserted, that the first species of reasoning alone is ever the cause of any action. As its proper province is the world of ideas, and as the will always places us in that of realities, demonstration and volition seem, upon that account, to be totally remov'd, from each other. . . . Abstract or demonstrative reasoning, therefore, never influences any   414
of our actions, but only as it directs our judgment concerning causes and effects; which leads us to the second operation of the understanding.

'Tis obvious, that when we have the prospect of pain or pleasure from any object, we feel a consequent emotion of aversion or propensity, and are carry'd to avoid or embrace what will give us this uneasiness or satisfaction. 'Tis also obvious, that this emotion rests not here, but making us cast our view on every side, comprehends whatever objects are connected with its original one by the relation of cause and effect. Here then reasoning takes place to discover this relation; and according as our reasoning varies, our actions receive a subsequent variation. But 'tis evident in this case, that the impulse arises not from reason, but is only directed by it. 'Tis from the prospect of pain or pleasure that the aversion or propensity arises towards any object: And these emotions extend themselves to the causes and effects of that object, as they are pointed out to us by reason and experience. . . .

Since reason alone can never produce any action, or give rise to volition, I infer, that the same faculty is as incapable of preventing volition, or of disputing the prefer-   415 ence with any passion or emotion.... Thus it appears, that the principle, which opposes our passion, cannot be the same with reason, and is only call'd so in an improper sense. We speak not strictly and philosophically when we talk of the combat of passion and of reason. Reason is, and ought only to be the slave of the passions, and can never pretend to any other office than to serve and obey them. As this opinion may appear somewhat extraordinary, it may not be improper to confirm it by some other considerations.

A passion is an original existence, or, if you will, modification of existence, and contains not any representative quality, which renders it a copy of any other existence or modification. When I am angry, I am actually possest with the passion, and in that emotion have no more a reference to any other object, than when I am thirsty, or sick, or more than five foot high. 'Tis impossible, therefore, that this passion can be oppos'd by, or be contradictory to truth and reason; since this contradiction consists in the disagreement of ideas, consider'd as copies, with those objects, which they represent.

What may at first occur on this head, is, that as nothing can be contrary to truth or reason, except what has a reference to it, and as the judgments of our understanding
416   only have this reference, it must follow, that passions can be contrary to reason only so far as they are *accompany'd* with some judgment or opinion. According to this principle, which is so obvious and natural, 'tis only in two senses, that any affection can be call'd unreasonable. First, When a passion, such as hope or fear, grief or joy, despair or security, is founded on the supposition of the existence of objects, which really do not exist. Secondly, When in exerting any passion in action, we chuse means insufficient for the design'd end, and deceive ourselves in our judgment of causes and effects.... 'Tis not contrary to reason to prefer the destruction of the whole world to the scratching of my finger. 'Tis not contrary to reason for me to chuse my total ruin, to prevent the least uneasiness of an *Indian* or person wholly unknown to me. 'Tis as little contrary to reason to prefer even my own acknowledg'd lesser good to my greater, and have a more ardent affection for the former than the latter.... In short, a passion must be accompany'd with some false judgment, in order to its being unreasonable; and even then 'tis not the passion, properly speaking, which is unreasonable, but the judgment....

Book III
Of Morals

Part 1
Of Virtue and Vice in General

Section 1
Moral distinctions not deriv'd from reason

456   ... Now as perceptions resolve themselves into two kinds, viz. *impressions* and *ideas*, this distinction gives rise to a question, with which we shall open up our present enquiry concerning morals, *Whether 'tis by means of our ideas or impressions we distinguish betwixt vice and virtue, and pronounce an action blameable or praise-worthy?*...

[Many] systems concur in the opinion, that morality, like truth, is discern'd merely by ideas, and by their juxta-position and comparison. In order, therefore, to judge of these systems, we need only consider, whether it be possible, from reason alone, to distinguish betwixt moral good and evil, or whether there must concur some other principles to enable us to make that distinction.... 457

Since morals ... have an influence on the actions and affections, it follows, that they cannot be deriv'd from reason; and that because reason alone, as we have already prov'd, can never have any such influence. Morals excite passions, and produce or prevent actions. Reason of itself is utterly impotent in this particular. The rules of morality, therefore, are not conclusions of our reason....

Reason is the discovery of truth or falshood. Truth or falshood consists in an agreement or disagreement either to the *real* relations of ideas, or to *real* existence and matter of fact. Whatever, therefore, is not susceptible of this agreement or disagreement, is incapable of being true or false, and can never be an object of our reason. Now 'tis evident our passions, volitions, and actions, are not susceptible of any such agreement or disagreement; being original facts and realities, compleat in themselves, and implying no reference to other passions, volitions, and actions. 'Tis impossible, therefore, they can be pronounced either true or false, and be either contrary or conformable to reason.... 458

There has been an opinion very industriously propagated by certain philosophers, that morality is susceptible of demonstration; and tho' no one has ever been able to advance a single step in those demonstrations; yet 'tis taken for granted, that this science may be brought to an equal certainty with geometry or algebra. Upon this supposition, vice and virtue must consist in some relations; since 'tis allow'd on all hands, that no matter of fact is capable of being demonstrated. Let us, therefore, begin with examining this hypothesis, and endeavour, if possible, to fix those moral qualities, which have been so long the objects of our fruitless researches.... 463

If you assert, that vice and virtue consist in relations susceptible of certainty and demonstration, you must confine yourself to those *four* relations, which alone admit of that degree of evidence; and in that case you run into absurdities, from which you will never be able to extricate yourself. For as you make the very essence of morality to lie in the relations, and as there is no one of these relations but what is applicable, not only to an irrational, but also to an inanimate object; it follows, that even such objects must be susceptible of merit or demerit. *Resemblance, contrariety, degrees in quality*, and *proportions in quantity and number*; all these relations belong as properly to matter, as to our actions, passions, and volitions. 'Tis unquestionable, therefore, that morality lies not in any of these relations, nor the sense of it in their discovery.... 464

Of all crimes that human creatures are capable of committing, the most horrid and unnatural is ingratitude, especially when it is committed against parents, and appears in the more flagrant instances of wounds and death. This is acknowledg'd by all mankind, philosophers as well as the people; the question only arises among philosophers, whether the guilt or moral deformity of this action be discover'd by demonstrative reasoning, or be felt by an internal sense, and by means of some sentiment, which the reflecting on such an action naturally occasions. This question will soon be decided against the former opinion, if we can shew the same relations in other objects, without the notion of any guilt or iniquity attending them.... To put the affair, therefore, to this trial, let us chuse any inanimate object, such as an oak or elm; 466
467

and let us suppose, that by the dropping of its seed, it produces a sapling below it, which springing up by degrees, at last overtops and destroys the parent tree: I ask, if in this instance there be wanting any relation, which is discoverable in parricide or ingratitude? Is not the one tree the cause of the other's existence; and the latter the cause of the destruction of the former, in the same manner as when a child murders his parent? 'Tis not sufficient to reply, that a choice or will is wanting. For in the case of parricide, a will does not give rise to any *different* relations, but is only the cause from which the action is deriv'd; and consequently produces the *same* relations, that in the oak or elm arise from some other principles. 'Tis a will or choice, that determines a man to kill his parent; and they are the laws of matter and motion, that determine a sapling to destroy the oak, from which it sprung. Here then the same relations have different causes; but still the relations are the same: And as their discovery is not in both cases attended with a notion of immorality, it follows, that that notion does not arise from such a discovery. . . .

468   Nor does this reasoning only prove, that morality consists not in any relations, that are the objects of science; but if examin'd, will prove with equal certainty, that it consists not in any *matter of fact*, which can be discover'd by the understanding. This is the *second* part of our argument; and if it can be made evident, we may conclude, that morality is not an object of reason. But can there be any difficulty in proving, that vice and virtue are not matters of fact, whose existence we can infer by reason? Take any action allow'd to be vicious: Wilful murder, for instance. Examine it in all lights, and see if you can find that matter of fact, or real existence, which you call *vice*. In whichever way you take it, you find only certain passions, motives, volitions and thoughts. There is no other matter of fact in the case. . . . You never can find it, till you turn your
469   reflexion into your own breast, and find a sentiment of disapprobation, which arises in you, towards this action. Here is a matter of fact; but 'tis the object of feeling, not of reason. It lies in yourself, not in the object. So that when you pronounce any action or character to be vicious, you mean nothing, but that from the constitution of your nature you have a feeling or sentiment of blame from the contemplation of it. Vice and virtue, therefore, may be compar'd to sounds, colours, heat and cold, which, according to modern philosophy, are not qualities in objects, but perceptions in the mind: And this discovery in morals, like that other in physics, is to be regarded as a considerable advancement of the speculative sciences; tho', like that too, it has little or no influence on practice. . . .

      I cannot forbear adding to these reasonings an observation, which may, perhaps, be found of some importance. In every system of morality, which I have hitherto met with, I have always remark'd, that the author proceeds for some time in the ordinary way of reasoning, and establishes the being of a God, or makes observations concerning human affairs; when of a sudden I am surpriz'd to find, that instead of the usual copulations of propositions, *is*, and *is not*, I meet with no proposition that is not connected with an *ought*, or an *ought not*. This change is imperceptible; but is, however, of the last consequence. For as this *ought*, or *ought not*, expresses some new relation or affirmation, 'tis necessary that it shou'd be observ'd and explain'd; and at the same time that a reason should be given, for what seems altogether inconceivable, how this new relation can be a deduction from others, which are entirely different from it. But as authors do not commonly use this precaution, I shall presume to recommend it to the
470   readers; and am persuaded, that this small attention wou'd subvert all the vulgar sys-

tems of morality, and let us see, that the distinction of vice and virtue is not founded merely on the relations of objects, nor is perceiv'd by reason.

Section 2

Moral distinctions deriv'd from a moral sense

Thus the course of the argument leads us to conclude, that since vice and virtue are not discoverable merely by reason, or the comparison of ideas, it must be by means of some impression or sentiment they occasion, that we are able to mark the difference betwixt them. . . . Morality, therefore, is more properly felt than judg'd of; tho' this feeling or sentiment is commonly so soft and gentle, that we are apt to confound it with an idea, according to our common custom of taking all things for the same, which have any near resemblance to each other.

The next question is, Of what nature are these impressions, and after what manner do they operate upon us? Here we cannot remain long in suspense, but must pronounce the impression arising from virtue, to be agreeable, and that proceeding from vice to be uneasy. Every moment's experience must convince us of this. There is no spectacle so fair and beautiful as a noble and generous action; nor any which gives us more abhorrence than one that is cruel and treacherous. . . .

Now since the distinguishing impressions, by which moral good or evil is known, are nothing but *particular* pains or pleasures; it follows, that in all enquiries concerning these moral distinctions, it will be sufficient to shew the principles, which make us feel a satisfaction or uneasiness from the survey of any character, in order to satisfy us why the character is laudable or blameable. An action, or sentiment, or character is virtuous or vicious; why? because its view causes a pleasure or uneasiness of a particular kind. . . . To have the sense of virtue, is nothing but to *feel* a satisfaction of a particular kind from the contemplation of a character. The very *feeling* constitutes our praise or admiration. . . .   471

Now it may . . . be objected to the present system, that if virtue and vice be determin'd by pleasure and pain, these qualities must, in every case, arise from the sensations; and consequently any object, whether animate or inanimate, rational or irrational, might become morally good or evil, provided it can excite a satisfaction or uneasiness. [But this objection has no force.] For, *first*, 'tis evident, that under the term *pleasure*, we   472 comprehend sensations, which are very different from each other, and which have only such a distant resemblance, as is requisite to make them be express'd by the same abstract term. A good composition of music and a bottle of good wine equally produce pleasure; and what is more, their goodness is determin'd merely by the pleasure. But shall we say upon that account, that the wine is harmonious, or the music of a good flavour? . . . Nor is every sentiment of pleasure or pain, which arises from characters and actions, of that *peculiar* kind, which makes us praise or condemn. The good qualities of an enemy are hurtful to us; but may still command our esteem and respect. 'Tis only when a character is considered in general, without reference to our particular interest, that it causes such a feeling or sentiment, as denominates it morally good or evil. 'Tis true, those sentiments, from interest and morals, are apt to be confounded, and naturally run into one another. It seldom happens, that we do not think an enemy vicious, and can distinguish betwixt his opposition to our interest and real villainy or baseness. But this hinders not, but that the sentiments are, in themselves, distinct. . . .

Part 2
Of Justice and Injustice

Section 1
Justice, whether a natural or artificial virtue?

477   I have already hinted, that our sense of every kind of virtue is not natural; but that there are some virtues, that produce pleasure and approbation by means of an artifice or contrivance, which arises from the circumstances and necessities of mankind. Of this kind I assert *justice* to be; and shall endeavour to defend this opinion by a short, and, I hope, convincing argument, before I examine the nature of the artifice, from which the sense of that virtue is derived.

'Tis evident, that when we praise any actions, we regard only the motives that produced them, and consider the actions as signs or indications of certain principles in the mind and temper. The external performance has no merit. We must look within to find the moral quality. This we cannot do directly; and therefore fix our attention on actions, as on external signs. But these actions are still considered as signs; and the ultimate object of our praise and approbation is the motive, that produc'd them. . . .

478   It appears, therefore, that all virtuous actions derive their merit only from virtuous motives, and are consider'd merely as signs of those motives. From this principle I conclude, that the first virtuous motive, which bestows a merit on any action, can never be a regard to the virtue of that action, but must be some other natural motive or principle. To suppose, that the mere regard to the virtue of the action, may be the first motive, which produc'd the action, and render'd it virtuous, is to reason in a circle. Before we can have such a regard, the action must be really virtuous; and this virtue must be deriv'd from some virtuous motive: And consequently the virtuous motive must be different from the regard to the virtue of the action. A virtuous motive is requisite to render an action virtuous. An action must be virtuous, before we can have a regard to its virtue. Some virtuous motive, therefore, must be antecedent to that regard.

Nor is this merely a metaphysical subtilty; but enters into all our reasonings in common life, tho' perhaps we may not be able to place it in such distinct philosophical terms. We blame a father for neglecting his child. Why? because it shews a want of natural affection, which is the duty of every parent. Were not natural affection a duty, the care of children cou'd not be a duty; and 'twere impossible we cou'd have the duty in our eye in the attention we give to our offspring. In this case, therefore, all men suppose a motive to the action distinct from a sense of duty. . . .

479   In short, it may be establish'd as an undoubted maxim, *that no action can be virtuous, or morally good, unless there be in human nature some motive to produce it, distinct from the sense of its morality.*

But may not the sense of morality or duty produce an action, without any other motive? I answer, It may: But this is no objection to the present doctrine. When any virtuous motive or principle is common in human nature, a person, who feels his heart devoid of that principle, may hate himself upon that account, and may perform the action without the motive, from a certain sense of duty, in order to acquire by practice, that virtuous principle, or at least, to disguise to himself, as much as possible, his want of it. A man that really feels no gratitude in his temper, is still pleas'd to perform grateful actions, and thinks he has, by that means, fulfill'd his duty. . . .

'Tis requisite, then, to find some motive to acts of justice and honesty, distinct from   480
our regard to the honesty; and in this lies the great difficulty. For shou'd we say, that
a concern for our private interest or reputation is the legitimate motive to all honest
actions; it wou'd follow, that wherever that concern ceases, honesty can no longer
have place. But 'tis certain, that self-love, when it acts at its liberty, instead of engaging
us to honest actions, is the source of all injustice and violence; nor can a man ever correct those vices, without correcting and restraining the *natural* movements of
that appetite.

But shou'd it be affirm'd, that the reason or motive of such actions is the *regard to
publick interest,* to which nothing is more contrary than examples of injustice and dishonesty; shou'd this be said, I wou'd propose the three following considerations, as worthy of our attention. *First,* public interest is not naturally attach'd to the observation
of the rules of justice; but is only connected with it, after an artificial convention for
the establishment of these rules, as shall be shewn more at large hereafter. *Secondly,* if
we suppose, that the loan was secret, and that it is necessary for the interest of the per-   481
son, that the money be restor'd in the same manner (as when the lender wou'd conceal
his riches) in that case the example ceases, and the public is no longer interested in
the actions of the borrower; tho' I suppose there is no moralist, who will affirm, that
the duty and obligation ceases. *Thirdly,* experience sufficiently proves, that men, in
the ordinary conduct of life, look not so far as the public interest, when they pay their
creditors, perform their promises, and abstain from theft, and robbery, and injustice of
every kind. That is a motive too remote and too sublime to affect the generality of
mankind, and operate with any force in actions so contrary to private interest as are
frequently those of justice and common honesty. . . .

If public benevolence, therefore, or a regard to the interests of mankind, cannot be   482
the original motive to justice, much less can *private benevolence,* or a *regard to the
interests of the party concern'd,* be this motive. For what if he be my enemy, and has given
me just cause to hate him? What if he be a vicious man, and deserves the hatred of
all mankind?. . . What if I be in necessity, and have urgent motives to acquire something to my family? In all these cases, the original motive to justice wou'd fail; and consequently the justice itself, and along with it all property, right, and obligation. . . .

From all this it follows, that we have naturally no real or universal motive for   483
observing the laws of equity, but the very equity and merit of that observance; and as
no action can be equitable or meritorious, where it cannot arise from some separate
motive, there is here an evident sophistry and reasoning in a circle. . . . We must allow,
that the sense of justice and injustice is not deriv'd from nature, but arises artificially,
tho' necessarily from education, and human conventions. . . .

Section 2

Of the origin of justice and property

We now proceed to examine [the question] *concerning the manner, in which the rules of*   484
justice are establish'd by the artifice of men. . . .

Of all the animals, with which this globe is peopled, there is none towards whom
nature seems, at first sight, to have exercis'd more cruelty than towards man, in the
numberless wants and necessities, with which she has loaded him, and in the slender
means, which she affords to the relieving these necessities. . . .

485   'Tis by society alone he is able to supply his defects, and raise himself up to an equality with his fellow-creatures, and even acquire a superiority above them. By society all his infirmities are compensated; and tho' in that situation his wants multiply every moment upon him, yet his abilities are still more augmented, and leave him in every respect more satisfied and happy, than 'tis possible for him, in his savage and solitary condition, ever to become. . . . By the conjunction of forces, our power is augmented: By the partition of employments, our ability encreases: And by mutual succour we are less expos'd to fortune and accidents. 'Tis by this additional *force, ability,* and *security,* that society becomes advantageous.

486   But in order to form society, 'tis requisite not only that it be advantageous, but also that men be sensible of its advantages; and 'tis impossible, in their wild uncultivated state, that by study and reflexion alone, they should ever be able to attain this knowledge. Most fortunately, therefore, there is conjoin'd to those necessities, whose remedies are remote and obscure, another necessity, which having a present and more obvious remedy, may justly be regarded as the first and original principle of human society. This necessity is no other than that natural appetite betwixt the sexes, which unites them together, and preserves their union, till a new tye takes place in their concern for their common offspring. This new concern becomes also a principle of union betwixt the parents and offspring, and forms a more numerous society. . . . In a little time, custom and habit operating on the tender minds of the children, makes them sensible of the advantages, which they may reap from society, as well as fashions them by degrees for it, by rubbing off those rough corners and untoward affections, which prevent their coalition. . . .

487   There are three different species of goods, which we are posses'd of; the internal satisfaction of our mind, the external advantages of our body, and the enjoyment of such possessions as we have acquir'd by our industry and good fortune. We are perfectly secure in the enjoyment of the first. The second may be ravish'd from us, but can be of no advantage to him who deprives us of them. The last only are both expos'd to the violence of others, and may be transferr'd without suffering any loss or alteration; while at the same time, there is not a sufficient quantity of them to supply every one's desires and necessities. As the improvement, therefore, of these goods is the chief advantage of society, so the *instability* of their possession, along with their *scarcity,* is the chief impediment. . . .

488   In the original frame of our mind, our strongest attention is confin'd to ourselves; our next is extended to our relations and acquaintance; and 'tis only the weakest which reaches to strangers and indifferent persons. This partiality, then, and unequal affection, must not only have an influence on our behaviour and conduct in society,

489   but even on our ideas of vice and virtue. . . . From all which it follows, that our natural uncultivated ideas of morality, instead of providing a remedy for the partiality of our affections, do rather conform themselves to that partiality, and give it an additional force and influence.

        The remedy, then, is not deriv'd from nature, but from *artifice;* or more properly speaking, nature provides a remedy in the judgment and understanding, for what is irregular and incommodious in the affections. . . . This can be done after no other manner, than by a convention enter'd into by all the members of the society to bestow stability on the possession of those external goods, and leave every one in the peaceable enjoyment of what he may acquire by his fortune and industry. By this means, every one knows what he may safely possess; and the passions are restrain'd in their partial and contradictory motions. Nor is such a restraint contrary to these passions; for if so, it cou'd never be enter'd into, nor maintain'd; but it is only contrary to their heedless and impetuous movement. Instead of departing from our own interest, or from that of our nearest friends, by abstaining from the possessions of others, we cannot better consult both these interests, than by such a convention; because it is by that means we maintain society, which is so necessary to their well-being and subsistence, as well as to our own.

Appendix

I had entertain'd some hopes, that however deficient our theory of the intellectual   633
world might be, it wou'd be free from those contradictions, and absurdities, which seem to attend every explication, that human reason can give of the material world. But upon a more strict review of the section concerning *personal identity*, I find myself involv'd in such a labyrinth, that, I must confess, I neither know how to correct my former opinions, nor how to render them consistent. If this be not a good *general* reason for scepticism, 'tis at least a sufficient one (if I were not already abundantly supplied) for me to entertain a diffidence and modesty in all my decisions. I shall propose the arguments on both sides, beginning with those that induc'd me to deny the strict and proper identity and simplicity of a self or thinking being.

When we talk of *self* or *substance*, we must have an idea annex'd to these terms, otherwise they are altogether unintelligible. Every idea is deriv'd from preceding impressions; and we have no impression of self or substance, as something simple and individual. We have, therefore, no idea of them in that sense.

Whatever is distinct, is distinguishable; and whatever is distinguishable, is separa-   634
ble by the thought or imagination. All perceptions are distinct. They are, therefore, distinguishable, and separable, and may be conceiv'd as separately existent, and may exist separately, without any contradiction or absurdity.

When I view this table and that chimney, nothing is present to me but particular perceptions, which are of a like nature with all the other perceptions. This is the doctrine of philosophers. But this table, which is present to me, and that chimney, may and do exist separately. This is the doctrine of the vulgar, and implies no contradiction. There is no contradiction, therefore, in extending the same doctrine to all the perceptions.

In general, the following reasoning seems satisfactory. All ideas are borrow'd from preceding perceptions. Our ideas of objects, therefore, are deriv'd from that source. Consequently no proposition can be intelligible or consistent with regard to objects, which is not so with regard to perceptions. But 'tis intelligible and consistent to say, that objects exist distinct and independent, without any common *simple* substance or subject of inhesion. This proposition, therefore, can never be absurd with regard to perceptions.

When I turn my reflexion on *myself*, I never can perceive this *self* without some one or more perceptions; nor can I ever perceive any thing but the perceptions. 'Tis the composition of these, therefore, which forms the self.

We can conceive a thinking being to have either many or few perceptions. Suppose the mind to be reduc'd even below the life of an oyster. Suppose it to have only one perception, as of thirst or hunger. Consider it in that situation. Do you conceive any thing but merely that perception? Have you any notion of *self* or *substance*? If not, the addition of other perceptions can never give you that notion.

635   The annihilation, which some people suppose to follow upon death, and which entirely destroys this self, is nothing but an extinction of all particular perceptions; love and hatred, pain and pleasure, thought and sensation. These therefore must be the same with self; since the one cannot survive the other.

Is *self* the same with *substance*? If it be, how can that question have place, concerning the subsistence of self, under a change of substance? If they be distinct, what is the difference betwixt them? For my part, I have a notion of neither, when conceiv'd distinct from particular perceptions.

Philosophers begin to be reconcil'd to the principle, *that we have no idea of external substance, distinct from the ideas of particular qualities.* This must pave the way for a like principle with regard to the mind, *that we have no notion of it, distinct from the particular perceptions.*

So far I seem to be attended with sufficient evidence. But having thus loosen'd all our particular perceptions, when I proceed to explain the principle of connexion, which binds them together, and makes us attribute to them a real simplicity and identity; I am sensible, that my account is very defective, and that nothing but the seeming evidence of the precedent reasonings cou'd have induc'd me to receive it. If perceptions are distinct existences, they form a whole only by being connected together. But no connexions among distinct existences are ever discoverable by human understanding. We only *feel* a connexion or a determination of the thought, to pass from one object to another. It follows, therefore, that the thought alone finds personal identity, when reflecting on the train of past perceptions, that compose a mind, the ideas of them are felt to be connected together, and naturally introduce each other. However extraordinary this conclusion may seem, it need not surprize us. Most philosophers seem inclin'd to think, that personal identity *arises* from consciousness; and consciousness is nothing but a reflected thought or perception. The present philosophy, therefore, has so far a promising aspect. But all my hopes vanish, when I come to explain the principles, that unite our successive perceptions in our thought or consciousness. I cannot discover any theory, which gives me satisfaction on this head.

636   In short there are two principles, which I cannot render consistent; nor is it in my power to renounce either of them, viz. *that all our distinct perceptions are distinct existences, and that the mind never perceives any real connexion among distinct existences.* Did our perceptions either inhere in something simple and individual, or did the mind perceive some real connexion among them, there wou'd be no difficulty in the case. For my part, I must plead the privilege of a sceptic, and confess, that this difficulty is too hard for my understanding. I pretend not, however, to pronounce it absolutely insuperable. Others, perhaps, or myself, upon more mature reflection, may discover some hypothesis, that will reconcile those contradictions. . . .

SELECTED BIBLIOGRAPHY

Hume, David. *Enquiries concerning Human Understanding and concerning the Principles of Morals.* Ed. L.A. Selby-Bigge, rev. P.H. Nidditch. New York: Oxford University Press, 1975.

———. *A Treatise of Human Nature.* Ed. L.A. Selby-Bigge, rev. P.H. Nidditch. New York: Oxford University Press, 1978.

Ayer, A.J. *Hume.* New York: Oxford University Press, 1980.

Chappell, V.C. *Hume: A Collection of Critical Essays.* Garden City, N.Y.: Doubleday, 1966.

Flew, Antony. *David Hume: Philosopher of Moral Science.* Oxford: Basil Blackwell, 1986.

Fogelin, Robert. *Hume's Skepticism in the Treatise of Human Nature.* London: Routledge, Chapman & Hall, 1985.

Harrison, Jonathan. *Hume's Moral Epistemology.* New York: Oxford University Press, 1976.

Livingston, Donald W. *Hume's Philosophy of Common Life.* Chicago: University of Chicago Press, 1985.

Mackie, J.L. *Hume's Moral Theory.* London: Routledge & Kegan Paul, 1980.

Mossner, Ernest Campbell. *The Life of David Hume.* New York: Oxford University Press, 1970.

Norton, David Fate. *David Hume, Common-Sense Moralist, Sceptical Metaphysician.* Princeton, N.J.: Princeton University Press, 1982.

Noxon, James. *Hume's Philosophical Development.* New York: Oxford University Press, 1973.

Penelhum, Terence. *Hume.* New York: St. Martin's Press, 1975.

Passmore, John. *Hume's Intentions.* Cambridge: Cambridge University Press, 1952.

Price, H.H. *Hume's Theory of the External World.* New York: Oxford University Press, 1963.

Smith, Norman Kemp. *The Philosophy of David Hume.* London: Macmillan, 1949.

Strawson, Galen. *The Secret Connexion: Causation, Realism, and David Hume.* New York: Oxford University Press, 1989.

Stroud, Barry. *Hume.* London: Routledge, Chapman & Hall, 1977.

Immanuel Kant

Immanuel Kant (1724–1804) was born in the East Prussian port of Königsberg, now Kaliningrad in the Soviet Union. His family were members of the Pietist movement, a Protestant group that emphasized the personal relation of each member to God and deemphasized the formal and institutional rites and practices of church religion. Kant was the first major post-Cartesian philosopher who was a full-time academic, and even for an academic his life was relatively staid. He apparently never ventured farther than some fifty miles from Königsberg in his life, despite being offered prestigious chairs at other universities. The punctual regularity of his daily walks is a matter of legend. The housewives of Königsberg reportedly set their clocks by these walks, and he missed his walk only once: when Jean-Jacques Rousseau's *Émile* so engrossed him that he could not bear to put it down. Kant's life is almost purely a life of the mind, a life filled with storms and triumphs befitting the most powerful philosophical mind of the modern era.

Kant enrolled at the university in Königsberg when he was sixteen and managed to study a far broader range of courses than was normally allowed. Afterward, he spent seven years as a private tutor to several different families near Königsberg. He used the time for a great deal of independent study, and soon after returning to Königsberg, he published the *Universal Natural History and Theory of the Heavens*. In this ground-breaking work, Kant attempted to show that Newton's laws would explain how our solar system and the heavens developed from a chaotic distribution of matter. This work ensured Kant a place as one of the founders of modern cosmology.

In 1755 Kant presented his dissertation to the university and later that year "habilitated" (qualified as a *Privatdozent*), which meant that he had a license to teach at the university but without salary. Because he had to support himself by collecting fees directly from the students who attended his lectures, Kant lectured a great deal and was apparently quite entertaining. For the next fifteen years Kant continued to earn a meager living by lecturing while waiting patiently for an appointment as a professor at the university. He published steadily on both philosophical and scientific topics and, under Rousseau's influence, broadened his horizons to larger social, moral, and political issues. Despite having been passed over several times at Königsberg, he continued to refuse appointments at several other universities.

Finally, in 1770 he received an appointment as professor of logic and metaphysics. His inaugural dissertation of that year marked a turning point in his career, for he started to leave behind the rationalist tradition within which he had been educated. Nonetheless, a long period of silence followed his appointment, though in his letters he kept promising to have his next book finished shortly. It was during this period that his reading of Hume awoke him "from his dogmatic slumbers." Just how much of Hume's work Kant had access to (he did not read English) has been widely debated, but it was clearly sufficient for him to appreciate, as virtually no one else at the time did, both the power and the danger of Hume's skeptical arguments.

In 1781 the *Critique of Pure Reason* finally appeared. Kant was fifty-seven at the time. Had he died before the first *Critique* appeared, he would have retained a small place in the history of philosophy as a good but secondary German rationalist. After the first *Critique*, philosophy could never be the same again. Kant, feeling the pressure of time on his aging shoulders, produced over the next fifteen years a body of work unsurpassed in sophistication and depth of insight and argument by any other philosopher. There were two more critiques: the *Critique of Practical Reason* (1787) and the *Critique of Judgment* (1790), the former Kant's analysis of the principles of ethics and the latter his analysis of the principles of aesthetics and teleology. He also produced a number of works applying his insights to particular questions and several shorter works that summarize his complex system, the *Prolegomena to Any Future Metaphysics* (1783) and the *Groundwork of the Metaphysic of Morals* (1785).

Philosophy

Kant faced two equally convincing yet contradictory philosophical positions, rationalism and empiricism. The rationalists claimed that humans could achieve wide-ranging metaphysical knowledge going well beyond the boundaries of sensory experience. Yet the rationalists had been unable to reach agreement about either the principles or the details of this metaphysical knowledge. The empiricists stringently denied the possibility of metaphysical knowledge, limiting all our knowledge to what could be derived from sensory experience. But in the end they could not justify the empirical knowledge we all take for granted: Hume had ended up unable to claim knowledge of anything other than his own current mental state, unable to claim knowledge of external things or even his own self.

It was easy to infer that both positions had to be wrong, but Kant's brilliance showed in his diagnosis of their error. He thought that they made essentially the *same* mistake—namely, both schools assumed that there was but one source of our knowledge. The rationalists intellectualized sensation, treating sensation and perception as but very confused episodes of thought, whereas the empiricists sensationalized thought, treating pure thought as but faint perception. With one momentous move Kant went beyond both, declaring that there were two independent and equally necessary sources of our knowledge: *intuition* (his word for the sensory aspect of experience, quite different from today's popular usage) and *understanding* (the faculty of concepts and judgment). "Thoughts without content are empty, intuitions without concepts are blind" [A 51/B 75].[1]

Besides this crucial insight into the plurality of the sources of our knowledge, Kant also made important revisions in the underlying framework that rationalists and empiricists shared, "the new way of ideas." Although everyone accepted the notion that some ideas (Kant calls them *representations*) are complex, little attention had been paid to the different forms of complexity. Kant drew a sharp distinction between concepts and judgments. Both concepts and judgments can be complex, but their structures differ significantly. For example, *the red ball* is a complex concept, in contrast with *The ball is red*, which is a judgment that asserts a content capable of truth or falsehood. Knowledge, Kant claims, is more than the possession of complex concepts, for knowledge is always judgmental in form. Kant thereby transformed the epistemological problem from that of tracing our complex ideas back to their simple elements and showing how they had been compounded to that of investigating the conditions under which judgments (assertions capable of truth and falsehood) are possible and justifiable.

Moreover, different kinds of judgments have different conditions. Kant distinguished analytic judgments, true because one of the parts of the judgment is contained in the other (e.g., "Brothers are male siblings"), from synthetic judgments, true not because of the internal relations of the parts but because of their relation to some other thing outside the judgment (e.g., "Immanuel Kant was born in 1724"). He then also distinguished a priori judgments, which are known to be true or false independently of experience, from a posteriori judgments, which can be known to be true or false only by reference to experience. These classifications do not coincide, Kant asserted. Everyone could agree that all analytic judgments are a priori and all a posteriori judgments are synthetic, but Kant insisted that there are synthetic a priori judgments and that any true assertions of metaphysics would be among them. All the principles philosophers have been interested in—that God exists; that the soul is simple, immortal, and free; even Hume's favorites: that every event has a cause, that there is a substance that persists through all change, that there is an external world extended in space—all such metaphysical assertions, if knowable at all, must be synthetic a priori judgments. They must be synthetic because they are clearly not just analytic; they go beyond simply unpacking the meaning of the terms involved. They must be a priori because none of them could be known by inductive inference from our experience. Metaphysical assertions make necessary and universal claims about the fundamental structures of reality, and no set of experiences could adequately justify such claims. This, there-

---

1. See "A Note on the Texts."

fore, becomes the central question of the *Critique*: How are synthetic a priori judgments possible?

Kant's answer is that both intuition and understanding have specific forms that place constraints on our knowledge, on what it is possible for us to experience. The forms of intuition are space and time, and the forms of understanding are the forms of judgment, for the understanding is the faculty by which we judge. Logic, Kant holds, shows that there are only a limited number of possible forms of judgment, and this provides a clue to the structure of our understanding. Anything we understand, we understand by making judgments about it, and hence everything we understand must be expressible using the forms of judgment. Our knowledge therefore necessarily assumes the form of judgments about objects located in space and/or time, and whatever conditions are necessary for being able to make judgments about spatiotemporal objects are conditions of all our knowledge. These forms of judgment applied to space and time are called the *categories* by Kant; they are the basic modes in which we must organize all our experience.

Kant uses this insight to defend the causal maxim that every event has a cause from Hume's attack by asserting, in his "Second Analogy of Experience," that the truth of the causal maxim is a necessary condition for being able to locate events in an objective temporal order. Kant turns his stratagem against the rationalists by pointing out that the metaphysical assertions they were most interested in (about God, freedom, and immortality) went beyond sensory experience and our intuitive faculty and therefore could not be defended in this way. Rationalist metaphysics could not be justified, though it could not be directly refuted either.

Kant's ultimate position is that we can have important synthetic a priori knowledge of the fundamental structures of the *phenomenal* world (the world as it appears to our intuition), but we can have no knowledge of the world as it is in itself, apart from our intuitive faculties.

The distinction Kant makes between the phenomenal world and the noumenal world (the world as it is in itself) has troubled many philosophers, but it is undoubtedly an essential part of Kant's philosophy. This is nowhere more evident than in his moral philosophy. By rejecting our pretense to know the world as it really is, Kant thought he was "denying knowledge to make room for faith." Leaving room for faith where knowledge could not be allowed is important, because the phenomenal realm, he thought, is a purely deterministic, mechanical realm. In such a realm there is no room for freedom and therefore no room for morality. Yet Kant was equally convinced that people could not help but view themselves as free, rational, moral agents. Kant's resolution to this dilemma was to say that though we could not ever claim to *know* that we are free, moral agents and in fact could show that as phenomenal beings we could not be free, we could nonetheless have faith that as we are in ourselves, our noumenal selves are free. That we are moral beings at all remains for Kant always a matter of faith.

Nevertheless, Kant's moral philosophy is every bit as deep, innovative, and influential as his theoretical philosophy. Kant believed that previous attempts to disclose the basis of morality, the ground of obligation, had failed badly. First, the ground of obligation had to be internal; an externally imposed "obligation" is coercive and no obligation at all unless it is internalized and accepted as binding no matter what the external consequences. Thus all attempts to understand morality as a system of external commands, whether divine commands or commands of the society or the rulers, necessarily fail. Second, attempts to ground morality in our sentiments or feelings also fail, for though "internal" in one sense, how we feel about things is always a contingent matter, radically relative to our background and upbringing. A coherent and consistent system of rules for action universally applicable to all moral agents could not be constructed on the basis of feelings. Truly universal rules for action must not be based on such contingencies of nature; they can have no other basis than the fact that we can govern ourselves by rules—the fact that we are rational. Morality is, for Kant, *practical reason*. Action governed by reason is moral action.

This does not mean that any action for which one has some reason is therefore morally justified. Satisfying a desire one just happens to have is a reason for action, but it is a reason for action conditioned on having that desire. For someone who does not share that condition, it is not a reason for action at all. "If you want to savor the unbridled majesty of nature, go to the Canadian Rockies" expresses a *hypothetical imperative*, an action-invoking command conditioned on some empirical desire. No hypothetical imperative ever expresses a commandment of morality, for moral commandments must be *unconditional*, or *categorical*. Only a command that binds regardless of one's desires can express a moral rule, and this is the source of the universality of moral rules. Kant believed that there could be only one categorical or unconditional imperative—namely, the commandment to act only on principles that themselves could be willed to be universal laws. The rational, moral agent acts in accordance with laws that he has given to himself and that apply equally well to everyone.

Kant gives several formulations of the categorical imperative that he claims are all equivalent (though that is a matter of some debate), but one formulation is a particularly telling expression of his contribution to ethics: "Act so that you treat humanity, whether in your own person or in the person of any other, never simply as a means but always at the same time as an end" [Ak. 429]. This means that you can never *use* someone for your own purposes without respecting that person's rational autonomy, his or her ability and right to determine a course of action and a set of goals in life, in accordance with the categorical imperative, without coercion from any outside force. Each person has infinite worth. With this formulation Kant gives the ultimate expression to the individualism characteristic of modern ethical and social thought, while also sketching a vision of mutually beneficial cooperative endeavor in which no one must debase one's own or another's independence and autonomy.

The Reading Context

Critique of Pure Reason

Kant had both his rationalist and empiricist predecessors in mind when he wrote the first *Critique*. At every turn he is interested in showing both *how much* and *how little* reason can accomplish on its own. Against the skepticism of the empiricists, he wanted to show that there were nontrivial, transcendental truths available to pure reason, truths that validated our right to claim empirical knowledge as well. But against the dogmatism of the rationalists, he wanted to demonstrate that reason yielded knowledge only in relation to our sensory experience. Therefore, in reading the *Critique*, try to understand how the positions he takes conflict or cohere with the positions of his predecessors.

Kant's terminology is somewhat difficult: He has been accused of drawing distinctions he does not use and using distinctions he does not draw. The fundamental terminology of the *Critique*, however, is laid out relatively straightforwardly in an important passage in which Kant distinguishes among the various kind of representations:

> The genus is *representation* in general (*repraesentatio*). Subordinate to it stands representation with consciousness (*perceptio*). A *perception* which relates solely to the subject as the modification of its state is *sensation* (*sensatio*), and objective perception is *knowledge* (*cognitio*). This is either *intuition* or *concept* (*intuitus vel conceptus*). The former relates immediately to the object and is single, the latter refers to it mediately by means of a feature which several things may have in common. The concept is either an *empirical* or a *pure concept*. (A 320/B 376–377)

The gist of this passage is that both intuition and concept are forms of knowledge and purport to relate to some (empirical) object. Sensation itself is not cognitive. Kant's problem is to distinguish more adequately than any of his predecessors the differences among sensations, intuitions, and concepts and the ways in which they are intrinsically related by their natures and extrinsically related in our judgments.

Another common source of confusion to beware of in reading Kant is that he often talks of *representations* without clarifying whether he is talking of "representings," the states of ours that represent, or "representeds" the contents of our representings. When you encounter *representation*, determine whether Kant has a representing or a represented in mind.

Groundwork of the Metaphysic of Morals

Suppose that two people see a small child drowning in a pond, and both go to rescue the child. Afterward, when asked why they attempted to save the child, one answers simply, "Because I had to, it was the right thing to do; the child could have drowned!" The other, equally sincerely, replies, "Well, I know the kid's dad is loaded, so I figured I'd probably at least get a healthy reward, if not a good job from it." Presumably, we can all immediately identify who the better person is. In the *Groundwork*, Kant wants to show us what this basic moral insight amounts to when all its implications are unpacked.

It is important to understand Kant's conception of a rational agent. For Kant, being rational, moral, and free or autonomous are all equivalent, and a fully rational being acts only on the basis of reasons, not on the basis of passions or inclinations. Acting on the basis of inclination is a form of slavery, of subjecting one's will to determination by external forces. Rational agents, furthermore, act on general principles—special pleading or treating similar cases differently are forms of irrationality. Morality is the system of general principles of action that rational beings, being rational, must respect. The source of these principles is none other than our own rational wills, so respect for the general principles of rational action entails respect for the foundation and source of those principles: rational agents, persons.

Kant seems excessively stringent in the discussions of his examples, but no one can doubt that he has given powerful formulations of a moral principle that lies deep in the heart of modern culture: persons are owed absolute respect.

A Note on the Texts

Kant's *Critique of Pure Reason* is one of the most difficult pieces in philosophy, yet it is also of crucial importance. Kant's own attempt to write a popularization of his doctrines in his *Prolegomena to Any Future Metaphysics* cannot be counted entirely successful. The *Critique* poses a daunting task to the translator, and Norman Kemp Smith's translation has held up quite well since its original publication. The *Critique*, originally published in 1781, was revised by Kant fairly substantially in 1787. There is a great deal of debate about the meaning and extent of the differences between the two editions, and Kemp Smith's translation includes both. The numbers in the margins prefaced by *A* and *B* refer to the pagination of the first and second editions, respectively. All references to the *Critique* use these page numbers.

The *Groundwork of the Metaphysic of Morals* first appeared in 1785. It has become a classic of ethical reflection, much more widely read than the *Critique of Practical Reason*, a more detailed and systematic work. References to the *Groundwork* standardly employ the pagination of the edition of Kant's works published by the Prussian (now German) Akademie der Wissenschaften. The pagination of the Akademie edition of the *Groundwork* is given in the margins of the selection.

Reading Questions

Critique of Pure Reason

1. What is metaphysics, according to Kant? What questions does it ask? Is it a science? What is the relation between metaphysics and a critique of pure reason?
2. What is Kant's Copernican revolution?
3. Define *a priori*, *a posteriori*, *analytic*, and *synthetic*. In what possible combinations can they occur?
4. Many have claimed that mathematical truths are analytic; some have claimed they are a posteriori. What arguments does Kant use to claim that they are synthetic a priori?
5. Either Kant's premises are analytic, in which case, if sound, his conclusions must also be analytic and hence empty, or his premises are synthetic a priori, in which case he is begging the question, or his premises are synthetic a posteriori, in which case his conclusions must be empirical hypotheses and not universally and necessarily true. Which is it?
6. Is there a difference between sensation and intuition? What is a *pure intuition*?
7. What does it mean to assert the empirical reality and the transcendental ideality of space?
8. How does Kant define *judgment*? How is the insight that knowledge is judgmental in form important in Kant's philosophy?
9. What is Kant's notion of *pure apperception*? Why must "I think" be able to accompany all my representations?
10. What is the difference between a subjective and an objective unity of consciousness? Between a subjective and an objective succession of representations?
11. How does Kant argue that "every event has a cause" is a synthetic a priori truth?

12. Although himself a transcendental idealist, Kant's *Critique* contains a refutation of idealism. What does he refute, and how?
13. Kant says that the great metaphysical questions concern "God, freedom, and immortality." What is Kant's position on each of these?

Groundwork of the Metaphysic of Morals

14. Under what conditions is an action morally good?
15. What is the difference between a hypothetical and a categorical imperative?
16. How can one tell what the maxim of an action is? What if there are numerous maxims under which one could perform a certain action?
17. What is the difference between a maxim one cannot think of as a universal law and a maxim one cannot will to be such a law?
18. Are there cases when, contrary to Kant, one may actually have an obligation to lie? For instance, if you lived in Nazi Germany and were hiding Jews in your attic, wouldn't you have had an obligation to lie to the Gestapo when they asked whether you knew of any Jews in the area?
19. By what right do we consider ourselves free, rational agents?

Critique of Pure Reason

Preface to First Edition

A vii   Human reason has this peculiar fate that in one species of its knowledge it is burdened by questions which, as prescribed by the very nature of reason itself, it is not able to ignore, but which, as transcending all its powers, it is also not able to answer.

    The perplexity into which it thus falls is not due to any fault of its own. It begins with principles which it has no option save to employ in the course of experience, and which this experience at the same time abundantly justifies it in using. Rising with their aid (since it is determined to this also by its own nature) to ever higher, ever more

A viii   remote, conditions, it soon becomes aware that in this way—the questions never ceasing—its work must always remain incomplete; and it therefore finds itself compelled to resort to principles which overstep all possible empirical employment, and which yet seem so unobjectionable that even ordinary consciousness readily accepts them. But by this procedure human reason precipitates itself into darkness and contradictions; and while it may indeed conjecture that these must be in some way due to concealed errors, it is not in a position to be able to detect them. For since the principles of which it is making use transcend the limits of experience, they are no longer subject to any empirical test. The battle-field of these endless controversies is called metaphysics. . . .

Preface to Second Edition

B vii   Whether the treatment of such knowledge as lies within the province of reason does or does not follow the secure path of a science, is easily to be determined from the outcome. For if after elaborate preparations, frequently renewed, it is brought to a stop immediately it nears its goal; if often it is compelled to retrace its steps and strike into some new line of approach; or again, if the various participants are unable to agree in any common plan of procedure, then we may rest assured that it is very far from having entered upon the secure path of a science, and is indeed a merely random groping. In these circumstances, we shall be rendering a service to reason should we succeed in discovering the path upon which it can securely travel, even if, as a result of so doing, much that is comprised in our original aims, adopted without reflection, may have to be abandoned as fruitless. . . .

B xiv   Metaphysics is a completely isolated speculative science of reason, which soars far above the teachings of experience, and in which reason is indeed meant to be its own pupil. Metaphysics rests on concepts alone—not, like mathematics, on their application to intuition. But though it is older than all other sciences, and would survive even if all the rest were swallowed up in the abyss of an all-destroying barbarism, it has not yet had the good fortune to enter upon the secure path of a science. For in it reason is perpetually being brought to a stand. . . .

From Immanuel Kant, *Critique of Pure Reason*, trans. Norman Kemp Smith (London: Macmillan, 1929). Reprinted with permission of Macmillan, London and Basingstoke. Copyright © 1969 by St. Martin's Press, Inc. Reprinted with the permission of St. Martin's Press, Inc.

What, then, is the reason why, in this field, the sure road to science has not *B xv*
hitherto been found? . . . If it be only that we have thus far failed to find the true path,
are there any indications to justify the hope that by renewed efforts we may have better
fortune than has fallen to our predecessors?

The examples of mathematics and natural science, which by a single and sudden *B xvi*
revolution have become what they now are, seem to me sufficiently remarkable to suggest our considering what may have been the essential features in the changed point
of view by which they have so greatly benefited. Their success should incline us, at
least by way of experiment, to imitate their procedure, so far as the analogy which, as
species of rational knowledge, they bear to metaphysics may permit. Hitherto it has
been assumed that all our knowledge must conform to objects. But all attempts to
extend our knowledge of objects by establishing something in regard to them *a priori*,
by means of concepts, have, on this assumption, ended in failure. We must therefore
make trial whether we may not have more success in the tasks of metaphysics, if we
suppose that objects must conform to our knowledge. This would agree better with
what is desired, namely, that it should be possible to have knowledge of objects *a priori*,
determining something in regard to them prior to their being given. We should then
be proceeding precisely on the lines of Copernicus' primary hypothesis. Failing of satisfactory progress in explaining the movements of the heavenly bodies on the supposition that they all revolved round the spectator, he tried whether he might not have
better success if he made the spectator to revolve and the stars to remain at rest. A *B xvii*
similar experiment can be tried in metaphysics, as regards the *intuition* of objects. If
intuition must conform to the constitution of the objects, I do not see how we could
know anything of the latter *a priori*; but if the object (as object of the senses) must conform to the constitution of our faculty of intuition, I have no difficulty in conceiving
such a possibility. Since I cannot rest in these intuitions if they are to become known,
but must relate them as representations to something as their object, and determine
this latter through them, either I must assume that the *concepts*, by means of which
I obtain this determination, conform to the object, or else I assume that the objects,
or what is the same thing, that the *experience* in which alone, as given objects, they
can be known, conform to the concepts. In the former case, I am again in the same
perplexity as to how I can know anything *a priori* in regard to the objects. In the latter
case the outlook is more hopeful. For experience is itself a species of knowledge which
involves understanding; and understanding has rules which I must presuppose as being
in me prior to objects being given to me, and therefore as being *a priori*. They find
expression in *a priori* concepts to which all objects of experience necessarily conform, *B xviii*
and with which they must agree. As regards objects which are thought solely through
reason, and indeed as necessary, but which can never—at least not in the manner in
which reason thinks them—be given in experience, the attempts at thinking them (for
they must admit of being thought) will furnish an excellent touchstone of what we are
adopting as our new method of thought, namely, that we can know *a priori* of things
only what we ourselves put into them.

This experiment succeeds as well as could be desired, and promises to metaphysics,
in its first part—the part that is occupied with those concepts *a priori* to which the corresponding objects, commensurate with them, can be given in experience—the secure
path of a science. For the new point of view enables us to explain how there can be *B xix*
knowledge *a priori*; and, in addition, to furnish satisfactory proofs of the laws which

form the *a priori* basis of nature, regarded as the sum of the objects of experience—neither achievement being possible on the procedure hitherto followed. But this deduction of our power of knowing *a priori*, in the first part of metaphysics, has a consequence which is startling, and which has the appearance of being highly prejudicial to the whole purpose of metaphysics, as dealt with in the second part. For we are brought to the conclusion that we can never transcend the limits of possible

B xx   experience, though that is precisely what this science is concerned, above all else, to achieve. This situation yields, however, just the very experiment by which, indirectly, we are enabled to prove the truth of this first estimate of our *a priori* knowledge of reason, namely, that such knowledge has to do only with appearances, and must leave the thing in itself as indeed real *per se*, but as not known by us. For what necessarily forces us to transcend the limits of experience and of all appearances is the *unconditioned*, which reason, by necessity and by right, demands in things in themselves, as required to complete the series of conditions. . . .

B xxii   This attempt to alter the procedure which has hitherto prevailed in metaphysics, by completely revolutionising it in accordance with the example set by the geometers and physicists, forms indeed the main purpose of this critique of pure speculative reason. It is a treatise on the method, not a system of the science itself. . . .

B xxv   So far, therefore, as our Critique limits speculative reason, it is indeed *negative*; but since it thereby removes an obstacle which stands in the way of the employment of practical reason, nay threatens to destroy it, it has in reality a *positive* and very important use. At least this is so, immediately we are convinced that there is an absolutely necessary *practical* employment of pure reason—the *moral*—in which it inevitably goes beyond the limits of sensibility. . . .

B xxvii   If our Critique is not in error in teaching that the object is to be taken *in a twofold sense*, namely as appearance and as thing in itself; if the deduction of the concepts of understanding is valid, and the principle of causality therefore applies only to things taken in the former sense, namely, in so far as they are objects of experience—these same objects, taken in the other sense, not being subject to the principle—then there

B xxviii   is no contradiction in supposing that one and the same will is, in the appearance, that is, in its visible acts, necessarily subject to the law of nature, and so far *not free*, while yet, as belonging to a thing in itself, it is not subject to that law, and is therefore *free*. My soul, viewed from the latter standpoint, cannot indeed be known by means of speculative reason (and still less through empirical observation); and freedom as a property of a being to which I attribute effects in the sensible world, is therefore also not knowable in any such fashion. For I should then have to know such a being as determined in its existence, and yet as not determined in time—which is impossible, since I cannot support my concept by any intuition. But though I cannot *know*, I can yet *think* freedom; that is to say, the representation of it is at least not self-contradictory, provided due account be taken of our critical distinction between the two modes of representation, the sensible and the intellectual, and of the resulting limitation of the pure concepts of understanding and of the principles which flow from them.

If we grant that morality necessarily presupposes freedom (in the strictest sense) as a property of our will; if, that is to say, we grant that it yields practical principles—original principles, proper to our reason—as *a priori data* of reason, and that this would

B xxix   be absolutely impossible save on the assumption of freedom; and if at the same time we grant that speculative reason has proved that such freedom does not allow of being thought, then the former supposition—that made on behalf of morality—would have to give way to this other contention, the opposite of which involves a palpable contradiction. For since it is only on the assumption of freedom that the negation of morality contains any contradiction, freedom, and with it morality, would have to yield to the mechanism of nature.

Morality does not, indeed, require that freedom should be understood, but only that it should not contradict itself, and so should at least allow of being thought, and that as thus thought it should place no obstacle in the way of a free act (viewed in another relation) likewise conforming to the mechanism of nature. The doctrine of morality and the doctrine of nature may each, therefore, make good its position. This, however, is only possible in so far as criticism has previously established our unavoidable ignorance of things in themselves, and has limited all that we can theoretically *know* to mere appearances.

This discussion as to the positive advantage of critical principles of pure reason can be similarly developed in regard to the concept of God and of the *simple nature* of our *soul*; but for the sake of brevity such further discussion may be omitted. [From what has already been said, it is evident that] even the *assumption*—as made on behalf of the necessary practical employment of my reason—of *God, freedom*, and *immortality* is not permissible unless at the same time speculative reason be deprived of its pretensions to transcendent insight. For in order to arrive at such insight it must make use of principles which, in fact, extend only to objects of possible experience, and which, if also applied to what cannot be an object of experience, always really change this into an appearance, thus rendering all *practical extension* of pure reason impossible. I have therefore found it necessary to deny *knowledge*, in order to make room for *faith*. . . .   B xxx

Introduction

I. The distinction between pure and empirical knowledge

There can be no doubt that all our knowledge begins with experience. For how should   B 1
our faculty of knowledge be awakened into action did not objects affecting our senses partly of themselves produce representations, partly arouse the activity of our understanding to compare these representations, and, by combining or separating them, work up the raw material of the sensible impressions into that knowledge of objects which is entitled experience? In the order of time, therefore, we have no knowledge antecedent to experience, and with experience all our knowledge begins.

But though all our knowledge begins with experience, it does not follow that it all arises out of experience. For it may well be that even our empirical knowledge is made up of what we receive through impressions and of what our own faculty of knowledge (sensible impressions serving merely as the occasion) supplies from itself. If our faculty of knowledge makes any such addition, it may be that we are not in a position to distinguish it from the raw material, until with long practice of attention we have become   B 2
skilled in separating it.

This, then, is a question which at least calls for closer examination, and does not allow of any off-hand answer:—whether there is any knowledge that is thus independent of experience and even of all impressions of the senses. Such knowledge is entitled *a priori*, and distinguished from the *empirical*, which has its sources *a posteriori*, that is, in experience. . . .

B 3 In what follows, therefore, we shall understand by *a priori* knowledge, not knowledge independent of this or that experience, but knowledge absolutely independent of all experience. Opposed to it is empirical knowledge, which is knowledge possible only *a posteriori*, that is, through experience. *A priori* modes of knowledge are entitled pure when there is no admixture of anything empirical. . . .

II. We are in possession of certain modes of a priori knowledge, and even the common understanding is never without them

What we here require is a criterion by which to distinguish with certainty between pure and empirical knowledge. Experience teaches us that a thing is so and so, but not that it cannot be otherwise. First, then, if we have a proposition which in being thought is thought as *necessary*, it is an *a priori* judgment; and if, besides, it is not derived from any proposition except one which also has the validity of a necessary judgment, it is an absolutely *a priori* judgment. Secondly, experience never confers on its judgments true or strict, but only assumed and comparative *universality*, through induction. We can properly only say, therefore, that, so far as we have hitherto

B 4 observed, there is no exception to this or that rule. If, then, a judgment is thought with strict universality, that is, in such manner that no exception is allowed as possible, it is not derived from experience, but is valid absolutely *a priori*. . . . Necessity and strict universality are thus sure criteria of *a priori* knowledge, and are inseparable from one another. . . .

Now it is easy to show that there actually are in human knowledge judgments which are necessary and in the strictest sense universal, and which are therefore pure *a priori* judgments. If an example from the sciences be desired, we have only to look to any of the propositions of mathematics; if we seek an example from the understand-

B 5 ing in its quite ordinary employment, the proposition, "every alteration must have a cause," will serve our purpose. . . .

Such *a priori* origin is manifest in certain concepts, no less than in judgments. If we remove from our empirical concept of a body, one by one, every feature in it which is [merely] empirical, the colour, the hardness or softness, the weight, even the impenetrability, there still remains the space which the body (now entirely vanished) occupied, and this cannot be removed. . . .

IV. The distinction between analytic and synthetic judgments

A 6 In all judgments in which the relation of a subject to the predicate is thought (I take
B 10 into consideration affirmative judgments only, the subsequent application to negative judgments being easily made), this relation is possible in two different ways. Either the predicate B belongs to the subject A, as something which is (covertly) contained in this concept A; or B lies outside the concept A, although it does indeed stand in con-

nection with it. In the one case I entitle the judgment analytic, in the other syn-   A 7
thetic. . . . The former, as adding nothing through the predicate to the concept of the   B 11
subject, but merely breaking it up into those constituent concepts that have all along
been thought in it, although confusedly, can also be entitled explicative. The latter,
on the other hand, add to the concept of the subject a predicate which has not been
in any wise thought in it, and which no analysis could possibly extract from it; and
they may therefore be entitled ampliative. If I say, for instance, "All bodies are
extended," this is an analytic judgment. For I do not require to go beyond the concept
which I connect with "body" in order to find extension as bound up with it. . . . But
when I say, "All bodies are heavy," the predicate is something quite different from anything that I think in the mere concept of body in general; and the addition of such
a predicate therefore yields a synthetic judgment.

Judgments of experience, as such, are one and all synthetic. . . . From the start I   B 12
can apprehend the concept of body analytically through the characters of extension,
impenetrability, figure, etc., all of which are thought in the concept. Now, however,
looking back on the experience from which I have derived this concept of body, and
finding weight to be invariably connected with the above characters, I attach it as a
predicate to the concept; and in doing so I attach it synthetically, and am therefore
extending my knowledge. The possibility of the synthesis of the predicate "weight"
with the concept of "body" thus rests upon experience. While the one concept is not
contained in the other, they yet belong to one another, though only contingently, as
parts of a whole, namely, of an experience which is itself a synthetic combination
of intuitions.

But in *a priori* synthetic judgments this help is entirely lacking. [I do not here have   A 9
the advantage of looking around in the field of experience.] Upon what, then, am I   B 13
to rely, when I seek to go beyond the concept A, and to know that another concept
B is connected with it? Through what is the synthesis made possible? . . .

V. In all theoretical sciences of reason synthetic a priori judgments are contained as principles

1. *All mathematical judgments, without exception, are synthetic.* This fact, though incon-
testably certain and in its consequences very important, has hitherto escaped the
notice of those who are engaged in the analysis of human reason, and is, indeed,
directly opposed to all their conjectures. For as it was found that all mathematical
inferences proceed in accordance with the principle of contradiction (which the
nature of all apodeictic certainty requires), it was supposed that the fundamental
propositions of the science can themselves be known to be true through that principle.
This is an erroneous view. For though a synthetic proposition can indeed be discerned
in accordance with the principle of contradiction, this can only be if another synthetic proposition is presupposed, and if it can then be apprehended as following from
this other proposition; it can never be so discerned in and by itself.

First of all, it has to be noted that mathematical propositions, strictly so called, are
always judgments *a priori*, not empirical; because they carry with them necessity,
which cannot be derived from experience. . . .   B 15

We might, indeed, at first suppose that the proposition $7 + 5 = 12$ is a merely analytic proposition, and follows by the principle of contradiction from the concept of a sum of 7 and 5. But if we look more closely we find that the concept of the sum of 7 and 5 contains nothing save the union of the two numbers into one, and in this no thought is being taken as to what that single number may be which combines both. The concept of 12 is by no means already thought in merely thinking this union of 7 and 5.... We have to go outside these concepts, and call in the aid of the intuition which corresponds to one of them, our five fingers, for instance....

B 16   Just as little is any fundamental proposition of pure geometry analytic. That the straight line between two points is the shortest, is a synthetic proposition. For my concept of *straight* contains nothing of quantity, but only of quality. The concept of the shortest is wholly an addition, and cannot be derived, through any process of analysis, from the concept of the straight line. Intuition, therefore, must here be called in; only by its aid is the synthesis possible....

B17   2. *Natural science (physics) contains* a priori *synthetic judgments as principles.* I need cite only two such judgments: that in all changes of the material world the quantity of matter remains unchanged; and that in all communication of motion, action and reaction must always be equal. Both propositions, it is evident, are not only necessary,

B 18   and therefore in their origin a priori, but also synthetic. For in the concept of matter I do not think its permanence, but only its presence in the space which it occupies....

3. *Metaphysics*, even if we look upon it as having hitherto failed in all its endeavours, is yet, owing to the nature of human reason, a quite indispensable science, and *ought to contain* a priori *synthetic knowledge.* For its business is not merely to analyse concepts which we make for ourselves a priori of things, and thereby to clarify them analytically, but to extend our a priori knowledge. And for this purpose we must employ principles which add to the given concept something that was not contained in it, and through a priori synthetic judgments venture out so far that experience is quite unable to follow us, as, for instance, in the proposition, that the world must have a first beginning, and such like. Thus metaphysics consists, at least *in intention*, entirely of a priori synthetic propositions.

VI. The general problem of pure reason

B 19   Now the proper problem of pure reason is contained in the question: How are *a priori synthetic judgments possible?*...

B 20   In the solution of the above problem, we are at the same time deciding as to the possibility of the employment of pure reason in establishing and developing all those sciences which contain a theoretical *a priori* knowledge of objects, and have therefore to answer the questions:

How is pure mathematics possible?
How is pure science of nature possible?

Since these sciences actually exist, it is quite proper to ask *how* they are possible;

B 21   for that they must be possible is proved by the fact that they exist. But the poor progress which has hitherto been made in metaphysics, and the fact that no system yet propounded can, in view of the essential purpose of metaphysics, be said really to exist, leaves everyone sufficient ground for doubting as to its possibility. . . .

TRANSCENDENTAL DOCTRINE OF ELEMENTS

First Part
Transcendental Aesthetic

§ 1

In whatever manner and by whatever means a cognition may relate to objects, *intuition* is that through which it is in immediate relation to them, and to which all thought as a means is directed. But intuition takes place only in so far as the object is given to us. This again is only possible, to man at least, in so far as the mind is affected in a certain way. The capacity (receptivity) for receiving representations through the mode in which we are affected by objects, is entitled *sensibility*. Objects are *given* to us by means of sensibility, and it alone yields us *intuitions*; they are *thought* through the understanding, and from the understanding arise *concepts*. But all thought must, directly or indirectly, by way of certain characters, relate ultimately to intuitions, and therefore, with us, to sensibility, because in no other way can an object be given to us.[1]

    The effect of an object upon the faculty of representation, so far as we are affected by it, is *sensation*. That intuition which is in relation to the object through sensation, is entitled *empirical*. The undetermined object of an empirical intuition is entitled *appearance*.

    That in the appearance which corresponds to sensation I term its *matter*; but that which so determines the manifold of appearance that it allows of being ordered in certain relations, I term the *form* of appearance. That in which alone the sensations can be posited and ordered in a certain form, cannot itself be sensation; and therefore, while the matter of all appearance is given to us *a posteriori* only, its form must lie ready for the sensations *a priori* in the mind, and so must allow of being considered apart from all sensation.

    I term all representations *pure* (in the transcendental sense) in which there is nothing that belongs to sensation. The pure form of sensible intuitions in general, in which all the manifold of intuition is intuited in certain relations, must be found in the mind *a priori*. This pure form of sensibility may also itself be called *pure intuition*. Thus, if I take away from the representation of a body that which the understanding thinks in regard to it, substance, force, divisibility, etc., and likewise what belongs to sensation, impenetrability, hardness, colour, etc., something still remains over from this empirical intuition, namely, extension and figure. These belong to pure intuition, which, even without any actual object of the senses or of sensation, exists in the mind *a priori* as a mere form of sensibility. . . .

A 19/
B 33

B 34
A 20

B 35

A 21

---

1. See the passage from A320/B377 cited in "The Reading Context" for further explanation of Kant's terminology.

Section 1
Space

§ 2 *Metaphysical exposition of this concept*

A 22/   By means of outer sense, a property of our mind, we represent to ourselves objects as
B 37   outside us, and all without exception in space. In space their shape, magnitude, and
relation to one another are determined or determinable. Inner sense, by means of
which the mind intuits itself or its inner state, yields indeed no intuition of the soul
A 23   itself as an object; but there is nevertheless a determinate form [namely, time] in
which alone the intuition of inner states is possible, and everything which belongs to
inner determinations is therefore represented in relations of time. Time cannot be
outwardly intuited, any more than space can be intuited as something in us. What,
then, are space and time? Are they real existences? Are they only determinations or
relations of things, yet such as would belong to things even if they were not intuited?
Or are space and time such that they belong only to the form of intuition, and there-
B38   fore to the subjective constitution of our mind, apart from which they could not be
ascribed to anything whatsoever? In order to obtain light upon these questions, let us
first give an exposition of the concept of space. By *exposition* (*expositio*) I mean the
clear, though not necessarily exhaustive, representation of that which belongs to a
concept: the exposition is *metaphysical* when it contains that which exhibits the concept *as given a priori*.

1. Space is not an empirical concept which has been derived from outer experiences. For in order that certain sensations be referred to something outside me (that
is, to something in another region of space from that in which I find myself), and similarly in order that I may be able to represent them as outside and alongside one
another, and accordingly as not only different but as in different places, the representation of space must be presupposed. The representation of space cannot, therefore, be
empirically obtained from the relations of outer appearance. On the contrary, this
outer experience is itself possible at all only through that representation.

A 24   2. Space is a necessary *a priori* representation, which underlies all outer intuitions.
We can never represent to ourselves the absence of space, though we can quite well
B39   think it as empty of objects. It must therefore be regarded as the condition of the possibility of appearances, and not as a determination dependent upon them. It is an
a priori representation, which necessarily underlies outer appearances.

3. Space is not a discursive or, as we say, general concept of relations of things in
A 25   general, but a pure intuition. For, in the first place, we can represent to ourselves only
one space; and if we speak of diverse spaces, we mean thereby only parts of one and
the same unique space. Secondly, these parts cannot precede the one all-embracing
space, as being, as it were, constituents out of which it can be composed; on the contrary, they can be thought only as *in* it. Space is essentially one; the manifold in it, and
therefore the general concept of spaces, depends solely on [the introduction of] limitations. Hence it follows that an *a priori*, and not an empirical, intuition underlies all
concepts of space. For kindred reasons, geometrical propositions, that, for instance, in
a triangle two sides together are greater than the third, can never be derived from the

general concepts of line and triangle, but only from intuition, and this indeed *a priori*, with apodeictic certainty.

4. Space is represented as an infinite given magnitude. Now every concept must be thought as a representation which is contained in an infinite number of different possible representations (as their common character), and which therefore contains these *under* itself; but no concept, as such, can be thought as containing an infinite number of representations *within* itself. It is in this latter way, however, that space is thought; for all the parts of space coexist *ad infinitum*. Consequently, the original representation of space is an *a priori* intuition, not a concept. . . .   B 40

§ 3 *Conclusions from the above concepts*

(*a*) Space does not represent any property of things in themselves, nor does it represent them in their relation to one another. That is to say, space does not represent any determination that attaches to the objects themselves, and which remains even when abstraction has been made of all the subjective conditions of intuition. . . .   A 26/ B 42

(*b*) Space is nothing but the form of all appearances of outer sense. It is the subjective condition of sensibility, under which alone outer intuition is possible for us. . . .

It is, therefore, solely from the human standpoint that we can speak of space, of extended things, etc. If we depart from the subjective condition under which alone we can have outer intuition, namely, liability to be affected by objects, the representation of space stands for nothing whatsoever. . . . Our exposition therefore establishes the *reality*, that is, the objective validity, of space in respect of whatever can be presented to us outwardly as object, but also at the same time the *ideality* of space in respect of things when they are considered in themselves through reason, that is, without regard to the constitution of our sensibility. We assert, then, the *empirical reality* of space, as regards all possible outer experience; and yet at the same time we assert its *transcendental ideality*—in other words, that it is nothing at all, immediately we withdraw the above condition, namely, its limitation to possible experience, and so look upon it as something that underlies things in themselves. . . .   A 28/ B 44

[*Kant gives parallel arguments to establish the status of time.*]

Time and space are, therefore, two sources of knowledge, from which bodies of *a priori* synthetic knowledge can be derived. (Pure mathematics is a brilliant example of such knowledge, especially as regards space and its relations.) Time and space, taken together, are the pure forms of all sensible intuition, and so are what make *a priori* synthetic propositions possible. But these *a priori* sources of knowledge, being merely conditions of our sensibility, just by this very fact determine their own limits, namely, that they apply to objects only in so far as objects are viewed as appearances, and do not present things as they are in themselves. This is the sole field of their validity; should we pass beyond it, no objective use can be made of them. This ideality of space and time leaves, however, the certainty of empirical knowledge unaffected, for we are equally sure of it, whether these forms necessarily inhere in things in themselves or only in our intuition of them. . . .   A 39 B 56

III. When I say that the intuition of outer objects and the self-intuition of the mind alike represent the objects and the mind, in space and in time, as they affect our senses, that is, as they appear, I do not mean to say that these objects are a mere *illu-*   B 69 sion. For in an appearance the objects, nay even the properties that we ascribe to them, are always regarded as something actually given. Since, however, in the relation of the given object to the subject, such properties depend upon the mode of intuition of the subject, this object as *appearance* is to be distinguished from itself as object *in itself*. Thus when I maintain that the quality of space and of time, in conformity with which, as a condition of their existence, I posit both bodies and my own soul, lies in my mode of intuition and not in those objects in themselves, I am not saying that bodies merely *seem* to be outside me, or that my soul only *seems* to be given in my self-consciousness. It would be my own fault, if out of that which I ought to reckon as appearance, I made

B 70   mere illusion. That does not follow as a consequence of our principle of the ideality of all our sensible intuitions—quite the contrary. It is only if we ascribe *objective reality* to these forms of representation, that it becomes impossible for us to prevent everything being thereby transformed into mere *illusion*. . . .

Second Part
Transcendental Logic

FIRST DIVISION
Transcendental Analytic

Book I
ANALYTIC OF CONCEPTS

Chapter 1
The Clue to the Discovery of All Pure Concepts of the Understanding

Section 3
The Pure Concepts of the Understanding, or Categories

§ 10

A 76/   General logic, as has been repeatedly said, abstracts from all content of knowledge,
B 102   and looks to some other source, whatever that may be, for the representations which it is to transform into concepts by process of analysis. Transcendental logic, on the
A 77   other hand, has lying before it a manifold of *a priori* sensibility, presented by transcendental aesthetic, as material for the concepts of pure understanding. In the absence of this material those concepts would be without any content, therefore entirely empty. Space and time contain a manifold of pure *a priori* intuition, but at the same time are conditions of the receptivity of our mind—conditions under which alone it can receive representations of objects, and which therefore must also always affect the concept of these objects. But if this manifold is to be known, the spontaneity of our thought requires that it be gone through in a certain way, taken up, and connected. This act I name *synthesis*.

B 103   By *synthesis*, in its most general sense, I understand the act of putting different representations together, and of grasping what is manifold in them in one [act of] knowledge. Such a synthesis is *pure*, if the manifold is not empirical but is given *a priori*, as is the manifold in space and time. Before we can analyse our representations, the representations must themselves be given, and therefore as regards *content* no concepts can first arise by way of analysis. Synthesis of a manifold (be it given empirically or *a priori*) is what first gives rise to knowledge. This knowledge may, indeed, at first, be crude and confused, and therefore in need of analysis. Still the synthesis is that which gathers the elements for knowledge, and unites them to [form] a certain content. It is to synthesis, therefore, that we must first direct our attention, if A 78 we would determine the first origin of our knowledge.

Synthesis in general, as we shall hereafter see, is the mere result of the power of imagination, a blind but indispensable function of the soul, without which we should have no knowledge whatsoever, but of which we are scarcely ever conscious. To bring this synthesis *to concepts* is a function which belongs to the understanding, and it is through this function of the understanding that we first obtain knowledge properly so called.

Pure synthesis, *represented in its most general aspect*, gives us the pure concept of the B 104 understanding. By this pure synthesis I understand that which rests upon a basis of *a priori* synthetic unity. Thus our counting, as is easily seen in the case of larger numbers, is a synthesis according to concepts, because it is executed according to a common ground of unity, as, for instance, the decade. In terms of this concept, the unity of the synthesis of the manifold is rendered necessary.

By means of analysis different representations are brought under one concept—a procedure treated of in general logic. What transcendental logic, on the other hand, teaches, is how we bring to concepts, not representations, but the *pure synthesis* of representations. What must first be given—with a view to the *a priori* knowledge of all objects—is the *manifold* of pure intuition; the second factor involved is the *synthesis* of A 79 this manifold by means of the imagination. But even this does not yet yield knowledge. The concepts which give *unity* to this pure synthesis, and which consist solely in the representation of this necessary synthetic unity, furnish the third requisite for the knowledge of an object; and they rest on the understanding.

The same function which gives unity to the various representations *in a judgment* also gives unity to the mere synthesis of various representations *in an intuition*; and this B 105 unity, in its most general expression, we entitle the pure concept of the understanding. The same understanding, through the same operations by which in concepts, by means of analytical unity, it produced the logical form of a judgment, also introduces a transcendental content into its representations, by means of the synthetic unity of the manifold in intuition in general. On this account we are entitled to call these representations pure concepts of the understanding, and to regard them as applying *a priori* to objects—a conclusion which general logic is not in a position to establish. . . .

These concepts we shall, with Aristotle, call *categories*, for our primary purpose is A 80 the same as his, although widely diverging from it in manner of execution.

Table of Categories B106

I
Of Quantity
Unity
Plurality
Totality

II	III
Of Quality	*Of Relation*
Reality	Of Inherence and Subsistence
Negation	(*substantia et accidens*)
Limitation	Of Causality and Dependence
	(cause and effect)
	Of Community (reciprocity
	between agent and patient)

IV
Of Modality
Possibility—Impossibility
Existence—Non-existence
Necessity—Contingency

This then is the list of all original pure concepts of synthesis that the understanding contains within itself *a priori*. . . .

Chapter 2
The Deduction of the Pure Concepts of Understanding

Section 1
The Principles of Any Transcendental Deduction

§ 14 *Transition to the transcendental deduction of the categories*

A 92/
B 124

B 125

A 93

B126

There are only two possible ways in which synthetic representations and their objects can establish connection, obtain necessary relation to one another, and, as it were, meet one another. Either the object alone must make the representation possible, or the representation alone must make the object possible. In the former case, this relation is only empirical, and the representation is never possible *a priori*. This is true of appearances, as regards that [element] in them which belongs to sensation. In the latter case, representation in itself does not produce its object in so far as *existence* is concerned, for we are not here speaking of its causality by means of the will. None the less the representation is *a priori* determinant of the object, if it be the case that only through the representation is it possible to *know* anything *as an object*. Now there are two conditions under which alone the knowledge of an object is possible, first, *intuition*, through which it is given, though only as appearance; secondly, *concept*, through which an object is thought corresponding to this intuition. It is evident from the [Aesthetic] that the first condition . . . does actually lie *a priori* in the mind as the formal ground of the objects. . . . The question now arises whether *a priori* concepts do not also serve as antecedent conditions under which alone anything can be, if not intuited, yet thought as object in general. In that case all empirical knowledge of objects would necessarily conform to such concepts, because only as thus presupposing them is anything possible as *object of experience*. Now all experience does indeed contain, in addition to the intuition of the senses through which something is given, a *concept* of an object as being thereby given, that is to say, as appearing. Concepts of objects in general thus underlie all empirical knowledge as its *a priori* conditions. The objective validity of the categories as *a priori* concepts rests, therefore, on the fact that, so far as the form of thought is concerned, through them alone does experience become possible. They relate of necessity and *a priori* to objects of experience, for the reason that only by means of them can any object whatsoever of experience be thought.

The transcendental deduction of all *a priori* concepts has thus a principle according A 94 to which the whole enquiry must be directed, namely, that they must be recognised as *a priori* conditions of the possibility of experience.... Concepts which yield the objective ground of the possibility of experience are for this very reason necessary....

Chapter 2
Deduction of the Pure Concepts of the Understanding
[As restated in second edition]

Section 2
Transcendental Deduction of the Pure Concepts of the Understanding

§ 15 The possibility of combination in general

The manifold of representations can be given in an intuition which is purely sensible, B 129 that is, nothing but receptivity; and the form of this intuition can lie *a priori* in our faculty of representation, without being anything more than the mode in which the subject is affected. But the combination (*conjunctio*) of a manifold in general can never come to us through the senses, and cannot, therefore, be already contained in the pure form of sensible intuition. For it is an act of spontaneity of the faculty of representa- B 130 tion; and since this faculty, to distinguish it from sensibility, must be entitled understanding, all combination—be we conscious of it or not, be it a combination of the manifold of intuition, empirical or non-empirical, or of various concepts—is an act of the understanding. To this act the general title "synthesis" may be assigned, as indicating that we cannot represent to ourselves anything as combined in the object which we have not ourselves previously combined, and that of all representations *combination* is the only one which cannot be given through objects....

§ 16 The original synthetic unity of apperception

It must be possible for the "I think" to accompany all my representations; for otherwise B 131 something would be represented in me which could not be thought at all, and that is B132 equivalent to saying that the representation would be impossible, or at least would be nothing to me. That representation which can be given prior to all thought is entitled intuition. All the manifold of intuition has, therefore, a necessary relation to the "I think" in the same subject in which this manifold is found. But this representation is an act of *spontaneity*, that is, it cannot be regarded as belonging to sensibility. I call it *pure apperception*, to distinguish it from empirical apperception.... The unity of this apperception I likewise entitle the *transcendental* unity of self-consciousness, in order to indicate the possibility of *a priori* knowledge arising from it. For the manifold representations, which are given in an intuition, would not be one and all *my* representations, if they did not all belong to one self-consciousness. As *my* representations (even if I am not conscious of them as such) they must conform to the condition under which alone they *can* stand together in one universal self-consciousness, because

B 133   otherwise they would not all without exception belong to me. From this original combination many consequences follow.

This thoroughgoing identity of the apperception of a manifold which is given in
intuition contains a synthesis of representations, and is possible only through the
consciousness of this synthesis. . . . Only in so far, therefore, as I can unite a manifold
of given representations in *one consciousness*, is it possible for me to represent to myself
the *identity of the consciousness in* [*i.e. throughout*] *these representations* . . . .

B 135   This principle of the necessary unity of apperception is itself, indeed, an identical,
and therefore analytic, proposition; nevertheless it reveals the necessity of a synthesis
of the manifold given in intuition, without which the thoroughgoing identity of self-
consciousness cannot be thought. . . .

§ 17 The principle of the synthetic unity is the supreme principle of all employment of the understanding

B 137   . . . *Understanding* is, to use general terms, *the faculty of knowledge*. This knowledge
consists in the determinate relation of given representations to an object; and an *object*
is that in the concept of which the manifold of a given intuition is *united*. Now all
unification of representations demands unity of consciousness in the synthesis of
them. Consequently it is the unity of consciousness that alone constitutes the relation
of representations to an object, and therefore their objective validity and the fact that
they are modes of knowledge; and upon it therefore rests the very possibility of the
understanding. . . .

§ 18 The objective unity of self-consciousness

B 139   The transcendental unity of apperception is that unity through which all the manifold
given in an intuition is united in a concept of the object. It is therefore entitled *objective*, and must be distinguished from the *subjective* unity of consciousness, which is a
determination of *inner sense*—through which the manifold of intuition for such [objec-
tive] combination is empirically given. Whether I can become *empirically* conscious of
the manifold as simultaneous or as successive depends on circumstances or empirical

B 140   conditions. . . . But the pure form of intuition in time, merely as intuition in general,
which contains a given manifold, is subject to the original unity of consciousness, simply through the necessary relation of the manifold of the intuition to the one "*I think*,"
and so through the pure synthesis of understanding which is the *a priori* underlying
ground of the empirical synthesis. . . .

§ 19 The logical form of all judgments consists in the objective unity of the apperception of the concepts which they contain

B141   . . . But if I investigate more precisely the relation of the given modes of knowledge in
any judgment, and distinguish it, as belonging to the understanding, from the relation
according to laws of the reproductive imagination, which has only subjective validity,
I find that a judgment is nothing but the manner in which given modes of knowledge
are brought to the objective unity of apperception. This is what is intended by the

B 142   copula "is." It is employed to distinguish the objective unity of given representations
from the subjective. It indicates their relation to original apperception, and its *neces-*

sary unity. It holds good even if the judgment is itself empirical, and therefore contingent, as, for example, in the judgment, "Bodies are heavy." I do not here assert that these representations *necessarily* belong *to one another* in the empirical intuition, but that they belong to one another *in virtue of the necessary unity* of apperception in the synthesis of intuitions. . . . Only in this way does there arise from this relation a *judgment*, that is, a relation which is *objectively valid*, and so can be adequately distinguished from a relation of the same representations that would have only subjective validity—as when they are connected according to laws of association. . . . Thus to say "The body is heavy" is not merely to state that the two representations have always been conjoined in my perception, however often that perception be repeated; what we are asserting is that they are combined *in the object*, no matter what the state of the subject may be.

§ 20 *All sensible intuitions are subject to the categories, as conditions under which alone their manifold can come together in one consciousness*

The manifold given in a sensible intuition is necessarily subject to the original synthetic unity of apperception, because in no other way is the *unity* of intuition possible (§ 17). But that act of understanding by which the manifold of given representations (be they intuitions or concepts) is brought under one apperception, is the logical function of judgment (cf. § 19). All the manifold, therefore, so far as it is given in a single empirical intuition, is *determined* in respect of one of the logical functions of judgment, and is thereby brought into one consciousness. Now the *categories* are just these functions of judgment, in so far as they are employed in determination of the manifold of a given intuition (cf. § 13). Consequently, the manifold in a given intuition is necessarily subject to the categories.

B 143

§ 26 *Transcendental deduction of the universally possible employment in experience of the pure concepts of the understanding*

. . . In the representations of space and time we have *a priori forms* of outer and inner sensible intuition; and to these the synthesis of apprehension of the manifold of appearance must always conform, because in no other way can the synthesis take place at all.[2] But space and time are represented *a priori* not merely as *forms* of sensible intuition, but as themselves *intuitions* which contain a manifold [of their own], and therefore are represented with the determination of the *unity* of this manifold (*vide* the Transcendental Aesthetic). Thus *unity of the synthesis* of the manifold, without or within us, and consequently also a *combination* to which everything that is to be represented as determined in space or in time must conform, is given *a priori* as the condition of the synthesis of all *apprehension*—not indeed in, but with these intuitions. This synthetic unity can be no other than the unity of the combination of the manifold of a given *intuition in general* in an original consciousness, in accordance with the categories, in so far as the combination is applied to our *sensible intuition*. All

B 160

B 161

2. First of all, I may draw attention to the fact that by *synthesis of apprehension* I understand that combination of the manifold in an empirical intuition, whereby perception, that is, empirical consciousness of the intuition (as appearance), is possible.

synthesis, therefore, even that which renders perception possible, is subject to the categories; and since experience is knowledge by means of connected perceptions, the categories are conditions of the possibility of experience, and are therefore valid *a priori* for all objects of experience. . . .

Book II
ANALYTIC OF PRINCIPLES

Chapter 2
The System of the Principles of Pure Understanding

Section 2
The Highest Principle of All Synthetic Judgments

A 154   The explanation of the possibility of synthetic judgments is a problem with which general logic has nothing to do. It need not even so much as know the problem by name. But in transcendental logic it is the most important of all questions; and indeed, if in treating of the possibility of synthetic *a priori* judgments we also take account of the conditions and scope of their validity, it is the only question with which it is concerned. For upon completion of this enquiry, transcendental logic is in a position completely to fulfil its ultimate purpose, that of determining the scope and limits of pure understanding. . . .

A 155/   Granted, then, that we must advance beyond a given concept in order to compare
B 194   it synthetically with another, a third something is necessary, as that wherein alone the synthesis of two concepts can be achieved. What, now, is this third something that is to be the medium of all synthetic judgments? There is only one whole in which all our representations are contained, namely, inner sense and its *a priori* form, time. The synthesis of representations rests on imagination; and their synthetic unity, which is required for judgment, on the unity of apperception. In these, therefore, [in inner sense, imagination, and apperception], we must look for the possibility of synthetic judgments; and since all three contain the sources of *a priori* representations, they must also account for the possibility of *pure* synthetic judgments. For these reasons they are, indeed, indispensably necessary for any knowledge of objects, which rests entirely on the synthesis of representations.

If knowledge is to have objective reality, that is, to relate to an object, and is to acquire meaning and significance in respect to it, the object must be capable of being in some manner given. Otherwise the concepts are empty; through them we have
B195   indeed thought, but in this thinking we have really known nothing; we have merely
A 156   played with representations. That an object be given (if this expression be taken, not as referring to some merely mediate process, but as signifying immediate presentation in intuition), means simply that the representation through which the object is thought relates to actual or possible experience. Even space and time, however free their concepts are from everything empirical, and however certain it is that they are represented in the mind completely *a priori*, would yet be without objective validity, senseless and meaningless, if their necessary application to the objects of experience were not established. . . . Apart from these objects of experience, they would be devoid of meaning. And so it is with concepts of every kind.

The *possibility of experience* is, then, what gives objective reality to all our *a priori* modes of knowledge. Experience, however, rests on the synthetic unity of appearances, that is, on a synthesis according to concepts of an object of appearances in general. Apart from such synthesis it would not be knowledge, but a rhapsody of perceptions that would not fit into any context according to rules of a completely interconnected (possible) consciousness, and so would not conform to the transcendental and neces- B 196 sary unity of apperception. Experience depends, therefore, upon *a priori* principles of its form, that is, upon universal rules of unity in the synthesis of appearances. Their A 157 objective reality, as necessary conditions of experience, and indeed of its very possibil- ity, can always be shown in experience. Apart from this relation synthetic *a priori* prin- ciples are completely impossible. For they have then no third something, that is, no object, in which the synthetic unity can exhibit the objective reality of its concepts....

The highest principle of all synthetic judgments is therefore this: every object A 158/ stands under the necessary conditions of synthetic unity of the manifold of intuition B 197 in a possible experience.

Synthetic *a priori* judgments are thus possible when we relate the formal conditions of *a priori* intuition, the synthesis of imagination and the necessary unity of this syn- thesis in a transcendental apperception, to a possible empirical knowledge in general. We then assert that the conditions of the *possibility of experience* in general are likewise conditions of the *possibility of the objects of experience*, and that for this reason they have objective validity in a synthetic *a priori* judgment.

Section 3
Systematic Representation of All the Synthetic Principles of Pure Understanding

3. Analogies of experience

A. First Analogy—*Principle of Permanence of Substance*: In all change of appearances A 182/ substance is permanent; its quantum in nature is neither increased nor diminished. B 224

Proof: All appearances are in time; and in it alone, as substratum (as permanent form of inner intuition), can either coexistence or succession be represented. Thus the time in which all change of appearances has to be thought, remains and does not change. B 225 For it is that in which, and as determinations of which, succession or coexistence can alone be represented. Now time cannot by itself be perceived. Consequently there must be found in the objects of perception, that is, in the appearances, the substratum which represents time in general; and all change or coexistence must, in being appre- hended, be perceived in this substratum, and through relation of the appearances to it. But the substratum of all that is real, that is, of all that belongs to the existence of things, is *substance*; and all that belongs to existence can be thought only as a determi- nation of substance. Consequently the permanent, in relation to which alone all time- relations of appearances can be determined, is substance in the [field of] appearance, that is, the real in appearance, and as the substrate of all change remains ever the same. And as it is thus unchangeable in its existence, its quantity in nature can be neither increased nor diminished.

Our *apprehension* of the manifold of appearance is always successive, and is there- fore always changing. Through it alone we can never determine whether this manifold, as object of experience, is coexistent or in sequence. For such determination we require an underlying ground which exists *at all times*, that is, something *abiding* and *permanent*, of which all change and coexistence are only so many ways (modes of time) in which the permanent exists. And simultaneity and succession being the only relations in time, it follows that only in the permanent are relations of time possible. In other words, the permanent is the *substratum* of the empirical representation of time itself; in it alone is any determination of time possible. Permanence, as the abiding correlate of all existence of appearances, of all change and of all concomitance, expresses time in general. For change does not affect time itself, but only appearances in time. (Coexistence is not a mode of time itself; for none of the parts of time coexist; they are all in succession to one another.) If we ascribe succession to time itself, we must think yet another time, in which the sequence would be possible. Only through the permanent does existence in different parts of the time-series acquire a magnitude which can be entitled duration. For in bare succession existence is always vanishing and recommencing, and never has the least magnitude. Without the permanent there is therefore no time-relation. Now time cannot be perceived in itself; the permanent in the appearances is therefore the substratum of all determination of time, and, as likewise follows, is also the condition of the possibility of all synthetic unity of perceptions, that is, of experience. All existence and all change in time have thus to be viewed as simply a mode of the existence of that which remains and persists. In all appearances the permanent is the object itself, that is, substance as phenomenon; everything, on the other hand, which changes or can change belongs only to the way in which substance or substances exist, and therefore to their determinations. . . .

B. Second Analogy—*Principle of Succession in Time, in Accordance with the Law of Causality*: All alterations take place in conformity with the law of the connection of cause and effect.

Proof: . . . I perceive that appearances follow one another, that is, that there is a state of things at one time the opposite of which was in the preceding time. Thus I am really connecting two perceptions in time. Now connection is not the work of mere sense and intuition, but is here the product of a synthetic faculty of imagination, which determines inner sense in respect of the time-relation. But imagination can connect these two states in two ways, so that either the one or the other precedes in time. For time cannot be perceived in itself, and what precedes and what follows cannot, therefore, by relation to it, be empirically determined in the object. I am conscious only that my imagination sets the one state before and the other after, not that the one state precedes the other in the object. In other words, the *objective relation* of appearances that follow upon one another is not to be determined through mere perception. In order that this relation be known as determined, the relation between the two states must be so thought that it is thereby determined as necessary which of them must be placed before, and which of them after, and that they cannot be placed in the reverse relation. But the concept which carries with it a necessity of synthetic unity can only be a pure concept that lies in the understanding, not in perception; and in this case it is the concept of the *relation of cause and effect*, the former of which determines the latter in time, as its consequence—not as in a sequence that may occur solely in the imagination (or that may not be perceived at all). Experience itself—in other words,

B 226

A 183

B 227

A 184

A 189/
B 233

B 234

empirical knowledge of appearances—is thus possible only in so far as we subject the succession of appearances, and therefore all alteration, to the law of causality; and, as likewise follows, the appearances, as objects of experience, are themselves possible only in conformity with the law.

The apprehension of the manifold of appearance is always successive. The representations of the parts follow upon one another. Whether they also follow one another in the object is a point which calls for further reflection, and which is not decided by the above statement. . . . The appearances, in so far as they are objects of consciousness simply in virtue of being representations, are not in any way distinct from their apprehension, that is, from their reception in the synthesis of imagination; and we must therefore agree that the manifold of appearances is always generated in the mind successively. Now if appearances were things in themselves, then since we have to deal solely with our representations, we could never determine from the succession of the representations how their manifold may be connected in the object. How things may be in themselves, apart from the representations through which they affect us, is entirely outside our sphere of knowledge. In spite, however, of the fact that the appearances are not things in themselves, and yet are what alone can be given to us to know, in spite also of the fact that their representation in apprehension is always successive, I have to show what sort of a connection in time belongs to the manifold in the appearances themselves. For instance, the apprehension of the manifold in the appearance of a house which stands before me is successive. The question then arises, whether the manifold of the house is also in itself successive. This, however, is what no one will grant. . . . That which lies in the successive apprehension is here viewed as representation, while the appearance which is given to me, notwithstanding that it is nothing but the sum of these representations, is viewed as their object; and my concept, which I derive from the representations of apprehension, has to agree with it. Since truth consists in the agreement of knowledge with the object, it will at once be seen that we can here enquire only regarding the formal conditions of empirical truth, and that appearance, in contradistinction to the representations of apprehension, can be represented as an object distinct from them only if it stands under a rule which distinguishes it from every other apprehension and necessitates some one particular mode of connection of the manifold. The object is *that* in the appearance which contains the condition of this necessary rule of apprehension.

Let us now proceed to our problem. That something happens, *i.e.* that something, or some state which did not previously exist, comes to be, cannot be perceived unless it is preceded by an appearance which does not contain in itself this state. . . . Every apprehension of an event is therefore a perception that follows upon another perception. But since, as I have above illustrated by reference to the appearance of a house, this likewise happens in all synthesis of apprehension, the apprehension of an event is not yet thereby distinguished from other apprehensions. But, as I also note, in an appearance which contains a happening (the preceding state of the perception we may entitle A, and the succeeding B) B can be apprehended only as following upon A; the perception A cannot follow upon B but only precede it. For instance, I see a ship move down stream. My perception of its lower position follows upon the perception of its position higher up in the stream, and it is impossible that in the apprehension of this appearance the ship should first be perceived lower down in the stream and afterwards higher up. The order in which the perceptions succeed one another in apprehension

A 199/
B 235

A 191/
B 236

B 237
A 192

is in this instance determined, and to this order apprehension is bound down. In the previous example of a house my perceptions could begin with the apprehension of the roof and end with the basement, or could begin from below and end above; and I could similarly apprehend the manifold of the empirical intuition either from right to left or from left to right. In the series of these perceptions there was thus no determinate order specifying at what point I must begin in order to connect the manifold empirically. But in the perception of an event there is always a rule that makes the order in which the perceptions (in the apprehension of this appearance) follow upon one another a *necessary* order.

In this case, therefore, we must derive the *subjective succession* of apprehension from the *objective succession* of appearances. Otherwise the order of apprehension is entirely undetermined, and does not distinguish one appearance from another. Since the subjective succession by itself is altogether arbitrary, it does not prove anything as to the manner in which the manifold is connected in the object. The objective succession will therefore consist in that order of the manifold of appearance according to which, *in conformity with a rule*, the apprehension of that which happens follows upon the apprehension of that which precedes. Thus only can I be justified in asserting, not merely of my apprehension, but of appearance itself, that a succession is to be met with in it. This is only another way of saying that I cannot arrange the apprehension otherwise than in this very succession. . . .

Let us suppose that there is nothing antecedent to an event, upon which it must follow according to rule. All succession of perception would then be only in the apprehension, that is, would be merely subjective, and would never enable us to determine objectively which perceptions are those that really precede and which are those that follow. We should then have only a play of representations, relating to no object; that is to say, it would not be possible through our perception to distinguish one appearance from another as regards relations of time. For the succession in our apprehension would always be one and the same, and there would be nothing in the appearance which so determines it that a certain sequence is rendered objectively necessary. I could not then assert that two states follow upon one another in the [field of] appearance, but only that one apprehension follows upon the other. That is something merely subjective, determining no object; and may not, therefore, be regarded as knowledge of any object, not even of an object in the [field of] appearance.

If, then, we experience that something happens, we in so doing always presuppose that something precedes it, on which it follows according to a rule. Otherwise I should not say of the object that it follows. For mere succession in my apprehension, if there be no rule determining the succession in relation to something that precedes, does not justify me in assuming any succession in the object. I render my subjective synthesis of apprehension objective only by reference to a rule in accordance with which the appearances in their succession, that is, as they happen, are determined by the preceding state. The experience of an event [*i.e.* of anything as *happening*] is itself possible only on this assumption. . . .

4. The postulates of empirical thoughts in general

Refutation of Idealism: Idealism—meaning thereby *material* idealism—is the theory which declares the existence of objects in space outside us either to be merely doubtful and indemonstrable or to be false and impossible. The former is the *problematic* idealism of Descartes, which holds that there is only one empirical assertion that is indubitably certain, namely, that "I am." The latter is the *dogmatic* idealism of Berkeley. He maintains that space, with all the things of which it is the inseparable condition, is something which is in itself impossible; and he therefore regards the things in space as merely imaginary entities. Dogmatic idealism is unavoidable, if space be interpreted as a property that must belong to things in themselves. For in that case space, and everything to which it serves as condition, is a non-entity. The ground on which this idealism rests has already been undermined by us in the Transcendental Aesthetic. Problematic idealism, which makes no such assertion, but merely pleads incapacity to prove, through immediate experience, any existence except our own, is, in so far as it allows of no decisive judgment until sufficient proof has been found, reasonable and in accordance with a thorough and philosophical mode of thought. The required proof must, therefore, show that we have *experience*, and not merely imagination of outer things; and this, it would seem, cannot be achieved save by proof that even our inner experience, which for Descartes is indubitable, is possible only on the assumption of outer experience.

B 275

Thesis: The mere, but empirically determined, consciousness of my own existence proves the existence of objects in space outside me.

Proof: I am conscious of my own existence as determined in time. All determination of time presupposes something *permanent* in perception. This permanent cannot, however, be something in me, since it is only through this permanent that my existence in time can itself be determined.[3] Thus perception of this permanent is possible only through a *thing* outside me and not through the mere *representation* of a thing outside me; and consequently the determination of my existence in time is possible only through the existence of actual things which I perceive outside me. Now consciousness [of my existence] in time is necessarily bound up with consciousness of the [condition of the] possibility of this time-determination; and it is therefore necessarily bound up with the existence of things outside me, as the condition of the time-determination. In other words, the consciousness of my existence is at the same time an immediate consciousness of the existence of other things outside me.

B 276

Note 1. It will be observed that in the foregoing proof the game played by idealism has been turned against itself, and with greater justice. Idealism assumed that the only immediate experience is inner experience, and that from it we can only *infer* outer things—and this, moreover, only in an untrustworthy manner, as in all cases where we are inferring from given effects to determinate causes. In this particular case, the cause of the representations, which we ascribe, perhaps falsely, to outer things, may lie in ourselves. But in the above proof it has been shown that outer experience is really immediate, and that only by means of it is inner experience—not indeed the consciousness of my own existence, but the determination of it in time—possible. Cer-

B 277

---

3. As stated by Kant in the Preface to [the second edition], this sentence should be altered as follows: "But this permanent cannot be an intuition in me. For all grounds of determination of my existence which are to be met with in me are representations; and as representations themselves require a permanent distinct from them, in relation to which their change, and so my existence in the time wherein they change, may be determined." [Trans. note.]

tainly, the representation "I am," which expresses the consciousness that can accompany all thought, immediately includes in itself the existence of a subject; but it does not so include any *knowledge* of that subject, and therefore also no empirical knowledge, that is, no experience of it. For this we require, in addition to the thought of something existing, also intuition, and in this case inner intuition, in respect of which, that is, of time, the subject must be determined. But in order so to determine it, outer objects are quite indispensable; and it therefore follows that inner experience is itself possible only mediately, and only through outer experience.

    Note 2. With this thesis all employment of our cognitive faculty in experience, in the determination of time, entirely agrees. Not only are we unable to perceive any determination of time save through change in outer relations (motion) relatively to the permanent in space (for instance, the motion of the sun relatively to objects on B 278 the earth), we have nothing permanent on which, as intuition, we can base the concept of a substance, save only *matter*; and even this permanence is not obtained from outer experience, but is presupposed *a priori* as a necessary condition of determination of time, and therefore also as a determination of inner sense in respect of [the determination of] our own existence through the existence of outer things. The consciousness of myself in the representation "I" is not an intuition, but a merely *intellectual* representation of the spontaneity of a thinking subject. This "I" has not, therefore, the least predicate of intuition, which, as permanent, might serve as correlate for the determination of time in inner sense—in the manner in which, for instance, *impenetrability* serves in our *empirical* intuition of matter. . . .

SECOND DIVISION
Transcendental Dialectic

Book II
THE DIALECTICAL INFERENCES OF PURE REASON

Chapter 1
The Paralogisms of Pure Reason
[*As restated in second edition*]

B 406   Since the proposition "I think" (taken problematically) contains the form of each and every judgment of understanding and accompanies all categories as their vehicle, it is evident that the inferences from it admit only of a transcendental employment of the understanding. And since this employment excludes any admixture of experience, we cannot, after what has been shown above, entertain any favourable anticipations in regard to its methods of procedure. We therefore propose to follow it, with a critical eye, through all the predicaments of pure psychology. But for the sake of brevity the examination had best proceed in an unbroken continuity. . . .

B 407   (1) In all judgments I am the *determining* subject of that relation which constitutes the judgment. That the "I", the "I" that thinks, can be regarded always as *subject*, and as something which does not belong to thought as a mere predicate, must be granted. It is an apodeictic and indeed *identical* proposition; but it does not mean that I, as *object*, am for myself a *self-subsistent* being or *substance*. The latter statement goes very far beyond the former, and demands for its proof data which are not to be met with in thought. . . .

(2) That the "I" of apperception, and therefore the "I" in every act of thought, is *one*, and cannot be resolved into a plurality of subjects, and consequently signifies a logically simple subject, is something already contained in the very concept of thought, and is therefore an analytic proposition. But this does not mean that the thinking "I"   B 408
is a simple *substance*. That proposition would be synthetic. The concept of substance always relates to intuitions which cannot in me be other than sensible, and which therefore lie entirely outside the field of the understanding and its thought. . . .

(3) The proposition, that in all the manifold of which I am conscious I am identical with myself, is likewise implied in the concepts themselves, and is therefore an analytic proposition. But this identity of the subject, of which I can be conscious in all my representations, does not concern any intuition of the subject, whereby it is given as object, and cannot therefore signify the identity of the person, if by that is understood the consciousness of the identity of one's own substance, as a thinking being, in all change of its states. . . .

(4) That I distinguish my own existence as that of a thinking being, from other   B 409
things outside me—among them my body—is likewise an analytic proposition; for *other* things are such as I think to be *distinct* from myself. But I do not thereby learn whether this consciousness of myself would be even possible apart from things outside me through which representations are given to me, and whether, therefore, I could exist merely as thinking being (*i.e.* without existing in human form).

The analysis, then, of the consciousness of myself in thought in general, yields nothing whatsoever towards the knowledge of myself as object. The logical exposition of thought in general has been mistaken for a metaphysical determination of the object. . . .

Chapter 2
The Antinomy of Pure Reason

Section 2
Antithetic of Pure Reason

The transcendental antithetic is an enquiry into the antinomy of pure reason, its causes and outcome. If in employing the principles of understanding we do not merely apply our reason to objects of experience, but venture to extend these principles   B 449
beyond the limits of experience, there arise *pseudo-rational* doctrines which can neither hope for confirmation in experience nor fear refutation by it. Each of them is not only in itself free from contradiction, but finds conditions of its necessity in the very nature of reason—only that, unfortunately, the assertion of the opposite has, on its side, grounds that are just as valid and necessary. . . .

A dialectical doctrine of pure reason must therefore be distinguished from all sophistical propositions in two respects. It must not refer to an arbitrary question such   A 422
as may be raised for some special purpose, but to one which human reason must necessarily encounter in its progress. And secondly, both it and its opposite must involve no mere artificial illusion such as at once vanishes upon detection, but a natural and unavoidable illusion, which even after it has ceased to beguile still continues to delude   B 450

though not to deceive us, and which though thus capable of being rendered harmless can never be eradicated. . . .

Third conflict of the transcendental ideas

A 444⎫
B 472⎭ *Thesis*: Causality in accordance with laws of nature is not the only causality from which the appearances of the world can one and all be derived. To explain these appearances it is necessary to assume that there is also another causality, that of freedom.

Proof of the Thesis: Let us assume that there is no other causality than that in accordance with laws of nature. This being so, everything which *takes place* presupposes a preceding state upon which it inevitably follows according to a rule. But the preceding state must itself be something which has taken place (having come to be in a time in which it previously was not); for if it had always existed, its consequence also would have always existed, and would not have only just arisen. The causality of the cause through which something takes place is itself, therefore, something that has *taken place*, which again presupposes, in accordance with the law of nature, a preceding state and its causality, and this in similar manner a still earlier state, and so on. If, therefore,
A 446⎫
B 474⎭ everything takes place solely in accordance with laws of nature, there will always be only a relative and never a first beginning, and consequently no completeness of the series on the side of the causes that arise the one from the other. But the law of nature is just this, that nothing takes place without a cause *sufficiently* determined *a priori*. The proposition that no causality is possible save in accordance with laws of nature, when taken in unlimited universality, is therefore self-contradictory; and this cannot, therefore, be regarded as the sole kind of causality.

We must, then, assume a causality through which something takes place, the cause of which is not itself determined, in accordance with necessary laws, by another cause antecedent to it, that is to say, an *absolute spontaneity* of the cause, whereby a series of appearances, which proceeds in accordance with laws of nature, begins *of itself*. This is transcendental freedom, without which, even in the [ordinary] course of nature, the series of appearances on the side of the causes can never be complete.

A 445⎫
B 473⎭ *Antithesis*: There is no freedom; everything in the world takes place solely in accordance with laws of nature.

Proof of the Antithesis: Assume that there is freedom in the transcendental sense, as a special kind of causality in accordance with which the events in the world can have come about, namely, a power of absolutely beginning a state, and therefore also of absolutely beginning a series of consequences of that state; it then follows that not only will a series have its absolute beginning in this spontaneity, but that the very determination of this spontaneity to originate the series, that is to say, the causality itself, will have an absolute beginning; there will be no antecedent through which this act, in taking place, is determined in accordance with fixed laws. But every beginning of action presupposes a state of the not yet acting cause; and a *dynamical* beginning of the action, if it is also a first beginning, presupposes a state which has no *causal* connection with the preceding state of the cause, that is to say, in nowise follows from it. Transcendental freedom thus stands opposed to the law of causality; and the kind of

---

4. The sequence of numbers A444/B472 to A447/B475 reflects the two-column format of the original text of this section.

connection which it assumes as holding between the successive states of the active causes renders all unity of experience impossible. It is not to be met with in any experience, and is therefore an empty thought-entity. $\left\{\begin{array}{l}\text{A 447}\\\text{B 475}\end{array}\right.$

In nature alone, therefore, [not in freedom], must we seek for the connection and order of cosmical events. Freedom (independence) from the laws of nature is no doubt a liberation from compulsion, but also from the guidance of all rules. For it is not permissible to say that the *laws* of freedom enter into the causality exhibited in the course of nature, and so take the place of natural laws. If freedom were determined in accordance with laws, it would not be freedom; it would simply be nature under another name. Nature and transcendental freedom differ as do conformity to law and lawlessness. Nature does indeed impose upon the understanding the exacting task of always seeking the origin of events ever higher in the series of causes, their causality being always conditioned. But in compensation it holds out the promise of thoroughgoing unity of experience in accordance with laws. The illusion of freedom, on the other hand, offers a point of rest to the enquiring understanding in the chain of causes, conducting it to an unconditioned causality which begins to act of itself. This causality is, however, blind, and abrogates those rules through which alone a completely coherent experience is possible.

Explanation of the cosmological idea of freedom in its connection with universal natural necessity

... That everything which happens has a cause, is a law of nature. Since the causality of this cause, that is, the *action* of the cause, is antecedent in time to the effect which has *ensued* upon it, it cannot itself have always existed, but must have *happened*, and *among the appearances* must have a cause by which it in turn is determined. Consequently, all events are empirically determined in an order of nature. Only in virtue of this law can appearances constitute a *nature* and become objects of experience. This law is a law of the understanding, from which no departure can be permitted, and from which no appearance may be exempted. To allow such exemption would be to set an appearance outside all possible experience, to distinguish it from all objects of possible experience, and so to make of it a mere thought-entity, a phantom of the brain.... $\left\{\begin{array}{l}\text{A 542}\\\text{B 570}\end{array}\right.$ $\left\{\begin{array}{l}\text{A 543}\\\text{B 571}\end{array}\right.$

The only question here is this:—Admitting that in the whole series of events there is nothing but natural necessity, is it yet possible to regard one and the same event as being in one aspect merely an effect of nature and in another aspect an effect due to freedom; or is there between these two kinds of causality a direct contradiction?

Among the causes in the [field of] appearance there certainly cannot be anything which could begin a series absolutely and of itself. Every action, [viewed] as appearance, in so far as it gives rise to an event, is itself an event or happening, and presupposes another state wherein its cause is to be found.... An *original* act, such as can by itself bring about what did not exist before, is not to be looked for in the causally connected appearances. $\left\{\begin{array}{l}\text{A 544}\\\text{B 572}\end{array}\right.$

Now granting that effects are appearances and that their cause is likewise appearance, is it necessary that the causality of their cause should be exclusively empirical? May it not rather be, that while for every effect in the [field of] appearance a connection with its cause in accordance with the laws of empirical causality is indeed required, this empirical causality, without the least violation of its connection with natural causes, is itself an effect of a causality that is not empirical but intelligible?...

The principle of the causal connection of appearances is required in order that we may be able to look for and to determine the natural conditions of natural events, that

is to say, their causes in the [field of] appearance. . . . These requirements are not in any way infringed, if we assume, even though the assumption should be a mere fiction, that some among the natural causes have a faculty which is intelligible only, inasmuch as its determination to action never rests upon empirical conditions, but solely on grounds of understanding. We must, of course, at the same time be able to assume that the *action* of these causes *in the [field of] appearance* is in conformity with all the laws of empirical causality. In this way the acting subject, as *causa phaenomenon*, would be bound up with nature through the indissoluble dependence of all its actions, and only as we ascend from the empirical object to the transcendental should we find that this subject, together with all its causality in the [field of] appearance, has in its *noumenon* certain conditions which must be regarded as purely intelligible. For if in determining in what ways appearances can serve as causes we follow the rules of nature, we need not concern ourselves what kind of ground for these appearances and their connection may have to be thought as existing in the transcendental subject, which is empirically unknown to us. This intelligible ground does not have to be considered in empirical

enquiries; it concerns only thought in the pure understanding; and although the effects of this thought and action of the pure understanding are to be met with in the appearances, these appearances must none the less be capable of complete causal explanation in terms of other appearances in accordance with natural laws. We have to take their strictly empirical character as the supreme ground of explanation, leaving entirely out of account their intelligible character (that is, the transcendental cause of their empirical character) as being completely unknown, save in so far as the empirical serves for its sensible sign.

Let us apply this to experience. Man is one of the appearances of the sensible world, and in so far one of the natural causes the causality of which must stand under empirical laws. Like all other things in nature, he must have an empirical character. This character we come to know through the powers and faculties which he reveals in his actions. In lifeless, or merely animal, nature we find no ground for thinking that any faculty is conditioned otherwise than in a merely sensible manner. Man, however, who knows all the rest of nature solely through the senses, knows himself also through pure apperception; and this, indeed, in acts and inner determinations which he cannot regard as impressions of the senses. He is thus to himself, on the one hand

phenomenon, and on the other hand, in respect of certain faculties the action of which cannot be ascribed to the receptivity of sensibility, a purely intelligible object. We entitle these faculties understanding and reason. The latter, in particular, we distinguish in a quite peculiar and especial way from all empirically conditioned powers. For it views its objects exclusively in the light of ideas, and in accordance with them determines the understanding, which then proceeds to make an empirical use of its own similarly pure concepts.

That our reason has causality, or that we at least represent it to ourselves as having causality, is evident from the *imperatives* which in all matters of conduct we impose as rules upon our active powers. "*Ought*" expresses a kind of necessity and of connection with grounds which is found nowhere else in the whole of nature. The understanding can know in nature only what is, what has been, or what will be. We cannot say that anything in nature *ought to be* other than what in all these time-relations it actually is. When we have the course of nature alone in view, "*ought*" has no meaning whatsoever. It is just as absurd to ask what ought to happen in the natural world as to ask what properties a circle ought to have. All that we are justified in asking is: what happens in nature? what are the properties of the circle?

This "*ought*" expresses a possible action the ground of which cannot be anything but a mere concept; whereas in the case of a merely natural action the ground must always be an appearance. The action to which the "*ought*" applies must indeed be possible under natural conditions. These conditions, however, do not play any part in determining the will itself, but only in determining the effect and its consequences in the [field of] appearance. No matter how many natural grounds or how many sensuous impulses may impel me to *will*, they can never give rise to the "*ought*," but only to a willing which, while very far from being necessary, is always conditioned; and the "*ought*" pronounced by reason confronts such willing with a limit and an end—nay more, forbids or authorises it. Whether what is willed be an object of mere sensibility (the pleasant) or of pure reason (the good), reason will not give way to any ground which is empirically given. Reason does not here follow the order of things as they present themselves in appearance, but frames for itself with perfect spontaneity an order of its own according to ideas, to which it adapts the empirical conditions, and according to which it declares actions to be necessary, even although they have never taken place, and perhaps never will take place. And at the same time reason also presupposes that it can have causality in regard to all these actions, since otherwise no empirical effects could be expected from its ideas. {A 548 / B 576

Now, in view of these considerations, let us take our stand, and regard it as at least possible for reason to have causality with respect to appearances. Reason though it be, it must none the less exhibit an empirical character. For every cause presupposes a rule according to which certain appearances follow as effects; and every rule requires uniformity in the effects. This uniformity is, indeed, that upon which the concept of cause (as a faculty) is based, and so far as it must be exhibited by mere appearances may be named the empirical character of the cause. This character is permanent, but its effects, according to variation in the concomitant and in part limiting conditions, appear in changeable forms. {A 549 / B 577

Thus the will of every man has an empirical character, which is nothing but a certain causality of his reason, so far as that causality exhibits, in its effects in the [field of] appearance, a rule from which we may gather what, in their kind and degrees, are the actions of reason and the grounds thereof, and so may form an estimate concerning the subjective principles of his will. Since this empirical character must itself be discovered from the appearances which are its effect and from the rule to which experience shows them to conform, it follows that all the actions of men in the [field of] appearance are determined in conformity with the order of nature, by their empirical character and by the other causes which co-operate with that character; and if we could exhaustively investigate all the appearances of men's wills, there would not be found a single human action which we could not predict with certainty, and recognise as proceeding necessarily from its antecedent conditions. So far, then, as regards this empirical character there is no freedom; and yet it is only in the light of this character that man can be studied—if, that is to say, we are simply *observing*, and in the manner of anthropology seeking to institute a physiological investigation into the motive causes of his actions. {A 550 / B 578

But when we consider these actions in their relation to reason—I do not mean speculative reason, by which we endeavour *to explain* their coming into being, but reason in so far as it is itself the cause *producing* them—if, that is to say, we compare them with [the standards of] reason in its *practical* bearing, we find a rule and order altogether different from the order of nature. For it may be that all that *has happened* in the course of nature, and in accordance with its empirical grounds must inevitably have happened, *ought not to have happened*. Sometimes, however, we find, or at least believe that we find, that the ideas of reason have in actual fact proved their causality in respect of the actions of men, as appearances; and that these actions have taken place, not because they were determined by empirical causes, but because they were determined by grounds of reason.

A 551
B 579

Granted, then, that reason may be asserted to have causality in respect of appearance, its action can still be said to be free, even although its empirical character (as a mode of sense) is completely and necessarily determined in all its detail. This empirical character is itself determined in the intelligible character (as a mode of thought). The latter, however, we do not know; we can only indicate its nature by means of appearances; and these really yield an immediate knowledge only of the mode of sense, the empirical character. . . . Pure reason, as a purely intelligible faculty, is not subject to the form of time, nor consequently to the conditions of succession in time.

A 552
B 580

The causality of reason in its intelligible character does not, in producing an effect, *arise* or begin to be at a certain time. For in that case it would itself be subject to the natural law of appearances, in accordance with which causal series are determined in time; and its causality would then be nature, not freedom. Thus all that we are justified in saying is that, if reason can have causality in respect of appearances, it is a faculty *through* which the sensible condition of an empirical series of effects first begins. For the condition which lies in reason is not sensible, and therefore does not itself begin to be. And thus what we failed to find in any empirical series is disclosed as being possible, namely, that the condition of a successive series of events may itself be empirically unconditioned. For here the condition is outside the series of appearances (in the intelligible), and therefore is not subject to any sensible condition, and to no time-determination through an antecedent cause. . . .

A 557
B 585

Thus in our judgments in regard to the causality of free actions, we can get as far as the intelligible cause, but not beyond it. We can know that it is free, that is, that it is determined independently of sensibility, and that in this way it may be the sensibly unconditioned condition of appearances. But to explain why in the given circumstances the intelligible character should give just these appearances and this empirical character transcends all the powers of our reason, indeed all its rights of questioning, just as if we were to ask why the transcendental object of our outer sensible intuition gives intuition in *space* only and not some other mode of intuition. But the problem which we have to solve does not require us to raise any such questions. Our problem was this only: whether freedom and natural necessity can exist without conflict in one and the same action; and this we have sufficiently answered. We have shown that since freedom may stand in relation to a quite different kind of conditions from those of natural necessity, the law of the latter does not affect the former, and that both may exist, independently of one another and without interfering with each other

The reader should be careful to observe that in what has been said our intention has not been to establish the *reality* of freedom as one of the faculties which contain

the cause of the appearances of our sensible world. For that enquiry, as it does not deal {A 558
with concepts alone, would not have been transcendental. And further, it could not {B 586
have been successful, since we can never infer from experience anything which cannot
be thought in accordance with the laws of experience. It has not even been our intention to prove the *possibility* of freedom. For in this also we should not have succeeded,
since we cannot from mere concepts *a priori* know the possibility of any real ground
and its causality. Freedom is here being treated only as a transcendental idea whereby
reason is led to think that it can begin the series of conditions in the [field of] appearance by means of the sensibly unconditioned, and so becomes involved in an antinomy with those very laws which it itself prescribes to the empirical employment of the
understanding. What we have alone been able to show, and what we have alone been
concerned to show, is that this antinomy rests on a sheer illusion, and that causality
through freedom is at least *not incompatible with* nature. . . .

Chapter 3
The Ideal of Pure Reason

Section 3
The Arguments of Speculative Reason in Proof of the Existence of a Supreme Being

There are only three possible ways of proving the existence   {A 590
of God by means of speculative reason   {B 618

All the paths leading to this goal begin either from determinate experience and the
specific constitution of the world of sense as thereby known, and ascend from it, in
accordance with laws of causality, to the supreme cause outside the world; or they start
from experience which is purely indeterminate, that is, from experience of existence
in general; or finally they abstract from all experience, and argue completely *a priori*,
from mere concepts, to the existence of a supreme cause. The first proof is the *physico-*   {A 591
theological, the second the *cosmological*, the third the *ontological*. There are, and there   {B 619
can be, no others.

I propose to show that reason is as little able to make progress on the one path, the
empirical, as on the other path, the transcendental, and that it stretches its wings in
vain in thus attempting to soar above the world of sense by the mere power of speculation. As regards the order in which these arguments should be dealt with, it will be
exactly the reverse of that which reason takes in the progress of its own development,
and therefore of that which we have ourselves followed in the above account. For it
will be shown that, although experience is what first gives occasion to this enquiry, it
is the *transcendental concept* which in all such endeavours marks out the goal that reason has set itself to attain, and which is indeed its sole guide in its efforts to achieve
that goal. I shall therefore begin with the examination of the transcendental proof,
and afterwards enquire what effect the addition of the empirical factor can have in
enhancing the force of the argument.

Section 4
The Impossibility of an Ontological Proof of the Existence of God

It is evident, from what has been said, that the concept of an absolutely necessary   {A 592
being is a concept of pure reason, that is, a mere idea the objective reality of which   {B 620

is very far from being proved by the fact that reason requires it. For the idea instructs us only in regard to a certain unattainable completeness, and so serves rather to limit the understanding than to extend it to new objects. But we are here faced by what is indeed strange and perplexing, namely, that while the inference from a given existence in general to some absolutely necessary being seems to be both imperative and legitimate, all those conditions under which alone the understanding can form a concept of such a necessity are so many obstacles in the way of our doing so. . . .

All the alleged examples are, without exception, taken from *judgments*, not from *things* and their existence. But the unconditioned necessity of judgments is not the same as an absolute necessity of things. The absolute necessity of the judgment is only a conditioned necessity of the thing, or of the predicate in the judgment. The [geometric] proposition does not declare that three angles are absolutely necessary, but that, under the condition that there is a triangle (that is, that a triangle is given), three angles will necessarily be found in it. So great, indeed, is the deluding influence exercised by this logical necessity that, by the simple device of forming an *a priori* concept of a thing in such a manner as to include existence within the scope of its meaning, we have supposed ourselves to have justified the conclusion that because existence necessarily belongs to the object of this concept—always under the condition that we posit the thing as given (as existing)—we are also of necessity, in accordance with the law of identity, required to posit the existence of its object, and that this being is therefore itself absolutely necessary—and this, to repeat, for the reason that the existence of this being has already been thought in a concept which is assumed arbitrarily and on condition that we posit its object.

If, in an identical proposition, I reject the predicate while retaining the subject, contradiction results; and I therefore say that the former belongs necessarily to the latter. But if we reject subject and predicate alike, there is no contradiction; for nothing is then left that can be contradicted. To posit a triangle, and yet to reject its three angles, is self-contradictory; but there is no contradiction in rejecting the triangle together with its three angles. The same holds true of the concept of an absolutely necessary being. If its existence is rejected, we reject the thing itself with all its predicates; and no question of contradiction can then arise. There is nothing outside it that would then be contradicted, since the necessity of the thing is not supposed to be derived from anything external; nor is there anything internal that would be contradicted, since in rejecting the thing itself we have at the same time rejected all its internal properties. "God is omnipotent" is a necessary judgment. The omnipotence cannot be rejected if we posit a Deity, that is, an infinite being; for the two concepts are identical. But if we say, "There is no God," neither the omnipotence nor any other of its predicates is given; they are one and all rejected together with the subject, and there is therefore not the least contradiction in such a judgment.

We have thus seen that if the predicate of a judgment is rejected together with the subject, no internal contradiction can result, and that this holds no matter what the predicate may be. The only way of evading this conclusion is to argue that there are subjects which cannot be removed, and must always remain. That, however, would only be another way of saying that there are absolutely necessary subjects; and that is the very assumption which I have called in question, and the possibility of which the above argument professes to establish. For I cannot form the least concept of a thing which, should it be rejected with all its predicates, leaves behind a contradiction; and in the absence of contradiction I have, through pure *a priori* concepts alone, no criterion of impossibility.

Notwithstanding all these general considerations, in which every one must concur, we may be challenged with a case which is brought forward as proof that in actual fact the contrary holds, namely, that there is one concept, and indeed only one, in reference to which the not-being or rejection of its object is in itself contradictory, namely, the concept of the *ens realissimum*. It is declared that it possesses all reality, and that we are justified in assuming that such a being is possible (the fact that a concept does not contradict itself by no means proves the possibility of its object: but the contrary assertion I am for the moment willing to allow). Now [the argument proceeds] "all reality" includes existence; existence is therefore contained in the concept of a thing that is possible. If, then, this thing is rejected, the internal possibility of the thing is rejected—which is self-contradictory.

{A 597
{B 625

My answer is as follows. There is already a contradiction in introducing the concept of existence—no matter under what title it may be disguised—into the concept of a thing which we profess to be thinking solely in reference to its possibility. If that be allowed as legitimate, a seeming victory has been won; but in actual fact nothing at all is said: the assertion is a mere tautology. We must ask: Is the proposition that *this or that thing* (which, whatever it may be, is allowed as possible) *exists*, an analytic or a synthetic proposition? If it is analytic, the assertion of the existence of the thing adds nothing to the thought of the thing; but in that case either the thought, which is in us, is the thing itself, or we have pre-supposed an existence as belonging to the realm of the possible, and have then, on that pretext, inferred its existence from its internal possibility—which is nothing but a miserable tautology. . . . But if, on the other hand, we admit, as every reasonable person must, that all existential propositions are synthetic, how can we profess to maintain that the predicate of existence cannot be rejected without contradiction? This is a feature which is found only in analytic propositions, and is indeed precisely what constitutes their analytic character.

{A 598
{B 626

I should have hoped to put an end to these idle and fruitless disputations in a direct manner, by an accurate determination of the concept of existence, had I not found that the illusion which is caused by the confusion of a logical with a real predicate (that is, with a predicate which determines a thing) is almost beyond correction. Anything we please can be made to serve as a logical predicate; the subject can even be predicated of itself; for logic abstracts from all content. But a *determining* predicate is a predicate which is added to the concept of the subject and enlarges it. Consequently, it must not be already contained in the concept.

"*Being*" is obviously not a real predicate; that is, it is not a concept of something which could be added to the concept of a thing. It is merely the positing of a thing, or of certain determinations, as existing in themselves. Logically, it is merely the copula of a judgment. The proposition, "God is omnipotent," contains two concepts, each of which has its object—God and omnipotence. The small word "is" adds no new predicate, but only serves to posit the predicate *in its relation* to the subject. If, now, we take the subject (God) with all its predicates (among which is omnipotence), and say "God is," or "There is a God," we attach no new predicate to the concept of God, but only posit the subject in itself with all its predicates, and indeed posit it as being an *object* that stands in relation to my *concept*. The content of both must be one and the same; nothing can have been added to the concept, which expresses merely what is

{A 599
{B 627

possible, by my thinking its object (through the expression "it is") as given absolutely. Otherwise stated, the real contains no more than the merely possible. A hundred real thalers do not contain the least coin more than a hundred possible thalers. For as the latter signify the concept, and the former the object and the positing of the object, should the former contain more than the latter, my concept would not, in that case, express the whole object, and would not therefore be an adequate concept of it. My financial position is, however, affected very differently by a hundred real thalers than it is by the mere concept of them (that is, of their possibility). For the object, as it actually exists, is not analytically contained in my concept, but is added to my concept (which is a determination of my state) synthetically; and yet the conceived hundred thalers are not themselves in the least increased through thus acquiring existence outside my concept.

A 600⎫
B 628⎭ By whatever and by however many predicates we may think a thing—even if we completely determine it—we do not make the least addition to the thing when we further declare that this thing *is*. Otherwise, it would not be exactly the same thing that exists, but something more than we had thought in the concept; and we could not, therefore, say that the exact object of my concept exists. . . .

A 602⎫
B 630⎭ The attempt to establish the existence of a supreme being by means of the famous ontological argument of Descartes is therefore merely so much labour and effort lost; we can no more extend our stock of [theoretical] insight by mere ideas, than a merchant can better his position by adding a few noughts to his cash account.

Section 5
The Impossibility of a Cosmological Proof of the Existence of God

A 604⎫
B 632⎭ . . . The *cosmological proof*, which we are now about to examine, retains the connection of absolute necessity with the highest reality, but instead of reasoning, like the former proof, from the highest reality to necessity of existence, it reasons from the previously given unconditioned necessity of some being to the unlimited reality of that being. It thus enters upon a course of reasoning which, whether rational or only pseudorational, is at any rate natural, and the most convincing not only for common sense but even for speculative understanding. . . . This proof, termed by Leibniz the proof *a contingentia mundi*, we shall now proceed to expound and examine.

It runs thus: If anything exists, an absolutely necessary being must also exist. Now I, at least, exist. Therefore an absolutely necessary being exists. The minor premiss
A 605⎫
B 633⎭ contains an experience, the major premiss the inference from there being any experience at all to the existence of the necessary. The proof therefore really begins with experience, and is not wholly *a priori* or ontological. . . . Since, in dealing with the objects of experience, the proof abstracts from all special properties through which this world may differ from any other possible world, the title also serves to distinguish it from the physico-theological proof, which is based upon observations of the particular properties of the world disclosed to us by our senses.

The proof then proceeds as follows: The necessary being can be determined in one way only, that is, by one out of each possible pair of opposed predicates. It must therefore be *completely* determined through its own concept. Now there is only one
A 606⎫
B 634⎭ possible concept which determines a thing completely *a priori*, namely, the concept of the *ens realissimum*. The concept of the *ens realissimum* is therefore the only concept

through which a necessary being can be thought. In other words, a supreme being necessarily exists.

In this cosmological argument there are combined so many pseudo-rational principles that speculative reason seems in this case to have brought to bear all the resources of its dialectical skill to produce the greatest possible transcendental illusion.... In order to lay a secure foundation for itself, this proof takes its stand on experience, and thereby makes profession of being distinct from the ontological proof, which puts its entire trust in pure *a priori* concepts. But the cosmological proof uses this experience only for a single step in the argument, namely, to conclude the existence of a necessary being. What properties this being may have, the empirical premiss cannot tell us. Reason therefore abandons experience altogether, and endeavours to discover from mere concepts what properties an absolutely necessary being must have, that is, which among all possible things contains in itself the conditions (*requisita*) essential to absolute necessity. Now these, it is supposed, are nowhere to be found save in the concept of an *ens realissimum*; and the conclusion is therefore drawn, that the *ens realissimum* is the absolutely necessary being. But it is evident that we are here presupposing that the concept of the highest reality is completely adequate to the concept of absolute necessity of existence; that is, that the latter can be inferred from the former. Now this is the proposition maintained by the ontological proof; it is here being assumed in the cosmological proof, and indeed made the basis of the proof; and yet it is an assumption with which this latter proof has professed to dispense.... Thus the so-called cosmological proof really owes any cogency which it may have to the ontological proof from mere concepts....

{ A 607
  B 635

I have stated that in this cosmological argument there lies hidden a whole nest of dialectical assumptions, which the transcendental critique can easily detect and destroy. These deceptive principles I shall merely enumerate, leaving to the reader, who by this time will be sufficiently expert in these matters, the task of investigating them further, and of refuting them.

{ A 609
  B 637

We find, for instance, (1) the transcendental principle whereby from the contingent we infer a cause. This principle is applicable only in the sensible world; outside that world it has no meaning whatsoever. For the mere intellectual concept of the contingent cannot give rise to any synthetic proposition, such as that of causality. The principle of causality has no meaning and no criterion for its application save only in the sensible world. But in the cosmological proof it is precisely in order to enable us to advance beyond the sensible world that it is employed. (2) The inference to a first cause, from the impossibility of an infinite series of causes, given one after the other, in the sensible world. The principles of the employment of reason do not justify this conclusion even within the world of experience, still less beyond this world in a realm into which this series can never be extended. (3) The unjustified self-satisfaction of reason in respect of the completion of this series. The removal of all the conditions without which no concept of necessity is possible is taken by reason to be a completion of the concept of the series, on the ground that we can then conceive nothing further. (4) The confusion between the logical possibility of a concept of all reality united into one (without inner contradiction) and the transcendental possibility of such a reality. In the case of the latter there is needed a principle to establish the practicability of such a synthesis, a principle which itself, however, can apply only to the field of possible experiences—etc....

{ A 610
  B 638

Section 6
The Impossibility of the Physico-theological Proof

If, then, neither the concept of things in general nor the experience of any *existence in general* can supply what is required, it remains only to try whether a *determinate experience*, the experience of the things of the present world, and the constitution and order of these, does not provide the basis of a proof which may help us to attain to an assured conviction of a supreme being. Such proof we propose to entitle the *physico-theological*. Should this attempt also fail, it must follow that no satisfactory proof of the existence of a being corresponding to our transcendental idea can be possible by pure speculative reason. . . .

The chief points of the physico-theological proof are as follows: (1) In the world we everywhere find clear signs of an order in accordance with a determinate purpose, carried out with great wisdom; and this in a universe which is indescribably varied in content and unlimited in extent. (2) This purposive order is quite alien to the things of the world, and only belongs to them contingently; that is to say, the diverse things could not of themselves have co-operated, by so great a combination of diverse means, to the fulfilment of determinate final purposes, had they not been chosen and designed for these purposes by an ordering rational principle in conformity with underlying ideas. (3) There exists, therefore, a sublime and wise cause (or more than one), which must be the cause of the world not merely as a blindly working all-powerful nature, by *fecundity*, but as intelligence, through *freedom*. (4) The unity of this cause may be inferred from the unity of the reciprocal relations existing between the parts of the world, as members of an artfully arranged structure—inferred with certainty in so far as our observation suffices for its verification, and beyond these limits with probability, in accordance with the principles of analogy.

We need not here criticise natural reason too strictly in regard to its conclusion from the analogy between certain natural products and what our human art produces when we do violence to nature, and constrain it to proceed not according to its own ends but in conformity with ours—appealing to the similarity of these particular natural products with houses, ships, watches. Nor need we here question its conclusion that there lies at the basis of nature a causality similar to that responsible for artificial products, namely, an understanding and a will; and that the inner possibility of a self-acting nature (which is what makes all art, and even, it may be, reason itself, possible) is therefore derived from another, though superhuman, art—a mode of reasoning which could not perhaps withstand a searching transcendental criticism. But at any rate we must admit that, if we are to specify a cause at all, we cannot here proceed more securely than by analogy with those purposive productions of which alone the cause and mode of action are fully known to us. Reason could never be justified in abandoning the causality which it knows for grounds of explanation which are obscure, of which it does not have any knowledge, and which are incapable of proof.

On this method of argument, the purposiveness and harmonious adaptation of so much in nature can suffice to prove the contingency of the form merely, not of the matter, that is, not of the substance in the world. To prove the latter we should have to demonstrate that the things in the world would not of themselves be capable of such order and harmony, in accordance with universal laws, if they were not *in their substance* the product of supreme wisdom. But to prove this we should require quite other grounds of proof than those which are derived from the analogy with human art. The utmost, therefore, that the argument can prove is an *architect* of the world who is always very much hampered by the adaptability of the material in which he works, not a *creator* of the world to whose idea everything is subject. This, however, is altogether inadequate to the lofty purpose which we have before our eyes, namely, the proof of an all-sufficient primordial being. To prove the contingency of matter itself, we should have to resort to a transcendental argument, and this is precisely what we have here set out to avoid.

The inference, therefore, is that the order and purposiveness everywhere observable throughout the world may be regarded as a completely contingent arrangement, and that we may argue to the existence of a cause *proportioned* to it. But the concept of this cause must enable us to know something quite *determinate* about it, and can therefore be no other than the concept of a being who possesses all might, wisdom, etc., in a word, all the perfection which is proper to an all-sufficient being. For the predicates— "very great," "astounding," "immeasurable" in power and excellence—give no determinate concept at all, and do not really tell us what the thing is in itself. They are only relative representations of the magnitude of the object, which the observer, in contemplating the world, compares with himself and with his capacity of comprehension, and which are equally terms of eulogy whether we be magnifying the object or be depreciating the observing subject in relation to that object. Where we are concerned with the magnitude (of the perfection) of a thing, there is no determinate concept except that which comprehends all possible perfection; and in that concept only the allness (*omnitudo*) of the reality is completely determined.

{A 628
{B 656

Now no one, I trust, will be so bold as to profess that he comprehends the relation of the magnitude of the world as he has observed it (alike as regards both extent and content) to omnipotence, of the world order to supreme wisdom, of the world unity to the absolute unity of its Author, etc. Physico-theology is therefore unable to give any determinate concept of the supreme cause of the world, and cannot therefore serve as the foundation of a theology which is itself in turn to form the basis of religion.

To advance to absolute totality by the empirical road is utterly impossible. None the less this is what is attempted in the physico-theological proof. . . .

Groundwork of the Metaphysic of Morals

Preface

387 Ancient Greek philosophy was divided into three sciences: *physics, ethics,* and *logic.* This division fits the nature of the subject perfectly, and there is no need to improve on it—except perhaps by adding the principle on which it is based. By so doing we may be able on the one hand to guarantee its completeness and on the other to determine correctly its necessary subdivisions.

All rational knowledge is either *material* and concerned with some object, or *formal* and concerned solely with the form of understanding and reason themselves—with the universal rules of thinking as such without regard to differences in its objects. Formal philosophy is called *logic;* while material philosophy, which has to do with determinate objects and with the laws to which they are subject, is in turn divided into two, since the laws in question are laws either of *nature* or of *freedom.* The science of the first is called *physics,* that of the second *ethics.* The former is also called natural philosophy, the latter moral philosophy.

Logic can have no empirical part—that is, no part in which the universal and necessary laws of thinking are based on grounds taken from experience.... As against this, both natural and moral philosophy can each have an empirical part, since the former has to formulate its laws for nature as an object of experience, and the latter for the will of man so far as affected by nature—the first set of laws being those in accor-

388 dance with which everything happens, the second being those in accordance with which everything ought to happen, although they also take into account the conditions under which what ought to happen very often does not happen.

All philosophy so far as it rests on the basis of experience can be called *empirical* philosophy. If it sets forth its doctrines as depending entirely on *a priori* principles, it can be called *pure* philosophy. The latter when wholly formal is called *logic;* but if it is confined to determinate objects of the understanding, it is then called *metaphysics.*

In this way there arises the Idea of a two-fold metaphysic—*a metaphysic of nature* and *a metaphysic of morals.* Thus physics will have its empirical part, but it will also have a rational one; and likewise ethics—although here the empirical part might be called specifically *practical anthropology,* while the rational part might properly be called *morals.*

All industries, arts, and crafts have gained by the division of labour.... Where tasks are not so distinguished and divided,...there industry is still sunk in utter barbarism.... Here, however, I confine myself to asking whether the nature of science does not always require that the empirical part should be scrupulously separated from the rational one, and that (empirical) physics proper should be prefaced by a metaphysic of nature, while practical anthropology should be prefaced by a metaphysic of morals—each metaphysic having to be scrupulously cleansed of every-

389 thing empirical if we are to know how much pure reason can accomplish in both cases and from what sources it can by itself draw its own *a priori* teaching....

From Immanuel Kant, *Groundwork of the Metaphysic of Morals,* trans. H.J. Paton (New York: Harper & Row, 1964), pp. 55–130. Reprinted with permission from Unwin Hyman Ltd.

Since my aim here is directed strictly to moral philosophy, I limit my proposed question to this point only—Do we not think it a matter of the utmost necessity to work out for once a pure moral philosophy completely cleansed of everything that can only be empirical and appropriate to anthropology? That there must be such a philosophy is already obvious from the common Idea of duty and from the laws of morality. Every one must admit that a law has to carry with it absolute necessity if it is to be valid morally—valid, that is, as a ground of obligation; that the command "Thou shalt not lie" could not hold merely for men, other rational beings having no obligation to abide by it—and similarly with all other genuine moral laws; that here consequently the ground of obligation must be looked for, not in the nature of man nor in the circumstances of the world in which he is placed, but solely a priori in the concepts of pure reason; and that every other precept based on principles of mere experience—and even a precept that may in a certain sense be considered universal, so far as it rests in its slightest part, perhaps only in its motive, on empirical grounds—can indeed be called a practical rule, but never a moral law.

Thus in practical knowledge as a whole, not only are moral laws, together with their principles, essentially different from all the rest in which there is some empirical element, but the whole of moral philosophy is based entirely on the part of it that is pure. When applied to man it does not borrow in the slightest from acquaintance with him (in anthropology), but gives him laws a priori as a rational being. These laws admittedly require in addition a power of judgement sharpened by experience, partly in order to distinguish the cases to which they apply, partly to procure for them admittance to the will of man and influence over practice; for man, affected as he is by so many inclinations, is capable of the Idea of a pure practical reason, but he has not so easily the power to realize the Idea in concreto in his conduct of life.

A metaphysic of morals is thus indispensably necessary, not merely in order to investigate, from motives of speculation, the source of practical principles which are present a priori in our reason, but because morals themselves remain exposed to corruption of all sorts as long as this guiding thread is lacking, this ultimate norm for correct moral judgement. For if any action is to be morally good, it is not enough that it should conform to the moral law—it must also be done for the sake of the moral law: where this is not so, the conformity is only too contingent and precarious, since the non-moral ground at work will now and then produce actions which accord with the law, but very often actions which transgress it. Now the moral law in its purity and genuineness (and in the field of action it is precisely this that matters most) is to be looked for nowhere else than in a pure philosophy. Hence pure philosophy (that is, metaphysics) must come first, and without it there can be no moral philosophy at all. . . . 390

Intending, as I do, to publish some day a metaphysic of morals, I issue this Ground-work in advance. For such a metaphysic there is strictly no other foundation than a critique of pure practical reason, just as for metaphysics there is no other foundation than the critique of pure speculative reason which I have already published. . . . 391

The sole aim of the present Groundwork is to seek out and establish the supreme principle of morality. . . . 392

The method I have adopted in this book is, I believe, one which will work best if we proceed analytically from common knowledge to the formulation of its supreme principle and then back again synthetically from an examination of this principle and its origins to the common knowledge in which we find its application. Hence the division turns out to be as follows:—

Chapter 1

Passage from Ordinary Rational Knowledge of Morality to Philosophical

393   It is impossible to conceive anything at all in the world, or even out of it, which can be taken as good without qualification, except a *good will.* Intelligence, wit, judgement, and any other talents of the mind we may care to name, or courage, resolution, and constancy of purpose, as qualities of *temperament,* are without doubt good and desirable in many respects; but they can also be extremely bad and hurtful when the will is not good which has to make use of these gifts of nature, and which for this reason has the term "*character*" applied to its peculiar quality. It is exactly the same with *gifts of fortune.* Power, wealth, honour, even health and that complete well-being and contentment with one's state which goes by the name of "*happiness*," produce boldness, and as a consequence often over-boldness as well, unless a good will is present by which their influence on the mind—and so too the whole principle of action—may be corrected and adjusted to universal ends; not to mention that a rational and impartial spectator can never feel approval in contemplating the uninterrupted prosperity of a being graced by no touch of a pure and good will, and that consequently a good will seems to constitute the indispensable condition of our very worthiness to be happy.

394   Some qualities are even helpful to this good will itself and can make its task very much easier. They have none the less no inner unconditioned worth, but rather presuppose a good will which sets a limit to the esteem in which they are rightly held and does not permit us to regard them as absolutely good. Moderation in affections and passions, self-control, and sober reflexion are not only good in many respects: they may even seem to constitute part of the *inner* worth of a person. Yet they are far from being properly described as good without qualification (however unconditionally they have been commended by the ancients). For without the principles of a good will they may become exceedingly bad; and the very coolness of a scoundrel makes him, not merely more dangerous, but also immediately more abominable in our eyes than we should have taken him to be without it.

A good will is not good because of what it effects or accomplishes—because of its fitness for attaining some proposed end: it is good through its willing alone—that is, good in itself. Considered in itself it is to be esteemed beyond comparison as far higher than anything it could ever bring about merely in order to favour some inclination or, if you like, the sum total of inclinations. Even if, by some special disfavour of destiny or by the niggardly endowment of step-motherly nature, this will is entirely lacking in power to carry out its intentions; if by its utmost effort it still accomplishes nothing, and only good will is left (not, admittedly, as a mere wish, but as the straining of every means so far as they are in our control); even then it would still shine like a jewel for its own sake as something which has its full value in itself. Its usefulness or fruitlessness can neither add to, nor subtract from, this value. . . .

In the natural constitution of an organic being—that is, of one contrived for the purpose of life—let us take it as a principle that in it no organ is to be found for any end unless it is also the most appropriate to that end and the best fitted for it. Suppose now that for a being possessed of reason and a will the real purpose of nature were his *preservation*, his *welfare*, or in a word his *happiness*. In that case nature would have hit on a very bad arrangement by choosing reason in the creature to carry out this purpose. For all the actions he has to perform with this end in view, and the whole rule of his behaviour, would have been mapped out for him far more accurately by instinct; and the end in question could have been maintained far more surely by instinct than it ever can be by reason. If reason should have been imparted to this favoured creature as well, it would have had to serve him only for contemplating the happy disposition of his nature, for admiring it, for enjoying it, and for being grateful to its beneficent Cause—not for subjecting his power of appetition to such feeble and defective guidance or for meddling incompetently with the purposes of nature. In a word, nature would have prevented reason from striking out into a *practical use* and from presuming, with its feeble vision, to think out for itself a plan for happiness and for the means to its attainment. Nature would herself have taken over the choice, not only of ends, but also of means, and would with wise precaution have entrusted both to instinct alone. . . .

395

For since reason is not sufficiently serviceable for guiding the will safely as regards its objects and the satisfaction of all our needs (which it in part even multiplies)—a purpose for which an implanted natural instinct would have led us much more surely; and since none the less reason has been imparted to us as a practical power—that is, as one which is to have influence on the *will*; its true function must be to produce a *will* which is *good*, not as a *means* to some further end, but *in itself*; and for this function reason was absolutely necessary in a world where nature, in distributing her aptitudes, has everywhere else gone to work in a purposive manner. Such a will need not on this account be the sole and complete good, but it must be the highest good and the condition of all the rest, even of all our demands for happiness. In that case we can easily reconcile with the wisdom of nature our observation that the cultivation of reason which is required for the first and unconditioned purpose may in many ways, at least in this life, restrict the attainment of the second purpose—namely, happiness—which is always conditioned; and indeed that it can even reduce happiness to less than zero without nature proceeding contrary to its purpose; for reason, which recognizes as its highest practical function the establishment of a good will, in attaining this end is capable only of its own peculiar kind of contentment—contentment in fulfilling a purpose which in turn is determined by reason alone, even if this fulfilment should often involve interference with the purposes of inclination.

396

We have now to elucidate the concept of a will estimable in itself and good apart from any further end. This concept, which is already present in a sound natural understanding and requires not so much to be taught as merely to be clarified, always holds the highest place in estimating the total worth of our actions and constitutes the condition of all the rest. We will therefore take up the concept of *duty*, which includes that of a good will, exposed, however, to certain subjective limitations and obstacles. These, so far from hiding a good will or disguising it, rather bring it out by contrast and make it shine forth more brightly.

397

I will here pass over all actions already recognized as contrary to duty, however useful they may be with a view to this or that end; for about these the question does not even arise whether they could have been done *for the sake of duty* inasmuch as they are directly opposed to it. . . . This distinction is far more difficult to perceive when the action accords with duty and the subject has in addition an *immediate* inclination to the action. . . .

To preserve one's life is a duty, and besides this every one has also an immediate inclination to do so. But on account of this the often anxious precautions taken by the greater part of mankind for this purpose have no inner worth, and the maxim of their action is without moral content. They do protect their lives *in conformity with duty*, but not *from the motive of duty*. When on the contrary, disappointments and hopeless misery have quite taken away the taste for life; when a wretched man, strong in soul and more angered at his fate than faint-hearted or cast down, longs for death and still preserves his life without loving it—not from inclination or fear but from duty; then indeed his maxim has a moral content.

To help others where one can is a duty, and besides this there are many spirits of so sympathetic a temper that, without any further motive of vanity or self-interest, they find an inner pleasure in spreading happiness around them and can take delight in the contentment of others as their own work. Yet I maintain that in such a case an action of this kind, however right and however amiable it may be, has still no genuinely moral worth. It stands on the same footing as other inclinations. . . . Suppose then that the mind of this friend of man were overclouded by sorrows of his own which extinguished all sympathy with the fate of others, but that he still had power to help those in distress, though no longer stirred by the need of others because sufficiently occupied with his own; and suppose that, when no longer moved by any inclination, he tears himself out of this deadly insensibility and does the action without any inclination for the sake of duty alone; then for the first time his action has its genuine moral worth. Still further: if nature had implanted little sympathy in this or that man's heart; if (being in other respects an honest fellow) he were cold in temperament and indifferent to the sufferings of others—perhaps because, being endowed with the special gift of patience and robust endurance in his own sufferings, he assumed the like in others or even demanded it; if such a man (who would in truth not be the worst product of nature) were not exactly fashioned by her to be a philanthropist, would he not still find in himself a source from which he might draw a worth far higher than any that a good-natured temperament can have? Assuredly he would. It is precisely in this that the worth of character begins to show—a moral worth and beyond all comparison the highest—namely, that he does good, not from inclination, but from duty. . . .

Our second proposition is this: An action done from duty has its moral worth, *not in the purpose* to be attained by it, but in the maxim in accordance with which it is decided upon; it depends therefore, not on the realization of the object of the action, but solely on the *principle* of *volition* in accordance with which, irrespective of all objects of the faculty of desire, the action has been performed. That the purposes we may have in our actions, and also their effects considered as ends and motives of the will, can give to actions no unconditioned and moral worth is clear from what has gone before. Where then can this worth be found if we are not to find it in the will's relation to the effect hoped for from the action? It can be found nowhere but in the *principle of the will*, irrespective of the ends which can be brought about by such an action; for between its *a priori* principle, which is formal, and its *a posteriori* motive, which is material, the will stands, so to speak, at a parting of the ways; and since it

398

399

400

must be determined by some principle, it will have to be determined by the formal principle of volition when an action is done from duty, where, as we have seen, every material principle is taken away from it.

Our third proposition, as an inference from the two preceding, I would express thus: *Duty is the necessity to act out of reverence for the law.* For an object as the effect of my proposed action I can have an *inclination*, but *never reverence*, precisely because it is merely the effect, and not the activity, of a will. Similarly for inclination as such, whether my own or that of another, I cannot have reverence: I can at most in the first case approve, and in the second case sometimes even love—that is, regard it as favourable to my own advantage. Only something which is conjoined with my will solely as a ground and never as an effect—something which does not serve my inclination, but outweighs it or at least leaves it entirely out of account in my choice—and therefore only bare law for its own sake, can be an object of reverence and therewith a command. Now an action done from duty has to set aside altogether the influence of inclination, and along with inclination every object of the will; so there is nothing left able to determine the will except objectively the *law* and subjectively *pure reverence* for this practical law, and therefore the maxim[1] of obeying this law even to the detriment of all my inclinations.   401

Thus the moral worth of an action does not depend on the result expected from it, and so too does not depend on any principle of action that needs to borrow its motive from this expected result. For all these results (agreeable states and even the promotion of happiness in others) could have been brought about by other causes as well, and consequently their production did not require the will of a rational being, in which, however, the highest and unconditioned good can alone be found. Therefore nothing but the *idea of the law* in itself, *which admittedly is present only in a rational being*—so far as it, and not an expected result, is the ground determining the will—can constitute that pre-eminent good which we call moral, a good which is already present in the person acting on this idea and has not to be awaited merely from the result.[2]

---

1. A *maxim* is the subjective principle of a volition: an objective principle (that is, one which would also serve subjectively as a practical principle for all rational beings if reason had full control over the faculty of desire) is a practical *law*. [All notes in the selection are Kant's.]

2. It might be urged against me that I have merely tried, under cover of the word "*reverence*," to take refuge in an obscure feeling instead of giving a clearly articulated answer to the question by means of a concept of reason. Yet although reverence is a feeling, it is not a feeling *received* through outside influence, but one *self-produced* by a rational concept, and therefore specifically distinct from feelings of the first kind, all of which can be reduced to inclination or fear. What I recognize immediately as law for me, I recognize with reverence, which means merely consciousness of the *subordination* of my will to a law without the mediation of external influences on my senses. Immediate determination of the will by the law and consciousness of this determination is called "*reverence*," so that reverence is regarded as the *effect* of the law on the subject and not as the *cause* of the law. Reverence is properly awareness of a value which demolishes my self-love. Hence there is something which is regarded neither as an object of inclination nor as an object of fear, though it has at the same time some analogy with both. The *object* of reverence is the *law* alone—that law which we impose *on ourselves* but yet as necessary in itself. Considered as a law, we are subject to it without any consultation of self-love; considered as self-imposed it is a consequence of our will. In the first respect it is analogous to fear, in the second to inclination. All reverence for a person is properly only reverence for the law (of honesty and so on) of which that person gives us an example. Because we regard the development of our talents as a duty, we see too in a man of talent a sort of *example of the law* (the law of becoming like him by practice), and this is what constitutes our reverence for him. All moral *interest*, so-called, consists solely in *reverence* for the law.

402   But what kind of law can this be the thought of which, even without regard to the
results expected from it, has to determine the will if this is to be called good absolutely
and without qualification? Since I have robbed the will of every inducement that
might arise for it as a consequence of obeying any particular law, nothing is left but the
conformity of actions to universal law as such, and this alone must serve the will as
its principle. That is to say, I ought never to act except in such a way *that I can also will
that my maxim should become a universal law.* Here bare conformity to universal law as
such (without having as its base any law prescribing particular actions) is what serves
the will as its principle, and must so serve it if duty is not to be everywhere an empty
delusion and a chimerical concept. The ordinary reason of mankind also agrees with
this completely in its practical judgments and always has the aforesaid principle before
its eyes.

       Take this question, for example. May I not, when I am hard pressed, make a promise
with the intention of not keeping it? Here I readily distinguish the two senses which
the question can have—Is it prudent, or is it right, to make a false promise? The first
no doubt can often be the case. I do indeed see that it is not enough for me to extricate
myself from present embarrassment by this subterfuge: I have to consider whether from
this lie there may not subsequently accrue to me much greater inconvenience than
that from which I now escape. . . . To tell the truth for the sake of duty is something
entirely different from doing so out of concern for inconvenient results; for in the first
case the concept of the action already contains in itself a law for me, while in the
second case I have first of all to look around elsewhere in order to see what effects may
403   be bound up with it for me. When I deviate from the principle of duty, this is quite
certainly bad; but if I desert my prudential maxim, this can often be greatly to my
advantage, though it is admittedly safer to stick to it. Suppose I seek, however, to learn
in the quickest way and yet unerringly how to solve the problem "Does a lying promise
accord with duty?" I have then to ask myself "Should I really be content that my maxim
(the maxim of getting out of a difficulty by a false promise) should hold as a universal
law (one valid both for myself and others)? And could I really say to myself that every
one may make a false promise if he finds himself in a difficulty from which he can
extricate himself in no other way?" I then become aware at once that I can indeed will
to lie, but I can by no means will a universal law of lying; for by such a law there could
properly be no promises at all, since it would be futile to profess a will for future action
to others who would not believe my profession or who, if they did so over-hastily, would
pay me back in like coin, and consequently my maxim, as soon as it was made a universal law, would be bound to annul itself.

       Thus I need no far-reaching ingenuity to find out what I have to do in order to pos-
sess a good will. Inexperienced in the course of world affairs and incapable of being
prepared for all the chances that happen in it, I ask myself only "Can you also will that
your maxim should become a universal law?" Where you cannot, it is to be rejected,
and that not because of a prospective loss to you or even to others, but because it cannot fit as a principle into a possible enactment of universal law. For such an enactment
reason compels my immediate reverence, into whose grounds (which the philosopher
may investigate) I have as yet no *insight*, although I do at least understand this much:
reverence is the assessment of a worth which far outweighs all the worth of what is
commended by inclination, and the necessity for me to act out of *pure* reverence for
the practical law is what constitutes duty, to which every other motive must give way
because it is the condition of a will good *in itself*, whose value is above all else.

In studying the moral knowledge of ordinary human reason we have now arrived at its first principle. This principle it admittedly does not conceive thus abstractly in its universal form; but it does always have it actually before its eyes and does use it as a norm of judgement. It would be easy to show here how human reason, with this com-   404
pass in hand, is well able to distinguish, in all cases that present themselves, what is good or evil, right or wrong—provided that, without the least attempt to teach it any-thing new, we merely make reason attend, as Socrates did, to its own principle; and how in consequence there is no need of science or philosophy for knowing what man has to do in order to be honest and good, and indeed to be wise and virtuous. It might even be surmised in advance that acquaintance with what every man is obliged to do, and so also to know, will be the affair of every man, even the most ordinary. . . .

Man feels in himself a powerful counterweight to all the commands of duty   405
presented to him by reason as so worthy of esteem—the counterweight of his needs and inclinations, whose total satisfaction he grasps under the name of "happiness." But reason, without promising anything to inclination, enjoins its commands relentlessly, and therefore, so to speak, with disregard and neglect of these turbulent and seemingly equitable claims (which refuse to be suppressed by any command). . . .

In this way the *common reason of mankind* is impelled, not by any need for specula-tion (which never assails it so long as it is content to be mere sound reason), but on practical grounds themselves, to leave its own sphere and take a step into the field of *practical philosophy*. It there seeks to acquire information and precise instruction about the source of its own principle, and about the correct function of this principle in com-parison with maxims based on need and inclination, in order that it may escape from the embarrassment of antagonistic claims and may avoid the risk of losing all genuine moral principles because of the ambiguity into which it easily falls. Thus ordinary reason, when cultivated in its practical use, gives rise insensibly to a *dialectic* which constrains it to seek help in philosophy, just as happens in its theoretical use; and con-sequently in the first case as little as in the second will it anywhere else than in a full critique of our reason be able to find peace.

Chapter 2

Passage from Popular Moral Philosophy to a Metaphysic of Morals

If so far we have drawn our concept of duty from the ordinary use of our practical rea-   406
son, it must by no means be inferred that we have treated it as a concept of experience. On the contrary, when we pay attention to our experience of human conduct, we meet frequent and—as we ourselves admit—justified complaints that we can adduce no certain examples of the spirit which acts out of pure duty, and that, although much may be done *in accordance with* the commands of *duty*, it remains doubtful whether it really is done *for the sake of duty* and so has a moral value. Hence at all times there have been philosophers who have absolutely denied the presence of this spirit in human actions and have ascribed everything to a more or less refined self-love. . . .

In actual fact it is absolutely impossible for experience to establish with complete   407
certainty a single case in which the maxim of an action in other respects right has rested solely on moral grounds and on the thought of one's duty. . . .

Nothing can protect us against a complete falling away from our Ideas of duty, or can preserve in the soul a grounded reverence for its law, except the clear conviction
408   that even if there never have been actions springing from such pure sources, the question at issue here is not whether this or that has happened; that, on the contrary, reason by itself and independently of all appearances commands what ought to happen; that consequently actions of which the world has perhaps hitherto given no example—actions whose practicability might well be doubted by those who rest everything on experience—are nevertheless commanded unrelentingly by reason; and that, for instance, although up to now there may have existed no loyal friend, pure loyalty in friendship can be no less required from every man, inasmuch as this duty, prior to all experience, is contained as duty in general in the Idea of a reason which determines the will by *a priori* grounds.

It may be added that unless we wish to deny to the concept of morality all truth and all relation to a possible object, we cannot dispute that its law is of such widespread significance as to hold, not merely for men, but for all *rational beings as such*—not merely subject to contingent conditions and exceptions, but *with absolute necessity*. It is therefore clear that no experience can give us occasion to infer even the possibility of such apodeictic laws. For by what right can we make what is perhaps valid only under the contingent conditions of humanity into an object of unlimited reverence as a universal precept for every rational nature? And how could laws for determining *our* will be taken as laws for determining the will of a rational being as such—and only because of this for determining ours—if these laws were merely empirical and did not have their source completely *a priori* in pure, but practical, reason?...

409   If there can be no genuine supreme principle of morality which is not grounded on pure reason alone independently of all experience, it should be unnecessary, I think, even to raise the question whether it is a good thing to set forth in general (*in abstracto*) these concepts which hold *a priori*....

410   Nevertheless such a completely isolated metaphysic of morals, mixed with no anthropology, no theology, no physics or hyperphysics, still less with occult qualities (which might be called hypophysical), is not only an indispensable substratum of all theoretical and precisely defined knowledge of duties, but is at the same time a desideratum of the utmost importance for the actual execution of moral precepts. Unmixed with the alien element of added empirical inducements, the pure thought of duty, and in general of the moral law, has by way of reason alone (which first learns from this that by itself it is able to be practical as well as theoretical) an influence on
411   the human heart so much more powerful than all the further impulsions capable of being called up from the field of experience that in the consciousness of its own dignity reason despises these impulsions and is able gradually to become their master. In place of this, a mixed moral philosophy, compounded of impulsions from feeling and inclination, and at the same time of rational concepts, must make the mind waver between motives which can be brought under no single principle and which can guide us only by mere accident to the good, but very often also to the evil.

From these considerations the following conclusions emerge. All moral concepts have their seat and origin in reason completely *a priori*, and indeed in the most ordinary human reason just as much as in the most highly speculative: they cannot be abstracted from any empirical, and therefore merely contingent, knowledge. In this purity of their origin is to be found their very worthiness to serve as supreme practical principles, and everything empirical added to them is just so much taken away from their genuine influence and from the absolute value of the corresponding actions. It is not only a requirement of the utmost necessity in respect of theory, where our concern is solely with speculation, but is also of the utmost practical importance, to draw these concepts and laws from pure reason, to set them forth pure and unmixed, and indeed to determine the extent of this whole practical, but pure, rational knowledge —that is, to determine the whole power of pure practical reason. We ought never—as speculative philosophy does allow and even at times finds necessary—to make principles depend on the special nature of human reason. Since moral laws have to hold for every rational being as such, we ought rather to derive our principles from the general concept of a rational being as such, and on this basis to expound the whole of ethics— which requires anthropology for its *application* to man—at first independently as pure philosophy, that is, entirely as metaphysics (which we can very well do in this wholly abstract kind of knowledge). We know well that without possessing such a metaphysics it is a futile endeavour, I will not say to determine accurately for speculative judgement the moral element of duty in all that accords with duty—but that it is impossible, even in ordinary and practical usage, particularly in that of moral instruction, to base morals on their genuine principles and so to bring about pure moral dispositions and engraft them on men's minds for the highest good of the world. . . .

412

Everything in nature works in accordance with laws. Only a rational being has the power to act *in accordance with his idea* of laws—that is, in accordance with principles —and only so has he a *will*. Since *reason* is required in order to derive actions from laws, the will is nothing but practical reason. If reason infallibly determines the will, then in a being of this kind the actions which are recognized to be objectively necessary are also subjectively necessary—that is to say, the will is then a power to choose *only that* which reason independently of inclination recognizes to be practically necessary, that is, to be good. But if reason solely by itself is not sufficient to determine the will; if the will is exposed also to subjective conditions (certain impulsions) which do not always harmonize with the objective ones; if, in a word, the will is not *in itself* completely in accord with reason (as actually happens in the case of men); then actions which are recognized to be objectively necessary are subjectively contingent, and the determining of such a will in accordance with objective laws is *necessitation*. That is to say, the relation of objective laws to a will not good through and through is conceived as one in which the will of a rational being, although it is determined by principles of reason, does not necessarily follow these principles in virtue of its own nature.

413

The conception of an objective principle so far as this principle is necessitating for a will is called a command (of reason), and the formula of this command is called an *Imperative*.

All imperatives are expressed by an *"ought"* (*Sollen*). By this they mark the relation of an objective law of reason to a will which is not necessarily determined by this law in virtue of its subjective constitution (the relation of necessitation). They say that something would be good to do or to leave undone; only they say it to a will which does not always do a thing because it has been informed that this is a good thing to do. The practically *good* is that which determines the will by concepts of reason, and therefore not by subjective causes, but objectively—that is, on grounds valid for every rational being as such. It is distinguished from the *pleasant* as that which influences the will, not as a principle of reason valid for every one, but solely through the medium of sensation by purely subjective causes valid only for the senses of this person or that.[3]

414   A perfectly good will would thus stand quite as much under objective laws (laws of the good), but it could not on this account be conceived as *necessitated* to act in conformity with law, since of itself, in accordance with its subjective constitution, it can be determined only by the concept of the good. Hence for the *divine* will, and in general for a *holy* will, there are no imperatives: "*I ought*" is here out of place, because "*I will*" is already of itself necessarily in harmony with the law. Imperatives are in consequence only formulae for expressing the relation of objective laws of willing to the subjective imperfection of the will of this or that rational being—for example, of the human will.

All *imperatives* command either *hypothetically* or *categorically*. Hypothetical imperatives declare a possible action to be practically necessary as a means to the attainment of something else that one wills (or that one may will). A categorical imperative would be one which represented an action as objectively necessary in itself apart from its relation to a further end.

Every practical law represents a possible action as good and therefore as necessary for a subject whose actions are determined by reason. Hence all imperatives are formulae for determining an action which is necessary in accordance with the principle of a will in some sense good. If the action would be good solely as a means *to something else*, the imperative is *hypothetical*; if the action is represented as good in itself and therefore as necessary, in virtue of its principle, for a will which of itself accords with reason, then the imperative is *categorical*.

An imperative therefore tells me which of my possible actions would be good; and it formulates a practical rule for a will that does not perform an action straight away because the action is good—whether because the subject does not always know that it is good or because, even if he did know this, he might still act on maxims contrary to the objective principles of practical reason. . . .

415   Since in early youth we do not know what ends may present themselves to us in the course of life, parents seek above all to make their children learn things *of many kinds*; they provide carefully for *skill* in the use of means to all sorts of *arbitrary* ends, of none of which can they be certain that it could not in the future become an actual purpose of their ward, while it is always *possible* that he might adopt it. Their care in this matter is so great that they commonly neglect on this account to form and correct the judgement of their children about the worth of the things which they might possibly adopt as ends.

---

3. The dependence of the power of appetition on sensations is called an inclination, and thus an inclination always indicates a *need*. The dependence of a contingently determinable will on principles of reason is called an *interest*. Hence an interest is found only where there is a dependent will which in itself is not always in accord with reason: to a divine will we cannot ascribe any interest. But even the human will can *take an interest* in something without therefore *acting from interest*. The first expression signifies *practical* interest in the action; the second *pathological* interest in the object of the action. The first indicates only dependence of the will on principles of reason by itself; the second its dependence on principles of reason at the service of inclination—that is to say, where reason merely supplies a practical rule for meeting the need of inclination. In the first case what interests me is the action; in the second case what interests me is the object of the action (so far as this object is pleasant to me). We have seen in Chapter I that in an action done for the sake of duty we must have regard, not to interest in the object, but to interest in the action itself and in its rational principle (namely, the law).

There is, however, *one* end that can be presupposed as actual in all rational beings (so far as they are dependent beings to whom imperatives apply); and thus there is one purpose which they not only *can* have, but which we can assume with certainty that they all *do* have by a natural necessity—the purpose, namely, of *happiness*. A hypothetical imperative which affirms the practical necessity of an action as a means to the furtherance of happiness is *assertoric*. We may represent it, not simply as necessary to an uncertain, merely possible purpose, but as necessary to a purpose which we can presuppose *a priori* and with certainty to be present in every man because it belongs to his very being. Now skill in the choice of means to one's own greatest well-being can be called *prudence*[4] in the narrowest sense. Thus an imperative concerned with the choice of means to one's own happiness—that is, a precept of prudence—still remains *hypothetical*: an action is commanded, not absolutely, but only as a means to a further purpose.

Finally, there is an imperative which, without being based on, and conditioned by, any further purpose to be attained by a certain line of conduct, enjoins this conduct immediately. This imperative is *categorical*. It is concerned, not with the matter of the action and its presumed results, but with its form and with the principle from which it follows; and what is essentially good in the action consists in the mental disposition, let the consequences be what they may. This imperative may be called the imperative of *morality*. . . .

The question now arises "How are all these imperatives possible?" This question does not ask how we can conceive the execution of an action commanded by the imperative, but merely how we can conceive the necessitation of the will expressed by the imperative in setting us a task. How an imperative of skill is possible requires no special discussion. Who wills the end, wills (so far as reason has decisive influence on his actions) also the means which are indispensably necessary and in his power. So far as willing is concerned, this proposition is analytic: for in my willing of an object as an effect there is already conceived the causality of myself as an acting cause—that is, the use of means; and from the concept of willing an end the imperative merely extracts the concept of actions necessary to this end. (Synthetic propositions are required in order to determine the means to a proposed end, but these are concerned, not with the reason for performing the act of will, but with the cause which produces the object.) That in order to divide a line into two equal parts on a sure principle I must from its ends describe two intersecting arcs—this is admittedly taught by mathematics only in synthetic propositions; but when I know that the aforesaid effect can be produced only by such an action, the proposition "If I fully will the effect, I also will the action required for it" is analytic; for it is one and the same thing to conceive something as an effect possible in a certain way through me and to conceive myself as acting in the same way with respect to it.

If it were only as easy to find a determinate concept of happiness, the imperatives of prudence would agree entirely with those of skill and would be equally analytic. For

416

417

---

4. The word "prudence" (*Klugheit*) is used in a double sense: in one sense it can have the name of "worldly wisdom" (*Weltklugheit*); in a second sense that of "personal wisdom" (*Privatklugheit*). The first is the skill of a man in influencing others in order to use them for his own ends. The second is sagacity in combining all these ends to his own lasting advantage. The latter is properly that to which the value of the former can itself be traced; and of him who is prudent in the first sense, but not in the second, we might better say that he is clever and astute, but on the whole imprudent.

418 here as there it could alike be said "Who wills the end, wills also (necessarily, if he accords with reason) the sole means which are in his power." Unfortunately, however, the concept of happiness is so indeterminate a concept that although every man wants to attain happiness, he can never say definitely and in unison with himself what it really is that he wants and wills. The reason for this is that all the elements which belong to the concept of happiness are without exception empirical—that is, they must be borrowed from experience; but that none the less there is required for the Idea of happiness an absolute whole, a maximum of well-being in my present, and in every future, state. Now it is impossible for the most intelligent, and at the same time most powerful, but nevertheless finite, being to form here a determinate concept of what he really wills. Is it riches that he wants? How much anxiety, envy, and pestering might he not bring in this way on his own head! Is it knowledge and insight? This might perhaps merely give him an eye so sharp that it would make evils at present hidden from him and yet unavoidable seem all the more frightful, or would add a load of still further needs to the desires which already give him trouble enough. . . . In short, he has no principle by which he is able to decide with complete certainty what will make him truly happy, since for this he would require omniscience. Thus we cannot act on determinate principles in order to be happy, but only on empirical counsels, for example, of diet, frugality, politeness, reserve, and so on—things which experience shows contribute most to well-being on the average. From this it follows that imperatives of prudence, speaking strictly, do not command at all—that is, cannot exhibit actions objectively as practically *necessary*; that they are rather to be taken as recommendations (*consilia*), than as commands (*praecepta*), of reason; that the problem of determining certainly and universally what action will promote the happiness of a rational being is completely insoluble; and consequently that in regard to this there is no imperative possible which in the strictest sense could command us to do what will make us happy, since happiness is an Ideal, not of reason, but of imagination—an Ideal

419 resting merely on empirical grounds, of which it is vain to expect that they should determine an action by which we could attain the totality of a series of consequences which is in fact infinite. Nevertheless, if we assume that the means to happiness could be discovered with certainty, this imperative of prudence would be an analytic practical proposition; for it differs from the imperative of skill only in this—that in the latter the end is merely possible, while in the former the end is given. In spite of this difference, since both command solely the means to something assumed to be willed as an end, the imperative which commands him who wills the end to will the means is in both cases analytic. Thus, there is likewise no difficulty in regard to the possibility of an imperative of prudence.

Beyond all doubt, the question "How is the imperative of *morality* possible?" is the only one in need of a solution; for it is in no way hypothetical, and consequently we cannot base the objective necessity which it affirms on any presupposition, as we can with hypothetical imperatives. . . .

420 We shall thus have to investigate the possibility of a *categorical* imperative entirely *a priori*, since here we do not enjoy the advantage of having its reality given in experience and so of being obliged merely to explain, and not to establish, its possibility. So much, however, can be seen provisionally—that the categorical imperative alone purports to be a practical *law*, while all the rest may be called *principles* of the will but not laws; for an action necessary merely in order to achieve an arbitrary

purpose can be considered as in itself contingent, and we can always escape from the precept if we abandon the purpose; whereas an unconditioned command does not leave it open to the will to do the opposite at its discretion and therefore alone carries with it that necessity which we demand from a law. . . .

In this task we wish first to enquire whether perhaps the mere concept of a categorical imperative may not also provide us with the formula containing the only proposition that can be a categorical imperative; for even when we know the purport of such an absolute command, the question of its possibility will still require a special and troublesome effort, which we postpone to the final chapter.

When I conceive a *hypothetical* imperative in general, I do not know beforehand what it will contain—until its condition is given. But if I conceive a *categorical* imperative, I know at once what it contains. For since besides the law this imperative contains only the necessity that our maxim[5] should conform to this law, while the law, as we have seen, contains no condition to limit it, there remains nothing over to which the maxim has to conform except the universality of a law as such; and it is this conformity alone that the imperative properly asserts to be necessary.   421

There is therefore only a single categorical imperative and it is this: "*Act only on that maxim through which you can at the same time will that it should become a universal law.*"

Now if all imperatives of duty can be derived from this one imperative as their principle, then even although we leave it unsettled whether what we call duty may not be an empty concept, we shall still be able to show at least what we understand by it and what the concept means.

Since the universality of the law governing the production of effects constitutes what is properly called nature in its most general sense (nature as regards its form)—that is, the existence of things so far as determined by universal laws—the universal imperative of duty may also run as follows: "*Act as if the maxim of your action were to become through your will a universal law of nature.*"

We will now enumerate a few duties, following their customary division into duties towards self and duties towards others and into perfect and imperfect duties.[6]

1. A man feels sick of life as the result of a series of misfortunes that has mounted to the point of despair, but he is still so far in possession of his reason as to ask himself   422
whether taking his own life may not be contrary to his duty to himself. He now applies the test "Can the maxim of my action really become a universal law of nature?" His maxim is "From self-love I make it my principle to shorten my life if its continuance threatens more evil than it promises pleasure." The only further question to ask is whether this principle of self-love can become a universal law of nature. It is then seen at once that a system of nature by whose law the very same feeling whose function (*Bestimmung*) is to stimulate the furtherance of life should actually destroy life would contradict itself and consequently could not subsist as a system of nature. Hence this

---

5. A *maxim* is a subjective principle of action and must be distinguished from an *objective principle*—namely, a practical law. The former contains a practical rule determined by reason in accordance with the conditions of the subject (often his ignorance or again his inclinations): it is thus a principle on which the subject acts. A law, on the other hand, is an objective principle valid for every rational being; and it is a principle on which he *ought to act*—that is, an imperative.

6. . . . I understand here by a perfect duty one which allows no exception in the interests of inclination, and so I recognize among *perfect duties*, not only outer ones, but also inner. . . .

maxim cannot possibly hold as a universal law of nature and is therefore entirely opposed to the supreme principle of all duty.

2. Another finds himself driven to borrowing money because of need. He well knows that he will not be able to pay it back; but he sees too that he will get no loan unless he gives a firm promise to pay it back within a fixed time. He is inclined to make such a promise; but he has still enough conscience to ask "Is it not unlawful and contrary to duty to get out of difficulties in this way?" Supposing, however, he did resolve to do so, the maxim of his action would run thus: "Whenever I believe myself short of money, I will borrow money and promise to pay it back, though I know that this will never be done." Now this principle of self-love or personal advantage is perhaps quite compatible with my own entire future welfare; only there remains the question "Is it right?" I therefore transform the demand of self-love into a universal law and frame my question thus: "How would things stand if my maxim became a universal law?" I then see straight away that this maxim can never rank as a universal law of nature and be self-consistent, but must necessarily contradict itself. For the universality of a law that every one believing himself to be in need can make any promise he pleases with the intention not to keep it would make promising, and the very purpose of promising, itself impossible, since no one would believe he was being promised anything, but would laugh at utterances of this kind as empty shams.

423   3. A third finds in himself a talent whose cultivation would make him a useful man for all sorts of purposes. But he sees himself in comfortable circumstances, and he prefers to give himself up to pleasure rather than to bother about increasing and improving his fortunate natural aptitudes. Yet he asks himself further "Does my maxim of neglecting my natural gifts, besides agreeing in itself with my tendency to indulgence, agree also with what is called duty?" He then sees that a system of nature could indeed always subsist under such a universal law, although (like the South Sea Islanders) every man should let his talents rust and should be bent on devoting his life solely to idleness, indulgence, procreation, and, in a word, to enjoyment. Only he cannot possibly *will* that this should become a universal law of nature or should be implanted in us as such a law by a natural instinct. For as a rational being he necessarily wills that all his powers should be developed, since they serve him, and are given him, for all sorts of possible ends.

4. Yet a *fourth* is himself flourishing, but he sees others who have to struggle with great hardships (and whom he could easily help); and he thinks "What does it matter to me? Let every one be as happy as Heaven wills or as he can make himself; I won't deprive him of anything; I won't even envy him; only I have no wish to contribute anything to his well-being or to his support in distress!" Now admittedly if such an attitude were a universal law of nature, mankind could get on perfectly well—better no doubt than if everybody prates about sympathy and goodwill, and even takes pains, on occasion, to practise them, but on the other hand cheats where he can, traffics in human rights, or violates them in other ways. But although it is possible that a universal law of nature could subsist in harmony with this maxim, yet it is impossible to *will* that such a principle should hold everywhere as a law of nature. For a will which decided in this way would be in a conflict with itself, since many a situation might arise in which the man needed love and sympathy from others, and in which, by such a law of nature sprung from his own will, he would rob himself of all hope of the help he wants for himself.

These are some of the many actual duties—or at least of what we take to be such—
whose derivation from the single principle cited above leaps to the eye. We must *be*   424
able to will that a maxim of our action should become a universal law—this is the
general canon for all moral judgement of action. Some actions are so constituted that
their maxim cannot even be *conceived* as a universal law of nature without contradiction, let alone be *willed* as what *ought* to become one. In the case of others we do not
find this inner impossibility, but it is still impossible to *will* that their maxim should
be raised to the universality of a law of nature, because such a will would contradict
itself. It is easily seen that the first kind of action is opposed to strict or narrow
(rigorous) duty, the second only to wider (meritorious) duty; and thus that by these
examples all duties—so far as the type of obligation is concerned (not the object of
dutiful action)—are fully set out in their dependence on our single principle.

If we now attend to ourselves whenever we transgress a duty, we find that we in fact
do not will that our maxim should become a universal law—since this is impossible for
us—but rather that its opposite should remain a law universally: we only take the
liberty of making an *exception* to it for ourselves (or even just for this once) to the
advantage of our inclination. Consequently if we weighed it all up from one and the
same point of view—that of reason—we should find a contradiction in our own will,
the contradiction that a certain principle should be objectively necessary as a universal law and yet subjectively should not hold universally but should admit of exceptions. Since, however, we first consider our action from the point of view of a will
wholly in accord with reason, and then consider precisely the same action from the
point of view of a will affected by inclination, there is here actually no contradiction,
but rather an opposition of inclination to the precept of reason (*antagonismus*),
whereby the universality of the principle (*universalitas*) is turned into a mere generality
(*generalitas*) so that the practical principle of reason may meet our maxim half-way.
This procedure, though in our own impartial judgement it cannot be justified, proves
none the less that we in fact recognize the validity of the categorical imperative and
(with all respect for it) merely permit ourselves a few exceptions which are, as we
pretend, inconsiderable and apparently forced upon us.

We have thus at least shown this much—that if duty is a concept which is to have   425
meaning and real legislative authority for our actions, this can be expressed only in
categorical imperatives and by no means in hypothetical ones. At the same time—and
this is already a great deal—we have set forth distinctly, and determinately for every
type of application, the content of the categorical imperative, which must contain the
principle of all duty (if there is to be such a thing at all). But we are still not so far
advanced as to prove *a priori* that there actually is an imperative of this kind—that
there is a practical law which by itself commands absolutely and without any further
motives, and that the following of this law is duty. . . .

Our question therefore is this: "Is it a necessary law *for all rational beings* always to   426
judge their actions by reference to those maxims of which they can themselves will
that they should serve as universal laws?" If there is such a law, it must already be connected (entirely *a priori*) with the concept of the will of a rational being as such. But
in order to discover this connexion we must, however much we may bristle, take a step
beyond it—that is, into metaphysics, although into a region of it different from that of
speculative philosophy, namely, the metaphysic of morals. In practical philosophy we   427
are not concerned with accepting reasons for what *happens*, but with accepting laws

of what *ought to happen*, even if it never does happen—that is, objective practical laws. And here we have no need to set up an enquiry as to the reasons why anything pleases or displeases; how the pleasure of mere sensation differs from taste, and whether the latter differs from a universal approval by reason; whereon feelings of pleasure and displeasure are based; how from these feelings there arise desires and inclinations; and how from these in turn, with the co-operation of reason, there arise maxims. All this belongs to empirical psychology, which would constitute the second part of the doctrine of nature, if we take this doctrine to be the *philosophy of nature* so far as grounded on *empirical laws*. Here, however, we are discussing objective practical laws, and consequently the relation of a will to itself as determined solely by reason. Everything related to the empirical then falls away of itself; for if *reason entirely by itself* determines conduct (and it is the possibility of this which we now wish to investigate), it must necessarily do so *a priori*.

The will is conceived as a power of determining oneself to action *in accordance with the idea of certain laws*. And such a power can be found only in rational beings. Now what serves the will as a subjective ground of its self-determination is an *end*; and this, if it is given by reason alone, must be equally valid for all rational beings. What, on the other hand, contains merely the ground of the possibility of an action whose effect is an end is called a *means*. . . . Practical principles are *formal* if they abstract from all subjective ends; they are *material*, on the other hand, if they are based on such ends and consequently on certain impulsions. Ends that a rational being adopts arbitrarily as *effects* of his action (material ends) are in every case only relative; for it is solely their relation to special characteristics in the subject's power of appetition which gives them their value. Hence this value can provide no universal principles, no principles valid and necessary for all rational beings and also for every volition—that is, no practical laws. Consequently all these relative ends can be the ground only of hypothetical imperatives.

Suppose, however, there were something *whose existence* has *in itself* an absolute value, something which as *an end in itself* could be a ground of determinate laws; then in it, and in it alone, would there be the ground of a possible categorical imperative—that is, of a practical law.

Now I say that man, and in general every rational being, exists as an end in himself, *not merely as a means* for arbitrary use by this or that will: he must in all his actions, whether they are directed to himself or to other rational beings, always be viewed *at the same time as an end*. All the objects of inclination have only a conditioned value; for if there were not these inclinations and the needs grounded on them, their object would be valueless. Inclinations themselves, as sources of needs, are so far from having an absolute value to make them desirable for their own sake that it must rather be the universal wish of every rational being to be wholly free from them. Thus the value of all objects that can *be produced* by our action is always conditioned. Beings whose existence depends, not on our will, but on nature, have none the less, if they are non-rational beings, only a relative value as means and are consequently called *things*. Rational beings, on the other hand, are called *persons* because their nature already marks them out as ends in themselves—that is, as something which ought not to be used merely as a means—and consequently imposes to that extent a limit on all arbitrary treatment of them (and is an object of reverence). Persons, therefore, are not merely subjective ends whose existence as an object of our actions has a value *for us*:

they are *objective ends*—that is, things whose existence is in itself an end, and indeed an end such that in its place we can put no other end to which they should serve *simply* as means; for unless this is so, nothing at all of *absolute* value would be found anywhere. But if all value were conditioned—that is, contingent—then no supreme principle could be found for reason at all.

If then there is to be a supreme practical principle and—so far as the human will is concerned—a categorical imperative, it must be such that from the idea of something which is necessarily an end for every one because it is an *end in itself* it forms an *objective* principle of the will and consequently can serve as a practical law. The ground   429
of this principle is: *Rational nature exists as an end in itself.* This is the way in which a man necessarily conceives his own existence: it is therefore so far a *subjective* principle of human actions. But it is also the way in which every other rational being conceives his existence on the same rational ground which is valid also for me;[7] hence it is at the same time an *objective* principle, from which, as a supreme practical ground, it must be possible to derive all laws for the will. The practical imperative will therefore be as follows: *Act in such a way that you always treat humanity, whether in your own person or in the person of any other, never simply as a means, but always at the same time as an end.* We will now consider whether this can be carried out in practice.

Let us keep to our previous examples.

First, as regards the concept of necessary duty to oneself, the man who contemplates suicide will ask "Can my action be compatible with the Idea of humanity *as an end in itself?*" If he does away with himself in order to escape from a painful situation, he is making use of a person merely as *a means* to maintain a tolerable state of affairs till the end of his life. But man is not a thing—not something to be used *merely* as a means: he must always in all his actions be regarded as an end in himself. Hence I cannot dispose of man in my person by maiming, spoiling, or killing. (A more precise determination of this principle in order to avoid all misunderstanding—for example, about having limbs amputated to save myself or about exposing my life to danger in order to preserve it, and so on—I must here forego: this question belongs to morals proper.)

Secondly, so far as necessary or strict duty to others is concerned, the man who has a mind to make a false promise to others will see at once that he is intending to make use of another man *merely as a means* to an end he does not share. For the man whom I seek to use for my own purposes by such a promise cannot possibly agree with my way of behaving to him, and so cannot himself share the end of the action. This incom-   430
patibility with the principle of duty to others leaps to the eye more obviously when we bring in examples of attempts on the freedom and property of others. For then it is manifest that a violator of the rights of man intends to use the person of others merely as a means without taking into consideration that, as rational beings, they ought always at the same time to be rated as ends—that is, only as beings who must themselves be able to share in the end of the very same action.

Thirdly, in regard to contingent (meritorious) duty to oneself, it is not enough that an action should refrain from conflicting with humanity in our own person as an end in itself: it must also *harmonize with this end.* Now there are in humanity capacities for

---

7. This proposition I put forward here as a postulate. The grounds for it will be found in the final chapter.

greater perfection which form part of nature's purpose for humanity in our person. To neglect these can admittedly be compatible with the *maintenance* of humanity as an end in itself, but not with the *promotion* of this end.

Fourthly, as regards meritorious duties to others, the natural end which all men seek is their own happiness. Now humanity could no doubt subsist if everybody contributed nothing to the happiness of others but at the same time refrained from deliberately impairing their happiness. This is, however, merely to agree negatively and not positively with *humanity as an end in itself* unless every one endeavours also, so far as in him lies, to further the ends of others. For the ends of a subject who is an end in himself must, if this conception is to have its *full* effect in me, be also, as far as possible, *my* ends.

431   This principle of humanity, and in general of every rational agent, *as an end in itself* (a principle which is the supreme limiting condition of every man's freedom of action) is not borrowed from experience; firstly, because it is universal, applying as it does to all rational beings as such, and no experience is adequate to determine universality; secondly, because in it humanity is conceived, not as an end of man (subjectively)— that is, as an object which, as a matter of fact, happens to be made an end—but as an objective end—one which, be our ends what they may, must, as a law, constitute the supreme limiting condition of all subjective ends and so must spring from pure reason. That is to say, the ground for every enactment of practical law lies *objectively in the rule* and in the form of universality which (according to our first principle) makes the rule capable of being a law (and indeed a law of nature); *subjectively*, however, it lies in the *end*; but (according to our second principle) the subject of all ends is to be found in every rational being as an end in himself. From this there now follows our third practical principle for the will—as the supreme condition of the will's conformity with universal practical reason—namely, the Idea *of the will of every rational being as a will which makes universal law.*

By this principle all maxims are repudiated which cannot accord with the will's own enactment of universal law. The will is therefore not merely subject to the law, but is so subject that it must be considered as also *making the law* for itself and precisely on this account as first of all subject to the law (of which it can regard itself as the author).

Imperatives as formulated above—namely, the imperative enjoining conformity of actions to universal law on the analogy of a *natural order* and that enjoining the universal *supremacy* of rational beings in themselves *as ends*—did, by the mere fact that they were represented as categorical, exclude from their sovereign authority every admixture of interest as a motive. They were, however, merely *assumed* to be categorical because we were bound to make this assumption if we wished to explain the concept of duty. That there were practical propositions which commanded categorically could not itself be proved, any more than it can be proved in this chapter generally; but one thing could have been done—namely, to show that in willing for the sake of duty renunciation of all interest, as the specific mark distinguishing a categorical from a hypothetical imperative, was expressed in the very imperative itself by means of some

432 determination inherent in it. This is what is done in the present third formulation of the principle—namely, in the Idea of the will of every rational being as *a will which makes universal law.*

Once we conceive a will of this kind, it becomes clear that while a will *which is sub-ject to law* may be bound to this law by some interest, nevertheless a will which is itself a supreme law-giver cannot possibly as such depend on any interest; for a will which is dependent in this way would itself require yet a further law in order to restrict the interest of self-love to the condition that this interest should itself be valid as a universal law.

Thus the *principle* that every human will is *a will which by all its maxims enacts univer-sal law*[8] — provided only that it were right in other ways — would be *well suited* to be a categorical imperative in this respect: that precisely because of the Idea of making universal law it is *based on no interest* and consequently can alone among all possible imperatives be *unconditioned*. . . .

We need not now wonder, when we look back upon all the previous efforts that have been made to discover the principle of morality, why they have one and all been bound to fail. Their authors saw man as tied to laws by his duty, but it never occurred to them that he is subject only to *laws which are made by himself* and yet are *universal*, and that he is bound only to act in conformity with a will which is his own but has as nature's purpose for it the function of making universal law. For when they thought of man merely as subject to a law (whatever it might be), the law had to carry with it some interest in order to attract or compel, because it did not spring as a law from *his own* will: in order to conform with the law his will had to be necessitated by *something else* to act in a certain way. This absolutely inevitable conclusion meant that all the labour spent in trying to find a supreme principle of duty was lost beyond recall; for what they discovered was never duty, but only the necessity of acting from a certain interest. This interest might be one's own or another's; but on such a view the impera-tive was bound to be always a conditioned one and could not possibly serve as a moral law. I will therefore call my principle the principle of the *Autonomy* of the will in con-trast with all others, which I consequently class under *Heteronomy*.

The concept of every rational being as one who must regard himself as making universal law by all the maxims of his will, and must seek to judge himself and his actions from this point of view, leads to a closely connected and very fruitful concept — namely, that of *a kingdom of ends*.

I understand by a "*kingdom*" a systematic union of different rational beings under common laws. Now since laws determine ends as regards their universal validity, we shall be able — if we abstract from the personal differences between rational beings, and also from all the content of their private ends — to conceive a whole of all ends in sys-tematic conjunction (a whole both of rational beings as ends in themselves and also of the personal ends which each may set before himself); that is, we shall be able to conceive a kingdom of ends which is possible in accordance with the above principles.

For rational beings all stand under the *law* that each of them should treat himself and all others, *never merely as a means*, but always *at the same time as an end in himself*. But by so doing there arises a systematic union of rational beings under common objective laws — that is, a kingdom. Since these laws are directed precisely to the rela-

433

---

8. I may be excused from bringing forward examples to illustrate this principle, since those which were first used as illustrations of the categorical imperative and its formula can all serve this purpose here.

tion of such beings to one another as ends and means, this kingdom can be called a kingdom of ends (which is admittedly only an Ideal).

A rational being belongs to the kingdom of ends as a *member*, when, although he makes its universal laws, he is also himself subject to these laws. He belongs to it as its *head*, when as the maker of laws he is himself subject to the will of no other. . . .

434   Thus morality consists in the relation of all action to the making of laws whereby alone a kingdom of ends is possible. This making of laws must be found in every rational being himself and must be able to spring from his will. The principle of his will is therefore never to perform an action except on a maxim such as can also be a universal law, and consequently such *that the will can regard itself as at the same time making universal law by means of its maxim.* Where maxims are not already by their very nature in harmony with this objective principle of rational beings as makers of universal law, the necessity of acting on this principle is practical necessitation—that is, *duty.* Duty does not apply to the head in a kingdom of ends, but it does apply to every member and to all members in equal measure. . . .

In the kingdom of ends everything has either a *price* or a *dignity.* If it has a price, something else can be put in its place as an *equivalent;* if it is exalted above all price and so admits of no equivalent, then it has a dignity.

What is relative to universal human inclinations and needs has a *market price;* what, even without presupposing a need, accords with a certain taste—that is, with 435 satisfaction in the mere purposeless play of our mental powers—has a *fancy price (Affektionspreis);* but that which constitutes the sole condition under which anything can be an end in itself has not merely a relative value—that is, a price—but has an intrinsic value—that is, *dignity.*

Now morality is the only condition under which a rational being can be an end in himself; for only through this is it possible to be a law-making member in a kingdom of ends. Therefore morality, and humanity so far as it is capable of morality, is the only thing which has dignity. Skill and diligence in work have a market price; wit, lively imagination, and humour have a fancy price; but fidelity to promises and kindness based on principle (not on instinct) have an intrinsic worth. In default of these, nature and art alike contain nothing to put in their place; for their worth consists, not in the effects which result from them, not in the advantage or profit they produce, but in the attitudes of mind—that is, in the maxims of the will—which are ready in this way to manifest themselves in action even if they are not favoured by success. . . .

436   Nothing can have a value other than that determined for it by the law. But the law-making which determines all value must for this reason have a dignity—that is, an unconditioned and incomparable worth—for the appreciation of which, as necessarily given by a rational being, the word *"reverence"* is the only becoming expression. *Autonomy* is therefore the ground of the dignity of human nature and of every rational nature. . . .

445   In order to prove that morality is no mere phantom of the brain—a conclusion which follows if the categorical imperative, and with it the autonomy of the will, is true and is absolutely necessary as an *a priori* principle—we require a *possible synthetic use of pure practical reason.* On such a use we cannot venture without prefacing it by a *critique* of this power of reason itself—a critique whose main features, so far as is sufficient for our purpose, we must outline in our final chapter.

Chapter 3

Passage from a Metaphysic of Morals to a Critique of Pure Practical Reason

The Concept of Freedom Is the Key to Explain Autonomy of the Will

Will is a kind of causality belonging to living beings so far as they are rational. *Freedom* 446
would then be the property this causality has of being able to work independently of
determination by alien causes; just as *natural necessity* is a property characterizing the
causality of all non-rational beings—the property of being determined to activity by
the influence of alien causes.

The above definition of freedom is *negative* and consequently unfruitful as a way of
grasping its essence; but there springs from it a *positive* concept, which, as positive, is
richer and more fruitful. The concept of causality carries with it that of *laws* (*Gesetze*)
in accordance with which, because of something we call a cause, something else—
namely, its effect—must be posited (*gesetzt*). Hence freedom of will, although it is not
the property of conforming to laws of nature, is not for this reason lawless: it must
rather be a causality conforming to immutable laws, though of a special kind; for
otherwise a free will would be self-contradictory. Natural necessity, as we have seen, is
a heteronomy of efficient causes; for every effect is possible only in conformity with
the law that something else determines the efficient cause to causal action. What else
then can freedom of will be but autonomy—that is, the property which will has of 447
being a law to itself? The proposition "Will is in all its actions a law to itself" expresses,
however, only the principle of acting on no maxim other than one which can have for
its object itself as at the same time a universal law. This is precisely the formula of the
categorical imperative and the principle of morality. Thus a free will and a will under
moral laws are one and the same.

Consequently if freedom of the will is presupposed, morality, together with its principle, follows by mere analysis of the concept of freedom. Nevertheless the principle
of morality is still a synthetic proposition, namely: "An absolutely good will is one
whose maxim can always have as its content itself considered as a universal law"; for
we cannot discover this characteristic of its maxim by analysing the concept of an
absolutely good will. Such synthetic propositions are possible only because two cognitions are bound to one another by their connexion with a third term in which both
of them are to be found. The *positive* concept of freedom furnishes this third term,
which cannot, as in the case of physical causes, be the nature of the sensible world (in
the concept of which there come together the concepts of something as cause and of
something else as effect in their relation to one another). What this third term is to
which freedom directs us and of which we have an Idea *a priori*, we are not yet in a position to show here straight away, nor can we as yet make intelligible the deduction of
the concept of freedom from pure practical reason and so the possibility of a categorical imperative: we require some further preparation.

Freedom Must Be Presupposed as a Property of the Will of All Rational Beings

It is not enough to ascribe freedom to our will, on whatever ground, unless we have
sufficient reason for attributing the same freedom to all rational beings as well. For

since morality is a law for us only as *rational beings*, it must be equally valid for all rational beings; and since it must be derived solely from the property of freedom, we have got to prove that freedom too is a property of the will of all rational beings. It is not enough to demonstrate freedom from certain alleged experiences of human nature (though to do this is in any case absolutely impossible and freedom can be demonstrated only *a priori*): we must prove that it belongs universally to the activity of rational beings endowed with a will. Now I assert that every being who cannot act except *under the Idea of freedom* is by this alone—from a practical point of view—really free; that is to say, for him all the laws inseparably bound up with freedom are valid just as much as if his will could be pronounced free in itself on grounds valid for theoretical philosophy.[9] And I maintain that to every rational being possessed of a will we must also lend the Idea of freedom as the only one under which he can act. For in such a being we conceive a reason which is practical—that is, which exercises causality in regard to its objects. But we cannot possibly conceive of a reason as being consciously directed from outside in regard to its judgements; for in that case the subject would attribute the determination of his power of judgement, not to his reason, but to an impulsion. Reason must look upon itself as the author of its own principles independently of alien influences. Therefore as practical reason, or as the will of a rational being, it must be regarded by itself as free; that is, the will of a rational being can be a will of his own only under the Idea of freedom, and such a will must therefore—from a practical point of view—be attributed to all rational beings.

The Interest Attached to the Ideas of Morality

We have at last traced the determinate concept of morality back to the Idea of freedom, but we have been quite unable to demonstrate freedom as something actual in ourselves and in human nature: we saw merely that we must presuppose it if we wish to conceive a being as rational and as endowed with consciousness of his causality in regard to actions—that is, as endowed with a will. Thus we find that on precisely the same ground we must attribute to every being endowed with reason and a will this property of determining himself to action under the Idea of his own freedom....

In this, we must frankly admit, there is shown a kind of circle, from which, as it seems, there is no way of escape. In the order of efficient causes we take ourselves to be free so that we may conceive ourselves to be under moral laws in the order of ends; and we then proceed to think of ourselves as subject to moral laws on the ground that we have described our will as free. Freedom and the will's enactment of its own laws are indeed both autonomy—and therefore are reciprocal concepts—but precisely for this reason one of them cannot be used to explain the other or to furnish its ground. It can at most be used for logical purposes in order to bring seemingly different ideas of the same object under a single concept (just as different fractions of equal value can be reduced to their simplest expression).

___

9. This method takes it as sufficient for our purpose if freedom is presupposed merely *as an Idea* by all rational beings in their actions; and I adopt it in order to avoid the obligation of having to prove freedom from a theoretical point of view as well. For even if this latter problem is left unsettled, the same laws as would bind a being who was really free are equally valid for a being who cannot act except under the Idea of his own freedom. In this way we can relieve ourselves of the burden which weighs upon theory.

One shift, however, still remains open to us. We can enquire whether we do not take one standpoint when by means of freedom we conceive ourselves as causes acting *a priori*, and another standpoint when we contemplate ourselves with reference to our actions as effects which we see before our eyes.

One observation is possible without any need for subtle reflexion and, we may assume, can be made by the most ordinary intelligence—no doubt in its own fashion through some obscure discrimination of the power of judgement known to it as "feel-   451 ing." The observation is this—that all ideas coming to us apart from our own volition (as do those of the senses) enable us to know objects only as they affect ourselves: what they may be in themselves remains unknown. Consequently, ideas of this kind, even with the greatest effort of attention and clarification brought to bear by understanding, serve only for knowledge of *appearances*, never of *things in themselves*. Once this distinction is made . . . it follows of itself that behind appearances we must admit and assume something else which is not appearance—namely, things in themselves— although, since we can never be acquainted with these, but only with the way in which they affect us, we must resign ourselves to the fact that we can never get any nearer to them and can never know what they are in themselves. This must yield us a distinction, however rough, between the *sensible world* and the *intelligible world*, the first of which can vary a great deal according to differences of sensibility in sundry observers, while the second, which is its ground, always remains the same. Even as regards himself—so far as man is acquainted with himself by inner sensation—he cannot claim to know what he is in himself. For since he does not, so to say, make himself, and since he acquires his concept of self not *a priori* but empirically, it is natural that even about himself he should get information through sense—that is, through inner sense—and consequently only through the mere appearance of his own nature and through the way in which his consciousness is affected. Yet beyond this character of himself as a subject made up, as it is, of mere appearances he must suppose there to be something else which is its ground—namely, his Ego as this may be constituted in itself; and thus as regards mere perception and the capacity for receiving sensations he must count himself as belonging to the *sensible world*, but as regards whatever there may be in him of pure activity (whatever comes into consciousness, not through affection of the senses, but immediately) he must count himself as belonging to the *intellectual world*, of which, however, he knows nothing further. . . .

Now man actually finds in himself a power which distinguishes him from all other   452 things—and even from himself so far as he is affected by objects. This power is *reason*. As pure spontaneity reason is elevated even above *understanding* in the following respect. Understanding—although it too is spontaneous activity and is not, like sense, confined to ideas which arise only when we are affected by things (and therefore are passive)—understanding cannot produce by its own activity any concepts other than those whose sole service is *to bring sensuous ideas under rules* and so to unite them in one consciousness: without this employment of sensibility it would think nothing at all. Reason, on the other hand—in what are called "Ideas"—shows a spontaneity so pure that it goes far beyond anything sensibility can offer: it manifests its highest function in distinguishing the sensible and intelligible worlds from one another and so in marking out limits for understanding itself.

Because of this a rational being must regard himself *qua intelligence* (and accordingly not on the side of his lower faculties) as belonging to the intelligible world, not to the sensible one. He has therefore two points of view from which he can regard himself and from which he can know laws governing the employment of his powers and consequently governing all his actions. He can consider himself *first*—so far as he belongs to the sensible world—to be under laws of nature (heteronomy); and *secondly* —so far as he belongs to the intelligible world—to be under laws which, being independent of nature, are not empirical but have their ground in reason alone....

453   The suspicion which we raised above is now removed—namely, that there might be a hidden circle in our inference from freedom to autonomy and from autonomy to the moral law; that in effect we had perhaps assumed the Idea of freedom only because of the moral law in order subsequently to infer the moral law in its turn from freedom; and that consequently we had been able to assign no ground at all for the moral law, but had merely assumed it by begging a principle which well-meaning souls will gladly concede us, but which we could never put forward as a demonstrable proposition. We see now that when we think of ourselves as free, we transfer ourselves into the intelligible world as members and recognize the autonomy of the will together with its consequence—morality; whereas when we think of ourselves as under obligation, we look upon ourselves as belonging to the sensible world and yet to the intelligible world at the same time.

How Is a Categorical Imperative Possible?

A rational being counts himself, *qua* intelligence, as belonging to the intelligible world, and solely *qua* efficient cause belonging to the intelligible world does he give to his causality the name of "*will.*" On the other side, however, he is conscious of himself as also a part of the sensible world, where his actions are encountered as mere appearances of this causality. Yet the possibility of these actions cannot be made intelligible by means of such causality, since with this we have no direct acquaintance; and instead these actions, as belonging to the sensible world, have to be understood as determined by other appearances—namely, by desires and inclinations. Hence, if I were solely a member of the intelligible world, all my actions would be in perfect conformity with the principle of the autonomy of a pure will; if I were solely a part of the sensible world, they would have to be taken as in complete conformity with the law of nature governing desires and inclinations—that is, with the heteronomy of nature.... *But the intelligible world contains the ground of the sensible world and therefore also of its laws*; and so in respect of my will, for which (as belonging entirely to the intelligible world) it gives laws immediately, it must also be conceived as containing such a ground. Hence, in spite of regarding myself from one point of view as a being

454   that belongs to the sensible world, I shall have to recognize that, *qua* intelligence, I am subject to the law in the Idea of freedom, and so to the autonomy of the will—and therefore I must look on the laws of the intelligible world as imperatives for me and on the actions which conform to this principle as duties....

461   Thus the question "How is a categorical imperative possible?" can be answered so far as we can supply the sole presupposition under which it is possible—namely, the Idea of freedom—and also so far as we can have insight into the necessity of this presupposition. This is sufficient for the *practical use* of reason—that is, for conviction of the *validity of this imperative,* and so too of the moral law. But how this presupposition itself is possible is never open to the insight of any human reason. Yet, on the

presupposition that the will of an intelligence is free, there follows necessarily its *autonomy* as the formal condition under which alone it can be determined. It is not only perfectly *possible* (as speculative philosophy can show) to presuppose such freedom of the will (without contradicting the principle that natural necessity governs the connexion of appearances in the sensible world); it is also *necessary*, without any further condition, for a rational being conscious of exercising causality by means of reason and so of having a will (which is distinct from desires) to make such freedom in practice—that is, in Idea—underlie all his voluntary actions as their condition. But *how* pure reason can be practical in itself without further motives drawn from some other source; that is, how the bare *principle of the universal validity of all its maxims as laws* (which would admittedly be the form of a pure practical reason) can by itself—without any matter (or object) of the will in which we could take some antecedent interest—supply a motive and create an interest which could be called purely *moral*; or, in other words, *how pure reason can be practical*—all human reason is totally incapable of explaining this, and all the effort and labour to seek such an explanation is wasted.

It is precisely the same as if I sought to fathom how freedom itself is possible as the causality of a will. There I abandon a philosophical basis of explanation, and I have no other. I could, no doubt, proceed to flutter about in the intelligible world, which still remains left to me—the world of intelligences; but although I have an *Idea* of it, which has its own good grounds, yet I have not the slightest *acquaintance* with such a world, nor can I ever attain such acquaintance by all the efforts of my natural power of reason. My Idea signifies only a "something" that remains over when I have excluded from the grounds determining my will everything that belongs to the world of sense: its sole purpose is to restrict the principle that all motives come from the field of sensibility, by setting bounds to this field and by showing that it does not comprise all in all within itself, but that there is still more beyond it; yet with this "more" I have no further acquaintance. Of the pure reason which conceives this Ideal, after I have set aside all matter—that is, all knowledge of objects—there remains nothing over for me except its form—namely, the practical law that maxims should be universally valid—and the corresponding conception of reason, in its relation to a purely intelligible world, as a possible efficient cause, that is, a cause determining the will. Here all sensuous motives must entirely fail; this Idea of an intelligible world would itself have to be the motive or to be that wherein reason originally took an interest. To make this comprehensible is, however, precisely the problem that we are unable to solve. . . .

SELECTED BIBLIOGRAPHY

Kant, Immanuel. *Critique of Practical Reason.* Trans. Lewis White Beck. Indianapolis: Bobbs-Merrill, 1956.

————. *Critique of Pure Reason.* Trans. Norman Kemp Smith. New York: St. Martin's Press, 1965.

————. *Groundwork of the Metaphysic of Morals.* Trans. H.J. Paton. New York: Harper & Row, 1964.

Allison, Henry E. *Kant's Transcendental Idealism: An Interpretation and Defense.* New Haven, Conn.: Yale University Press, 1983.

Aune, Bruce. *Kant's Theory of Morals.* Princeton, N.J.: Princeton University Press, 1979.

Broad, C.D. *Kant: An Introduction.* Cambridge: Cambridge University Press, 1978.

Cassirer, Ernst. *Kant's Life and Thought.* Trans. James Haden. New Haven, Conn.: Yale University Press, 1981.

Deleuze, Gilles. *Kant's Critical Philosophy: The Doctrine of the Faculties.* Trans. Hugh Tomlinson and Barbara Habberjam. Minneapolis: University of Minnesota Press, 1984.

Ewing, A.C. *A Short Commentary on Kant's "Critique of Pure Reason."* Chicago: University of Chicago Press, 1967.

Gram, Moltke. *Kant: Disputed Questions.* 2d ed. Atascadero, Calif.: Ridgeview, 1984.

Kemp, Jonathan. *The Philosophy of Kant.* New York: Oxford University Press, 1968.

Körner, Stephan. *Kant.* rev. ed. New Haven, Conn.: Yale University Press, 1982.

Martin, Gottfried. *Kant's Metaphysics and Theory of Science.* Trans. P.G. Lucas. Manchester: Manchester University Press, 1955.

Murphy, Jeffrie G. *Kant: The Philosophy of Right.* London: Macmillan, 1970.

Nell, Onora. *Acting on Principle: An Essay in Kantian Ethics.* New York: Columbia University Press, 1975.

Paton, H.J. *The Categorical Imperative: A Study in Kant's Moral Philosophy.* New York: Harper & Row, 1965.

Ross, W.D. *Kant's Ethical Theory: A Commentary on the "Grundlegung zur Metaphysik der Sitten."* Oxford: Clarendon Press, 1954.

Scruton, Roger, *Kant.* New York: Oxford University Press, 1982.

Sullivan, Roger. *Kant's Moral Theory.* Cambridge: Cambridge University Press, 1989.

Walker, R.C.S. *Kant.* London: Routledge, Chapman & Hall, 1978.

————. *Kant on Pure Reason.* New York: Oxford University Press, 1982.

Walsh, W.H. *Kant's Criticism of Metaphysics.* Chicago: University of Chicago Press, 1976.

Werkmeister, W.H. *Kant: The Architectonic and Development of His Philosophy.* La Salle, Ill.: Open Court, 1980.

Wolff, Robert Paul. *The Autonomy of Reason.* New York: Harper & Row, 1973.

————. *Kant's Theory of Mental Activity.* Cambridge, Mass.: Harvard University Press, 1963.

NINETEENTH-CENTURY PHILOSOPHY

Histories of philosophy tell a fairly univocal and coherent story about the era from René Descartes to Immanuel Kant, but philosophy after Kant seems to explode in many different directions, and it becomes very difficult to see any unitary line of development among the various schools of thought.

It is perhaps misleading to place Kant at the root of the explosive differences among nineteenth-century philosophers. One philosopher who dominated the early parts of the nineteenth century has not even been included in this anthology: Georg Wilhelm Friedrich Hegel (1770–1831). Hegel represents the culmination of the German idealism begun by Kant, and he constructed a philosophical system that in its sweep and depth can be rivaled only by Plato, Aristotle, and Kant. Unfortunately, Hegel's writing is extremely involuted and dense. Reluctantly, I have left Hegel out of this anthology, committed as he was to the idea that every part of his system can be understood only in the context of the whole, selections are unintelligible without an understanding of his system as a whole.

Much of nineteenth-century philosophy was a reaction to Hegel, whose all-encompassing system deified reason but denied that reason could ever be ahistorical and pure. Hegel's God, the Absolute, is the self-developing world system, coming to self-consciousness in humanity's growing awareness of its own historical development. In Hegel's totalizing system, the tasks of both philosophy and history are accomplished, and further historical or philosophical development seems impossible.

But neither history nor philosophy ceased after Hegel's death in 1831. Indeed, the rate of change in society increased, and philosophy remained sensitive to such developments. The old political order had been decisively defeated at the end of the eighteenth century in two major revolutions, the American and the French. The American Revolution was significant because it established a nonmonarchical, republican government that embodied many of the ideals of the Enlightenment. At its inception, the French Revolution was also seen as an embodiment of the political philosophy of the Enlightenment, but the excesses of the Terror and the emergence of the Napoleonic empire belied major flaws in Enlightenment theories. Whereas the American Revolution had been an essentially well-behaved, middle-class revolt, the French peasantry went to horrendous, anarchic extremes. Napoleon, who had forged a superior army out of social disarray, accomplished the conquest of Europe, rewrote its laws, and restructured its map, with tremendous repercussions, even for philosophy.

Not only were political structures changing rapidly, but the socioeconomic structures were shifting swiftly as well. Europe and North America were industrializing. The sudden growth of the urban centers and their factories afforded undreamed-of riches for some and unconscionable squalor for most others. The old feudalistic social order, abolished by the French Revolution, was replaced with a new capitalist order. But many observers questioned whether ordinary people were any better off than they had been.

The rate of growth in scientific knowledge also began to increase appreciably during the nineteenth century. Though physics had apparently been mastered by Newton in the seventeenth century, the other sciences were much slower in gaining their footing. Electricity and magnetism opened up new fields in physics; John Dalton, Dmitry Mendeleyev, and others solidified theoretical chemistry; physiology made great strides; and the social sciences—psychology, anthropology, and sociology—emerged as autonomous disciplines in the nineteenth century. The most influential scientific work of the nineteenth century, however, was undoubtedly Charles Darwin's *On the Origin of Species*, in which he meticulously laid out his case for the theory of evolution. Darwin demonstrated how the diversity and complexity of living things could arise by natural processes. Until his theory of evolution, there had been little evidence against the doctrines of special creation and little reason not to believe that organic life was entirely distinct from other material forms. This explosion in scientific knowledge, especially the theory of evolution, needed to be accommodated in any philosophical understanding of the place of humans in the world.

In Germany, which enjoyed a golden age of philosophical speculation between Kant and Hegel, one had to break free of Hegel's vision in order to go on with philosophy. Denmark's Søren Kierkegaard (1813–1855), another philosopher whose absence from this collection is most regrettable, turned against all rationalistic systems and focused on the existential problem of a human individual trying to live a life of faith in a world where God no longer converses casually with us. The "Young Hegelians," a group of radical thinkers that arose in Berlin and included David Strauss, Ludwig Feuerbach, Bruno Bauer, and Karl Marx, turned against Hegel's idealistic presuppositions and insisted that the reality of the world is not spiritual, as Hegel contended, but material. A true understanding of the world would be an understanding of its material constitution, in particular, the material constitution of the social world. Such an understanding would not be merely retrospective, as Hegel thought, but revolutionary: if we understood the material, productive forces that form society, we could change them.

Later in the century Nietzsche took Hegel's historicization of reason seriously and, influenced as well by Darwin's theory of evolution, argued that the goals and values humanity has hitherto pursued must be fundamentally revalued. Elsewhere in Germany, which had lagged behind France and England intellectually through most of the seventeenth and eighteenth centuries, there was a tremendous explosion of scientific and intellectual culture, and the German universities established themselves at the forefront of learning.

Germany, however, was not the only intellectually vital culture during that era. England, the leading commercial power of the world, commanded a vast empire that contained an untold treasure of knowledge. Represented in this volume by John Stuart Mill, it is perhaps fitting that Mill, the great heir to the proud tradition of British empiricism, did not hold a university post but like many learned Victorians pursued his wide-ranging intellectual endeavors while holding down a significant bureaucratic position. Otherwise noticeable in nineteenth-century British thought was the work of Augustus De Morgan, George Boole, W. S. Jevons, and John Venn, who set the stage for the blossoming of modern formal logic at the turn of the century. By the end of the nineteenth century, British universities were in the grasp of a neo-Hegelian revival, led F. H. Bradley, T. H. Green, Bernard Bosanquet, and others. This aberration in the otherwise solid tradition of empiricism lasted only until Bertrand Russell and G. E. Moore reasserted the empirical tradition at the turn of the twentieth century.

It was during the nineteenth century that the United States began defining its own particular philosophical culture. Numerous influences came together: the British tradition of Locke, Hume, and Thomas Reid; the German idealists (many Kant or Hegel clubs were scattered across the country); various religious traditions; and America's self-image as a down-to-earth, can-do society at the forefront of social and technological change. The distinctively American philosophical tradition—pragmatism—looks back to Charles Sanders Peirce as its founder. Extremely well read in the history of philosophy, Peirce was also a ground-breaking logician and a practicing scientist of significant accomplishment. Supported by his friend William James, the leading psychologist of the era, Peirce's pragmatic theory of meaning and his application of logical analysis to philosophical questions defined a style and set of concerns that still pervade American philosophy.

If there is a summation of nineteenth-century views of knowledge, reality, and the good life, it is that it was essentially a time in which all the old assumptions were brought into question. In metaphysics and epistemology a major disagreement arose between the positivists and the idealists. The positivists believed that science would eventually be able to answer all worthwhile questions; all speculation, whether religious or philosophical, would eventually be replaced by the solid, empirical truths of science. Epistemology, they held, is just the theory of scientific method. While the nineteenth century witnessed a rapid increase in scientific knowledge, it also marked the high point of the grand idealist systems that maintained the metaphysical priority of the spiritual over the material. No longer able to dismiss science, the idealists insisted that science reveals to us only a fraction of all there is to know: there is a higher, spiritual point of view from which the partiality of scientific knowledge is evident.

The Darwinian revolution itself had two contrary effects. To many thinkers it demonstrated the continuity of the human (and consequently the spiritual) with the natural and the material; to others it simply reinforced the inability of the empirical sciences to understand the spiritual. Could the empirical sciences answer *all* our questions, or must some questions remain beyond their purview? Could the sciences be the final measure of what is and what is not, or could we be assured of the existence of some things (perhaps God, or our minds) quite independently of the sciences?

Nowhere is the range of nineteenth-century thought more evident than in its reflections on the good life. The success of the American Revolution strengthened the convictions of those who retained the ideals of the Enlightenment. The success of Napoleon strengthened those who thought that the masses needed strong, even absolute leaders. Social conditions were changing at an unprecedented rate with the industrialization of Western Europe and North America. Reactions ranged from Marx's dedication to overcoming the alienation of the proletariat, those masses of laborers that were fodder for the factories, by erecting a society in which the bureaucratic apparatus of the state would wither away, to Friedrich Nietzsche's elitist disdain for the "herd" in the hope that something higher might emerge from humankind. Mill's middle-of-the-road, classical liberalism, with its insistence that the role of the government is both to maximize the general welfare and to protect individual liberties, became a powerful force for reform in nineteenth-century Britain and has continued to influence democratic governments worldwide.

SELECTED BIBLIOGRAPHY

Beiser, Frederick. *The Fate of Reason*. Cambridge, Mass.: Harvard University Press, 1987.

Cassirer, Ernst. *The Problem of Knowledge: Philosophy, Science, and History since Hegel*. New Haven, Conn.: Yale University Press, 1950.

Kolakowski, Leszek. *The Alienation of Reason: A History of Postivist Thought*. Garden City, N.Y.: Doubleday, 1967.

Lowith, Karl. *From Hegel to Nietzsche: The Revolution in Nineteenth-Century Thought*. Trans. David Green. London: Constable, 1965.

Mandelbaum, Maurice. *History, Man and Reason: A Study in Nineteenth-Century Thought*. Baltimore: Johns Hopkins Press, 1971.

Mead, George Herbert. *Movements of Thought in the Nineteenth Century*. Ed. Merritt Moore. Chicago: University of Chicago Press, 1936.

Royce, Josiah. *The Spirit of Modern Philosophy*. Boston: Houghton Mifflin, 1892.

Schacht, Richard. *Hegel and After*. Pittsburgh: University of Pittsburgh Press, 1975.

Scruton, Roger. *From Descartes to Wittgenstein: A Short History of Modern Philosophy*. New York: Harper & Row, 1981.

Solomon, Robert C. *From Rationalism to Existentialism: The Existentialists and Their Nineteenth-Century Backgrounds*. New York: Humanities Press, 1978.

_____. *History and Human Nature: A Philosophical Review of European Philosophy and Culture, 1750–1850*. Orlando, Fla.: Harcourt Brace Jovanovich, 1979.

Karl Marx

Karl Marx (1818–1883) was born in Trier, a city with Roman roots in the German wine-growing Mosel River valley. His family was of Jewish descent, but his father converted to Protestantism in order to preserve his job as a lawyer. His father was a man of the Enlightenment who introduced his son to Voltaire and Gotthold Lessing. Later Marx was also deeply influenced by his future father-in-law, Baron Ludwig von Westphalen, who was enamored of romantic literature and introduced him to Shakespeare, Homer, and Dante.

When he finished high school, Marx enrolled at the university in Bonn (at that time a sleepy little college town on the Rhine) to study law but spent much of his time drinking, dueling, and writing poetry to Jenny von Westphalen. In 1836 he transferred his studies to the University of Berlin, a far larger school in a major cosmopolitan center. Berlin was the center of Hegelian philosophy, which had pervaded most of Germany, and Marx soon abandoned the law in favor of philosophy. He threw himself into his studies and joined the *Doktorklub*, a group of radical Young Hegelians led by Bruno Bauer that attacked the orthodoxies of the era. His doctoral dissertation compared Democratean and Epicurean atomism (Democritus and Epicurus were Graeco-Roman proponents of atomism), and Marx briefly considered a career teaching philosophy. But a project he undertook with Bauer to inspire the young radicals to more strident activity led to Bauer's dismissal from the university and ultimately closed off the possibility of an academic career for Marx.

447

Offered the opportunity to write for the newly established liberal journal *Rheinische Zeitung*, Marx took up journalism and became the chief editor of the journal ten months later. His own description of his career, encapsulated in the "Preface to *On the Critique of Political Economy*," reprinted here, summarizes his further development until 1859. After 1843 he spent little time in his native Germany, where his leftist radicalism placed him in jeopardy. First he moved to Paris, where he wrote the *Economic and Philosophical Manuscripts*, then to Brussels, and finally, after an interlude in Germany during the tumult of 1848 and 1849 (when revolts erupted in numerous German principalities, mostly aimed at securing some form of democratic constitution), to London, where he lived in dire poverty. What he earned from writing for the *New York Tribune* was supplemented by his friend and collaborator Friedrich Engels, and neither Karl nor his wife Jenny von Westphalen Marx was able to manage money well.

In 1857 Marx composed a manuscript outlining, in more than eight hundred pages, the work that was to be his definitive statement on political economy. Of the six parts of that projected work, only the first volume of the first part—volume 1 of *Capital*—was brought to completion by Marx. Volumes 2 and 3 of part 1 were left in manuscript form to be edited by Engels. Marx never began the other five parts. A compulsive perfectionist, he could not let anything sit for more than a few days without deciding that it was deficient and needed to be reworked. Another reason was that Marx devoted a good deal of time to the cause of workers, both by writing polemics defending his vision of the cause and attacking other views, and by helping found and run the International Workingman's Association.

No philosopher has had a greater impact on the political world than Marx. Until the astounding events of late 1989, approximately one-third of the world's population lived under a government that claimed ideological descent from Marx, but a massive reassessment of Marxist ideologies is currently under way. Is the death of East Bloc communism the death of Marx's philosophy or is it at last the freeing of that philosophy from a prison of misinterpretation, misapplication, and outright perversion? Only a sober and critical reading of Marx's own texts can reveal the answer.

Philosophy

Though his early training was in philosophy, for most of his working life Marx would probably not have described himself as a philosopher but rather as a scientist (in the broader, German sense of the *Wissenschaftler*), economist, and revolutionary politician. It is certainly easier to find directly and recognizably philosophical passages in his earlier works, such as the ones included in this text.

But Marx never left philosophy behind, for his entire corpus is deeply informed with a philosophical viewpoint, a set of fundamental assumptions and methodological precepts from which the ultimate coherence of his thought derives. He never abandoned the methodological lessons learned from Hegel: no concept can be understood or explained without exhibiting its essential interconnections, both positive and negative, to other concepts, and philosophical analysis must always begin from a whole that is already present, at least in outline, and seek to expose the internal structural relationships that constitute that whole. Marx also held tight to what he had learned from

Feuerbach and the other Young Hegelians: the fundamental relationships are real, historical, material relationships among individual people and the surrounding nature in which they sustain themselves; the whole to be analyzed, therefore, is not the absolute idea—the megalomaniacal projection of humanity's own ideals—but the complex conditions under which we must produce our being, that is, the structures of social reality and the forces of production. And Marx's vision of what a fully humane society would have to be like drew from numerous influences: Kant, Voltaire, and the Enlightenment; Hegel; French socialism; romanticism. Marx is an applied philosopher who never lost sight of the fact that "philosophers have only *interpreted* the world in various ways; the point is to *change* it."

At the center of Marx's concern is the free human individual. What differentiates him from so many other philosophers is his understanding of the conditions required by humans to achieve freedom and individuality. In contrast to the earlier social contract theorists, who treated humans as fully formed individuals on their own, apart from society, Marx believed that humans must necessarily emerge from and reflect the particular social conditions in which they live. And though it was not the sole determinant, economic structures (the modes of production and of trade) are the most important determinants of the social and cultural conditions within which individuals express their being. Universal free individuality is possible only under certain social and economic arrangements—namely, communism, the abolition of private property.

For Marx these beliefs were more than philosophical views; they were scientific truths that arose from a painstaking effort at understanding historical change. Marx's efforts to promote communism reflected his belief that capitalism, like feudalism before it, contained the seeds of its own demise and would be followed by a more equitable, and in any case inevitable, reordering of society.

The Reading Context

Marx is among the most difficult of philosophical writers for North American readers, not so much because of his writing style but because readers sometimes have difficulty distancing Karl Marx from Marxism. Marxism, however, has been molded by many figures besides Marx—Engels, Lenin, Stalin, Trotsky, and Mao, among others. To give Marx's own thought a fair hearing, the reader must keep in mind that in his use of the term *communism* Marx meant it to designate the idealized political state in which human potential is fulfilled, not what called itself communism in Stalinist Russia, Maoist China, Castro's Cuba, or even Gorbachev's restructured USSR.

Marx's primary goal was the construction of a society in which human potential could achieve its maximal fulfillment. His diagnosis of the obstructions preventing such fulfillment and his conception of the situation in which that fulfillment could be achieved both have their roots in the Enlightenment, as do the political ideals of North American democracy. Marx was influenced by Hegel and early European socialism in ways that North American political thought never was. His driving motivations in the face of the desperate conditions of the mid-nineteenth-century proletariat are readily understandable—indeed, shared—by any sympathetic soul.

Read Marx's own words at first as if you were unaware of all that has been done in his name.

A Note on the Texts

The *Economic and Philosophical Manuscripts* were written in the summer of 1844 but not published until 1932. Their first publication aroused renewed interest in Marx's debt to Hegel and captured a more humanistic side of Marx than his later writings, which focused more exclusively on the economics of capitalism. The "Theses on Feuerbach" were originally jotted down as notes in March 1845 and were first published as an appendix to Friedrich Engels's book *Ludwig Feuerbach and the End of Classical German Philosophy*. *The German Ideology*, written in collaboration with Friedrich Engels in 1845–1846, was originally refused by several publishers. Much of it is highly polemical, and Marx and Engels, having both worked out their own position more fully and sufficiently vented their ire, let it lie unpublished. Only in the 1930s did their editors reconstruct the complete text and publish it. The "Preface to *On the Critique of Political Economy*," one of the classic statements of the thesis of historical materialism, is from a precursor of Marx's great work, *Capital*.

Reading Questions

1. Why does Marx claim that workers become poorer as they produce more?
2. What three aspects of alienated labor does Marx describe? How are they interrelated?
3. What is the life activity peculiar to humanity? What is the effect of alienated labor on it?
4. Compare Marx's explanation of the nature of private property with Locke's.
5. Describe the conditions under which labor would not be alienated.
6. Why does Marx state that his premises are real individuals, their actions, and the material conditions of life?
7. What would Marx say about the idea of a social contract as found in Hobbes or Locke?
8. What role in his materialist history does Marx attribute to consciousness?
9. What role in the development of communism does the state play?
10. How does Marx envision life under pure communism?

Economic and Philosophical Manuscripts of 1844

Alienated Labor

We . . . have to grasp the essential connection among private property, greed, division of labor, capital and land-ownership, and the connection of exchange with competition, of value with the devaluation of men, of monopoly with competition, etc., and of this whole alienation with the *money*-system.

Let us not put ourselves in a fictitious primordial state like a political economist trying to clarify things. Such a primordial state clarifies nothing. It merely pushes the issue into a gray, misty distance. It acknowledges as a fact or event what it should deduce, namely, the necessary relation between two things for example, between division of labor and exchange. In such a manner theology explains the origin of evil by the fall of man. That is, it asserts as a fact in the form of history what it should explain.

We proceed from a *present* fact of political economy.

The worker becomes poorer the more wealth he produces, the more his production increases in power and extent. The worker becomes a cheaper commodity the more commodities he produces. The *increase in value* of the world of things is directly proportional to the *decrease in value* of the human world. Labor not only produces commodities. It also produces itself and the worker as a *commodity*, and indeed in the same proportion as it produces commodities in general.

This fact simply indicates that the object which labor produces, its product, stands opposed to it as an *alien thing*, as a *power independent* of the producer. The product of labor is labor embodied and made objective in a thing. It is the *objectification* of labor. The realization of labor is its objectification. In the viewpoint of political economy this realization of labor appears as the *diminution* of the worker, the objectification as the *loss of and subservience to the object*, and the appropriation as *alienation* [*Entfremdung*], as externalization [*Entäusserung*].

So much does the realization of labor appear as diminution that the worker is diminished to the point of starvation. So much does objectification appear as loss of the object that the worker is robbed of the most essential objects not only of life but also of work. Indeed, work itself becomes a thing of which he can take possession only with the greatest effort and with the most unpredictable interruptions. So much does the appropriation of the object appear as alienation that the more objects the worker produces, the fewer he can own and the more he falls under the domination of his product, of capital.

All these consequences follow from the fact that the worker is related to the *product of his labor* as to an *alien* object. For it is clear according to this premise: The more the worker exerts himself, the more powerful becomes the alien objective world which he fashions against himself, the poorer he and his inner world become, the less there is that belongs to him. It is the same in religion. The more man attributes to God, the less he retains in himself. The worker puts his life into the object; then it no longer belongs to him but to the object. . . .

From *Writings of the Young Marx on Philosophy and Society*, ed. and trans. Loyd D. Easton and Kurt H. Guddat (Garden City, NY: Doubleday, 1967), pp. 288–402. Reprinted with the kind permission of Loyd D. Easton and Mrs. Kurt H. Guddat.

(The alienation of the worker in his object is expressed according to the laws of political economy as follows: the more the worker produces, the less he has to consume; the more values he creates the more worthless and unworthy he becomes; the better shaped his product, the more misshapen is he; the more civilized his product, the more barbaric is the worker; the more powerful the work, the more powerless becomes the worker; the more intelligence the work has, the more witless is the worker and the more he becomes a slave of nature.)

Political economy conceals the alienation in the nature of labor by ignoring the direct relationship between the worker (labor) *and production.* To be sure, labor produces marvels for the wealthy but it produces deprivation for the worker. It produces palaces, but hovels for the worker. It produces beauty, but mutilation for the worker. It displaces labor through machines, but it throws some workers back into barbarous labor and turns others into machines. It produces intelligence, but for the worker it produces imbecility and cretinism. . . .

Up to now we have considered the alienation, the externalization of the worker only from one side: his *relationship to the products of his labor.* But alienation is shown not only in the result but also in the *process of production,* in the *producing activity* itself. How could the worker stand in an alien relationship to the product of his activity if he did not alienate himself from himself in the very act of production? After all, the product is only the résumé of activity, of production. If the product of work is externalization, production itself must be active externalization, externalization of activity, activity of externalization. Only alienation—and externalization in the activity of labor itself—is summarized in the alienation of the object of labor.

What constitutes the externalization of labor?

First is the fact that labor is *external* to the laborer—that is, it is not part of his nature—and that the worker does not affirm himself in his work but denies himself, feels miserable and unhappy, develops no free physical and mental energy but mortifies his flesh and ruins his mind. The worker, therefore feels at ease only outside work, and during work he is outside himself. He is at home when he is not working and when he is working he is not at home. His work, therefore, is not voluntary, but coerced, *forced labor.* It is not the satisfaction of a need but only a *means* to satisfy other needs. Its alien character is obvious from the fact that as soon as no physical or other pressure exists, labor is avoided like the plague. . . . Finally, the external nature of work for the worker appears in the fact that it is not his own but another person's, that in work he does not belong to himself but to someone else. . . .

The result, therefore, is that man (the worker) feels that he is acting freely only in his animal functions—eating, drinking, and procreating, or at most in his shelter and finery—while in his human functions he feels only like an animal. The animalistic becomes the human and the human the animalistic.

To be sure, eating, drinking, and procreation are genuine human functions. In abstraction, however, and separated from the remaining sphere of human activities and turned into final and sole ends, they are animal functions.

We have considered labor, the act of alienation of practical human activity, in two aspects: (1) the relationship of the worker to the *product of labor* as an alien object dominating him. This relationship is at the same time the relationship to the sensuous external world, to natural objects as an alien world hostile to him; (2) the relationship of labor to the *act of production* in *labor.* This relationship is that of the worker to his own activity as alien and not belonging to him. . . .

We have now to derive a third aspect of *alienated labor* from the two previous ones.

Man is a species-being [*Gattungswesen*] not only in that he practically and theoretically makes his own species as well as that of other things his object, but also—and this is only another expression for the same thing—in that as present and living species he considers himself to be a universal and consequently free being.

The life of the species in man as in animals is physical in that man, (like the animal) lives by inorganic nature. And as man is more universal than the animal, the realm of inorganic nature by which he lives is more universal. As plants, animals, minerals, air, light, etc., in theory form a part of human consciousness, partly as objects of natural science, partly as objects of art—his spiritual inorganic nature or spiritual means of life which he first must prepare for enjoyment and assimilation—so they also form in practice a part of human life and human activity. . . . The universality of man appears in practice in the universality which makes the whole of nature his *inorganic* body: (1) as a direct means of life, and (2) as the matter, object, and instrument of his life activity. . . .

In alienating (1) nature from man, and (2) man from himself, his own active function, his life activity, alienated labor also alienates the *species* from him; it makes *species-life* the means of individual life. In the first place it alienates species-life and the individual life, and secondly it turns the latter in its abstraction into the purpose of the former, also in its abstract and alienated form.

For labor, *life activity*, and *productive life* appear to man at first only as a *means* to satisfy a need, the need to maintain physical existence. Productive life, however, is species-life. It is life begetting life. In the mode of life activity lies the entire character of a species, its species-character; and free conscious activity is the species-character of man. Life itself appears only as a *means of life*.

The animal is immediately one with its life activity, not distinct from it. The animal is *its life activity*. Man makes his life activity itself into an object of will and consciousness. He has conscious life activity. . . . Conscious life activity distinguishes man immediately from the life activity of the animal. Only thereby is he a species-being. Or rather, he is only a conscious being—that is, his own life is an object for him—since he is a species-being. Only on that account is his activity free activity. Alienated labor reverses the relationship in that man, since he is a conscious being, makes his life activity, his *essence*, only a means for his *existence*.

The practical creation of an *objective world*, the *treatment* of inorganic nature, is proof that man is a conscious species-being, that is, a being which is related to its species as to its own essence or is related to itself as a species-being. To be sure animals also produce. They build themselves nests, dwelling places, like the bees, beavers, ants, etc. But the animal produces only what is immediately necessary for itself or its young. It produces in a one-sided way while man produces universally. The animal produces under the domination of immediate physical need while man produces free of physical need and only genuinely so in freedom from such need. The animal only produces itself while man reproduces the whole of nature. The animal's product belongs immediately to its physical body while man is free when he confronts his product. The animal builds only according to the standard and need of the species to which it belongs while man knows how to produce according to the standard of any species and at all times knows how to apply an intrinsic standard to the object. Thus man creates also according to the laws of beauty.

In the treatment of the objective world, therefore, man proves himself to be genuinely a *species-being*. This production is his active species-life. Through it nature appears as *his* work and his actuality. The object of labor is thus the *objectification of man's species-life*: he produces himself not only intellectually, as in consciousness, but also actively in a real sense and sees himself in a world he made. In taking from man the object of his production, alienated labor takes from his *species-life*, his actual and objective existence as a species. It changes his superiority to the animal to inferiority, since he is deprived of nature, his inorganic body. . . .

A direct consequence of man's alienation from the product of his work, from his life activity, and from his species-existence, is the *alienation of man* from *man*. When man confronts himself, he confronts *other* men. What holds true of man's relationship to his work, to the product of his work, and to himself, also holds true of man's relationship to other men, to their labor, and the object of their labor.

In general, the statement that man is alienated from his species-existence means that one man is alienated from another just as each man is alienated from human nature. . . .

Let us now see further how the concept of alienated, externalized labor must express and represent itself in actuality.

If the product of labor is alien to me, confronts me as an alien power, to whom then does it belong?

If my own activity does not belong to me, if it is an alien and forced activity, to whom then does it belong?

To a being *other* than myself.

Who is this being?

Gods? To be sure, in early times the main production, for example, the building of temples in Egypt, India, and Mexico, appears to be in the service of the gods, just as the product belongs to the gods. But gods alone were never workmasters. The same is true of *nature*. And what a contradiction it would be if the more man subjugates nature through his work and the more the miracles of gods are rendered superfluous by the marvels of industry, man should renounce his joy in producing and the enjoyment of his product for love of these powers.

The *alien* being who owns labor and the product of labor, whom labor serves and whom the product of labor satisfies can only be *man* himself.

That the product of labor does not belong to the worker and an alien power confronts him is possible only because this product belongs to *a man other than the worker*. If his activity is torment for him, it must be the *pleasure* and the life-enjoyment for another. . . .

If man is related to the product of his labor, to his objectified labor, as to an *alien*, hostile, powerful object independent of him, he is so related that another alien, hostile, powerful man independent of him is the lord of this object. If he is unfree in relation to his own activity, he is related to it as bonded activity, activity under the domination, coercion, and yoke of another man. . . .

Thus through *alienated externalized labor* does the worker create the relation to this work of man alienated to labor and standing outside it. The relation of the worker to labor produces the relation of the capitalist to labor, or whatever one wishes to call the lord of labor. *Private property* is thus product, result, and necessary consequence of *externalized labor*, of the external relation of the worker to nature and to himself.

Private property thus is derived, through analysis, from the concept of *externalized labor*, that is, *externalized man*, alienated labor, alienated life, and *alienated* man. . . .

The analysis of this idea shows that though private property appears to be the ground and cause of externalized labor, it is rather a consequence of externalized labor, just as gods are *originally* not the cause but the effect of an aberration of the human mind. Later this relationship reverses.

Only at the final culmination of the development of private property does this, its secret, reappear—namely, that on the one hand it is the *product* of externalized labor and that secondly it is the *means* through which labor externalizes itself, the *realization of this externalization*.

Therefore we also perceive that *wages* and *private property* are identical: for when the product, the object of labor, pays for the labor itself, wages are only a necessary consequence of the alienation of labor. In wages labor appears not as an end in itself but as the servant of wages. . . .

An enforced *raising* of *wages* . . . would therefore be nothing but a *better slave-salary* and would not achieve either for the worker or for labor human significance and dignity.

Even the *equality of wages*, as advanced by Proudhon, would only convert the relation of the contemporary worker to his work into the relation of all men to labor. Society would then be conceived as an abstract capitalist.

Wages are a direct result of alienated labor, and alienated labor is the direct cause of private property. The downfall of one is necessarily the downfall of the other. . . .

From the relation of alienated labor to private property it follows further that the emancipation of society from private property, etc., from servitude, is expressed in its *political* form as the *emancipation of workers*, not as though it is only a question of their emancipation but because in their emancipation is contained universal human emancipation. It is contained in their emancipation because the whole of human servitude is involved in the relation of worker to production, and all relations of servitude are only modifications and consequences of the worker's relation to production. . . .

Theses on Feuerbach

(1)

The chief defect of all previous materialism (including Feuerbach's) is that the object, actuality, sensuousness is conceived only in the form of the *object or perception* [*Anschauung*], but not as *sensuous human activity, practice* [*Praxis*], not subjectively. Hence in opposition to materialism the *active* side was developed by idealism—but only abstractly since idealism naturally does not know actual, sensuous activity as such. Feuerbach wants sensuous objects actually different from thought objects: but he does not comprehend human activity itself as *objective*. Hence in *The Essence of Christianity* he regards only the theoretical attitude as the truly human attitude, while practice is understood and fixed only in its dirtily Jewish form of appearance. Consequently he does not comprehend the significance of "revolutionary," of "practical-critical" activity.

(2)

The question whether human thinking can reach objective truth—is not a question of theory but a *practical* question. In practice man must prove the truth, that is, actuality and power, this-sidedness of his thinking. The dispute about the actuality or non-actuality of thinking—thinking isolated from practice—is a purely *scholastic* question.

(3)

The materialistic doctrine concerning the change of circumstances and education forgets that circumstances are changed by men and that the educator must himself be educated. Hence this doctrine must divide society into two parts—one of which towers above [as in Robert Owen, Engels added].

The coincidence of the change of circumstances and of human activity or self-change can be comprehended and rationally understood only as *revolutionary practice*.

(4)

Feuerbach starts out from the fact of religious self-alienation, the duplication of the world into a religious and secular world. His work consists in resolving the religious world into its secular basis. But the fact that the secular basis becomes separate from itself and establishes an independent realm in the clouds can only be explained by the cleavage and self-contradictoriness of the secular basis. Thus the latter must itself be both understood in its contradiction and revolutionized in practice. For instance, after the earthly family is found to be the secret of the holy family, the former must then be theoretically and practically nullified.

(5)

Feuerbach, not satisfied with *abstract thinking*, wants *perception*; but he does not comprehend sensuousness as *practical*, human-sensuous activity.

From *Writings of the Young Marx on Philosophy and Science*, ed. and trans. Loyd D. Easton and Kurt H. Guddat (Garden City, NY: Doubleday, 1967), pp. 403–407. Reprinted with the kind permission of Loyd D. Easton and Mrs. Kurt H. Guddat.

(6)

Feuerbach resolves the religious essence into the *human* essence. But the essence of man is no abstraction inhering in each single individual. In its actuality it is the ensemble of social relationships.

Feuerbach, who does not go into the criticism of this actual essence, is hence compelled

1. to abstract from the historical process and to establish religious feeling as something self-contained, and to presuppose an abstract—*isolated*—human individual;

2. to view the essence of man merely as "species," as the inner, dumb generality which unites the many individuals *naturally*.

(7)

Feuerbach does not see, consequently, that "religious feeling" is itself a social product and that the abstract individual he analyzes belongs to a particular form of society.

(8)

All social life is essentially *practical*. All mysteries which lead theory to mysticism find their rational solution in human practice and the comprehension of this practice.

(9)

The highest point attained by perceptual materialism, that is, materialism that does not comprehend sensuousness as practical activity, is the view of separate individuals and civil society.

(10)

The standpoint of the old materialism is civil society; the standpoint of the new is human society or socialized humanity.

(11)

The philosophers have only *interpreted* the world in various ways; the point is to *change* it.

The German Ideology

The premises from which we start are not arbitrary; they are no dogmas but rather actual premises from which abstraction can be made only in imagination. They are the real individuals, their actions, and their material conditions of life, those which they find existing as well as those which they produce through their actions. These premises can be substantiated in a purely empirical way.

The first premise of all human history, of course, is the existence of living human individuals. The first fact to be established, then, is the physical organization of these individuals and their consequent relationship to the rest of nature. Of course, we cannot discuss here the physical nature of man or the natural conditions in which man finds himself—geological, orohydrographical, climatic, and others. All historiography must proceed from these natural bases and their modification in the course of history through the actions of men.

Man can be distinguished from the animal by consciousness, religion, or anything else you please. He begins to distinguish himself from the animal the moment he begins to *produce* his means of subsistence, a step required by his physical organization. By producing food, man indirectly produces his material life itself.

The way in which man produces his food depends first of all on the nature of the means of subsistence that he finds and has to reproduce. This mode of production must not be viewed simply as reproduction of the physical existence of individuals. Rather it is a definite form of their activity, a definite way of expressing their life, a definite *mode of life*. As individuals express their life, so they are. What they are, therefore, coincides with what they produce, with *what* they produce and *how* they produce. The nature of individuals thus depends on the material conditions which determine their production.

This production begins with *population growth* which in turn presupposes *interaction* [*Verkehr*] among individuals. The form of such interaction is again determined by production. . . .

The different stages of development in the division of labor are just so many different forms of ownership; that is, the stage in the division of labor also determines the relations of individuals to one another so far as the material, instrument, and product of labor are concerned.

The first form of ownership is tribal ownership. It corresponds to the undeveloped stage of production where people live by hunting and fishing, by breeding animals or, in the highest stage, by agriculture. . . . The division of labor at this stage is still very undeveloped and confined to extending the natural division of labor in the family. . . .

The second form is the ancient communal and state ownership which proceeds especially from the union of several tribes into a *city* by agreement or by conquest; this form is still accompanied by slavery. Alongside communal ownership there already develops movable, and later even immovable, private property, but as an abnormal form subordinate to communal ownership. . . . Hence the whole social structure based

From *Writings of the Young Marx on Philosophy and Society*, ed. and trans. Loyd D. Easton and Kurt H. Guddat (Garden City, N.Y.: Doubleday, 1967), pp. 408–431. Reprinted with the kind permission of Loyd D. Easton and Mrs. Kurt H. Guddat.

on communal ownership and with it the power of the people decline as immovable private property develops. The division of labor is developed to a larger extent. We already find antagonism between town and country and later antagonism between states representing urban interests and those representing rural interests. Within the cities themselves we find the antagonism between industry and maritime commerce. The class relation between citizens and slaves is then fully developed. . . .

The third form is feudal or estate ownership. Antiquity started out from the *town* and the small territory around it; the Middle Ages started out from the *country*. This different starting-point was caused by the sparse population at that time, scattered over a large area and receiving no large population increase from the conquerors. . . .

This feudal organization of land ownership had its counterpart in the *towns* in the form of corporate property, the feudal organization of the trades. Property consisted mainly in the labor of each individual. The necessity for association against the organized robber nobility, the need for communal markets in an age when the industrialist was at the same time a merchant, the growing competition of escaped serfs pouring into the rising cities, and the feudal structure of the whole country gave rise to *guilds*. . . .

The main form of property during the feudal times consisted on the one hand of landed property with serf labor and on the other hand, individual labor with small capital controlling the labor of journeymen. The organization of both was determined by the limited conditions of production: small-scale, primitive cultivation of land and industry based on crafts. There was little division of labor when feudalism was at its peak. . . .

The fact is, then, that definite individuals who are productively active in a specific way enter into these definite social and political relations. In each particular instance, empirical observation must show empirically, without any mystification or speculation, the connection of the social and political structure with production. The social structure and the state continually evolve out of the life-process of definite individuals, but individuals not as they may appear in their own or other people's imagination but rather as they *really* are, that is, as they work, produce materially, and act under definite material limitations, presuppositions, and conditions independent of their will.

The production of ideas, of conceptions, of consciousness is directly interwoven with the material activity and the material relationships of men; it is the language of actual life. Conceiving, thinking, and the intellectual relationships of men appear here as the direct result of their material behavior. The same applies to intellectual production as manifested in a people's language of politics, law, morality, religion, metaphysics, etc. Men are the producers of their conceptions, ideas, etc., but these are real, active men, as they are conditioned by a definite development of their productive forces and of the relationships corresponding to these up to their highest forms. Consciousness can never be anything else except conscious existence, and the existence of men is their actual life-process. . . .

In direct contrast to German philosophy, which descends from heaven to earth, here one ascends from earth to heaven. In other words, to arrive at man in the flesh, one does not set out from what men say, imagine, or conceive, nor from man as he is described, thought about, imagined, or conceived. Rather one sets out from real, active men and their actual life-process and demonstrates the development of ideological reflexes and echoes of that process. The phantoms formed in the human brain, too, are necessary sublimations of man's material life-process which is empirically verifiable and connected with material premises. Morality, religion, metaphysics, and all the rest of ideology and their corresponding forms of consciousness no longer seem to be independent. They have no history or development. Rather, men who develop their material production and their material relationships alter their thinking and the products of their thinking along with their real existence. Consciousness does not determine life, but life determines consciousness. . . .

In dealing with Germans devoid of premises, we must begin by stating the first premise of all human existence, and hence of all history, the premise, namely, that men must be able to live in order to be able "to make history." But life involves above all eating and drinking, shelter, clothing, and many other things. The first historical act is thus the production of the means to satisfy these needs, the production of material life itself. This is a historical act, a fundamental condition of all history which must be fulfilled in order to sustain human life every day and every hour, today as well as thousands of years ago. . . . The first principle therefore in any theory of history is to observe this fundamental fact in its entire significance and all its implications and to attribute to this fact its due importance. . . .

The second point is that once a need is satisfied, which requires the action of satisfying and the acquisition of the instrument for this purpose, new needs arise. The production of new needs is the first historical act. . . .

The third circumstance entering into historical development from the very beginning is the fact that men who daily remake their own lives begin to make other men, begin to propagate: the relation between husband and wife, parents and children, the *family*. The family, initially the only social relationship, becomes later a subordinate relationship (except in Germany) when increased needs produce new social relations and an increased population creates new needs. . . . These three aspects of social activity are not to be taken as three different stages, but just for what they are, three aspects. . . .

The production of life, of one's own life in labor and of another in procreation, now appears as a double relationship: on the one hand as a natural relationship, on the other as a social one. The latter is social in the sense that individuals co-operate, no matter under what conditions, in what manner, and for what purpose. Consequently a certain mode of production or industrial stage is always combined with a certain mode of co-operation or social stage, and this mode of co-operation is itself a "productive force." We observe in addition that the multitude of productive forces accessible to men determines the nature of society and that the "history of mankind" must always be studied and treated in relation to the history of industry and exchange. . . .

Having considered four moments, four aspects of the primary historical relationships, we now find that man also possesses "consciousness." But this consciousness is not inherent, not "pure." From the start the "spirit" bears the curse of being "burdened" with matter which makes its appearance in the form of agitated layers of air, sounds, in short, in the form of language. Language is as old as consciousness. It *is* practical consciousness which exists also for other men and hence exists for me personally as well. Language, like consciousness, only arises from the need and necessity of relationships with other men. Where a relationship exists, it exists for me. The animal has no "*relations*" with anything, no relations at all. Its relation to others does not exist as a relation. Consciousness is thus from the very beginning a social product and will remain so as long as men exist. At first consciousness is concerned only with the *immediate* sensuous environment and a limited relationship with other persons and things outside the individual who is becoming conscious of himself. . . . On the other hand it is consciousness of the necessity to come in contact with other individuals; it is the beginning of man's consciousness of the fact that he lives in a society. This beginning is as animalistic as social life itself at this stage. It is the mere consciousness of being a member of a flock, and the only difference between sheep and man is that man possesses consciousness instead of instinct, or in other words his instinct is more conscious.

This sheeplike or tribal consciousness receives further development and formation through increased productivity, the increase of needs, and what is fundamental to both, the increase of population. Along with these, division of labor develops which originally was nothing but the division of labor in the sexual act, then that type of division of labor which comes about spontaneously or "naturally" because of natural predisposition (e.g. physical strength), needs, accidents, etc., etc. The division of labor is a true division only from the moment a division of material and mental labor appears. From this moment on consciousness can really boast of being something other than consciousness of existing practice, of *really* representing something without representing something real. From this moment on consciousness can emancipate itself from the world and proceed to the formation of "pure" theory, theology, philosophy, ethics, etc. But even if this theory, theology, philosophy, ethics, etc., comes into conflict with existing relations, this can only occur because existing social relations have come into conflict with the existing force of production. . . .

Moreover it does not make any difference what consciousness starts to do on its own. The only result we obtain from all such muck is that these three moments—the force of production, the state of society, and consciousness—can and must come into conflict with one another because the *division of labor* implies the possibility, indeed the necessity, that intellectual and material activity—enjoyment and labor, production and consumption—are given to different individuals, and the only possibility of their not coming into conflict lies in again transcending the division of labor. It is self-evident that words such as "specters," "bonds," "higher being," "concept," "scruple," are only the idealistic, spiritual expression, the apparent conception of the isolated individual, the image of very empirical fetters and restrictions within which the mode of production of life and the related form of interaction move.

With the division [*Teilung*] of labor, in which all these conflicts are implicit and which is based on the natural division of labor in the family and the partition of society into individual families opposing one another, there is at the same time distribution [*Verteilung*], indeed *unequal* distribution, both quantitative and qualitative, of labor and its products, hence property which has its first form, its nucleus, in the family where wife and children are the slaves of the man. The latent slavery in the family, though still very crude, is the first property. Even at this initial stage, however, it corresponds perfectly to the definition of modern economists who call it the power of controlling the labor of others.

Furthermore, the division of labor implies the conflict between the interest of the individual or the individual family and the communal interest of all individuals having contact with one another. The communal interest does not exist only in the imagination, as something "general," but first of all in reality, as a mutual interdependence of those individuals among whom the labor is divided. And finally, the division of labor offers us the first example for the fact that man's own act becomes an alien power opposed to him and enslaving him instead of being controlled by him—as long as man remains in natural society, as long as a split exists between the particular and the common interest, and as long as the activity is not voluntarily but naturally divided. For as soon as labor is distributed, each person has a particular, exclusive area of activity which is imposed on him and from which he cannot escape. He is a hunter, a fisherman, a herdsman, or a critical critic, and he must remain so if he does not want to lose his means of livelihood. In communist society, however, where nobody has an exclusive area of activity and each can train himself in any branch he wishes, society regulates the general production, making it possible for me to do one thing today and another tomorrow, to hunt in the morning, fish in the afternoon, breed cattle in the evening, criticize after dinner, just as I like, without ever becoming a hunter, a fisherman, a herdsman, or a critic. This fixation of social activity, this consolidation of our own products into an objective power above us, growing out of our control, thwarting our expectations, and nullifying our calculations, is one of the chief factors in historical development so far, [(nine lines deleted and illegible)]

<[beside previous paragraph][1] Out of this very contradiction between the interest of the individual and that of the community the latter takes an independent form as the *State*, separated from the real interests of individual and community, and at the same time as an illusory communal life, but always based on the real bonds present in every family and every tribal conglomeration, . . . and particularly based, as we intend to show later, on the classes already determined by the division of labor, classes which form in any such mass of people and of which one dominates all the others. It follows from this that all struggles within the State, the struggle between democracy, aristocracy and monarchy, the struggle for franchise, etc., etc., are nothing but the illusory forms in which the real struggles of different classes are carried out among one another. . . . Furthermore, it follows that every class striving to gain control—even when such control means the transcendence of the entire old form of society and of control itself, as is the case with the proletariat—must first win political power in order to represent its interest in turn as the universal interest, something which the class is forced to do immediately.> . . .

<<This *"alienation,"* to use a term which the philosophers will understand, can be abolished only on the basis of two *practical* premises. To become an "intolerable" power, that is, a power against which men make a revolution, it must have made the great mass of humanity "propertyless" and this at the same time in contradiction to an existing world of wealth and culture, both of which presuppose a great increase in productive power and a high degree of its development. On the other hand, this development of productive forces (which already implies the actual empirical existence of men on a *world-historical* rather than local scale) is an absolutely necessary practical premise

---

1. Double pointed brackets [indicate] adjacent addenda in Marx's handwriting in the right column of the manuscript page. Each manuscript page is halved lengthwise into two columns, the left filled with most of the text in Engels' script—he wrote more smoothly and quickly than Marx—from joint dictation. Single pointed brackets [indicate] adjacent addenda in Engels' writing in the right column of the manuscript page. [Trans. note]

because, without it, *want* is merely made general, and with *destitution* the struggle for necessities and all the old muck would necessarily be reproduced; and furthermore, because only with this universal development of productive forces is a *universal* commerce among men established which produces in all nations simultaneously the phenomenon of a "propertyless" mass (universal competition), makes each nation dependent on the revolutions of the others, and finally replaces local individuals with *world-historical*, empirically universal individuals. Without this, (1) communism could only exist locally; (2) the *forces* of interaction themselves could not have developed as *universal* and thus intolerable powers, but would have remained homebred, superstitious "conditions"; (3) any extension of interaction would abolish local communism. Empirically, communism is only possible as the act of dominant peoples "all at once" and simultaneously, which presupposes the universal development of productive power and worldwide interaction linked with communism. Besides, the mass of *propertyless* workers—labor power on a mass scale cut off from capital or even limited satisfaction, and hence no longer just temporarily deprived of work as a secure source of life—presupposes a *world market* through competition.>>....

In history up to the present it is certainly an empirical fact that separate individuals, with the broadening of their activity into world-historical activity, have become more and more enslaved to a power alien to them..., a power which has become increasingly great and finally turns out to be the *world market*. But it is just as empirically established that by the overthrow of the existing state of society by the communist revolution (more about this below) and the abolition of private property which is identical with it, this alien power so baffling to German theoreticians will be dissolved. Then the liberation of each single individual will be accomplished to the extent that history becomes world history. Hence it is clear that the real intellectual wealth of the individual depends entirely on the wealth of his real connections. Only in this way will separate individuals be liberated from the various national and local barriers, be brought into practical connection with the material and intellectual production of the whole world, and be able to enjoy this all-sided production of the whole earth (the creations of man). *All-around* dependence, that natural form of the *world-historical* co-operation of individuals, will be transformed by the communist revolution into the control and conscious governance of these powers, which, born of the interaction of men, have until now overawed and governed men as powers completely alien to them....

In all revolutions up till now the mode of activity remained unchanged, and it was only a question of a different distribution of this activity, a new distribution of labor to other persons. But the communist revolution is directed against the preceding *mode* of activity, does away with *labor*, and abolishes the rule of all classes along with the classes themselves, because it is accomplished by the class which society no longer recognizes as a class and is itself the expression of the dissolution of all classes, nationalities, etc....

A Contribution to the Critique of Political Economy

Preface

. . . I was taking up law, which study, however, I only pursued as a subordinate subject along with philosophy and history. In the year 1842–43, as editor of the *Rheinische Zeitung*, I experienced for the first time the embarrassment of having to take part in discussions on so-called material interests. The proceedings of the Rhenish Landtag on thefts of wood and parcelling of landed property, the official polemic which Herr von Schaper, then *Oberpräsident* of the Rhine Province, opened against the *Rheinische Zeitung* on the conditions of the Moselle peasantry, and finally debates on free trade and protective tariffs gave the first incentive to my occupation with economic questions. . . .

The first work which I undertook for a solution of the doubts which assailed me was a critical review of the Hegelian philosophy of law, a work the introduction to which appeared in 1844 in the *Deutsch-Französische Jahrbücher*, published in Paris. My investigation led to the result that legal relations such as forms of state are to be grasped neither from themselves nor from the so-called general development of the human mind, but rather have their roots in the material conditions of life. . . . The general result at which I arrived and which, once won, served as a guiding thread for my studies, can be briefly formulated as follows: In the social production of their life, men enter into definite relations that are indispensable and independent of their will; these relations of production correspond to a definite stage of development of their material forces of production. The sum total of these relations of production constitutes the economic structure of society—the real foundation, on which rises a legal and political superstructure and to which correspond definite forms of social consciousness. The mode of production of material life determines the social, political and intellectual life process in general. It is not the consciousness of men that determines their being, but, on the contrary, their social being that determines their consciousness. At a certain stage of their development, the material productive forces in society come in conflict with the existing relations of production, or—what is but a legal expression for the same thing—with the property relations within which they have been at work before. From forms of development of the productive forces these relations turn into their fetters. Then begins an epoch of social revolution. With the change of the economic foundation the entire immense superstructure is more or less rapidly transformed. In considering such transformations a distinction should always be made between the material transformation of the economic conditions of production, which can be determined with the precision of natural science, and the legal, political, religious, aesthetic or philosophic—in short, ideological forms in which men become conscious of this conflict and fight it out. Just as our opinion of an individual is not based on what he thinks of himself, so can we not judge of such a period of transformation by its own consciousness; on the contrary, this consciousness must be explained rather from the contradictions of material life, from the existing conflict

From *Marx and Engels: Selected Works*, 2d Eng. ed. 2 vols. (London: Lawrence & Wishart, 1947), pp. 299–301. Reprinted by permission of International Publishers Co., Inc.

between the social productive forces and the relations of production. No social order ever disappears before all the productive forces for which there is room in it have been developed; and new, higher relations of production never appear before the material conditions of their existence have matured in the womb of the old society itself. Therefore, mankind always sets itself only such tasks as it can solve; since, looking at the matter more closely, we will always find that the task itself arises only when the material conditions necessary for its solution already exist or are at least in the process of formation. In broad outlines we can designate the Asiatic, the ancient, the feudal, and the modern bourgeois modes of production as so many progressive epochs in the economic formation of society. The bourgeois relations of production are the last antagonistic form of the social process of production—antagonistic not in the sense of individual antagonism, but of one arising from the social conditions of life of the individuals; at the same time the productive forces developing in the womb of bourgeois society create the material conditions for the solution of that antagonism. This social formation constitutes, therefore, the closing chapter of the prehistoric stage of human society. . . .

SELECTED BIBLIOGRAPHY

Marx, Karl. *Capital. A Critique of Political Economy.* 3 vols. Ed. Friedrich Engels. New York: International Publishers, 1967.

_____. *Karl Marx and Frederick Engels: Selected Works in One Volume.* New York: International Publishers, 1968.

_____. *Karl Marx: Selected Writings.* Ed. D. McLellan. New York: Oxford University Press, 1977.

Avineri, Shlomo. *Social and Political Thought of Karl Marx.* Cambridge: Cambridge University Press, 1971

Bottomore, Tom, ed. *Interpretations of Marx.* Oxford: Basil Blackwell, 1988.

_____. *Karl Marx.* Oxford: Basil Blackwell, 1979.

Buchanan, Allen E. *Marx and Justice: The Radical Critique of Liberalism.* Totowa, N.J.: Rowman & Littlefield, 1982.

Cohen, G.A. *Karl Marx's Theory of History.* Princeton, N.J.: Princeton University Press, 1980.

Elster, Jon. *An Introduction to Marx.* Cambridge: Cambridge University Press, 1986.

_____. *Making Sense of Marx.* Cambridge: Cambridge University Press, 1985.

Kolakowski, Leszek. *Main Currents of Marxism.* 3 vols. Trans. P.S. Falla. New York: Oxford University Press, 1978.

Mazlish, Bruce. *The Meaning of Karl Marx.* New York: Oxford University Press, 1987.

McBride, William. *The Philosophy of Marx.* New York: St. Martin's Press, 1977.

McLellan, David. *Karl Marx.* London: Fontana, 1976.

Meszaros, Istvan. *Marx's Theory of Alienation.* London: Merlin Press, 1970.

Roemer, John, ed. *Analytical Marxism.* Cambridge: Cambridge University Press, 1986.

Singer, Peter. *Marx.* New York: Oxford University Press, 1980.

Suchting, W.A. *Marx and Philosophy.* New York: NYU Press, 1986.

Wood, Allen. *Karl Marx.* London: Routledge, Chapman & Hall, 1981.

John Stuart Mill

John Stuart Mill (1806–1873) was the first son of James Mill, a Scot who had come to London to try his hand at writing for a living. Soon after his first son was born, two important events determined James Mill's future course: he set to writing *The History of British India*, a work that would take a dozen years to complete, and he made the acquaintance of Jeremy Bentham, the patriarch of utilitarianism, a man who devoted his entire life to the careful exposition of the principles on which all legislation and morality should be founded. The time James Mill devoted to his history of India prevented him from holding steady, remunerative employment, so the growing family was never easy for money. From the older, much better situated Bentham, James received significant aid, both financial and intellectual; more important, he also received a cause. James became the purest disciple of Bentham, fighting to promulgate his philosophy, agitating for social change, and even raising his family in strict accordance with Benthamite precepts.

The story of young John Mill's education is seed for a great deal of speculation. His father never sent him to school but took complete charge of the boy's learning. He began Greek at age three, Latin and arithmetic at eight, logic at twelve, and political economy at thirteen. The young boy's reading list was quite daunting. James and young John shared a study, James at work on the history of India, John at his lessons. John was expected to write summaries and comments on his reading and each day during their long afternoon walks to report orally on what he had learned. John's facility in written

467

and oral presentation as well as his keen analytical skills clearly owed a great deal to this arduous regimen, but he later admitted, "I never was a boy; never played at cricket; it is better to let Nature have her way." In 1820, now fourteen years old, Mill spent a year in France, living with Bentham's brother.

When he returned, his basic education now complete, he was introduced to the central works of Bentham's philosophy—it was time to begin his indoctrination in the cause. As some consideration also had to be given to a suitable career, he began to read law in the office of John Austin, probably the greatest British jurist of the nineteenth century. At this point John Mill became active in several different groups of young men devoted to debate, to utilitarian principles, to stimulating human progress. In 1818, after the publication of his history of India, James Mill was appointed assistant examiner at the East India Company, which essentially controlled all trade with India. This solved James's financial problems, and he advanced quickly in the company and secured a post for his son in 1823. Mill followed his father's path and remained with the East India Company until 1858.

These years of "youthful propagandism" were busy and culminated in 1826, when, probably exhausted from his busy schedule of work, writing, debating, and editing Bentham's *Rationale of Judicial Evidence* (a ponderous job, given Bentham's style), Mill experienced a "mental crisis." Asking himself, "Suppose that all your objects in life were realized; that all the changes in institutions and opinions which you are looking forward to, could be completely effected at this very instant: would this be a great joy and happiness to you?" he found that his answer was no. This sent Mill into a deep depression, for he thought he had lost the ability to feel, to respond emotionally to anything. Nevertheless, he managed to carry on with his work and his writing. Fortunately, this state did not last too long. Reading a book of French memoirs, a particular passage moved him to tears, and finding himself not bereft of all feeling, Mill began to emerge from his despondency. Had his father's driving, rigorous educational plan provoked the crisis? What sources of strength pulled him out of it? Whatever interpretation one gives the episode, the Mill that arose from his depression was a broader man. James Mill and the Benthamites had a deep distrust of emotion and sentiment, but after his personal crisis, John Mill recognized the importance of feelings in any fully human life and sought to enrich the philosophy he had inherited to take account of this inescapable fact. Mill was never again a pure disciple of Benthamite principles. Rather, he attempted to appropriate the artistic and individualistic emphases of such romantics as Samuel Taylor Coleridge and Thomas Carlyle and meld them with the liberal, utilitarian framework he never abandoned.

In 1830 Mill was introduced to Mrs. Harriet Taylor, wife of a London merchant. Twenty-two years old, vivacious and intelligent, she enchanted Mill, and he, a handsome young man of obviously superior capacities, similarly entranced her. Mrs. Taylor and Mill became constant companions, creating a scandal among society that endured for many years. Both Mill and Mrs. Taylor professed innocence, and Harriet never divorced her husband, though she and Mill were inseparable. In 1851, a respectable two years after John Taylor's death, Mill and Harriet married. Mill was thoroughly devoted to her and attributed to her the highest level of insight, sensitivity, and intelligence. The somewhat scandalous circumstances of his life led Mill to restrict the circle of his companions and to devote himself more fully to his writing.

Mill's first major book, *A System of Logic*, was published in 1843. In it he continues the tradition of British empiricism marked out by Locke and Hume. Although not widely read today, it was a tremendously influential work that could not be ignored by any English-speaking thinker in the nineteenth century. The *Principles of Political Economy* followed in 1848. Mill retired from the East India Company in 1858, the same year in which his beloved Harriet died. Other than a brief term in Parliament from 1865 to 1868, the remainder of his life was spent in writing. *On Liberty*, a consideration of the extent of the individual's right versus the government's, appeared in 1859. *Utilitarianism*, a restatement of the fundamental principles of his moral philosophy, appeared in 1863. The year 1865 saw the publication of *An Examination of Sir William Hamilton's Philosophy* and *August Comte and Positivism*. The *Subjection of Women*, though written earlier with his wife, appeared in 1869, as did Mill's revision of his father's book *Analysis of the Human Mind*. His autobiography, written in 1861, was published after his death in 1873.

Throughout his life Mill also wrote shorter essays and reviews and maintained voluminous correspondence with many of the leading thinkers of the day. His massive collected works document a powerful mind that sought to do justice to all the opinions it encountered, a mind for which truth was always the sole cause.

Philosophy

As the heir of Locke and Hume, Mill was committed to the notion that the association of ideas (a principle that had in the meantime been developed and applied still more thoroughly by David Hartley and James Mill) was the fundamental principle of all activities of the human mind. All our concepts, beliefs, and judgments are acquired or constructed in accordance with a set of principles governing the ways in which the ideas given to us through experience are recalled and combined. The depth of his empiricism is most tellingly shown by his defense, in his *Logic*, of the claim that even the truths of arithmetic are highly abstract *empirical* claims justified by the evidence of our senses. Unlike Hume, Mill did not draw skeptical conclusions from his empiricism. His attempts to justify the employment of inductive methods have drawn a great deal of criticism, but his analysis of the actual methods employed in the natural and the moral (humanistic) sciences were very influential in science as well as philosophy.

In his ethical philosophy Mill is utilitarian, the direct descendent of Jeremy Bentham, though by no means a slavish disciple. What they share is allegiance to the utilitarian maxim that the right act is the one that maximizes the welfare of the greatest number of sentient beings. Mill and Bentham differ, however, in their applications of this principle. Bentham is a psychological hedonist; our fundamental motivation, he believes, is always the attainment of pleasure and the avoidance of pain. The goodness of alternative actions could be assessed by subjecting them to a "hedonic calculus" in which the amount, duration, certainty, and breadth (among other factors) of the resultant pleasures and pains could be estimated, summed, and compared. The role of social and governmental institutions and laws is to ensure that those actions for or against the general interest are sufficiently rewarded or punished to motivate us to take or avoid them.

In his adaptation of this doctrine, Mill introduces a distinction among *kinds* of pleasure—some pleasures are of a higher kind than others: "It is better to be a human being dissatisfied than a pig satisfied." Distinguishing kinds of pleasure that are then incommensurable rules out any kind of "hedonic calculus," but Mill also recognized that the factors involved in utilitarian decision making are beyond calculation. In order to be able to make reliable judgments about what to do, we have to rely on the wisdom of the ages summed up in the moral principles we are all taught from infancy—be honest, keep your promises, don't kill innocent people, and so forth. There is some controversy about whether Mill intended us always to go by such rules, using the utilitarian principle only to assess the rules themselves (a position called *rule utilitarianism*), or whether he intended those rules just as convenient but nonbinding summaries of what would probably be revealed by a more thorough and searching examination in accordance with the utilitarian principle (*act utilitarianism*).

Mill's ethics is another expression of his deep-seated empiricism, for a fully executed utilitarianism would make ethics an empirical discipline. What makes people happy is a matter of empirical investigation, and progress in the sciences will leave us in an ever better position to assess the consequences of our actions and choose the actions that will truly maximize the welfare of all. In this way utilitarianism is an extremely optimistic doctrine. Despite the power and influence it has attained in the twentieth century, the difficulties utilitarianism faces in providing plausible analyses of moral right, justice, and the legitimate differences among individuals have kept it from the universal assent Mill hoped for.

The Reading Context

Although Mill was one of the more accessible stylists of his day, reading him now can be difficult, for the average sentence length in Victorian England was more than three times the length of the average sentence in contemporary American English.

Mill was a superb polemicist, but he was never overly strident. Instead of castigating his opponents or belittling their opinions, he sought points of agreement with them, connections that might bridge gaps and permit a satisfactory resolution of differences or least keep open that possibility. This reconciliationist temper cost Mill a number of friends and a leadership role among the hard-core Benthamites (or philosophical radicals, as they were sometimes called). An important key to understanding Mill as you read him is to understand the opposing views he is trying to reconcile. Each of the changes he makes in orthodox Benthamite utilitarianism is intended to accommodate some important insight of the opposition, thereby not just correcting utilitarian doctrine but also, Mill hopes, bringing the opposition into the fold.

A Note on the Text

Utilitarianism was first published in *Fraser's Magazine* in 1861 and subsequently reissued as a separate volume. The text here is that of the fourth edition, the last published during Mill's life and under his supervision.

Reading Questions

1. What does Mill think is the highest good? How does he attempt to prove that it is?
2. How does Mill define *utilitarianism*?
3. Does Mill end up begging the question by requiring that judgments about the relative worth of different pleasures be made by "competent judges"?
4. In what does a good life consist, according to Mill?
5. What role does Mill assign to the accepted rules of morality? When we act, should we simply look to the rule of morality commonly invoked in such situations, or must we always refer to the utilitarian maxim in making our decisions?
6. How does Mill think the abstract theory of utilitarianism can engage our personal motivations sufficiently to bind us to actions in accordance with its law?
7. *Visible* means "can be seen"; *desirable* means "should be desired." Is this difference sufficient to refute Mill's argument that happiness is the only thing desirable as an end?
8. The utilitarian is commanded to maximize general welfare or happiness. Is there a principle to guide the utilitarian in the *distribution* of happiness or welfare? Why would one need such a principle?
9. Is Mill's theory of justice convincing? Can Mill make room for the notion of a fundamental *right*?

Utilitarianism

Chapter 1
General Remarks

. . . From the dawn of philosophy, the question concerning the *summum bonum*, or, what is the same thing, concerning the foundation of morality, has been accounted the main problem in speculative thought, has occupied the most gifted intellects, and divided them into sects and schools, carrying on a vigorous warfare against one another. And after more than two thousand years the same discussions continue, philosophers are still ranged under the same contending banners, and neither thinkers nor mankind at large seem nearer to being unanimous on the subject, than when the youth Socrates listened to the old Protagoras, and asserted (if Plato's dialogue be grounded on a real conversation) the theory of utilitarianism against the popular morality of the so-called sophist.

It is true that similar confusion and uncertainty, and in some cases similar discordance, exist respecting the first principles of all the sciences, not excepting that which is deemed the most certain of them, mathematics; without much impairing, generally indeed without impairing at all, the trustworthiness of the conclusions of those sciences. An apparent anomaly, the explanation of which is, that the detailed doctrines of a science are not usually deduced from, nor depend for their evidence upon, what are called its first principles. . . . The truths which are ultimately accepted as the first principles of a science, are really the last results of metaphysical analysis, practised on the elementary notions with which the science is conversant; and their relation to the science is not that of foundations to an edifice, but of roots to a tree, which may perform their office equally well though they be never dug down to and exposed to light. But though in science the particular truths precede the general theory, the contrary might be expected to be the case with a practical art, such as morals or legislation. All action is for the sake of some end, and rules of action, it seems natural to suppose, must take their whole character and colour from the end to which they are subservient. When we engage in a pursuit, a clear and precise conception of what we are pursuing would seem to be the first thing we need, instead of the last we are to look forward to. A test of right and wrong must be the means, one would think, of ascertaining what is right or wrong, and not a consequence of having already ascertained it.

The difficulty is not avoided by having recourse to the popular theory of a natural faculty, a sense or instinct, informing us of right and wrong. For—besides that the existence of such a moral instinct is itself one of the matters in dispute—those believers in it who have any pretensions to philosophy, have been obliged to abandon the idea that it discerns what is right or wrong in the particular case in hand, as our other senses discern the sight or sound actually present. Our moral faculty, according to all those of its interpreters who are entitled to the name of thinkers, supplies us only with the general principles of moral judgments; it is a branch of our reason, not of our sensitive faculty; and must be looked to for the abstract doctrines of morality, not for perception of it in the concrete. The intuitive, no less than what may be termed the inductive, school of ethics, insists on the necessity of general laws. They both agree that the morality of an individual action is not a question of direct perception, but of the application of a law to an individual case. They recognise also, to a great extent, the same moral laws; but differ as to their evidence, and the source from which they derive their authority. According to the one opinion, the principles of morals are evident *à priori*, requiring nothing to command assent, except that the meaning of the terms be understood. According to the other doctrine, right and wrong, as well as truth and falsehood, are questions of observation and experience. But both hold equally that morality must be deduced from principles. . . . Yet they seldom attempt to make out a list of the *à priori* principles which are to serve as the premises of the science; still more rarely do they make any effort to reduce those various principles to one first principle, or common ground of obligation. They either assume the ordinary precepts of morals as of *à priori* authority, or they lay down as the common groundwork of those maxims, some generality much less obviously authoritative than the maxims themselves, and which has never succeeded in gaining popular acceptance. Yet to support their pretensions there ought either to be some one fundamental principle or law, at the root of all morality, or if there be several, there should be a determinate order of precedence among them; and the one principle, or the rule for deciding between the various principles when they conflict, ought to be self-evident. . . .

Although the non-existence of an acknowledged first principle has made ethics not so much a guide as a consecration of men's actual sentiments, still, as men's sentiments, both of favour and of aversion, are greatly influenced by what they suppose to be the effects of things upon their happiness, the principle of utility, or as Bentham latterly called it, the greatest happiness principle, has had a large share in forming the moral doctrines even of those who most scornfully reject its authority. Nor is there any school of thought which refuses to admit that the influence of actions on happiness is a most material and even predominant consideration in many of the details of morals, however unwilling to acknowledge it as the fundamental principle of morality, and the source of moral obligation. . . . [Kant lays down] an universal first principle as the origin and ground of moral obligation; it is this:—"So act that the rule on which thou actest would admit of being adopted as a law by all rational beings." But when he begins to deduce from this precept any of the actual duties of morality, he fails, almost grotesquely, to show that there would be any contradiction, any logical (not to say physical) impossibility, in the adoption by all rational beings of the most outrageously immoral rules of conduct. All he shows is that the *consequences* of their universal adoption would be such as no one would choose to incur.

On the present occasion, I shall, without further discussion of the other theories, attempt to contribute something towards the understanding and appreciation of the Utilitarian or Happiness theory, and towards such proof as it is susceptible of. It is evident that this cannot be proof in the ordinary and popular meaning of the term. Questions of ultimate ends are not amenable to direct proof. Whatever can be proved to be good, must be so by being shown to be a means to something admitted to be good without proof. The medical art is proved to be good, by its conducing to health; but how is it possible to prove that health is good? The art of music is good, for the reason, among others, that it produces pleasure; but what proof is it possible to give that pleasure is good? . . . There is a larger meaning of the word proof, in which this question is as amenable to it as any other of the disputed questions of philosophy. The subject is within the cognizance of the rational faculty; and neither does that faculty deal with it solely in the way of intuition. Considerations may be presented capable of determining the intellect either to give or withhold its assent to the doctrine; and this is equivalent to proof.

Chapter 2
What Utilitarianism Is

A passing remark is all that needs be given to the ignorant blunder of supposing that those who stand up for utility as the test of right and wrong, use the term in that restricted and merely colloquial sense in which utility is opposed to pleasure. . . . Those who know anything about the matter are aware that every writer, from Epicurus to Bentham, who maintained the theory of utility, meant by it, not something to be contradistinguished from pleasure, but pleasure itself, together with exemption from pain; and instead of opposing the useful to the agreeable or the ornamental, have always declared that the useful means these, among other things. . . .

The creed which accepts as the foundation of morals, Utility, or the Greatest Happiness Principle, holds that actions are right in proportion as they tend to promote happiness, wrong as they tend to produce the reverse of happiness. By happiness is intended pleasure, and the absence of pain; by unhappiness, pain, and the privation of pleasure. To give a clear view of the moral standard set up by the theory, much more requires to be said; in particular, what things it includes in the ideas of pain and pleasure; and to what extent this is left an open question. But these supplementary explanations do not affect the theory of life on which this theory of morality is grounded—namely, that pleasure, and freedom from pain, are the only things desirable as ends; and that all desirable things (which are as numerous in the utilitarian as in any other scheme) are desirable either for the pleasure inherent in themselves, or as means to the promotion of pleasure and the prevention of pain.

Now, such a theory of life excites in many minds, and among them in some of the most estimable in feeling and purpose, inveterate dislike. To suppose that life has (as they express it) no higher end than pleasure—no better and nobler object of desire and pursuit—they designate as utterly mean and grovelling; as a doctrine worthy only of swine. . . .

When thus attacked, the Epicureans have always answered, that it is not they, but their accusers, who represent human nature in a degrading light; since the accusation supposes human beings to be capable of no pleasures except those of which swine are capable. If this supposition were true, the charge could not be gainsaid, but would then be no longer an imputation; for if the sources of pleasure were precisely the same to human beings and to swine, the rule of life which is good enough for the one would be good enough for the other. The comparison of the Epicurean life to that of beasts is felt as degrading, precisely because a beast's pleasures do not satisfy a human being's conceptions of happiness. Human beings have faculties more elevated than the animal appetites, and when once made conscious of them, do not regard anything as happiness which does not include their gratification. . . . It must be admitted, however, that utilitarian writers in general have placed the superiority of mental over bodily pleasures chiefly in the greater permanency, safety, uncostliness, &c., of the former—that is, in their circumstantial advantages rather than in their intrinsic nature. And on all these points utilitarians have fully proved their case; but they might have taken the other, and, as it may be called, higher ground, with entire consistency. It is quite compatible with the principle of utility to recognise the fact, that some *kinds* of pleasure are more desirable and more valuable than others. It would be absurd that while, in estimating all other things, quality is considered as well as quantity, the estimation of pleasures should be supposed to depend on quantity alone. . . .

Of two pleasures, if there be one to which all or almost all who have experience of both give a decided preference, irrespective of any feeling of moral obligation to prefer it, that is the more desirable pleasure. If one of the two is, by those who are competently acquainted with both, placed so far above the other that they prefer it, even though knowing it to be attended with a greater amount of discontent, and would not resign it for any quantity of the other pleasure which their nature is capable of, we are justified in ascribing to the preferred enjoyment a superiority in quality, so far outweighing quantity as to render it, in comparison, of small account.

Now it is an unquestionable fact that those who are equally acquainted with, and equally capable of appreciating and enjoying, both, do give a most marked preference to the manner of existence which employs their higher faculties. Few human creatures would consent to be changed into any of the lower animals, for a promise of the fullest allowance of a beast's pleasures; no intelligent human being would consent to be a fool, no instructed person would be an ignoramus, no person of feeling and conscience would be selfish and base, even though they should be persuaded that the fool, the dunce, or the rascal is better satisfied with his lot than they are with theirs. They would not resign what they possess more than he, for the most complete satisfaction of all the desires which they have in common with him. . . . We may give what explanation we please of this unwillingness; . . . but its most appropriate appellation is a sense of dignity, which all human beings possess in one form or other, and in some, though by no means in exact, proportion to their higher faculties, and which is so essential a part of the happiness of those in whom it is strong, that nothing which conflicts with it could be, otherwise than momentarily, an object of desire to them. Whoever supposes that this preference takes place at a sacrifice of happiness—that the superior being, in anything like equal circumstances, is not happier than the inferior—confounds the two very different ideas, of happiness, and content. . . . It is better to be a human being dissatisfied than a pig satisfied; better to be Socrates dissatisfied than a fool satisfied. And if the fool, or the pig, is of a different opinion, it is because they only know their own side of the question. The other party to the comparison knows both sides.

It may be objected, that many who are capable of the higher pleasures, occasionally, under the influence of temptation, postpone them to the lower. But this is quite compatible with a full appreciation of the intrinsic superiority of the higher. Men often, from infirmity of character, make their election for the nearer good, though they know it to be the less valuable; and this no less when the choice is between two bodily pleasures, than when it is between bodily and mental. They pursue sensual indulgences to the injury of health, though perfectly aware that health is the greater good. . . . Capacity for the nobler feelings is in most natures a very tender plant, easily killed, not only by hostile influences, but by mere want of sustenance; and in the majority of young persons it speedily dies away if the occupations to which their position in life has devoted them, and the society into which it has thrown them, are not favourable to keeping that higher capacity in exercise. . . . It may be questioned whether any one who has remained equally susceptible to both classes of pleasures, ever knowingly and calmly preferred the lower; though many, in all ages, have broken down in an ineffectual attempt to combine both.

From this verdict of the only competent judges, I apprehend there can be no appeal. On a question which is the best worth having of two pleasures, or which of two modes of existence is the most grateful to the feelings, apart from its moral attributes and from its consequences, the judgment of those who are qualified by knowledge of both, or, if they differ, that of the majority among them, must be admitted as final. And there needs be the less hesitation to accept this judgment respecting the quality of pleasures, since there is no other tribunal to be referred to even on the question of quantity. What means are there of determining which is the acutest of two pains, or the intensest of two pleasurable sensations, except the general suffrage of those who are familiar with both?. . . What is there to decide whether a particular pleasure is worth purchasing at the cost of a particular pain, except the feelings and judgment of the experienced? When, therefore, those feelings and judgment declare the pleasures derived from the higher faculties to be preferable *in kind*, apart from the question of intensity, to those of which the animal nature, disjoined from the higher faculties, is susceptible, they are entitled on this subject to the same regard.

I have dwelt on this point, as being a necessary part of a perfectly just conception of Utility or Happiness, considered as the directive rule of human conduct. But it is by no means an indispensable condition to the acceptance of the utilitarian standard; for that standard is not the agent's own greatest happiness, but the greatest amount of happiness altogether; and if it may possibly be doubted whether a noble character is always the happier for its nobleness, there can be no doubt that it makes other people happier, and that the world in general is immensely a gainer by it. Utilitarianism, therefore, could only attain its end by the general cultivation of nobleness of character, even if each individual were only benefited by the nobleness of others, and his own, so far as happiness is concerned, were a sheer deduction from the benefit. But the bare enunciation of such an absurdity as this last, renders refutation superfluous. . . .

Against [utilitarianism], however, arises another class of objectors, who say that happiness, in any form, cannot be the rational purpose of human life and action; because, in the first place, it is unattainable: and they contemptuously ask, What right hast thou to be happy? a question which Mr. Carlyle clenches by the addition, What right, a short time ago, hadst thou even *to be*? Next, they say that men can do *without* happiness; that all noble human beings have felt this, and could not have become noble but by learning the lesson of Entsagen, or renunciation. . . .

The first of these objections would go to the root of the matter were it well founded; for if no happiness is to be had at all by human beings, the attainment of it cannot be the end of morality, or of any rational conduct. Though, even in that case, something might still be said for the utilitarian theory; since utility includes not solely the pursuit of happiness, but the prevention or mitigation of unhappiness; and if the former aim be chimerical, there will be all the greater scope and more imperative need for the latter, so long at least as mankind think fit to live. . . . When, however, it is thus positively asserted to be impossible that human life should be happy, the assertion, if not something like a verbal quibble, is at least an exaggeration. If by happiness be meant a continuity of highly pleasurable excitement, it is evident enough that this is impossible. A state of exalted pleasure lasts only moments, or in some cases, and with some intermissions, hours or days, and is the occasional brilliant flash of enjoyment, not its permanent and steady flame. Of this the philosophers who have taught that happiness is the end of life were as fully aware as those who taunt them. The happiness which they meant was not a life of rapture; but moments of such, in an existence made up of few and transitory pains, many and various pleasures, with a decided predominance of the active over the passive, and having as the foundation of the whole, not to expect more from life than it is capable of bestowing. . . . And such an existence is even now the lot of many, during some considerable portion of their lives. The present wretched education, and wretched social arrangements, are the only real hindrance to its being attainable by almost all. . . .

The main constituents of a satisfied life appear to be two, either of which by itself is often found sufficient for the purpose: tranquillity, and excitement. With much tranquillity, many find that they can be content with very little pleasure: with much excitement, many can reconcile themselves to a considerable quantity of pain. . . . The two are so far from being incompatible that they are in natural alliance, the prolongation of either being a preparation for, and exciting a wish for, the other. . . . When people who are tolerably fortunate in their outward lot do not find in life sufficient enjoyment to make it valuable to them, the cause generally is, caring for nobody but themselves. To those who have neither public nor private affections, the excitements of life are much curtailed, and in any case dwindle in value as the time approaches when all selfish interests must be terminated by death: while those who leave after them objects of personal affection, and especially those who have also cultivated a fellow-feeling with the collective interests of mankind, retain as lively an interest in life on the eve of death as in the vigour of youth and health. Next to selfishness, the principal cause which makes life unsatisfactory, is want of mental cultivation. A cultivated mind . . . finds sources of inexhaustible interest in all that surrounds it; in the objects of nature, the achievements of art, the imaginations of poetry, the incidents of history, the ways of mankind past and present, and their prospects in the future. . . .

In a world in which there is so much to interest, so much to enjoy, and so much also to correct and improve, every one who has this moderate amount of moral and intellectual requisites is capable of an existence which may be called enviable; and unless such a person, through bad laws, or subjection to the will of others, is denied the liberty to use the sources of happiness within his reach, he will not fail to find this enviable existence, if he escape the positive evils of life, the great sources of physical and mental suffering—such as indigence, disease, and the unkindness, worthlessness, or premature loss of objects of affection. The main stress of the problem lies, therefore, in the contest with these calamities, from which it is a rare good fortune entirely to escape; which, as things now are, cannot be obviated, and often cannot be in any material degree mitigated. Yet no one whose opinion deserves a moment's considera-tion can doubt that most of the great positive evils of the world are in themselves removable, and will, if human affairs continue to improve, be in the end reduced within narrow limits. . . .

And this leads to the true estimation of what is said by the objectors concerning the possibility, and the obligation, of learning to do without happiness. Unquestiona-bly it is possible to do without happiness; it is done involuntarily by nineteen-twentieths of mankind, even in those parts of our present world which are least deep in barbarism; and it often has to be done voluntarily by the hero or the martyr, for the sake of something which he prizes more than his individual happiness. But this something, what is it, unless the happiness of others, or some of the requisites of happiness?...

Though it is only in a very imperfect state of the world's arrangements that any one can best serve the happiness of others by the absolute sacrifice of his own; yet so long as the world is in that imperfect state, I fully acknowledge that the readiness to make such a sacrifice is the highest virtue which can be found in man. I will add, that in this condition of the world, paradoxical as the assertion may be, the conscious ability to do without happiness gives the best prospect of realizing such happiness as is attainable. For nothing except that consciousness can raise a person above the chances of life, by making him feel that, let fate and fortune do their worst, they have not power to subdue him....

I must again repeat, what the assailants of utilitarianism seldom have the justice to acknowledge, that the happiness which forms the utilitarian standard of what is right in conduct, is not the agent's own happiness, but that of all concerned. As between his own happiness and that of others, utilitarianism requires him to be as strictly impartial as a disinterested and benevolent spectator. In the golden rule of Jesus of Nazareth, we read the complete spirit of the ethics of utility. To do as one would be done by, and to love one's neighbour as oneself, constitute the ideal perfection of utilitarian morality....

The objectors to utilitarianism cannot always be charged with representing it in a discreditable light. On the contrary, those among them who entertain anything like a just idea of its disinterested character, sometimes find fault with its standard as being too high for humanity. They say it is exacting too much to require that people shall always act from the inducement of promoting the general interests of society. But this is to mistake the very meaning of a standard of morals, and to confound the rule of action with the motive of it. It is the business of ethics to tell us what are our duties, or by what test we may know them; but no system of ethics requires that the sole motive of all we do shall be a feeling of duty; on the contrary, ninety-nine hundredths of all our actions are done from other motives, and rightly so done, if the rule of duty does not condemn them. It is the more unjust to utilitarianism that this particular misapprehension should be made a ground of objection to it, inasmuch as utilitarian moralists have gone beyond almost all others in affirming that the motive has nothing to do with the morality of the action, though much with the worth of the agent. He who saves a fellow creature from drowning does what is morally right, whether his motive be duty, or the hope of being paid for his trouble: he who betrays the friend that trusts him, is guilty of a crime, even if his object be to serve another friend to whom he is under greater obligations.... The great majority of good actions are intended, not for the benefit of the world, but for that of individuals, of which the good of the world is made up; and the thoughts of the most virtuous man need not on these occasions travel beyond the particular persons concerned, except so far as is necessary to assure himself that in benefiting them he is not violating the rights—that is, the legitimate and authorized expectations—of any one else. The multiplication of happiness is, according to the utilitarian ethics, the object of virtue: the occasions on which any person (except one in a thousand) has it in his power to do this on an extended scale, in other words, to be a public benefactor, are but exceptional; and on these occasions alone is he called on to consider public utility; in every other case, private utility, the interest or happiness of some few persons, is all he has to attend to. Those alone the influence of whose actions extends to society in general, need concern themselves habitually about so large an object. . . .

It is often affirmed that utilitarianism renders men cold and unsympathizing; that it chills their moral feelings towards individuals; that it makes them regard only the dry and hard consideration of the consequences of actions, not taking into their moral estimate the qualities from which those actions emanate. If the assertion means that they do not allow their judgment respecting the rightness or wrongness of an action to be influenced by their opinion of the qualities of the person who does it, this is a complaint not against utilitarianism, but against having any standard of morality at all; for certainly no known ethical standard decides an action to be good or bad because it is done by a good or a bad man, still less because done by an amiable, a brave, or a benevolent man, or the contrary. These considerations are relevant, not to the estimation of actions, but of persons; and there is nothing in the utilitarian theory inconsistent with the fact that there are other things which interest us in persons besides the rightness and wrongness of their actions. . . . Utilitarians are quite aware that there are other desirable possessions and qualities besides virtue, and are perfectly willing to allow to all of them their full worth. They are also aware that a right action does not necessarily indicate a virtuous character, and that actions which are blameable often proceed from qualities entitled to praise. When this is apparent in any particular case, it modifies their estimation, not certainly of the act, but of the agent. I grant that they are, notwithstanding, of opinion, that in the long run the best proof of a good character is good actions; and resolutely refuse to consider any mental disposition as good, of which the predominant tendency is to produce bad conduct. . . .

We not uncommonly hear the doctrine of utility inveighed against as a *godless* doctrine. If it be necessary to say anything at all against so mere an assumption, we may say that the question depends upon what idea we have formed of the moral character of the Deity. If it be a true belief that God desires, above all things, the happiness of his creatures, and that this was his purpose in their creation, utility is not only not a godless doctrine, but more profoundly religious than any other. If it be meant that utilitarianism does not recognise the revealed will of God as the supreme law of morals, I answer, that an utilitarian who believes in the perfect goodness and wisdom of God, necessarily believes that whatever God has thought fit to reveal on the subject of morals, must fulfil the requirements of utility in a supreme degree. But others besides utilitarians have been of opinion that the Christian revelation was intended, and is fitted, to inform the hearts and minds of mankind with a spirit which should enable them to find for themselves what is right, and incline them to do it when found, rather than to tell them, except in a very general way, what it is: and that we need a doctrine of ethics, carefully followed out, to *interpret* to us the will of God. . . .

Again, defenders of utility often find themselves called upon to reply to such objections as this—that there is not time, previous to action, for calculating and weighing the effects of any line of conduct on the general happiness. This is exactly as if any one were to say that it is impossible to guide our conduct by Christianity, because there is not time, on every occasion on which anything has to be done, to read through the Old and New Testaments. The answer to the objection is, that there has been ample time, namely the whole past duration of the human species. During all that time mankind have been learning by experience the tendencies of actions; on which experience all the prudence, as well as all the morality of life, is dependent. People talk as if the commencement of this course of experience had hitherto been put off, and as if, at the moment when some man feels tempted to meddle with the property or life of another, he had to begin considering for the first time whether murder and theft are injurious to human happiness. Even then I do not think that he would find the question very puzzling; but, at all events, the matter is now done to his hand.... There is no difficulty in proving any ethical standard whatever to work ill, if we suppose universal idiocy to be conjoined with it; but on any hypothesis short of that, mankind must by this time have acquired positive beliefs as to the effects of some actions on their happiness; and the beliefs which have thus come down are the rules of morality for the multitude, and for the philosopher until he has succeeded in finding better. That philosophers might easily do this, even now, on many subjects; that the received code of ethics is by no means of divine right; and that mankind have still much to learn as to the effects of actions on the general happiness, I admit, or rather, earnestly maintain.... But to consider the rules of morality as improvable, is one thing; to pass over the intermediate generalizations entirely, and endeavour to test each individual action directly by the first principle, is another. It is a strange notion that the acknowledgment of a first principle is inconsistent with the admission of secondary ones.... The proposition that happiness is the end and aim of morality, does not mean that no road ought to be laid down to that goal, or that persons going thither should not be advised to take one direction rather than another.... Whatever we adopt as the fundamental principle of morality, we require subordinate principles to apply it by: the impossibility of doing without them, being common to all systems, can afford no argument against any one in particular: but gravely to argue as if no such secondary principles could be had, and as if mankind had remained till now, and always must remain, without drawing any general conclusions from the experience of human life, is as high a pitch, I think, as absurdity has ever reached in philosophical controversy....

It is not the fault of any creed, but of the complicated nature of human affairs, that rules of conduct cannot be so framed as to require no exceptions, and that hardly any kind of action can safely be laid down as either always obligatory or always condemnable. There is no ethical creed which does not temper the rigidity of its laws, by giving a certain latitude, under the moral responsibility of the agent, for accommodation to peculiarities of circumstances; and under every creed, at the opening thus made, self-deception and dishonest casuistry get in. There exists no moral system under which there do not arise unequivocal cases of conflicting obligation. These are the real difficulties, the knotty points both in the theory of ethics, and in the conscientious guidance of personal conduct. They are overcome practically with greater or with less success according to the intellect and virtue of the individual.... If utility is the ultimate source of moral obligations, utility may be invoked to decide between them when their demands are incompatible. Though the application of the standard may be difficult, it is better than none at all: while in other systems, the moral laws all claiming independent authority, there is no common umpire entitled to interfere between them; their claims to precedence one over another rest on little better than sophistry, and unless determined, as they generally are, by the unacknowledged influence of considerations of utility, afford a free scope for the action of personal desires and partialities....

Chapter 3
Of the Ultimate Sanction of the Principle of Utility

The question is often asked, and properly so, in regard to any supposed moral standard—What is its sanction? what are the motives to obey it? or more specifically, what is the source of its obligation? whence does it derive its binding force? It is a necessary part of moral philosophy to provide the answer to this question; which, though frequently assuming the shape of an objection to the utilitarian morality, as if it had some special applicability to that above others, really arises in regard to all standards. It arises, in fact, whenever a person is called on to *adopt* a standard, or refer morality to any basis on which he has not been accustomed to rest it. For the customary morality, that which education and opinion have consecrated, is the only one which presents itself to the mind with the feeling of being *in itself* obligatory; and when a person is asked to believe that this morality *derives* its obligation from some general principle round which custom has not thrown the same halo, the assertion is to him a paradox; the supposed corollaries seem to have a more binding force than the original theorem; the superstructure seems to stand better without, than with, what is represented as its foundation. He says to himself, I feel that I am bound not to rob or murder, betray or deceive; but why am I bound to promote the general happiness? If my own happiness lies in something else, why may I not give that the preference?

If the view adopted by the utilitarian philosophy of the nature of the moral sense be correct, this difficulty will always present itself, until the influences which form moral character have taken the same hold of the principle which they have taken of some of the consequences—until, by the improvement of education, the feeling of unity with our fellow creatures shall be (what it cannot be doubted that Christ intended it to be) as deeply rooted in our character, and to our own consciousness as completely a part of our nature, as the horror of crime is in an ordinarily well-brought-up young person. . . .

The principle of utility either has, or there is no reason why it might not have, all the sanctions which belong to any other system of morals. Those sanctions are either external or internal. Of the external sanctions it is not necessary to speak at any length. They are, the hope of favour and the fear of displeasure from our fellow creatures or from the Ruler of the Universe, along with whatever we may have of sympathy or affection for them, or of love and awe of Him, inclining us to do his will independently of selfish consequences. There is evidently no reason why all these motives for observance should not attach themselves to the utilitarian morality, as completely and as powerfully as to any other. . . .

So far as to external sanctions. The internal sanction of duty, whatever our standard of duty may be, is one and the same—a feeling in our own mind; a pain, more or less intense, attendant on violation of duty, which in properly-cultivated moral natures rises, in the more serious cases, into shrinking from it as an impossibility. This feeling, when disinterested, and connecting itself with the pure idea of duty, and not with some particular form of it, or with any of the merely accessory circumstances, is the essence of Conscience. . . . Its binding force, however, consists in the existence of a mass of feeling which must be broken through in order to do what violates our standard of right, and which, if we do nevertheless violate that standard, will probably have to be encountered afterwards in the form of remorse. Whatever theory we have of the nature or origin of conscience, this is what essentially constitutes it.

The ultimate sanction, therefore, of all morality (external motives apart) being a subjective feeling in our own minds, I see nothing embarrassing to those whose standard is utility, in the question, what is the sanction of that particular standard? We may answer, the same as of all other moral standards—the conscientious feelings of mankind. Undoubtedly this sanction has no binding efficacy on those who do not possess the feelings it appeals to; but neither will these persons be more obedient to any other moral principle than to the utilitarian one. . . .

There is, I am aware, a disposition to believe that a person who sees in moral obligation a transcendental fact, an objective reality belonging to the province of "Things in themselves," is likely to be more obedient to it than one who believes it to be entirely subjective, having its seat in human consciousness only. But whatever a person's opinion may be on this point of Ontology, the force he is really urged by is his own subjective feeling, and is exactly measured by its strength. No one's belief that Duty is an objective reality is stronger than the belief that God is so; yet the belief in God, apart from the expectation of actual reward and punishment, only operates on conduct through, and in proportion to, the subjective religious feeling. The sanction, so far as it is disinterested, is always in the mind itself; and the notion therefore of the transcendental moralists must be, that this sanction will not exist *in* the mind unless it is believed to have its root out of the mind; and that if a person is able to say to himself, This which is restraining me, and which is called my conscience, is only a feeling in my own mind, he may possibly draw the conclusion that when the feeling ceases the obligation ceases, and that if he find the feeling inconvenient, he may disregard it, and endeavour to get rid of it. But is this danger confined to the utilitarian morality? Does the belief that moral obligation has its seat outside the mind make the feeling of it too strong to be got rid of? The fact is so far otherwise, that all moralists admit and lament the ease with which, in the generality of minds, conscience can be silenced or stifled. . . .

If, as is my own belief, the moral feelings are not innate, but acquired, they are not for that reason the less natural. It is natural to man to speak, to reason, to build cities, to cultivate the ground, though these are acquired faculties. The moral feelings are not indeed a part of our nature, in the sense of being in any perceptible degree present in all of us; but this, unhappily, is a fact admitted by those who believe the most strenuously in their transcendental origin. Like the other acquired capacities above referred to, the moral faculty, if not a part of our nature, is a natural outgrowth from it; capable, like them, in a certain small degree, of springing up spontaneously; and susceptible of being brought by cultivation to a high degree of development. Unhappily it is also susceptible, by a sufficient use of the external sanctions and of the force of early impressions, of being cultivated in almost any direction: so that there is hardly anything so absurd or so mischievous that it may not, by means of these influences, be made to act on the human mind with all the authority of conscience. . . .

But moral associations which are wholly of artificial creation, when intellectual culture goes on, yield by degrees to the dissolving force of analysis: and if the feeling of duty, when associated with utility, would appear equally arbitrary. . . if there were not . . . a natural basis of sentiment for utilitarian morality, it might well happen that this association also, even after it had been implanted by education, might be analysed away.

But there *is* this basis of powerful natural sentiment; and this it is which, when once the general happiness is recognised as the ethical standard, will constitute the strength of the utilitarian morality. This firm foundation is that of the social feelings of mankind; the desire to be in unity with our fellow creatures, which is already a powerful principle in human nature, and happily one of those which tend to become stronger, even without express inculcation, from the influences of advancing civilization. The social state is at once so natural, so necessary, and so habitual to man, that, except in some unusual circumstances or by an effort of voluntary abstraction, he never conceives himself otherwise than as a member of a body; and this association is riveted more and more, as mankind are further removed from the state of savage independence. Any condition, therefore, which is essential to a state of society, becomes more and more an inseparable part of every person's conception of the state of things which he is born into, and which is the destiny of a human being. Now, society between human beings, except in the relation of master and slave, is manifestly impossible on any other footing than that the interests of all are to be consulted. Society between equals can only exist on the understanding that the interests of all are to be regarded equally. . . . They are under a necessity of conceiving themselves as at least abstaining from all the grosser injuries, and (if only for their own protection) living in a state of constant protest against them. They are also familiar with the fact of co-operating with others, and proposing to themselves a collective, not an individual, interest, as the aim (at least for the time being) of their actions. So long as they are co-operating, their ends are identified with those of others; there is at least a temporary feeling that the interests of others are their own interests. Not only does all strengthening of social ties, and all healthy growth of society, give to each individual a stronger personal interest in practically consulting the welfare of others; it also leads him to identify his *feelings* more and more with their good, or at least with an ever greater degree of practical consideration for it. He comes, as though instinctively, to be conscious of himself as a being who *of course* pays regard to others. The good of others becomes to him a thing naturally and necessarily to be attended to, like any of the physical conditions of our existence. . . .

This feeling in most individuals is much inferior in strength to their selfish feelings, and is often wanting altogether. But to those who have it, it possesses all the characters of a natural feeling. It does not present itself to their minds as a superstition of education, or a law despotically imposed by the power of society, but as an attribute which it would not be well for them to be without. This conviction is the ultimate sanction of the greatest-happiness morality. This it is which makes any mind, of well-developed feelings, work with, and not against, the outward motives to care for others, afforded by what I have called the external sanctions; and when those sanctions are wanting, or act in an opposite direction, constitutes in itself a powerful internal binding force, in proportion to the sensitiveness and thoughtfulness of the character; since few but those whose mind is a moral blank, could bear to lay out their course of life on the plan of paying no regard to others except so far as their own private interest compels.

Chapter 4
Of What Sort of Proof the Principle of Utility Is Susceptible

It has already been remarked, that questions of ultimate ends do not admit of proof, in the ordinary acceptation of the term. To be incapable of proof by reasoning is common to all first principles; to the first premises of our knowledge, as well as to those of our conduct. But the former, being matters of fact, may be the subject of a direct appeal to the faculties which judge of fact—namely, our senses, and our internal consciousness. Can an appeal be made to be same faculties on questions of practical ends? Or by what other faculty is cognizance taken of them?

Questions about ends are, in other words, questions what things are desirable. The utilitarian doctrine is, that happiness is desirable, and the only thing desirable, as an end; all other things being only desirable as means to that end. What ought to be required of this doctrine—what conditions is it requisite that the doctrine should fulfil—to make good its claim to be believed?

The only proof capable of being given that an object is visible, is that people actually see it. The only proof that a sound is audible, is that people hear it: and so of the other sources of our experience. In like manner, I apprehend, the sole evidence it is possible to produce that anything is desirable, is that people do actually desire it. If the end which the utilitarian doctrine proposes to itself were not, in theory and in practice, acknowledged to be an end, nothing could ever convince any person that it was so. No reason can be given why the general happiness is desirable, except that each person, so far as he believes it to be attainable, desires his own happiness. This, however, being a fact, we have not only all the proof which the case admits of, but all which it is possible to require, that happiness is a good: that each person's happiness is a good to that person, and the general happiness, therefore, a good to the aggregate of all persons. Happiness has made out its title as *one* of the ends of conduct, and consequently one of the criteria of morality.

But it has not, by this alone, proved itself to be the sole criterion. To do that, it would seem, by the same rule, necessary to show, not only that people desire happiness, but that they never desire anything else. Now it is palpable that they do desire things which, in common language, are decidedly distinguished from happiness. They desire, for example, virtue, and the absence of vice, no less really than pleasure and the absence of pain. The desire of virtue is not as universal, but it is as authentic a fact, as the desire of happiness. And hence the opponents of the utilitarian standard deem that they have a right to infer that there are other ends of human action besides happiness, and that happiness is not the standard of approbation and disapprobation.

But does the utilitarian doctrine deny that people desire virtue, or maintain that virtue is not a thing to be desired? The very reverse. It maintains not only that virtue is to be desired, but that it is to be desired disinterestedly, for itself. Whatever may be the opinion of utilitarian moralists as to the original conditions by which virtue is made virtue; however they may believe (as they do) that actions and dispositions are only virtuous because they promote another end than virtue; yet this being granted, and it having been decided, from considerations of this description, what is virtuous, they not only place virtue at the very head of the things which are good as means to the ultimate end, but they also recognise as a psychological fact the possibility of its being, to the individual, a good in itself, without looking to any end beyond it; and hold, that the mind is not in a right state, not in a state conformable to Utility, not in the state most conducive to the general happiness, unless it does love virtue in this manner—as a thing desirable in itself, even although, in the individual instance, it should not produce those other desirable consequences which it tends to produce, and on account of which it is held to be virtue. This opinion is not, in the smallest degree, a departure from the Happiness principle. The ingredients of happiness are very various, and each of them is desirable in itself, and not merely when considered as swelling an aggregate. The principle of utility does not mean that any given pleasure, as music, for instance, or any given exemption from pain, as for example health, are to be looked upon as means to a collective something termed happiness, and to be desired on that account. They are desired and desirable in and for themselves; besides being means, they are a part of the end. Virtue, according to the utilitarian doctrine, is not naturally and originally part of the end, but it is capable of becoming so; and in those who love it disinterestedly it has become so, and is desired and cherished, not as a means to happiness, but as a part of their happiness. . . .

What was once desired as an instrument for the attainment of happiness, has come to be desired for its own sake. In being desired for its own sake it is, however, desired as *part* of happiness. The person is made, or thinks he would be made, happy by its mere possession; and is made unhappy by failure to obtain it. The desire of it is not a different thing from the desire of happiness, any more than the love of music, or the desire of health. They are included in happiness. They are some of the elements of which the desire of happiness is made up. Happiness is not an abstract idea, but a concrete whole; and these are some of its parts. And the utilitarian standard sanctions and approves their being so. Life would be a poor thing, very ill provided with sources of happiness, if there were not this provision of nature, by which things originally indifferent, but conducive to, or otherwise associated with, the satisfaction of our primitive desires, become in themselves sources of pleasure more valuable than the primitive pleasures. . . .

Virtue, according to the utilitarian conception, is a good of this description. There was no original desire of it, or motive to it, save its conduciveness to pleasure, and especially to protection from pain. But through the association thus formed, it may be felt a good in itself, and desired as such with as great intensity as any other good; and with this difference between it and the love of money, of power, or of fame, that all of these may, and often do, render the individual noxious to the other members of the society to which he belongs, whereas there is nothing which makes him so much a blessing to them as the cultivation of the disinterested love of virtue. And consequently, the utilitarian standard, while it tolerates and approves those other acquired desires, up to the point beyond which they would be more injurious to the general happiness than promotive of it, enjoins and requires the cultivation of the love of virtue up to the greatest strength possible, as being above all things important to the general happiness.

It results from the preceding considerations, that there is in reality nothing desired except happiness. Whatever is desired otherwise than as a means to some end beyond itself, and ultimately to happiness, is desired as itself a part of happiness, and is not desired for itself until it has become so. . . .

And now to decide . . . whether mankind do desire nothing for itself but that which is a pleasure to them, or of which the absence is a pain; we have evidently arrived at a question of fact and experience, dependent, like all similar questions, upon evidence. It can only be determined by practised self-consciousness and self-observation, assisted by observation of others. I believe that these sources of evidence, impartially consulted, will declare that desiring a thing and finding it pleasant, aversion to it and thinking of it as painful, are phenomena entirely inseparable, or rather two parts of the same phenomenon; in strictness of language, two different modes of naming the same psychological fact: that to think of an object as desirable (unless for the sake of its consequences), and to think of it as pleasant, are one and the same thing; and that to desire anything, except in proportion as the idea of it is pleasant, is a physical and metaphysical impossibility. . . .

Chapter 5
On the Connexion between Justice and Utility

In all ages of speculation, one of the strongest obstacles to the reception of the doctrine that Utility or Happiness is the criterion of right and wrong, has been drawn from the idea of Justice. The powerful sentiment, and apparently clear perception, which that word recalls with a rapidity and certainty resembling an instinct, have seemed to the majority of thinkers to point to an inherent quality in things; to show that the Just must have an existence in Nature as something absolute — generically distinct from every variety of the Expedient, and, in idea, opposed to it, though (as is commonly acknowledged) never, in the long run, disjoined from it in fact.

In the case of this, as of our other moral sentiments, there is no necessary connexion between the question of its origin, and that of its binding force. That a feeling is bestowed on us by Nature, does not necessarily legitimate all its promptings. The feeling of justice might be a peculiar instinct, and might yet require, like our other instincts, to be controlled and enlightened by a higher reason. . . . For the purpose of this inquiry, it is practically important to consider whether the feeling itself, of justice and injustice, is *sui generis* like our sensations of colour and taste, or a derivative feeling, formed by a combination of others. . . . Inasmuch as the subjective mental feeling of Justice is different from that which commonly attaches to simple expediency, and, except in extreme cases of the latter, is far more imperative in its demands, people find it difficult to see, in Justice, only a particular kind or branch of general utility, and think that its superior binding force requires a totally different origin.

To throw light upon this question, it is necessary to attempt to ascertain what is the distinguishing character of justice, or of injustice. . . . If, in everything which men are accustomed to characterize as just or unjust, some one common attribute or collection of attributes is always present, we may judge whether this particular attribute or combination of attributes would be capable of gathering round it a sentiment of that peculiar character and intensity by virtue of the general laws of our emotional constitution, or whether the sentiment is inexplicable, and requires to be regarded as a special provision of Nature. If we find the former to be the case, we shall, in resolving this question, have resolved also the main problem: if the latter, we shall have to seek for some other mode of investigating it.

To find the common attributes of a variety of objects, it is necessary to begin by surveying the objects themselves in the concrete. Let us therefore advert successively to the various modes of action, and arrangements of human affairs, which are classed, by universal or widely spread opinion, as Just or as Unjust. . . .

In the first place, it is mostly considered unjust to deprive any one of his personal liberty, his property, or any other thing which belongs to him by law. Here, therefore, is one instance of the application of the terms just and unjust in a perfectly definite sense, namely, that it is just to respect, unjust to violate, the *legal rights* of any one. . . .

Secondly; the legal rights of which he is deprived, may be rights which *ought* not to have belonged to him; in other words, the law which confers on him these rights, may be a bad law. When it is so, . . . opinions will differ as to the justice or injustice of infringing it. . . . Among these diversities of opinion, it seems to be universally admitted that there may be unjust laws, and that law, consequently, is not the ultimate criterion of justice. . . . When, however, a law is thought to be unjust, it seems always to be regarded as being so in the same way in which a breach of law is unjust, namely, by infringing somebody's right; which, as it cannot in this case be a legal right, receives a different appellation, and is called a moral right. We may say, therefore, that a second case of injustice consists in taking or withholding from any person that to which he has a *moral right*. . . .

It is confessedly unjust to *break faith* with any one: to violate an engagement, either express or implied, or disappoint expectations raised by our own conduct, at least if we have raised those expectations knowingly and voluntarily. . . .

It is by universal admission, inconsistent with justice to be *partial*; to show favour or preference to one person over another, in matters to which favour and preference do not properly apply. Impartiality, however, does not seem to be regarded as a duty in itself, but rather as instrumental to some other duty; for it is admitted that favour and preference are not always censurable, and indeed the cases in which they are con-demned are rather the exception than the rule. . . . Impartiality, in short, as an obliga-tion of justice, may be said to mean, being exclusively influenced by the considera-tions which it is supposed ought to influence the particular case in hand; and resisting the solicitation of any motives which prompt to conduct different from what those considerations would dictate. . . .

In our survey of the various popular acceptations of justice, the term appeared gener-ally to involve the idea of a personal right—a claim on the part of one or more individuals, like that which the law gives when it confers a proprietary or other legal right. Whether the injustice consists in depriving a person of a possession, or in break-ing faith with him, or in treating him worse than he deserves, or worse than other peo-ple who have no greater claims, in each case the supposition implies two things—a wrong done, and some assignable person who is wronged. Injustice may also be done by treating a person better than others; but the wrong in this case is to his competitors, who are also assignable persons. It seems to me that this feature in the case—a right in some person, correlative to the moral obligation—constitutes the specific difference between justice, and generosity or beneficence. Justice implies something which it is not only right to do, and wrong not to do, but which some individual person can claim from us as his moral right. No one has a moral right to our generosity or beneficence, because we are not morally bound to practise those virtues towards any given individual. . . .

Having thus endeavoured to determine the distinctive elements which enter into the composition of the idea of justice, we are ready to enter on the inquiry, whether the feeling, which accompanies the idea, is attached to it by a special dispensa-tion of nature, or whether it could have grown up, by any known laws, out of the idea itself; and in particular, whether it can have originated in considerations of general expediency.

I conceive that the sentiment itself does not arise from anything which would com-monly, or correctly, be termed an idea of expediency; but that though, the sentiment does not, whatever is moral in it does.

We have seen that the two essential ingredients in the sentiment of justice are, the desire to punish a person who has done harm, and the knowledge or belief that there is some definite individual or individuals to whom harm has been done.

Now it appears to me, that the desire to punish a person who has done harm to some individual, is a spontaneous outgrowth from two sentiments, both in the highest degree natural, and which either are or resemble instincts; the impulse of self-defence, and the feeling of sympathy.

It is natural to resent, and to repel or retaliate, any harm done or attempted against ourselves, or against those with whom we sympathize. The origin of this sentiment it is not necessary here to discuss. Whether it be an instinct or a result of intelligence, it is, we know, common to all animal nature. . . . Human beings, on this point, only differ from other animals in two particulars. First, in being capable of sympathizing, not solely with their offspring, or, like some of the more noble animals, with some superior animal who is kind to them, but with all human, and even with all sentient, beings. Secondly, in having a more developed intelligence, which gives a wider range to the whole of their sentiments, whether self-regarding or sympathetic. . . .

The sentiment of justice, in that one of its elements which consists of the desire to punish, is thus, I conceive, the natural feeling of retaliation or vengeance, rendered by intellect and sympathy applicable to those injuries, that is, to those hurts, which wound us through, or in common with, society at large. This sentiment, in itself, has nothing moral in it; what is moral is, the exclusive subordination of it to the social sympathies, so as to wait on and obey their call. . . .

To recapitulate: the idea of justice supposes two things; a rule of conduct, and a sentiment which sanctions the rule. The first must be supposed common to all mankind, and intended for their good. The other (the sentiment) is a desire that punishment may be suffered by those who infringe the rule. There is involved, in addition, the conception of some definite person who suffers by the infringement; whose rights (to use the expression appropriated to the case) are violated by it. And the sentiment of justice appears to me to be, the animal desire to repel or retaliate a hurt or damage to oneself, or to those with whom one sympathizes, widened so as to include all persons, by the human capacity of enlarged sympathy, and the human conception of intelligent self-interest. From the latter elements, the feeling derives its morality; from the former, its peculiar impressiveness, and energy of self-assertion. . . .

To have a right, then, is, I conceive, to have something which society ought to defend me in the possession of. If the objector goes on to ask why it ought, I can give him no other reason than general utility. If that expression does not seem to convey a sufficient feeling of the strength of the obligation, nor to account for the peculiar energy of the feeling, it is because there goes to the composition of the sentiment, not a rational only but also an animal element, the thirst for retaliation; and this thirst derives its intensity, as well as its moral justification, from the extraordinarily important and impressive kind of utility which is concerned. The interest involved is that of security, to every one's feelings the most vital of all interests. . . .

The equal claim of everybody to happiness in the estimation of the moralist and the legislator, involves an equal claim to all the means of happiness, except in so far as the inevitable conditions of human life, and the general interest, in which that of every individual is included, set limits to the maxim; and those limits ought to be strictly construed. . . . All persons are deemed to have a *right* to equality of treatment, except when some recognised social expediency requires the reverse. And hence all social inequalities which have ceased to be considered expedient, assume the character not of simple inexpediency, but of injustice, and appear so tyrannical, that people are apt to wonder how they ever could have been tolerated. . . . The entire history of social improvement has been a series of transitions, by which one custom or institution after another, from being a supposed primary necessity of social existence, has passed into the rank of an universally stigmatized injustice and tyranny. So it has been with the distinctions of slaves and freemen, nobles and serfs, patricians and plebeians; and so it will be, and in part already is, with the aristocracies of colour, race, and sex.

It appears from what has been said, that justice is a name for certain moral requirements, which, regarded collectively, stand higher in the scale of social utility, and are therefore of more paramount obligation, than any others; though particular cases may occur in which some other social duty is so important, as to overrule any one of the general maxims of justice. Thus, to save a life, it may not only be allowable, but a duty, to steal, or take by force, the necessary food or medicine, or to kidnap, and compel to officiate, the only qualified medical practitioner. In such cases, as we do not call anything justice which is not a virtue, we usually say, not that justice must give way to some other moral principle, but that what is just in ordinary cases is, by reason of that other principle, not just in the particular case. By this useful accommodation of language, the character of indefeasibility attributed to justice is kept up, and we are saved from the necessity of maintaining that there can be laudable injustice.

The considerations which have now been adduced resolve, I conceive, the only real difficulty in the utilitarian theory of morals. . . . Justice remains the appropriate name for certain social utilities which are vastly more important, and therefore more absolute and imperative, than any others are as a class (though not more so than others may be in particular cases); and which, therefore, ought to be, as well as naturally are, guarded by a sentiment not only different in degree, but also in kind; distinguished from the milder feeling which attaches to the mere idea of promoting human pleasure or convenience, at once by the more definite nature of its commands, and by the sterner character of its sanctions.

SELECTED BIBLIOGRAPHY

Mill, John Stuart, *The Collected Works of John Stuart Mill*. Toronto: University of Toronto Press, 1963–.

Anschutz, R.P. *The Philosophy of John Stuart Mill*. Oxford: Clarendon Press, 1953.

Berger, Frederick R. *Happiness, Justice, and Freedom: The Moral and Political Philosophy of John Stuart Mill*. Berkeley: University of California Press, 1984.

Britton, Karl. *John Stuart Mill*. Harmondsworth, England: Penguin, 1953.

Douglas, Charles. *John Stuart Mill: A Study of His Philosophy*. London: Blackwood & Sons, 1895.

Duncan, Graeme Campbell. *Marx and Mill: Two Views of Social Conflict and Social Harmony*. Cambridge: Cambridge University Press, 1973.

Halévy, Elie. *The Growth of Philosophic Radicalism*. Trans. Mary Morris. Boston: Beacon Press, 1955.

Mazlish, Bruce. *James and John Stuart Mill: Father and Son in the Nineteenth Century*. New York: Basic Books, 1975.

Miller, H.B., and Williams, W.H., ed. *The Limits of Utilitarianism*. Minneapolis: University of Minnesota Press, 1982.

Plamenatz, John. *The English Utilitarians*, 2d ed. Oxford: Basil Blackwell, 1958.

Quinton, Anthony. *Utilitarian Ethics*. New York: St. Martin's Press, 1973.

Ryan, Alan. *John Stuart Mill*, 2nd ed. Atlantic Highlands, N.J.: Humanities Press, 1989.

_____. *J.S. Mill*. London: Routledge & Kegan Paul, 1974.

Schneewind, J.B. *Mill: A Collection of Critical Essays*. Garden City, N.Y.: Doubleday, 1968.

Semmel, Bernard. *John Stuart Mill and the Pursuit of Virtue*. New Haven, Conn.: Yale University Press, 1984.

Thomas, William. *J.S. Mill*. New York: Oxford University Press, 1985.

Friedrich Nietzsche

Friedrich Nietzsche (1844–1900) was born in Prussia of devout Lutheran parents, the son of a minister and the grandson of two more ministers. Nietzsche's father went insane four years later (a fate that awaited Nietzsche as well—though probably not because of any genetic inheritance), and two years after that, Nietzsche's younger brother also died, leaving Nietzsche to be raised in an extended family that was entirely female.

He received a strong classical education at Pforta, a boarding school near Naumberg, and went on to study theology and classical philology at the University of Bonn in 1864. He soon abandoned theology and followed Professor Friedrich Ritschl to Leipzig, where he continued his work in philology and also studied philosophy, reading Immanuel Kant, Arthur Schopenhauer, and Friedrich Lange's *History of Materialism*. Ritschl, one of the leading classicists of the day, became increasingly impressed with Nietzsche's talents, and, though Nietzsche was still a student, his work began to be published in several journals. In 1867 Nietzsche interrupted his studies to perform his year of mandatory military service. It was also during his Leipzig period that Nietzsche became a devotee of the work of Richard Wagner, the composer.

In 1869 the professorship of classical philology at the university of Basel, Switzerland, opened up, and thanks to Ritschl's strong recommendation, the young Nietzsche was appointed to the position. He had not yet written his dissertation, but Ritschl

491

arranged for the University of Leipzig to award him a doctorate on the basis of the work he had already published. He thus became one of the youngest professors ever to occupy a chair at a European university.

Not long after his arrival in Basel, however, Nietzsche asked for a leave in order to serve as a medical orderly during the Franco-Prussian War. A collapse from dysentery and diphtheria caused his discharge from the service, his health seriously undermined. From then on, Nietzsche was subject to periodic bouts of illness that left him quite weak. In any case, he was not terribly comfortable in the rather sedate life of a classics professor but sought higher and wider horizons. These he found in Richard Wagner, whom he visited often in nearby Lucerne and to whom he became increasingly devoted. Wagner was a powerful force, a supreme egoist utterly convinced of his own genius, who had developed a romantic ideology to support his artistic endeavors. Nietzsche's first philosophical work, *The Birth of Tragedy*, appeared in 1872. From that time on, with the exception of the period from 1875 to 1878, Nietzsche published steadily in philosophy. He slowly grew more and more distanced from the early influences of Schopenhauer and Wagner and more appreciative of Charles Darwin. After breaking with Wagner in 1878 and resigning from the university shortly thereafter because of his declining health, Nietzsche's publication rate increased and his charac-teristic philosophical views took a more definite shape. Between 1878 and 1889 he published a book a year. By this point, writing was his life.

In January 1889 Nietzsche saw a cabman flogging a horse; he ran to protect the animal and collapsed, his arms flung about the horse's neck. Carried back to his room, he awoke some time later and began sending letters all over Europe signed "Dionysus" or "The Crucified." Suffering from a complete mental collapse, probably the final stages of a syphilitic infection contracted years earlier, Nietzsche was confined to a psy-chiatric institution, where he lived, deranged, for eleven more years.

Philosophy

Nietzsche is difficult to write about, in part because he himself wrote so well. His aphoristic style is tremendously refreshing and provocative: it challenges and teases the reader at every turn with its high rhetoric, penetrating insight, and biting humor. An iconoclast, Nietzsche sets out to shake up our worldview from top to bottom. There is little that escapes his withering and often caustic criticism. Yet how to piece together a coherent picture of the positive vision that drives Nietzsche remains elusive. Most scholarly treatments of Nietzsche's philosophy seem but staid recitations that do little justice to the genius that bursts forth from Nietzsche's own pages and that fall short of tying all of his writing together into a coherent whole.

The *Genealogy of Morals* (1887) consists of three essays, of which the second is reprinted here. The *Genealogy* began as an expansion of a similarly titled section in an earlier book, *Beyond Good and Evil*, published in 1886. One of the most accessible of Nietzsche's works in that decade, it must be seen in the context of Nietzsche's pro-gram for a *revaluation of all values*. As a critic of conventional morality, Nietzsche is far more radical than most, for he does not rest content with trying to systematize the received (generally and traditionally accepted) morality. Nor does he attempt to find for it a firmer foundation on the basis of which morality can be reconstructed in puri-fied form. Nietzsche challenges the root assumptions of the received morality, the fundamental values that pervade it. In the *Genealogy of Morals*, Nietzsche outlines a view of the genesis and development of morality that differs sharply from the traditional views that morality is either a dictate of the deity, a product of pure reason, or founded in some sentiment natural to the human mind.

The hypothesis that Nietzsche defends in the *Genealogy* is that the set of rules that constitute modern Western morality actually represent a subtle and insidious program by which weaker humans can band together to dominate strong-willed, independent souls, what Nietzsche calls *slave morality*. The weak protect themselves at the cost of the strong, and this seems counter to biological imperatives that rule nature— biological imperatives that Nietzsche reinterprets as the drive of an all-encompassing will to power. But the transcendentalized slave morality that the weak have developed to protect themselves from the strong does have its role to play in the larger scheme: it trains humankind, regularizes it, deepens it through the tortures of guilt. But soon will come a time when the strongest, now fortified with the lessons of the slave morality, will once again break free of this oppressive heritage and go beyond morality, beyond good and evil. Humanity is just a bridge to a still higher being that awaits us in the future.

In viewing human morality as the expression of the primordial will to power under a certain set of social circumstances, Nietzsche opens up the possibility that morality is itself a naturally developing phenomenon that can be superseded. In fact, Nietzsche goes much further and suggests that all our values—even the value of truth itself—could be overcome and abandoned. Nietzsche vividly challenges us to realize that all our values represent choices, choices that could be made differently.

Nietzsche's insights into the human psyche and the structure of our social relationships prefigure many of Freud's ideas and seem far less radical in the late twentieth century than when they were first formulated. Even if we have slowly begun to appreciate a Nietzschean analysis of the human psyche and social behavior, there is still much in Nietzsche that is deeply disturbing, particularly his emphasis on humanity's need for and enjoyment of inflicting pain on others, and his attitudes toward women.

The Reading Context

An influential recent commentator on Nietzsche writes:

> Nietzsche takes the world as if it were a text and the things within it as if they were the characters and other fictional entities of which texts consist. He can thus see them all as a vast sum of essentially interrelated objects. Each one of these is already the product of an earlier grouping or interpretation, and each grouping affects and is affected by all the others. Genealogy concerns itself with these groupings and with the paths that connect them. Every path it traces reveals, where only facts were visible before, an earlier interpretation with its own purposes and values, its own will to power. And in doing so, each genealogical account itself embodies its own interests and manifests its own will to power.[1]

---

1. Alexander Nehamas, *Nietzsche: Life as Literature* (Cambridge, Mass.: Harvard University Press, 1985), pp. 104–105.

In reading the selection, try to diagnose what interests and will to power are manifested in Nietzsche's genealogical account.

A Note on the Text

The selection reprinted here is the second of the three essays in *On the Genealogy of Morals*, written and published in 1887. The *Genealogy* was originally written as an expansion of and supplement to some of the themes in Nietzsche's earlier book, *Beyond Good and Evil*. The first essay in the *Genealogy*, " 'Good and Evil,' 'Good and Bad,' " lays out his distinction between master and slave moralities. The third essay, "What Do Ascetic Ideals Mean?" explores the role slave morality has played in the development of the human race.

Reading Questions

1. How does one gain the "right to make promises"? What kind of beings would not have such a right? Do all humans have this right?
2. What are the characteristics of the autonomous person or *sovereign individual*?
3. What is the relationship between the conscience of the *sovereign individual* and the consciousness of guilt, "bad conscience"?
4. At one point in the essay Nietzsche claims that it is mere sentimentalism to think that society began with a contract, yet he also wants to claim that social institutions such as punishment, which make society possible, do have their origin in a contract. Is this a contradiction?
5. Nietzsche claims that all suffering is bearable as long as it is not senseless. Have we therefore invented a sense for our sufferings?
6. How does one create a value?
7. Does Nietzsche believe that the world has a purpose? What is it to have meaning? What is the will to power?
8. Why do we punish? Are the reasons for which we punish sufficient to justify punishment? Are any grounds sufficient to justify punishment? What effect does punishment actually have?
9. Given Nietzsche's picture of the barbarian, conqueror race, how can we make sense of the claim that there is some sort of natural organization governing their interactions?
10. Why is Nietzsche so confident that the "true redeemer" will come, *must* come?

On the Genealogy of Morals
A Polemic

Second Essay
"Guilt," "Bad Conscience," and the Like

1

To breed an animal *with the right to make promises*—is not this the paradoxical task that nature has set itself in the case of man? is it not the real problem regarding man?

That this problem has been solved to a large extent must seem all the more remarkable to anyone who appreciates the strength of the opposing force, that of *forgetfulness*. Forgetting is no mere *vis inertiae* [inertial force] as the superficial imagine; it is rather an active and in the strictest sense positive faculty of repression, that is responsible for the fact that what we experience and absorb enters our consciousness as little while we are digesting it (one might call the process "inpsychation") as does the thousandfold process, involved in physical nourishment—so-called "incorporation." To close the doors and windows of consciousness for a time; to remain undisturbed by the noise and struggle of our underworld of utility organs working with and against one another; a little quietness, a little *tabula rasa* [clean slate] of the consciousness, to make room for new things, above all for the nobler functions and functionaries, for regulation, foresight, premeditation (for our organism is an oligarchy)—that is the purpose of active forgetfulness, which is like a doorkeeper, a preserver of psychic order, repose, and etiquette: so that it will be immediately obvious how there could be no happiness, no cheerfulness, no hope, no pride, no *present*, without forgetfulness. The man in whom this apparatus of repression is damaged and ceases to function properly may be compared (and more than merely compared) with a dyspeptic—he cannot "have done" with anything.

Now this animal which needs to be forgetful, in which forgetting represents a force, a form of *robust* health, has bred in itself an opposing faculty, a memory, with the aid of which forgetfulness is abrogated in certain cases—namely in those cases where promises are made. This involves no mere passive inability to rid oneself of an impression, no mere indigestion through a once-pledged word with which one cannot "have done," but an active *desire* not to rid oneself, a desire for the continuance of something desired once, a real *memory of the will*: so that between the original "I will," "I shall do this" and the actual discharge of the will, its *act*, a world of strange new things, circumstances, even acts of will may be interposed without breaking this long chain of will. But how many things this presupposes! To ordain the future in advance in this way, man must first have learned to distinguish necessary events from chance ones, to think causally, to see and anticipate distant eventualities as if they belonged to the present, to decide with certainty what is the goal and what he means to it, and in general be able to calculate and compute. Man himself must first of all have become *calculable*,

From Friedrich Nietzsche, *On the Genealogy of Morals* (1887), trans. and ed. Walter Kaufmann (New York: Random House, 1967), pp. 493–532. Copyright © Random House, Inc. Reprinted with permission from Random House, Inc.

regular, necessary, even in his own image of himself, if he is to be able to stand security for *his own future,* which is what one who promises does!

2

This precisely is the long story of how *responsibility* originated. The task of breeding an animal with the right to make promises evidently embraces and presupposes as a preparatory task that one first *makes* men to a certain degree necessary, uniform, like among like, regular, and consequently calculable. The tremendous labor of that which I have called "morality of mores"—the labor performed by man upon himself during the greater part of the existence of the human race, his entire *prehistoric* labor, finds in this its meaning, its great justification, notwithstanding the severity, tyranny, stupidity, and idiocy involved in it: with the aid of the morality of mores and the social strait-jacket, man was actually *made* calculable.

If we place ourselves at the end of this tremendous process, where the tree at last brings forth fruit, where society and the morality of custom at last reveal *what* they have simply been the means to: then we discover that the ripest fruit is the *sovereign individual,* like only to himself, liberated again from morality of custom, autonomous and supramoral (for "autonomous" and "moral" are mutually exclusive), in short, the man who has his own independent, protracted will and the *right to make promises*—and in him a proud consciousness, quivering in every muscle, of what has at length been achieved and become flesh in him, a consciousness of his own power and freedom, a sensation of mankind come to completion. This emancipated individual, with the actual *right* to make promises, this master of a *free* will, this sovereign man—how should he not be aware of his superiority over all those who lack the right to make promises and stand as their own guarantors, of how much trust, how much fear, how much reverence he arouses—he *"deserves"* all three—and of how this mastery over himself also necessarily gives him mastery over circumstances, over nature, and over all more short-willed and unreliable creatures? The "free" man, the possessor of a protracted and unbreakable will, also possesses his *measure of value:* looking out upon others from himself, he honors or he despises; and just as he is bound to honor his peers, the strong and reliable (those with the *right* to make promises)—that is, all those who promise like sovereigns, reluctantly, rarely, slowly, who are chary of trusting, whose trust is a mark of *distinction,* who give their word as something that can be relied on because they know themselves strong enough to maintain it in the face of accidents, even "in the face of fate"—he is bound to reserve a kick for the feeble windbags who promise without the right to do so, and a rod for the liar who breaks his word even at the moment he utters it. The proud awareness of the extraordinary privilege of *responsibility,* the consciousness of this rare freedom, this power over oneself and over fate, has in his case penetrated to the profoundest depths and become instinct, the dominating instinct. What will he call this dominating instinct, supposing he feels the need to give it a name? The answer is beyond doubt: this sovereign man calls it his *conscience.*

3

His conscience?—It is easy to guess that the concept of "conscience" that we here encounter in its highest, almost astonishing, manifestation, has a long history and variety of forms behind it. To possess the right to stand security for oneself and to do so with pride, thus to possess also the *right to affirm oneself*—this, as has been said, is a ripe fruit, but also a *late* fruit: how long must this fruit have hung on the tree, unripe and sour! And for a much longer time nothing whatever was to be seen of any such fruit: no one could have promised its appearance, although everything in the tree was preparing for and growing toward it!

"How can one create a memory for the human animal? How can one impress something upon this partly obtuse, partly flighty mind, attuned only to the passing moment, in such a way that it will stay there?"

One can well believe that the answers and methods for solving this primeval problem were not precisely gentle; perhaps indeed there was nothing more fearful and uncanny in the whole prehistory of man than his *mnemotechnics*. "If something is to stay in the memory it must be burned in: only that which never ceases to *hurt* stays in the memory"—this is a main clause of the oldest (unhappily also the most enduring) psychology on earth. One might even say that wherever on earth solemnity, seriousness, mystery, and gloomy coloring still distinguish the life of man and a people, something of the terror that formerly attended all promises, pledges, and vows on earth is *still effective*: the past, the longest, deepest and sternest past, breathes upon us and rises up in us whenever we become "serious." Man could never do without blood, torture, and sacrifices when he felt the need to create a memory for himself; the most dreadful sacrifices and pledges (sacrifices of the first-born among them), the most repulsive mutilations (castration, for example), the cruelest rites of all the religious cults (and all religions are at the deepest level systems of cruelties)—all this has its origin in the instinct that realized that pain is the most powerful aid to mnemonics.

In a certain sense, the whole of asceticism belongs here: a few ideas are to be rendered inextinguishable, ever-present, unforgetable, "fixed," with the aim of hypnotising the entire nervous and intellectual system with these "fixed ideas"—and ascetic procedures and modes of life are means of freeing these ideas from the competition of all other ideas, so as to make them "unforgettable." The worse man's memory has been, the more fearful has been the appearance of his customs; the severity of the penal code provides an especially significant measure of the degree of effort needed to overcome forgetfulness and to impose a few primitive demands of social existence as *present realities* upon these slaves of momentary affect and desire.

We Germans certainly do not regard ourselves as a particularly cruel and hard-hearted people, still less as a particularly frivolous one, living only for the day; but one has only to look at our former codes of punishments to understand what effort it costs on this earth to breed a "nation of thinkers" (which is to say, *the* nation in Europe in which one still finds today the maximum of trust, seriousness, lack of taste, and matter-of-factness—and with these qualities one has the right to breed every kind of European mandarin). . . . With the aid of such procedures one finally remembers five or six "I will not's," in regard to which one had given one's *promise* so as to participate in the advantages of society—and it was indeed with the aid of this kind of memory that one at last came "to reason"! Ah, reason, seriousness, mastery over the affects, the whole somber thing called reflection, all these prerogatives and showpieces of man: how dearly they have been bought! how much blood and cruelty lie at the bottom of all "good things"!

4

But how did that other "somber thing," the consciousness of guilt, the "bad con-science," come into the world?—And at this point we return to the genealogists of morals. To say it again—or haven't I said it yet?—they are worthless. A brief span of experience that is merely one's own, merely modern; no knowledge or will to knowledge of the past; even less of historical instinct, of that "second sight" needed here above all—and yet they undertake history of morality: it stands to reason that their results stay at a more than respectful distance from the truth. Have these genealo-gists of morals had even the remotest suspicion that, for example, the major moral con-cept *Schuld* [guilt] has its origin in the very material concept *Schulden* [debts]?[1] Or that punishment, as requital, evolved quite independently of any presupposition concern-ing freedom or nonfreedom of the will?—to such an extent, indeed, that a *high* degree of humanity had to be attained before the animal "man" began even to make the much more primitive distinctions between "intentional," "negligent," "accidental," "account-able," and their opposites and to take them into account when determining punish-ments. The idea, now so obvious, apparently so natural, even unavoidable, that had to serve as the explanation of how the sense of justice ever appeared on earth—"the criminal deserves punishment *because* he could have acted differently"—is in fact an extremely late and subtle form of human judgment and inference: whoever transposes it to the beginning is guilty of a crude misunderstanding of the psychology of more primitive mankind. Throughout the greater part of human history punishment was *not* imposed *because* one held the wrongdoer responsible for his deed, thus *not* on the presupposition that only the guilty one should be punished: rather, as parents still pun-ish their children, from anger at some harm or injury, vented on the one who caused it—but this anger is held in check and modified by the idea that every injury has its *equivalent* and can actually be paid back, even if only through the *pain* of the culprit. And whence did this primeval, deeply rooted, perhaps by now ineradicable idea draw its power—this idea of an equivalence between injury and pain? I have already divulged it: in the contractual relationship between *creditor* and *debtor*, which is as old as the idea of "legal subjects" and in turn points back to the fundamental forms of buy-ing, selling, barter, trade, and traffic.

5

When we contemplate these contractual relationships, to be sure, we feel considerable suspicion and repugnance toward those men of the past who created or permitted them. This was to be expected from what we have previously noted. It was here that *promises* were made; it was here that a memory had to be *made* for those who promised; it is here, one suspects, that we shall find a great deal of severity, cruelty, and pain. To inspire trust in his promise to repay, to provide a guarantee of the seriousness and sanc-tity of his promise, to impress repayment as a duty, an obligation upon his own con-science, the debtor made a contract with the creditor and pledged that if he should fail to repay he would substitute something else that he "possessed," something he had

---

1. The German equivalent of "guilt" is *Schuld*; and the German for "debt(s)" is *Schuld(en)*. "Innocent" is *unschuldig*; "debtor" is *Schuldner*; and so forth. [All footnotes in this selection are the translator's.]

control over; for example, his body, his wife, his freedom, or even his bliss after death, the salvation of his soul, ultimately his peace in the grave. . . . Above all, however, the creditor could inflict every kind of indignity and torture upon the body of the debtor; for example, cut from it as much as seemed commensurate with the size of the debt— and everywhere and from early times one had exact evaluations, *legal* evaluations, of the individual limbs and parts of the body from this point of view, some of them going into horrible and minute detail. I consider it as an advance, as evidence of a freer, more generous, *more Roman* conception of law when the Twelve Tables of Rome decreed it a matter of indifference how much or how little the creditor cut off in such cases: "*si plus minusve secuerunt, ne fraude esto.*"[2]

Let us be clear as to the logic of this form of compensation: it is strange enough. An equivalence is provided by the creditor's receiving, in place of a literal compensation for an injury (thus in place of money, land, possessions of any kind), a recompense in the form of a kind of *pleasure*—the pleasure of being allowed to vent his power freely upon one who is powerless, the voluptuous pleasure "*de faire le mal pour le plaisir de le faire*,"[3] the enjoyment of violation. This enjoyment will be the greater the lower the creditor stands in the social order, and can easily appear to him as a most delicious morsel, indeed as a foretaste of higher rank. In "punishing" the debtor, the creditor participates in a *right of the masters*: at last he, too, may experience for once the exalted sensation of being allowed to despise and mistreat someone as "beneath him"—or at least, if the actual power and administration of punishment has already passed to the "authorities," to *see* him despised and mistreated. The compensation, then, consists in a warrant for and title to cruelty.—

6

It was in *this* sphere then, the sphere of legal obligations, that the moral conceptual world of "guilt," "conscience," "duty," "sacredness of duty" had its origin: its beginnings were, like the beginnings of everything great on earth, soaked in blood thoroughly and for a long time. And might one not add that, fundamentally, this world has never since lost a certain odor of blood and torture? (Not even in good old Kant: the categorical imperative smells of cruelty.) It was here, too, that that uncanny intertwining of the ideas "guilt and suffering" was first effected—and by now they may well be inseparable. To ask it again: to what extent can suffering balance debts or guilt?[4] To the extent that to *make* suffer was in the highest degree pleasurable, to the extent that the injured party exchanged for the loss he had sustained, including the displeasure caused by the loss, an extraordinary counterbalancing pleasure: that of *making* suffer. . . . This is offered only as a conjecture; for the depths of such subterranean things are difficult to fathom, besides being painful; and whoever clumsily interposes the concept of "revenge" does not enhance his insight into the matter but further veils and darkens it (—for revenge merely leads us back to the same problem: "how can making suffer constitute a compensation?").

---

2. If they have secured more or less, let that be no crime.

3. Of doing evil for the pleasure of doing it.

4. "Debts or guilt": "*Schulden.*"

It seems to me that the delicacy and even more the tartuffery of tame domestic animals (which is to say modern men, which is to say us) resists a really vivid comprehension of the degree to which *cruelty* constituted the great festival pleasure of more primitive men and was indeed an ingredient of almost every one of their pleasures; and how naïvely, how innocently their thirst for cruelty manifested itself, how, as a matter of principle, they posited "disinterested malice" . . . as a *normal* quality of man—and thus as something to which the conscience *says* Yes! . . . To see others suffer does one good, to make others suffer even more: this is a hard saying but an ancient, mighty, human, all-too-human principle to which even the apes might subscribe; for it has been said that in devising bizarre cruelties they anticipate man and are, as it were, his "prelude." Without cruelty there is no festival: thus the longest and most ancient part of human history teaches—and in punishment there is so much that is *festive!*—

7

With this idea, by the way, I am by no means concerned to furnish our pessimists with more grist for their discordant and creaking mills of life-satiety. On the contrary, let me declare expressly that in the days when mankind was not yet ashamed of its cruelty, life on earth was more cheerful than it is now that pessimists exist. The darkening of the sky above mankind has deepened in step with the increase in man's feeling of shame *at man*. The weary pessimistic glance, mistrust of the riddle of life, the icy No of disgust with life—these do not characterize the most *evil* epochs of the human race: rather do they first step into the light of day as the swamp weeds they are when the swamp to which they belong comes into being—I mean the morbid softening and moralization through which the animal "man" finally learns to be ashamed of all his instincts. On his way to becoming an "angel" (to employ no uglier word) man has evolved that queasy stomach and coated tongue through which not only the joy and innocence of the animal but life itself has become repugnant to him—so that he sometimes holds his nose in his own presence and, with Pope Innocent the Third, disapprovingly catalogues his own repellent aspects ("impure begetting, disgusting means of nutrition in his mother's womb, baseness of the matter out of which man evolves, hideous stink, secretion of saliva, urine, and filth").

Today, when suffering is always brought forward as the principal argument *against* existence, as the worst question mark, one does well to recall the ages in which the opposite opinion prevailed because men were unwilling to refrain from *making* suffer and saw in it an enchantment of the first order, a genuine seduction *to* life. . . .

What really arouses indignation against suffering is not suffering as such but the senselessness of suffering: but neither for the Christian, who has interpreted a whole mysterious machinery of salvation into suffering, nor for the naïve man of more ancient times, who understood all suffering in relation to the spectator of it or the causer of it, was there any such thing as *senseless* suffering. So as to abolish hidden, undetected, unwitnessed suffering from the world and honestly to deny it, one was in the past virtually compelled to invent gods and genii of all the heights and depths, in short something that roams even in secret, hidden places, sees even in the dark, and will not easily let an interesting painful spectacle pass unnoticed. For it was with the aid of such inventions that life then knew how to work the trick which it has always known how to work, that of justifying itself, of justifying its "evil." Nowadays it might require other auxiliary inventions (for example, life as a riddle, life as an epistemological problem). "Every evil the sight of which edifies a god is justified": thus spoke the primitive logic of feeling—and was it, indeed, only primitive?... With what eyes do you think Homer made his gods look down upon the destinies of men? What was at bottom the ultimate meaning of Trojan Wars and other such tragic terrors? There can be no doubt whatever: they were intended as *festival plays* for the gods; and, insofar as the poet is in these matters of a more "godlike" disposition than other men, no doubt also as festival plays for the poets.

It was in the same way that the moral philosophers of Greece later imagined the eyes of God looking down upon the moral struggle, upon the heroism and self-torture of the virtuous: the "Herakles of duty" was on a stage and knew himself to be; virtue without a witness was something unthinkable for this nation of actors. Surely, that philosophers' invention, so bold and so fateful, which was then first devised for Europe, the invention of "free will," of the absolute spontaneity of man in good and in evil, was devised above all to furnish a right to the idea that the interest of the gods in man, in human virtue, *could never be exhausted*. There must never be any lack of real novelty, of really unprecedented tensions, complications, and catastrophies on the stage of the earth: the course of a completely deterministic world would have been predictable for the gods and they would have quickly grown weary of it—reason enough for those *friends of the gods*, the philosophers, not to inflict such a deterministic world on their gods!...

8

To return to our investigation: the feeling of guilt, of personal obligation, had its origin, as we saw, in the oldest and most primitive personal relationship, that between buyer and seller, creditor and debtor: it was here that one person first encountered another person, that one person first *measured himself* against another. No grade of civilization, however low, has yet been discovered in which something of this relationship has not been noticeable. Setting prices, determining values, contriving equivalences, exchanging—these preoccupied the earliest thinking of man to so great an extent that in a certain sense they constitute thinking *as such*; here it was that the oldest kind of astuteness developed; here likewise, we may suppose, did human pride, the feeling of superiority in relation to other animals, have its first beginnings. Perhaps our word "man" (*manas*) still expresses something of precisely *this* feeling of self-satisfaction: man designated himself as the creature that measures values, evaluates and measures, as the "valuating animal as such."

Buying and selling, together with their psychological appurtenances, are older even than the beginnings of any kind of social forms of organization and alliances: it was rather out of the most rudimentary form of personal legal rights that the budding sense of exchange, contract, guilt, right, obligation, settlement, first *transferred* itself to the coarsest and most elementary social complexes (in their relations with other similar complexes), together with the custom of comparing, measuring, and calculating power against power. The eye was now focused on this perspective; and with that blunt consistency characteristic of the thinking of primitive mankind, which is hard to set in motion but then proceeds inexorably in the same direction, one forthwith arrived at the great generalization, "everything has its price; *all* things can be paid for"—the oldest and naïvest moral canon of *justice*, the beginning of all "good-naturedness," all "fairness," all "good will," all "objectivity" on earth. Justice on this elementary level is the good will among parties of approximately equal power to come to terms with one another, to reach an "understanding" by means of a settlement—and to *compel* parties of lesser power to reach a settlement among themselves.—

9

Still retaining the criteria of prehistory (this prehistory is in any case present in all ages or may always reappear): the community, too, stands to its members in that same vital basic relation, that of the creditor to his debtors. One lives in a community, one enjoys the advantages of a communality (oh what advantages! we sometimes underrate them today), one dwells protected, cared for, in peace and trustfulness, without fear of certain injuries and hostile acts to which the man *outside*, the "man without peace," is exposed—a German will understand the original connotations of *Elend*[5]—since one has bound and pledged oneself to the community precisely with a view to injuries and hostile acts. What will happen *if this pledge is broken*? The community, the disappointed creditor, will get what repayment it can, one may depend on that. The direct harm caused by the culprit is here a minor matter; quite apart from this, the lawbreaker is above all a "breaker," a breaker of his contract and his word *with the whole* in respect to all the benefits and comforts of communal life of which he has hitherto had a share. The lawbreaker is a debtor who has not merely failed to make good the advantages and advance payments bestowed upon him but has actually attacked his creditor: therefore he is not only deprived henceforth of all these advantages and benefits, as is fair—he is also reminded *what these benefits are really worth*. The wrath of the disappointed creditor, the community, throws him back again into the savage and outlaw state against which he has hitherto been protected: it thrusts him away—and now every kind of hostility may be vented upon him. "Punishment" at this level of civilization is simply a copy, a *mimus*, of the normal attitude toward a hated, disarmed, prostrated enemy, who has lost not only every right and protection, but all hope of quarter as well; it is thus the rights of war and the victory celebration of the *vae victis*![6] in all their mercilessness and cruelty—which explains why it is that war itself (including the warlike sacrificial cult) has provided all the *forms* that punishment has assumed throughout history.

10

As its power increases, a community ceases to take the individual's transgressions so seriously, because they can no longer be considered as dangerous and destructive to the whole as they were formerly: the malefactor is no longer "set beyond the pale of peace" and thrust out; universal anger may not be vented upon him as unrestrainedly as before—on the contrary, the whole from now on carefully defends the malefactor against this anger, especially that of those he has directly harmed, and takes him under its protection. A compromise with the anger of those directly injured by the criminal; an effort to localize the affair and to prevent it from causing any further, let alone a

---

5. Misery; originally, exile.
6. Woe to the losers!

general, disturbance; attempts to discover equivalents and to settle the whole matter (*compositio*); above all, the increasingly definite will to treat every crime as in some sense *dischargeable*, and thus at least to a certain extent to *isolate* the criminal and his deed from one another—these traits become more and more clearly visible as the penal law evolves. As the power and self-confidence of a community increase, the penal law always becomes more moderate; every weakening or imperiling of the former brings with it a restoration of the harsher forms of the latter. The "creditor" always becomes more humane to the extent that he has grown richer; finally, how much injury he can endure without suffering from it becomes the actual *measure* of his wealth. It is not unthinkable that a society might attain such a *consciousness of power* that it could allow itself the noblest luxury possible to it—letting those who harm it go *unpunished*. "What are my parasites to me?" it might say. "May they live and prosper: I am strong enough for that!"

The justice which began with, "everything is dischargeable, everything must be discharged," ends by winking and letting those incapable of discharging their debt go free: it ends, as does every good thing on earth, by *overcoming itself*. This self-overcoming of justice: one knows the beautiful name it has given itself—*mercy*; it goes without saying that mercy remains the privilege of the most powerful man, or better, his—beyond the law.

11

Here a word in repudiation of attempts that have lately been made to seek the origin of justice in quite a different sphere—namely in that of *ressentiment*. To the psychologists first of all, presuming they would like to study *ressentiment* close up for once, I would say: this plant blooms best today among anarchists and anti-Semites—where it has always bloomed, in hidden places, like the violet, though with a different odor. And as like must always produce like, it causes us no surprise to see a repetition in such circles of attempts often made before to sanctify *revenge* under the name of *justice*—as if justice were at bottom merely a further development of the feeling of being aggrieved—and to rehabilitate not only revenge but all *reactive* affects in general. To the latter as such I would be the last to raise any objection: in respect to the entire biological problem (in relation to which the value of these affects has hitherto been underrated) it even seems to me to constitute a *service*. All I draw attention to is the circumstance that it is the spirit of *ressentiment* itself out of which this new nuance of scientific fairness (for the benefit of hatred, envy, jealousy, mistrust, rancor, and revenge) proceeds. For this "scientific fairness" immediately ceases and gives way to accents of deadly enmity and prejudice once it is a question of dealing with another group of affects, affects that, it seems to me, are of even greater biological value than those reactive affects and consequently deserve even more to be *scientifically* evaluated and esteemed: namely, the truly *active* affects, such as lust for power, avarice, and the like. . . .

So much against this tendency in general: as for Dühring's[7] specific proposition that the home of justice is to be sought in the sphere of the reactive feelings, one is obliged for truth's sake to counter it with a blunt antithesis: the *last* sphere to be

---

7. Eugen Dühring (1833–1901), a prolific German philosopher and political economist, was among other things an impassioned patriot and anti-Semite and hated the cosmopolitan Goethe and the Greeks.

conquered by the spirit of justice is the sphere of the reactive feelings! When it really happens that the just man remains just even toward those who have harmed him (and not merely cold, temperate, remote, indifferent: being just is always a *positive* attitude), when the exalted, clear objectivity, as penetrating as it is mild, of the eye of justice and *judging* is not dimmed even under the assault of personal injury, derision, and calumny, this is a piece of perfection and supreme mastery on earth—something it would be prudent not to expect or to *believe* in too readily. On the average, a small dose of aggression, malice, or insinuation certainly suffices to drive the blood into the eyes—and fairness out of the eyes—of even the most upright people. The active, aggressive, arrogant man is still a hundred steps closer to justice than the reactive man; for he has absolutely no need to take a false and prejudiced view of the object before him in the way the reactive man does and is bound to do. For that reason the aggressive man, as the stronger, nobler, more courageous, has in fact also had at all times a *freer* eye, a *better* conscience on his side: conversely, one can see who has the invention of the "bad conscience" on his conscience—the man of *ressentiment!*

Finally, one only has to look at history: in which sphere has the entire administration of law hitherto been at home—also the need for law? In the sphere of reactive men, perhaps? By no means: rather in that of the active, strong, spontaneous, aggressive. From a historical point of view, law represents on earth . . . the struggle *against* the reactive feelings, the war conducted against them on the part of the active and aggressive powers who employed some of their strength to impose measure and bounds upon the excesses of the reactive pathos and to compel it to come to terms. Wherever justice is practiced and maintained one sees a stronger power seeking a means of putting an end to the senseless raging of *ressentiment* among the weaker powers that stand under it (whether they be groups or individuals)—partly by taking the object of *ressentiment* out of the hands of revenge, partly by substituting for revenge the struggle against the enemies of peace and order, partly by devising and in some cases imposing settlements, partly by elevating certain equivalents for injuries into norms to which from then on *ressentiment* is once and for all directed. The most decisive act, however, that the supreme power performs and accomplishes against the predominance of grudges and rancor—it always takes this action as soon as it is in any way strong enough to do so—is the institution of *law*, the imperative declaration of what in general counts as permitted, as just, in its eyes, and what counts as forbidden, as unjust: once it has instituted the law, it treats violence and capricious acts on the part of individuals or entire groups as offenses against the law, as rebellion against the supreme power itself, and thus leads the feelings of its subjects away from the direct injury caused by such offenses; and in the long run it thus attains the reverse of that which is desired by all revenge that is fastened exclusively to the viewpoint of the person injured: from now on the eye is trained to an ever more *impersonal* evaluation of the deed, and this applies even to the eye of the injured person himself (although last of all, as remarked above).

"Just" and "unjust" exist, accordingly, only after the institution of the law (and *not*, as Dühring would have it, after the perpetration of the injury). To speak of just or unjust *in itself* is quite senseless; *in itself*, of course, no injury, assault, exploitation, destruction can be "unjust," since life operates *essentially*, that is in its basic functions, through injury, assault, exploitation, destruction and simply cannot be thought of at all without this character. One must indeed grant something even more unpalatable: that, from the highest biological standpoint, legal conditions can never be other than *exceptional conditions*, since they constitute a partial restriction of the will of life, which is bent upon power, and are subordinate to its total goal as a single means: namely, as a means of creating *greater* units of power. A legal order thought of as sovereign and universal, not as a means in the struggle between power-complexes but as a means of *preventing* all struggle in general—perhaps after the communistic cliché of Dühring, that every will must consider every other will its equal—would be a principle *hostile to life*, an agent of the dissolution and destruction of man, an attempt to assassinate the future of man, a sign of weariness, a secret path to nothingness.—

12

Yet a word on the origin and the purpose of punishment—two problems that are separate, or ought to be separate: unfortunately, they are usually confounded. How have previous genealogists of morals set about solving these problems? Naïvely, as has always been their way: they seek out some "purpose" in punishment, for example, revenge or deterrence, then guilelessly place this purpose at the beginning as *causa fiendi*[8] of punishment, and—have done. The "purpose of law," however, is absolutely the last thing to employ in the history of the origin of law: on the contrary, there is for historiography of any kind no more important proposition than the one it took such effort to establish but which really *ought to be* established now: the cause of the origin of a thing and its eventual utility, its actual employment and place in a system of purposes, lie worlds apart; whatever exists, having somehow come into being, is again and again reinterpreted to new ends, taken over, transformed, and redirected by some power superior to it; all events in the organic world are a subduing, a *becoming master*, and all subduing and becoming master involves a fresh interpretation, an adaptation through which any previous "meaning" and "purpose" are necessarily obscured or even obliterated. . . .

Thus one also imagined that punishment was devised for punishing. But purposes and utilities are only *signs* that a will to power has become master of something less powerful and imposed upon it the character of a function; and the entire history of a "thing," an organ, a custom can in this way be a continuous sign-chain of ever new interpretations and adaptations whose causes do not even have to be related to one another but, on the contrary, in some cases succeed and alternate with one another in a purely chance fashion. The "evolution" of a thing, a custom, an organ is thus by no means its *progressus* toward a goal, even less a logical *progressus* by the shortest route and with the smallest expenditure of force—but a succession of more or less profound, more or less mutually independent processes of subduing, plus the resistances they encounter, the attempts at transformation for the purpose of defense and reaction, and the results of successful counteractions. The form is fluid, but the "meaning" is even more so.

The case is the same even within each individual organism: with every real growth in the whole, the "meaning" of the individual organs also changes; in certain circumstances their partial destruction, a reduction in their numbers (for example, through the disappearance of intermediary members) can be a sign of increasing strength and

---

8. The cause of the origin.

perfection. It is not too much to say that even a partial *diminution of utility*, an atrophying and degeneration, a loss of meaning and purposiveness—in short, death—is among the conditions of an actual *progressus*, which always appears in the shape of a will and way to *greater power* and is always carried through at the expense of numerous smaller powers. The magnitude of an "advance" can even be measured by the mass of things that had to be sacrificed to it; mankind in the mass sacrificed to the prosperity of a single *stronger* species of man—that *would* be an advance.

I emphasize this major point of historical method all the more because it is in fundamental opposition to the now prevalent instinct and taste which would rather be reconciled even to the absolute fortuitousness, even the mechanistic senselessness of all events than to the theory that in all events a *will to power* is operating. The democratic idiosyncrasy which opposes everything that dominates and wants to dominate, the modern *misarchism*[9] (to coin an ugly word for an ugly thing) has permeated the realm of the spirit and disguised itself in the most spiritual forms to such a degree that today it has forced its way, has acquired the *right* to force its way into the strictest, apparently most objective sciences; indeed, it seems to me to have already taken charge of all physiology and theory of life—to the detriment of life, as goes without saying, since it has robbed it of a fundamental concept, that of *activity*. Under the influence of the above-mentioned idiosyncrasy, one places instead "adaptation" in the foreground, that is to say, an activity of the second rank, a mere reactivity. . . . Thus the essence of life, its *will to power*, is ignored; one overlooks the essential priority of the spontaneous, aggressive, expansive, form-giving forces that give new interpretations and directions, although "adaptation" follows only after this. . . .

13

To return to our subject, namely *punishment*, one must distinguish two aspects: on the one hand, that in it which is relatively *enduring*, the custom, the act, the "drama," a certain strict sequence of procedures; on the other, that in it which is *fluid*, the meaning, the purpose, the expectation associated with the performance of such procedures. In accordance with the previously developed major point of historical method, it is assumed without further ado that the procedure itself will be something older, earlier than its employment in punishment, that the latter is *projected* and interpreted *into* the procedure (which has long existed but been employed in another sense), in short, that the case is *not* as has hitherto been assumed by our naïve genealogists of law and morals, who have one and all thought of the procedure as *invented* for the purpose of punishing, just as one formerly thought of the hand as invented for the purpose of grasping.

As for the other element in punishment, the fluid element, its "meaning," in a very late condition of culture (for example, in modern Europe) the concept "punishment" possesses in fact not *one* meaning but a whole synthesis of "meanings": the previous history of punishment in general, the history of its employment for the most various purposes, finally crystallizes into a kind of unity that is hard to disentangle, hard to analyze and, as must be emphasized especially, totally *indefinable*. (Today it is impossi-

---

9. Hatred of rule or government.

ble to say for certain *why* people are really punished: all concepts in which an entire process is semiotically concentrated elude definition; only that which has no history is definable.). . . .

To give at least an idea of how uncertain, how supplemental, how accidental "the meaning" of punishment is, and how one and the same procedure can be employed, interpreted, adapted to ends that differ fundamentally, I set down here the pattern that has emerged from consideration of relatively few chance instances I have noted. Punishment as a means of rendering harmless, of preventing further harm. Punishment as recompense to the injured party for the harm done, rendered in any form (even in that of a compensating affect). Punishment as the isolation of a disturbance of equilibrium, so as to guard against any further spread of the disturbance. Punishment as a means of inspiring fear of those who determine and execute the punishment. Punishment as a kind of repayment for the advantages the criminal has enjoyed hitherto (for example, when he is employed as a slave in the mines). Punishment as the expulsion of a degenerate element (in some cases, of an entire branch, as in Chinese law: thus as a means of preserving the purity of a race or maintaining a social type). Punishment as a festival, namely as the rape and mockery of a finally defeated enemy. Punishment as the making of a memory, whether for him who suffers the punishment—so-called "improvement"—or for those who witness its execution. . . .

14

This list is certainly not complete; it is clear that punishment is overdetermined by utilities of all kinds. All the more reason, then, for deducting from it a *supposed* utility that, to be sure, counts in the popular consciousness as the most essential one—belief in punishment, which for several reasons is tottering today, always finds its strongest support in this. Punishment is supposed to possess the value of awakening the *feeling of guilt* in the guilty person; one seeks in it the actual *instrumentum* of that psychical reaction called "bad conscience," "sting of conscience." Thus one misunderstands psychology and the reality of things even as they apply today: how much more as they applied during the greater part of man's history, his prehistory!

It is precisely among criminals and convicts that the sting of conscience is extremely rare; prisons and penitentiaries are *not* the kind of hotbed in which this species of gnawing worm is likely to flourish: all conscientious observers are agreed on that, in many cases unwillingly enough and contrary to their own inclinations. Generally speaking, punishment makes men hard and cold; it concentrates; it sharpens the feeling of alienation; it strengthens the power of resistance. If it happens that punishment destroys the vital energy and brings about a miserable prostration and self-abasement, such a result is certainly even less pleasant than the usual effects of punishment—characterized by dry and gloomy seriousness.

If we consider those millennia *before* the history of man, we may unhesitatingly assert that it was precisely through punishment that the development of the feeling of guilt was most powerfully *hindered*—at least in the victims upon whom the punitive force was vented. For we must not underrate the extent to which the sight of the judicial and executive procedures prevents the criminal from considering his deed, the type of his action *as such*, reprehensible: for he sees exactly the same kind of actions practiced in the service of justice and approved of and practiced with a good conscience: spying, deception, bribery, setting traps, the whole cunning and underhand art of police and prosecution, plus robbery, violence, defamation, imprisonment, torture, murder, practiced as a matter of principle and without even emotion to excuse them, which are pronounced characteristics of the various forms of punishment—all of them therefore actions which his judges in no way condemn and repudiate *as such*, but only when they are applied and directed to certain particular ends.

The "bad conscience," this most uncanny and most interesting plant of all our earthly vegetation, did *not* grow on this soil; indeed, during the greater part of the past the judges and punishers themselves were *not at all* conscious of dealing with a "guilty person." But with an instigator of harm, with an irresponsible piece of fate. And the person upon whom punishment subsequently descended, again like a piece of fate, suffered no "inward pain" other than that induced by the sudden appearance of something unforeseen, a dreadful natural event, a plunging, crushing rock that one cannot fight.

15

. . . If there existed any criticism of the deed in those days, it was prudence that criticized the deed: the actual *effect* of punishment must beyond question be sought above all in a heightening of prudence, in an extending of the memory, in a will henceforth to go to work more cautiously, mistrustfully, secretly, in the insight that one is definitely too weak for many things, in a kind of improvement in self-criticism. That which can in general be attained through punishment, in men and in animals, is an increase of fear, a heightening of prudence, mastery of the desires: thus punishment *tames* men, but it does not make them "better"—one might with more justice assert the opposite. ("Injury makes one prudent," says the proverb: insofar as it makes one prudent it also makes one bad. Fortunately, it frequently makes people stupid.)

16

At this point I can no longer avoid giving a first, provisional statement of my own hypothesis concerning the origin of the "bad conscience": it may sound rather strange and needs to be pondered, lived with, and slept on for a long time. I regard the bad conscience as the serious illness that man was bound to contract under the stress of the most fundamental change he ever experienced—that change which occurred when he found himself finally enclosed within the walls of society and of peace. The situation that faced sea animals when they were compelled to become land animals or perish was the same as that which faced these semi-animals, well adapted to the wilderness, to war, to prowling, to adventure: suddenly all their instincts were disvalued and "suspended." From now on they had to walk on their feet and "bear themselves" whereas hitherto they had been borne by the water: a dreadful heaviness lay upon them. They felt unable to cope with the simplest undertakings; in this new world they no longer possessed their former guides, their regulating, unconscious and infallible drives: they were reduced to thinking, inferring, reckoning, co-ordinating cause and effect, these unfortunate creatures; they were reduced to their "consciousness," their weakest and most infallible organ! I believe there has never been such a feeling of misery on earth, such a leaden discomfort—and at the same time the old instincts had not suddenly ceased to make their usual demands! Only it was hardly or rarely possible to humor them: as a rule they had to seek new and, as it were, subterranean gratifications.

All instincts that do not discharge themselves outwardly *turn inward*—this is what I call the *internalization* of man: thus it was that man first developed what was later called his "soul." The entire inner world, originally as thin as if it were stretched between two membranes, expanded and extended itself, acquired depth, breadth, and height, in the same measure as outward discharge was *inhibited*. Those fearful bulwarks with which the political organization protected itself against the old instincts of freedom—punishments belong among these bulwarks—brought about that all those instincts of wild, free, prowling man turned backward *against man himself*. Hostility, cruelty, joy in persecuting, in attacking, in change, in destruction—all this turned against the possessors of such instincts: *that* is the origin of the "bad conscience."

The man who, from lack of external enemies and resistances and forcibly confined to the oppressive narrowness and punctiliousness of custom, impatiently lacerated, persecuted, gnawed at, assaulted, and maltreated himself; this animal that rubbed itself raw against the bars of its cage as one tried to "tame" it; this deprived creature, racked with homesickness for the wild, who had to turn himself into an adventure, a torture chamber, an uncertain and dangerous wilderness—this fool, this yearning and desperate prisoner became the inventor of the "bad conscience." But thus began the gravest and uncanniest illness, from which humanity has not yet recovered, man's suffering *of man, of himself*—the result of a forcible sundering from his animal past, as it were a leap and plunge into new surroundings and conditions of existence, a declaration of war against the old instincts upon which his strength, joy, and terribleness had rested hitherto.

Let us add at once that, on the other hand, the existence on earth of an animal soul turned against itself, taking sides against itself, was something so new, profound, unheard of, enigmatic, contradictory, *and pregnant with a future* that the aspect of the earth was essentially altered. Indeed, divine spectators were needed to do justice to the spectacle that thus began and the end of which is not yet in sight—a spectacle too subtle, too marvelous, too paradoxical to be played senselessly unobserved on some ludicrous planet! From now on, man is *included* among the most unexpected and exciting lucky throws in the dice game of Heraclitus' "great child," be he called Zeus or chance; he gives rise to an interest, a tension, a hope, almost a certainty, as if with him something were announcing and preparing itself, as if man were not a goal but only a way, an episode, a bridge, a great promise.—

17

Among the presuppositions of this hypothesis concerning the origin of the bad conscience is, first, that the change referred to was not a gradual or voluntary one and did not represent an organic adaptation to new conditions but a break, a leap, a compulsion, an ineluctable disaster which precluded all struggle and even all *ressentiment*. Secondly, however, that the welding of a hitherto unchecked and shapeless populace into a firm form was not only instituted by an act of violence but also carried to its conclusion by nothing but acts of violence—that the oldest "state" thus appeared as a fearful tyranny, as an oppressive and remorseless machine, and went on working until this raw material of people and semi-animals was at last not only thoroughly kneaded and pliant but also *formed*.

I employed the word "state": it is obvious what is meant—some pack of blond beasts of prey, a conqueror and master race which, organized for war and with the ability to organize, unhesitatingly lays its terrible claws upon a populace perhaps tremendously superior in numbers but still formless and nomad. That is after all how the "state" began on earth: I think that sentimentalism which would have it begin with "contract" has been disposed of. He who can command, he who is by nature "master," he who is violent in act and bearing—what has he to do with contracts! One does not reckon with such natures; they come like fate, without reason, consideration, or pretext; they appear as lightning appears, too terrible, too sudden, too convincing, too "different" even to be hated. Their work is an instinctive creation and imposition of forms; they are the most involuntary, unconscious artists there are—wherever they appear something new soon arises, a ruling structure that *lives*, in which parts and functions are delimited and co-ordinated, in which nothing whatever finds a place that has not first been assigned a "meaning" in relation to the whole. They do not know what guilt, responsibility, or consideration are, these born organizers; they exemplify that terrible artists' egoism that has the look of bronze and knows itself justified to all eternity in its "work," like a mother in her child. It is not in *them* that the "bad conscience" developed, that goes without saying—but it would not have developed *without them*, this ugly growth, it would be lacking if a tremendous quantity of freedom had not been expelled from the world, or at least from the visible world, and made as it were *latent* under their hammer blows and artists' violence. This *instinct for freedom* forcibly made latent—we have seen it already—this instinct for freedom pushed back and repressed, incarcerated within and finally able to discharge and vent itself only on itself: that, and that alone, is what the *bad conscience* is in its beginnings.

18

One should guard against thinking lightly of this phenomenon merely on account of its initial painfulness and ugliness. For fundamentally it is the same active force that is at work on a grander scale in those artists of violence and organizers who build states, and that here, internally, on a smaller and pettier scale, directed backward, in the "labyrinth of the breast," to use Goethe's expression, creates for itself a bad conscience and builds negative ideals—namely, the *instinct for freedom* (in my language: the will to power); only here the material upon which the form-giving and ravishing nature of this force vents itself is man himself, his whole ancient animal self—and *not*, as in that greater and more obvious phenomenon, some *other* man, *other* men. This secret self-ravishment, this artists' cruelty, this delight in imposing a form upon oneself as a hard, recalcitrant, suffering material and in burning a will, a critique, a contradiction, a contempt, a No into it, this uncanny, dreadfully joyous labor of a soul voluntarily at odds with itself that makes itself suffer out of joy in making suffer—eventually this entire *active* "bad conscience"—you will have guessed it—as the womb of all ideal and imaginative phenomena, also brought to light an abundance of strange new beauty and affirmation, and perhaps beauty itself.—After all, what would be "beautiful" if the contradiction had not first become conscious of itself, if the ugly had not first said to itself: "I am ugly"?

This hint will at least make less enigmatic the enigma of how contradictory concepts such as *selflessness, self-denial, self-sacrifice* can suggest an ideal, a kind of beauty. . . .

So much for the present about the origin of the moral value of the "unegoistic," about the soil from which this value grew: only the bad conscience, only the will to self-maltreatment provided the conditions for the *value* of the unegoistic.—

19

The bad conscience is an illness, there is no doubt about that, but an illness as pregnancy is an illness. Let us seek out the conditions under which this illness has reached its most terrible and most sublime height; we shall see what it really was that thus entered the world. But for that one needs endurance—and first of all we must go back again to an earlier point of view. . . .

Within the original tribal community—we are speaking of primeval times—the living generation always recognized a juridical duty toward earlier generations, and especially toward the earliest, which founded the tribe (and by no means a merely sentimental obligation. . . .) The conviction reigns that it is only through the sacrifices and accomplishments of the ancestors that the tribe *exists*—and that one has to *pay them back* with sacrifices and accomplishments: one thus recognizes a *debt* that constantly grows greater, since these forebears never cease, in their continued existence as powerful spirits, to accord the tribe new advantages and new strength. . . .

The *fear* of the ancestor and his power, the consciousness of indebtedness to him, increases, according to this kind of logic, in exactly the same measure as the power of the tribe itself increases, as the tribe itself grows ever more victorious, independent, honored, and feared. By no means the other way round! Every step toward the decline of a tribe, every misfortune, every sign of degeneration, of coming disintegration always *diminishes* fear of the spirit of its founder and produces a meaner impression of his cunning, foresight, and present power. If one imagines this rude kind of logic carried to its end, then the ancestors of the *most powerful* tribes are bound eventually to grow to monstrous dimensions through the imagination of growing fear and to recede into the darkness of the divinely uncanny and unimaginable: in the end the ancestor must necessarily be transfigured into a *god*. Perhaps this is even the origin of gods, an origin therefore out of *fear*! . . .

20

History shows that the consciousness of being in debt to the deity did not by any means come to an end together with the organization of communities on the basis of blood relationship. . . . The guilty feeling of indebtedness to the divinity continued to grow for several millennia—always in the same measure as the concept of God and the feeling for divinity increased on earth and was carried to the heights. . . .

The advent of the Christian God, as the maximum god attained so far, was therefore accompanied by the maximum feeling of guilty indebtedness on earth. Presuming we have gradually entered upon the *reverse* course, there is no small probability that with the irresistible decline of faith in the Christian God there is now also a considerable decline in mankind's feeling of guilt; indeed, the prospect cannot be dismissed that the complete and definitive victory of atheism might free mankind of this whole feeling of guilty indebtedness toward its origin, its *causa prima* [first cause]. Atheism and a kind of *second innocence* belong together.—

21

So much for a first brief preliminary on the connection of the concepts "guilt" and "duty" with religious presuppositions: I have up to now deliberately ignored the moralization of these concepts (their pushing back into the conscience; more precisely, the involvement of the *bad* conscience with the concept of god); and at the end of the last section I even spoke as if this moralization had not taken place at all, and as if these concepts were now necessarily doomed since their presupposition, the faith in our "creditor," in God, had disappeared. The reality is, to a fearful degree, otherwise.

The moralization of the concepts guilt and duty, their being pushed back into the *bad* conscience, actually involves an attempt to *reverse* the direction of the development described above, or at least to bring it to a halt: the *aim* now is to preclude pessimistically, once and for all, the prospect of a final discharge; the *aim* now is to make the glance recoil disconsolately from an iron impossibility; the *aim* now is to turn back the concepts "guilt" and "duty"—back against whom? There can be no doubt: against the "debtor" first of all, in whom from now on the bad conscience is firmly rooted, eating into him and spreading within him like a polyp, until at last the irredeemable debt gives rise to the conception of irredeemable penance, the idea that it cannot be discharged ("*eternal* punishment"). Finally, however, they are turned back against the "creditor," too: whether we think of the *causa prima* of man, the beginning of the human race, its primal ancestor who is from now on burdened with a curse ("Adam," "original sin," "unfreedom of the will"), or of nature from whose womb mankind arose and into whom the principle of evil is projected from now on ("the diabolizing of nature"), or of existence in general, which is now considered *worthless as such* (nihilistic withdrawal from it, a desire for nothingness or a desire for its antithesis, for a different mode of being, Buddhism and the like)—suddenly we stand before the paradoxical and horrifying expedient that afforded temporary relief for tormented humanity, that stroke of genius on the part of Christianity: God himself sacrifices himself for the guilt of mankind, God himself makes payment to himself, God as the only being who can redeem man from what has become unredeemable for man himself—the creditor sacrifices himself for his debtor, out of *love* (can one credit that?), out of love for his debtor!—

22

You will have guessed *what* has really happened here, *beneath* all this: that will to self-tormenting, that repressed cruelty of the animal-man made inward and scared back into himself, the creature imprisoned in the "state" so as to be tamed, who invented the bad conscience in order to hurt himself after the *more natural* vent for this desire to hurt had been blocked—this man of the bad conscience has seized upon the presupposition of religion so as to drive his self-torture to its most gruesome pitch of severity and rigor. Guilt before *God*: this thought becomes an instrument of torture to him. He apprehends in "God" the ultimate antithesis of his own ineluctable animal instincts; he reinterprets these animal instincts themselves as a form of guilt before God (as hostility, rebellion, insurrection against the "Lord," the "father," the primal ancestor and origin of the world); he stretches himself upon the contradiction "God" and "Devil"; he ejects from himself all his denial of himself, of his nature, naturalness, and actuality, in the form of an affirmation, as something existent, corporeal, real, as God, as the holiness of God, as God the Judge, as God the Hangman, as the beyond, as eternity, as torment without end, as hell, as the immeasurability of punishment and guilt.

In this psychical cruelty there resides a madness of the will which is absolutely unexampled: the *will* of man to find himself guilty and reprehensible to a degree that can never be atoned for; his *will* to think himself punished without any possibility of the punishment becoming equal to the guilt; his *will* to infect and poison the fundamental ground of things with the problem of punishment and guilt so as to cut off once and for all his own exit from this labyrinth of "fixed ideas"; his *will* to erect an ideal—that of the "holy God"—and in the face of it to feel the palpable certainty of his own absolute unworthiness. Oh this insane, pathetic beast—man! What ideas he has, what unnaturalness, what paroxysms of nonsense, what *bestiality of thought* erupts as soon as he is prevented just a little from being a *beast in deed*! . . .

23

This should dispose once and for all of the question of how the "holy God" originated.

That the conception of gods *in itself* need not lead to the degradation of the imagination that we had to consider briefly, that there are *nobler* uses for the invention of gods than for the self-crucifixion and self-violation of man in which Europe over the past millennia achieved its distinctive mastery—that is fortunately revealed even by a mere glance at the *Greek gods*, those reflections of noble and autocratic men, in whom *the animal* in man felt deified and did *not* lacerate itself, did *not* rage against itself! For the longest time these Greeks used their gods precisely so as to ward off the "bad conscience," so as to be able to rejoice in their freedom of soul—the very opposite of the use to which Christianity put its God. They went *very far* in this direction, these splendid and lion-hearted children; and no less an authority than the Homeric Zeus himself occasionally gives them to understand that they are making things too easy for themselves. "Strange!" he says once—the case is that of Aegisthus, a *very* bad case—

> Strange how these mortals so loudly complain of the gods!
> *We alone produce evil*, they say; yet themselves
> Make themselves wretched through folly, even counter to fate.[10]

Yet one can see and hear how even this Olympian spectator and judge is far from holding a grudge against them or thinking ill of them on that account: "how *foolish* they are!" he thinks when he observes the misdeeds of mortals—and "foolishness," "folly," a little "disturbance in the head," this much even the Greeks of the strongest, bravest age conceded of themselves as the reason for much that was bad and calamitous—foolishness, *not* sin! do you grasp that?

Even this disturbance in the head, however, presented a problem: "how is it possible? how could it actually have happened to heads such as *we* have, we men of aristocratic descent, of the best society, happy, well-constituted, noble, and virtuous?"—thus noble Greeks asked themselves for centuries in the face of every incomprehensible atrocity or wantonness with which one of their kind had polluted himself.

---

10. *Odyssey* 1, ll. 32–34.

"He must have been deluded by a *god*," they concluded finally, shaking their heads. . . . This expedient is *typical* of the Greeks. . . . In this way the gods served in those days to justify man to a certain extent even in his wickedness, they served as the originators of evil—in those days they took upon themselves, not the punishment but, what is *nobler*, the guilt.

24

I end up with three question marks; that seems plain. "What are you really doing, erecting an ideal or knocking one down?" I may perhaps be asked.

But have you ever asked yourselves sufficiently how much the erection of *every* ideal on earth has cost? How much reality has had to be misunderstood and slandered, how many lies have had to be sanctified, how many consciences disturbed, how much "God" sacrificed every time? If a temple is to be erected *a temple must be destroyed*: that is the law—let anyone who can show me a case in which it is not fulfilled!

We modern men are the heirs of the conscience-vivisection and self-torture of millennia: this is what we have practiced longest, it is our distinctive art perhaps, and in any case our subtlety in which we have acquired a refined taste. Man has all too long had an "evil eye" for his natural inclinations, so that they have finally become insepara-ble from his "bad conscience." An attempt at the reverse would *in itself* be possible—but who is strong enough for it?—that is, to wed the bad conscience to all the *unnatural* inclinations, all those aspirations to the beyond, to that which runs counter to sense, instinct, nature, animal, in short all ideals hitherto, which are one and all hostile to life and ideals that slander the world. To whom should one turn today with *such* hopes and demands?

One would have precisely the *good* men against one; and, of course, the comforta-ble, the reconciled, the vain, the sentimental, the weary.

What gives greater offense, what separates one more fundamentally, than to reveal something of the severity and respect with which one treats oneself? And on the other hand—how accommodating, how friendly all the world is toward us as soon as we act as all the world does and "let ourselves go" like all the world!

The attainment of this goal would require a *different* kind of spirit from that likely to appear in this present age: spirits strengthened by war and victory, for whom con-quest, adventure, danger, and even pain have become needs; it would require habitua-tion to the keen air of the heights, to winter journeys, to ice and mountains in every sense; it would require even a kind of sublime wickedness, an ultimate, supremely self-confident mischievousness in knowledge that goes with great health; it would require, in brief and alas, precisely this *great health*!

Is this even possible today?—But some day, in a stronger age than this decaying, self-doubting present, he must yet come to us, the *redeeming* man of great love and con-tempt, the creative spirit whose compelling strength will not let him rest in any aloof-ness or any beyond, whose isolation is misunderstood by the people as if it were flight *from* reality—while it is only his absorption, immersion, penetration *into* reality, so that, when he one day emerges again into the light, he may bring home the *redemption* of this reality: its redemption from the curse that the hitherto reigning ideal has laid upon it. This man of the future, who will redeem us not only from the hitherto reigning ideal but also from that which was bound to grow out of it, the great nausea, the will to nothingness, nihilism; this bell-stroke of noon and of the great decision that liberates the will again and restores its goal to the earth and his hope to man; this Antichrist and antinihilist; this victor over God and nothingness—*he must come one day.*—

25

But what am I saying? Enough! Enough! At this point it behooves me only to be silent; or I shall usurp that to which only one younger, "heavier with future," and stronger than I has a right—that to which only *Zarathustra* has a right, *Zarathustra the godless.*—

SELECTED BIBLIOGRAPHY

Nietzsche, Friedrich. *The Basic Writings of Nietzsche*. New York: Random House, 1968.

_____. *The Portable Nietzsche*. New York: Viking Penguin, 1968.

Allison, David B. *The New Nietzsche: Contemporary Styles of Interpretation*. Cambridge, Mass.: MIT Press, 1985.

Danto, Arthur. *Nietzsche as Philosopher*. New York: Macmillan, 1965.

Deleuze, Gilles. *Nietzsche and Philosophy*. Trans. Hugh Tomlinson. New York: Columbia University Press, 1983.

Hollingdale, R.J. *Nietzsche*. London: Routledge, Chapman & Hall, 1986.

Kaufmann, Walter. *Nietzsche: Philosopher, Psychologist, Antichrist*, 4th ed. Princeton, N.J.: Princeton University Press, 1975.

Lampert, Laurence. *Nietzsche's Teaching: An Interpretation of "Thus Spoke Zarathustra."* New Haven, Conn.: Yale University Press, 1987.

Magnus, Bernd. *Nietzsche's Existential Imperative*. Bloomington: Indiana University Press, 1978.

Morgan, George Allen. *What Nietzsche Means*. Cambridge, Mass.: Harvard University Press, 1941.

Nehamas, Alexander. *Nietzsche: Life as Literature*. Cambridge, Mass.: Harvard University Press, 1985.

Schacht, Richard. *Nietzsche*. London: Routledge, Chapman & Hall, 1983.

Solomon, Robert C. *Nietzsche: A Collection of Critical Essays*. Garden City, N.Y.: Doubleday, 1973.

Solomon, Robert C., and K.M. Higgins. *Reading Nietzsche*. New York: Oxford University Press, 1988.

Strong, Tracy B. *Friedrich Nietzsche and the Politics of Transfiguration*. Berkeley: University of California Press, 1976.

Charles Sanders Peirce

Charles Sanders Peirce (1839–1914) was born in Cambridge, Massachusetts. His father, Benjamin Peirce, was a professor of mathematics at Harvard College and one of the leading mathematicians of the day. Charles was a very bright child, always interested in puzzles, codes, chess problems, and the like, and he began studying chemistry at the age of eight, quite of his own accord. His father took a great deal of interest in young Charles's education, posing various problems and examples until Charles could tease out some general principle that would allow a solution. Benjamin undertook to train the child's powers of concentration and sensory discrimination, but Charles later complained that insufficient attention had been paid to training his "moral self-control," which was to cause trouble for him later in life.

Peirce entered Harvard in 1855 but did not do very well in his formal course of studies, graduating seventy-first in a class of ninety-one in 1859. It was during this time that his mind turned to philosophy. His father read and discussed Immanuel Kant's *Critique of Pure Reason* with him, and Peirce soon undertook a regimen of studying it for two hours every day. In 1861 he took a job with the U.S. Coast and Geodetic Survey, a connection he maintained for thirty years. He took an M.A. and then an Sc.B. (the first ever granted) from Harvard in chemistry. Despite his uninspiring undergraduate record, his intellect impressed many, and he gave several courses of lectures at Harvard, first on the philosophy of science in 1864–1865, then in philosophy in 1869–1870, and on logic in 1871–1872.

517

Peirce's work for the Coast and Geodetic Survey took him to many different places, but most of his time was spent doing basic science rather than survey work. He studied the properties of light (the only book he published in his lifetime was *Photometric Researches* in 1878) and became an important authority on pendulums and gravity. He was also the first to suggest using the wave length of light as a standard unit of measure. His work in philosophy is deeply imbued with a thorough knowledge not just of the important scientific results of his time but also of the methods that define and constitute science.

The centerpiece of Peirce's philosophical work is logic—not construed merely as the theory of valid inference but as the theory of the conditions for signification and truth. As early as 1867, picking up George Boole's work on the mathematical treatment of logic, Peirce introduced some important extensions and refinements. He went on to found the study of the logic of relations, the most significant precursor of modern mathematical logic, and also made important contributions to set theory, probability theory, and other fields. The large book on logic that Peirce did manage to finish never found a publisher, but he worked tirelessly throughout his career on problems in logic while also working extensively and at the highest level in mathematics. But even less of his mathematical writing was ever published, so many of his discoveries were rediscovered by others. Thus he did not leave as profound an impression on later mathematics as he did on logic.

Although Peirce's distinctive philosophical opinions started forming early in his career, they began to jell into a well-ordered system under the impetus of the "metaphysical club" he helped organize in Cambridge in the 1870s. Among its members was Oliver Wendell Holmes, the great jurist. But the members who most influenced and inspired Peirce were William James, brother of the novelist Henry James and soon to become the leading presence in American philosophy and psychology, and Chauncey Wright, an admirer of John Stuart Mill's empiricism who was Peirce's toughest interlocutor. It was in the fortnightly discussions of this group that Peirce's pragmatism took shape.

In 1862 Peirce married Harriet Fay, an intelligent and well-respected daughter of a prominent New England family, but the marriage did not last long. Although Peirce did not divorce Harriet until 1883, he claimed she deserted him in 1876. He later married Juliette Froisy, from Nancy, France, who remained with him until his death.

Peirce taught only sporadically. Besides his early lectures at Harvard, he taught from 1879 to 1884 at Johns Hopkins University, where he and his students compiled an important early work in formal logic. His lifelong friend and colleague, William James, who appreciated Peirce's peculiar genius more than his less farsighted colleagues did, arranged for him to lecture periodically at Harvard. Why Peirce never secured a permanent academic post had much to do with the fact that he was not easy to get along with. A proud man, sure of his talents and often impatient with lesser minds, he was easily offended and quite emotional, with a tendency to forget appointments and other external matters. He was either unwilling to make the little compromises getting along in academia required or genuinely incapable of making them. Furthermore, his divorce was not a pretty affair, particularly because Harriet Fay was so popular. His reputation suffered from the divorce, and Peirce's career never recovered.

His inability to secure a permanent academic post condemned Peirce to penury, especially after he resigned from the Coast and Geodetic Survey in 1891. He supported himself by writing definitions for the *Century Cyclopedia*, book reviews for the *Nation*, and other literary odd-jobs. Several times he applied for foundation support, but never with success. William James repeatedly came to the rescue by arranging lectures at Harvard and finally by collecting a small fund from Peirce's friends and former students, on the proceeds of which Peirce was able to survive. Throughout these difficult times Peirce worked steadily, averaging about two thousand words a day on philosophical, logicomathematical, scientific, literary, and historical subjects of all kinds. In his final years Peirce was an isolated and sickly man, wracked with cancer, still revising his reams of unpublished papers, unknown and unappreciated except by those who were able to see beyond the published snippets a powerful, insightful, and systematic mind.

After Peirce's death in 1914, William James arranged for Harvard to buy Peirce's papers from his widow. The mass of material he compiled remained in large part unavailable to the broader public until an edition of the most important pieces was published in the 1930s. Since that time Peirce has gained increasing recognition as one of America's greatest and most original philosophers.

Philosophy

Peirce is known as the founder of pragmatism, the school of philosophical thought that is distinctively American. Peircean pragmatism is essentially a doctrine about the meanings of concepts, or, rather, a methodological rule for investigating their meanings: "Consider what effects, that might conceivably have practical bearings, we conceive the object of our conception to have. Then, our conception of these effects is the whole of our conception of the object." The meanings of our terms (for instance, *pain, mass, soul*) are best investigated by thinking about what effects, what empirically ascertainable changes and results, they imply.

Other pragmatists, notably William James, reinterpreted Peirce's pragmatic principle as a doctrine not about the proper method of investigating meanings but about truth—coarsely put, that what is true is "what works." Peirce rejected this form of pragmatism as ultimately irrationalistic and referred to his version as "pragmaticism," "which is ugly enough to be safe from kidnappers." Truth is still a problematic concept for Peirce, however, for he rejects the standard correspondence interpretation of truth, the idea that a sentence is true if and only if it corresponds with the facts. Instead, truth is a regulative idea, according to Peirce: it is what the ultimate community of inquirers would agree on.

That Peirce's pragmatic principle is a methodological rule about meaning is no accident, for at the very heart of his philosophy is the theory of signs, where his groundbreaking work in formal logic and his reflections on the problems of epistemology and metaphysics come together. Understanding how our thoughts and words can mean or represent other things to other people is crucial to understanding what the objects of our thoughts are and how we can know of them.

The essay included here does not explain Peirce's entire theory of signs or its use in his metaphysics and epistemology. Peirce's systematic philosophy, like Leibniz's, is difficult to piece together from his scattered writings, but he stands interestingly between the grand metaphysical systems of Kant and Georg Wilhelm Friedrich Hegel and the antimetaphysical analysis of language and logic popular in the twentieth century. His work in logic and the theory of signs, as well as the central role he gives the investigation of meaning and the importance of the methods of the sciences, are all perfectly in tune with twentieth-century analytic philosophy. But Peirce did not shy away from strong metaphysical convictions: he was a Scotistic realist (i.e., he believed that universals have genuine reality in the objects of the world) who thought that the universe was evolving toward a state of perfect orderliness and beauty. He was a system builder convinced that he could delineate the fundamental structures of reality, just as Kant and Hegel had tried to do.

The Reading Context

Like John Locke's *Essay concerning Human Understanding* almost two hundred years earlier, Peirce's reflections on "how to make our ideas clear" began in a discussion group. In both cases it became evident that serious discussion of philosophical issues requires some agreement about the tools and the medium of philosophy, namely, our conceptions and the language we express them in.

Like most such attempts to clarify the notion of meaning or the idea of an idea, Peirce's pragmatic theory of meaning can perhaps best be tested by applying it to itself. Suppose you, the reader, take Peirce's pragmatic maxim seriously and try to clarify its meaning. Consider, then, what practical effects his pragmatic principle may have. What consequences for the practice of science would accepting the pragmatic maxim entail—for politics, art, religion, philosophy itself? If the consequences are not always clear, should you conclude that you don't yet understand the maxim or that Peirce's own principle is still too indeterminate, still itself unclear?

A Note on the Text

Although little of Peirce's writing was published during his life, this essay did originally appear in *Popular Science Monthly* in 1878. It was later revised for inclusion in a larger book Peirce planned but never published. The selection text is drawn from volume 5 of the standard edition of Peirce's works, the *Collected Papers*, originally published in the 1930s from the papers Peirce's widow sold to Harvard University. All the paragraphs in this edition are numbered, and citations standardly refer to the volume and paragraph number: for example, 5.389 indicates volume 5, paragraph 389.

Reading Questions

1. What does Peirce think is wrong with the traditional conception of clear and distinct ideas?
2. What does Peirce say is the purpose of thought?
3. How does Peirce draw the distinction between the mediately and the immediately conscious?
4. How does Peirce characterize belief?

5. How does Peirce derive his pragmatic maxim?
6. Peirce believes that there would be nothing false in the claim that untouched diamonds are perfectly soft. Nonetheless, he does not make this claim. Why?
7. What methods for ascertaining the truth does Peirce find in our history? Which one does he accept?
8. How does Peirce define reality? Is it consistent with his belief that "the question of what would occur under circumstances which do not actually arise is not a question of fact"?

How to Make Our Ideas Clear

1. Clearness and Distinctness

388. Whoever has looked into a modern treatise on logic of the common sort, will doubtless remember the two distinctions between *clear* and *obscure* conceptions, and between *distinct* and *confused* conceptions. They have lain in the books now for nigh two centuries, unimproved and unmodified, and are generally reckoned by logicians as among the gems of their doctrine.

389. A clear idea is defined as one which is so apprehended that it will be recognized wherever it is met with, and so that no other will be mistaken for it. If it fails of this clearness, it is said to be obscure.

This is rather a neat bit of philosophical terminology; yet, since it is clearness that they were defining, I wish the logicians had made their definition a little more plain. Never to fail to recognize an idea, and under no circumstances to mistake another for it, let it come in how recondite a form it may, would indeed imply such prodigious force and clearness of intellect as is seldom met with in this world. On the other hand, merely to have such an acquaintance with the idea as to have become familiar with it, and to have lost all hesitancy in recognizing it in ordinary cases, hardly seems to deserve the name of clearness of apprehension, since after all it only amounts to a subjective feeling of mastery which may be entirely mistaken. I take it, however, that when the logicians speak of "clearness," they mean nothing more than such a familiarity with an idea, since they regard the quality as but a small merit, which needs to be supplemented by another, which they call *distinctness*.

390. A distinct idea is defined as one which contains nothing which is not clear. This is technical language; by the *contents* of an idea logicians understand whatever is contained in its definition. So that an idea is *distinctly* apprehended, according to them, when we give a precise definition of it, in abstract terms. Here the professional logicians leave the subject; and I would not have troubled the reader with what they have to say, if it were not such a striking example of how they have been slumbering through ages of intellectual activity, listlessly disregarding the enginery of modern thought, and never dreaming of applying its lessons to the improvement of logic. It is easy to show that the doctrine that familiar use and abstract distinctness make the perfection of apprehension has its only true place in philosophies which have long been extinct; and it is now time to formulate the method of attaining to a more perfect clearness of thought, such as we see and admire in the thinkers of our own time.

391. When Descartes set about the reconstruction of philosophy, his first step was to (theoretically) permit skepticism and to discard the practice of the schoolmen of looking to authority as the ultimate source of truth. That done, he sought a more natural fountain of true principles, and thought he found it in the human mind; thus passing, in the directest way, from the method of authority to that of apriority. . . .

Self-consciousness was to furnish us with our fundamental truths, and to decide what was agreeable to reason. But since, evidently, not all ideas are true, he was led to note, as the first condition of infallibility, that they must be clear. The distinction between an idea *seeming* clear and really being so, never occurred to him. Trusting to introspection, as he did, even for a knowledge of external things, why should he question its testimony in respect to the contents of our own minds? But then, I suppose, seeing men, who seemed to be quite clear and positive, holding opposite opinions upon fundamental principles, he was further led to say that clearness of ideas is not sufficient, but that they need also to be distinct, i.e., to have nothing unclear about them. What he probably meant by this (for he did not explain himself with precision) was, that they must sustain the test of dialectical examination; that they must not only seem clear at the outset, but that discussion must never be able to bring to light points of obscurity connected with them.

392. Such was the distinction of Descartes, and one sees that it was precisely on the level of his philosophy. It was somewhat developed by Leibniz. This great and singular genius was as remarkable for what he failed to see as for what he saw. . . . He did not understand that the machinery of the mind can only transform knowledge, but never originate it, unless it be fed with facts of observation. He thus missed the most essential point of the Cartesian philosophy, which is, that to accept propositions which seem perfectly evident to us is a thing which, whether it be logical or illogical, we cannot help doing. Instead of regarding the matter in this way, he sought to reduce the first principles of science to two classes, those which cannot be denied without self-contradiction, and those which result from the principle of sufficient reason (of which more anon), and was apparently unaware of the great difference between his position and that of Descartes. . . . It was quite natural, therefore, that on observing that the method of Descartes labored under the difficulty that we may seem to ourselves to have clear apprehensions of ideas which in truth are very hazy, no better remedy occurred to him than to require an abstract definition of every important term. Accordingly, in adopting the distinction of *clear* and *distinct* notions, he described the latter quality as the clear apprehension of everything contained in the definition; and the books have ever since copied his words. . . . Our existing beliefs can be set in order by this process, and order is an essential element of intellectual economy, as of every other. It may be acknowledged, therefore, that the books are right in making familiarity with a notion the first step toward clearness of apprehension, and the defining of it the second. But in omitting all mention of any higher perspicuity of thought, they simply mirror a philosophy which was exploded a hundred years ago. That much-admired "ornament of logic"—the doctrine of clearness and distinctness—may be pretty enough, but it is high time to relegate to our cabinet of curiosities the antique *bijou*, and to wear about us something better adapted to modern uses.

393. The very first lesson that we have a right to demand that logic shall teach us is, how to make our ideas clear; and a most important one it is, depreciated only by minds who stand in need of it. To known what we think, to be masters of our own meaning, will make a solid foundation for great and weighty thought. . . . It is terrible to see how a single unclear idea, a single formula without meaning, lurking in a young man's head, will sometimes act like an obstruction of inert matter in an artery, hindering the nutrition of the brain, and condemning its victim to pine away in the fullness of his intellectual vigor and in the midst of intellectual plenty. . . .

2. The Pragmatic Maxim

394. [My principles] . . . lead, at once, to a method of reaching a clearness of thought of higher grade than the "distinctness" of the logicians. . . . The action of thought is excited by the irritation of doubt, and ceases when belief is attained; so that the production of belief is the sole function of thought. All these words, however, are too strong for my purpose. . . . Doubt and Belief, as the words are commonly employed, relate to religious or other grave discussions. But here I use them to designate the starting of any question, no matter how small or how great, and the resolution of it. If, for instance, in a horse-car, I pull out my purse and find a five-cent nickel and five coppers, I decide, while my hand is going to the purse, in which way I will pay my fare. To call such a question Doubt, and my decision Belief, is certainly to use words very disproportionate to the occasion. To speak of such a doubt as causing an irritation which needs to be appeased, suggests a temper which is uncomfortable to the verge of insanity. Yet, looking at the matter minutely, it must be admitted that, if there is the least hesitation as to whether I shall pay the five coppers or the nickel (as there will be sure to be, unless I act from some previously contracted habit in the matter), though irritation is too strong a word, yet I am excited to such small mental activity as may be necessary to deciding how I shall act. Most frequently doubts arise from some indecision, however momentary, in our action. Sometimes it is not so. I have, for example, to wait in a railway-station, and to pass the time I read the advertisements on the walls. I compare the advantages of different trains and different routes which I never expect to take, merely fancying myself to be in a state of hesitancy, because I am bored with having nothing to trouble me. Feigned hesitancy, whether feigned for mere amusement or with a lofty purpose, plays a great part in the production of scientific inquiry. . . .

395. In this process we observe two sorts of elements of consciousness, the distinction between which may best be made clear by means of an illustration. In a piece of music there are the separate notes, and there is the air. A single tone may be prolonged for an hour or a day, and it exists as perfectly in each second of that time as in the whole taken together; so that, as long as it is sounding, it might be present to a sense from which everything in the past was as completely absent as the future itself. But it is different with the air, the performance of which occupies a certain time, during the portions of which only portions of it are played. It consists in an orderliness in the succession of sounds which strike the ear at different times; and to perceive it there must be some continuity of consciousness which makes the events of a lapse of time present to us. We certainly only perceive the air by hearing the separate notes; yet we cannot be said to directly hear it, for we hear only what is present at the instant, and an orderliness of succession cannot exist in an instant. These two sorts of objects, what we are *immediately* conscious of and what we are *mediately* conscious of, are found in all consciousness. Some elements (the sensations) are completely present at every instant so long as they last, while others (like thought) are actions having beginning, middle, and end, and consist in a congruence in the succession of sensations which flow through the mind. They cannot be immediately present to us, but must cover some portion of the past or future. Thought is a thread of melody running through the succession of our sensations.

396. We may add that just as a piece of music may be written in parts, each part having its own air, so various systems of relationship of succession subsist together

between the same sensations. These different systems are distinguished by having different motives, ideas, or functions. Thought is only one such system, for its sole motive, idea, and function is to produce belief, and whatever does not concern that purpose belongs to some other system of relations. The action of thinking may incidentally have other results; it may serve to amuse us, for example. . . . But the soul and meaning of thought, abstracted from the other elements which accompany it, though it may be voluntarily thwarted, can never be made to direct itself toward anything but the production of belief. Thought in action has for its only possible motive the attainment of thought at rest; and whatever does not refer to belief is no part of the thought itself.

397. And what, then, is belief? It is the demi-cadence which closes a musical phrase in the symphony of our intellectual life. We have seen that it has just three properties: First, it is something that we are aware of; second, it appeases the irritation of doubt; and, third, it involves the establishment in our nature of a rule of action, or, say for short, a *habit*. As it appeases the irritation of doubt, which is the motive for thinking, thought relaxes, and comes to rest for a moment when belief is reached. But, since belief is a rule for action, the application of which involves further doubt and further thought, at the same time that it is a stopping-place, it is also a new starting-place for thought. That is why I have permitted myself to call it thought at rest, although thought is essentially an action. The *final* upshot of thinking is the exercise of volition, and of this thought no longer forms a part; but belief is only a stadium of mental action, an effect upon our nature due to thought, which will influence future thinking.

398. The essence of belief is the establishment of a habit; and different beliefs are distinguished by the different modes of action to which they give rise. If beliefs do not differ in this respect, if they appease the same doubt by producing the same rule of action, then no mere differences in the manner of consciousness of them can make them different beliefs, any more than playing a tune in different keys is playing different tunes. Imaginary distinctions are often drawn between beliefs which differ only in their mode of expression. . . . One singular deception of this sort, which often occurs, is to mistake the sensation produced by our own unclearness of thought for a character of the object we are thinking. Instead of perceiving that the obscurity is purely subjective, we fancy that we contemplate a quality of the object which is essentially mysterious; and if our conception be afterward presented to us in a clear form we do not recognize it as the same, owing to the absence of the feeling of unintelligibility. So long as this deception lasts, it obviously puts an impassable barrier in the way of perspicuous thinking; so that it equally interests the opponents of rational thought to perpetuate it, and its adherents to guard against it. . . .

400. From all these sophisms we shall be perfectly safe so long as we reflect that the whole function of thought is to produce habits of action; and that whatever there is connected with a thought, but irrelevant to its purpose, is an accretion to it, but no part of it. If there be a unity among our sensations which has no reference to how we shall act on a given occasion, as when we listen to a piece of music, why we do not call that thinking. To develop its meaning, we have, therefore, simply to determine what habits it produces, for what a thing means is simply what habits it involves. Now, the identity of a habit depends on how it might lead us to act, not merely under such circumstances as are likely to arise, but under such as might possibly occur, no matter

how improbable they may be. What the habit is depends on *when* and *how* it causes us to act. As for the *when*, every stimulus to action is derived from perception; as for the *how*, every purpose of action is to produce some sensible result. Thus, we come down to what is tangible and conceivably practical, as the root of every real distinction of thought, no matter how subtle it may be; and there is no distinction of meaning so fine as to consist in anything but a possible difference of practice.

401. To see what this principle leads to, consider in the light of it such a doctrine as that of transubstantiation. The Protestant churches generally hold that the elements of the sacrament are flesh and blood only in a tropical sense; they nourish our souls as meat and the juice of it would our bodies. But the Catholics maintain that they are literally just meat and blood; although they possess all the sensible qualities of wafer-cakes and diluted wine. But we can have no conception of wine except what may enter into a belief, either—

1. That this, that, or the other, is wine; or,
2. That wine possesses certain properties.

Such beliefs are nothing but self-notifications that we should, upon occasion, act in regard to such things as we believe to be wine according to the qualities which we believe wine to possess. The occasion of such action would be some sensible perception, the motive of it to produce some sensible result. Thus our action has exclusive reference to what affects the senses, our habit has the same bearing as our action, our belief the same as our habit, our conception the same as our belief; and we can consequently mean nothing by wine but what has certain effects, direct or indirect, upon our senses; and to talk of something as having all the sensible characters of wine, yet being in reality blood, is senseless jargon. . . .

402. It appears, then, that the rule for attaining the third grade of clearness of apprehension is as follows: Consider what effects, that might conceivably have practical bearings, we conceive the object of our conception to have. Then, our conception of these effects is the whole of our conception of the object.[1]

3. Some Applications of the Pragmatic Maxim

403. Let us illustrate this rule by some examples; and, to begin with the simplest one possible, let us ask what we mean by calling a thing *hard*. Evidently that it will not be scratched by many other substances. The whole conception of this quality, as of every other, lies in its conceived effects. There is absolutely no difference between a hard thing and a soft thing so long as they are not brought to the test. Suppose, then, that a diamond could be crystallized in the midst of a cushion of soft cotton, and should

---

1. Note that in these three lines one finds, "conceivably," "conceive," "conception," "conception," "conception." . . . This employment five times over of derivatives of *concipere* must then have had a purpose. In point of fact it had two. One was to show that I was speaking of meaning in no other sense than that of *intellectual purport*. The other was to avoid all danger of being understood as attempting to explain a concept by percepts, images, schemata, or by anything but concepts. I did not, therefore, mean to say that acts, which are more strictly singular than anything, could constitute the purport, or adequate proper interpretation, of any symbol. . . . Pragmaticism makes thinking to consist in the living inferential metaboly of symbols whose purport lies in conditional general resolutions to act. [All notes in this selection are Peirce's.]

remain there until it was finally burned up. Would it be false to say that that diamond was soft? This seems a foolish question, and would be so, in fact, except in the realm of logic. There such questions are often of the greatest utility as serving to bring logical principles into sharper relief than real discussions every could. . . . We may, in the present case, modify our question, and ask what prevents us from saying that all hard bodies remain perfectly soft until they are touched, when their hardness increases with the pressure until they are scratched. Reflection will show that the reply is this: there would be no *falsity* in such modes of speech. They would involve a modification of our present usage of speech with regard to the words hard and soft, but not of their meanings. For they represent no fact to be different from what it is; only they involve arrangements of facts which would be exceedingly maladroit. This leads us to remark that the question of what would occur under circumstances which do not actually arise is not a question of fact, but only of the most perspicuous arrangement of them. For example, the question of free-will and fate in its simplest form, stripped of verbiage, is something like this: I have done something of which I am ashamed: could I, by an effort of the will, have resisted the temptation, and done otherwise? The philosophical reply is, that this is not a question of fact, but only of the arrangement of facts. . . .

404. [Let] us undertake an account of the idea of Force in general. This is the great conception which, developed in the early part of the seventeenth century from the rude idea of a cause, and constantly improved upon since, has shown us how to explain all the changes of motion which bodies experience, and how to think about all physical phenomena; which has given birth to modern science, and changed the face of the globe; and which, aside from its more special uses, has played a principal part in directing the course of modern thought, and in furthering modern social development. It is, therefore, worth some pains to comprehend it. According to our rule, we must begin by asking what is the immediate use of thinking about force; and the answer is, that we thus account for changes of motion. If bodies were left to themselves, without the intervention of forces, every motion would continue unchanged both in velocity and in direction. Furthermore, change of motion never takes place abruptly; if its direction is changed, it is always through a curve without angles; if its velocity alters, it is by degrees. The gradual changes which are constantly taking place are conceived by geometers to be compounded together according to the rules of the parallelogram of forces. . . .

If the actual changes of motion which the different particles of bodies experience are each resolved in its appropriate way, each component acceleration is precisely such as is prescribed by a certain law of Nature, according to which bodies, in the relative positions which the bodies in question actually have at the moment,[2] always receive certain accelerations, which, being compounded by geometrical addition, give the acceleration which the body actually experiences.

This is the only fact which the idea of force represents, and whoever will take the trouble clearly to apprehend what this fact is, perfectly comprehends what force is. Whether we ought to say that a force is an acceleration, or that it *causes* an acceleration, is a mere question of propriety of language, which has no more to do with our real meaning than the difference between the French idiom "*Il fait froid*" and its

---

2. Possibly the velocities also have to be taken into account.

English equivalent "*It is cold.*" Yet it is surprising to see how this simple affair has muddled men's minds. In how many profound treatises is not force spoken of as a "mysterious entity," which seems to be only a way of confessing that the author despairs of ever getting a clear notion of what the word means! In a recent admired work on *Analytic Mechanics*[3] it is stated that we understand precisely the effect of force, but what force itself is we do not understand! This is simply a self-contradiction. The idea which the word force excites in our minds has no other function than to affect our actions, and these actions can have no reference to force otherwise than through its effects. Consequently, if we know what the effects of force are, we are acquainted with every fact which is implied in saying that a force exists, and there is nothing more to know. . . .

4. Reality

405. Let us now approach the subject of logic, and consider a conception which particularly concerns it, that of *reality*. Taking clearness in the sense of familiarity, no idea could be clearer than this. Every child uses it with perfect confidence, never dreaming that he does not understand it. As for clearness in its second grade, however, it would probably puzzle most men, even among those of a reflective turn of mind, to give an abstract definition of the real. Yet such a definition may perhaps be reached by considering the points of difference between reality and its opposite, fiction. A figment is a product of somebody's imagination; it has such characters as his thought impresses upon it. That those characters are independent of how you or I think is an external reality. There are, however, phenomena within our own minds, dependent upon our thought, which are at the same time real in the sense that we really think them. But though their characters depend on how we think, they do not depend on what we think those characters to be. Thus, a dream has a real existence as a mental phenomenon, if somebody has really dreamt it; that he dreamt so and so, does not depend on what anybody thinks was dreamt, but is completely independent of all opinion on the subject. On the other hand, considering, not the fact of dreaming, but the thing dreamt, it retains its peculiarities by virtue of no other fact than that it was dreamt to possess them. Thus we may define the real as that whose characters are independent of what anybody may think them to be.

406. But, however satisfactory such a definition may be found, it would be a great mistake to suppose that it makes the idea of reality perfectly clear. Here, then, let us apply our rules. According to them, reality, like every other quality, consists in the peculiar sensible effects which things partaking of it produce. The only effect which real things have is to cause belief, for all the sensations which they excite emerge into consciousness in the form of beliefs. The question therefore is, how is true belief (or belief in the real) distinguished from false belief (or belief in fiction). Now, as we have seen in the former paper, the ideas of truth and falsehood, in their full development, appertain exclusively to the experiential method of settling opinion. . . .

---

3. Kirchhoff's *Vorlesungen über math. Physik*, Bd. I, Vorrede.

407. . . . All the followers of science are animated by a cheerful hope that the processes of investigation, if only pushed far enough, will give one certain solution to each question to which they apply it. One man may investigate the velocity of light by studying the transits of Venus and the aberration of the stars; another by the oppositions of Mars and the eclipses of Jupiter's satellites; a third by the method of Fizeau; a fourth by that of Foucault; a fifth by the motions of the curves of Lissajoux; a sixth, a seventh, an eighth, and a ninth, may follow the different methods of comparing the measures of statical and dynamical electricity. They may at first obtain different results, but, as each perfects his method and his processes, the results are found to move steadily together toward a destined centre. So with all scientific research. Different minds may set out with the most antagonistic views, but the progress of investigation carries them by a force outside of themselves to one and the same conclusion. This activity of thought by which we are carried, not where we wish, but to a foreordained goal, is like the operation of destiny. No modification of the point of view taken, no selection of other facts for study, no natural bent of mind even, can enable a man to escape the predestinate opinion. This great hope is embodied in the conception of truth and reality. The opinion which is fated[4] to be ultimately agreed to by all who investigate, is what we mean by the truth, and the object represented in this opinion is the real. That is the way I would explain reality.

408. But it may be said that this view is directly opposed to the abstract definition which we have given of reality, inasmuch as it makes the characters of the real depend on what is ultimately thought about them. But the answer to this is that, on the one hand, reality is independent, not necessarily of thought in general, but only of what you or I or any finite number of men may think about it; and that, on the other hand, though the object of the final opinion depends on what that opinion is, yet what that opinion is does not depend on what you or I or any man thinks. Our perversity and that of others may indefinitely postpone the settlement of opinion; it might even conceivably cause an arbitrary proposition to be universally accepted as long as the human race should last. Yet even that would not change the nature of the belief, which alone could be the result of investigation carried sufficiently far; and if, after the extinction of our race, another should arise with faculties and disposition for investigation, that true opinion must be the one which they would ultimately come to. "Truth crushed to earth shall rise again," and the opinion which would finally result from investigation does not depend on how anybody may actually think. But the reality of that which is real does depend on the real fact that investigation is destined to lead, at last, if continued long enough, to a belief in it.

409. But I may be asked what I have to say to all the minute facts of history, forgotten never to be recovered, to the lost books of the ancients, to the buried secrets.

"Full many a gem of purest ray serene
   The dark, unfathomed caves of ocean bear;
Full many a flower is born to blush unseen,
   And waste its sweetness on the desert air."

---

4. Fate means merely that which is sure to come true, and can nohow be avoided. It is a superstition to suppose that a certain sort of events are ever fated, and it is another to suppose that the word fate can never be freed from its superstitious taint. We are all fated to die.

Do these things not really exist because they are hopelessly beyond the reach of our knowledge? And then, after the universe is dead (according to the prediction of some scientists), and all life has ceased forever, will not the shock of atoms continue though there will be no mind to know it? To this I reply that, though in no possible state of knowledge can any number be great enough to express the relation between the amount of what rests unknown to the amount of the known, yet it is unphilosophical to suppose that, with regard to any given question (which has any clear meaning), investigation would not bring forth a solution of it, if it were carried far enough. Who would have said, a few years ago, that we could ever know of what substances stars are made whose light may have been longer in reaching us than the human race has existed? Who can be sure of what we shall not know in a few hundred years? Who can guess what would be the result of continuing the pursuit of science for ten thousand years, with the activity of the last hundred? And if it were to go on for a million, or a billion, or any number of years you please, how is it possible to say that there is any question which might not ultimately be solved?

But it may be objected, "Why make so much of these remote considerations, especially when it is your principle that only practical distinctions have a meaning?" Well, I must confess that it makes very little difference whether we say that a stone on the bottom of the ocean, in complete darkness, is brilliant or not—that is to say, that it *probably* makes no difference, remembering always that that stone *may* be fished up tomorrow. But that there are gems at the bottom of the sea, flowers in the untraveled desert, etc., are propositions which, like that about a diamond being hard when it is not pressed, concern much more the arrangement of our language than they do the meaning of our ideas. . . .

SELECTED BIBLIOGRAPHY

Peirce, Charles Sanders. *Collected Papers of Charles Sanders Peirce* (8 vols.), ed. Charles Hartshorne, Paul Weiss, and Arthur W. Burks. Cambridge, Mass.: Harvard University Press, 1931–1958.

Ayer, A.J. *The Origins of Pragmatism*. San Francisco: Freeman Cooper, 1968.

Gallie, W.G. *Peirce and Pragmatism*. Harmondsworth, England: Penguin, 1952.

Hookway, Christopher. *Peirce*. London: Routledge, Chapman & Hall, 1985.

Murphy, Murray G. *Development of Peirce's Philosophy*. Cambridge, Mass.: Harvard University Press, 1961.

Reilly, Francis E. *Charles Peirce's Theory of Scientific Method*. New York: Forham University Press, 1970.

Scheffler, Israel. *Four Pragmatists: A Critical Introduction to Peirce, James, Mead, and Dewey*. New York: Humanities Press, 1974.

Thayer, H.S. *Meaning and Action: A Critical History of Pragmatism*. Indianapolis: Bobbs-Merrill, 1968.

Thompson, Manley. *The Pragmatic Philosophy of C.S. Peirce*. Chicago: University of Chicago Press, 1953.

TWENTIETH-CENTURY PHILOSOPHY

Our view of Western philosophy in the twentieth century is obscured by the proximity of its object; since the filter of time has had no chance to sort out the most important contributions to philosophy in our own era, we run the double danger of missing the forest for the trees and of not being able to tell a mountain from a molehill—both consequences of not being able to stand back far enough to gain a perspective on the whole.

The currently popular caricature of twentieth-century Western philosophy divides it into two "mainstreams," one primarily located on the European continent, the other in English-speaking, Anglo-American lands.

European philosophy (if one can indeed speak of but one) is in many ways an extension of the Continental philosophies of the nineteenth century—Immanuel Kant, Georg Wilhelm Friedrich Hegel, Karl Marx, Søren Kierkegaard, Friedrich Nietzsche—as well as the philosophers they influenced. The major new development in twentieth-century Continental philosophy is the rise of phenomenology. The phenomenological method, as originally described, demands that we focus on the pure *experience* of some object, event, or state of affairs (and emphasizes that experience is always *of something*), without considering its veracity or whether that object of experience actually exists. Then by considering possible variations in the experience, one can explore the conceptual boundaries of that kind of object of experience, leading at last to an intuition or understanding of the essence of that object. Precisely because it is a *method*, it is not a *doctrine*. Nonetheless, the actual structure of the phenomenological method, its goals, and its competence have all been questioned or revised by subsequent practitioners.

Although numerous philosophers were involved in the early development and spread of phenomenology, the German-educated Edmund Husserl was the leading figure in this movement. He is represented here by his early essay "Philosophy as Rigorous Science." Husserl was originally concerned with the foundations of logic and mathematics, but many of the more important applications of the phenomenological method have applied it to the analysis of perception, aesthetic or moral experience, and even more broadly, human experience in general. Starting in Germany, where such noted philosophers as Martin Heidegger, Hans-Georg Gadamer, and Roman Ingarden were deeply influenced by phenomenology, this philosophical method spread across the Continent. In France, Jean-Paul Sartre, Simone de Beauvoir, Maurice Merleau-Ponty, and Gaston Bachelard, among others, practiced this method. Jose Ortega y Gasset in Spain and Nichola Abbagnano in Italy were also influenced by Husserl.

The Anglo-American tradition, analytic philosophy, is less connected to nineteenth-century philosophy than the Continental traditions, for it began as a revolt against the neo-Hegelianism that had seized Britain at the end of the nineteenth century. In many ways it is a reassertion of the long tradition of British empiricism, but with an important difference. Twentieth-century empiricism has been called the "new way of words," in contrast to John Locke's new way of ideas, because of the central role that language, as the mediator of our contact with the world, assumes in its methodology. Thus the careful analysis of language, its structure, and its use is the central focus of analytic philosophy.

The two men generally regarded as the founders of the analytic tradition are Bertrand Russell (1872–1970) and G.E. Moore (1873–1958). Russell was deeply involved in the development of modern symbolic logic. He saw in the powerful systems of modern logic a privileged language in which philosophical problems could be cleanly stated and solved. Moore, though not reliant on the methods of modern logic, was similarly convinced that the solution to most philosophical problems could be found by paying extremely careful attention to the statement of the problem and the statement of its proposed solutions.

Although Russell and Moore remain commanding figures in the Anglo-American tradition, the Austrian Ludwig Wittgenstein represents analytic philosophy in this book. Wittgenstein was a pupil of Russell's, and his early book, the *Tractatus Logico-Philosophicus*, was heavily stamped with Russell's influence. Wittgenstein was also deeply admired by Moore, to whose chair in philosophy at Cambridge he succeeded.

There are two important subdivisions within analytic philosophy as practiced through about 1960: *ideal-language* theory, which sought to uncover or construct an ideal language that would mirror reality, and *ordinary-language* philosophy, which maintained that natural languages like English are already as ideal as can be found if one only pays sufficient attention to the subtleties and complexities of the language. Wittgenstein played a major role in both of these subdivisions, moving from the ideal-language toward the ordinary-language type of philosophy.

The spread of analytic philosophy was not a matter of simple British hegemony. The American philosophical scene was quite diverse at the beginning of this century, and the British style of analytic philosophy was not accepted immediately. It did, however, blend well with the emphasis on questions of meaning and truth and the emphasis on logic espoused by such pragmatists as Charles Sanders Peirce and C.I. Lewis. Initially, the analytic tradition found a strong reception on the Continent. Because of its use of modern symbolic logic, its concern with problems in the foundations of mathematics, and the attention it pays to the methods of the empirical sciences, it attracted a number of adherents on the Continent who were trained in the sciences. These thinkers, the logical positivists, employed the techniques of modern logical analysis in their attempt to replace metaphysical speculation with sound, scientific procedure. The spread of the analytic tradition on the Continent was cut short by the rise of fascism, for many of its leading proponents were either liberals, left-leaning, or Jewish. The subsequent dispersion of such powerful thinkers as Rudolph Carnap, Hans Reichenbach, Carl Hempel, Herbert Feigl, and Otto Neurath throughout the Anglo-American world contributed significantly to making analytic philosophy the dominant form in the English-speaking parts of the globe.

There is little doubt that the split between the Continental and the Anglo-American schools of philosophy was exacerbated by World War II, but that cannot suffice to explain its endurance. A number of leading figures of the Frankfurt school of critical theory, a group combining socialist and Marxist thought with Freudian analyses of human and social psychology, also were forced out of Germany and settled in New York City (founding the New School for Social Research). Yet this group, comprised of such notables as Theodor Adorno, Max Horkheimer, and Erich Fromm, left relatively little impression on American philosophy when they decided to return to Germany in the 1950s. Once back in Europe, the Frankfurt school easily regained its influential position, aided by its current principal spokesperson, Jürgen Habermas.

Turning from the sociology (or geography) of contemporary philosophy to consider the central topics in philosophy, the differences between the Continental and Anglo-American traditions seem less marked. The major figures of both traditions, Husserl on the Continent and Gottlob Frege and Russell in the analytic tradition, originally focused on problems in the philosophy of the mathematics. Tremendous developments in the nineteenth century had overthrown the standard conceptions of the nature of mathematics, and Husserl, Frege, Russell, and Wittgenstein were all deeply interested in reestablishing a sound philosophical foundation for the discipline.

This interest placed both metaphysical and epistemological concerns at the very core of these two movements, for seeking the foundations of mathematics requires questioning the objects of mathematical assertions, the grounds for our knowledge of mathematical truths, and the relation of mathematics to the empirical sciences and to human thought.

In twentieth-century epistemology, numerous debates have occurred about the nature of the foundation of our knowledge and whether such a foundation even exists. Is our knowledge a structure built on a self-evident or indubitable foundation in what is given to us perceptually, or is our knowledge more like a raft, floating without determinate anchor in the world, kept afloat by its own internal integrity? Is there a large realm of the a priori, a special domain open to the pure investigations of mathematicians and philosophers, or is there no purely a priori knowledge at all?

In metaphysics, a constant theme throughout this century has been the competence of the empirical sciences. One group, the scientific realists, has maintained that "science is the measure of what is, that it is, and what is not, that it is not." They hold that the ultimate nature and structure of the world are matters of empirical investigation and empirical theory. Those who reject scientific realism, however, vary significantly in their grounds but usually claim that science, as a relatively late-blooming human activity, is based on commonsense concepts that cannot be replaced or overridden by scientific constructs. Science is a revision of our understanding of the world, but science cannot force us to revise our understanding so radically that the fundamental experiences on which science is built must ultimately be rejected. The fundamental experiences used in science therefore retain priority over the deliverances of science. Depending on what one takes the fundamental objects of experience to be, this kind of argument can support (1) phenomenalism, in which sense data are the primary objects of the world; (2) a metaphysics based on "prepredicative lived experience," in which the meaningful structures of the lived world as directly revealed to us in consciousness are accorded metaphysical priority; or (3) a form of commonsense realism, in which the commonsense world of medium-sized objects retains metaphysical priority over the world of fields, particles, and wave packets offered to us by science.

The status of the mind and its relation to the body have also been a central focus of metaphysical thought in the twentieth century. Idealists deny the existence of matter or body, materialists deny the existence of minds, and dualists insist on the independent existence of both. The analytic tradition has been particularly fascinated with materialism—the notion that a complete story of the world need mention only material bodies, their properties and relations. But an objection to such a position—and this is a viewpoint shared widely on the Continent—is that such an accounting of the world would exclude the notion of a subjectivity that experiences the world. This form of posing the clash between materialism and its opponents emphasizes the difficulty of constructing a balanced account of the relations between the objective and the subjective aspects of the world, a problem that bedevils both traditions.

The two traditions have also differed significantly in their approaches to reflection on the good life. In analytic philosophy there have been some major efforts at refining and defending both the utilitarian position found in John Stuart Mill and the social contract tradition found in Thomas Hobbes, Locke, and Kant. The selection by John Rawls included here represents an effort by the most influential of contemporary analytic social philosophers to elaborate a refined social contract theory. Rawls's efforts are firmly rooted in the tradition of liberal European thought, but like much of contemporary analytic ethical philosophy, it is highly academic. Only since the mid-1970s have Anglo-American philosophers turned their attention to significant applied problems in ethics, such as the morality of abortion, capital punishment, or nuclear deterrence.

Reflection on the good life on the Continent, in contrast, has long been characterized by real-world concerns. Tossed amid the trauma of two world wars fought principally on European soil, positioned between two superpowers, Continental philosophers have found it only natural to abandon the theoretical speculations of the ivory tower for the activism of the streets. One of Europe's most committed and active philosophers, Simone de Beauvoir, represents Continental ethics in this anthology.

De Beauvoir is also the sole female in this collection, a sad fact that reflects the male dominance of the Western philosophical tradition. Yes, there have been female philosophers: both René Descartes and Gottfried Wilhelm Leibniz, for instance, had philosophically important female correspondents, Princess Elizabeth of Bohemia and Queen Sophie Charlotte of Prussia, respectively. But for reasons that have nothing to do with innate talent, women have not made widely recognized and influential contributions to mainstream philosophy until this century. Slowly, headway is now being made against this sorry legacy, and a number of important female philosophers (or rather, a number of important philosophers who are females) have emerged, L. Susan Stebbing, Susanne K. Langer, Hanna Arendt, Elizabeth Anscombe, Ruth Barcan Marcus, Amelie Oksenberg Rorty, among them.

Just what it is that divides the Continental and Anglo-American traditions remains open to investigation. Some have claimed that it is really little more than a difference in style, for there is no doubt that the two traditions have distinct vocabularies and differ in their styles of presentation. The most vehement members of each group, however, sometimes even refuse to recognize as philosophy what the other group produces. Thankfully, there are some indications that such an extreme division between the two schools is being overcome. Increased communication and familiarity are the first steps in reuniting philosophy.

SELECTED BIBLIOGRAPHY

Ayer, A.J. *Philosophy in the Twentieth Century*. London: Weidenfeld & Nicolson, 1982.

_____. *Russell and Moore*. London: Macmillan, 1971.

Bochenski, I.M. *Contemporary European Philosophy*. Berkeley: University of California Press, 1956.

Bubner, Rüdiger. *Modern German Philosophy*. Trans. Eric Mathews. Cambridge: Cambridge University Press, 1981.

Descombes, Vincent. *Modern French Philosophy*. Trans. L. Scott-Fox and J.M. Harding. Cambridge: Cambridge University Press, 1980.

Feigl, Herbert, and Wilfrid Sellars. *Readings in Philosophical Analysis*. New York: Appleton-Century-Crofts, 1949.

Hanfling, Oswald. *Essential Readings in Logical Positivism*. Oxford: Basil Blackwell, 1981.

Landgrebe, Ludwig. *Major Problems in Contemporary European Philosophy: From Dilthey to Heidegger*. Trans. Kurt F. Reinhardt. New York: Frederick Unger, 1966.

Macquarrie, John. *Existentialism*. Harmondsworth, England: Penguin, 1973.

Passmore, John. *A Hundred Years of Philosophy*. Harmondsworth, England: Penguin, 1968.

_____. *Recent Philosophers*. London: Duckworth, 1985.

Rorty, Richard, ed. *The Linguistic Turn*. Chicago: University of Chicago Press, 1967.

Schrader, George Alfred, ed. *Existential Philosophers: Kierkegaard to Merleau-Ponty*. New York: McGraw-Hill, 1967.

Spiegleberg, Herbert. *The Phenomenological Movement: A Historical Introduction*, 3d ed. Boston: Martinus Nijhoff, 1982.

Urmson, J.O. *Philosophical Analysis: Its Development between the Two World Wars*. New York: Oxford University Press, 1956.

Warnock, G.J. *English Philosophy since 1900*. New York: Oxford University Press, 1958.

Warnock, Mary. *Ethics since 1900*, 3d ed. New York: Oxford University Press, 1978.

Edmund Husserl

Edmund Husserl (1859–1938) was born in Moravia, then a part of the Austro-Hungarian Empire, now a part of Czechoslovakia. His parents were middle-class Jews, though Husserl later converted to Protestantism. He studied mathematics and physics at the University of Leipzig, then at the University of Berlin under the famous mathematician Karl Weierstrass. In 1881 he went to Vienna, where he completed his doctorate, after which he returned briefly to Berlin to serve as Weierstrass's assistant.

In 1884, upon returning to Vienna for further studies, Husserl started attending the lectures of Franz Brentano, an important figure in both philosophy and psychology. Brentano's lectures captivated him, and he determined to devote the rest of his life to philosophy. Brentano is most commonly remembered today for his attempt to distinguish between psychological and physical phenomena on the basis of the fact that psychological phenomena are directed at some object, event, or state of affairs. Thus when I think, I think *of* something, or I think *that* something is the case. When I hope or fear, I hope *that* something will happen, or I fear *that* it will. What is peculiar about the relationship of thought to its object is that the object of a thought does not need to exist. I can think of unicorns even though they do not exist. We signal the special status of the object of our thoughts by calling it an *intentional object*. Since physical relations can exist only when the objects themselves exist, relation to an intentional object (a relation that could exist even if the intentional object does not exist) cannot be a physical relation. Brentano then claimed (though there is some debate whether this is a faithful characterization of his views) that being related to an intentional object is distinctive of the psychological. Husserl built on Brentano's insight that psychological states always have an intentional object.

Husserl served as a *Privatdozent* (which means that he was not paid a regular faculty salary but collected money individually from the students who attended his lectures) at the University of Halle in Germany from 1887 to 1901. He turned his attention to the philosophical foundations of mathematics, which had been thrown into question by several important developments in nineteenth-century mathematics, especially the discovery of alternative, non-Euclidean geometries. Husserl's first attempt, in the *Philosophy of Arithmetic*, to provide a foundation for mathematics—that is, to provide a coherent explanation of what mathematical assertions are about, why they are true, and how they can be justified—was a form of *psychologism*. Psychologism grounds mathematics in our own psychology, taking mathematical assertions to be generalizations about our experience or the ways in which we tend to think. Further reflection, aided by a hefty critique of his book by Gottlob Frege (1848–1925), a great logician who influenced the analytic school of philosophy, convinced Husserl that this was the wrong approach. He elaborated his critique of psychologism and began working out his new phenomenological method in his *Logical Investigations* (1900–1901).

Husserl moved to a position at the University of Göttingen in late 1901. There he worked steadily, extending and deepening his conception of his new method, to which he gave a first systematic statement in 1907. He published little during this period, and recognition of his work came only slowly, but he worked out his ideas in his lectures and established the basis of phenomenology. This period of incubation came to an end with the publication in the early 1910s of "Philosophy as Rigorous Science," a popular work aimed at proclaiming the domain of his philosophy, and *Ideas*, a difficult core volume in which Husserl laid out many of the details of the phenomenological method.

In 1916 Husserl finally received the recognition he had so missed and was named a full professor at the University of Freiburg. However, the loss of his son Wolfgang at the battle of Verdun immediately afterward prevented Husserl from savoring this achievement. Although he published few books during his lifetime, he worked ceaselessly and produced mountains of material, much of which has been published posthumously. Devoted to philosophy, Husserl made a deep impression on his students precisely because of his intense commitment and the earnestness with which he attacked his discipline. Still, he was a sympathetic teacher who worked hard to make his views clear to his students.

Husserl retired in 1928 but did not cease working. In the 1930s he recognized the coming crisis in Europe and suffered under the Nazi repression because of his Jewish heritage, though he died in 1938 before coming to any physical harm. In the face of the growing irrationality of the European scene, Husserl produced his last work, *The Crisis of European Sciences and Phenomenology*, showing how phenomenology, which until then had been hermetically academic, might help overcome the broader social malaise tormenting Europe.

Philosophy

Although Husserl tackles numerous philosophical problems, the overriding concerns of most of his works are the philosopher's task and how best to accomplish it. Considering that he spent thousands of manuscript pages investigating these problems in detail, the brief summary given here cannot do him full justice, but the flavor of his philosophy will become apparent.

Phenomenology means, etymologically, the study of phenomena. Husserl uses *phenomenon* in a very specific way, however. Any intentional object of consciousness is a phenomenon. (This usage recalls Immanuel Kant's but does not duplicate it.) To investigate something out there in the world (e.g., time or religious worship) is to engage in empirical science (e.g., physics or the sociology or psychology of religion). To investigate a phenomenon—an intentional object of consciousness as it appears within consciousness—is not empirical science. There may be an empirical science of consciousness, which would worry about consciousness's relations to the world, but the internal structures of the objects of consciousness as such are not objects of empirical investigation.

The first move in the phenomenological method is to ensure that one is dealing with pure phenomena, and this is accomplished through *phenomenological reduction*, the bracketing off of all questions about the existence of the object of consciousness and its actual relations to other things in order to focus solely on the object as it appears within consciousness. Having isolated the pure phenomenon, one then employs the technique of *eidetic variation*, imagining changes to the phenomenon, in order to ascertain the boundaries of the phenomenon. This process culminates in an *eidetic intuition*, an intuition of the essence of the phenomenon. Thus a phenomenology of religious worship would first bracket off any worries about the existence of God or the existence of particular religious traditions and go straight to the description of the nature and content of one's consciousness in worship. By exploring variations of that experience, one would eventually come to see what makes religious worship what it is, how it differs from hero worship or mere fetishism, and how it differs from religious ritual or religious disputation.

Husserl elaborated, refined, and improved that basic method many times over, so this is little more than a caricature. Nevertheless, one can see that although it can be applied to virtually any kind of experience, its most significant results will come when it is applied to the most general features of our consciousness, especially the reflexive application of this method to the essence of consciousness and experience itself. It is under this rubric that Husserl thinks phenomenology will provide the foundation for knowledge and the sciences generally, for it will demonstrate to us the essential structures of experience itself.

The Reading Context

Husserl was concerned to show that philosophy is an autonomous and legitimate field of inquiry in its own right and that it can be as rigorously scientific as any discipline. He takes pains to distinguish philosophy from other sciences in order to demonstrate its autonomy and to explain its proper methodology, but he clearly devotes the greatest energy to distinguishing philosophy from psychology. This is itself very revealing; across the English Channel, the early Wittgenstein needed to take equal pains to distinguish philosophy not from psychology but from *logic*.

A constant throughout Husserl's career was his conviction that philosophy had to be an intensely subjective affair, not in the sense that philosophy was a matter of subjective opinion but that philosophy was about the very structure of subjectivity (i.e., consciousness). The phenomenological method is an attempt to purge consciousness of the purely subjective, to understand one's own understanding with a clear, cold, objective eye. Husserl knew well the difficulty of such a task, and the depth and sincerity of his devotion to philosophy made a tremendous impression on his students.

A question to keep in mind as you read is: Has Husserl successfully delimited a field of research distinct from the other sciences, with a methodology peculiar to it, capable of rigor and certainty?

A Note on the Text

"Philosophy as Rigorous Science" first appeared in the journal *Logos* in 1911. It was an important precursor of Husserl's first fully developed statement of the phenomenological method in *Ideas*, published two years later.

Reading Questions

1. What criteria must a discipline satisfy in order to be a science?
2. What are the defining characteristics of naturalism? How does Husserl argue that it is self-refuting?
3. Is it preferable to attempt to embed the natural sciences within a higher-level view of human consciousness and activity or to embed the understanding of human consciousness and activity within a broader natural science? Differently put, should we expect natural science to tell us what consciousness is, or should we look to the pure investigation (or self-investigation) of consciousness to determine what science is?
4. What is the difference between a *psychology* of consciousness and a *phenomenology* of consciousness?
5. What is the difference between *phenomenon* and *nature*?
6. What is it to "see" an essence "immediately"? What are the objects of such a vision? Why isn't this just another form of experience and thus another empirical method?
7. Must our ordinary psychological knowledge be grounded on concepts or essences capable of scientific precision?
8. What is historicism? What arguments does Husserl mount against it?
9. What is the value of *Weltanschauung* philosophies, according to Husserl? Why can Husserl not rest content with such a philosophy?

Philosophy as Rigorous Science

From its earliest beginnings philosophy has claimed to be rigorous science. What is more, it has claimed to be the science that satisfies the loftiest theoretical needs and renders possible from an ethico-religious point of view a life regulated by pure rational norms. This claim has been pressed with sometimes more, sometimes less energy, but it has never been completely abandoned, not even during those times when interest in and capacity for pure theory were in danger of atrophying, or when religious forces restricted freedom of theoretical investigation.

During no period of its development has philosophy been capable of living up to this claim of being rigorous science; not even in its most recent period, when—despite the multiplicity and contradictory character of its philosophical orientations—it has followed from the Renaissance up to the present an essentially unitary line of development. It is, in fact, the dominant characteristic of modern philosophy that, rather than surrender itself naïvely to the philosophical impulse, it will by means of critical reflection and by ever more profound methodological investigation constitute itself as rigorous science. But the only mature fruit of these efforts has been to secure first the foundation and then the independence of rigorous natural and humanistic sciences along with new purely mathematical disciplines. Philosophy itself, in the particular sense that only now has become distinguished, lacked as much as ever the character of rigorous science. The very meaning of the distinction remained without scientifically secure determination. The question of philosophy's relation to the natural and humanistic sciences—whether the specifically philosophical element of its work, essentially related as it is to nature and the human spirit, demands fundamentally new attitudes, that in turn involve fundamentally peculiar goals and methods; whether as a result the philosophical takes us, as it were, into a new dimension, or whether it performs its function on the same level as the empirical sciences of nature and of the human spirit—all this is to this day disputed. It shows that even the proper sense of philosophical problems has not been made scientifically clear.

Thus philosophy, according to its historical purpose the loftiest and most rigorous of all sciences, representing as it does humanity's imperishable demand for pure and absolute knowledge (and what is inseparably one with that, its demand for pure and absolute valuing and willing), is incapable of assuming the form of rigorous science. Philosophy, whose vocation is to teach us how to carry on the eternal work of humanity, is utterly incapable of teaching in an objectively valid manner. . . . What is that but an admission of philosophy's unscientific character? As far as science, real science, extends, so far can one teach and learn, and this everywhere in the same sense. . . . In all cases it is based on self-activity, on an inner reproduction, in their relationships as grounds and consequences, of the rational insights gained by creative spirits. One cannot learn philosophy, because here there are no such insights objectively grasped and grounded, or to put it in another way, because here the problems, methods, and theories have not been clearly defined conceptually, their sense has not been fully clarified.

From Edmund Husserl, *Phenomenology and the Crisis of Philosophy*, trans. Quentin Lauer. English Translation © 1965 by Quentin Lauer. Reprinted by permission of HarperCollins Publishers.

I do not say that philosophy is an imperfect science; I say simply that it is not yet a science at all, that as science it has not yet begun. . . . All sciences are imperfect, even the much-admired exact sciences. On the one hand they are incomplete, because the limitless horizon of open problems, which will never let the drive toward knowledge rest, lies before them; and on the other hand they have a variety of defects in their already developed doctrinal content, there remain evidences here and there of a lack of clarity or perfection in the systematic ordering of proofs and theories. Nevertheless they do have a doctrinal content that is constantly growing and branching out in new directions. No reasonable person will doubt the objective truth or the objectively grounded probability of the wonderful theories of mathematics and the natural sciences. Here there is, by and large, no room for private "opinions," "notions," or "points of view." To the extent that there are such in particular instances, the science in question is not established as such but is in the process of becoming a science and is in general so judged.[1]

The imperfection of philosophy is of an entirely different sort from that of the other sciences as just described. It does not have at its disposal a merely incomplete and, in particular instances, imperfect doctrinal system; it simply has none whatever. Each and every question is herein controverted, every position is a matter of individual conviction, of the interpretation given by a school, of a "point of view."

It may well be that the proposals presented in the world-renowned scientific works of philosophy in ancient and modern times are based on serious, even colossal intellectual activity. More than that, it may in large measure be work done in advance for the future establishment of scientifically strict doctrinal systems; but for the moment, nothing in them is recognizable as a basis for philosophical science, nor is there any prospect of cutting out, as it were, with the critical scissors here and there a fragment of philosophical doctrine. . . .

The question immediately arises whether philosophy is to continue envisioning the goal of being a rigorous science, whether it can or must want to be so. . . . What meaning should be given to the "system" for which we yearn, which is supposed to gleam as an ideal before us in the lowlands where we are doing our investigative work? . . . Is it to be a philosophical system of doctrine that, after the gigantic preparatory work of generations, really begins from the ground up with a foundation free of doubt and rises up like any skillful construction, wherein stone is set upon stone, each as solid as the other, in accord with directive insights? . . .

The revolutions decisive for the progress of philosophy are those in which the claim of former philosophies to be scientific are discredited by a critique of their pretended scientific procedure. . . . First of all, thought concentrates all its energy on decisively clarifying, by means of systematic examination, the conditions of strict science that in

---

1. Obviously I am not thinking here of the philosophico-mathematical and scientific-philosophical controversies that, when closely examined, do involve not merely isolated points in the subject matter but the very "sense" of the entire scientific accomplishment of the disciplines in question. These controversies can and must remain distinct from the disciplines themselves, and in this way they are, in fact, a matter of indifference to the majority of those who pursue these disciplines. Perhaps the word philosophy, in connection with the titles of all sciences, signifies a genus of investigation that in a certain sense gives to them all a new dimension and thereby a final perfection. At the same time, however, the word dimension indicates something else: rigorous science is still rigorous science, doctrinal content remains doctrinal content, even when the transition to this new dimension has not been achieved. [Husserl's note.]

former philosophies were naïvely overlooked or misunderstood, in order thereafter to attempt to construct anew a structure of philosophical doctrine. Such a fully conscious will for rigorous science dominated the Socratic-Platonic revolution of philosophy and also the scientific reactions against Scholasticism, especially the Cartesian revolution. Its impulse carries over to the great philosophies of the seventeenth and eighteenth centuries; it renews itself with most radical vigor in Kant's critique of reason and still dominates Fichte's philosophizing. Again and again research is directed toward true beginnings, decisive formulation of problems, and correct methods.

Only with romantic philosophy does a change occur. However much Hegel insists on the absolute validity of his method and his doctrine, still his system lacks a critique of reason, which is the foremost prerequisite for being scientific in philosophy. In this connection it is clear that this philosophy, like romantic philosophy in general, acted in the years that followed either to weaken or to adulterate the impulse toward the constitution of rigorous philosophical science. . . .

The following arguments are based on the conviction that the highest interests of human culture demand the development of a rigorously scientific philosophy; consequently, if a philosophical revolution in our times is to be justified, it must without fail be animated by the purpose of laying a new foundation for philosophy in the sense of strict science. This purpose is by no means foreign to the present age. It is fully alive precisely in the naturalism that dominates the age. From the start, naturalism sets out with a firm determination to realize the ideal of a rigorously scientific reform of philosophy. It even believes at all times, both in its earlier and in its modern forms, that it has already realized this idea. But all this takes place, when we look at it from the standpoint of principle, in a form that from the ground up is replete with erroneous theory; and from a practical point of view this means a growing danger for our culture. It is important today to engage in a radical criticism of naturalistic philosophy. . . .

However, with regard to the remarkable revolution in our times, it is in fact—and in that it is justified—anti-naturalistic in its orientation. Still under the influence of historicism, it seems to desire a departure from the lines of scientific philosophy and a turn toward mere *Weltanschauung* philosophy. The second part of this study is devoted to an exposé, based on principles, of the differences between these two philosophies and to an evaluation of their respective justifications.

Naturalistic Philosophy

Naturalism is a phenomenon consequent upon the discovery of nature, which is to say, nature considered as a unity of spatio-temporal being subject to exact laws of nature. With the gradual realization of this idea in constantly new natural sciences that guarantee strict knowledge regarding many matters, naturalism proceeds to expand more and more. In a very similar fashion historicism developed later, consequent upon the "discovery of history," constantly guaranteeing new humanistic sciences. In accord with each one's dominant habit of interpretation, the natural scientist has the tendency to look upon everything as nature, and the humanistic scientist sees everything as "spirit," as a historical creation; by the same token, both are inclined to falsify the sense of what cannot be seen in their way. Thus the naturalist, to consider him in particular, sees only nature, and primarily physical nature. Whatever is is either itself physical, belonging to the unified totality of physical nature, or it is in fact psychical, but then merely as a variable dependent on the physical, at best a secondary "parallel accompaniment." Whatever is belongs to psychophysical nature, which is to say that it is univocally determined by rigid laws. . . .

Characteristic of all forms of extreme and consistent naturalism . . . is on one hand the naturalizing of consciousness, including all intentionally immanent data of consciousness, and on the other the naturalizing of ideas and consequently of all absolute ideals and norms.

From the latter point of view, without realizing it, naturalism refutes itself. If we take an exemplary index of all ideality, formal logic, then the formal-logical principles, the so-called "laws of thought," are interpreted by naturalism as natural laws of thinking. That this brings with it the sort of absurdity that characterizes every theory of scepticism in the fullest sense has elsewhere been demonstrated in detail. One can submit naturalistic axiology and practical philosophy (including ethics) as well as naturalistic practice to a radical criticism of the same sort. For theoretical absurdities are inevitably followed by absurdities (evident inconsistencies) in actual theoretical, axiological, and ethical ways of acting. The naturalist is, one can safely say, idealist and objectivist in the way he acts. He is dominated by the purpose of making scientifically known (i.e., in a way that compels any rational individual) whatever is genuine truth, the genuinely beautiful and good; he wants to know how to determine what is its universal essence and the method by which it is to be obtained in the particular case. He believes that through natural science and through a philosophy based on the same science the goal has for the most part been attained, and with all the enthusiasm that such a consciousness gives, he has installed himself as teacher and practical reformer in regard to the true, the good, and the beautiful, from the standpoint of natural science. He is, however, an idealist who sets up and (so he thinks) justifies theories, which deny precisely what he presupposes in his idealistic way of acting, whether it be in constructing theories or in justifying and recommending values or practical norms as the most beautiful and the best. . . . The naturalist teaches, preaches, moralizes, reforms. . . . But he denies what every sermon, every demand, if it is to have a meaning, presupposes. The only thing is, he does not preach in express terms that the only rational thing to do is to deny reason, as well theoretical as axiological and practical reason. He would, in fact, banish that sort of thing far from him. The absurdity is not in his case evident, but remains hidden from him because he naturalizes reason. . . .

Since naturalism, which wanted to establish philosophy both on a basis of strict science and as a strict science, appears completely discredited, now the aim of its method seems to be discredited too, and all the more so because among non-naturalists, too, there is a widespread tendency to look upon positive science as the only strict science and to recognize as scientific philosophy only one that is based on this sort of science. That, however, is also only prejudice, and it would be a fundamental error to want for that reason to deviate from the line of strict science. . . . There is, perhaps, in all modern life no more powerfully, more irresistibly progressing idea than that of science. Nothing will hinder its victorious advance. In fact, with regard to its legitimate aims, it is all-embracing. Looked upon in its ideal perfection, it would be reason itself, which could have no other authority equal or superior to itself. There belong in the domain of strict science all the theoretical, axiological, and practical ideals that naturalism, by giving them a new empirical meaning, at the same time falsifies.

Still, general convictions carry little weight when one cannot give them a foundation; hopes for a science signify little if one is incapable of envisioning a path to its goals. If, then, the idea of a philosophy as a rigorous science of the aforesaid problems and of all problems essentially related to them is not to remain without force, we must have before our eyes clear possibilities of realizing it. Through a clarification of the problems and through penetration into their pure sense, the methods adequate to these problems, because demanded by their very essence, must impose themselves on us.... For this purpose the otherwise useful and indispensable refutation of naturalism based on its consequences accomplishes very little for us.

It is altogether different when we engage in the necessary positive and hence principiant criticism of its foundation, methods and accomplishments....

We are concerned with a method and a discipline whereby this philosophy [naturalism] believes that it has definitely attained the rank of an exact science. So sure is it of this that it looks down disdainfully on all other modes of philosophizing.... If we ask about exact though as yet scarcely developed philosophy ... we are shown psychophysical and, above all, experimental psychology, to which, of course, no one can deny the rank of strict science. This, they tell us, is the long-sought scientific psychology, that has at last become a fact. Logic and epistemology, aesthetics, ethics, and pedagogy have finally obtained their scientific foundation through it; they are in fact already on the way toward being transformed into experimental disciplines. In addition, strict psychology is obviously the foundation for all humanistic sciences and not less even for metaphysics. With regard to this last, of course, it is not the preferential foundation, since to the same extent physical natural science also has a share in supplying a foundation for this general theory of reality.

In answer to this, these are our objections. First of all, ... psychology in general, as a factual science, is not calculated to lay the foundations of those philosophical disciplines that have to do with the pure principles for the establishing of norms, of pure logic, pure axiology, and practical discipline. We can spare ourselves a more detailed exposition: ... [but] much can be said against epistemological psychologism and physicism, whereof something should be indicated here.

All natural science is naïve in regard to its point of departure. The nature that it will investigate is for it simply there.... We perceive them, we describe them by means of simple empirical judgments. It is the aim of natural science to know these unquestioned data in an objectively valid, strictly scientific manner. The same is true in regard to nature in the broader, psycho-physical sense, or in regard to the sciences that investigate it—in particular, therefore, in regard to psychology. The psychical does not constitute a world for itself; it is given as an ego or as the experience of an ego (by the way, in a very different sense), and this sort of thing reveals itself empirically as bound to certain physical things called bodies. This, too, is a self-evident pre-datum.

It is the task of psychology to explore this psychic element scientifically within the psychophysical nexus of nature (the nexus in which, without question, it occurs), to determine it in an objectively valid way, to discover the laws according to which it develops and changes, comes into being and disappears. Every psychological determination is by that very fact psychophysical, which is to say in the broadest sense (which we retain from now on), that it has a never-failing physical connotation.... To eliminate the relation to nature would deprive the psychical of its character as an objectively and temporally determinable fact of nature, in short, of its character as a psychological fact. Then let us hold fast to this: every psychological judgment involves the existential positing of physical nature, whether expressly or not.

As a result, the following is clear: should there be decisive arguments to prove that physical natural science cannot be philosophy in the specific sense of the word, can never in any way serve as a foundation for philosophy, and can achieve a philosophical value for the purposes of metaphysics only on the basis of a prior philosophy, then all such arguments must be equally applicable to psychology.

Now, there is by no means a lack of such arguments. It is sufficient merely to recall the "naïveté" with which, according to what was said above, natural science accepts nature as given. . . . It is true, of course, that natural science is, in its own way, very critical. Isolated experience, even when it is accumulated, is still worth little to it. It is in the methodical disposition and connection of experiences, in the interplay of experience and thought, which has its rigid logical laws, that valid experience is distinguished from invalid, that each experience is accorded its level of validity, and that objectively valid knowledge as such, knowledge of nature, is worked out. Still, no matter how satisfactory this kind of critique of experience may be, as long as we remain within natural science and think according to its point of view, a completely different critique of experience is still possible and indispensable, a critique that places in question all experience as such and the sort of thinking proper to empirical science.

How can experience as consciousness give or contact an object? How can experiences be mutually legitimated or corrected by means of each other, and not merely replace each other or confirm each other subjectively? How can the play of a consciousness whose logic is empirical make objectively valid statements, valid for things that are in and for themselves? Why are the playing rules, so to speak, of consciousness not irrelevant for things? How is natural science to be comprehensible in absolutely every case, to the extent that it pretends at every step to posit and to know a nature that is in itself—in itself in opposition to the subjective flow of consciousness? All these questions become riddles as soon as reflection on them becomes serious. It is well known that theory of knowledge is the discipline that wants to answer such questions, and also that . . . this discipline has not answered in a manner scientifically clear, unanimous, and decisive.

It requires only a rigorous consistency in maintaining the level of this problematic (a consistency missing, it is true, in all theories of knowledge up to the present) to see clearly the absurdity of a theory of knowledge based on natural science, and thus, too, of any psychological theory of knowledge. If certain riddles are, generally speaking, inherent in principle to natural science, then it is self-evident that the solution of these riddles according to premises and conclusions in principle transcends natural science. To expect from natural science itself the solution of any one of the problems inherent in it as such . . . is to be involved in a vicious circle. . . .

Further: if knowledge theory will nevertheless investigate the problems of the relationship between consciousness and being, it can have before its eyes only being as the correlate of consciousness, as something "intended" after the manner of consciousness: as perceived, remembered, expected, represented pictorially, imagined, identified, distinguished, believed, opined, evaluated, etc. It is clear, then, that the investigation must be directed toward a scientific essential knowledge of consciousness, toward that which consciousness itself "is" according to its essence in all its distinguishable forms. At the same time, however, the investigation must be directed toward what consciousness "means," as well as toward the different ways in which—in accord with the essence of the aforementioned forms—it intends the objective, now clearly, now obscurely, now by presenting or by presentifying, now symbolically or pictorially, now simply, now mediated in thought, now in this or that mode of attention, and so in countless other forms, and how ultimately it "demonstrates" the objective as that which is "validly," "really."

Every type of object that is to be the object of a rational proposition, of a prescientific and then of a scientific cognition, must manifest itself in knowledge, thus in consciousness itself, and it must permit being brought to givenness, in accord with the sense of all knowledge. All types of consciousness, in the way they are, so to speak, teleologically ordered under the title of knowledge and, even more, in the way they are grouped according to the various object categories—considered as the groups of cognitive functions that especially correspond to these categories—must permit being studied in their essential connection and in their relation back to the forms of the consciousness of givenness belonging to them. . . .

What it means, that objectivity is, and manifests itself cognitively as so being, must precisely become evident purely from consciousness itself, and thereby it must become completely understandable. And for that is required a study of consciousness in its entirety, since according to all its forms it enters into possible cognitive functions. To the extent, however, that every consciousness is "consciousness-of," the essential study of consciousness includes also that of consciousness-meaning and consciousness-objectivity as such. To study any kind of objectivity whatever according to its general essence (a study that can pursue interests far removed from those of knowledge theory and the investigation of consciousness) means to concern oneself with objectivity's modes of givenness and to exhaust its essential content in the processes of "clarification" proper to it. Even if the orientation is not that which is directed toward the kinds of consciousness and an essential investigation of them, still the method of clarification is such that even here reflection on the modes of being intended and of being given cannot be avoided. In any case, however, the clarification of all fundamental kinds of objectivities is for its part indispensable for the essential analysis of consciousness, and as a result is included in it, but primarily in an epistemological analysis, that finds its task precisely in the investigation of correlations. Consequently we include all such studies, even though relatively they are to be distinguished, under the title "phenomenological."

With this we meet a science of whose extraordinary extent our contemporaries have as yet no concept; a science, it is true, of consciousness that is still not psychology; a phenomenology of consciousness as opposed to a natural science about consciousness. . . . Psychology is concerned with "empirical consciousness," with consciousness from the empirical point of view, as an empirical being in the ensemble of nature, whereas phenomenology is concerned with "pure" consciousness, i.e., consciousness from the phenomenological point of view.

If this is correct, the result would then be—without taking away from the truth that psychology is not nor can be any more philosophy than the physical science of nature can—that for essential reasons psychology must be more closely related to philosophy (i.e., through the medium of phenomenology) and must in its destiny remain most intimately bound up with philosophy. Finally, it would be possible to foresee that any psychologistic theory of knowledge must owe its existence to the fact that, missing the proper sense of the epistemological problematic, it is a victim of a presumably facile confusion between pure and empirical consciousness. To put the same in another way: it "naturalizes" pure consciousness. . . .

There is food for thought in the fact that everything psychical (to the extent that it is taken in that full concretion wherein it must be, both for psychology and for phenomenology, the first object of investigation), has the character of a more or less complex "consciousness-of"; in the fact that this "consciousness-of" has a confusing fullness of forms; that all expressions that at the beginning of the investigation could help toward making clearly understandable and toward describing objectively are fluid and ambiguous, and that as a result the first beginning can obviously only be to uncover the crudest equivocations that immediately become evident. A definitive fixation of scientific language presupposes the complete analysis of phenomena—a goal that lies in the dim distance—and so long as this has not been accomplished, the progress of the investigation, too, looked at from the outside, moves to a great extent in the form of demonstrating new ambiguities, distinguishable now for the first time, ambiguities in the very concepts that presumably were already fixed in the preceding investigations. That is obviously inevitable, because it is rooted in the nature of things. It is on this basis that one should judge the depth of understanding manifested in the disdainful way the professional guardians of the exactness and scientific character of psychology speak of "merely verbal," merely "grammatical," and "scholastic" analysis.

In the epoch of vigorous reaction against Scholasticism the war cry was: "Away with empty word analyses! We must question things themselves. Back to experience, to seeing, which alone can give to our words sense and rational justification." Very much to the point! But what, then, are things? And what sort of experience is it to which we must return in psychology? Are they perhaps the statements we get from subjects in answer to our questions? And is the interpretation of their statements the "experience" of the psychical? The experimentalists themselves will say that that is merely a secondary experience, that the primary lies in the subject himself, and that with the experimenting and interpreting psychologists it must be in their own former self-perceptions, that for good reasons are not and must not be introspections. . . .

The psychologists think that they owe all their psychological knowledge to experience, thus to those naïve recollections or to empathetic penetration into recollections, which by virtue of the methodical art of the experiment are to become foundations for empirical conclusions. Nevertheless the description of the naïve empirical data, along with the immanent analysis and conceptional grasp that go hand in hand with this description, is affected by virtue of a fund of concepts whose scientific value is decisive for all further methodical steps. These remain—as is evidenced by a bit of reflection—by the very nature of experimental questioning and method, constantly untouched in the further procedure, and they enter into the final result, which means into the empirical judgment, with its claim to be scientific. On the other hand, their scientific value cannot be there from the beginning, nor can it stem from the experiences of the subject or of the psychologist himself, no matter how many of them are heaped up; it can in fact be obtained logically from no empirical determinations whatever. And here is the place for phenomenological analysis of essence, which, however strange and unsympathetic it may sound to the naturalistic psychologist, can in no way be an empirical analysis. . . .

In description we employ the words perception, recollection, imaginative representation, enunciation, etc. What a wealth of immanent components does a single such word indicate, components that we, "grasping" what is described, impose on it without having found them in it analytically. Is it sufficient to use these words in the popular sense, in the vague, completely chaotic sense they have taken on, we know not how, in the "history" of consciousness? And even if we were to know it, what good is this history to do us, how is that to change the fact that vague concepts are simply vague and, by virtue of this character proper to them, obviously unscientific? So long as we have no better, we may use them in the confidence that with them enough crude distinctions for the practical aims of life have been attained. But does a psychology that leaves the concepts that determine its objects without scientific fixation, without methodical elaboration, have a claim to "exactness"? No more, obviously, than would a physics that would be satisfied with the everyday concepts of heavy, warm, mass, etc. Modern psychology no longer wants to be a science of the "soul" but rather of "psychical phenomena." If that is what it wants, then it must be able to describe and determine these phenomena with conceptual rigor. It must have acquired the necessary rigorous concepts by methodical work. Where is this methodical work accomplished in "exact" psychology? We seek for it in vain throughout its vast literature.

The question as to how natural, "confused" experience can become scientific experience, as to how one can arrive at the determination of objectively valid empirical judgments, is the cardinal methodological question of every empirical science. It does not have to be put and answered in the abstract, and in any case it does not have to be answered purely philosophically. Historically it finds an answer in practice, in that the genial pioneers of empirical science grasp intuitively and in the concrete the sense of the necessary empirical method and, by pursuing it faithfully in an accessible sphere of experience, realize a fragment of objectively valid empirical determination, thus getting the science started. The motive for their procedure they owe not to any revelation but to penetrating the sense of the experiences themselves, or the sense of the "being" in them. For, although already "given," in "vague" experience it is given only "confusedly." Consequently the question imposes itself: How are things really? How are they to be determined with objective validity? How, that is, by what better "experiences" and how are they to be improved—by what method?

The phenomenal had to elude psychology because of its naturalistic point of view as well as its zeal to imitate the natural sciences and to see experimental procedures as the main point. In its laborious, frequently very keen considerations on the possibilities of psychophysical experiment, in proposing empirical arrangements of experiments, in constructing the finest apparatus, in discovering possible sources of error, etc., it has still neglected to pursue the question more profoundly, i.e., how, by what method, can those concepts that enter essentially into psychological judgments be brought from the state of confusion to that of clarity and objective validity. It has neglected to consider to what extent the psychical, rather than being the presentation of a nature, has an essence proper to itself to be rigorously and in full adequation investigated prior to any psychophysics. It has not considered what lies in the "sense" of psychological experience and what "demands" being (in the sense of the psychical) of itself makes on method.

What has constantly confused empirical psychology since its beginnings in the eighteenth century is thus the deceptive image of a scientific method modeled on that of the physicochemical method. There is a sure conviction that the method of all empirical sciences, considered in its universal principles, is one and the same, thus that it is the same in psychology as in the science of physical nature. . . . It is not without significance that the fathers of experimentally exact psychology were physiologists and physicists. The true method follows the nature of the things to be investigated and not our prejudices and preconceptions. From the vague subjectivity of things in their naïvely sensible appearance natural science laboriously brings out objective things with exact objective characteristics. Thus, they tell themselves, psychology must bring that which is psychologically vague in naïve interpretation to objectively valid determination. The objective method accomplishes this, and it is evident that this is the same as the experimental method brilliantly guaranteed in natural science by countless successes. . . .

Only the spatiotemporal world of bodies is nature in the significant sense of that word. All other individual being, i.e., the psychical, is nature in a secondary sense, a fact that determines basically essential differences between the methods of natural science and psychology. In principle, only corporeal being can be experienced in a number of direct experiences, i.e., perceptions, as individually identical. Hence, only this being can, if the perceptions are thought of as distributed among various "subjects," be experienced by many subjects as individually identical and be described as intersubjectively the same. The same realities (things, procedures, etc.) are present to the eyes of all and can be determined by all of us according to their "nature." Their "nature," however, denotes: presenting themselves in experience according to diversely varying "subjective appearances."

Nevertheless, they stand there as temporal unities of enduring or changing properties, and they stand there as incorporated in the totality of one corporeal world that binds them all together, with its one space and its one time. They are what they are only in this unity; only in the causal relation to or connection with each other do they retain their individual identity (substance), and this they retain as that which carries "real properties." All physically real properties are causal. Every corporeal being is subject to laws of possible changes, and these laws concern the identical, the thing, not by itself but in the unified, actual, and possible totality of the one nature. Each physical thing has its nature . . . by virtue of being the union point of causalities within the one all-nature. Real properties . . . are a title for the possibilities of transformation of something identical, possibilities preindicated according to the laws of causality. And thus this identical, with regard to what it is, is determinable only by recourse to these laws. Realities, however, are given as unities of immediate experience, as unities of diverse sensible appearances. Stabilities, changes, and relationships of change (all of which can be grasped sensibly) direct cognition everywhere, and function for it like a "vague" medium in which the true, objective, physically exact nature presents itself, a medium through which thought (as empirically scientific thought) determines and constructs what is true.[2]

---

2. It should be noted that this medium of phenomenality, wherein the observation and thought of natural science constantly moves, is not treated as a scientific theme by the latter. It is the new sciences, psychology (to which belongs a good portion of physiology) and phenomenology, that are concerned with this theme. [Husserl's note.]

All that is not something one attributes to the things of experience and to the experience of things. Rather it is something belonging inseparably to the essences of things in such a way that every intuitive and consistent investigation of what a thing in truth is (a thing which as experienced always appears as something, a being, determined and at the same time determinable, and which nevertheless, as appearances and their circumstances vary, is constantly appearing as a different being) necessarily leads to causal connections and terminates in the determination of corresponding objective properties subject to law. Natural science, then, simply follows consistently the sense of what the thing so to speak pretends to be as experienced. . . .

Let us now turn to the "world" of the "psychical," and let us confine ourselves to "psychical phenomena," which the new psychology looks upon as its field of objects— i.e., in beginning we leave out of consideration problems relative to the soul and to the ego. We ask, then, whether in every perception of the psychical, just as in the sense of every physical experience and of every perception of the real, there is included "nature"-objectivity? We soon see that the relationships in the sphere of the psychical are totally different from those in the physical sphere. The psychical is divided (to speak metaphorically and not metaphysically) into monads that have no windows and are in communication only through empathy. Psychical being, being as "phenomenon," is in principle not a unity that could be experienced in several separate perceptions as individually identical, not even in perceptions of the same subject. In the psychical sphere there is, in other words, no distinction between appearance and being, and if nature is a being that appears in appearances, still appearances themselves (which the psychologist certainly looks upon as psychical) do not constitute a being which itself appears by means of appearances lying behind it—as every reflection on the perception of any appearance whatever makes evident. It is then clear: there is, properly speaking, only one nature, the one that appears in the appearances of things. Everything that in the broadest sense of psychology we call a psychical phenomenon, when looked at in and for itself, is precisely phenomenon and not nature.

A phenomenon, then, is no "substantial" unity; it has no "real properties," it knows no real parts, no real changes, and no causality; all these words are here understood in the sense proper to natural science. To attribute a nature to phenomena, to investigate their real component parts, their causal connections—that is pure absurdity, no better than if one wanted to ask about the causal properties, connections, etc. of numbers. It is the absurdity of naturalizing something whose essence excludes the kind of being that nature has. A thing is what it is, and it remains in its identity forever: nature is eternal. Whatever in the way of real properties or modifications of properties belongs in truth to a thing (to the thing of nature, not to the sensible thing of practical life, the thing "as it appears sensibly") can be determined with objective validity and confirmed or corrected in constantly new experiences. On the other hand, something psychical, a "phenomenon," comes and goes; it retains no enduring, identical being that would be objectively determinable as such in the sense of natural science, e.g., as objectively divisible into components, "analysable" in the proper sense.

What psychical being "is," experience cannot say in the same sense that it can with regard to the physical. The psychical is simply not experienced as something that appears; . . . it appears as itself through itself, in an absolute flow, as now and already "fading away," clearly recognizable as constantly sinking back into a "having been." The psychical can also be a "recalled," and thus in a certain modified way an "experienced";

and in the "recalled" lies a "having been perceived." It can also be a "repeatedly recalled," in recollections that are united in an act of consciousness which in turn is conscious of the recollections themselves as recalled or as still retained. In this connection, and in this alone, can the a priori psychical, in so far as it is the identical of such "repetitions," be "experienced" and identified as being. Everything psychical which is thus an "experienced" is, then, as we can say with equal evidence, ordered in an overall connection, in a "monadic" unity of consciousness, a unity that in itself has nothing at all to do with nature, with space and time or substantiality and causality, but has its thoroughly peculiar "forms." It is a flow of phenomena, unlimited at both ends, traversed by an intentional line that is, as it were, the index of the all-pervading unity. . . .

Now, to what extent is something like rational investigation and valid statement possible in this sphere? . . . It goes without saying that research will be meaningful here precisely when it directs itself purely to the sense of the experiences, which are given as experiences of the "psychical," and when thereby it accepts and tries to determine the "psychical" exactly as it demands, as it were, to be accepted and determined, when it is seen—above all where one admits no absurd naturalizings. One must, it was said, take phenomena as they give themselves, i.e., as this flowing "having consciousness," intending, appearing, as this foreground and background "having consciousness." . . . All that bears the title "consciousness-of" and that "has" a "meaning," "intends" something "objective," which latter—whether from one standpoint or other it is to be called "fiction" or "reality"—permits being described as something "immanently objective," "intended as such," and intended in one or another mode of intending.

That one can here investigate and make statements, and do so on the basis of evidence, adapting oneself to the sense of this sphere of "experience," is absolutely evident. Admittedly, it is fidelity to the demands indicated above that constitutes the difficulty. On the single-mindedness and purity of the "phenomenological" attitude depends entirely the consistency or absurdity of the investigations that are here to be carried out. We do not easily overcome the inborn habit of living and thinking according to the naturalistic attitude, and thus of naturalistically adulterating the psychical. . . .

If the immanently psychical is not nature in itself but the respondent of nature, what are we seeking for in it as its "being"? If it is not determinable in "objective" identity as the substantial unity of real properties that must be grasped over and over again and be determined and confirmed in accordance with science and experience, if it is not to be withdrawn from the eternal flux, if it is incapable of becoming the object of an intersubjective evaluation—then what is there in it that we can seize upon, determine, and fix as an objective unity? This, however, is understood as meaning that we remain in the pure phenomenological sphere and leave out of account relationships to nature and to the body experienced as a thing. The answer, then, is that if phenomena have no nature, they still have an essence, which can be grasped and adequately determined in an immediate seeing. All the statements that describe the phenomena in direct concepts do so, to the degree that they are valid, by means of concepts of essence, that is, by conceptual significations of words that must permit of being redeemed in an essential intuition.

It is necessary to be accurate in our understanding of this ultimate foundation of all psychological method. The spell of the naturalistic point of view, to which all of us at the outset are subject and which makes us incapable of prescinding from nature and hence, too, of making the psychical an object of intuitive investigation from the pure rather than from the psychophysical point of view, has here blocked the road to a great science unparalleled in its fecundity, a science which is on the one hand the fundamental condition for a completely scientific psychology and on the other the field for the genuine critique of reason. The spell of inborn naturalism also consists in the fact that it makes it so difficult for all of us to see "essences," or "ideas" —or rather, since in fact we do, so to speak, constantly see them, for us to let them have the peculiar value which is theirs instead of absurdly naturalizing them. Intuiting essences conceals no more difficulties or "mystical" secrets than does perception. When we bring "color" to full intuitive clarity, to givenness for ourselves, then the datum is an "essence"; and when we likewise in pure intuition—looking, say, at one perception after another—bring to givenness for ourselves what "perception" is, perception in itself (this identical character of any number of flowing singular perceptions), then we have intuitively grasped the essence of perception. . . . To the extent that the intuition is a pure one that involves no transient connotations, to the same extent is the intuited essence an adequately intuited one, an absolutely given one. Thus the field dominated by pure intuition includes the entire sphere that the psychologist reserves to himself as the sphere of "psychical phenomena," provided that he takes them merely by themselves, in pure immanence. That the "essences" grasped in essential intuition permit, at least to a very great extent, of being fixed in definitive concepts and thereby afford possibilities of definitive and in their own way absolutely valid objective statements, is evident to anyone free of prejudice. The ultimate differences of color, its finest nuances, may defy fixation, but "color" as distinguished from "sound" provides a sure difference, than which there is in the world no surer. And such absolutely distinguishable—better, fixable—essences are not only those whose very "content" is of the senses, appearances ("apparitions," phantoms, and the like), but also the essences of whatever is psychical in the pregnant sense, of all ego "acts" or ego states, which correspond to well-known headings such as perception, imagination, recollection, judgment, emotion, will—with all their countless particular forms. . . . Every psychological heading such as perception or will designates a most extensive area of "consciousness analyses," i.e., of investigations into essences. There is question here of a field that in extent can be compared only with natural science—however extraordinary this may sound.

Now, it is of decisive significance to know that essential intuition is in no way "experience" in the sense of perception, recollection, and equivalent acts; further, that it is in no way an empirical generalization whose sense it is to posit existentially at the same time the individual being of empirical details. Intuition grasps essence as essential being, and in no way posits being-there. In accord with this, knowledge of essence is by no means matter-of-fact knowledge, including not the slightest shade of affirmation regarding an individual (e.g., natural) being-there. The foundation, or better, the point of departure for an essential intuition (e.g., of the essence of perception, recollection, judgment, etc.) can be a perception of a perception, of a recollection, of a judgment, etc., but it can also be a mere—but mere—imagination, so long as it is clear, even though obviously as such not an experience, that is, grasps no being-there. . . . Obviously essences can also be vaguely represented, let us say represented in symbol and falsely posited; then they are merely conjectural essences, involving contradiction, as is shown by the transition to an intuition of their inconsistency. It is possible, however, that their vague position will be shown to be valid by a return to the intuition of the essence in its givenness.

Every judgment which achieves in definitive, adequately constructed concepts an adequate experience of what is contained in essences, experiencing how essences of a certain genus or particularity are connected with others—how, for example, "intuition" and "empty intention," "imagination" and "perception," "concept" and "intuition" unite with each other; how they are on the basis of such and such essential components necessarily "unifiable," corresponding to each other (let us say) as "intention" and "fulfillment," or on the contrary cannot be united, founding as they do a "consciousness of deception," etc.—every judgment of this kind is an absolute, generally valid cognition, and as such it is a kind of essential judgment that it would be absurd to want to justify, confirm, or refute by experience. It fixes a "relation of idea," an a priori in the authentic sense that Hume, it is true, had before his eyes but which necessarily escaped him because of his positivistic confusion of essence and "idea"—as the opposite of "impression.". . .

The whole thing, however, depends on one's seeing and making entirely one's own the truth that just as immediately as one can hear a sound, so one can intuit an "essence"—the essence "sound," the essence "appearance of thing," the essence "apparition," the essence "pictorial representation," the essence "judgment" or "will," etc.—and in the intuition one can make an essential judgment. On the other hand, however, it depends on one's protecting himself from the Humean confusion and accordingly not confounding phenomenological intuition with "introspection," with interior experience—in short, with acts that posit not essences but individual details corresponding to them.

Pure phenomenology as science, so long as it is pure and makes no use of the existential positing of nature, can only be essence investigation, and not at all an investigation of being-there; all "introspection" and every judgment based on such "experience" falls outside its framework. The particular can in its immanence be posited only as this—this disappearing perception, recollection, etc.—and if need be, can be brought under the strict essential concepts resulting from essential analysis. . . . Phenomenology can recognize with objective validity only essences and essential relations, and thereby it can accomplish and decisively accomplish whatever is necessary for a correct understanding of all empirical cognition and of all cognition whatsoever: the clarification of the "origin" of all formal-logical and natural-logical principles (and whatever other guiding "principles" there may be) and of all the problems involved in correlating "being" (being of nature, being of value, etc.) and consciousness, problems intimately connected with the aforementioned principles.

Let us now turn to the psychophysical attitude. Therein the "psychical," with the entire essence proper to it, receives an orientation to a body and to the unity of physical nature. What is grasped in immanent perception and interpreted as essentially so qualified, enters into relation to the sensibly perceived and consequently to nature. Only through this orientation does it gain an indirect natural objectivity, mediately a position in space and in nature's time (the kind we measure by clocks). To a certain but not more precisely determined extent, the experiential "dependence" on the physical provides a means of determining intersubjectively the psychical as individual being and at the same time of investigating psychophysical relationships to a progressively more thorough extent. That is the domain of "psychology as natural science," which according to the literal sense is psycho-physical psychology, which is hence, obviously in contrast to phenomenology, an empirical science.

Not without misgivings, it is true, does one consider psychology, the science of the "psychical," merely as a science of "psychical phenomena" and of their connections with the body. But in fact psychology is everywhere accompanied by those inborn and inevitable objectivations whose correlates are the empirical unities man and beast, and, on the other hand, soul, personality, or character, i.e., disposition of personality. Still, for our purposes it is not necessary to pursue the essential analysis of these unity constructions nor the problem of how they by themselves determine the task of psychology. After all, it immediately becomes sufficiently clear that these unities are of a kind that is in principle different from the realities of nature. . . . Only the basic substrate "human body," and not man himself, is a unity of real appearance; and above all, personality, character, etc. are not such unities. With all such unities we are evidently referred back to the immanent vital unity of the respective "consciousness flow" and to morphological peculiarities that distinguish the various immanent unities of this sort. Consequently, all psychological knowledge, too, even where it is related primarily to human individualities, characters, and dispositions, finds itself referred back to those unities of consciousness, and thereby to the study of the phenomena themselves and of their implications. . . .

All psychological knowledge in the ordinary sense presupposes essential knowledge of the psychical, and that the hope of investigating the essence of recollection, judgment, will, etc. by means of casual inner perceptions or experiences, in order thereby to acquire the strict concepts that alone can give scientific value to the designation of the psychical in psycho-physical statements and to these statements themselves—that such a hope would be the height of absurdity. . . .

After the foregoing explanations it is clear, and it will, as I have good reason to hope, soon be more generally recognized, that a really adequate empirical science of the psychical in its relations to nature can be realized only when psychology is constructed on the base of a systematic phenomenology. . . .

It is hoped that our criticism will have made it clear that to recognize naturalism as a fundamentally erroneous philosophy still does not mean giving up the idea of a rigorously scientific philosophy, a "philosophy from the ground up." The critical separation of the psychological and phenomenological methods shows that the latter is the true way to a scientific theory of reason and, by the same token, to an adequate psychology.

In accord with our plan, we now turn to a critique of historicism and to a discussion of *Weltanschauung* philosophy.

Historicism and *Weltanschauung* Philosophy

Historicism takes its position in the factual sphere of the empirical life of the spirit. To the extent that it posits this latter absolutely, without exactly naturalizing it, . . . there arises a relativism that has a close affinity to naturalistic psychologism and runs into similar sceptical difficulties. Here we are interested only in what is characteristic of historical scepticism, and we want to familiarize ourselves more thoroughly with it.

Every spiritual formation—taking the term in its widest possible sense, which can include every kind of social unity, ultimately the unity of the individual itself and also every kind of cultural formation—has its intimate structure, its typology, its marvelous wealth of external and internal forms which in the stream of spirit-life itself grow and transform themselves, and in the very manner of the transformation again cause to come forward differences in structure and type. In the visible outer world the structure and typology of organic development afford us exact analogies. Therein there are no enduring species and no construction of the same out of enduring organic elements. Whatever seems to be enduring is but a stream of development. If by interior intuition we enter vitally into the unity of spirit-life, we can get a feeling for the motivations at play therein and consequently "understand" the essence and development of the spiritual structure in question, in its dependence on a spiritually motivated unity and development. In this manner everything historical becomes for us "understandable," "explicable," in the "being" peculiar to it, which is precisely "spiritual being," a unity of interiorly self-questioning moments of a sense and at the same time a unity of intelligible structuration and development according to inner motivation. Thus in this manner also art, religion, morals, etc. can be intuitively investigated, and likewise the *Weltanschauung* that stands so close to them and at the same time is expressed in them. It is this *Weltanschauung* that, when it takes on the forms of science and after the manner of science lays claim to objective validity, is customarily called metaphysics, or even philosophy. With a view to such a philosophy there arises the enormous task of thoroughly investigating its morphological structure and typology as well as its developmental connections and of making historically understandable the spiritual motivations that determine its essence, by reliving them from within. That there are significant and in fact wonderful things to be accomplished from this point of view is shown by W. Dilthey's writings, especially the most recently published study on the types of *Weltanschauung*.[3]

Up to this point we have obviously been speaking of historical science, not of historicism. We shall grasp most easily the motives that impel toward the latter if in a few sentences we follow Dilthey's presentation. We read as follows: "Among the reasons that constantly give new nourishment to scepticism, one of the most effective is the anarchy of philosophical systems" (p. 3). "Much deeper, however, than the sceptical conclusions based on the contradictoriness of human opinions go the doubts that have attached themselves to the progressive development of historical consciousness" (p. 4). "The theory of development (as a theory of evolution based on natural science, bound up with a knowledge of cultural structures based on developmental history) is necessarily linked to the knowledge of the relativity proper to the historical life form. In face of the view that embraces the earth and all past events, the absolute validity of any particular form of life-interpretation, of religion, and of philosophy disappears. Thus the formation of a historical consciousness destroys more thoroughly than does surveying the disagreement of systems a belief in the universal validity of any of the philosophies that have undertaken to express in a compelling manner the coherence of the world by an ensemble of concepts" (p. 6).

---

3. W. Dilthey et al., *Weltanschauung, Philosophie und Religion in Darstellungen* (Berlin: Reichel, 1911). [Ed.'s note.]

The factual truth of what is said here is obviously indubitable. The question is, however, whether it can be justified when taken as universal in principle. Of course, *Weltanschauung* and *Weltanschauung* philosophy are cultural formations that come and go in the stream of human development, with the consequences that their spiritual content is definitely motivated in the given historical relationships. But the same is true of the strict sciences. Do they for that reason lack objective validity? A thoroughly extreme historicist will perhaps answer in the affirmative. In doing so he will point to changes in scientific views—how what is today accepted as a proved theory is recognized tomorrow as worthless, how some call certain things laws that others call mere hypotheses and still others vague guesses, etc. Does that mean that in view of this constant change in scientific views we would actually have no right to speak of sciences as objectively valid unities instead of merely as cultural formations? It is easy to see that historicism, if consistently carried through, carries over into extreme sceptical subjectivism. The ideas of truth, theory, and science would then, like all ideas, lose their absolute validity. That an idea has validity would mean that it is a factual construction of spirit which is held as valid and which in its contingent validity determines thought. There would be no unqualified validity, or validity-in-itself, which is what it is even if no one has achieved it and though no historical humanity will ever achieve it. Thus too there would then be no validity to the principle of contradiction nor to any logic, which latter is nevertheless still in full vigor in our time. The result, perhaps, will be that the logical principles of noncontradiction will be transformed into their opposites. And to go even further, all the propositions we have just enunciated and even the possibilities that we have weighed and claimed as constantly valid would in themselves have no validity, etc. It is not necessary to go further here and to repeat discussions already given in another place. We shall certainly have said enough to obtain recognition that no matter what great difficulties the relation between a sort of fluid worth and objective validity, between science as a cultural phenomenon and science as a valid systematic theory, may offer an understanding concerned with clarifying them, the distinction and opposition must be recognized. If, however, we have admitted science as a valid idea, what reason would we still have not to consider similar differences between the historically worthwhile and the historically valid as at least an open possibility—whether or not we can understand this idea in the light of a critique of reason? The science of history, or simply empirical humanistic science in general, can of itself decide nothing, either in a positive or in a negative sense, as to whether a distinction is to be made between art as a cultural formation and valid art, between historical and valid law, and finally between historical and valid philosophy. . . . Historical facts of development, even the most general facts concerning the manner of development proper to systems as such, may be reasons, good reasons. Still, historical reasons can produce only historical consequences. The desire either to prove or to refute ideas on the basis of facts is nonsense—according to the quotation Kant used: *ex pumice aquam* [(getting) water from a stone]. . . .

It can as historical science in no way prove even the affirmation that up to the present there has been no scientific philosophy; it can do so only from other sources of knowledge, and they are clearly philosophical sources. For it is clear that philosophical criticism, too, in so far as it is really to lay claim to validity, is philosophy and that its sense implies the ideal possibility of a systematic philosophy as a strict science. The unconditional affirmation that any scientific philosophy is a chimaera, based on the argument that the alleged efforts of millennia make probable the intrinsic impossibility of such a philosophy, is erroneous not merely because to draw a conclusion regarding an unlimited future from a few millennia of higher culture would not be a good induction, but erroneous as an absolute absurdity, like $2 \times 2 = 5$. And this is for the indicated reason: if there is something there whose objective validity philosophical criticism can refute, then there is also an area within which something can be grounded as objectively valid. . . . If criticism proves that philosophy in its historical growth has operated with confused concepts, has been guilty of mixed concepts and specious conclusions, then if one does not wish to fall into nonsense, that very fact makes it undeniable that, ideally speaking, the concepts are capable of being pointed, clarified, distinguished, that in the given area correct conclusions can be drawn. Any correct, profoundly penetrating criticism itself provides means for advancing and ideally points to correct goals, thereby indicating an objectively valid science. To this would obviously be added that the historical untenableness of a spiritual formation as a fact has nothing to do with its untenableness from the standpoint of validity. . . .

We pass now to evaluating the sense and justification of *Weltanschauung* philosophy, in order thereafter to compare it with philosophy as a rigorous science. . . . The majority of *Weltanschauung* philosophers . . . esteem very highly the worth of this sort of philosophy, which wants precisely to be rather *Weltanschauung* than science of the world, and they esteem it all the more highly the more, precisely under the influence of historicism, they look sceptically at the orientation toward strict philosophical world science. Their motives, that at the same time more exactly determined the sense of *Weltanschauung* philosophy, are approximately the following:

Every great philosophy is not only a historical fact, but in the development of humanity's life of the spirit it has a great, even unique teleological function, that of being the highest elevation of the life experience, education, and wisdom of its time. Let us linger awhile over the clarification of these concepts.

Experience as a personal habitus is the residue of acts belonging to a natural experimental attitude, acts that have occurred during the course of life. This habitus is essentially conditioned by the manner in which the personality, as this particular individuality, lets itself be motivated by acts of its own experience, and not less by the manner in which it lets experiences transmitted by others work on it by agreeing with it or rejecting it. [These] acts . . . can be cognitions of natural existence of every kind, either simple perceptions or other acts of immediately intuitive cognition, or the acts of thought based on these at different levels of logical elaboration and confirmation. But that does not go far enough. We also have experiences of art works and of other beauty values, and no less of ethical values, whether on the basis of our own ethical conduct or of looking into that of others; and likewise of real goods, practical utilities, technical applications. In short, we have not only theoretical but also axiological and practical experiences. Analysis shows that these latter refer back to vital experiences of evaluating and willing as their intuitive foundation. . . . The man of many-sided experience, or as we also say, the "cultivated man," has not only experience of the world but also religious, aesthetic, ethical, political, practico-technical, and other kinds of experience, or "culture." With regard to particularly high levels of value, there is the old-fashioned word "wisdom" (wisdom of the world, wisdom of world and life), and most of all, the now-beloved expressions "world view" and "life view," or simply *Weltanschauung*.

We shall have to look upon wisdom, or *Weltanschauung*, in this sense as an essential component of that still more valuable human habitus that comes before us in the idea of perfect virtue and designates habitual ability with regard to all the orientations of human attitudes, whether cognitional, evaluational, or volitional. For evidently hand in hand with this ability goes the well-developed capacity to judge rationally regarding the objectivities proper to these attitudes, regarding the world about us, regarding values, real goods, deeds, etc., or the capacity to justify expressly one's attitudes. That, however, presupposes wisdom and belongs to its higher forms.

Wisdom, or *Weltanschauung*, in this determined sense, which includes a variety of types and grades of value, is—and this needs no further explanation—no mere accomplishment of the isolated personality (this latter would moreover be an abstraction); rather it belongs to the cultural community and to the time, and with regard to its most pronounced forms there is a good sense in which one can speak not only of the culture and *Weltanschauung* of a determined individual but also of that of the time. This is particularly true of the forms we are now to treat. . . .

In so far . . . as the vital and hence most persuasive cultural motives of the time are not only conceptually grasped but also logically unfolded and otherwise elaborated in thought, in so far as the results thus obtained are brought, in interplay with additional intuitions and insights, to scientific unification and consistent completion, there develops an extraordinary extension and elevation of the originally unconceptualized wisdom. There develops a *Weltanschauung* philosophy, which in the great systems . . . affords as well as possible a solution and satisfactory explanation to the theoretical, axiological, and practical inconsistencies of life that experience, wisdom, mere world and life view, can only imperfectly overcome. . . .

In so far as the value of *Weltanschauung* philosophy . . . is primarily conditioned by the value of wisdom and the striving for wisdom, it is hardly necessary to consider in particular the goal it sets itself. If one makes the concept of wisdom as wide as we have made it, then it certainly expresses an essential component in the ideal of that perfect ability achievable in accord with the measure proper to the respective phase in humanity's life, in other words, a relatively perfect adumbration of the idea of humanity. . . .

From the natural reflections on the best ways to achieve the lofty goal of humanity and consequently at the same time the lofty goal of perfect wisdom, there has grown up, as is known, a technique—that of the virtuous or able man. If it is as usual defined as the art of correct conduct, it obviously comes to the same thing. For consistently able conduct, which is certainly meant, leads back to the able, practical character, and this presupposes habitual perfection from the intellectual and axiological point of view. Again, conscious striving for perfection presupposes striving for universal wisdom. In regard to content, this discipline directs the one striving to the various groups of values, those present in the sciences, the arts, religion, etc. that every individual in his conduct has to recognize as intersubjective and unifying validities; and one of the highest of these values is the idea of this wisdom and perfect ability itself. . . .

Now that we have seen to it that full justice has been accorded to the high value of *Weltanschauung* philosophy, it might seem that nothing should keep us from unconditionally recommending the striving toward such a philosophy.

Still, perhaps it can be shown that in regard to the idea of philosophy, other values—and from certain points of view, higher ones—must be satisfied, which is to say, those of a philosophical science. The following should be taken into account. Our consideration takes place from the standpoint of the high scientific culture of our time, which is a time for mighty forces of objectified strict sciences. For modern consciousness the ideas of culture, or *Weltanschauung*, and science—understood as practical ideas—have been sharply separated, and from now on they remain separated for all eternity. . . . The historical philosophies were certainly *Weltanschauung* philosophies, in so far as the wisdom drive ruled their creators; but they were just as much scientific philosophies, in so far as the goal of scientific philosophy was also alive in them. The two goals were either not at all or not sharply distinguished. . . . Since the constitution of a supratemporal universality of strict sciences, that situation has fundamentally changed. Generations upon generations work enthusiastically on the mighty structure of science and add to it their modest building blocks, always conscious that the structure is endless, by no means ever to be finished. *Weltanschauung*, too, is an "idea," but of a goal lying in the finite, in principle to be realized in an individual life by way of constant approach, just like morality, which would certainly lose its sense if it were the idea of an eternal that would be in principle transfinite.

Thus *Weltanschauung* philosophy and scientific philosophy are sharply distinguished as two ideas, related in a certain manner to each other but not to be confused. . . . Nevertheless, it can be said that the realization of these ideas (presupposing realizations of both) would approach each other asymptotically in the infinite and coincide, should we want to represent to ourselves the infinite of science metaphorically as an "infinitely distant point." . . .

If we take the two distinct ideas as contents of life goals, then accordingly, in opposition to the aspiration proper to *Weltanschauung*, an entirely different research aspiration is possible. This latter, though fully conscious that science can in no wise be the complete creation of the individual, still devotes its fullest energies to promoting, in cooperation with men of like mind, the break-through and gradual progress of a scientific philosophy. The big problem at present is, apart from clearly distinguishing them, to make a relative evaluation of these goals and thereby of their practical unifiability. . . .

Of course, every exact scholar constructs for himself *Anschauungen*; by his views, his guesses, his opinions, he looks beyond what has been firmly established, but only with methodical intent, in order to plan new fragments of strict doctrine. This attitude does not preclude, as the investigator of nature himself knows quite well, that experience in the prescientific sense—though in connection with scientific insights—plays an important role within the technique proper to natural science. Technical tasks want to be done, the house, the machine is to be built; there can be no waiting until natural science can give exact information on all that concerns them. The technician, therefore, as a practical man, decides otherwise than the theoretician of natural science. From the latter he takes doctrine, from life he takes "experience."

The situation is not quite the same in regard to scientific philosophy, precisely because as yet not even a beginning of scientifically rigorous doctrine has been developed, and the philosophy handed down historically as well as that conceived in a living development, each representing itself as such a doctrine, are at most scientific half-fabrications, or indistinguished mixtures of *Weltanschauung* and theoretical knowledge. On the other hand, here too we unfortunately cannot wait. Philosophical necessity as a need for *Weltanschauung* forces us. This need becomes constantly greater the wider the circle of positive sciences is extended. The extraordinary fullness of scientifically "explained" facts that they bestow on us cannot help us, since in principle, along with all the sciences, they bring in a dimension of riddles whose solutions become for us a vital question. The natural sciences have not in a single instance unraveled for us actual reality, the reality in which we live, move, and are. The general belief that it is their function to accomplish this and that they are merely not yet far enough advanced, the opinion that they can accomplish this—in principle—has revealed itself to those with more profound insight as a superstition. The necessary separation between natural science and philosophy—in principle, a differently oriented science, though in some fields essentially related to natural science—is in process of being established and clarified. As Lotze puts it, "To calculate the course of the world does not mean to understand it." In this direction, however, we are no better off with the humanistic sciences. To "understand" humanity's spirit-life is certainly a great and beautiful thing. But unfortunately even this understanding cannot help us, and it must not be confused with the philosophical understanding that is to unravel for us the riddles of the world and of life.

The spiritual need of our time has, in fact, become unbearable. Would that it were only theoretical lack of clarity regarding the sense of the "reality" investigated in the natural and humanistic sciences that disturbed our peace—e.g., to what extent is being in the ultimate sense understood in them, what is to be looked on as such "absolute" being, and whether this sort of thing is knowable at all. Far more than this, it is the most radical vital need that afflicts us, a need that leaves no point of our lives untouched. All life is taking a position, and all taking of position is subject to a must—that of doing justice to validity and invalidity according to alleged norms of absolute validation. So long as these norms were not attacked, were threatened and ridiculed by no scepticism, there was only one vital question: how best to satisfy these norms in practice. But how is it now, when any and every norm is controverted or empirically falsified and robbed of its ideal validity? Naturalists and historicists fight about *Weltanschauung*, and yet both are at work on different sides to misinterpret ideas as facts and to transform all reality, all life, into an incomprehensible, idealess confusion of "facts." The superstition of the fact is common to them all.

It is certain that we cannot wait. We have to take a position, we must bestir ourselves to harmonize the disharmonies in our attitude to reality—to the reality of life, which has significance for us and in which we should have significance—into a rational, even though unscientific, "world-and-life-view." And if the *Weltanschauung* philosopher helps us greatly in this, should we not thank him?

No matter how much truth there is in what has just been asserted, no matter how little we should like to miss the exaltation and consolation old and new philosophies offer us, still it must be insisted that we remain aware of the responsibility we have in regard to humanity. . . . The need here has its source in science. But only science can definitively overcome the need that has its source in science. If the sceptical criticism of naturalists and historicists dissolves genuine objective validity in all fields of obligation into nonsense, if unclear and disagreeing, even though naturally developed, reflective concepts and consequently equivocal and erroneous problems impede the understanding of actuality and the possibility of a rational attitude toward it, if a special but (for a large class of sciences) required methodical attitude becomes a matter of routine so that it is incapable of being transformed into other attitudes, and if depressing absurdities in the interpretation of the world are connected with such prejudices, then there is only one remedy for these and all similar evils: a scientific critique and in addition a radical science, rising from below, based on sure foundations, and progressing according to the most rigorous methods—the philosophical science for which we speak here. *Weltanschauungen* can engage in controversy; only science can decide, and its decision bears the stamp of eternity.

And so whatever be the direction the new transformation of philosophy may take, without question it must not give up its will to be rigorous science. Rather as theoretical science it must oppose itself to the practical aspiration toward *Weltanschauung* and quite consciously separate itself from this aspiration. . . .

SELECTED BIBLIOGRAPHY

Husserl, Edmund. *Cartesian Meditations: An Introduction to Phenomenology*. Trans. Dorion Cairns. Boston: Martinus Nijhoff, 1960.

_____. *The Crisis of European Sciences and Transcendental Phenomenology: An Introduction to Phenomenological Philosophy*. Trans. David Carr. Evanston, Ill.: Northwestern University Press, 1970.

_____. *Husserl: Shorter Works*. Ed. Peter McCormick and Frederick Elliston. Notre Dame, Ind.: University of Notre Dame Press, 1981.

_____. *Ideas*. Trans. F. Kersten. Boston: Martinus Nijhoff, 1982.

Boer, Theodore de. *The Development of Husserl's Thought*. Trans. Theodore Plantinga. The Hague: Martinus Nijhoff, 1978.

Carr, David. *Interpreting Husserl*. The Hague: Martinus Nijhoff, 1978.

Edie, James M. *Edmund Husserl's Phenomenology: A Critical Commentary*. Bloomington: Indiana University Press, 1987.

Elliston, Frederick, and Peter McCormick, eds. *Husserl: Expositions and Appraisals*. Notre Dame, Ind.: University of Notre Dame Press, 1978.

Elveton, R.O., ed. *The Philosophy of Husserl: Selected Critical Readings*. Chicago: Quadrangle Books, 1970.

Kockelmans, Joseph J. *A First Introduction to Husserl's Phenomenology*. Pittsburgh: Duquesne University Press, 1967.

_____, ed. *Phenomenology: The Philosophy of Edmund Husserl and Its Interpretations*. Garden City, N.Y.: Doubleday, 1967.

Kolakowski, Leszek. *Husserl and the Search for Certitude*. Chicago: University of Chicago Press, 1987.

Levin, David M. *Reason and Evidence in Husserl's Phenomenology*. Evanston, Ill.: Northwestern University Press, 1970.

Levinas, Emmanuel. *The Theory of Intuition in Husserl's Phenomenology*. Evanston, Ill.: Northwestern University Press, 1973.

Mohanty, J. *Husserl and Frege*. Bloomington: Indiana University Press, 1982.

Natanson, Maurice. *Edmund Husserl: Philosopher of Infinite Tasks*. Evanston, Ill.: Northwestern University Press, 1973.

Ricoeur, Paul. *Husserl: An Analysis of His Phenomenology*. Trans. Edward Ballard and Lester Embree. Evanston, Ill.: Northwestern University Press, 1967.

Smith, David Woodruff, and Ronald McIntyre. *Husserl and Intentionality: A Study of Mind, Meaning, and Language*. Boston: Reidel, 1982.

Ludwig Wittgenstein

Ludwig Wittgenstein (1889–1951) was born of a wealthy Austrian family. Several of his brothers committed suicide; another, Paul, whose right arm was shot off in World War I, became a world-famous pianist, inspiring many great composers to write pieces for the left hand. Until Ludwig was fourteen he was educated at home. He was originally trained in aeronautical engineering, first in Berlin and then in Manchester, England, but his engineering studies led to an interest in mathematics, which in turn led to an interest in the foundations of mathematics and logic. Bertrand Russell's *Principles of Mathematics* introduced him to the work of Gottlob Frege, a great German logician, who personally encouraged Wittgenstein to study logic and philosophy with Russell at Cambridge. So Wittgenstein in 1912 and 1913 spent five terms at Cambridge, where he deeply impressed both Russell and G.E. Moore, the founders of what is now called analytic philosophy.

Wittgenstein then retreated to Norway, to a hut that he built himself, where he worked on the notebooks that would grow into the *Tractatus Logico-Philosophicus*, his only philosophical book published during his lifetime. When World War I broke out, Wittgenstein enlisted in the Austrian army, where he served as a machine gunner, first on the eastern front, then in the Tyrol. During his leaves he assembled the *Tractatus* by organizing the best thoughts from his notebooks. He was taken prisoner by the Italians in 1918, but managed to send copies of his work to Frege and Russell. Russell undertook to write a preface and get it published. The work appeared in Germany in 1921 and in a bilingual German-English edition shortly thereafter. Because Wittgenstein was convinced that the *Tractatus* solved all real philosophical problems, he gave up philosophy to pursue other things.

Wittgenstein had become quite wealthy after the death of his father in 1912, who had been a major figure in the Austrian steel industry. After the war, however, reportedly influenced by reading Tolstoy, Wittgenstein divested himself of his wealth, splitting it among the rest of his family. Having completed the *Tractatus*, he enrolled in a teacher-training college and from 1920 to 1926 taught elementary school in several small Austrian villages. But he was desperately unhappy. Raised in high Viennese society and educated among the most powerful minds of the era, he could not find among the villagers companionship adequate to his needs. He then abandoned teaching to become a monastery gardener and also spent time designing and supervising the construction of a house for his sister. During this period, back in Vienna, he met Moritz Schlick, who had just become professor of the history and philosophy of the inductive sciences at the university. Schlick was the organizing force behind a group of philosophers, mathematicians, and scientists (including Rudolph Carnap, Friedrich Waismann, and Herbert Feigl) that later became known as the Vienna Circle and had a tremendous impact on contemporary philosophy. Under this influence (and the visits paid him from Cambridge by Frank Ramsey, a young British philosopher and logician), Wittgenstein's interest in philosophy revived.

Wittgenstein began to doubt whether he had in fact resolved everything in the *Tractatus*, and Ramsey convinced him to return to Cambridge in 1929. There he submitted the *Tractatus*—already proclaimed an epochal work—as his doctoral dissertation. Russell and Moore, the grand old men of the analytic movement, formed his examination committee; remarked Moore, "It is my personal opinion that Mr. Wittgenstein's thesis is a work of genius; but, be that as it may, it is certainly up to the standard required for the Cambridge degree of Doctor of Philosophy." Wittgenstein began lecturing at Cambridge in 1930, working steadily on several books that were published only posthumously (*Philosophische Bemerkungen; Philosophische Grammatik*) and moving progressively away from his Tractarian views. In 1935, after a trip to the Soviet Union, he again took to his Norwegian retreat and worked there on the *Philosophical Investigations*, the first of his books to be published posthumously and considered the major work of his later period. In 1939 Wittgenstein succeeded to Moore's chair of philosophy at Cambridge, but he spent the war years as a medical orderly and laboratory assistant in a British hospital. (Characteristically, he told no one that he was also a professor of philosophy.) In 1947, after only two years of active service as a professor, he resigned, quite unhappy with the formal academic routine. He lived for a short time in Ireland and visited the United States in 1949, in which year he learned that he had cancer. His last two years were spent in Oxford and Cambridge.

Throughout his years at Cambridge, Wittgenstein made a remarkable impression on many of his students. His apartment was furnished monastically: a bed, a table, a lamp, and some deck chairs. He shunned most public events, although after his classes he would relax by going to the movies, always sitting in the front row. During his classes he would sit in the middle of the room and, without notes, think through his concerns aloud, often pausing for long periods to think, at other times passionately questioning his audience. His intensity intimidated many, and his relationships with colleagues were often ticklish, for he held a low opinion of most academics. He was impatient with those who could not keep up with his thoughts, and he was often harshly self-critical. His students were absolutely devoted to him, however; they often mimicked his telltale mannerisms later in their own classes. Someone who shunned all "schools of thought" and whose own thought was markedly independent, Wittgenstein became the focus of a near cultish following.

Philosophy

Were there two Wittgensteins or one? The later Wittgenstein rejected many of the positions of the early Wittgenstein, but was the change a radical break, creating a philosophical viewpoint of an entirely different kind, or was it a matter of significant evolution and adjustment that nonetheless stays within a common framework? Wittgenstein scholars differ sharply on this issue, but his works are the high points of two different phases of analytic philosophy.

The early Wittgenstein, working within the framework established by the pioneering work in symbolic logic of Frege, Russell, and Alfred North Whitehead, sought to uncover the true logical form that he believed lay at the heart of all language. His central insight here was that propositions are, in their own way, *pictures* of facts. A fact is itself a complex of objects, and propositions are complexes of simple names. When there is a rule-governed relationship by which we can read off the arrangement of objects from the arrangement of names, the proposition pictures the fact. At first this doesn't seem to tally with our understanding of normal sentences in English, for in the sentence *The cube is square*, what object does the word *is* name? (For that matter, what object does *the* or *square* name?) But the true logical form of our language is hidden by its superficial grammar, which is constrained to be linear and compelled for obvious reasons to use names to designate complex objects, not just simple objects. In order to uncover the true logical form of a sentence such as *The cube is square*, we would have to analyze it until the only names that occur in the analysis are names of atomic objects, which are so arranged as to show us what it is for the cube to be square.

Much of the *Tractatus* is quite technical, demonstrating techniques of analyzing sentences. It emerges from Wittgenstein's position that language can only describe the world—the totality of facts. Sentences that do not themselves describe the world but perform some other job, such as stating the rules that govern our descriptions of the world or prescribing or proscribing some action, cannot, therefore, be propositions. Such things simply cannot be said, though Wittgenstein believes that they can be shown. Science can say everything sayable; among the things that cannot be said are statements of ethics, religion, and philosophy itself. This is why, according to Wittgenstein, the *Tractatus* itself is really nonsense; one who has understood it must realize that it is an effort to say things that cannot be said. The reader must, Wittgenstein says, "throw away the ladder after he has climbed up it." (6.54)[1]

The Tractarian view of language as an ideal, crystalline, logical medium in which, if we but understood its true form well enough, only sensible things could be said and

---

1. Wittgenstein's reference system is explained on the first page of the selection.

metaphysical statements, indeed anything that went beyond the reach of science, could not even be mouthed, exercised a tremendous influence, especially on the logical positivists in the Vienna Circle and in Berlin. Wittgenstein became a hero for them, though he never really sympathized with positivism, the doctrine that science is the ultimate arbiter of all questions. The positivists thought that his arguments showed that the sciences reigned supreme, for they said everything sayable and therefore everything important; metaphysics and other such obscurantist babble (as they would call it) was revealed to be mere nonsense, a snare and a delusion. Yet for Wittgenstein the conclusion of his work ran in quite the opposite direction: the most important things in life were simply unsayable. If the sciences could say nothing about values, the self, or even logical form—well, so much the worse for the sciences.

The root change between the early and the later Wittgenstein is a realization of the manifold purposes language can serve and of the great variety of ways of meaning. One story, perhaps apocryphal, recounts that Wittgenstein was talking with his friend Piero Sraffa about meaning, sticking fairly close to the Tractarian doctrine, when Sraffa, a Cambridge economist, made a contemptuous gesture with his hand and said, "Eh!" Wittgenstein, stunned, realized that what Saffra had done was perfectly meaningful, yet pictured nothing.

Part of this shift in Wittgenstein's interests is a turn from what it is for a sentence to mean something (in the *Tractatus*) to what it is for a *person* to mean something. Thus the *Philosophical Investigations* is as important a work in the philosophy of mind as in the philosophy of language.

Just as the metaphor of picturing dominates the reflections in the *Tractatus*, the metaphor of a language game dominates the *Investigations*. What makes a phrase meaningful? Wittgenstein abandons the idea that there is any single relationship between words and things that constitutes meaningfulness; rather, words are meaningful because of what we *do* with them, the patterns of behavior with which they are connected. What makes a certain object a chess pawn? Certainly not its shape or its composition—though there is a standard pawn shape, plenty of fancy chess sets use little statues for pawns, and there is no reason why automobiles driving on a grid of Kansas counties couldn't serve as perfectly good chess pieces. An object is a chess pawn because it is treated according to certain rules that dictate how it can move according to the rules of the game. But then, what is it to treat something in accordance with a rule, or more basically, what is it to follow a rule? Following a rule doesn't have to mean formulating the rule explicitly in one's head and then controlling one's behavior to obey the rule—in fact, that *could not* be what following a rule means, because formulating an expression explicitly involves following the rules governing language.

Both the early and the later Wittgenstein believed that everything is in order in such natural languages as English. However, the Tractarian philosopher believed that this was because there is a pure unitary logical system hidden in our language. Philosophical problems arise when the superficial form of language confuses us. (For example, when we say "It's raining," what does *it* refer to? Is there some thing that rains?) It is the job of the philosopher to expose the true logical form of what we say, and in doing so all our philosophical problems will be resolved. But the later Wittgenstein rejects the idea that there is a homogenous, systematic logical form to be discovered at the heart of all language and meaning. He still believes that natural languages are perfectly in order and that philosophical problems arise when we get confused about what is going on with our language. Now the therapy for philosophical confusion is not discovery of the true logical form, however, but an understanding of how that piece of language functions in its context. The assumption that all language works the same way is one of the sources of philosophical confusion, so we need to be on our guard to notice and appreciate the differences in the way language is used.

The two central works of Wittgenstein's corpus, the *Tractatus* and the *Investigations*, were written in a similar manner—assembled by rearranging notebook entries—but stylistically they are worlds apart. Yet both the terse austerity of the *Tractatus* and the conversational loquacity of the *Investigations* challenge readers to think along with the text, to wrestle through the problems on their own. Perhaps one reason for Wittgenstein's prominence in twentieth-century philosophy is that his works challenge one to *do* philosophy (rather than just read about it) in a way that few others have been able to achieve.

The Reading Context

Tractatus Logico-Philosophicus

Wittgenstein's cryptic remarks can be quite frustrating to read—especially since he admits that they are, strictly speaking, nonsense (6.54) and since he seems to hold his work in an arrogantly low esteem:

> The *truth* of the thoughts that are here set forth seems to me unassailable and definitive. I therefore believe myself to have found, on all essential points, the final solution of the problems. And if I am not mistaken in this belief, then the second thing in which the value of this work consists is that it shows how little is achieved when these problems are solved.[2]

Wittgenstein does not want so much to impart truths to his reader as to provoke in his reader a train of thoughts leading to a shared insight. What he writes is a trail of clues leading to the insight. The *Tractatus* is therefore a kind of mystery book. The evidence, in one sense, is all there, but it needs to be interpreted; the connections need to be made, the implications drawn out. It is difficult to find a more challenging book, but for all its Spartan rigor, it can be as engrossing as the most intricately plotted thriller.

Philosophical Investigations

Less cryptic on the surface than the oracular pronouncements of the *Tractatus*, the little stories and reflections that fill the pages of the *Investigations* can be equally baffling. Each story has a moral, but Wittgenstein rarely points out the moral explicitly. Consequently, each of the numerous commentators on this book disagrees with the others about the precise morals Wittgenstein intended. But particular doctrines are not that important to Wittgenstein: in response to his own question, "What is your aim in philosophy?" he answers, "To shew the fly the way out of the fly-bottle" (309).

---

2. Ludwig Wittgenstein, *Tractatus Logico-Philosophicus*, trans. D.F. Pears and B.F. McGuiness (London: Routledge & Kegan Paul, 1961), p. 5.

Philosophical problems and puzzles are not to be solved so much as dissolved by increasing our understanding of the manifold varieties of language use. Thus understanding Wittgenstein is less a matter of learning doctrines than of learning how to unravel the complexities hidden in our ordinary conceptions of things.

A Note on the Texts

The *Tractatus Logico-Philosophicus* was assembled by Wittgenstein during World War I from remarks in his notebooks and finished during a leave in 1918. The manuscript was in Wittgenstein's knapsack when he was taken prisoner later that year. It was first published in 1921 in German; a bilingual edition in English and German, with an introduction by Bertrand Russell and translated by Frank Ramsey and C.K. Ogden, followed in 1922. It was retranslated by David Pears and B.F. McGuiness in 1960 and further revised in 1974.

The *Philosophical Investigations*, though not published in Wittgenstein's lifetime, was the only book other than the *Tractatus* that he intended to publish. The first part, from which the selections included here are drawn, was finished by 1945; it was not published until 1953. Since Wittgenstein numbered the paragraphs in the first part of the book, citations conform to his numbering scheme.

Reading Questions

Tractatus Logico-Philosophicus

1. What is the difference between a totality of facts and a totality of things?
2. What would count as an object for Wittgenstein? Are they not only colorless but also tasteless and without size, solidity, or texture?
3. What is a picture? In what sense is a picture a *fact* and not an object? What is a picture's form? Can there be negative pictures, pictures of something not being the case?
4. What is the difference between a proposition, a propositional sign, and a significant proposition?
5. If the limits of my language are the limits of my world, does this mean I must live in a different world from anyone who speaks a different language?
6. Is there room for ethical reflection in a Tractarian world?
7. Does the fact that, on its own terms, the propositions of the *Tractatus* are nonsense, to be discarded after having been understood, mean that the position of the book is self-defeating? How can we understand its propositions if they are nonsense?

Philosophical Investigations

8. What is a "language-game"? Why does Wittgenstein spend so much time discussing simple language-games?
9. What criticisms does the author of the *Philosophical Investigations* make of the *Tractatus*?

10. How does Wittgenstein's notion of a family resemblance compare to Plato's notion of a Form?
11. Does Wittgenstein think that anyone who utters a sentence and means or understands it must be operating a calculus according to definite rules? What reasons does he give?
12. What does Wittgenstein think a philosophical problem is? How do philosophical problems get solved?
13. Does Wittgenstein still think in the *Philosophical Investigations* that an ideal language is achievable?
14. What is going on when someone follows a rule? Must there be something special going on in the person's head? How can one tell which rule is being followed?
15. Is obeying a rule a form of interpretation of that rule?
16. Could there be a private language? Why?

Tractatus Logico-Philosophicus

1[1]	The world is all that is the case.
1.1	The world is the totality of facts, not of things.
1.11	The world is determined by the facts, and by their being *all* the facts.
1.12	For the totality of facts determines what is the case, and also whatever is not the case.
1.13	The facts in logical space are the world.
1.2	The world divides into facts.
1.21	Each item can be the case or not the case while everything else remains the same.
2	What is the case—a fact—is the existence of states of affairs.
2.01	A state of affairs (a state of things) is a combination of objects (things).
2.011	It is essential to things that they should be possible constituents of states of affairs.
2.012	In logic nothing is accidental: if a thing *can* occur in a state of affairs, the possibility of the state of affairs must be written into the thing itself.
2.0121	It would seem to be a sort of accident, if it turned out that a situation would fit a thing that could already exist entirely on its own.

If things can occur in states of affairs, this possibility must be in them from the beginning.

(Nothing in the province of logic can be merely possible. Logic deals with every possibility and all possibilities are its facts.)

Just as we are quite unable to imagine spatial objects outside space or temporal objects outside time, so too there is *no* object that we can imagine excluded from the possibility of combining with others.

If I can imagine objects combined in states of affairs, I cannot imagine them excluded from the *possibility* of such combinations. . . .

2.013	Each thing is, as it were, in a space of possible states of affairs. This space I can imagine empty, but I cannot imagine the thing without the space. . . .
2.014	Objects contain the possibility of all situations.
2.0141	The possibility of its occurring in states of affairs is the form of an object.
2.02	Objects are simple.
2.0201	Every statement about complexes can be resolved into a statement about their constituents and into the propositions that describe the complexes completely.
2.021	Objects make up the substance of the world. That is why they cannot be composite. . . .
2.022	It is obvious that an imagined world, however different it may be from the real one, must have *something*—a form—in common with it.

From Ludwig Wittgenstein, *Tractatus Logico-Philosophicus*, trans D.F. Pears and B.F. McGuiness (London: Routledge & Kegan Paul, 1961), pp. 5–74. Reprinted by permission of Routledge, International Thomson Publishing.

1. The decimal numbers assigned to the individual propositions indicate the logical importance of the propositions, the stress laid on them in my exposition. The propositions n.1, n.2, n.3, etc. are comments on proposition no. n; the propositions n.m1, n.m2, etc. are comments on proposition no. n.m; and so on. [Wittgenstein's note.]

2.023	Objects are just what constitute this unalterable form.
2.0231	The substance of the world *can* only determine a form, and not any material properties. For it is only by means of propositions that material properties are represented—only by the configuration of objects that they are produced....
2.024	Substance is what subsists independently of what is the case.
2.025	It is form and content.
2.0251	Space, time, and colour (being coloured) are forms of objects.
2.026	There must be objects, if the world is to have an unalterable form.
2.027	Objects, the unalterable, and the subsistent are one and the same.
2.0271	Objects are what is unalterable and subsistent; their configuration is what is changing and unstable....
2.03	In a state of affairs objects fit into one another like the links of a chain.
2.031	In a state of affairs objects stand in a determinate relation to one another.
2.032	The determinate way in which objects are connected in a state of affairs is the structure of the state of affairs.
2.033	Form is the possibility of structure....
2.04	The totality of existing states of affairs is the world.
2.05	The totality of existing states of affairs also determines which states of affairs do not exist.
2.06	The existence and non-existence of states of affairs is reality. (We also call the existence of states of affairs a positive fact, and their non-existence a negative fact.)
2.061	States of affairs are independent of one another....
2.1	We picture facts to ourselves.
2.11	A picture presents a situation in logical space, the existence and non-existence of states of affairs.
2.12	A picture is a model of reality.
2.13	In a picture objects have the elements of the picture corresponding to them.
2.131	In a picture the elements of the picture are the representatives of the objects.
2.14	What constitutes a picture is that its elements are related to one another in a determinate way.
2.141	A picture is a fact.
2.15	The fact that the elements of a picture are related to one another in a determinate way represents that things are related to one another in the same way. Let us call this connexion of its elements the structure of the picture, and let us call the possibility of this structure the pictorial form of the picture....
2.16	If a fact is to be a picture, it must have something in common with what it depicts.
2.17	What a picture must have in common with reality, in order to be able to depict it—correctly or incorrectly—in the way it does, is its pictorial form.
2.171	A picture can depict any reality whose form it has. A spatial picture can depict anything spatial, a coloured one anything coloured, etc.

2.172   A picture cannot, however, depict its pictorial form: it displays it. . . .

2.18   What any picture, of whatever form, must have in common with reality, in order to be able to depict it—correctly or incorrectly—in any way at all, is logical form, i.e. the form of reality. . . .

2.2   A picture has logico-pictorial form in common with what it depicts.

2.201   A picture depicts reality by representing a possibility of existence and non-existence of states of affairs.

2.202   A picture represents a possible situation in logical space. . . .

2.21   A picture agrees with reality or fails to agree; it is correct or incorrect, true or false.

2.22   What a picture represents it represents independently of its truth or falsity, by means of its pictorial form.

2.221   What a picture represents is its sense.

2.222   The agreement or disagreement of its sense with reality constitutes its truth or falsity.

2.223   In order to tell whether a picture is true or false we must compare it with reality.

2.224   It is impossible to tell from the picture alone whether it is true or false. . . .

3   A logical picture of facts is a thought.

3.001   "A state of affairs is thinkable": what this means is that we can picture it to ourselves.

3.01   The totality of true thoughts is a picture of the world.

3.02   A thought contains the possibility of the situation of which it is the thought. What is thinkable is possible too.

3.03   Thought can never be of anything illogical, since, if it were, we should have to think illogically. . . .

3.1   In a proposition a thought finds an expression that can be perceived by the senses.

3.11   We use the perceptible sign of a proposition (spoken or written, etc.) as a projection of a possible situation.

         The method of projection is to think of the sense of the proposition.

3.12   I call the sign with which we express a thought a propositional sign.—And a proposition is a propositional sign in its projective relation to the world.

3.13   A proposition includes all that the projection includes, but not what is projected.

         Therefore, though what is projected is not itself included, its possibility is.

         A proposition, therefore, does not actually contain its sense, but does contain the possibility of expressing it.

         ("The content of a proposition" means the content of a proposition that has sense.)

         A proposition contains the form, but not the content, of its sense.

3.14   What constitutes a propositional sign is that in it its elements (the words) stand in a determinate relation to one another.

         A propositional sign is a fact. . . .

3.142   Only facts can express a sense, a set of names cannot.

3.143   Although a propositional sign is a fact, this is obscured by the usual form of expression in writing or print.

For in a printed proposition, for example, no essential difference is apparent between a propositional sign and a word. . . .

3.1432   Instead of, "The complex sign '*aRb*' says that *a* stands to *b* in the relation *R*," we ought to put, "That '*a*' stands to '*b*' in a certain relation says that *aRb*". . .

3.2   In a proposition a thought can be expressed in such a way that elements of the propositional sign correspond to the objects of the thought. . . .

3.21   The configuration of objects in a situation corresponds to the configuration of simple signs in the propositional sign.

3.22   In a proposition a name is the representative of an object. . . .

3.23   The requirement that simple signs be possible is the requirement that sense be determinate.

3.24   A proposition about a complex stands in an internal relation to a proposition about a constituent of the complex.

          A complex can be given only by its description, which will be right or wrong. A proposition that mentions a complex will not be nonsensical, if the complex does not exist, but simply false.

          When a propositional element signifies a complex, this can be seen from an indeterminateness in the propositions in which it occurs. In such cases we *know* that the proposition leaves something undetermined. (In fact the notation for generality *contains* a prototype.)

          The contraction of a symbol for a complex into a simple symbol can be expressed in a definition.

3.25   A proposition has one and only one complete analysis. . . .

3.26   A name cannot be dissected any further by means of a definition: it is a primitive sign. . . .

3.3   Only propositions have sense; only in the nexus of a proposition does a name have meaning.

3.31   I call any part of a proposition that characterizes its sense an expression (or a symbol).

          (A proposition is itself an expression.)

          Everything essential to their sense that propositions can have in common with one another is an expression.

          An expression is the mark of a form and a content. . . .

3.32   A sign is what can be perceived of a symbol.

3.321   So one and the same sign (written or spoken, etc.) can be common to two different symbols—in which case they will signify in different ways.

3.322   Our use of the same sign to signify two different objects can never indicate a common characteristic of the two, if we use it with two different *modes of signification*. For the sign, of course, is arbitrary. So we could choose two different signs instead, and then what would be left in common on the signifying side?

3.323   In everyday language it very frequently happens that the same word has different modes of signification—and so belongs to different symbols—or that two words that have different modes of signification are employed in propositions in what is superficially the same way.

          Thus the word "is" figures as the copula, as a sign for identity, and as an expression for existence; "exist" figures as an intransitive verb like "go," and "identical" as an adjective; we speak of *something*, but also of *something's* happening.

(In the proposition, "Green is green"—where the first word is the proper name of a person and the last an adjective—these words to not merely have different meanings: they are *different symbols*.)

3.324 In this way the most fundamental confusions are easily produced (the whole of philosophy is full of them).

3.325 In order to avoid such errors we must make use of a sign-language that excludes them by not using the same sign for different symbols and by not using in a superficially similar way signs that have different modes of signification: that is to say, a sign-language that is governed by *logical* grammar—by logical syntax. . . .

3.328 If a sign is *useless*, it is meaningless. That is the point of Occam's maxim.

(If everything behaves as if a sign had meaning, then it does have meaning.)

3.33 In logical syntax the meaning of a sign should never play a role. It must be possible to establish logical syntax without mentioning the *meaning* of a sign: *only* the description of expressions may be presupposed. . . .

3.332 No proposition can make a statement about itself, because a propositional sign cannot be contained in itself (that is the whole of the "theory of types"). . . .

3.34 A proposition possesses essential and accidental features.

Accidental features are those that result from the particular way in which the propositional sign is produced. Essential features are those without which the proposition could not express its sense.

3.341 So what is essential in a proposition is what all propositions that can express the same sense have in common.

And similarly, in general, what is essential in a symbol is what all symbols that can serve the same purpose have in common. . . .

3.4 A proposition determines a place in logical space. The existence of this logical place is guaranteed by the mere existence of the constituents—by the existence of the proposition with a sense. . . .

3.42 A proposition can determine only one place in logical space: nevertheless the whole of logical space must already be given by it.

(Otherwise negation, logical sum, logical product, etc., would introduce more and more new elements—in coordination.)

(The logical scaffolding surrounding a picture determines logical space. The force of a proposition reaches through the whole of logical space.)

3.5 A propositional sign, applied and thought out, is a thought.

4 A thought is a proposition with a sense.

4.001 The totality of propositions is language.

4.002 Man possesses the ability to construct languages capable of expressing every sense, without having any idea how each word has meaning or what its meaning is—just as people speak without knowing how the individual sounds are produced.

Everyday language is a part of the human organism and is no less complicated than it.

It is not humanly possible to gather immediately from it what the logic of language is.

Language disguises thought. So much so, that from the outward form of the clothing it is impossible to infer the form of the thought beneath it, because the outward form of the clothing is not designed to reveal the form of the body, but for entirely different purposes.

The tacit conventions on which the understanding of everyday language depends are enormously complicated.

4.003　　Most of the propositions and questions to be found in philosophical works are not false but nonsensical. Consequently we cannot give any answer to questions of this kind, but can only point out that they are nonsensical. Most of the propositions and questions of philosophers arise from our failure to understand the logic of our language.

(They belong to the same class as the question whether the good is more or less identical than the beautiful.)

And it is not surprising that the deepest problems are in fact *not* problems at all.

4.0031　　All philosophy is a "critique of language." . . . It was Russell who performed the service of showing that the apparent logical form of a proposition need not be its real one.

4.01　　A proposition is a picture of reality. A proposition is a model of reality as we imagine it. . . .

4.02　　We can see this from the fact that we understand the sense of a propositional sign without its having been explained to us. . . .

4.022　　A proposition *shows* its sense.

A proposition *shows* how things stand *if* it is true. And it *says that* they do so stand. . . .

4.024　　To understand a proposition means to know what is the case if it is true.

(One can understand it, therefore, without knowing whether it is true.)

It is understood by anyone who understands its constituents. . . .

4.03　　A proposition must use old expressions to communicate a new sense.

A proposition communicates a situation to us, and so it must be *essentially* connected with the situation.

And the connexion is precisely that it is its logical picture.

A proposition states something only in so far as it is a picture. . . .

4.0312　　The possibility of propositions is based on the principle that objects have signs as their representatives.

My fundamental idea is that the "logical constants" are not representatives; that there can be no representatives of the *logic* of facts. . . .

4.04　　In a proposition there must be exactly as many distinguishable parts as in the situation that it represents.

The two must possess the same logical (mathematical) multiplicity. . . .

4.05　　Reality is compared with propositions.

4.06　　A proposition can be true or false only in virtue of being a picture of reality. . . .

4.1　　Propositions represent the existence and non-existence of states of affairs.

4.11　　The totality of true propositions is the whole of natural science (or the whole corpus of the natural sciences).

4.111   Philosophy is not one of the natural sciences.
            (The word "philosophy" must mean something whose place is above or below the natural sciences, not beside them.)

4.112   Philosophy aims at the logical clarification of thoughts.
            Philosophy is not a body of doctrine but an activity.
            A philosophical work consists essentially of elucidations.
            Philosophy does not result in "philosophical propositions," but rather in the clarification of propositions.
            Without philosophy thoughts are, as it were, cloudy and indistinct: its task is to make them clear and to give them sharp boundaries.

4.1121   Psychology is no more closely related to philosophy than any other natural science.
            Theory of knowledge is the philosophy of psychology. . . .

4.113   Philosophy sets limits to the much disputed sphere of natural science. . . .

4.12   Propositions can represent the whole of reality, but they cannot represent what they must have in common with reality in order to be able to represent it—logical form.
            In order to be able to represent logical form, we should have to be able to station ourselves with propositions somewhere outside logic, that is to say outside the world.

4.121   Propositions cannot represent logical form: it is mirrored in them.
            What finds its reflection in language, language cannot represent.
            What expresses *itself* in language, *we* cannot express by means of language.
            Propositions *show* the logical form of reality.
            They display it. . . .

4.1212   What *can* be shown, *cannot* be said. . . .

5.6   *The limits of my language* mean the limits of my world.

5.61   Logic pervades the world: the limits of the world are also its limits.
            So we cannot say in logic, "The world has this in it, and this, but not that."
            For that would appear to presuppose that we were excluding certain possibilities, and this cannot be the case, since it would require that logic should go beyond the limits of the world; for only in that way could it view those limits from the other side as well.
            We cannot think what we cannot think; so what we cannot think we cannot *say* either.

5.62   This remark provides the key to the problem, how much truth there is in solipsism.
            For what the solipsist *means* is quite correct; only it cannot be *said*, but makes itself manifest.
            The world is *my* world: this is manifest in the fact that the limits of *language* (of that language which alone I understand) mean the limits of *my* world.

5.621   The world and life are one.

5.63   I am my world. (The microcosm.)

5.631   There is no such thing as the subject that thinks or entertains ideas.
            If I wrote a book called *The World as I found it*, I should have to include a report on my body, and should have to say which parts were subordinate

to my will, and which were not, etc., this being a method of isolating the subject, or rather of showing that in an important sense there is no subject; for it alone could *not* be mentioned in that book.—

5.632   The subject does not belong to the world: rather, it is a limit of the world.

5.633   Where in the world is a metaphysical subject to be found?

You will say that this is exactly like the case of the eye and the visual field. But really you do *not* see the eye.

And nothing *in the visual field* allows you to infer that it is seen by an eye. . . .

5.634   This is connected with the fact than no part of our experience is at the same time a priori.

Whatever we see could be other than it is.

Whatever we can describe at all could be other than it is.

There is no a priori order of things.

5.64   Here it can be seen that solipsism, when its implications are followed out strictly, coincides with pure realism. The self of solipsism shrinks to a point without extension, and there remains the reality co-ordinated with it.

5.641   Thus there really is a sense in which philosophy can talk about the self in a non-psychological way.

What brings the self into philosophy is the fact that the "world is my world."

The philosophical self is not the human being, not the human body, or the human soul, with which psychology deals, but rather the metaphysical subject, the limit of the world—not a part of it. . . .

6.3   The exploration of logic means the exploration of *everything that is subject to law*. And outside logic everything is accidental.

6.31   The so-called law of induction cannot possibly be a law of logic, since it is obviously a proposition with sense.—Nor, therefore, can it be an a priori law.

6.32   The law of causality is not a law but the form of a law. . . .

6.341   Newtonian mechanics, for example, imposes a unified form on the description of the world. Let us imagine a white surface with irregular black spots on it. We then say that whatever kind of picture these make, I can always approximate as closely as I wish to the description of it by covering the surface with a sufficiently fine square mesh, and then saying of every square whether it is black or white. In this way I shall have imposed a unified form on the description of the surface. The form is optional, since I could have achieved the same result by using a net with a triangular or hexagonal mesh. Possibly the use of a triangular mesh would have made the description simpler: that is to say, it might be that we could describe the surface more accurately with a coarse triangular mesh than with a fine square mesh (or conversely), and so on. The different nets correspond to different systems for describing the world. Mechanics determines one form of description of the world by saying that all propositions used in the description of the world must be obtained in a given way from a given set of propositions—the axioms of mechanics. It thus supplies the bricks for building the edifice of science, and it says, "Any building that you want to erect, whatever it may be, must somehow be constructed with these bricks, and with these alone." . . .

6.342   And now we can see the relative position of logic and mechanics. (The net might also consist of more than one kind of mesh: e.g. we could use both triangles and hexagons.) The possibility of describing a picture like the one mentioned above with a net of a given form tells us *nothing* about the picture. (For that is true of all such pictures.) But what *does* characterize the picture is that it can be described *completely* by a particular net with a *particular* size of mesh. . . .

6.343   Mechanics is an attempt to construct according to a single plan all the *true* propositions that we need for the description of the world. . . .

6.36   If there were a law of causality, it might be put in the following way: There are laws of nature.
        But of course that cannot be said: it makes itself manifest. . . .

6.362   What can be described can happen too: and what the law of causality is meant to exclude cannot even be described.

6.363   The procedure of induction consists in accepting as true the *simplest* law that can be reconciled with our experiences.

6.3631 This procedure, however, has no logical justification but only a psychological one.
        It is clear that there are no grounds for believing that the simplest eventuality will in fact be realized.

6.36311 It is an hypothesis that the sun will rise tomorrow: and this means that we do not *know* whether it will rise.

6.37   The whole modern conception of the world is founded on the illusion that the so-called laws of nature are the explanations of natural phenomena.

6.372   Thus people today stop at the laws of nature, treating them as something inviolable, just as God and Fate were treated in past ages.
        And in fact both are right and both wrong: though the view of the ancients is clearer in so far as they have a clear and acknowledged terminus, while the modern system tries to make it look as if *everything* were explained.

6.4   All propositions are of equal value.

6.41   The sense of the world must lie outside the world. In the world everything is as it is, and everything happens as it does happen: *in* it no value exists— and if it did exist, it would have no value.
        If there is any value that does have value, it must lie outside the whole sphere of what happens and is the case. For all that happens and is the case is accidental.
        What makes it non-accidental cannot lie *within* the world, since if it did it would itself be accidental.
        It must lie outside the world.

6.42   So too it is impossible for there to be propositions of ethics.
        Propositions can express nothing that is higher.

6.421   It is clear that ethics cannot be put into words.
        Ethics is transcendental.
        (Ethics and aesthetics are one and the same.)

6.422   When an ethical law of the form, "Thou shalt . . . ," is laid down, one's first thought is, "And what if I do not do it?" It is clear, however, that ethics has nothing to do with punishment and reward in the usual sense of the terms. So our question about the *consequences* of an action must be unimportant.—At least those consequences should not be events. For there must be something right about the question we posed. There must indeed be some kind of ethical reward and ethical punishment, but they must reside in the action itself.

(And it is also clear that the reward must be something pleasant and the punishment something unpleasant.)

6.43 If the good or bad exercise of the will does alter the world, it can alter only the limits of the world, not the facts—not what can be expressed by means of language.

In short the effect must be that it becomes an altogether different world. It must, so to speak, wax and wane as a whole.

The world of the happy man is a different one from that of the unhappy man.

6.431 So too at death the world does not alter, but comes to an end.

6.4311 Death is not an event in life: we do not live to experience death.

If we take eternity to mean not infinite temporal duration but timelessness, then eternal life belongs to those who live in the present.

Our life has no end in just the way in which our visual field has no limits.

6.4312 Not only is there no guarantee of the temporal immortality of the human soul, that is to say of its eternal survival after death; but, in any case, this assumption completely fails to accomplish the purpose for which it has always been intended. Or is some riddle solved by my surviving for ever? Is not this eternal life itself as much of a riddle as our present life? The solution of the riddle of life in space and time lies *outside* space and time. . . .

6.432 *How* things are in the world is a matter of complete indifference for what is higher. God does not reveal himself *in* the world. . . .

6.44 It is not *how* things are in the world that is mystical, but *that* it exists.

6.45 To view the world sub specie aeterni is to view it as a whole—a limited whole.

Feeling the world as a limited whole—it is this that is mystical.

6.5 When the answer cannot be put into words, neither can the question be put into words.

The riddle does not exist.

If a question can be framed at all, it is also *possible* to answer it.

6.51 Scepticism is *not* irrefutable, but obviously nonsensical, when it tries to raise doubts where no questions can be asked.

For doubt can exist only where a question exists, a question only where an answer exists, and an answer only where something *can be said*.

6.52 We feel that even when all *possible* scientific questions have been answered, the problems of life remain completely untouched. Of course there are then no questions left, and this itself is the answer.

6.521 The solution of the problem of life is seen in the vanishing of the problem.

(Is not this the reason why those who have found after a long period of doubt that the sense of life became clear to them have then been unable to say what constituted that sense?)

6.522   There are, indeed, things that cannot be put into words. They *make themselves manifest.* They are what is mystical.

6.53   The correct method in philosophy would really be the following: to say nothing except what can be said, i.e. propositions of natural science—i.e. something that has nothing to do with philosophy—and then, whenever someone else wanted to say something metaphysical, to demonstrate to him that he had failed to give a meaning to certain signs in his propositions. Although it would not be satisfying to the other person—he would not have the feeling that we were teaching him philosophy—*this* method would be the only strictly correct one.

6.54   My propositions serve as elucidations in the following way: anyone who understands me eventually recognizes them as nonsensical, when he has used them—as steps—to climb up beyond them. (He must, so to speak, throw away the ladder after he has climbed up it.)

     He must transcend these propositions, and then he will see the world aright.

7   What we cannot speak about we must pass over in silence.

Philosophical Investigations

1. "When they [my elders] named some object, and accordingly moved towards something, I saw this and I grasped that the thing was called by the sound they uttered when they meant to point it out. Their intention was shewn by their bodily movements, as it were the natural language of all peoples: the expression of the face, the play of the eyes, the movement of other parts of the body, and the tone of voice which expresses our state of mind in seeking, having, rejecting, or avoiding something. Thus, as I heard words repeatedly used in their proper places in various sentences, I gradually learnt to understand what objects they signified; and after I had trained my mouth to form these signs, I used them to express my own desires." (Augustine, *Confessions* 1:8)

These words, it seems to me, give us a particular picture of the essence of human language. It is this: the individual words in language name objects—sentences are combinations of such names.——In this picture of language we find the roots of the following idea: Every word has a meaning. This meaning is correlated with the word. It is the object for which the word stands.

Augustine does not speak of there being any difference between kinds of word. If you describe the learning of language in this way you are, I believe, thinking primarily of nouns like "table," "chair," "bread," and of people's names, and only secondarily of the names of certain actions and properties; and of the remaining kinds of word as something that will take care of itself.

Now think of the following use of language: I send someone shopping. I give him a slip marked "five red apples." He takes the slip to the shopkeeper, who opens the drawer marked "apples"; then he looks up the word "red" in a table and finds a colour sample opposite it; then he says the series of cardinal numbers—I assume that he knows them by heart—up to the word "five" and for each number he takes an apple of the same colour as the sample out of the drawer.——It is in this and similar ways that one operates with words.——"But how does he know where and how he is to look up the word 'red' and what he is to do with the word 'five'?"——Well, I assume that he *acts* as I have described. Explanations come to an end somewhere.—But what is the meaning of the word "five"?—No such thing was in question here, only how the world "five" is used.

2. That philosophical concept of meaning has its place in a primitive idea of the way language functions. But one can also say that it is the idea of a language more primitive than ours.

Let us imagine a language for which the description given by Augustine is right. The language is meant to serve for communication between a builder A and an assistant B. A is building with building-stones: there are blocks, pillars, slabs and beams. B has to pass the stones, and that in the order in which A needs them. For this purpose they use a language consisting of the words "block," "pillar," "slab," "beam." A calls them out;—B brings the stone which he has learnt to bring at such-and-such a call.—— Conceive this as a complete primitive language.

From Ludwig Wittgenstein, *Philosophical Investigations* (3d ed.), trans. G.E.M. Anscombe (London: Basil Blackwell & Mott, 1958). Reprinted by permission of the publisher.

3. Augustine, we might say, does describe a system of communication; only not everything that we call language is this system. And one has to say this in many cases where the question arises "Is this an appropriate description or not?" The answer is: "Yes, it is appropriate, but only for this narrowly circumscribed region, not for the whole of what you were claiming to describe."

It is as if someone were to say: "A game consists in moving objects about on a surface according to certain rules . . ."—and we replied: You seem to be thinking of board games, but there are others. You can make your definition correct by expressly restricting it to those games. . . .

6. We could imagine that the language of §2 was the *whole* language of A and B; even the whole language of a tribe. The children are brought up to perform *these* actions, to use *these* words as they do so, and to react in *this* way to the words of others.

An important part of the training will consist in the teacher's pointing to the objects, directing the child's attention to them, and at the same time uttering a word; for instance, the word "slab" as he points to that shape. (I do not want to call this "ostensive definition," because the child cannot as yet *ask* what the name is. I will call it "ostensive teaching of words."— —I say that it will form an important part of the training, because it is so with human beings; not because it could not be imagined otherwise.) This ostensive teaching of words can be said to establish an association between the word and the thing. But what does this mean? Well, it can mean various things; but one very likely thinks first of all that a picture of the object comes before the child's mind when it hears the word. But now, if this does happen—is it the purpose of the word?—Yes, it *can* be the purpose.—I can imagine such a use of words (of series of sounds). (Uttering a word is like striking a note on the keyboard of the imagination.) But in the language of §2 it is *not* the purpose of the words to evoke images. (It may, of course, be discovered that that helps to attain the actual purpose.)

But if the ostensive teaching has this effect,—am I to say that it effects an understanding of the word? Don't you understand the call "Slab!" if you act upon it in such-and-such a way?—Doubtless the ostensive teaching helped to bring this about; but only together with a particular training. With different training the same ostensive teaching of these words would have effected a quite different understanding.

"I set the brake up by connecting up rod and lever."—Yes, given the whole of the rest of the mechanism. Only in conjunction with that is it a brake-lever, and separated from its support it is not even a lever; it may be anything, or nothing.

7. In the practice of the use of language (2) one party calls out the words, the other acts on them. In instruction in the language the following process will occur: the learner *names* the objects; that is, he utters the word when the teacher points to the stone.—And there will be this still simpler exercise: the pupil repeats the words after the teacher— —both of these being processes resembling language.

We can also think of the whole process of using words in (2) as one of those games by means of which children learn their native language. I will call these games "language-games" and will sometimes speak of a primitive language as a language-game.

And the processes of naming the stones and of repeating words after someone might also be called language-games. Think of much of the use of words in games like ring-a-ring-a-roses.

I shall also call the whole, consisting of language and the actions into which it is woven, the "language-game."

8. Let us now look at an expansion of language (2). Besides the four words "block," "pillar," etc., let it contain a series of words used as the shopkeeper in (1) used the numerals (it can be the series of letters of the alphabet); further, let there be two words, which may as well be "there" and "this" (because this roughly indicates their purpose), that are used in connexion with a pointing gesture; and finally a number of colour samples. A gives an order like "d—slab—there." At the same time he shews the assistant a colour sample, and when he says "there" he points to a place on the building site. From the stock of slabs B takes one for each letter of the alphabet up to "d," of the same colour as the sample, and brings them to the place indicated by A.—On other occasions A gives the order "this—there." At "this" he points to a building stone. And so on. . . .

13. When we say: "Every word in language signifies something" we have so far said *nothing whatever*; unless we have explained exactly what distinction we wish to make. (It might be, of course, that we wanted to distinguish the words of language (8) from words "without meaning" such as occur in Lewis Carroll's poems, or words like "Lilliburlero" in songs.)

14. Imagine someone's saying: "*All* tools serve to modify something. Thus the hammer modifies the position of the nail, the saw the shape of the board, and so on."—And what is modified by the rule, the glue-pot, the nails?—"Our knowledge of a thing's length, the temperature of the glue, and the solidity of the box."——Would anything be gained by this assimilation of expressions?—. . .

18. Do not be troubled by the fact that languages (2) and (8) consist only of orders. If you want to say that this shews them to be incomplete, ask yourself whether our language is complete;—whether it was so before the symbolism of chemistry and the notation of the infinitesimal calculus were incorporated in it; for these are, so to speak, suburbs of our language. (And how many houses or streets does it take before a town begins to be a town?) Our language can be seen as an ancient city: a maze of little streets and squares, of old and new houses, and of houses with additions from various periods; and this surrounded by a multitude of new boroughs with straight regular streets and uniform houses.

19. It is easy to imagine a language consisting only of orders and reports in battle.—Or a language consisting only of questions and expressions for answering yes and no. And innumerable others.——And to imagine a language means to imagine a form of life.

But what about this: is the call "Slab!" in example (2) a sentence or a word?—If a word, surely it has not the same meaning as the like-sounding word of our ordinary language, for in §2 it is a call. But if a sentence, it is surely not the elliptical sentence: "Slab!" of our language.——As far as the first question goes you can call "Slab!" a word and also a sentence; perhaps it could be appropriately called a "degenerate sentence" (as one speaks of a degenerate hyperbola); in fact it *is* our "elliptical" sentence.—But that is surely only a shortened form of the sentence "Bring me a slab," and there is no such sentence in example (2).—But why should I not on the contrary have called the sentence "Bring me a slab" a *lengthening* of the sentence "Slab!"—Because if you shout "Slab!" you really mean: "Bring me a slab."—But how do you do this: how do you *mean that* while you *say* "Slab!"? . . .

21. Imagine a language-game in which A asks and B reports the number of slabs or blocks in a pile, or the colours and shapes of the building-stones that are stacked in such-and-such a place.—Such a report might run: "Five slabs." Now what is the differ-

ence between the report or statement "Five slabs" and the order "Five slabs!"?—Well, it is the part which uttering these words plays in the language-game. No doubt the tone of voice and the look with which they are uttered, and much else besides, will also be different. But we could also imagine the tone's being the same—for an order and a report can be spoken in a *variety* of tones of voice and with various expressions of face—the difference being only in the application. . . .

23. But how many kinds of sentence are there? Say assertion, question, and command?—There are *countless* kinds: countless different kinds of use of what we call "symbols," "words," "sentences." And this multiplicity is not something fixed, given once for all; but new types of language, new language-games, as we may say, come into existence, and others become obsolete and get forgotten. (We can get a *rough picture* of this from the changes in mathematics.)

Here the term "language-*game*" is meant to bring into prominence the fact that the *speaking* of language is part of an activity, or of a form of life.

Review the multiplicity of language-games in the following examples, and in others:

Giving orders, and obeying them—
Describing the appearance of an object, or giving its measurements—
Constructing an object from a description (a drawing)—
Reporting an event—
Speculating about an event—
Forming and testing a hypothesis—
Presenting the results of an experiment in tables and diagrams—
Making up a story; and reading it—
Play-acting—
Singing catches—
Guessing riddles—
Making a joke; telling it—
Solving a problem in practical arithmetic—
Translating from one language into another—
Asking, thanking, cursing, greeting, praying.

—It is interesting to compare the multiplicity of the tools in language and of the ways they are used, the multiplicity of kinds of word and sentence, with what logicians have said about the structure of language. (Including the author of the *Tractatus Logico-Philosophicus*.). . .

46. What lies behind the idea that names really signify simples?—

Socrates says in the Theaetetus: "If I make no mistake, I have heard some people say this: there is no definition of the primary elements—so to speak —out of which we and everything else are composed; for everything that exists in its own right can only be *named*, no other determination is possible, neither that it *is* nor that it is *not*. . . . But what exists in its own right has to be . . . named without any other determination. In consequence it is impossible to give an account of any primary element; for it, nothing is possible but the bare name; its name is all it has. But just as what consists of these primary elements is itself complex, so the names of the elements become descriptive language by being compounded together. For the essence of speech is the composition of names."

Both Russell's "individuals" and my "objects" (*Tractatus Logico-Philosophicus*) were such primary elements.

47. But what are the simple constituent parts of which reality is composed?—What are the simple constituent parts of a chair?—The bits of wood of which it is made? Or the molecules, or the atoms?—"Simple" means: not composite. And here the point is: in what sense "composite"? It makes no sense at all to speak absolutely of the "simple parts of a chair."

Again: Does my visual image of this tree, of this chair, consist of parts? And what are its simple component parts? Multi-colouredness is one kind of complexity; another is, for example, that of a broken outline composed of straight bits. And a curve can be said to be composed of an ascending and a descending segment. . . .

To the *philosophical* question: "Is the visual image of this tree composite, and what are its component parts?" the correct answer is: "That depends on what you understand by 'composite.'" (And that is of course not an answer but a rejection of the question.). . .

65. Here we come up against the great question that lies behind all these considerations.—For someone might object against me: "You take the easy way out! You talk about all sorts of language-games, but have nowhere said what the essence of a language-game, and hence of language, is: what is common to all these activities, and what makes them into language or parts of language. So you let yourself off the very part of the investigation that once gave you yourself most headache, the part about the *general form of propositions* and of language."

And this is true.—Instead of producing something common to all that we call language, I am saying that these phenomena have no one thing in common which makes us use the same word for all,—but that they are *related* to one another in many different ways. And it is because of this relationship, or these relationships, that we call them all "language." I will try to explain this.

66. Consider for example the proceedings that we call "games." I mean board-games, card-games, ball-games, Olympic games, and so on. What is common to them all?—Don't say: "There *must* be something common, or they would not be called 'games'"—but *look and see* whether there is anything common to all.—For if you look at them you will not see something that is common to *all*, but similarities, relationships, and a whole series of them at that. To repeat: don't think, but look!—Look for example at board-games, with their multifarious relationships. Now pass to card-games; here you find many correspondences with the first group, but many common features drop out, and others appear. When we pass next to ball-games, much that is common is retained, but much is lost.—Are they all "amusing"? Compare chess with noughts and crosses [tic-tac-toe]. Or is there always winning and losing, or competition between players? Think of patience. In ball games there is winning and losing; but when a child throws his ball at the wall and catches it again, this feature has disappeared. Look at the parts played by skill and luck; and at the difference between skill in chess and skill in tennis. Think now of games like ring-a-ring-a-roses; here is the element of amusement, but how many other characteristic features have disappeared! And we can go through the many, many other groups of games in the same way; can see how similarities crop up and disappear.

And the result of this examination is: we see a complicated network of similarities overlapping and criss-crossing: sometimes overall similarities, sometimes similarities of detail.

67. I can think of no better expression to characterize these similarities than "family resemblances"; for the various resemblances between members of a family: build, features, colour of eyes, gait, temperament, etc. etc. overlap and criss-cross in the same way.—And I shall say: "games" form a family. . . .

70. "But if the concept 'game' is uncircumscribed like that, you don't really know what you mean by a 'game.' "——When I give the description: "The ground was quite covered with plants"—do you want to say I don't know what I am talking about until I can give a definition of a plant?

My meaning would be explained by, say, a drawing and the words "The ground looked roughly like this." Perhaps I even say "it looked *exactly* like this."—Then were just *this* grass and *these* leaves there, arranged just like this? No, that is not what it means. And I should not accept any picture as exact in *this* sense.

71. One might say that the concept "game" is a concept with blurred edges.—"But is a blurred concept a concept at all?"—Is an indistinct photograph a picture of a person at all? Is it even always an advantage to replace an indistinct picture by a sharp one? Isn't the indistinct one often exactly what we need?. . .

Is it senseless to say: "Stand roughly there"? Suppose that I were standing with someone in a city square and said that. As I say it I do not draw any kind of boundary, but perhaps point with my hand—as if I were indicating a particular *spot*. And this is just how one might explain to someone what a game is. One gives examples and intends them to be taken in a particular way.—I do not, however, mean by this that he is supposed to see in those examples that common thing which I—for some reason—was unable to express; but that he is now to *employ* those examples in a particular way. Here giving examples is not an *indirect* means of explaining—in default of a better. For any general definition can be misunderstood too. The point is that *this* is how we play the game. (I mean the language-game with the word "game.") . . .

75. What does it mean to know what a game is? What does it mean, to know it and not be able to say it? Is this knowledge somehow equivalent to an unformulated definition? So that if it were formulated I should be able to recognize it as the expression of my knowledge? Isn't my knowledge, my concept of a game, completely expressed in the explanations that I could give? That is, in my describing examples of various kinds of game; shewing how all sorts of other games can be constructed on the analogy of these; saying that I should scarcely include this or this among games; and so on. . . .

81. F.P. Ramsey once emphasized in conversation with me that logic was a "normative science." I do not know exactly what he had in mind, but it was doubtless closely related to what only dawned on me later: namely, that in philosophy we often *compare* the use of words with games and calculi which have fixed rules, but cannot say that someone who is using language *must* be playing such a game.——But if you say that our languages only *approximate* to such calculi you are standing on the very brink of a misunderstanding. For then it may look as if what we were talking about were an *ideal* language. As if our logic were, so to speak, a logic for a vacuum.—Whereas logic does not treat of language—or of thought—in the sense in which a natural science treats of a natural phenomenon, and the most that can be said is that we *construct* ideal languages. But here the word "ideal" is liable to mislead, for it sounds as if these languages were better, more perfect, than our everyday language; and as if it took the logician to shew people at last what a proper sentence looked like.

All this, however, can only appear in the right light when one has attained greater clarity about the concepts of understanding, meaning, and thinking. For it will then also become clear what can lead us (and did lead me) to think that if anyone utters a sentence and *means* or *understands* it he is operating a calculus according to definite rules. . . .

89. These considerations bring us up to the problem: In what sense is logic something sublime?

For there seemed to pertain to logic a peculiar depth—a universal significance. Logic lay, it seemed, at the bottom of all the sciences.—For logical investigation explores the nature of all things. It seeks to see to the bottom of things and is not meant to concern itself whether what actually happens is this or that.——It takes its rise, not from an interest in the facts of nature, nor from a need to grasp causal connexions: but from an urge to understand the basis, or essence, of everything empirical. Not, however, as if to this end we had to hunt out new facts; it is, rather, of the essence of our investigation that we do not seek to learn anything *new* by it. We want to *understand* something that is already in plain view. For *this* is what we seem in some sense not to understand.

Augustine says in the *Confessions* "quid est ergo tempus? si nemo ex me quaerat scio; si quaerenti explicare velim, nescio" [What then is time? If no one asks me, I know; if I want to explain it to a questioner, I do not know.].—This could not be said about a question of natural science ("What is the specific gravity of hydrogen?" for instance). Something that we know when no one asks us, but no longer know when we are supposed to give an account of it, is something that we need to *remind* ourselves of. (And it is obviously something of which for some reason it is difficult to remind oneself.)

90. We feel as if we had to *penetrate* phenomena: our investigation, however, is directed not towards phenomena, but, as one might say, towards the "*possibilities*" of phenomena. We remind ourselves, that is to say, of the *kind of statement* that we make about phenomena. Thus Augustine recalls to mind the different statements that are made about the duration, past present or future, of events. (These are, of course, not *philosophical* statements about time, the past, the present and the future.)

Our investigation is therefore a grammatical one. Such an investigation sheds light on our problem by clearing misunderstandings away. Misunderstandings concerning the use of words, caused, among other things, by certain analogies between the forms of expression in different regions of language.—Some of them can be removed by substituting one form of expression for another; this may be called an "analysis" of our forms of expression, for the process is sometimes like one of taking a thing apart.

91. But now it may come to look as if there were something like a final analysis of our forms of language, and so a *single* completely resolved form of every expression. That is, as if our usual forms of expression were, essentially, unanalysed; as if there were something hidden in them that had to be brought to light. When this is done the expression is completely clarified and our problem solved.

It can also be put like this: we eliminate misunderstandings by making our expressions more exact; but now it may look as if we were moving towards a particular state, a state of complete exactness; and as if this were the real goal of our investigation. . . .

98. On the one hand it is clear that every sentence in our language "is in order as it is." That is to say, we are not *striving after* an ideal, as if our ordinary vague sentences had not yet got a quite unexceptionable sense, and a perfect language awaited con-

struction by us.—On the other hand it seems clear that where there is sense there must be perfect order.——So there must be perfect order even in the vaguest sentence.

99. The sense of a sentence—one would like to say—may, of course, leave this or that open, but the sentence must nevertheless have *a* definite sense. An indefinite sense—that would really not be a sense *at all*.—This is like: An indefinite boundary is not really a boundary at all. Here one thinks perhaps: if I say "I have locked the man up fast in the room—there is only one door left open"—then I simply haven't locked him in at all; his being locked in is a sham. One would be inclined to say here: "You haven't done anything at all." An enclosure with a hole in it is as good as *none*.—But is that true?

100. "But still, it isn't a game, if there is some vagueness *in the rules*."—But *does* this prevent its being a game?—"Perhaps you'll call it a game, but at any rate it certainly isn't a perfect game." This means: it has impurities, and what I am interested in at present is the pure article.—But I want to say: we misunderstood the role of the ideal in our language. That is to say: we too should call it a game, only we are dazzled by the ideal and therefore fail to see the actual use of the word "game" clearly. . . .

108. We see that what we call "sentence" and "language" has not the formal unity that I imagined, but is the family of structures more or less related to one another.—— But what becomes of logic now? Its rigour seems to be giving way here.—But in that case doesn't logic altogether disappear?—For how can it lose its rigour? Of course not by our bargaining any of its rigour out of it.—The *preconceived idea* of crystalline purity can only be removed by turning our whole examination round. (One might say: the axis of reference of our examination must be rotated, but about the fixed point of our real need.)

The philosophy of logic speaks of sentences and words in exactly the sense in which we speak of them in ordinary life when we say e.g. "Here is a Chinese sentence," or "No, that only looks like writing; it is actually just an ornament" and so on.

We are talking about the spatial and temporal phenomenon of language, not about some non-spatial, nontemporal phantasm. [Note in margin: Only it is possible to be interested in a phenomenon in a variety of ways]. But we talk about it as we do about the pieces in chess when we are stating the rules of the game, not describing their physical properties.

The question "What is a word really?" is analogous to "What is a piece in chess?"

109. It was true to say that our considerations could not be scientific ones. . . . We must do away with all *explanation*, and description alone must take its place. And this description gets its light, that is to say its purpose, from the philosophical problems. These are, of course, not empirical problems; they are solved, rather, by looking into the workings of our language, and that in such a way as to make us recognize those workings: *in despite of* an urge to misunderstand them. The problems are solved, not by giving new information, but by arranging what we have always known. Philosophy is a battle against the bewitchment of our intelligence by means of language. . . .

119. The results of philosophy are the uncovering of one or another piece of plain nonsense and of bumps that the understanding has got by running its head up against the limits of language. These bumps make us see the value of the discovery. . . .

143. Let us now examine the following kind of language-game: when A gives an order B has to write down series of signs according to a certain formation rule.

The first of these series is meant to be that of the natural numbers in decimal notation.—How does he get to understand this notation?—First of all series of numbers will be written down for him and he will be required to copy them. (Do not balk at the expression "series of numbers"; it is not being used wrongly here.) And here already there is a normal and an abnormal learner's reaction.—At first perhaps we guide his hand in writing out the series 0 to 9; but then the *possibility of getting him to understand* will depend on his going on to write it down independently.—And here we can imagine, e.g., that he does copy the figures independently, but not in the right order: he writes sometimes one sometimes another at random. And then communication stops at *that* point.—Or again, he makes "*mistakes*" in the order.—The difference between this and the first case will of course be one of frequency.—Or he makes a *systematic* mistake; for example, he copies every other number, or he copies the series 0, 1, 2, 3, 4, 5, . . . like this: 1, 0, 3, 2, 5, 4, ... Here we shall almost be tempted to say that he has understood *wrong*.

Notice, however, that there is no sharp distinction between a random mistake and a systematic one. That is, between what you are inclined to call "random" and what "systematic."

Perhaps it is possible to wean him from the systematic mistake (as from a bad habit). Or perhaps one accepts his way of copying and tries to teach him ours as an offshoot, a variant of his.—And here too our pupil's capacity to learn may come to an end. . . .

145. Suppose the pupil now writes the series 0 to 9 to our satisfaction.—And this will only be the case when he is often successful, not if he does it right once in a hundred attempts. Now I continue the series and draw his attention to the recurrence of the first series in the units; and then to its recurrence in the tens. (Which only means that I use particular emphases, underline figures, write them one under another in such-and-such ways, and similar things.)—And now at some point he continues the series independently—or he does not.—But why do you say that? so much is obvious!—Of course; I only wished to say: the effect of any further *explanation* depends on his *reaction*.

Now, however, let us suppose that after some efforts on the teacher's part he continues the series correctly, that is, as we do it. So now we can say he has mastered the system.—But how far need he continue the series for us to have the right to say that? Clearly you cannot state a limit here.

146. Suppose I now ask: "Has he understood the system where he continues the series to the hundredth place?" Or—if I should not speak of "understanding" in connection with our primitive language-game: Has he got the system, if he continues the series correctly so far?—Perhaps you will say here: to have got the system (or, again, to understand it) can't consist in continuing the series up to *this* or *that* number: *that* is only applying one's understanding. The understanding itself is a state which is the *source* of the correct use.

What is one really thinking of here? Isn't one thinking of the derivation of a series from its algebraic formula? Or at least of something analogous? . . . The point is, we can think of more than *one* application of an algebraic formula; and every type of application can in turn be formulated algebraically; but naturally this does not get us any further.—The application is still a criterion of understanding. . . .

150. The grammar of the word "knows" is evidently closely related to that of "can," "is able to." But also closely related to that of "understands." ("Mastery" of a technique,)

151. But there is also *this* use of the word "to know": we say "Now I know!"—and similarly "Now I can do it!" and "Now I understand!"

Let us imagine the following example: A writes series of numbers down; B watches him and tries to find a law for the sequence of numbers. If he succeeds he exclaims: "Now I can go on!"—So this capacity, this understanding, is something that makes its appearance in a moment. So let us try and see what it is that makes its appearance here.—A has written down the numbers 1, 5, 11, 19, 29; at this point B says he knows how to go on. What happened here? Various things may have happened; for example, while A was slowly putting one number after another, B was occupied with trying various algebraic formulae on the numbers which had been written down. After A had written the number 19 B tried the formula $a_n = n^2 + n - 1$; and the next number confirmed his hypothesis.

Or again, B does not think of formulae. He watches A writing his numbers down with a certain feeling of tension, and all sorts of vague thoughts go through his head. Finally he asks himself: "What is the series of differences?" He finds the series 4, 6, 8, 10 and says: Now I can go on.

Or he watches and says "Yes, I know *that* series"—and continues it, just as he would have done if A had written down the series 1, 3, 5, 7, 9.—Or he says nothing at all and simply continues the series. Perhaps he had what may be called the sensation "that's easy!" (Such a sensation is, for example, that of a light quick intake of breath, as when one is slightly startled.)

152. But are the processes which I have described here *understanding*?

"B understands the principle of the series" surely doesn't mean simply: the formula $a_n = \ldots$ " occurs to B. For it is perfectly imaginable that the formula should occur to him and that he should nevertheless not understand. "He understands" must have more in it than: the formula occurs to him. And equally, more than any of those more or less characteristic *accompaniments* or manifestations of understanding. . . .

179. Let us return to our case (151). It is clear that we should not say B had the right to say the words "Now I know how to go on," just because he thought of the formula— unless experience shewed that there was a connexion between thinking of the formula—saying it, writing it down—and actually continuing the series. And obviously such a connexion does exist.—And now one might think that the sentence "I can go on" meant "I have an experience which I know empirically to lead to the continuation of the series." But does B mean that when he says he can go on? Does that sentence come to his mind, or is he ready to produce it in explanation of what he meant?

(a) "Understanding a word": a state. But a *mental* state?—Depression, excitement, pain, are called mental states. Carry out a grammatical investigation as follows: we say

"He was depressed the whole day."

"He was in great excitement the whole day."

"He has been in continuous pain since yesterday."—

We also say "Since yesterday I have understood this word." "Continuously," though?—To be sure, one can speak of an interruption of understanding. But in what cases? Compare: "When did your pains get less?" and "When did you stop understanding that word?"

(b) Suppose it were asked: "*When* do you know how to play chess? All the time? or just while you are making a move? And the *whole* of chess during each move?"—How queer that knowing how to play chess should take such a short time, and a game so much longer!

No. The words "Now I know how to go on" were correctly used when he thought of the formula: that is, given such circumstances as that he had learnt algebra, had used such formulae before.—But that does not mean that his statement is only short for a description of all the circumstances which constitute the scene for our language-game.—Think how we learn to use the expressions "Now I know how to go on," "Now I can go on" and others; in what family of language-games we learn their use.

We can also imagine the case where nothing at all occurred in B's mind except that he suddenly said "Now I know how to go on"—perhaps with a feeling of relief; and that he did in fact go on working out the series without using the formula. And in this case too we should say—in certain circumstances—that he did know how to go on.

180. *This is how these words are used.* It would be quite misleading, in this last case, for instance, to call the words a "description of a mental state."—One might rather call them a "signal"; and we judge whether it was rightly employed by what he goes on to do. . . .

185. Let us return to our example (143). Now—judged by the usual criteria—the pupil has mastered the series of natural numbers. Next we teach him to write down other series of cardinal numbers and get him to the point of writing down series of the form

$$o, n, 2n, 3n, \text{etc.}$$

at an order of the form "$+n$"; so at the order "$+1$" he writes down the series of natural numbers.—Let us suppose we have done exercises and given him tests up to 1000.

Now we get the pupil to continue a series (say + 2) beyond 1000—and he writes 1000, 1004, 1008, 1012.

We say to him: "Look what you've done!"—He doesn't understand. We say: "You were meant to add *two*: look how you begin the series!"—He answers: "Yes, isn't it right? I thought that was how I was *meant* to do it."——Or suppose he pointed to the series and said: "But I went on in the same way."—It would now be no use to say: "But can't you see . . . ?"—and repeat the old examples and explanations.—In such a case we might say, perhaps: It comes natural to this person to understand our order with our explanations as *we* should understand the order: "Add 2 up to 1000, 4 up to 2000, 6 up to 3000 and so on."

Such a case would present similarities with one in which a person naturally reacted to the gesture of pointing with the hand by looking in the direction of the line from finger-tip to wrist, not from wrist to finger-tip.

186. "What you are saying, then, comes to this: a new insight—intuition—is needed at every step to carry out the order "$+n$" correctly."—To carry it out correctly! How is it decided what is the right step to take at any particular stage?—"The right step is the one that accords with the order—as it was *meant*."—So when you gave the order + 2 you meant that he was to write 1002 after 1000—and did you also mean that he should write 1868 after 1866, and 100036 after 100034, and so on—an infinite number of such propositions?—"No: what I meant was, that he should write the next but one number after *every* number that he wrote; and from this all those propositions follow in turn."—But that is just what is in question: what, at any stage, does follow from that sentence. Or, again, what, at any stage we are to call "being in accord" with that sentence (and with the *mean*-ing you then put into the sentence—whatever that may

have consisted in). It would almost be more correct to say, not that an intuition was needed at every stage, but that a new decision was needed at every stage.

187. "But I already knew, at the time when I gave the order, that he ought to write 1002 after 1000."—Certainly; and you can also say you *meant* it then; only you should not let yourself be misled by the grammar of the words "know" and "mean." For you don't want to say that you thought of the step from 1000 to 1002 at that time—and even if you did think of this step, still you did not think of other ones. When you said "I already knew at the time . . ." that meant something like: "If I had then been asked what number should be written after 1000, I should have replied '1002.'" And that I don't doubt. This assumption is rather of the same kind as: "If he had fallen into the water then, I should have jumped in after him."—Now, what was wrong with your idea?

188. Here I should first of all like to say: your idea was that that act of meaning the order had in its own way already traversed all those steps: that when you meant it your mind as it were flew ahead and took all the steps before you physically arrived at this or that one.

Thus you were inclined to use such expressions as: "The steps are *really* already taken, even before I take them in writing or orally or in thought." And it seemed as if they were in some *unique* way predetermined, anticipated—as only the act of meaning can anticipate reality. . . .

198. "But how can a rule shew me what I have to do at *this* point? Whatever I do is, on some interpretation, in accord with the rule."—That is not what we ought to say, but rather: any interpretation still hangs in the air along with what it interprets, and cannot give it any support. Interpretations by themselves do not determine meaning.

"Then can whatever I do be brought into accord with the rule?"—Let me ask this: what has the expression of a rule—say a sign-post—got to do with my actions? What sort of connexion is there here?—Well, perhaps this one: I have been trained to react to this sign in a particular way, and now I do so react to it.

But that is only to give a causal connexion; to tell how it has come about that we now go by the sign-post; not what this going-by-the-sign really consists in. On the contrary; I have further indicated that a person goes by a sign-post only in so far as there exists a regular use of sign-posts, a custom.

199. Is what we call "obeying a rule" something that it would be possible for only *one* man to do, and to do only *once* in his life?—This is of course a note on the grammar of the expression "to obey a rule."

It is not possible that there should have been only one occasion on which someone obeyed a rule. It is not possible that there should have been only one occasion on which a report was made, an order given or understood; and so on.—To obey a rule, to make a report, to give an order, to play a game of chess, are *customs* (uses, institutions).

To understand a sentence means to understand a language. To understand a language means to be master of a technique. . . .

201. This was our paradox: no course of action could be determined by a rule, because every course of action can be made out to accord with the rule. The answer was: if everything can be made out to accord with the rule, then it can also be made out to conflict with it. And so there would be neither accord nor conflict here.

It can be seen that there is a misunderstanding here from the mere fact that in the course of our argument we give one interpretation after another; as if each one contented us at least for a moment, until we thought of yet another standing behind it.

What this shews is that there is a way of grasping a rule which is *not* an *interpretation*, but which is exhibited in what we call "obeying the rule" and "going against it" in actual cases.

Hence there is an inclination to say: every action according to the rule is an interpretation. But we ought to restrict the term "interpretation" to the substitution of one expression of the rule for another.

202. And hence also "obeying a rule" is a practice. And to *think* one is obeying a rule is not to obey a rule. Hence it is not possible to obey a rule "privately": otherwise thinking one was obeying a rule would be the same thing as obeying it. . . .

205. "But it is just the queer thing about *intention*, about the mental process, that the existence of a custom, of a technique, is not necessary to it. That, for example, it is imaginable that two people should play chess in a world in which otherwise no games existed; and even that they should begin a game of chess—and then be interrupted."

But isn't chess defined by its rules? And how are these rules present in the mind of the person who is intending to play chess?

206. Following a rule is analogous to obeying an order. We are trained to do so; we react to an order in a particular way. But what if one person reacts in one way and another in another to the order and the training? Which one is right?

Suppose you came as an explorer into an unknown country with a language quite strange to you. In what circumstances would you say that the people there gave orders, understood them, obeyed them, rebelled against them, and so on?

The common behaviour of mankind is the system of reference by means of which we interpret an unknown language.

207. Let us imagine that the people in that country carried on the usual human activities and in the course of them employed, apparently, an articulate language. If we watch their behaviour we find it intelligible, it seems 'logical'. But when we try to learn their language we find it impossible to do so. For there is no regular connexion between what they say, the sounds they make, and their actions; but still these sounds are not superfluous, for if we gag one of the people, it has the same consequences as with us; without the sounds their actions fall into confusion—as I feel like putting it.

Are we to say that these people have a language: orders, reports, and the rest?

There is not enough regularity for us to call it "language."

208. Then am I defining "order" and "rule" by means of "regularity"?—How do I explain the meaning of "regular," "uniform," "same" to anyone?—I shall explain these words to someone who, say, only speaks French by means of the corresponding French words. But if a person has not yet got the *concepts*, I shall teach him to use the words by means of *examples* and by *practice*.—And when I do this I do not communicate less to him than I know myself.

In the course of this teaching I shall shew him the same colours, the same lengths, the same shapes, I shall make him find them and produce them, and so on. I shall, for instance, get him to continue an ornamental pattern uniformly when told to do so.— And also to continue progressions. And so, for example, when given: . . . . . . to go on: . . . .

I do it, he does it after me; and I influence him by expressions of agreement, rejection, expectation, encouragement. I let him go his way, or hold him back; and so on.

Imagine witnessing such teaching. None of the words would be explained by means of itself; there would be no logical circle.

The expressions "and so on," "and so on ad infinitum" are also explained in this teaching. A gesture, among other things, might serve this purpose. The gesture that means "go on like this," or "and so on" has a function comparable to that of pointing to an object or a place. . . .

Teaching which is not meant to apply to anything but the examples given is different from that which "*points beyond*" them. . . .

217. "How am I able to obey a rule?—if this is not a question about causes, then it is about the justification for my following the rule in the way I do.

If I have exhausted the justifications I have reached bedrock, and my spade is turned. Then I am inclined to say: "this is simply what I do."

(Remember that we sometimes demand definitions for the sake not of their content, but of their form. Our requirement is an architectural one; the definition a kind of ornamental coping that supports nothing.). . .

219. "All the steps are really already taken" means: I no longer have any choice. The rule, once stamped with a particular meaning, traces the lines along which it is to be followed through the whole of space.— —But if something of this sort really were the case, how would it help?

No; my description only made sense if it was to be understood symbolically.—I should have said: *This is how it strikes me.*

When I obey a rule, I do not choose.

I obey the rule *blindly*. . . .

238. The rule can only seem to me to produce all its consequences in advance if I draw them as a *matter of course*. As much as it is a matter of course for me to call this colour "blue." (Criteria for the fact that something is "a matter of course" for me.)

239. How is he to know what colour he is to pick out when he hears "red"?—Quite simple: he is to take the colour whose image occurs to him when he hears the word.—But how is he to know which colour it is "whose image occurs to him"? Is a further criterion needed for that? (There is indeed such a procedure as choosing the colour which occurs to one when one hears the word ". . .")

" 'Red' means the colour that occurs to me when I hear the word 'red' "—would be a *definition*. Not an explanation of *what it is* to use a word as a name.

240. Disputes do not break out (among mathematicians, say) over the question whether a rule has been obeyed or not. People don't come to blows over it, for example. That is part of the framework on which the working of our language is based (for example, in giving descriptions).

241. "So you are saying that human agreement decides what is true and what is false?"—It is what human beings *say* that is true and false; and they agree in the *language* they use. That is not agreement in opinions but in form of life.

242. If language is to be a means of communication there must be agreement not only in definitions but also (queer as this may sound) in judgments. This seems to abolish logic, but does not do so.—It is one thing to describe methods of measurement, and another to obtain and state results of measurement. But what we call "measuring" is partly determined by a certain constancy in results of measurement. . . .

244. How do words *refer* to sensations?—There doesn't seem to be any problem here; don't we talk about sensations every day, and give them names? But how is the connexion between the name and the thing named set up? This question is the same as: how does a human being learn the meaning of the names of sensations?—of the word "pain" for example. Here is one possibility: words are connected with the primitive, the

natural, expressions of the sensation and used in their place. A child has hurt himself and he cries; and then adults talk to him and teach him exclamations and, later, sentences. They teach the child new pain-behaviour.

"So you are saying that the word 'pain' really means crying?"—On the contrary: the verbal expression of pain replaces crying and does not describe it. . . .

246. In what sense are my sensations *private?*—Well, only I can know whether I am really in pain; another person can only surmise it.—In one way this is wrong, and in another nonsense. If we are using the word "to know" as it is normally used (and how else are we to use it?), then other people very often know when I am in pain.—Yes, but all the same not with the certainty with which I know it myself!—It can't be said of me at all (except perhaps as a joke) that I *know* I am in pain. What is it supposed to mean—except perhaps that I *am* in pain?

Other people cannot be said to learn of my sensations *only* from my behaviour,—for I cannot be said to learn of them. I *have* them.

The truth is: it makes sense to say about other people that they doubt whether I am in pain; but not to say it about myself. . . .

257. "What would it be like if human beings shewed no outward signs of pain (did not groan, grimace, etc.)? Then it would be impossible to teach a child the use of the word 'tooth-ache.' "—Well, let's assume the child is a genius and itself invents a name for the sensation!—But then, of course, he couldn't make himself understood when he used the word.—So does he understand the name, without being able to explain its meaning to anyone?—But what does it mean to say that he has "named his pain"?—How has he done this naming of pain?! And whatever he did, what was its purpose?—When one says "He gave a name to his sensation" one forgets that a great deal of stage-setting in the language is presupposed if the mere act of naming is to make sense. And when we speak of someone's having given a name to pain, what is presupposed is the existence of the grammar of the word "pain"; it shews the post where the new word is stationed.

258. Let us imagine the following case. I want to keep a diary about the recurrence of a certain sensation. To this end I associate it with the sign "S" and write this sign in a calendar for every day on which I have the sensation.— —I will remark first of all that a definition of the sign cannot be formulated.—But still I can give myself a kind of ostensive definition.—How? Can I point to the sensation? Not in the ordinary sense. But I speak, or write the sign down, and at the same time I concentrate my attention on the sensation—and so, as it were, point to it inwardly.—But what is this ceremony for? for that is all it seems to be! A definition surely serves to establish the meaning of a sign.—Well, that is done precisely by the concentrating of my attention; for in this way I impress on myself the connexion between the sign and the sensation.—But "I impress it on myself" can only mean: this process brings it about that I remember the connexion *right* in the future. But in the present case I have no criterion of correctness. One would like to say: whatever is going to seem right to me is right. And that only means that here we can't talk about "right." . . .

304. "But you will surely admit that there is a difference between pain-behaviour accompanied by pain and pain-behaviour without any pain?"—Admit it? What greater difference could there be?—"And yet you again and again reach the conclusion that the sensation itself is a *nothing*."—Not at all. It is not a *something*, but not a *nothing* either! The conclusion was only that a nothing would serve just as well as a something about

which nothing could be said. We have only rejected the grammar which tries to force itself on us here.

The paradox disappears only if we make a radical break with the idea that language always functions in one way, always serves the same purpose: to convey thoughts— which may be about houses, pains, good and evil, or anything else you please.

305. "But you surely cannot deny that, for example, in remembering, an inner process takes place."—What gives the impression that we want to deny anything? When one says "Still, an inner process does take place here"—one wants to go on: "After all, you *see* it." And it is this inner process that one means by the word "remembering."—The impression that we wanted to deny something arises from our setting our faces against the picture of the "inner process." What we deny is that the picture of the inner process gives us the correct idea of the use of the word "to remember." We say that this picture with its ramifications stands in the way of our seeing the use of the word as it is. . . .

309. What is your aim in philosophy?—To shew the fly the way out of the fly-bottle. . . .

SELECTED BIBLIOGRAPHY

Wittgenstein, Ludwig. *Philosophical Investigations*, 3d ed. Trans. G.E.M. Anscombe. New York: Macmillan, 1958.

_____. *Tractatus Logico-Philosophicus*. Trans. D.F. Pears and B.F. McGuiness. London: Routledge & Kegan Paul, 1961.

Ayer, A.J. *Wittgenstein*. New York: Random House, 1985.

Baker, G.P., and P.M.S. Hacker. *Wittgenstein: Understanding and Meaning*. Chicago: University of Chicago Press, 1980.

Black, Max. *A Companion to Wittgenstein's "Tractatus."* Ithaca, N.Y.: Cornell University Press, 1964.

Fogelin, Robert J. *Wittgenstein*. Boston: Routledge & Kegan Paul, 1976.

Grayling, A.C. *Wittgenstein*. New York: Oxford University Press, 1988.

Hallett, Garth. *A Companion to Wittgenstein's "Philosophical Investigations."* Ithaca, N.Y.: Cornell University Press, 1977.

Hartnack, Justus. *Wittgenstein and Modern Philosophy*. Trans. Maurice Cranston. New York: NYU Press, 1965.

Kenny, Anthony. *Wittgenstein*. Cambridge, Mass.: Harvard University Press, 1973.

Kripke, Saul A. *Wittgenstein on Rules and Private Language*. Cambridge, Mass.: Harvard University Press, 1982.

Mounce, H.O. *Wittgenstein's "Tractatus": An Introduction*. Chicago: University of Chicago Press, 1981.

Pears, David. *The False Prison* (2 vols.). New York: Oxford University Press, 1987, 1988.

_____. *Ludwig Wittgenstein*. New York: Viking Penguin, 1970.

Russell, Bertrand Arthur William. *Logic and Knowledge*. Ed. Robert Marsh. London: Allen & Unwin, 1956.

Simone de Beauvoir

Simone de Beauvoir (1908–1986) was born in Paris of a wealthy family whose fortunes were in decline. Unaware of any financial strains until adolescence, Simone was very happy in her early years. As she confesses, she was a "dutiful daughter" who basked in the love of her mother and God. Her parents emphasized her education, putting ever more value on her spiritual qualities and intellectual accomplishments as the family's material circumstances worsened. Simone made a distinction early on between the spiritual and the intellectual, reflecting, no doubt, the tension between her mother's deep Catholicism and her father's religious skepticism.

With adolescence Simone came to the realization that God, who had seemed such a palpable presence earlier in her life, did not exist and that she was therefore entirely mortal, condemned to die. This rebellion against her mother's influence was soon matched by an increasing rejection of her father's very conservative politics and values. A troubling, lonely period in Beauvoir's life, she took solace in the companionship of "Zaza," Elizabeth Mabille, her best friend, and by dedicating her life to the service of humanity, initially through a movement to bring intellectual culture to the working classes. When her father announced bitterly that since he could afford no dowry, his daughters could not marry and would have to work for their living, he simply affirmed a decision Simone had made long before: she would never marry, never have children—she would write.

Beauvoir was a brilliant student and took her degree in literature and philosophy from the Sorbonne in 1927. She began practice teaching in philosophy at a boys' *lycée* in Paris (the first woman to do so) and then decided to pursue postgraduate work in philosophy. She entered the *École Normale Supérieure*, where she quickly established herself as an estimable colleague among the cream of the French educational system. One of the star pupils and a ringleader of the young intellectuals at the school was Jean-Paul Sartre, three years Beauvoir's senior, more worldly, very self-assured, and utterly convinced of his literary calling. When Sartre and his colleague Paul Nizan invited Beauvoir to study with them for the final examination, Sartre and Beauvoir became inseparable almost at once. They finished first and second in the examinations (Sartre was first, but he'd already failed once). Wrote Beauvoir, "Sartre corresponded exactly to the dream companion I had longed for since I was fifteen: he was the double in whom I found all my burning aspirations raised to the pitch of incandescence. I should always be able to share everything with him" (Memoirs 366).

Beauvoir and Sartre's relationship endured throughout their lives. They never married, they each engaged in serious relations with other people, yet they remained steady companions and constant coworkers. Sartre achieved greater immediate literary and philosophical fame, but as time progresses, Beauvoir is emerging ever more clearly as a major figure in Western letters.

After her studies, Beauvoir taught philosophy at several schools, first in Marseilles, then in Rouen, and finally in Paris. And she wrote. Her first novel, completed in 1932, was never published. A collection of short stories, *When Things of the Spirit Come First*, was also rejected by several publishers, though it was finally brought to print forty years later. Her first successful novel, *She Came to Stay*, begun in 1937 and published in 1943, was an imaginative recasting of the love triangle she, Sartre, and Olga Kosakiewicz had lived for the previous three years. Beauvoir's best writing, other than her philosophical pieces, draws heavily from her own life. Her best novels are imaginative transformations of the people and the situations she knew from the inside, and her four-volume autobiography stands as a major landmark of the genre. Although not gifted with an imagination that could create original worlds of her own, she could capture the spirit of her age and milieu as few writers could. The 1930s were for Beauvoir an inward time in which she sought and found her own literary voice.

World War II abruptly changed all that. It became clear to her that the bohemian life of the artist living at the margins of society was no longer acceptable. Beauvoir, together with Sartre, who had spent several months early in the war as a prisoner of war, began to involve themselves in the French resistance. They played but a small role, for only the communists had an organization strong enough to support active and ongoing resistance work. Although they were attracted to the communists' critique of bourgeois culture, Sartre and Beauvoir criticized them for downplaying the importance of individual freedom. For the rest of their lives the two danced a delicate tango with communism, alternately supporting and attacking it as the tenor of world communism mutated.

Sartre and Beauvoir found themselves increasingly at the center of French intellectual life. Sartre's massive treatise *Being and Nothingness* was published during the war; his play *The Flies* was a great success. Simone's first novel finally appeared in 1943 and was followed in 1945 (with great acclaim) by *The Blood of Others*, based on her experience with the resistance. They published important articles in *Combat*, the underground journal edited by Albert Camus. Beauvoir and Sartre suddenly found themselves identified as the leaders of a new movement called existentialism. This philosophical and cultural movement emphasized the individual's inalienable freedom and a corresponding responsibility for one's personal situation. It took root in part because the end of the war brought a tremendous feeling of combined optimism and cynicism: so much had been destroyed that it was hoped that an entirely new social fabric could be woven, but it was also clear from the war that for every hero who fought oppression, there was an enemy collaborator as well.

Together with several others, notably Maurice Merleau-Ponty, Sartre and Beauvoir founded a new journal, *Les Temps modernes* (*Modern Times*), as the organ of the new French left. *The Ethics of Ambiguity*, from which the selection included here is taken, appeared originally in *Les Temps modernes* as an attempt to elaborate an existentialist ethic, something Sartre himself had promised to do but never actually undertook.

In the late 1940s, approaching forty herself, Beauvoir, who had always considered herself "one of the guys" even though she had long been the lone female in most situations, turned in the course of her ongoing self-examination to consider how her own femininity had affected her. Her realization that she had grown up in a world thoroughly defined by males was a revelation, since it was also clear that there was nothing *natural* in this state of affairs. She recognized that the marginalization of women, the assumption that they are essentially "other," that they are defined in terms of their relations to the independent male, is a cultural construct not rooted in any unalterable fact. *The Second Sex*, published in 1949, incited a firestorm of criticism. Her frank discussions of motherhood, sex, and abortion shocked many. The book still draws fire today, now from both sides, for feminists have castigated it for accepting the identification of the masculine with the positive and prescribing an increased masculinization of women rather than revaluing the female itself. But it stands as a monumental work in the history of feminist thought, inspiring many to begin to fight an oppression they had not even understood they suffered.

By the early 1950s Beauvoir had settled the pattern of her life. Truly an engaged intellectual, she lent her voice to many causes, traveled extensively, wrote steadily—novels, political essays, accounts of her travels, her autobiography. Her cause was always freedom—freedom from the constraints of petty bourgeois society, freedom from colonial rule, freedom from oppression, whether capitalist or communist. As she and Sartre grew older, they grew more radical in many ways, and less and less trusting of any social institutions, all of which employ forms of domination. The stand she and Sartre took in the late 1950s and early 1960s in support of Algeria's liberation from France threatened their safety, emotions ran so high about the issue. In the Paris student revolt of 1968 Beauvoir and Sartre sided with the students, standing on street corners handing out leaflets. In the 1970s Beauvoir threw her energies increasingly into feminist causes, supporting women's rights to contraception and abortion. Increasingly, though, Sartre's failing health demanded her attention. When he died in 1980, she characteristically worked herself out of her depression at the loss of her lifelong companion by writing about him.

Philosophy

The existentialist movement was never a unified school of thought sharing a common doctrine. Even Sartre and Beauvoir accepted the title "existentialist" with some reluctance. With roots in the writings of Søren Kierkegaard and Friedrich Nietzsche, existentialist thought takes many different forms in the writings of Gabriel Marcel, Martin Heidegger, Maurice Merleau-Ponty, Albert Camus, and others. French existentialism was particularly blessed by the writerly skills of its proponents (although Sartre's *Being and Nothingness* is as crabbed a work as any piece of High German transcendentalism).

Because of the rather extreme diversity of the so-called existentialists, it is difficult to pin down themes common to existential thought, but the following capture the heart of the movement:

Humanity is sick. The sickness is not physical but metaphysical: we are not at home with ourselves; our existence and our essence cannot be brought into full coincidence; we are and experience ourselves as a *lack*.

Our sickness is a lack of self. Our selves are always in process, never complete, until we die. To be human is to be incomplete, open toward the future, able to accept or reject one's past. The self is always in danger, from without, under the force of circumstances, and from within, since there is nothing that sustains our efforts other than our own determination.

We are sick because we are free. Our freedom is the openness to the past and the future that defines human reality. However constraining circumstances may be, the meaning of our actions cannot be dictated absolutely from without, either by sheer physical necessity or by forces of external domination. It is precisely because we are free that we have a self and that the self is a problem for us. To be human, to have a self, is to face the problem of the meaning of one's existence; only a free being can confront that problem, and every free being must confront the problem or flee it in bad faith.

Our sickness arises from our attempts to evade or escape our freedom. The realization of one's freedom, containing as it does the realization of one's responsibility as well, is a frightening affair. We realize our freedom in *angst*, anxiety, for we realize then our ultimate aloneness in the world, that our lives are up to us. An all-too-common reaction to this realization is the attempt to evade this terrifying freedom by seeking to contract one's being into an already formed package, to treat one's self as already fixed—bad faith. Paradoxically, even an insistence on one's freedom can be a form of bad faith, for one's freedom is itself always a problematic aspect of one's self. One's freedom, though inescapable, is not itself a fixed commodity, ready-made and reliable. One's freedom must itself be conquered and made one's own, lest its self-evasion destroy it.

Our freedom is inescapable. Freedom is the human condition. Even the "escape" of suicide is undertaken freely. True, one is always in a situation that lies beyond one's choice, but the meaning of that situation, particularly one's way of being in the situation—enthusiastic acceptance, reluctant acquiescence, stubborn resistance—is still open. Any being for whom no freedom at all exists is not a human being.

A healthy freedom is possible. The existentialists were often criticized as pessimists about human nature, but all have held out the possibility of a healthy freedom. They disagree significantly on how such a freedom could be constituted, though. Theistic existentialists insist that a healthy freedom is possible only through turning to God and acknowledging him as the ground of all being. Atheistic existentialists, like Beauvoir and Sartre, proclaim religion another form of bad faith and seek to delineate a notion of an authentic human existence that, by taking situated freedom as its own value, seeks neither escape from freedom nor escape into freedom.

The Reading Context

Simone de Beauvoir faced a formidable challenge in writing *The Ethics of Ambiguity*, for in his grand statement of French existentialism, Jean-Paul Sartre had attributed to humankind a ruling desire for unambiguous determinateness. In Sartre's terms, each person desires to be the in-itself-for-itself—that is, to be something that simply is what it is and yet retains the distance from itself that is essential to being self-conscious—and the only thing that could be such is the impossible construct God. Furthermore, claimed Sartre, most of us are deeply imbued with the spirit of seriousness, which he says has two characteristics: "It considers values as transcendent givens independent of human subjectivity, and it transfers the quality of 'desirable' from the ontological structure of things to their simply material constitution." Existentialism opposes these two tendencies. Treating objects as having value because of what they are made of independent of their relation to and role within human lives is a mistake, Sartre argues. He concludes:

> Many men, in fact, know that the goal of their pursuit is being; and to the extent that they possess this knowledge, they refrain from appropriating things for their own sake and try to realize the symbolic appropriation of their being-in-itself. But to the extent that this attempt still shares in the spirit of seriousness and that these men can still believe that their mission of effecting the existence of the in-itself-for-itself is written in things, they are condemned to despair; for they discover at the same time that all human activities are equivalent (for they all tend to sacrifice man in order that the self-cause may arise) and that all are on principle doomed to failure. Thus it amounts to the same thing whether one gets drunk alone or is a leader of nations. If one of these activities takes precedence over the other, this will not be because of its real goal but because of the degree of consciousness which it possesses of its ideal goal; and in this case it will be the quietism of the solitary drunkard which will take precedence over the vain agitation of the leader of nations.[1]

Beauvoir took on the task of showing that within the confines of this existential outlook, a coherent ethic is still possible.

A Note on the Text

The Ethics of Ambiguity originally appeared in *Les Temps modernes*, the journal edited by Beauvoir, Sartre, and Merleau-Ponty, as a series of three essays. It was in part a response to the hefty criticisms of Sartre's *Being and Nothingness*, for numerous critics argued that the existentialism sketched out there could not support a coherent ethical view. Sartre himself promised a book on the subject but never wrote it. Beauvoir demonstrates in these essays the ethical force of the existential movement and in the process puts her own indelible stamp on existential thought.

---

1. Jean-Paul Sartre, *Being and Nothingness*, trans. Hazel Barnes (New York: Philosophical Library, 1956), p. 627.

Reading Questions

1. What is the "tragic ambiguity" of the human condition? How have humans tried to evade or escape this ambiguity?
2. In what sense is a human being a "useless passion"? Why doesn't Beauvoir think this means that our situation is hopeless?
3. By saying that an "existentialist conversion" "prevents any possibility of failure," is Beauvoir contradicting her earlier dictum that the possibility of failure is essential to ethics?
4. How does Beauvoir argue that freedom is a value implicit in the human condition even if there are no unconditional, intrinsic values?
5. Why, in order to realize my own freedom, must I also will the freedom of others?
6. If ethical deliberation cannot escape ambiguity, why is it even worth engaging in?
7. How would an existentialist ethical deliberation differ from a utilitarian or Kantian deliberation about the same dilemma?
8. Is an existentialist utopia possible? What would it be like?

The Ethics of Ambiguity

"Life in itself is neither good nor evil.
It is the place of good and evil,
according to what you make it."

Montaigne

1. Ambiguity and Freedom

"The continuous work of our life," says Montaigne, "is to build death.". . . Man knows and thinks this tragic ambivalence which the animal and the plant merely undergo. A new paradox is thereby introduced into his destiny. "Rational animal," "thinking reed," he escapes from his natural condition without, however, freeing himself from it. He is still a part of this world of which he is a consciousness. He asserts himself as a pure internality against which no external power can take hold, and he also experiences himself as a thing crushed by the dark weight of other things. At every moment he can grasp the non-temporal truth of his existence. But between the past which no longer is and the future which is not yet, this moment when he exists is nothing. This privilege, which he alone possesses, of being a sovereign and unique subject amidst a universe of objects, is what he shares with all his fellow-men. In turn an object for others, he is nothing more than an individual in the collectivity on which he depends.

As long as there have been men and they have lived, they have all felt this tragic ambiguity of their condition, but as long as there have been philosophers and they have thought, most of them have tried to mask it. They have striven to reduce mind to matter, or to reabsorb matter into mind, or to merge them within a single substance. Those who have accepted the dualism have established a hierarchy between body and soul which permits of considering as negligible the part of the self which cannot be saved. They have denied death, either by integrating it with life or by promising to man immortality. Or, again they have denied life, considering it as a veil of illusion beneath which is hidden the truth of Nirvana.

And the ethics which they have proposed to their disciples has always pursued the same goal. It has been a matter of eliminating the ambiguity by making oneself pure inwardness or pure externality, by escaping from the sensible world or by being engulfed in it, by yielding to eternity or enclosing oneself in the pure moment. Hegel, with more ingenuity, tried to reject none of the aspects of man's condition and to reconcile them all. . . .

At the present time there still exist many doctrines which choose to leave in the shadow certain troubling aspects of a too complex situation. But their attempt to lie to us is in vain. Cowardice doesn't pay. Those reasonable metaphysics, those consoling ethics with which they would like to entice us only accentuate the disorder from which we suffer. Men of today seem to feel more acutely than ever the paradox of their

From Simone de Beauvoir, *The Ethics of Ambiguity*, trans. Bernard Frechtman (New York: Philosophical Library, 1948), pp. 7–34, 129–159. Reprinted by permission of the Philosophical Library.

condition. They know themselves to be the supreme end to which all action should be subordinated, but the exigencies of action force them to treat one another as instruments or obstacles, as means. The more widespread their mastery of the world, the more they find themselves crushed by uncontrollable forces. Though they are masters of the atomic bomb, yet it is created only to destroy them. . . . Since we do not succeed in fleeing it, let us therefore try to look the truth in the face. Let us try to assume our fundamental ambiguity. It is in the knowledge of the genuine conditions of our life that we must draw our strength to live and our reason for acting.

From the very beginning, existentialism defined itself as a philosophy of ambiguity. . . . But it is also claimed that existentialism is a philosophy of the absurd and of despair. It encloses man in a sterile anguish, in an empty subjectivity. It is incapable of furnishing him with any principle for making choices. Let him do as he pleases. In any case, the game is lost. Does not Sartre declare, in effect, that man is a "useless passion," that he tries in vain to realize the synthesis of the for-oneself and the in-oneself, to make himself God? It is true. But it is also true that the most optimistic ethics have all begun by emphasizing the element of failure involved in the condition of man; without failure, no ethics; for a being who, from the very start, would be an exact coincidence with himself, in a perfect plenitude, the notion of having-to-be would have no meaning. One does not offer an ethics to a God. . . . This means that there can be a having-to-be only for a being who, according to the existentialist definition, questions himself in his being, a being who is at a distance from himself and who has to be his being.

Well and good. But it is still necessary for the failure to be surmounted, and existentialist ontology does not allow this hope. Man's passion is useless; he has no means for becoming the being that he is not. That too is true. . . .

The failure described in *Being and Nothingness* is definitive, but it is also ambiguous. Man, Sartre tells us, is "a being who *makes himself* a lack of being *in order that there might be being*." That means, first of all, that his passion is not inflicted upon him from without. He chooses it. It is his very being and, as such, does not imply the idea of unhappiness. If this choice is considered as useless, it is because there exists no absolute value before the passion of man, outside of it, in relation to which one might distinguish the useless from the useful. The word "useful" has not yet received a meaning on [this] level of description. . . . It can be defined only in the human world established by man's projects and the ends he sets up. In the original helplessness from which man surges up, nothing is useful, nothing is useless. It must therefore be understood that the passion to which man has acquiesced finds no external justification. No outside appeal, no objective necessity permits of its being called useful. It *has* no reason to will itself. But this does not mean that it can not justify itself, that it can not *give itself* reasons for being that it does not *have*. And indeed . . . man makes himself this lack of being *in order that* there might be being. The term *in order that* clearly indicates an intentionality. It is not in vain that man nullifies being. Thanks to him, being is disclosed and he desires this disclosure. There is an original type of attachment to being which is not the relationship "wanting to be" but rather "wanting to disclose being." Now, here there is not failure, but rather success. This end, which man proposes to himself by making himself lack of being, is, in effect, realized by him. By uprooting himself from the world, man makes himself present to the world and makes the world present to him. . . . This means that man, in his vain attempt to *be* God, makes himself exist *as* man, and if he is satisfied with this existence, he coincides exactly with himself. It is not granted him to exist without tending toward this being which he will never be. But it is possible for him to want this tension even with the failure which it involves. His being is lack of being, but this lack has a way of being which is precisely existence.... Man makes himself a lack, but he can deny the lack as lack and affirm himself as a positive existence. He then assumes the failure. And the condemned action, insofar as it is an effort to be, finds its validity insofar as it is a manifestation of existence.... The failure is not surpassed, but assumed. Existence asserts itself as an absolute which must seek its justification within itself and not suppress itself, even though it may be lost by preserving itself. To attain his truth, man must not attempt to dispel the ambiguity of his being but, on the contrary, accept the task of realizing it. He rejoins himself only to the extent that he agrees to remain at a distance from himself. This conversion is sharply distinguished from the Stoic conversion in that it does not claim to oppose to the sensible universe a formal freedom which is without content. To exist genuinely is not to deny this spontaneous movement of my transcendence, but only to refuse to lose myself in it. Existentialist conversion should rather be compared to Husserlian reduction: let man put his will to be "in parentheses" and he will thereby be brought to the consciousness of his true condition. And just as phenomenological reduction prevents the errors of dogmatism by suspending all affirmation concerning the mode of reality of the external world, whose flesh and bone presence the reduction does not, however, contest, so existentialist conversion does not suppress my instincts, desires, plans, and passions. It merely prevents any possibility of failure by refusing to set up as absolutes the ends toward which my transcendence thrusts itself, and by considering them in their connection with the freedom which projects them.

The first implication of such an attitude is that the genuine man will not agree to recognize any foreign absolute. When a man projects into an ideal heaven that impossible synthesis of the for-itself and the in-itself that is called God, it is because he wishes the regard of this existing Being to change his existence into being; but if he agrees not to be in order to exist genuinely, he will abandon the dream of an inhuman objectivity. He will understand that it is not a matter of being right in the eyes of a God, but of being right in his own eyes. Renouncing the thought of seeking the guarantee for his existence outside of himself, he will also refuse to believe in unconditioned values which would set themselves up athwart his freedom like things. Value is this lacking-being of which freedom *makes itself* a lack; and it is because the latter makes itself a lack that value appears. It is desire which creates the desirable, and the project which sets up the end. It is human existence which makes values spring up in the world on the basis of which it will be able to judge the enterprise in which it will be engaged. But first it locates itself beyond any pessimism, as beyond any optimism, for the fact of its original springing forth is a pure contingency. Before existence there is no more reason to exist than not to exist.... And the truth is that outside of existence there is nobody. Man exists. For him it is not a question of wondering whether his presence in the world is useful, whether life is worth the trouble of being lived. These questions make no sense. It is a matter of knowing whether he wants to live and under what conditions.

But if man is free to define for himself the conditions of a life which is valid in his own eyes, can he not choose whatever he likes and act however he likes? Dostoievsky asserted, "If God does not exist, everything is permitted." Today's believers use this formula for their own advantage. To re-establish man at the heart of his destiny is, they claim, to repudiate all ethics. However, far from God's absence authorizing all license, the contrary is the case, because man is abandoned on the earth, because his acts are definitive, absolute engagements. He bears the responsibility for a world which is not the work of a strange power, but of himself, where his defeats are inscribed, and his victories as well. A God can pardon, efface, and compensate. But if God does not exist, man's faults are inexpiable. If it is claimed that, whatever the case may be, this earthly stake has no importance, this is precisely because one invokes that inhuman objectivity which we declined at the start. One cannot start by saying that our earthly destiny *has* or *has not* importance, for it depends upon us to give it importance. It is up to man to make it important to be a man, and he alone can feel his success or failure. And if it is again said that nothing forces him to try to justify his being in this way, then one is playing upon the notion of freedom in a dishonest way. The believer is also free to sin. The divine law is imposed upon him only from the moment he decides to save his soul. . . .

However, even among the proponents of secular ethics, there are many who charge existentialism with offering no objective content to the moral act. It is said that this philosophy is subjective, even solipsistic. If he is once enclosed within himself, how can man get out? But there too we have a great deal of dishonesty. . . .

For existentialism, it is not impersonal universal man who is the source of values, but the plurality of concrete, particular men projecting themselves toward their ends on the basis of situations whose particularity is as radical and as irreducible as subjectivity itself. How could men, originally separated, get together?

And, indeed, we are coming to the real situation of the problem. But to state it is not to demonstrate that it cannot be resolved. . . . The ethics which have given solutions by effacing the fact of the separation of men are not valid precisely because there *is* this separation. An ethics of ambiguity will be one which will refuse to deny *a priori* that separate existants can, at the same time, be bound to each other, that their individual freedoms can forge laws valid for all. . . .

The characteristic feature of all ethics is to consider human life as a game that can be won or lost and to teach man the means of winning. Now, we have seen that the original scheme of man is ambiguous: he wants to be, and to the extent that he coincides with this wish, he fails. All the plans in which this will to be is actualized are condemned; and the ends circumscribed by these plans remain mirages. Human transcendence is vainly engulfed in those miscarried attempts. But man also wills himself to be a disclosure of being, and if he coincides with this wish, he wins, for the fact is that the world becomes present by his presence in it. But the disclosure implies a perpetual tension to keep being at a certain distance, to tear oneself from the world, and to assert oneself as a freedom. To wish for the disclosure of the world and to assert oneself as freedom are one and the same movement. Freedom is the source from which all significations and all values spring. It is the original condition of all justification of existence. The man who seeks to justify his life must want freedom itself absolutely and above everything else. . . . It is necessarily summoned up by the values which it sets up and through which it sets itself up. It cannot establish a denial of itself, for in denying itself, it would deny the possibility of any foundation. To will oneself moral and to will oneself free are one and the same decision. . . .

Now, Sartre declares that every man is free, that there is no way of his not being free. When he wants to escape his destiny, he is still freely fleeing it. Does not this presence of a so to speak natural freedom contradict the notion of ethical freedom? What meaning can there be in the words *to will oneself* free, since at the beginning we *are* free? It is contradictory to set freedom up as something conquered if at first it is something given.

This objection would mean something only if freedom were a thing or a quality naturally attached to a thing. Then, in effect, one would either have it or not have it. But the fact is that it merges with the very movement of this ambiguous reality which is called existence and which *is* only by making itself be; to such an extent that it is precisely only by having to be conquered that it gives itself. To will oneself free is to effect the transition from nature to morality by establishing a genuine freedom on the original upsurge of our existence.

Every man is originally free, in the sense that he spontaneously casts himself into the world. But if we consider this spontaneity in its facticity, it appears to us only as a pure contingency, an upsurging as stupid as the clinamen of the Epicurean atom which turned up at any moment whatsoever from any direction whatsoever. And it was quite necessary for the atom to arrive somewhere. But its movement was not justified by this result which had not been chosen. It remained absurd. Thus, human spontaneity always projects itself toward something. The psychoanalyst discovers a meaning even in abortive acts and attacks of hysteria. But in order for this meaning to justify the transcendence which discloses it, it must itself be founded, which it will never be if I do not choose to found it myself. Now, I can evade this choice. We have said that it would be contradictory deliberately to will oneself not free. But one can choose not to will himself free. In laziness, heedlessness, capriciousness, cowardice, impatience, one contests the meaning of the project at the very moment that one defines it. The spontaneity of the subject is then merely a vain living palpitation, its movement toward the object is a flight, and itself is an absence. To convert the absence into presence, to convert my flight into will, I must assume my project positively. It is not a matter of retiring into the completely inner and, moreover, abstract movement of a given spontaneity, but of adhering to the concrete and particular movement by which this spontaneity defines itself by thrusting itself toward an end. It is through this end that it sets up that my spontaneity confirms itself by reflecting upon itself. Then, by a single movement, my will, establishing the content of the act, is legitimized by it. . . . But this justification requires a constant tension. My project is never founded; it founds itself. To avoid the anguish of this permanent choice, one may attempt to flee into the object itself, to engulf one's own presence in it. In the servitude of the serious, the original spontaneity strives to deny itself. It strives in vain, and meanwhile it then fails to fulfill itself as moral freedom.

We have just described only the subjective and formal aspect of this freedom. But we also ought to ask ourselves whether one can will oneself free in any matter, whatsoever it may be. It must first be observed that this will is developed in the course of time. It is in time that the goal is pursued and that freedom confirms itself. And this assumes that it is realized as a unity in the unfolding of time. One escapes the absurdity of the clinamen only by escaping the absurdity of the pure moment. An existence would be unable to found itself if moment by moment it crumbled into nothingness. That is why no moral question presents itself to the child as long as he is still incapable of recognizing himself in the past or seeing himself in the future. It is only when the moments of his life begin to be organized into behaviour that he can decide and choose. The value of the chosen end is confirmed and, reciprocally, the genuineness of the choice is manifested concretely through patience, courage, and fidelity. If I leave behind an act which I have accomplished, it becomes a thing by falling into the past. It is no longer anything but a stupid and opaque fact. In order to prevent this metamorphosis, I must ceaselessly return to it and justify it in the unity of the project in which I am engaged. Setting up the movement of my transcendence requires that I never let it uselessly fall back upon itself, that I prolong it indefinitely. Thus I can not genuinely desire an end today without desiring it through my whole existence, insofar as it is the future of this present moment and insofar as it is the surpassed past of days to come. To will is to engage myself to persevere in my will.... Thus, a creative freedom develops happily without ever congealing into unjustified facticity. The creator leans upon anterior creations in order to create the possibility of new creations. His present project embraces the past and places confidence in the freedom to come, a confidence which is never disappointed. It discloses being at the end of a further disclosure. At each moment freedom is confirmed through all creation.

However, man does not create the world. He succeeds in disclosing it only through the resistance which the world opposes to him. The will is defined only by raising obstacles, and by the contingency of facticity certain obstacles let themselves be conquered, and others do not. This is what Descartes expressed when he said that the freedom of man is infinite, but his power is limited. How can the presence of these limits be reconciled with the idea of a freedom confirming itself as a unity and an indefinite movement?

In the face of an obstacle which it is impossible to overcome, stubbornness is stupid. If I persist in beating my fist against a stone wall, my freedom exhausts itself in this useless gesture without succeeding in giving itself a content. It debases itself in a vain contingency. Yet, there is hardly a sadder virtue than resignation.... We could indeed assert our freedom against all constraint if we agreed to renounce the particularity of our projects. If a door refuses to open, let us accept not opening it and there we are free. But by doing that, one manages only to save an abstract notion of freedom. It is emptied of all content and all truth....

The truth is that in order for my freedom not to risk coming to grief against the obstacle which its very engagement has raised, in order that it might still pursue its movement in the face of the failure, it must, by giving itself a particular content, aim by means of it at an end which is nothing else but precisely the free movement of existence. Popular opinion is quite right in admiring a man who, having been ruined or having suffered an accident, knows how to gain the upper hand, that is, renew his engagement in the world, thereby strongly asserting the independence of freedom in relation to thing.... But this act of passing beyond is conceivable only if what the content has in view is not to bar up the future, but, on the contrary, to plan new possibilities. This brings us back by another route to what we had already indicated. My freedom must not seek to trap being but to disclose it. The disclosure is the transition from being to existence. The goal which my freedom aims at is conquering existence across the always inadequate density of being.

However, such salvation is only possible if, despite obstacles and failures, a man preserves the disposal of his future, if the situation opens up more possibilities to him.

In case his transcendence is cut off from his goal or there is no longer any hold on objects which might give it a valid content, his spontaneity is dissipated without founding anything. Then he may not justify his existence positively and he feels its contingency with wretched disgust. There is no more obnoxious way to punish a man than to force him to perform acts which make no sense to him, as when one empties and fills the same ditch indefinitely, when one makes soldiers who are being punished march up and down, or when one forces a schoolboy to copy lines. . . . A freedom cannot will itself without willing itself as an indefinite movement. It must absolutely reject the constraints which arrest its drive toward itself. This rejection takes on a positive aspect when the constraint is natural. One rejects the illness by curing it. But it again assumes the negative aspect of revolt when the oppressor is a human freedom. . . . But revolt, insofar as it is pure negative movement, remains abstract. It is fulfilled as freedom only by returning to the positive, that is, by giving itself a content through action, escape, political struggle, revolution. Human transcendence then seeks, with the destruction of the given situation, the whole future which will flow from its victory. It resumes its indefinite rapport with itself. There are limited situations where this return to the positive is impossible, where the future is radically blocked off. Revolt can then be achieved only in the definitive rejection of the imposed situation, in suicide.

It can be seen that, on the one hand, freedom can always save itself, for it is realized as a disclosure of existence through its very failures, and it can again confirm itself by a death freely chosen. But, on the other hand, the situations which it discloses through its project toward itself do not appear as equivalents. It regards as privileged situations those which permit it to realize itself as indefinite movement; that is, it wishes to pass beyond everything which limits its power; and yet, this power is always limited. Thus, just as life is identified with the will-to-live, freedom always appears as a movement of liberation. It is only by prolonging itself through the freedom of others that it manages to surpass death itself and to realize itself as an indefinite unity. . . . If man wishes to save his existence, as only he himself can do, his original spontaneity must be raised to the height of moral freedom by taking itself as an end through the disclosure of a particular content.

But a new question is immediately raised. If man has one and only one way to save his existence, how can he choose not to choose it in all cases? How is a bad willing possible? We meet with this problem in all ethics, since it is precisely the possibility of a perverted willing which gives a meaning to the idea of virtue. . . . Unlike Kant, we do not see man as being essentially a positive will. On the contrary, he is first defined as a negativity. He is first at a distance from himself. He can coincide with himself only by agreeing never to rejoin himself. There is within him a perpetual playing with the negative, and he thereby escapes himself, he escapes his freedom. And it is precisely because an evil will is here possible that the words "to will oneself free" have a meaning. Therefore, not only do we assert that the existentialist doctrine permits the elaboration of an ethics, but it even appears to us as the only philosophy in which an ethics has its place. For, in a metaphysics of transcendence, in the classical sense of the term, evil is reduced to error; and in humanistic philosophies it is impossible to account for it, man being defined as complete in a complete world. Existentialism alone gives— like religions—a real role to evil, and it is this, perhaps, which make its judgments so gloomy. Men do not like to feel themselves in danger. Yet, it is because there are real dangers, real failures and real earthly damnation that words like victory, wisdom, or joy have meaning. Nothing is decided in advance, and it is because man has something to lose and because he can lose that he can also win. . . .

5. Ambiguity

The notion of ambiguity must not be confused with that of absurdity. To declare that existence is absurd is to deny that it can ever be given a meaning; to say that it is ambiguous is to assert that its meaning is never fixed, that it must be constantly won. Absurdity challenges every ethics; but also the finished rationalization of the real would leave no room for ethics; it is because man's condition is ambiguous that he seeks, through failure and outrageousness, to save his existence. . . .

What must be done, practically? Which action is good? Which is bad? To ask such a question is also to fall into a naive abstraction. We don't ask the physicist, "Which hypotheses are true?" Nor the artist, "By what procedures does one produce a work whose beauty is guaranteed?" Ethics does not furnish recipes any more than do science and art. One can merely propose methods. Thus, in science the fundamental problem is to make the idea adequate to its content and the law adequate to the facts; the logician finds that in the case where the pressure of the given fact bursts the concept which serves to comprehend it, one is obliged to invent another concept; but he can not define *a priori* the moment of invention, still less foresee it. Analogously, one may say that in the case where the content of the action falsifies its meaning, one must modify not the meaning, which is here willed absolutely, but the content itself; however, it is impossible to determine this relationship between meaning and content abstractly and universally: there must be a trial and decision in each case. But likewise just as the physicist finds it profitable to reflect on the conditions of scientific invention and the artist on those of artistic creation without expecting any ready-made solutions to come from these reflections, it is useful for the man of action to find out under what conditions his undertakings are valid. We are going to see that on this basis new perspectives are disclosed.

In the first place, it seems to us that the individual as such is one of the ends at which our action must aim. Here we are at one with the point of view of Christian charity, the Epicurean cult of friendship, and Kantian moralism which treats each man as an end. He interests us not merely as a member of a class, a nation, or a collectivity, but as an individual man. . . . However, it must not be forgotten that there is a concrete bond between freedom and existence; . . . in order for the idea of liberation to have a concrete meaning, the joy of existence must be asserted in each one, at every instant; the movement toward freedom assumes its real, flesh and blood figure in the world by thickening into pleasure, into happiness. If the satisfaction of an old man drinking a glass of wine counts for nothing, then production and wealth are only hollow myths. . . . If we do not love life on our own account and through others, it is futile to seek to justify it in any way. . . .

Just what is meant by the expression "to love others"? What is meant by taking them as ends? In any event, it is evident that we are not going to decide to fulfill the will of every man. There are cases where a man positively wants evil, that is, the enslavement of other men, and he must then be fought. It also happens that, without harming anyone, he flees from his own freedom, seeking passionately and alone to attain the being which constantly eludes him. If he asks for our help, are we to give it to him? We blame a man who helps a drug addict intoxicate himself or a desperate man commit suicide, for we think that rash behavior of this sort is an attempt of the individual against his own freedom; he must be made aware of his error and put in the presence of the real demands of his freedom. Well and good. But what if he persists?. . . . Besides, I am in no position to make decisions of this sort indiscriminately; the example of the unknown person who throws himself in to the Seine and whom I hesitate whether or not to fish out is quite abstract; in the absence of a concrete bond with this desperate person my choice will never be anything but a contingent facticity. If I find myself in a position to do violence to a child, or to a melancholic, sick, or distraught person the reason is that I also find myself charged with his upbringing, his happiness, and his health: I am a parent, a teacher, a nurse, a doctor, or a friend. . . . So, by a tacit agreement, by the very fact that I am solicited, the strictness of my decision is accepted or even desired; the more seriously I accept my responsibilities, the more justified it is. That is why love authorizes severities which are not granted to indifference. What makes the problem so complex is that, on the one hand, one must not make himself an accomplice of that flight from freedom that is found in heedlessness, caprice, mania, and passion, and that, on the other hand, it is the abortive movement of man toward being which is his very existence, it is through the failure which he has assumed that he asserts himself as a freedom. To want to prohibit a man from error is to forbid him to fulfill his own existence, it is to deprive him of life. . . . We object to the inquisitors who want to create faith and virtue from without; we object to all forms of fascism which seek to fashion the happiness of man from without; and also the paternalism which thinks that it has done something for man by prohibiting him from certain possibilities of temptation, whereas what is necessary is to give him reasons for resisting it. . . .

Thus, we can set up point number one: the good of an individual or a group of individuals requires that it be taken as an absolute end of our action; but we are not authorized to decide upon this end *a priori*. The fact is that no behavior is ever authorized to begin with, and one of the concrete consequences of existentialist ethics is the rejection of all the previous justifications which might be drawn from the civilization, the age, and the culture; it is the rejection of every principle of authority. To put it positively, the precept will be to treat the other (to the extent that he is the only one concerned, which is the moment that we are considering at present) as a freedom so that his end may be freedom; in using this conducting-wire one will have to incur the risk, in each case, of inventing an original solution. Out of disappointment in love a young girl takes an overdose of pheno-barbital; in the morning friends find her dying, they call a doctor, she is saved; later on she becomes a happy mother of a family; her friends were right in considering her suicide as a hasty and heedless act and in putting her into position to reject it or return to it freely. But in asylums one sees melancholic patients who have tried to commit suicide twenty times, who devote their freedom to seeking the means of escaping their jailers and of putting an end to their intolerable anguish; the doctor who gives them a friendly pat on the shoulder is their tyrant and their torturer. . . . What makes the problem more complex is that the freedom of one man almost always concerns that of other individuals. Here is a married couple who persist in living in a hovel; if one does not succeed in giving them the desire to live in a more healthful dwelling, they must be allowed to follow their preferences; but the situation changes if they have children; the freedom of the parents would be the ruin of their sons, and as freedom and the future are on the side of the latter, these are the ones who must first be taken into account. The Other is multiple, and on the basis of this new questions arise.

One might first wonder for whom we are seeking freedom and happiness. When raised in this way, the problem is abstract; the answer will, therefore, be arbitrary, and the arbitrary always involves outrage.... But man is man only through situations whose particularity is precisely a universal fact. There are men who expect help from certain men and not from others, and these expectations define privileged lines of action. It is fitting that the negro fight for the negro, the Jew for the Jew, the proletarian for the proletarian, and the Spaniard in Spain....

But it is then that we find in concrete form the conflicts which we have described abstractly; for the cause of freedom can triumph only through particular sacrifices. And certainly there are hierarchies among the goods desired by men: one will not hesitate to sacrifice the comfort, luxury, and leisure of certain men to assure the liberation of certain others; but when it is a question of choosing among freedoms, how shall we decide?

Let us repeat, one can only indicate a method here. The first point is always to consider what genuine human interest fills the abstract form which one proposes as the action's end. Politics always puts forward Ideas: Nation, Empire, Union, Economy, etc. But none of these forms has value in itself; it has it only insofar as it involves concrete individuals. If a nation can assert itself proudly only to the detriment of its members, if a union can be created only to the detriment of those it is trying to unite, the nation or the union must be rejected. We repudiate all idealisms, mysticisms, etcetera which prefer a Form to man himself. But the matter becomes really agonizing when it is a question of a Cause which genuinely serves man....

Thus, we challenge every condemnation as well as every *a priori* justification of the violence practised with a view to a valid end. They must be legitimized concretely. A calm, mathematical calculation is here impossible.... On the one hand, one can multiply a probability infinitely without ever reaching certainty; but yet, practically, it ends by merging with this asymptote: in our private life as in our collective life there is no other truth than a statistical one. On the other hand, the interests at stake do not allow themselves to be put into an equation; the suffering of one man, that of a million men, are incommensurable with the conquests realized by millions of others, present death is incommensurable with the life to come.... One finds himself back at the anguish of free decision. And that is why political choice is an ethical choice: it is a wager as well as a decision; one bets on the chances and risks of the measure under consideration; but whether chances and risks must be assumed or not in the given circumstances must be decided without help, and in so doing one sets up values....

Conclusion

Is this kind of ethics individualistic or not? Yes, if one means by that that it accords to the individual an absolute value and that it recognizes in him alone the power of laying the foundations of his own existence. It is individualism in the sense in which the wisdom of the ancients, the Christian ethics of salvation, and the Kantian ideal of virtue also merit this name; it is opposed to the totalitarian doctrines which raise up beyond man the mirage of Mankind. But it is not solipsistic, since the individual is defined only by his relationship to the world and to other individuals; he exists only by transcending himself, and his freedom can be achieved only through the freedom of others. He justifies his existence by a movement which, like freedom, springs from his heart but which leads outside of him.

This individualism does not lead to the anarchy of personal whim. Man is free; but he finds his law in his very freedom. First, he must assume his freedom and not flee it; he assumes it by a constructive movement: one does not exist without doing something; and also by a negative movement which rejects oppression for oneself and others. In construction, as in rejection, it is a matter of reconquering freedom on the contingent facticity of existence, that is, of taking the given, which, at the start, *is there* without any reason, as something willed by man. A conquest of this kind is never finished; the contingency remains. . . . This does not mean that one should consent to failure, but rather one must consent to struggle against it without respite. . . .

Let men attach value to words, forms, colors, mathematical theorems, physical laws, and athletic prowess; let them accord value to one another in love and friendship, and the objects, the events, and the men immediately *have* this value; they have it absolutely. It is possible that a man may refuse to love anything on earth; he will prove this refusal and he will carry it out by suicide. If he lives, the reason is that, whatever he may say, there still remains in him some attachment to existence; his life will be commensurate with this attachment; it will justify itself to the extent that it genuinely justifies the world.

This justification, though open upon the entire universe through time and space, will always be finite. Whatever one may do, one never realizes anything but a limited work, like existence itself which tries to establish itself through that work and which death also limits. It is the assertion of our finiteness which doubtless gives the doctrine which we have just evoked its austerity and, in some eyes, its sadness. . . . Existentialism proposes no evasion. On the contrary, its ethics is experienced in the truth of life, and it then appears as the only proposition of salvation which one can address to men. Taking on its own account Descartes' revolt against the evil genius, the pride of the thinking reed in the face of the universe which crushes him, it asserts that, despite his limits, through them, it is up to each one to fulfill his existence as an absolute. Regardless of the staggering dimensions of the world about us, the density of our ignorance, the risks of catastrophes to come, and our individual weakness within the immense collectivity, the fact remains that we are absolutely free today if we choose to will our existence in its finiteness, a finiteness which is open on the infinite. And in fact, any man who has known real loves, real revolts, real desires, and real will knows quite well that he has no need of any outside guarantee to be sure of his goals; their certitude comes from his own drive. There is a very old saying which goes: "Do what you must, come what may." That amounts to saying in a different way that the result is not external to the good will which fulfills itself in aiming at it. If it came to be that each man did what he must, existence would be saved in each one without there being any need of dreaming of a paradise where all would be reconciled in death.

SELECTED BIBLIOGRAPHY

Beauvoir, Simone de. *The Coming of Age*. Trans. Patrick O'Brian. New York: Putnam, 1972.

_____. *The Ethics of Ambiguity*. Trans. Bernard Frechtman. New York: Philosophical Library, 1948.

_____. *Force of Circumstance*. Trans. Richard Howard. New York: Putnam, 1965.

_____. *Memoirs of a Dutiful Daughter*. Trans. James Kirkup. New York: Harper & Row, 1974.

_____. *The Second Sex*. Trans. H.M. Parshley. New York: Knopf, 1953.

Barnes, Hazel. *An Existentialist Ethics*. New York: Knopf, 1967.

Bieber Konrad. *Simone de Beauvoir*. Boston: Twayne, 1979.

Detmer, David. *Freedom as a Value: A Critique of the Ethical Theory of Jean-Paul Sartre*. La Salle, Ill.: Open Court, 1988.

Howells, Christina. *Sartre: The Necessity of Freedom*. Cambridge: Cambridge University Press, 1988.

Keefe, Terry. *Simone de Beauvoir: A Study of Her Writings*. Totowa, N.J.: Barnes & Noble, 1983.

Leighton, Jean. *Simone de Beauvoir on Women*. Rutherford, N.J.: Fairleigh Dickinson University Press, 1975.

Marcel, Gabriel. *The Philosophy of Existentialism*. Trans. Manya Harari. Secaucus, N.J.: Citadel Press, 1956.

Olafson, Frederick. *Principles and Persons: An Ethical Interpretation of Existentialism*. Baltimore: Johns Hopkins Press, 1967.

Sartre, Jean-Paul. *Being and Nothingness*. Trans. Hazel Barnes. New York: Philosophical Library, 1956.

Warnock, Mary. *Existentialist Ethics*. New York: St. Martin's Press, 1967.

Whitmarsh, Anne. *Simone de Beauvoir and the Limits of Commitment*. Cambridge: Cambridge University Press, 1981.

John Rawls

Born in Baltimore in 1921, John Rawls is the only philosopher represented in this book who is still living. He attended the Kent School and then Princeton University. After serving as a platoon sergeant in the Pacific theater during World War II, Rawls returned to Princeton, where he completed his Ph.D. He has since taught at Princeton, Cornell, MIT, and Harvard, where he is presently James Bryant Conant University Professor of Philosophy. Not a prolific writer, he published his views slowly in a series of articles spanning the 1950s and 1960s. The book in which he would lay out his position in full was eagerly anticipated, though by the time the work finally appeared it came almost as an anticlimax, for drafts of various chapters had circulated privately for years. Nonetheless, his sole book, *A Theory of Justice*, rekindled concern with social theory, for it constituted a large-scale, coherent theory of the legitimate ends and means of social organization in the tradition of Thomas Hobbes, John Locke, and Immanuel Kant.

Political and social philosophy were moribund in Anglo-American analytic philosophy during the first two-thirds of the twentieth century. The dominant schools within the analytic tradition could say little about the proper forms of social organization or the proper uses of political power. Logical positivism, with its conviction that only scientifically answerable questions were legitimate, tended to treat attributions of value as nonrational, emotive affairs. This left little room for rational and philosophical treatments of the important issues in social and political philosophy. So-called

619

ordinary-language philosophy, with its conviction that philosophical problems were puzzles to be solved (or rather dissolved) by paying close attention to the logic of ordinary discourse, seemed tied to the status quo and incapable of considering the full range of social and political alternatives. To the extent that there was any reflection on social and political questions, the utilitarian heirs of John Stuart Mill, Henry Sidgwick, and G.E. Moore dominated the field.

Rawls's revival of the social contract tradition of Hobbes, Locke, and Kant breathed new life into classical political theory and generated an unbelievable response: now that his theory as a whole was available for scrutiny, everyone, it seemed, was either extending Rawls's work or criticizing it.

In the short essay included here, Rawls summarizes the principal theses of his theory and situates them with regard to the contract tradition. Before discussing his two principles, it is important to note that Rawls believes that there is a fundamentally objective measure of the goods that societies need to protect. These primary social goods include "rights, liberties and opportunities, income and wealth, and the social bases of self-respect." The problem of justice is in large degree a problem of the fair distribution of these primary social goods.

Rawls's two principles establish that the fundamental values in the society he envisions are freedom and equality of treatment. The first principle, which always has priority over the second, is that "each person has an equal right to the most extensive scheme of equal basic liberties compatible with a similar scheme of liberties for all." This means that there is a presumption against restrictions on anyone; the only acceptable reason for denying a liberty is that it could not be part of a system of liberties that would be open and acceptable to all. More colloquially, your right to swing your arms stops at my nose. This principle also establishes that everyone is to be treated equally.

The second principle qualifies the first by stating the conditions under which inequalities within society can be justified. "Social and economic inequalities are to meet two conditions: they must be (a) to the greatest expected benefit of the least advantaged; and (b) attached to offices and positions open to all under conditions of fair opportunity." Often called the "difference principle," this condition dictates that the only reason for permitting an inequality (such as different income levels for different people) is that it is expected ultimately to be in the best interest of the worst-off members of the society. Society should constantly strive to improve as much as possible the situation of the least advantaged. Society can offer incentives by permitting inequalities, but these must ultimately be to the best advantage of the worst-off and available to everyone.

The basic insights behind these two principles are fairly commonsensical, yet if we acted on these principles in a concerted fashion, our social and governmental structures would probably need major revision. These two principles, which Rawls defends as the principles of justice, represent only the tip of the iceberg in his work, however, for their defense and explication is quite an intricate affair.

In his book, Rawls goes on to sketch the form social institutions that accord with his principles would have to take, either a liberal constitutional democracy with a competitive economy or perhaps a liberal socialism. He also devotes a part of his book to moral psychology, the grounding of his theory of justice in human emotions and our goals and hopes. It is important for the validation of his theory, Rawls feels, that a society embodying his principles would generate a desire among its members to support and defend those principles.

Rawls's work unites a deeply informed social and historical sense with the latest methods of economic and game-theoretic analysis. Whether his work will remain required reading for all philosophers a hundred years from now we cannot be sure, but it is essential in contemporary social thought.

The Reading Context

Much of Rawls's writing is abstract. To ensure comprehension, try to apply Rawls's principles to concrete cases that you are familiar with. Are the tremendous differences in wages and salaries between lawyers and teachers, doctors and plumbers, and baseball players and garbage collectors justifiable according to Rawls's principles? Do Rawls's principles have important consequences for such issues as school desegregation, prison reform, and the extent and nature of welfare, Head Start, and other public assistance programs? What would a Rawlsian tax structure be like?

A Note on the Text

This short essay, published in 1975, is an attempt by Rawls to lay out in simple, direct terms the fundamental ideas of his book *A Theory of Justice*, published four years earlier.

Reading Questions

1. Does the "well-ordered society" that Rawls describes correspond to your vision of a well-ordered society? Does the description of the members of this well-ordered society fit *you*? Are you pleased or displeased with the degree of fit?
2. Does the requirement that the public conception of justice be based on *reasonable* beliefs or that its application be a matter of *rational* procedures play any real role in Rawls's theory? Would it suffice if the conception of justice and its application are simply widely agreed on, however irrational they may be?
3. What is the purpose of the principles of justice? What is the subject of those principles?
4. Rawls's second principle establishes the condition under which inequalities are permissible. Is each particular inequality (e.g., the difference in salaries between the janitor, the president of the United States, and the CEO of General Motors) to be judged against this principle, or does the principle apply primarily to general *types* of inequalities (e.g., between janitors and CEOs in general)?
5. What would you include as the social primary goods? Is it hopelessly utopian to think that we could come up with some index of such goods by which to measure relative advantage?
6. How does Rawls defend himself against the claim that the second principle (the difference principle) is biased toward the least favored people in society?

A Conception of Equality

My aim in this paper is to give a brief account of the conception of equality that underlies the view expressed in my book *A Theory of Justice* and the principles considered there. I hope to state the fundamental intuitive idea simply and informally. . . .

I

When fully articulated, any conception of justice expresses a conception of the person, of the relations between persons, and of the general structure and ends of social cooperation. To accept the principles that represent a conception of justice is at the same time to accept an ideal of the person; and in acting from these principles we realize such an ideal. Let us begin, then, by trying to describe the kind of person we might want to be and the form of society we might wish to live in and to shape our interests and character. In this way we arrive at the notion of a well-ordered society. I shall first describe this notion and then use it to explain a Kantian conception of equality.

First of all, a well-ordered society is effectively regulated by a public conception of justice. That is, it is a society all of whose members accept, and know that the others accept, the same principles (the same conception) of justice. It is also the case that basic social institutions and their arrangement into one scheme (the basic structure) actually satisfy, and are on good grounds believed by everyone to satisfy, these principles. Finally, publicity also implies that the public conception is founded on reasonable beliefs that have been established by generally accepted methods of inquiry; and the same is true of the application of its principles to basic social arrangements. This last aspect of publicity does not mean that everyone holds the same religious, moral, and theoretical beliefs; on the contrary, there are assumed to be sharp and indeed irreconcilable differences on such questions. But at the same time there is a shared understanding that the principles of justice, and their application to the basic structure of society, should be determined by considerations and evidence that are supported by rational procedures commonly recognized.

Second, I suppose that the members of a well-ordered society are, and view themselves as free and equal moral persons. They are moral persons in that, once they have reached the age of reason, each has, and views the others as having, a realized sense of justice; and this sentiment informs their conduct for the most part. That they are equal is expressed by the supposition that they each have, and view themselves as having a right to equal respect and consideration in determining the principles by which the basic arrangements of their society are to be regulated. Finally, we express their being free by stipulating that they each have, and view themselves as having, fundamental aims and higher-order interests (a conception of their good) in the name of which it is legitimate to make claims on one another in the design of their institutions. At the same time, as free persons they do not think of themselves as inevitably

---

Reprinted with permission from *The Cambridge Review* (February 1975), pp. 94–99. The original title was "A Kantian Conception of Equality."

bound to, or as identical with, the pursuity of any particular array of fundamental interests that they may have at any given time; instead, they conceive of themselves as capable of revising and altering these final ends and they give priority to preserving their liberty in this regard.

In addition, I assume that a well-ordered society is stable relative to its conception of justice. This means that social institutions generate an effective supporting sense of justice. Regarding society as a going concern, its members acquire as they grow up an allegiance to the public conception and this allegiance usually overcomes the temptations and strains of social life.

Now we are here concerned with a conception of justice and the idea of equality that belongs to it. Thus, let us suppose that a well-ordered society exists under circumstances of justice. These necessitate some conception of justice and give point to its special role. First, moderate scarcity obtains. This means that although social cooperation is productive and mutually advantageous (one person's or group's gain need not be another's loss), natural resources and the state of technology are such that the fruits of joint efforts fall short of the claims that people make. And second, persons and associations have contrary conceptions of the good that lead them to make conflicting claims on one another; and they also hold opposing religious, philosophical, and moral convictions (on matters the public conception leaves open) as well as different ways of evaluating arguments and evidence in many important cases. Given these circumstances, the members of a well-ordered society are not indifferent as to how the benefits produced by their cooperation are distributed. A set of principles is required to judge between social arrangements that shape this division of advantages. Thus the role of the principles of justice is to assign rights and duties in the basic structure of society and to specify the manner in which institutions are to influence the overall distribution of the returns from social cooperation. The basic structure is the primary subject of justice and that to which the principles of justice in the first instance apply.

It is perhaps useful to observe that the notion of a well-ordered society is an extension of the idea of religious toleration. Consider a pluralistic society, divided along religious, ethnic, or cultural lines in which the various groups have reached a firm understanding on the scheme of principles to regulate their fundamental institutions. While they have deep differences about other things, there is public agreement on this framework of principles and citizens are attached to it. A well-ordered society had not attained social harmony in all things, if indeed that would be desirable; but it has achieved a large measure of justice and established a basis for civic friendship, which makes people's secure association together possible.

II

The notion of a well-ordered society assumes that the basic structure, the fundamental social institutions and their arrangement into one scheme, is the primary subject of justice. What is the reason for this assumption? First of all, any discussion of social justice must take the nature of the basic structure into account. Suppose we begin with the initially attractive idea that the social process should be allowed to develop over time as free agreements fairly arrived at and fully honoured require. Straight-away we need an account of when agreements are free and the conditions under which they are reached are fair. In addition, while these conditions may be satisfied at an earlier time, the accumulated results of agreements in conjunction with social and historical contingencies are likely to change institutions and opportunities so that the conditions for free and fair agreements no longer hold. The basic structure specifies the background conditions against which the actions of individuals, groups, and associations take place. Unless this structure is regulated and corrected so as to be just over time, the social process with its procedures and outcomes is no longer just, however free and fair particular transactions may look to us when viewed by themselves. We recognize this principle when we say that the distribution resulting from voluntary market transactions will not in general be fair unless the antecedent distribution of income and wealth and the structure of the market is fair. Thus we seem forced to start with an account of a just basic structure. It's as if the most important agreement is that which establishes the principles that must be acknowledged ahead of time, as it were. To agree to them now, when everyone knows their present situation, would enable some to take unfair advantage of social and natural contingencies, and of the results of historical accidents and accumulations.

Other considerations also support taking the basic structure as the primary subject of justice. It has always been recognized that the social system shapes the desires and aspirations of its members; it determines in large part the kind of persons they want to be as well as the kind of persons they are. Thus an economic system is not only an institutional device for satisfying existing wants and desires but a way of fashioning wants and desires in the future. By what principles are we to regulate a scheme of institutions that has such fundamental consequences for our view of ourselves and for our interests and aims? This question becomes all the more crucial when we consider that the basic structure contains social and economic inequalities. I assume that these are necessary, or highly advantageous, for various reasons: they are required to maintain and to run social arrangements, or to serve as incentives; or perhaps they are a way to put resources in the hands of those who can make the best social use of them, and so on. In any case, given these inequalities, individuals' life prospects are bound to be importantly affected by their family and class origins, by their natural endowments and the chance contingencies of their (particularly early) development, and by other accidents over the course of their lives. The social structure, therefore, limits people's ambitions and hopes in different ways, for they will with reason view themselves in part according to their place in it and take into account the means and opportunities they can realistically expect.

 The justice of the basic structure is, then, of predominant importance. The first problem of justice is to determine the principles to regulate inequalities and to adjust the profound and long-lasting effects of social, natural, and historical contingencies, particularly since these contingencies combined with inequalities generate tendencies that, when left to themselves, are sharply at odds with the freedom and equality appropriate for a well-ordered society. In view of the special role of the basic structure, we cannot assume that the principles suitable to it are natural applications, or even extensions, of the familiar principles governing the actions of individuals and associations in everyday life which take place within its framework. Most likely we shall have to loosen ourselves from our ordinary perspective and take a more comprehensive viewpoint.

III

I shall now state and explain two principles of justice, and then discuss the appropriateness of these principles for a well-ordered society. They read as follows:

1. Each person has an equal right to the most extensive scheme of equal basic liberties compatible with a similar scheme of liberties for all.
2. Social and economic inequalities are to meet two conditions: they must be (a) to the greatest expected benefit of the least advantaged; and (b) attached to offices and positions open to all under conditions of fair opportunity.

The first of these principles is to take priority over the second; and the measure of benefit to the least advantaged is specified in terms of an index of social primary goods. These goods I define roughly as rights, liberties and opportunities, income and wealth, and the social bases of self-respect. Individuals are assumed to want these goods whatever else they want, or whatever their final ends. The least advantaged are defined very roughly, as they overlap between those who are least favored by each of the three main kinds of contingencies. Thus this group includes persons whose family and class origins are more disadvantaged than others, whose natural endowments have permitted them to fare less well, and whose fortune and luck have been relatively less favorable, all within the normal range (as noted below) and with the relevant measures based on social primary goods. Various refinements are no doubt necessary, but this definition of the least advantaged suitably expresses the link with the problem of contingency and should suffice for our purposes here.

I also suppose that everyone has physical needs and psychological capacities within the normal range, so that the problems of special health care and of how to treat the mentally defective do not arise. Besides prematurely introducing difficult questions that may take us beyond the theory of justice, the consideration of these hard cases can distract our moral perception by leading us to think of people distant from us whose fate arouses pity and anxiety. Whereas the first problem of justice concerns the relations among those who in the normal course of things are full and active participants in society and directly or indirectly associated together over the whole course of their life.

Now the members of a well-ordered society are free and equal; so let us first consider the fittingness of the two principles to their freedom, and then to their equality. These principles reflect two aspects of their freedom, namely, liberty, and responsibility, which I take up in turn. In regard to liberty, recall that people in a well-ordered society view themselves as having fundamental aims and interests which they must protect, if this is possible. It is partly in the name of these interests that they have a right to equal consideration and respect in the design of their society. A familiar historical example is the religious interest; the interest in the integrity of the person, freedom from psychological oppression, and from physical assault and dismemberment is another. The notion of a well-ordered society leaves open what particular expression these interests take; only their general form is specified. But individuals do have interests of the requisite kind and the basic liberties necessary for their protection are guaranteed by the first principle.

It is essential to observe that these liberties are given by a list of liberties; important among these are freedom of thought and liberty of conscience, freedom of the person, and political liberty. These liberties have a central range of application within which they can be limited and compromised only when they conflict with other basic liberties. Since they may be limited when they clash with one another, none of these liberties is absolute; but however they are adjusted to form one system, this system is to be the same for all. It is difficult, perhaps impossible, to give a complete definition of these liberties independently from the particular circumstances, social, economic, and technological, of a given well-ordered society. Yet the hypothesis is that the general form of such a list could be devised with sufficient exactness to sustain this conception of justice. Of course, liberties not on the list, for example, the right to own certain kinds of property (e.g., means of production), and freedom of contract as understood by the doctrine of laissez-faire, are not basic: and so they are not protected by the priority of the first principle.

One reason, then, for holding the two principles suitable for a well-ordered society is that they assure the protection of the fundamental interests that members of such a society are presumed to have. Further reasons for this conclusion can be given by describing in more detail the notion of a free person. Thus we may suppose that such persons regard themselves as having a highest-order interest in how all their other interests, including even their fundamental ones, are shaped and regulated by social institutions. As I noted earlier, they do not think of themselves as unavoidably tied to any particular array of fundamental interests; instead they view themselves as capable of revising and changing these final ends. They wish, therefore, to give priority to their liberty to do this, and so their original allegiance and continued devotion to their ends are to be formed and affirmed under conditions that are free. Or, expressed another way, members of a well-ordered society are viewed as responsible for their fundamental interests and ends. While as members of particular associations some may decide in practice to yield much of this responsibility to others, the basic structure cannot be arranged so as to prevent people from developing their capacity to be responsible, or to obstruct their exercise of it once they attain it. Social arrangements must respect their autonomy and this points to the appropriateness of the two principles.

IV

These last remarks about responsibility may be elaborated further in connection with the role of social primary goods. As already stated, these are things that people in a well-ordered society may be presumed to want, whatever their final ends. And the two principles assess the basic structure in terms of certain of these goods: rights, liberties, and opportunities, income and wealth, and the social bases of self-respect. The latter are features of the basic structure that may reasonably be expected to affect people's self-respect and self-esteem (these are not the same) in important ways. Part (a) of the second principle (the difference principle, or as economists prefer to say, the maximum criterion) uses an index of these goods to determine the least advantaged. Now certainly there are difficulties in working out a satisfactory index, but I shall leave these aside. Two points are particularly relevant here: first, social primary goods are certain objective characteristics of social institutions and of people's situation with respect to them; and second, the same index of these goods is used to compare everyone's social circumstances. It is clear, then, that although the index provides a basis for interpersonal comparisons for the purposes of justice, it is not a measure of individuals' overall satisfaction or dissatisfaction. Of course, the precise weights adopted in such an index cannot be laid down ahead of time, for these should be adjusted, to some degree at least, in view of social conditions. What can be settled initially is certain constraints on these weights, as illustrated by the priority of the first principle.

Now, that the responsibility of free persons is implicit in the use of primary goods can be seen in the following way. We are assuming that people are able to control and to revise their wants and desires in the light of circumstances and that they are to have responsibility for doing so, provided that the principles of justice are fulfilled, as they are in a well-ordered society. Persons do not take their wants and desires as determined by happenings beyond their control. We are not, so to speak, assailed by them, as we are perhaps by disease and illness so that wants and desires fail to support claims to the means of satisfaction in the way that disease and illness support claims to medicine and treatment.

Of course, it is not suggested that people must modify their desires and ends whatever their circumstances. The doctrine of primary goods does not demand the stoic virtues. Society, for its part, bears the responsibility for upholding the principles of justice and secures for everyone a fair share of primary goods (as determined by the difference principle) within a framework of equal liberty and fair equality of opportunity. It is within the limits of this division of responsibility that individuals and associations are expected to form and moderate their aims and wants. Thus among the members of a well-ordered society there is an understanding that as citizens they will press claims for only certain kinds of things, as allowed for by the principles of justice. Passionate convictions and zealous aspirations do not, as such, give anyone a claim upon social resources or the design of social institutions. For the purposes of justice, the appropriate basis of interpersonal comparisons is the index of primary goods and not strength of feeling or intensity of desire. The theory of primary goods is an extension of the notion of needs, which are distinct from aspirations and desires. One might say, then, that as citizens the members of a well-ordered society collectively take responsibility for dealing justly with one another founded on a public and objective measure of (extended) needs, while as individuals and members of associations they take responsibility for their preferences and devotions.

V

I now take up the appropriateness of two principles in view of the equality of the members of a well-ordered society. The principles of equal liberty and fair opportunity (part (b) of the second principle) are a natural expression of this equality; and I assume, therefore, that such a society is one in which some form of democracy exists. Thus our question is by what principle can members of a democratic society permit the tendencies of the basic structure to be deeply affected by social chance, and natural and historical contingencies.

Now since we are regarding citizens as free and equal moral persons (the priority of the first principle of equal liberty gives institutional expression to this), the obvious starting point is to suppose that all other social primary goods, and in particular income and wealth, should be equal: everyone should have an equal share. But society must take organizational requirements and economic efficiency into account. So it is unreasonable to stop at equal division. The basic structure should allow inequalities so long as these improve everyone's situation, including that of the least advantaged, provided these inequalities are consistent with equal liberty and fair opportunity. Because we start from equal shares, those who benefit least have, so to speak, a veto; and thus we arrive at the difference principle. Taking equality as the basis of comparison, those who have gained more must do so on terms that are justifiable to those who have gained the least.

In explaining this principle, several matters should be kept in mind. First of all, it applies in the first instance to the main public principles and policies that regulate social and economic inequalities. It is used to adjust the system of entitlements and rewards, and the standards and precepts that this system employs. Thus the difference principle holds, for example, for income and property taxation, for fiscal and economic policy; it does not apply to particular transactions or distributions, nor, in general, to small-scale and local decisions, but rather to the background against which these take place. No observable pattern is required of actual distributions, nor even any measure of the degree of equality (such as the Gini coefficient) that might be computed from these. What is enjoined is that the inequalities make a functional contribution to those least favoured. Finally, the aim is not to eliminate the various contingencies for some such contingencies seem inevitable. Thus, even if an equal distribution of natural assets seemed more in keeping with the equality of free persons, the question of redistributing these assets (were this conceivable) does not arise, since it is incompatible with the integrity of the person. Nor need we make any specific assumptions about how great these variations are; we only suppose that, as realized in later life, they are influenced by all three kinds of contingencies. The question, then, is by what criterion a democratic society is to organize cooperation and arrange the system of entitlements that encourages and rewards productive efforts. We have a right to our natural abilities and a right to whatever we become entitled to by taking part in a fair social process. The problem is to characterize this process.

At first sight, it may appear that the difference principle is arbitrarily biased towards the least favored. But suppose, for simplicity, that there are only two groups, one significantly more fortunate than the other. Society could maximize the expectations of either group but not both, since we can maximize with respect to only one aim at a time. It seems plain that society should not do the best it can for those initially more advantaged; so if we reject the difference principle, we must prefer maximizing some weighted mean of the two expectations. But how should this weighted mean be specified? Should society proceed as if we had an equal chance of being in either group (in proportion to their size) and determine the mean that maximizes this purely hypothetical expectation? Now it is true that we sometimes agree to draw lots but normally only to things that cannot be appropriately divided or else cannot be enjoyed or suffered in common. And we are willing to use the lottery principle even in matters of lasting importance if there is no other way out. (Consider the example of conscription.) But to appeal to it in regulating the basic structure itself would be extraordinary. There is no necessity for society as an enduring system to invoke the lottery principle in this case; nor is there any reason for free and equal persons to allow their relations over the whole course of their life to be significantly affected by contingencies to the greater advantage of those already favored by these accidents. No one had an antecedent claim to be benefitted in this way; and so to maximize a weighted mean is, so to speak, to favour the more fortunate twice over. Society can, however, adopt the difference principle to arrange inequalities so that social and natural contingencies are efficiently used to the benefit of all, taking equal division as a benchmark. So while natural assets cannot be divided evenly, or directly enjoyed or suffered in common, the results of their productive efforts can be allocated in ways consistent with an initial equality. Those favored by social and natural contingencies regard themselves as already compensated, as it were, by advantages to which no one (including themselves) had a prior claim. Thus they think the difference principle appropriate for regulating the system of entitlements and inequalities. . . .

SELECTED BIBLIOGRAPHY

Rawls, John. *A Theory of Justice.* Cambridge, MA: Harvard University Press, 1971.

Barry, Brian. *The Liberal Theory of Justice: A Critical Examination of the Principal Doctrines in "A Theory of Justice."* New York: Oxford University Press, 1973.

Blocker, H. Gene, and Elizabeth H. Smith, eds. *John Rawls' Theory of Social Justice: An Introduction.* Athens: Ohio University Press, 1985.

Daniels, Norman. *Reading Rawls: Critical Studies of "A Theory of Justice."* New York: Basic Books, 1974.

Martin, Rex. *Rawls and Rights.* Lawrence: University Press of Kansas, 1985.

Nozick, Robert. *Anarchy, State and Utopia.* New York: Basic Books, 1974.

Richards, David A.J. *A Theory of Reasons for Action.* Oxford: Clarendon Press, 1971.

Wolff, Robert Paul. *Understanding Rawls: A Reconstruction and Critique of "A Theory of Justice."* Princeton, N.J.: Princeton University Press, 1977.

GLOSSARY

Abstract/Concrete. To think about something abstractly is to consider an aspect of it apart from many of its actual relations and properties. An abstract idea omits traits that distinguish individual referents of the idea from each other, preserving only what they have in common. To think about something concretely is to consider it with full regard to its many relations and properties.

Accident. (1) In scholastic philosophy, something that has no independent existence but must inhere in a substance. (2) In Aristotle, a nonessential property.

Actuality/Potentiality. For Aristotle, actuality is the realization of some form, which also entails having causes and effects. Potentiality is the power to change form.

Alienation. [*Entfremdung*] Originally applied in English to property when sold or otherwise dissociated from its owner, it has come to mean the distancing of something from its proper nature, especially in Hegelian and Marxist contexts.

Altruism/Egoism. The altruist asserts the validity and the necessity of having interests in others for their own sake. The egoist claims that our only interests are self-interests.

Ambiguous. Having two or more distinct meanings; e.g., the word *bank* is ambiguous, for it means both "land bordering a river" and "institution for financial deposits." Not the same as *vagueness*.

Analytic/Synthetic. Different definitions of analyticity have been proposed: (1) A statement is analytically true if and only if the concept of the predicate is contained in the concept of the subject. (2) A statement is analytically true if and only if its denial is equivalent to a contradiction. (3) A statement is analytically true if and only if it is true in virtue of the meanings of the words in it. In all cases, a synthetic truth is any truth that is not analytic.

Antinomy. A paradox or contradiction.

Aperion. The Greek term for the unlimited or the indeterminate.

Apodictic. An apodictic judgment asserts that something is either necessary or impossible. It is capable of being established by a priori proof.

Aporetic. Raising questions, problems, and objections without necessarily providing an answer.

A Posteriori. *See* A Priori/A Posteriori.

Apperception. Self-consciousness or self-awareness.

A Priori/A Posteriori. Something a priori is knowable without reference to experience (except for whatever experience may be necessary to understand the words). Any English speaker who understands the words knows that "Brothers are male siblings" is true. A posteriori knowledge, in contrast, requires some experience. "Harry drives a red Chevy" cannot be known simply by understanding the sentence; at some point someone has to look and see.

Argument. A set of declarative sentences, some of which purport to support others. A deductive argument purports to be such that if the premises are true, the conclusion must be true. An inductive argument purports only to show that the conclusion is more likely given the premises.

Autonomy. Self-governance.

Axiology. The study of the nature, types, and criteria of values and value judgments.

Axiom. A statement assumed true without further supporting argument, from which other statements are derived.

Beg the question. In an argument, to assume the proposition that is to be established by the argument.

Cartesian. Of or relating to René Descartes.

Categorical Imperative. An imperative that commands universally and without condition, making no assumptions about the agent's desires or interests.

Category. In Aristotle, one of the ten basic modes of being. In Kant, an item in his logical classification of the forms of judgments applied to our forms of intuition. In general, a fundamental form of being or of expression.

Certain. (1) Necessary, impossible to be false. (2) Beyond all doubt. (3) Inevitable.

Clear and Distinct. An idea is said to be clear by Descartes if it is present and patently evident to an attentive mind; an idea is distinct when it is so precise and different from all other ideas as to contain only what is clear. According to Leibniz, a clear idea is sufficient to enable one to recognize the thing represented; a distinct idea enables one to enumerate the characteristics required to distinguish the thing from others.

Commodity. An item transferrable or alienable for a price.

Compatibilism. The view that determinism (physical or psychological) is consistent with human freedom.

Concrete. *See* Abstract/Concrete.

Consistent. Two statements are consistent if it is possible for them both to be true at the same moment. Two states of affairs are consistent if they can both exist simultaneously.

Contiguous. Immediately next to, adjacent.

Contingent. In logic, a sentence is contingent if neither it nor its denial is contradictory.

Contradiction. The simultaneous assertion and denial of the same statement; any statement equivalent to "*p* and not *p*."

Contrary. Two statements so related that both may be false, but only one can be true. (E.g., "All apples are sweet" and "No apples are sweet" can both be false if some but not all apples are sweet. They cannot both be true.)

Cosmological Argument. The argument for God's existence based on the existence of contingent, finite things and the impossibility of an infinite series of causes.

Deductive Argument. An argument that purports to be such that if the premises are true, the conclusion must be true, or in which it is impossible for the premises to be true and the conclusion false.

Demonstration. A deductive proof of a thesis. A demonstrative truth is a truth capable of proof by demonstration from a priori premises.

Determinism. The doctrine that every event in the universe is strictly determined by the prior total state of the universe.

Dogma. A belief or set of beliefs accepted without rational support, usually on the basis of tradition or authority.

Dualism. The doctrine that there are two independent types of substance, usually material substance and mental substance. It is a special case of *pluralism* and contrasted with *monism*.

Egoism. *See* Altruism/Egoism.

Eidos. Term used by Plato to denote the forms or ideas, the eternal, unchangeable objects of reason (*nous*), in which sensible particulars can participate.

Eminent Reality. *See* Formal/Objective/Eminent Reality.

Empirical. Based on experience.

Empiricism. The school of thought whose central thesis is that all knowledge, or at least all knowledge of fact, is based on experience. What counts as an experience and what form the basing relation takes varies in different branches of the school.

Enlightenment. The period from the late seventeenth to the late eighteenth century in which high intellectual culture was characterized by the rejection of tradition and authority as sufficient grounds for our beliefs or behavior, the acceptance of rational and empirical modes of inquiry as the only justifiable methods, and the belief in the perfectibility of mankind given sufficient understanding of human nature and its situation in the world.

Epistemology. The branch of philosophy concerned with the theory of knowledge—the analysis of the concept of knowledge, the investigation of the structure of justification, the scope of knowledge, skepticism, and the like.

Epoche. The bracketing off or suspension of all considerations regarding existence.

Essence. The set of properties or whatever in virtue of which something is what it is.

Ethics. Broadly, the study of the fundamental principles and concepts of our search for the good life. The science of right character or conduct.

Faculty. An ability, function, or power; sometimes the mechanism or seat of such an ability or function.

Fallacy. An error in reasoning or inference.

Form. In Plato, a common translation of *eidos*, also translated as *idea*. For Aristotle, a form is something that, within a particular kind of matter, yields an individual with a determinate mode of being. In Kant, a mode of relation among representations.

Formal/Objective/Eminent Reality. In Descartes, to possess formal reality is to exist as a substance or as an accident of a substance. To have objective reality is to exist as a content of a mental representation. Eminent reality is relational; X contains the reality of Y eminently if and only if X can produce Y. For example, unicorns are not formal realities, though they have objective reality (in our thoughts about unicorns), and they are contained eminently in God, since he could create them if he chose.

Game Theory. A mathematical theory of decisions in gamelike situations under conditions of uncertainty.

Generalization. A statement that asserts something of a whole class of objects.

Hedonism. In its psychological version, the doctrine that procuring pleasure and avoiding pain are the sole motivations for which people ultimately act. In ethics, the doctrine that pleasure and pain are the ultimate touchstones for all ethical values.

Historicism. Most often used to describe a relativistic position claiming that the categories of human thought evolve through history and that all judgments must be assessed and/or understood relative to some historical framework.

Hylomorphism. The doctrine that every substance is composed of matter and form.

Idea. (1) In Plato, an archetype or immaterial pattern of which the members of any natural class are but imperfect copies and by participation in which they have their being. (2) In early modern philosophy (the "new way of ideas"), an immediate object of thought: what one feels when one feels or thinks when one thinks; whatever is in one's understanding and directly present to cognitive consciousness. (3) In Kant, a conception of reason, the object of which transcends all possible experience.

Idealism. The doctrine that the sole fundamental substances or ultimate realities of the world are minds. Transcendental idealism is the doctrine that nature insofar as we can know it is dependent on our minds but leaves open the question as to whether there is a mind-independent reality apart from our knowledge.

Induction. The form of reasoning in which a general principle or law is inferred from observed particular instances. More generally, any argument form in which the truth of the conclusion is claimed to be made more probable by the premises.

Innate Ideas. Concepts or ideas possessed by the mind antecedent to and independent of any experience.

Instrumental Good. A good whose goodness is derivative from its contribution toward the realization of some further good; good as a means, not as an end.

Intrinsic Good. Good in itself, without regard to anything else.

Intuition. A noninferential cognitive state; either the noninferential knowledge of a truth or the immediate knowledge of some object. In Kant, an intuition is a cognitive state immediately related to a sensory object.

Knowledge. Several kinds of knowledge have been distinguished: (1) Knowledge *that*, knowledge of some fact. The classical analysis of this form of knowledge says that *S* knows that *p* if and only if (a) *S* believes that *p*, (b) *S* is justified in believing that *p*, and (c) *p* is true. There is good reason to doubt that these conditions are sufficient for knowledge. (2) Knowledge *of*, knowledge by acquaintance. Some philosophers have claimed that knowledge by acquaintance is independent of knowledge *that* and more basic; others that all knowledge by acquaintance can be analyzed into knowledge *that*. (3) Knowledge *how*.

Libertarianism. In metaphysics, the view that the will is not causally determined. In political philosophy, the view that the government that governs least, governs best.

Logic. The study of the principles of valid argument. More broadly, the study of the structures of thought and language that make truth and validity possible.

Manichaeism. A religious movement founded in the third century by the Persian Mani, who saw the world as a struggle between two independent and equally fundamental principles, one good and one evil.

Materialism. The doctrine that everything that exists is either matter or dependent on and reducible to matter.

Matter. In Aristotle, the indeterminate stuff or potentiality that receives determination by being imbued with a form. In modern thought, it is usually contrasted with *mind* and is seen as the ultimate subject of mechanical laws. Matter occupies space, has mass, and is capable of motion and rest.

Maxim. In Kant, a subjective rule of conduct, a policy by which one intends to govern one's own actions.

Mechanism. The doctrine that the geometric and motive properties of things are sufficient for the complete explanation of all natural phenomena.

Metaphysics. Derived originally from the title given by his editors to the book of Aristotle's placed after the *Physics*, it has come to denote an area of philosophic inquiry with a disparate subject matter. The heart of metaphysics is ontology, the study of being or existence, but numerous other topics are often treated under the rubric of metaphysics, such as free will and determinism, causation, and the nature of necessity.

Mind. That by virtue of which one thinks, perceives, feels, or wills.

Monism. In its strictest form, the doctrine that there is one and only one substance in the world. More broadly, the doctrine that there is only one kind of substance in the world.

Mysticism. The belief that the world is not rationally or discursively comprehensible but can be grasped in particular states or experiences in which there is a direct apprehension of or unification with the world.

Naturalism. (1) The doctrine that everything in the world is natural; supernatural causes or beings do not exist. (2) The position in ethics that normative terms can be defined by completely natural properties.

Natural Theology. What can be known of God on the basis of reason and sensory experience.

Necessary. A sentence is logically necessary if its denial is equivalent to a contradiction. An event is physically necessary if, given the antecedent state of the world, the occurrence of the event follows by the (true) laws of nature.

Necessary Condition. *A* is a necessary condition of *B* if and only if *B* could not be true without *A*. Clouds are a necessary condition of precipitation. *See* Sufficient Condition.

Noumenon. In Kant, whatever exists as it is in itself independently of our knowledge; that which can be the object only of a purely intellectual intuition.

Nous. The Greek term for reason or intellect, the faculty of mind by virtue of which we can cognize necessary and eternal truths.

Objective Reality. *See* Formal/Objective/Eminent Reality.

Omnipotent. All-powerful.

Omniscient. All-knowing.

Ontology. The study of being or existence. Ontologists question what it is to exist and what varieties of existence there may be. Trees exist, numbers exist, pains exist—but all in the same way? And what about nonbeing—does it exist?

Panpsychism. The doctrine that everything in nature is conscious to some degree.

Pantheism. The doctrine that God is the entirety of existence.

Pelagianism. A heretical Christian doctrine promulgated by the fifth-century British monk Pelagius, who denied original sin and maintained that humanity can, of its own free will and without the intervention of God's grace, strip itself of sin and attain eternal life.

Phenomenalism. The doctrine that statements about material objects can be translated without remainder into statements about actual and possible sense experiences.

Phenomenology. A philosophical method developed and championed principally by Husserl.

Phenomenon. (1) An appearance or immediate object of experience, as distinguished from a thing in itself. (2) Any perceivable object or event; often used more broadly to refer to any event at all. In Kant, phenomena are the objects of our thought and sensory experience.

Pluralism. The doctrine that there are multiple fundamental beings (substantival pluralism) or kinds of being in the world.

Positivism. A doctrine launched by Auguste Comte that proclaims the triumph of science over all religion and metaphysics and promulgates a view of science as a set of purely descriptive generalizations about experienceable events.

Potentiality. *See* Actuality/Potentiality.

Primary/Secondary Qualities. Primary qualities are properties that things have on their own, without relation to subjectivity. Secondary qualities are the dispositional properties things have to excite certain experiences in us.

Psychologism. The doctrine that psychology is the foundation of our knowledge and that the proper method of knowing this foundation is introspection.

Pyrrhonism. A strong skepticism (named for Pyrrho, c. 365–275 B.C.E., a Greek generally regarded as the earliest systematic skeptic).

Rationalism. A doctrine popular in the seventeenth century. It claims that it is possible to obtain a knowledge of the nature of what exists by the use of reason alone and that such knowledge forms one complete system (like Euclid's geometry) resting on innately known truths. More broadly, the belief in the systematic explicability of all aspects of the world. More generally, a belief in the supremacy of reason.

Real. Existing in or pertaining to things and not merely words or thought, independent of any person's thought about the subject.

Realism. Ontological realism (in medieval philosophy) is the view that universals (or Platonic forms) are real, substantial existences independent of the individuals that exemplify them and the minds that think them. In modern philosophy, realism is the view that physical objects exist external to and independently of minds. The doctrine that we have immediate knowledge through perception of such independent existences is also sometimes called realism.

Relativism. The doctrine that truth depends on the standards employed. Ethical relativism relativizes right and wrong to either a subjective or a societal standard.

Representationalism. The doctrine that the mind relates to its objects through the medium of an internal symbolic scheme that itself bears a semantic relation to the objects in the world—that is, that in thought and perception the mind relates immediately to a (mental) object that represents the mediate object of thought.

Self-evident. Known to be true without other supporting justification.

Skepticism. Doubt or rejection of some form of knowledge. Skepticism can vary in strength and in scope. The strongest skepticism maintains that knowledge is impossible; a moderately strong skepticism maintains that though possible, knowledge does not in fact exist; the weakest skepticism simply doubts that knowledge is as widespread as generally thought. Global skepticism is skepticism about our knowledge of anything; more restricted skepticisms question our knowledge in specific areas, such as theology or the empirical sciences.

Solipsism. The philosophical doctrine that there is only one existent, namely, the proponent of the doctrine, and that all other things exist solely as contents of that person's consciousness.

Sophists. Ancient Greek philosophy and rhetoric teachers who took pay for teaching virtue, government, the winning of law suits, and other intellectual skills.

Sophrosyne. The quality of wise moderation.

Soul. Among the Greeks, the principle of life. In Christian theology, the immortal principle of personhood. In Cartesian doctrine, a substantial, nonextended, thinking substance.

Species-Being. As originally used by Feuerbach and later adopted by Marx, the peculiarly human awareness of ourselves as members of our species, as having a common nature.

Substance. A term used by many but used precisely by few. Among its meanings are these: (1) The ultimate subject of predication, which can never itself be predicated of something else. (2) That which exists independently of any other existent. (3) That which endures through change.

Sufficient Condition. *A* is a sufficient condition of *B* if and only if the truth or existence of *A* guarantees the truth or existence of *B*. Rain is a sufficient condition of the presence of clouds. *See* Necessary Condition.

Synthetic. *See* Analytic/Synthetic.

Teleology. Purpose or goal; the doctrine of final causation.

Transcendent. Beyond experience or beyond the world.

Transcendental. (1) Of or related to the transcendent. (2) In Aristotelian philosophy, extending beyond the bounds of a single category. (3) In Kant, relating to the possibility of a priori knowledge.

Universalizability. Any moral judgment, it is widely thought, must be an instance of a general rule or principle; hence any particular moral judgment must be universalizable into such a rule.

Utilitarianism. The moral theory, originally propounded by Jeremy Bentham and James and John Stuart Mill, that the standard of rightness in action is producing the greatest balance of pleasure over pain (or happiness over unhappiness) for all affected by an action, counting each person equally.

Vagueness. An indeterminacy in the meaning or conditions of applicability of a term. Not the same as *ambiguous*. *Bald* is a vague term, for there is no determinate number of hairs that demarcates the bald and the hairy. Most ordinary descriptive terms are vague to some degree.

Valid. (1) In logic, validity is a property of deductive arguments in which it is impossible for the premises to be true and the conclusion false. (2) More generally, to be valid is to be worthy of respect or to possess a legitimate, though not necessarily overriding, weight in some consideration.

Weltanschauung. Worldview, an entire and relatively complete way of understanding and interpreting the world.